Seventh Edition

APPLIED PSYCHOLOGY IN HUMAN RESOURCE MANAGEMENT

Wayne F. Cascio
The Business School
University of Colorado Denver

Herman Aguinis
Kelley School of Business
Indiana University

Prentice Hall
Boston   Columbus   Indianapolis   New York   San Francisco   Upper Saddle River
Amsterdam   Cape Town   Dubai   London   Madrid   Milan   Munich   Paris   Montreal   Toronto
Delhi   Mexico City   Sao Paulo   Sydney   Hong Kong   Seoul   Singapore   Taipei   Tokyo

*To my Mother and Dad
Whose generosity and self-sacrifice enabled me
to have what they did not*

—WC

*To my wife, Heidi, and my daughters Hannah Miriam
and Naomi Rebecca, whose patience, love, and support
have made this book possible*

—HA

Editorial Director: Sally Yagan
Editor in Chief: Eric Svendsen
Acquisitions Editor: Jennifer M. Collins
Editorial Project Manager: Susie Abraham
Director of Marketing: Patrice Jones
Marketing Manager: Nikki Jones
Marketing Assistant: Ian Gold
Project Manager: Renata Butera
Operations Specialist: Renata Butera
Creative Art Director: Jayne Conte

Cover Designer: Bruce Kenselaar
Cover Art: Getty Images, Inc.
Full-Service Project Management:
   Hema Latha, Integra Software Services
Composition: Integra Software Services
Printer/Binder: Hamilton Printing Co.
Cover Printer: Lehigh-Phoenix Color,
   Hagerstown
Text Font: 10/12 Times

Credits and acknowledgments borrowed from other sources and reproduced, with permission, in this textbook appear on appropriate page within the text.

Library of Congress Cataloging-in-Publication Data

Cascio, Wayne F.
   Applied psychology in human resource management/Wayne F. Cascio, Herman Aguinis.
      p. cm.
   Includes bibligraphical references and index.
   ISBN-13: 978-0-13-609095-3
   ISBN-10: 0-13-609095-8
   1. Personal management—Psychological aspects.   2. Psychology, Industrial.   3. Personnel management—
   United States.   4. Psychological, Industrial—United States.   I. Aguinis, Herman, 1966–   II. Title
HF5549.C297 2011
658.3001'9—dc22

                                                          2009043551

10 9 8 7 6 5 4 3 2

Prentice Hall
is an imprint of

www.pearsonhighered.com

ISBN 10:   0-13-609095-8
ISBN 13: 978-0-13-609095-3

CONTENTS

PREFACE

NEW TO THIS EDITION

In preparing this seventh edition, we reviewed a total of 5,881 journal articles and extracted 826 from the following 21 journals: *Academy of Management Journal, Academy of Management Review, Human Performance, International Journal of Selection and Assessment, Journal of Applied Psychology, Journal of Vocational Behavior, Organizational Behavior and Human Performance, Organizational Research Methods, Personnel Psychology, American Psychologist, Annual Review of Psychology, Human Relations, Human Resource Management, Journal of Management, Journal of Occupational and Organizational Psychology, Journal of Organizational Behavior, European Journal of Psychological Assessment, European Journal of Work and Organizational Psychology, Academy of Management Executive/AOM Perspectives, HRMagazine, Harvard Business Review,* and the *APA Handbook of I/O Psychology.*

After completing the revision, we deleted a total of 174 citations from the sixth edition and added 546 to the seventh, including many from the popular press. Reflecting these additions in content, the new edition is 6.8 percent longer than the last. Before we get to the new features in each chapter, however, there are two cross-chapter issues that we want you to know about. One, we incorporated a new feature into every chapter, namely "Evidence-Based Implications for Practice." Second, relative to previous editions, we reversed the order of Chapters 13 ("Decision Making for Selection") and 14 ("Managerial Selection"). We relabeled Chapter 14 as "Decision Making for Selection" and Chapter 12 as "Selection Methods: Part I." So the order is now: Chapter 12—"Selection Methods: Part I," Chapter 13—"Selection Methods: Part II," and Chapter 14—"Decision Making for Selection." Here is a chapter-by-chapter rundown of some new features.

Chapter 1

- Considered the impact of outsourcing on product and service markets, as well as on the people who produce those products and services
- Emphasized that high technology cannot substitute for skill in managing the people who use the high technology
- Used Accenture's innovative approach in training a globally dispersed workforce to illustrate the need for comprehensive training policies that focus on organizational needs three to five years out

Chapter 2

- Highlighted the difference in approach between the former Immigration and Naturalization Service (imposition of civil fines on employers who hired illegal aliens) and today's Immigration and Customs Enforcement (ICE, which relies heavily on criminal prosecutions and the seizure of company assets) to gain compliance with the nation's immigration laws
- Explained a key requirement of the ADA Amendments Act, effective January 1, 2009, to identify a qualified individual
- Updated preventive actions employers can take to avoid sexual harassment charges, in light of recent court rulings and research
- Offered practical guidance to employers about implementing "English-only" rules

Chapter 3

- Three basic ideas provide the foundation of this chapter, and they have not changed: *utility theory*, which insists that costs and expected consequences of decisions always be taken into account; *open-systems theory*, which regards organizations as open systems in continual interaction with multiple, dynamic environments; and the *employment process as a network of sequential, interdependent decisions*

Chapter 4

- Introduced the concept of *in situ* performance, that is, specification of the broad range of effects—situational, contextual, strategic, and environmental—that may affect individual, team, or organizational performance

Chapter 5

- Provided examples of the implementation of performance management systems in actual organizations, such as Microsoft Corporation

- Emphasized the importance of context (i.e., organizational, cultural, interpersonal relationships) in the performance-management process. This helps students to understand that performance management is both a technical/measurement and an interpersonal/emotional issue

Chapter 6

- Developed a decision tree for choosing an appropriate process for developing parallel-form tests
- Discussed scale coarseness, its relationship to measurement error, and its detrimental impact on resulting correlation coefficients (i.e., lack of measurement precision)

Chapter 7

- Provided step-by-step recommendations on how to conduct a content validation study that follows the best scientific guidelines and is legally defensible
- Included updates regarding meta-analysis, validity generalization, and synthetic validity
- Described an empirical, Bayes-analysis approach to validation

Chapter 8

- Challenged the established conclusion that test bias does not exist, and, if it does exist, it favors minority-group members
- Distinguished between the social concept of test fairness and the psychometric concept of test bias
- Presented a procedure for anticipating consequences in terms of selection errors and adverse impact when using a particular test with a particular sample
- Expanded recommendations to minimize adverse impact

Chapter 9

- Added new information about strategies for assessing the content-oriented validity of minimum qualifications for education and experience
- Incorporated the latest information about the use of frame-of-reference training in personality- based job analysis
- Added recent applications of the O*Net database of occupational information to forecast three different types of adult literacy (which may be more critical than education in determining wages)

Chapter 10

- Revised the treatment of strategic planning
- Added a new model that shows the relationship of HR strategy to the broader strategy of a business
- Provided new information about IBM's technology-powered staff-deployment tool called "Workforce Management Initiative"
- Completely revised and updated the section on leadership-succession planning, with in-depth treatment of 3M Company as an example
- Completely revised the treatment of CEO succession
- Completely revised the treatment of workforce-demand forecasting
- Provided guidelines to help assess when "buying" talent is more effective than "making" it

Chapter 11

- Added a comprehensive, multistage model of the recruitment process
- Included the latest findings with respect to planning, managing, and evaluating recruitment operations, especially with respect to new technology and Internet-based recruitment
- Described the ingenious methods that Whirlpool and IBM use to attract MBAs
- Updated findings regarding realistic job previews and job search from the applicant's perspective

Chapter 12

- Offered guidance on conducting telephone-based reference checks
- Included alternative ways to measure integrity, such as conditional reasoning and situational-judgment tests

- Addressed the equivalence of face-to-face versus videotaped interviews
- Presented the latest research regarding the effects of type of interview and interviewee's personality and other characteristics on an interviewer's hiring recommendation

Chapter 13

- Extensively revised sections on cognitive-ability testing and personality, including a discussion of new ways to measure personality (e.g., conditional reasoning), techniques for addressing faking in self-report personality tests, and newly proposed personality constructs, such as core self-evaluations
- Presented the latest research regarding race-based differences in various types of tests used for managerial selection (e.g., work samples and situational-judgment tests)

Chapter 14

- Discussed the implications of a multiple-hurdle approach for criterion-related validity estimation
- Presented revised guidelines for setting cutoff scores

Chapter 15

- Described technology-driven instruction (Web, PDA, or MP3 player) that has made training economically feasible to provide to individuals outside an organization's own employees (e.g., to customers and suppliers)
- Presented current findings on team-based training, such as Crew Resource Management training
- Included transfer-of-training research findings that apply to individuals and teams
- Described research on self-regulation to maintain changes in behavior over time
- Addressed the side effects of goal setting
- Included new findings regarding the mechanism that seems to drive behavior modeling, as well as more precise statements about the effects of behavior modeling

Chapter 16

- Illustrated the effects of time on transfer to the job and the perceived applicability of training
- Considered the advantages and disadvantages of ROI
- Presented a comprehensive framework for influencing managerial decisions with program-evaluation data
- Discussed the upward bias in effect sizes when single-group, pretest–posttest evaluation designs are used to assess training outcomes
- Added a new, quasi-experimental research design, the nonequivalent dependent variable design, along with its advantages and disadvantages

Chapter 17

- Completely revised and updated the treatment of the effects of globalization and technology on organizations and people
- Updated the treatment of culture and of Hofstede's work on country-level cultural differences
- Included current findings regarding international validity generalization for general mental ability and personality as predictors of success in overseas assignments
- Incorporated both quantitative (meta-analytic) and qualitative reviews of the effects of cross-cultural training on a variety of outcomes
- Identified key differences between performance management in domestic and international contexts, and provided research-based guidelines for its implementation
- Updated the treatment of three key aspects of repatriation: planning, career management, and compensation

Chapter 18

- Expanded this chapter to include the broader area of organizational responsibility, which subsumes ethical issues
- Described the role of HRM researchers and practitioners in organizational responsibility, including directions for future research and practice

Like its first six editions, this book is an interdisciplinary-oriented, research-based HR text. As in the past, our subject matter is personnel psychology—the application of psychological research and theory to human resource management (HRM) in organizations. As an applied area of psychology, personnel psychology seeks to make organizations more effective and more satisfying as places to work.

Personnel psychology represents the overlap between psychology and HRM. It is a subfield within HRM, excluding, for example, such topics as labor law, compensation and benefits, safety, and industrial relations. Personnel psychology is also a subfield along with industrial and organizational (I/O) psychology—the study of the behavior of men and women in work settings. Today, with the tremendous growth of I/O psychology in many directions, HRM is appropriately considered only one of many areas to which I/O psychologists have turned their attention.

As in the first six editions, we have included material of a decidedly theoretical, statistical, or psychometric nature. No doubt some readers will criticize the book on these grounds and charge that "things just aren't done that way in the real world." Perhaps not, for we agree that some of the ideas in the book are used by very few organizations. However, many topics in earlier editions that may have seemed "far out" are now considered "mainstream"—for example, validity generalization, statistical power analysis, and situational interviews. The book is designed to be forward looking and progressive, and, even though some of the material is presented in a conventional manner, with a dose of statistical, psychometric, or psychological theory thrown in, we believe that, in the last analysis, nothing is more practical.

In writing this book, we make two assumptions about our readers: (1) They are familiar with the general problems of HRM or I/O psychology, and (2) they have some background in fundamental statistics—at least enough to understand statistical procedures on a conceptual level, and preferably enough to compute and interpret tests of statistical significance. As in earlier editions, our goals are (1) to challenge the field to advance rather than simply to document past practice, (2) to present a model toward which professionals should aim, and (3) to present scientific procedure and fundamental theory so that the serious student can develop a solid foundation on which to build a broad base of knowledge.

Our overall objective is to integrate psychological theory with tools and methods that will enable the student or professional to translate theory into practice effectively. We are well aware that in the complex, dynamic environment in which we live and work, scientific and technological advances are occurring faster than ever before. Hence, education must be a lifelong effort if one is to avoid what Armer (1970) calls the "Paul Principle": Over time, people become uneducated and therefore incompetent to perform at a level at which they once performed adequately. If the book projects this one message, then the HR profession will be enriched immeasurably.

The response to the first six editions of this book in psychology departments and in business and professional schools has been particularly gratifying. However, new ideas and research findings in all the areas covered by the book made a seventh edition necessary in order to reflect the state of the art in personnel psychology. We have tried to do just that, as reflected in the new content, and we have added many new references.

We would be remiss if we did not acknowledge the moral support and encouragement of our families throughout the project. Their love and devotion make good times better and bad times a little easier to take.

Wayne Cascio
Denver, Colorado

Herman Aguinis
Bloomington, Indiana

Organizations, Work, and Applied Psychology

At a Glance

Organizations are all around us—businesses, hospitals, political parties, government and nongovernment organizations, social clubs, churches, Boy and Girl Scouts, and Little Leagues, just to name a few. Each organization has its own particular set of objectives, and, in order to function effectively, each organization must subdivide its overall objectives into various jobs. Jobs differ in their requirements. Likewise, people differ in aptitudes, abilities, and interests, and along many other dimensions. Faced with such variability in people and jobs, programs for the efficient use of human resources are essential.

As we move further into the Information Age, *job security* (the belief that one will retain employment with the same organization until retirement) has become less important to workers than *employment security* (having the kinds of skills that employers in the labor market are willing to pay for). Hence, workplace training and development activities will be top priorities for organizations and their people. Demographic changes in society will make recruitment and staffing key considerations for many organizations. Diversity at work will be a major theme as the composition of the workforce changes.

Guided by the fundamental assumption that in a free society every individual has a basic and inalienable right to compete for any job for which he or she is qualified, we turn to a consideration of how applied psychology can contribute to a wiser, more humane use of our human resources. If present technological, social, and economic indicators predict future concerns, applied psychology will play an increasingly significant role in the world of work in the twenty-first century.

THE PERVASIVENESS OF ORGANIZATIONS

Throughout the course of our lives, each of us is deeply touched by organizations of one form or another. In the normal course of events, a child will be exposed to a school organization, a church or a religious organization, and perhaps a Little League or a Boy or Girl Scout organization, as well as the social organization of the local community. After leaving the school organization, the young person may choose to join a military, business, or government organization, and as his or her career unfolds, the person probably will move across several different organizations. The point is simply that our everyday lives are inseparably intertwined with organizational memberships of one form or another.

What common characteristics unite these various activities under the collective label "organization"? The question is not an easy one to answer. Many different definitions of organization have

FIGURE 1-1 Inputs to organizations.

been suggested, and each definition reflects the background and theoretical point of view of its author with respect to what is relevant and/or important. Yet certain fundamental elements recur in these definitions.

In general, an organization is a collection of people working together in a division of labor to achieve a common purpose (Hitt, Miller, & Collela, 2009). Another useful concept views an organization as a system of inputs, throughputs, and outputs. Inputs (raw materials) are imported from the outside environment, transformed or modified (e.g., every day tons of steel are molded into automobile bodies), and finally exported or sold back into the environment as outputs (finished products). Although there are many inputs to organizations (energy, raw materials, information, etc.), people are the basic ingredients of *all* organizations, and social relationships are the cohesive bonds that tie them together (see Figure 1-1).

This book is about people as members and resources of organizations and about what applied psychology can contribute toward helping organizations make the wisest, most humane use of human resources. *Personnel psychology, a subfield of applied psychology, is concerned with individual differences in behavior and job performance and with methods for measuring and predicting such differences.* In the following sections, we will consider some of the sources of these differences.

Differences in Jobs

In examining the world of work, one is immediately awed by the vast array of goods and services that have been and are being produced as a result of organized effort. This great variety ranges from the manufacture of tangible products—such as food, automobiles, plastics, paper, textiles, and glassware—to the provision of less tangible services—such as legal counsel, health care, police and fire protection, and education. Thousands of jobs are part of our work-a-day world, and the variety of task and human requirements necessary to carry out this work is staggering. Faced with such variability in jobs and their requirements on the one hand, and with people and their individual patterns of values, aspirations, interests, and abilities on the other, programs for the efficient use of human resources are essential.

Differences in Performance

People represent substantial investments by firms—as is immediately evident when one stops to consider the costs of recruiting, selecting, placing, and training as many people as there are organizational roles to fill. But psychology's first law is that people are different. People differ in size, weight, and other physical dimensions, as well as in aptitudes, abilities, personality, interests, and a myriad of other psychological dimensions. People also differ greatly in the extent to which they are willing and able to commit their energies and resources to the attainment of organizational objectives.

If we observe a group of individuals doing the same kind of work, it will soon be evident that some are more effective workers than others. For example, if we observe a group of carpenters building cabinets, we will notice that some work faster than others, make fewer mistakes than others, and seem to enjoy their work more than others. These observations pose a question of psychological interest: Why? That is, what "people differences" cause these "work differences"? Perhaps these variations in effectiveness are due to differences in abilities. Some of the carpenters may be stronger, have keener eyesight, and have more finely developed motor coordination than others. Perhaps another reason for the observed differences in behavior is motivation. At any given point in time, the strength of forces impelling an individual to put forth effort on a given task, or to reach a certain goal, may vary drastically. In other words, differences in individual performance on any task, or on any job, could be due to differences in ability, or to differences in motivation, or to both. This has clear implications for the optimal use of individual talents in our society.

A Utopian Ideal

In an idealized existence, our goal would be to assess each individual's aptitudes, abilities, personality, and interests; to profile these characteristics; and then to place all individuals in jobs perfectly suited to them and to society. Each individual would make the best and wisest possible use of his or her talents, while in the aggregate, society would be making maximal use of its most precious resource.

Alas, this ideal falls far short in practice. The many, and often gross, mismatches between individual capabilities and organizational roles are glaringly obvious even to the most casual observer—history PhDs are driving taxicabs for lack of professional work, and young people full of enthusiasm, drive, and intelligence are placed in monotonous, routine, dead-end jobs.

Point of View

In any presentation of issues, it is useful to make explicit underlying assumptions. The following assumptions have influenced the presentation of this book:

1. In a free society, every individual, regardless of race, age, gender, disability, religion, national origin, or other characteristics, has a fundamental and inalienable right to compete for any job for which he or she is qualified.
2. Society can and should do a better job of making the wisest and most humane use of its human resources.
3. Individuals working in the field of human resources and managers responsible for making employment decisions must be as technically competent and well informed as possible, since their decisions will materially affect the course of individual livelihoods and lives. Personnel psychology holds considerable potential for improving the caliber of human resource management (HRM) in organizations. Several recent developments have combined to stimulate this growing awareness. After first describing what personnel psychology is, we will consider the nature of some of these developments.

PERSONNEL PSYCHOLOGY IN PERSPECTIVE

People have always been subjects of inquiry by psychologists, and the behavior of people at work has been the particular subject matter of industrial and organizational (I/O) psychology. Yet sciences and subdisciplines within sciences are distinguished not so much by the subject matter they study as by the questions they ask. Thus, both the social psychologist and the engineering psychologist are concerned with studying people. The engineering psychologist is concerned with the human aspects of the design of tools, machines, work spaces, information systems, and aspects of the work environment. The social psychologist studies power and influence, attitude change, communication in groups, and individual and group social behavior.

Personnel psychology is a subfield within I/O psychology. It is an applied discipline that focuses on individual differences in behavior and job performance and on methods of measuring and predicting such differences. Some of the major areas of interest to personnel psychologists include job analysis and job evaluation; recruitment, screening, and selection; training and development; and performance management.

Personnel psychology also represents the overlap between psychology and HRM. HRM is concerned with the management of staffing, retention, development, adjustment, and change in order to achieve both individual and organizational objectives (Cascio, 2010). As a subfield of HRM, personnel psychology excludes, for example, such topics as labor and compensation law, organization theory, industrial medicine, collective bargaining, and employee benefits. Psychologists have already made substantial contributions to the field of HRM; in fact, most of the empirical knowledge available in such areas as motivation, leadership, and staffing is due to their work. Over the past decade, dramatic changes in markets, technology, organizational designs, and the respective roles of managers and workers have inspired renewed emphasis on and interest in personnel psychology (Cascio, 2003a; 2008). The following sections consider each of these in more detail. Figure 1-2 illustrates them graphically.

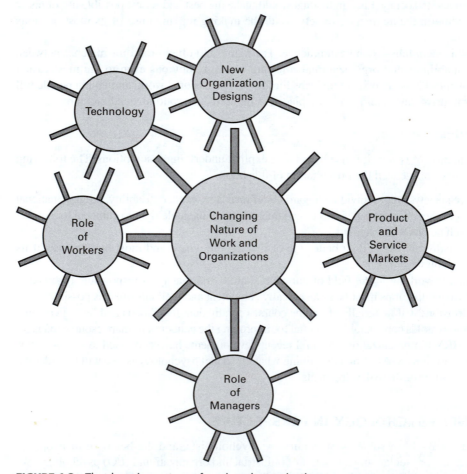

FIGURE 1-2   The changing nature of work and organizations.

The Changing Nature of Product and Service Markets

Globalization, a defining characteristic of economic life in the twenty-first century, refers to commerce without borders, along with the interdependence of business operations in different locations. Indeed, in a world where the transfer of capital, goods, and, increasingly, labor, occurs almost seamlessly, globalization is bringing tremendous changes, both positive and negative, for billions of people around the world. From just-in-time inventories to nanotechnologies, the pace of change is accelerating as a 24/7 culture pervades society. Product and service markets have truly become globalized.

To facilitate globalization, some films consider outsourcing. Genpact, Accenture, IBM Services, and similar big outsourcing specialists dispatch teams that meticulously dissect the workflow of an entire department—HR, finance, or information technology department. The team then helps build a new IT platform, redesigns all processes, and administers programs, acting as a virtual subsidiary. The contractor then disperses work among global networks of staff ranging from the United States, to Asia, to Eastern Europe (Engardio, 2006). Such structural changes have far-reaching consequences that are beneficial for the global economy but promise more frequent career changes for U.S. workers.

Against this backdrop, growing ethnic and regional tensions, coupled with the ever-present threat of terrorism, increase the chances of further geopolitical conflict. Nevertheless, economic interdependence among the world's countries will continue. Global corporations will continue to be created through mergers and acquisitions of unparalleled scope. These megacorporations will achieve immense economies of scale and compete for goods, capital, and labor on a global basis. As a result, prices will drop, and consumers will have more options than ever (Bhagwati, 2007).

The results of accelerated global competition have been almost beyond comprehension—free political debate throughout the former Soviet empire, democratic reforms in Central and South America, the integration of the European community, the North American Free Trade Agreement, and an explosion of free market entrepreneurship in southern China. In short, the free markets and free labor markets that the United States has enjoyed throughout its history have now become a global passion.

However, it takes more than trade agreements, technology, capital investment, and infrastructure to deliver world-class products and services. It also takes the skills, ingenuity, and creativity of a competent, well-trained workforce. Workers with the most advanced skills create higher-value products and services and reap the biggest rewards. Attracting, developing, and retaining talent in a culture that supports and nurtures ongoing learning is a continuing challenge for all organizations. Human resource professionals are at the epicenter of that effort.

IMPACT ON JOBS AND THE PSYCHOLOGICAL CONTRACT   The job churning that characterized the labor market in the 1990s and early twenty-first century has not let up. If anything, its pace has accelerated (Schwartz, 2009). Both white- and blue-collar jobs aren't being lost *temporarily* because of a recession; rather, they are being wiped out *permanently* as a result of new technology, improved machinery, and new ways of organizing work (Cascio, 2003b; Friedman, 2005, 2008). These changes have had, and will continue to have, dramatic effects on organizations and their people.

Corporate downsizing has become entrenched in American culture since the 1980s, but it was not always so. It was not until the final 20 years of the twentieth century that such downsizing and the loss of the perceived "psychological contract" of lifelong employment with a single employer in the public and private sectors of the economy came to characterize many corporate cultures and the American workforce (Cascio, 1993b, 2002). The psychological contract refers to an unwritten agreement in which the employee and employer develop expectations about their mutual relationship (Payne, Culbertson, & Boswell, 2008; Rousseau, 1995). For example, absent just cause, the employee expects not to be terminated involuntarily, and the employer expects the employee to perform to the best of his or her ability.

Stability and predictability characterized the old psychological contract. In the 1970s, for example, workers held an average of three to four jobs during their working lives. Change and uncertainty, however, are hallmarks of the new psychological contract. Soon workers will hold 7–10 jobs during their working lives. Job-hopping no longer holds the same stigma as it once did. Indeed, the massive downsizing of employees has made job mobility the norm, rather than the exception. This has led workers operating under the new psychological contract to expect more temporary employment relationships. Paternalism on the part of companies has given way to self-reliance on the part of employees, and also to a decrease in satisfaction, commitment, intentions to stay, and perceptions of an organization's trustworthiness, honesty, and concern for its employees (Lester, Kickul, Bergmann, & De Meuse, 2003; Osterman, 2009). Indeed, our views of hard work, loyalty, and managing as a career will probably never be the same.

Effects of Technology on Organizations and People

Millions of workers use networked computers every day, along with other products of the digital age, such as cellular phones, personal digital assistants, and e-mail. Anything digital is borderless, and, therefore, distance means nothing if you have a digital infrastructure (Grove, 2003). The digital revolution is breaking down departmental barriers, enhancing the sharing of vast amounts of information, creating "virtual offices" for workers on the go, collapsing product-development cycles, and changing the ways that organizations service customers and relate to their suppliers and to their employees (King, 2008). To succeed and prosper in a world where nothing is constant except the increasingly rapid pace of change, companies need motivated, technically literate workers who are willing to train continually.

There is also a dark side to new technology, as workers may be bombarded with mass junk e-mail (spam), company computer networks may be attacked by hackers who can wreak havoc on the ability of an organization to function, and employees' privacy may be compromised. One study estimated that an avalanche of spam may be costing companies as much as $874 a year per worker (Baker, 2003). Like other new developments, there are negatives as well as positives associated with new technology, and they need to be acknowledged.

A caveat is in order here, however. It relates to the common assumption that since production and service processes have become more sophisticated, high technology can substitute for skill in managing a workforce. Beware of such a "logic trap." On the contrary, as Lawler and O'Toole (2006) noted, "it takes extremely competent people . . . to create and deliver the complex services and products that are keys to success in the global economy . . . (organizations) need to develop systems and practices that attract, retain, and develop skilled, educated, and talented managers . . . (for) we are at the dawn of the Age of Human Capital" (p. 35). Ideally, therefore, technology will help workers make decisions in organizations that encourage them to do so (Ansberry, 2003b). However, organizations of the future will look very different from organizations of the past, as the next section illustrates.

Changes in the Structure and Design of Organizations

Many factors are driving change, but none is more important than the rise of Internet technologies. Like the steam engine or the assembly line, the Web has already become an advance with revolutionary consequences, most of which we have only begun to feel. The Web gives everyone in the organization, from the lowliest clerk to the chairman of the board, the ability to access a mind-boggling array of information—instantaneously from anywhere. Instead of seeping out over months or years, ideas can be zapped around the globe in the blink of an eye. That means that twenty-first-century organizations must adapt to management via the Web. They must be predicated on constant change, not stability; organized around networks, not rigid hierarchies; built on shifting partnerships and alliances, not self-sufficiency; and constructed on technological advantages, not bricks and mortar (Cascio, 2010). Twenty-first-century organizations are global in orientation, and all about speed. They are characterized by terms such as "virtual," "boundaryless," and "flexible," with no guarantees to workers or managers.

This approach to organizing is no short-term fad. The fact is that organizations are becoming leaner and leaner, with better and better trained "multispecialists"—those who have in-depth knowledge about a number of different aspects of the business. Eschewing narrow specialists or broad generalists, organizations of the future will come to rely on cross-trained multispecialists in order to get things done. One such group whose role is changing dramatically is that of managers.

The Changing Role of the Manager

In the traditional hierarchy that once made up most bureaucratic organizations, rules were simple. Managers ruled by *command* from the top (essentially one-way communication), used rigid *controls* to ensure that fragmented tasks (grouped into clearly defined jobs) could be coordinated effectively, and partitioned information into neat *compartments*—departments, units, and functions. Information was (and is) power, and, at least in some cases, managers clung to power by hoarding information. This approach to organizing—that is, 3-C logic—was geared to achieve three objectives: stability, predictability, and efficiency.

In today's reengineered, hypercompetitive work environment, the autocratic, top-down command-and-control approach is out of step with the competitive realities that many organizations face. To survive, organizations have to be able to respond quickly to shifting market conditions. In this kind of an environment, a key task for all managers, especially top managers, is to articulate a vision of what their organizations stand for, what they are trying to accomplish, and how they compete for business in the marketplace. Managers need to be able to explain and communicate how their organizations create value. The next step is to translate that value-creation story into everything that is done, including the implications for employee knowledge and behavior, and to use it as a benchmark to assess progress over time.

A large and growing number of organizations now recognize that they need to emphasize workplace democracy in order to achieve the vision. This involves breaking down barriers, sharing information, using a collaborative approach to problem solving, and orienting employees toward continuous learning and improvement. For many managers, these kinds of skills simply weren't needed in organizations designed and structured under 3-C logic.

Does this imply that we are moving toward a universal model of organizational and leadership effectiveness? Hardly. Contingency theories of leadership such as path-goal theory (House & Mitchell, 1974), normative decision theory (Vroom & Yetton, 1973), and LPC contingency theory (Fiedler, 1967) suggest that an autocratic style is appropriate in some situations. In recent years, many organizations (e.g., DuPont, Royal Dutch Shell) have instituted formal information-sharing and workplace-education programs that reduce or eliminate a key condition that makes autocratic leadership appropriate—workers who lack the information or knowledge needed to make meaningful suggestions or decisions. More often, today's networked, interdependent, culturally diverse organizations require transformational leadership (Avolio et al., 2003; Bass & Riggio, 2006). Leaders who are to transform followers to bring out their creativity, imagination, and best efforts require well-developed interpersonal skills, founded on an understanding of human behavior in organizations. Such strategic leadership is particularly effective under unstable or uncertain conditions (Colbert, Kristof-Brown, Bradley, & Barrick, 2008; Waldman et al., 2001). I/O psychologists are well positioned to help managers develop those kinds of skills.

In addition, although by no means universal, much of the work that results in a product, service, or decision is now done in teams—*intact, identifiable social systems (even if small or temporary) whose members have the authority to manage their own task and interpersonal processes as they carry out their work.* Such teams go by a variety of names—autonomous work groups, process teams, self-managing work teams, and so on (see Figure 1-3). All of this implies a radical reorientation from the traditional view of a manager's work.

FIGURE 1-3   Teams are now, and will continue to be, a key feature of organizations.

In this kind of an environment, workers are acting more like managers, and managers more like workers. The managerial roles of "controllers," "planners," and "inspectors" are being replaced by "coaches," "facilitators," and "mentors" (Srivastava, Bartol, & Locke, 2006; Wellins, Byham, & Wilson, 1991). This doesn't just happen—it requires good interpersonal skills, continuous learning, and an organizational culture that supports and encourages both.

Flattened hierarchies also mean that there are fewer managers in the first place. The empowered worker will be a defining feature of such organizations.

The Empowered Worker—No Passing Fad

It should be clear by now that we are in the midst of a revolution—a revolution at work. Change isn't coming only from large, high-profile companies doing high-technology work. It has also permeated unglamorous, low-tech work. As an example, consider Cincinnati-based Cintas Corporation (Box 1-1), which outfits the employees of some of North America's leading corporations (Cintas Corporation, 2009; Henkoff, 1994; Siehl & Hessell, 1999).

Twenty-first-century organizations, both large and small, differ dramatically in structure, design, and demographics from those of even a decade ago. Demographically, they are far more diverse. They comprise more women at all levels; more multiethnic, multicultural workers; older workers; more workers with disabilities; robots; and contingent workers. Paternalism is out; self-reliance is in. There is constant pressure to do more with less and a steady emphasis on

---

BOX 1-1

HRM in Action—Cintas Corporation

Cintas doesn't just hire people to drive trucks, deliver clean uniforms, and pick up dirty ones. Rather, its concept of "customer service representatives" (CSRs) extends much further. They are mini-entrepreneurs who design their own routes, manage their own accounts, and, to a large extent, determine the size of their paychecks.

Cintas ties compensation almost entirely to measures of customer satisfaction. Lose a customer on your watch and your salary sinks. CSR pay is nearly twice the industry average. In practice, Cintas rarely loses a customer; its annual defection rate is less than 1 percent. Employees don't leave either; turnover is a low 7 percent. To a large extent, this is because Cintas spends considerable time and effort on selecting employees—those who take pride in their work and are exceedingly neat and outgoing. In all, 46 different ethnic groups are represented at Cintas, and its company culture is built on a foundation of high ethical standards, trust, and cooperation.

Cintas is the world's largest supplier of corporate-identity uniforms, with more than 800,000 clients. In addition, it provides a broad range of business solutions, including facility, document-management, and fire-protection services. As of 2009, *Fortune* magazine named Cintas as one of "World's Most Admired Companies." Said CEO Scott Farmer, "Our achievement as a company is testament to the achievement of our Cintas employee-partners who represent our company in the plant and in the field. All are focused on our principal objective: 'We will exceed our customers' expectations to maximize the long-term value of Cintas for its shareholders and working partners.'"

How has Cintas done? Sales and profits have increased for 39 consecutive years. In a gesture that reflects its strong culture, Cintas has shared more than $176 million with its employee-partners over the past decade.

---

empowerment, cross-training, personal flexibility, self-managed work teams, and continuous learning. Workers today have to be able to adapt to changing circumstances and to be prepared for multiple careers. I/O psychologists are helping to educate prospective, current, and former workers to these new realities. In the future, they will be expected to do much more, as we shall see, but first let's consider some organizational responses to these new realities.

Implications for Organizations and Their People

What do these trends imply for the ways that organizations will compete for business? In a world where virtually every factor that affects the production of goods or the delivery of services—capital, equipment, technology, and information—is available to every player in the global economy, the one factor that doesn't routinely move across national borders is a nation's workforce. Today the quality of a nation's workforce is a crucial determinant of its ability to compete and win in world markets.

Human resources can be sources of sustained competitive advantage as long as they meet three basic requirements: (1) They add positive economic benefits to the process of producing goods or delivering services; (2) the skills of the workforce are distinguishable from those of competitors (e.g., through education and workplace learning); and (3) such skills are not easily duplicated (Barney, 1991). A human resource system (the set of interrelated processes designed to attract, develop, and maintain human resources) can either enhance or destroy this potential competitive advantage (Lado & Wilson, 1994).

Perhaps a quote attributed to Albert Einstein, the famous physicist, best captures the position of this book. After the first atomic reaction in 1942, Einstein remarked: "Everything has changed, except our way of thinking" (*Workplace*, 1993, p. 2). As I/O psychology in general, and personnel psychology in particular, moves forward into the twenty-first century, our greatest challenge will be to change the way we think about organizations and their people. The remainder of this book will help you do that.

Trends such as these have intensified the demand for comprehensive training policies that focus training efforts on organizational needs three to five years out. Here's an example: Accenture puts 400 of its most promising managers through a special leadership development program. They are assigned to groups that can include Irish, Chinese, Belgians, and Filipinos, and specialists in fields such as finance, marketing, and technology. Over 10 months, teams meet in different international locations. As part of the program, they pick a project—developing a new Web page, say—and learn how to tap the company's worldwide talent pool to complete it (Engardio, 2007). None of this is simple or easily done, and it may take several years to become fully integrated into a business.

From the perspective of employees, programs like these are especially valuable because *job* security (the belief that one will retain employment with the same organization until retirement) has become less important to workers than *employment* security (having the kinds of skills that employers in the labor market are willing to pay for). Demographic changes in society are making recruitment and staffing top priorities for many organizations. Diversity at work is a major theme as the composition of the workforce changes. Consider, for example, that more than half of the U.S. workforce now consists of racial and ethnic minorities, immigrants, and women. White, native-born males, though still dominant, are themselves a statistical minority. The so-called mainstream is now almost as diverse as the society at large. In short, a diverse workforce is not something a company *ought* to have; it's something all companies do have or soon will have.

In addition to demographic changes, we are witnessing sweeping changes in the nature of work and its impact on workers and society. The following potential problems could surface (Colvin, 2003; Engardio, 2007; Howard, 1995):

- *Insecurity*—ongoing employment downsizing; "offshoring" of skilled jobs in services, such as financial analysis, software design, and tax preparation.
- *Uncertainty*—constant change, multiple reporting relationships, inability to forecast the future.
- *Stress*—competing demands, long work hours, exhaustion, lack of separation between work and nonwork activities, global competition.
- *Social friction*—two-tiered society, sharp differences in opportunities based on ability, insufficient work for the low skilled.

On the other hand, work could provide the following compensations:

- *Challenge*—endless opportunities for stretching, growing, developing skills, keeping interested.
- *Creativity*—opportunities to generate novel solutions to emerging problems, self-expression.
- *Flexibility*—individualized careers and person–organization contracts, personal time and space arrangements, multiple careers.
- *Control*—empowerment, responsibility for making decisions and directing one's life.
- *Interrelatedness*—global communication and "virtual connectedness," group and team collaboration, end of isolation.

The future world of work will not be a place for the timid, the insecure, or the low skilled. For those who thrive on challenge, responsibility, and risk taking, security will come from seizing opportunities to adapt and to develop new competencies (Gunz & Peiperl, 2007; Hall & Mirvis, 1995). The need for competent HR professionals with broad training in a variety of areas has never been greater.

PLAN OF THE BOOK

In Chapter 2, we will explore a pivotal issue in HRM today: legal requirements for fair employment practice. In particular, we will emphasize the constitutional basis for civil rights legislation and the judicial interpretation of Title VII of the 1964 Civil Rights Act. The remainder of the book will focus in greater depth on some of the major issues in contemporary personnel psychology.

Each chapter will outline the nature of the topic under consideration, survey past practice and research findings, describe present issues and procedures, and, where relevant, indicate future trends and new directions for research.

The goal of Chapters 3 through 5 is to provide the reader with a strategy for viewing the employment-decision process and an appreciation of the problems associated with assessing its outcomes. Chapter 3 presents an integrative model in which the major areas of personnel psychology are seen as a network of sequential, interdependent decisions. The model will then provide a structure for the rest of the book, as well as a conceptual framework from which to view the complex process of matching individuals and jobs.

In Chapter 4, we will focus on one of the most persistent and critical problems in the field of personnel psychology, that of developing and applying adequate performance criteria. A thorough understanding and appreciation of the criterion problem is essential, for it is relevant to all other areas of HRM, especially to performance management.

In Chapter 5, we will examine current methods, issues, and problems associated with the performance-management process, of which performance appraisal is a key component. The objective of performance management is to improve performance at the level of the individual or team every day.

The first part of the book presents fundamental concepts in applied measurement that underlie all employment decisions. Chapters 6 and 7 represent the core of personnel psychology—measurement and validation of individual differences. After comparing and contrasting physical and psychological measurement, we will consider the requirements of good measurement (reliability and validity) and the practical interpretation and evaluation of measurement procedures. As a capstone to this part of the text, Chapter 8 is devoted entirely to a consideration of the issue of fairness in employment decisions. Taken together, Chapters 2 through 8 provide a sound basis for a fuller appreciation of the topics covered in the remainder of the book.

In order to provide a job-relevant basis for employment decisions, information on jobs, work, and workforce planning is essential. This is the purpose of Chapters 9 and 10. In Chapter 9, we will examine job analysis (the study of the work to be done, the skills needed, and the training required of the individual jobholder). It is the touchstone for all employment decisions. In Chapter 10, we will consider the emerging area of workforce planning. The goal of a workforce-planning system is to anticipate future staffing requirements of an organization and, based on an inventory of present employees, to establish action programs (e.g., in recruitment, training, and career path planning) to prepare individuals for future jobs. The emphasis of the chapter will be on tying current workforce-planning theory to practice.

Chapters 11 through 14 are concerned with staffing—specifically, recruitment and selection. In Chapter 11, we consider the theoretical and practical aspects of recruitment, emphasizing both traditional and Web-based strategies. Chapter 12 is the first of two chapters on selection methods. Its particular focus is on nontest techniques such as personal-history data and employment interviews. Chapter 13 is the second chapter on selection methods, with particular emphasis on managerial selection. Chapter 14 demonstrates how material from the previous three chapters can be integrated into alternative strategies for making selection decisions.

Chapters 15 and 16 focus on the design, implementation, and evaluation of training and development activities for individuals and teams, colocated as well as virtual. These topics have drawn special attention in HRM, especially in light of the need to develop skills continually in a dynamic business environment. We consider these issues with the conviction that a considerable reservoir of human potential for productivity improvement, among managers as well as nonmanagers, remains to be tapped.

The last part of the book comprises Chapters 17 and 18. Chapter 17, "International Dimensions of Applied Psychology," reflects the increasing role of globalization. Globalization

Evidence-Based Implications for Practice

Organizations are all around us, but over time how we think about them has changed dramatically. Consider just a few such changes.

- Product and service markets are global, 24/7/365. New, Internet-based organizations are "born global," and labor markets in every region of the world now compete against each other for foreign direct investment. The result: globally dispersed workforces.
- The influence of factors such as technology, notably digitization and the Internet, has changed the work and personal lives of millions of people.
- Given the massive downsizing that has occurred worldwide in the past few years, the stability and predictability of the old psychological contract have given way to uncertainty, change, and the need for self-reliance.
- The ability to work in teams is more important than ever, but those teams may be spread geographically all over the world. Diversity has been woven into the very fabric of workplaces everywhere, spawning the need for information sharing, tolerance, and cultural understanding in order to prosper.

implies more, not less, contact with cultures other than one's own. Personnel psychology has much to contribute, from identifying international management potential early on to selecting, training, developing, and managing the careers of expatriates.

Finally, Chapter 18 addresses a variety of organizational responsibility and ethical issues in HRM. Corporate scandals, including those associated with Enron, Siemens, Worldcom, and Tyco, just to name a few, have called public attention to the crisis in ethics at all levels of organizations (Byrne, 2002; Crawford & Esterl, 2007; Dougherty, 2008). While there are no easy answers to many ethical questions, public discussion of them is essential if genuine progress is to be made. Moreover, HR departments are primary resources for ethical policies. Now that we have considered the "big picture," let us begin our treatment in Chapter 2 by examining the legal environment within which employment decisions are made.

Discussion Questions

1. Why is employment security more important to most workers than job security?
2. How have globalized product and service markets affected organizations and workers?
3. Discuss some of the changes that have occurred in the perceptions that workers and organizations have about each other in light of the massive downsizing that has taken place during the past decade.
4. How does information technology change the roles of managers and workers?
5. Describe some potential problems and opportunities presented by the changing nature of work.

2

The Law and Human Resource Management

At a Glance

Comprehensive employment-related legislation, combined with increased motivation on the part of individuals to rectify unfair employment practices, makes the legal aspects of employment one of the most dominant issues in HRM today. All three branches of the federal government have been actively involved in ongoing efforts to guarantee equal employment opportunity as a fundamental individual right, regardless of race, color, age, gender, religion, national origin, or disability.

All aspects of the employment relationship, including initial screening, recruitment, selection, placement, compensation, training, promotion, and performance management, have been addressed by legislative and executive pronouncements and by legal interpretations from the courts. With growing regularity, I/O psychologists and HR professionals are being called on to work with attorneys, the courts, and federal regulatory agencies. It is imperative, therefore, to understand thoroughly the rights as well as obligations of individuals and employers under the law and to ensure that these are translated into everyday practice in accordance with legal guidelines promulgated by federal regulatory agencies. Affirmative action as a matter of public policy has become a fact of modern organizational life. To ignore it is to risk serious economic, human, and social costs.

Every public opinion poll based on representative national samples drawn between 1950 and the present shows that a majority of Americans—black, brown, and white—support EEO and reject differential treatment based on race, regardless of its alleged purposes or results. There is agreement about the ends to be achieved, but there is disagreement about the means to be used (Von Drehle, 2003). EEO has been, and is still, an emotionally charged issue. Congress has provided sound legal bases for effecting changes in EEO through sweeping civil rights legislation. Subsequently, thousands of dissatisfied groups and individuals have won substantial redress on many issues by availing themselves of their legal rights. The combination of the motivation to rectify perceived inequities and an easily available legal framework for doing so has made the legal aspects of the employment relationship a dominant issue in HRM today.

It is imperative, therefore, that I/O psychologists and HR professionals understand the rights and obligations of individuals and employers in this most delicate area. They must be able to work with attorneys (and vice versa), for neither can succeed alone. Each group has a great deal to contribute in order to identify vulnerable employment policies and practices, to make required adjustments in them, and thus to minimize the likelihood of time-consuming and expensive litigation. Let us begin, therefore, with an overview of the legal system, legal terminology, important laws and court decisions, and underlying legal and scientific issues.

THE LEGAL SYSTEM

Above the complicated network of local, state, and federal laws, the United States Constitution stands as the supreme law of the land. Certain powers and limitations are prescribed to the federal government by the Constitution; those powers not given to the federal government are considered to be reserved for the states. The states, in turn, have their own constitutions that are subject to, and must remain consistent with, the U.S. Constitution.

While certain activities are regulated exclusively by the federal government (e.g., interstate commerce), other areas are subject to concurrent regulation by federal and state governments (e.g., equal employment opportunity). It should be emphasized, however, that in the event of a conflict between a state law and the U.S. Constitution (or the laws enacted by Congress in accordance with it), the federal requirements take precedence. Thus, any state or local law that violates the Constitution or federal law is, in effect, unconstitutional. Therefore, it is no defense to argue that one is acting according to such a state or local law.

The legislative branch of government (Congress) enacts laws, called **statutes**, which are considered primary authority. Court decisions and the decisions and guidelines of regulatory agencies are not laws, but interpretations of laws for given situations in which the law is not specific. Nevertheless, these interpretations form a complex fabric of legal opinion and precedent that must be given great deference by the public.

Let us consider the judicial system, one of the three main branches of government (along with the executive and legislative branches), more closely. The judicial power of the United States is vested "in one Supreme Court and in such inferior courts as Congress may from time to time ordain and establish" according to Article III of the Constitution. The system of "inferior" (i.e., lower) courts includes the U.S. District Courts, the federal trial courts in each state. These courts hear cases that fall under federal jurisdiction, usually either cases between citizens of different states or cases relevant to the Constitution or federal law.

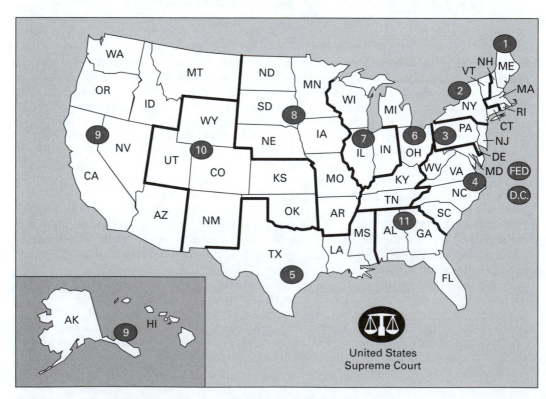

FIGURE 2-1   The system of federal appellate courts in the United States.

Decisions of these lower federal courts may be appealed to 1 of 12 U.S. Courts of Appeals, corresponding to the geographical region or "circuit" in which the case arose (see Figure 2-1). In turn, these courts' decisions may be appealed to the U.S. Supreme Court—not as a matter of right, but only when the Supreme Court feels that the case warrants a decision at the highest level. Generally the Supreme Court will grant **certiorari** (review) when two or more circuit courts have reached different conclusions on the same point of law or when a major question of constitutional interpretation is involved. If the Supreme Court denies a petition for a **writ of certiorari**, then the lower court's decision is binding.

The state court structure parallels the federal court structure, with state district courts at the lowest level, followed by state appellate (review) courts, and finally by a state supreme court. State supreme court decisions may be reviewed by the U.S. Supreme Court where a question of federal law is involved or where the judicial power of the United States extends as defined by the U.S. Constitution. In all other instances, the state supreme court decision is final.

Equal Employment Opportunity (EEO) complaints may take any one of several alternative routes (see Figure 2-2). By far the simplest and least costly alternative is to arrive at an informal,

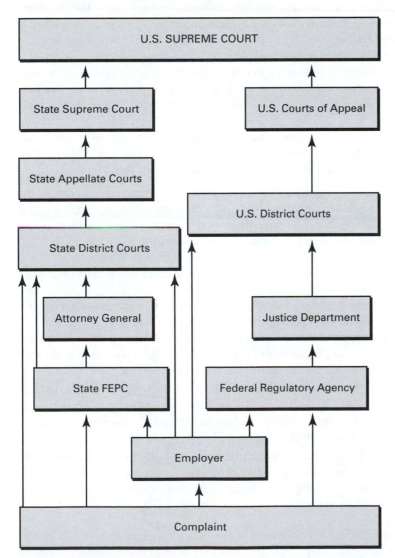

FIGURE 2-2 Possible legal routes for complaints against an employer's employment practices.
Source: Seberhagen, L. W., McCollum, M. D., & Churchill, C. D. (1972). Legal aspects of personnel selection in the public service. International Personnel Mgmt Assoc.

out-of-court settlement with the employer. Often, however, the employer does not have an established mechanism for dealing with such problems. Or, if such a mechanism does exist, employees or other complainants are unaware of it or are not encouraged to use it. So the complainant must choose more formal legal means, such as contacting state and local fair employment-practice commissions (where they exist), federal regulatory agencies (e.g., Equal Employment Opportunity Commission or the Office of Federal Contract Compliance Programs), or the federal and state district courts. At this stage, however, solutions become time consuming and expensive. Litigation is a luxury that few can afford. Perhaps the wisest course of action an employer can take is to establish a sound internal complaint system to deal with problems before they escalate to formal legal proceedings.

UNFAIR DISCRIMINATION: WHAT IS IT?

No law has ever attempted to define precisely the term *discrimination*. However, in the employment context, it can be viewed broadly as the giving of an unfair advantage (or disadvantage) to the members of a particular group in comparison to the members of other groups. The disadvantage usually results in a denial or restriction of employment opportunities or in an inequality in the terms or benefits of employment.

It is important to note that whenever there are more candidates than available positions, it is necessary to select some candidates in preference to others. Selection implies exclusion. As long as the exclusion is based on what can be demonstrated to be job-related criteria, however, that kind of discrimination is entirely proper. It is only when candidates are excluded on a prohibited basis not related to the job (e.g., age, race, gender, or disability) that unlawful and unfair discrimination exists. Despite federal and state laws on these issues, they represent the basis of an enormous volume of court cases, indicating that stereotypes and prejudices do not die quickly or easily. Discrimination is a subtle and complex phenomenon that may assume two broad forms:

1. *Unequal (disparate) treatment* is based on an *intention to discriminate*, including the intention to *retaliate* against a person who opposes discrimination, who has brought charges, or who has participated in an investigation or hearing. There are three major subtheories of discrimination within the disparate-treatment theory:

    1. Cases that rely on *direct evidence* of the intention to discriminate. Such cases are proven with direct evidence of
       • Pure bias based on an open expression of hatred, disrespect, or inequality, knowingly directed against members of a particular group.
       • Blanket exclusionary policies—for example, deliberate exclusion of an individual whose disability (e.g., an impairment of her ability to walk) has nothing to do with the requirements of the job she is applying for (financial analyst).
    2. Cases that are proved through *circumstantial evidence* of the intention to discriminate (see *Schwager v. Sun Oil Co. of Pa.*, p. 34), including those that rely on statistical evidence as a method of circumstantially proving the intention to discriminate systematically against classes of individuals.
    3. *Mixed-motive* cases (a hybrid theory) that often rely on both direct evidence of the intention to discriminate on some impermissible basis (e.g., sex, race, or disability) and proof that the employer's stated legitimate basis for its employment decision is actually just a pretext for illegal discrimination.

2. *Adverse impact (unintentional) discrimination* occurs when identical standards or procedures are applied to everyone, despite the fact that they lead to a substantial difference in employment outcomes (e.g., selection, promotion, and layoffs) for the members of a

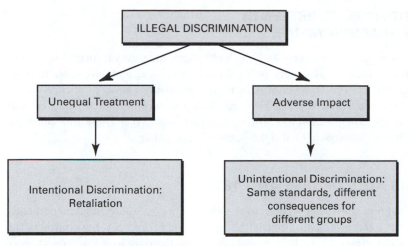

FIGURE 2-3   Major forms of illegal discrimination.

particular group *and* they are unrelated to success on a job. For example: use of a minimum height requirement of 5' 8" for police cadets. This requirement would have an adverse impact on Asians, Hispanics, and women. The policy is neutral on its face, but has an adverse impact. To use it, an employer would need to show that applicants must meet the height requirement in order to be able to perform the job.

These two forms of illegal discrimination are illustrated graphically in Figure 2-3.

LEGAL FRAMEWORK FOR CIVIL RIGHTS REQUIREMENTS

Employers in the public and private sectors, employment agencies, unions, and joint labor–management committees controlling apprentice programs are subject to the various nondiscrimination **laws**. Government contractors and subcontractors are subject to **executive orders**. Many business organizations are employers as well as government contractors and, therefore, are directly subject *both* to nondiscrimination laws and to executive orders. While it is beyond the scope of this chapter to analyze all the legal requirements pertaining to EEO, HR professionals should at least understand the major legal principles as articulated in the following laws of broad scope:

- The U.S. Constitution—Thirteenth and Fourteenth Amendments
- The Civil Rights Acts of 1866 and 1871
- The Equal Pay Act of 1963
- Title VII of the Civil Rights Act of 1964 (as amended by the Equal Employment Opportunity Act of 1972)
- The Age Discrimination in Employment Act of 1967 (as amended in 1986)
- The Immigration Reform and Control Act of 1986
- The Americans with Disabilities Act of 1990
- The Civil Rights Act of 1991
- The Family and Medical Leave Act of 1993

In addition, there are laws of limited application:

- Executive Orders 11246, 11375, and 11478
- The Rehabilitation Act of 1973
- Vietnam Era Veterans Readjustment Act of 1974
- The Uniformed Services Employment and Reemployment Rights Act of 1994

THE U.S. CONSTITUTION—THIRTEENTH AND FOURTEENTH AMENDMENTS

The Thirteenth Amendment prohibits slavery and involuntary servitude. Any form of discrimination may be considered an incident of slavery or involuntary servitude, and thus liable to legal action under this Amendment. The Fourteenth Amendment guarantees equal protection of the law for all citizens. Both the Thirteenth and Fourteenth Amendments granted Congress the constitutional power to enact legislation to enforce their provisions. It is from this source of constitutional power that all subsequent civil rights legislation originates.

THE CIVIL RIGHTS ACTS OF 1866 AND 1871

These laws were enacted based on the provisions of the Thirteenth and Fourteenth Amendments. The Civil Rights Act of 1866 grants all citizens the right to make and enforce contracts for employment, and the Civil Rights Act of 1871 grants all citizens the right to sue in federal court if they feel they have been deprived of any rights or privileges guaranteed by the Constitution and laws. It applies only to "persons within the jurisdiction of the United States," and does not extend to discriminatory conduct occurring overseas (Peikes & Mitchell, 2006).

Until recently, both of these laws were viewed narrowly as tools for Reconstruction era racial problems. This is no longer so. In *Johnson v. Railway Express Agency* (1975), the Supreme Court held that while Section 1981 of the Civil Rights Act of 1866 on its face relates primarily to racial discrimination in the making and enforcement of contracts, it also provides a federal remedy against discrimination in private employment on the basis of race. It is a powerful remedy. The Civil Rights Act of 1991 amended the Civil Rights Act of 1866 so that workers are protected from intentional discrimination in *all* aspects of employment, not just hiring and promotion. The Civil Rights Act of 1866 allows for jury trials and for compensatory and punitive damages[1] for victims of *intentional* racial and ethnic discrimination, and it covers both large and small employers, even those with fewer than 15 employees. A recent Supreme Court decision also permits employees to sue for retaliation under this law (Smith, 2008).

The 1866 law also has been used to broaden the definition of racial discrimination originally applied to African Americans. In a unanimous decision, the Supreme Court ruled in 1987 that race was equated with ethnicity during the legislative debate after the Civil War, and, therefore, Arabs, Jews, and other ethnic groups thought of as "white" are not barred from suing under the 1866 law. The Court held that Congress intended to protect identifiable classes of persons who are subjected to intentional discrimination solely because of their ancestry or ethnic characteristics. Under the law, therefore, race involves more than just skin pigment ("Civil Rights," 1987).

EQUAL PAY FOR EQUAL WORK REGARDLESS OF SEX

Equal Pay Act of 1963

This Act was passed as an amendment to the Fair Labor Standards Act (FLSA) of 1938. For those employers already subject to the FLSA, the Equal Pay Act requires that men and women working for the same establishment be paid the same rate of pay for work that is substantially equal in skill, effort, responsibility, and working conditions. Pay differentials are legal and appropriate if they

---

[1] Punitive damages are awarded in civil cases to punish or deter a defendant's conduct. They are separate from compensatory damages, which are intended to reimburse a plaintiff for injuries or harm.

are based on seniority, merit, systems that measure the quality or quantity of work, or any factor other than sex (e.g., shift differentials, completion of a job-related training program).

The Equal Employment Opportunity Commission (EEOC) administers the Equal Pay Act, the first in a series of federal civil-rights laws passed during the 1960s. Wages withheld in violation of its provisions are viewed as unpaid minimum wages or unpaid overtime compensation under the FLSA. The EEOC receives about 1,000 equal-pay complaints per year, and, in 2008, it won $9.6 million for aggrieved individuals, excluding monetary benefits obtained through litigation (EEOC, 2009a). For individual companies, the price can be quite high, because in correcting any inequity under the Act, a company must ordinarily raise the lower rate. For example, in 2005 Morgan Stanley settled a sex-discrimination lawsuit filed by the EEOC for $54 million (Stites, 2005).

Equal Pay for Jobs of Comparable Worth

When women dominate an occupational field (such as nursing or secretarial work), the rate of pay for jobs in that field tends to be lower than the pay that men receive when they are the dominant incumbents (e.g., in construction or skilled trades). Is the market biased against jobs held mostly by women? Should jobs dominated by women and jobs dominated by men be paid equally if they are of "comparable" worth to an employer? Answering the latter question involves the knotty problem of how to make valid and accurate comparisons of the relative worth of unlike jobs. The key difference between the Equal Pay Act and the comparable worth standard is this: The Equal Pay Act requires equal pay for men and women who do work that is *substantially equal*. Comparable worth would require equal pay for work of *equal value* to an employer (e.g., librarian and electrician).

The crux of the issue is this: Are women underpaid for their work, or do they merely hold those jobs that are worth relatively less? Existing federal laws do not support the comparable-worth standard. However, several states and cities have enacted laws that require a comparable-worth standard for public employees (Milkovich & Newman, 2008).

The ultimate resolution of the comparable-worth controversy remains to be seen, but there is an inescapable irony to the whole episode: The Equal Pay Act was passed for the express purpose of eliminating gender as a basis for the payment of wages. Comparable worth, by its very nature, *requires* that some jobs be labeled "male" and others "female." In so doing, it makes gender the fundamental consideration in the payment of wages.

Is it possible that the goals of comparable worth can be accomplished through normal labor-market processes? Court decisions to date imply that pay differentials between dissimilar jobs will not be prohibited if the differences can be shown to be based on the content of the work, the value of that work to organizational objectives, and the employer's ability to attract and retain employees in competitive external labor markets (Milkovich & Newman, 2008). In short, the appropriate response is to remove the barriers to equal pay for equal work, not to abolish supply and demand.

EQUAL EMPLOYMENT OPPORTUNITY

Title VII of the Civil Rights Act of 1964

The Civil Rights Act of 1964 is divided into several sections or titles, each dealing with a particular facet of discrimination (e.g., voting rights, public accommodations, and public education). For our purposes, Title VII is particularly relevant.

Title VII (as amended by the Equal Employment Opportunity Act of 1972) has been the principal body of federal legislation in the area of fair employment. It established the EEOC to ensure compliance with the law by employers, employment agencies, and labor organizations. We will consider the organization and operation of the EEOC in greater detail in a later section.

Nondiscrimination on the Basis of Race, Color, Religion, Sex, or National Origin

Employers are bound by the provisions of Section 703(a) of Title VII as amended, which states:

> It shall be an unlawful employment practice for an employer—(1) to fail or to refuse to hire or to discharge any individual or otherwise to discriminate against any individual with respect to his compensation, terms, conditions, or privileges of employment, because of such individual's race, color, religion, sex, or national origin; or (2) to limit, segregate, or classify his employees or applicants for employment in any way which would deprive or tend to deprive any individual of employment opportunities or otherwise adversely affect his status as an employee, because of such individual's race, color, religion, sex, or national origin.

Note that race and color are not synonymous. Under federal law discriminating against people because of the shade of their skin—so-called intrarace or appearance discrimination—is distinct from, but just as illegal as, racial discrimination. For example, whites can be guilty of color discrimination, but not racial discrimination, if they favor hiring light-skinned over dark-skinned blacks. This issue is growing in importance as the sheer number of racial blends increases (Valbrun, 2003).

Apprenticeship Programs, Retaliation, and Employment Advertising

Section 703(b) of Title VII states:

> It shall be an unlawful employment practice for any employer, labor organization, or joint labor-management committee controlling apprenticeship or other training or retraining, including on-the-job training programs, to discriminate against any individual because of his race, color, religion, sex, or national origin in admission to, or employment in, any program established to provide apprenticeship or other training.

A further provision of Title VII, Section 704(a), prohibits discrimination against an employee or applicant because he or she has opposed an unlawful employment practice or made a charge, testified, assisted, or participated in a Title VII investigation, proceeding, or hearing. Finally, Section 704(b) prohibits notices or advertisements relating to employment from indicating any preference, limitation, specification, or discrimination on any of the prohibited factors unless it is in relation to a bona fide occupational qualification (see p. 21).

Prior to 1972, Title VII was primarily aimed at private employers with 25 or more employees, labor organizations with 25 or more members, and private employment agencies. In 1973, the Equal Employment Opportunity Act expanded this coverage to public and private employers (including state and local governments and public and private educational institutions) with 15 or more employees, labor organizations with 15 or more members, and both public and private employment agencies. These amendments provide broad coverage under Title VII, with the following exceptions: (1) private clubs, (2) places of employment connected with an Indian reservation, and (3) religious organizations (which are allowed to discriminate because of religion) [Title VII, Sections 701(a), 702, and 703(i)]. The U.S. Office of Personnel Management and the Merit Systems Protection Board, rather than the EEOC, monitor nondiscrimination and affirmative action programs of the federal government. Affirmative action involves a proactive examination of whether equality of opportunity exists. If it does not, a plan is implemented for taking concrete measures to eliminate the barriers and to establish true equality (Crosby, Iyer, Clayton, & Downing, 2003).

Suspension of Government Contracts and Back-Pay Awards

Two other provisions of the 1972 law are noteworthy. First, denial, termination, or suspension of government contracts is proscribed (without a special hearing) if an employer has and is following an affirmative action plan accepted by the federal government for the same facility within the past 12 months. Second, back-pay awards in Title VII cases are limited to two years *prior to the filing of a charge*. Thus, if a woman filed a Title VII charge in 2004, but the matter continued through investigation, conciliation, trial, and appeal until 2008, she might be entitled to as much as six years of back pay, from 2002 (two years prior to the filing of her charge) to 2008 (assuming the matter was resolved in her favor).

In addition to its basic objective of protecting various minority groups against discrimination in employment, Title VII extends the prohibition against sex discrimination to all aspects of the employment relationship. At the same time, several specific exemptions to the provisions of Title VII were written into the law itself. Among these are the following.

Bona Fide Occupational Qualifications

Classification or discrimination in employment according to race, religion, sex, or national origin is permissible when such qualification is a bona fide occupational qualification "reasonably necessary to the operation of that particular business or enterprise." The burden of proof rests with the employer to demonstrate this, and, as we shall see, the courts interpret Bona Fide Occupational Qualifications (BFOQs) quite narrowly (Thompson, 2008). Preferences of the employer, coworkers, or clients are irrelevant, and BFOQ is not a viable defense to a race claim under Title VII.

Seniority Systems

Bona fide seniority or merit systems and incentive pay systems are lawful "provided that such differences are not the result of an intention to discriminate."

Preemployment Inquiries

Such inquiries—for example, regarding sex and race—are permissible as long as they are not used as bases for discrimination. In addition, certain inquiries are necessary to meet the reporting requirements of the federal regulatory agencies and to ensure compliance with the law. Applicants provide this information on a voluntary basis.

Testing

An employer may give or act on any professionally developed ability test, provided the test is not used as a vehicle to discriminate on the basis of race, color, religion, sex, or national origin. We will examine this issue in greater detail in a later section.

Preferential Treatment

It is unlawful to interpret Title VII as requiring the granting of preferential treatment to individuals or groups because of their race, color, religion, sex, or national origin on account of existing imbalances. Such imbalances may exist with respect to differences between the total number or percentage of similar persons employed by an employer, or admitted to or employed in any training or apprenticeship program, and the total number or percentage of such persons in any geographical area or in the available workforce in any geographical area (see *Wards Cove Packing v. Antonio*, 1989).

Veterans Preference Rights

These are not repealed or modified in any way by Title VII. In a 1979 ruling (*Personnel Administrator of Massachusetts v. Feeney*, 1979), the Supreme Court held that while veterans

FIGURE 2-4   The six exemptions to Title VII coverage.

preference rights do have an adverse impact on women's job opportunities, this is not caused by an *intent* to discriminate against women. Both male and female veterans receive the same preferential treatment, and male nonveterans are at the same disadvantage as female nonveterans.

National Security

When it is deemed necessary to protect the national security, discrimination (e.g., against members of the Communist Party) is permitted under Title VII.

These exemptions are summarized in Figure 2-4. Initially it appeared that these exemptions would significantly blunt the overall impact of the law. However, it soon became clear that they would be interpreted very narrowly both by the EEOC and by the courts.

AGE DISCRIMINATION IN EMPLOYMENT ACT OF 1967

Just as Title VII prohibits discrimination in employment on the basis of race, color, sex, religion, or national origin, the Age Discrimination in Employment Act (ADEA) requires employers to provide EEO on the basis of age. As amended in 1986, the ADEA specifically proscribes discrimination on the basis of age for employees age 40 and over unless the employer can demonstrate that age is a BFOQ for the job in question. If a company claims that the layoffs were based on factors other than age, such as performance criteria or needed skills, the Supreme Court has ruled that the employer bears the burden of proving that its policy was, in fact, based on those nonage factors (Biskupic, 2008). This law is administered by the EEOC; in 2008 the agency won $82.8 million for aggrieved individuals, excluding monetary benefits obtained through litigation (EEOC, 2009b).

A key objective of this law is to prevent financially troubled companies from singling out older employees when there are cutbacks. However, the EEOC has ruled that when there are cutbacks, older employees can waive their rights to sue under this law (e.g., in return for sweetened benefits for early retirement). Under the Older Workers Benefit Protection Act, an individual employee who does not have a pending claim has 21 days to consider such a waiver (45 days if terminated during a group reduction in force or if leaving voluntarily through a group incentive program), and seven days after signing to revoke it. On the other hand, courts have made clear that severance agreements will be upheld against challenges when agreements follow the rules and are written clearly and in a manner that will enable employees to understand what it is that they are agreeing to (*Parsons v. Pioneer Hi-Bred Int'l Inc.*, 2006).

THE IMMIGRATION REFORM AND CONTROL ACT OF 1986

This law applies to every employer in the United States—no matter how small—as well as to every employee—whether full-time, part-time, temporary, or seasonal. The Act makes the enforcement of national immigration policy the job of every employer. It requires (1) that employers not hire or continue to employ aliens who are not legally authorized to work in the United States; and (2) that within three days of the hire date employers verify the identity and work authorization of every new employee, and then sign (under penalty of perjury) a form I-9, attesting that the employee is lawfully eligible to work in the United States.

Experts advise firms to make copies of whatever documentation they accept for an individual's employment, such as a work visa or Social Security card. In addition, to show a good-faith effort to abide by the law, employers should do a self-audit of all I-9 forms, not just those of a particular ethnic group (Ladika, 2006).

Under this law, employers may not discriminate on the basis of national origin, but when two applicants are equally qualified, an employer may choose a U.S. citizen over a non-U.S. citizen. Penalties for noncompliance are severe. For example, failure to comply with the verification rules can result in fines ranging from $100 to $1,000 for *each* employee whose identity and work authorization have not been verified. The law also provides for criminal sanctions for employers who engage in a pattern of violations.

While the former Immigration and Naturalization Service focused on imposing civil fines on employers who hired illegal aliens, today Immigration and Customs Enforcement (ICE) relies heavily on criminal prosecutions and the seizure of company assets to gain compliance with the nation's immigration laws. In fiscal year 2007, ICE secured fines and judgments of more than $30 million against employers whose hiring processes violate the law, while making 863 criminal arrests (primarily of company owners and managers who knowingly employed illegal workers) and 4,077 administrative arrests (primarily of illegal immigrants on the job) (U.S. Immigration and Customs Enforcement, 2008; Krell, 2007).

THE AMERICANS WITH DISABILITIES ACT OF 1990

Almost 13 percent of people ages 21 to 64 in the United States have at least one disability—a percentage that more than doubles, to 30.2 percent, for people ages 65 to 74. At the same time, the employment rate for working-age people with disabilities remains only half that of those without disabilities (37.7 percent versus 79.7 percent) (Wells, 2008). Passed to protect people with disabilities from discrimination in employment, transportation, and public accommodation, the ADA applies to all employers with 15 or more employees.

As a general rule, the ADA prohibits an employer from discriminating against a "qualified individual with a disability." A "qualified individual" is one who is able to perform the "essential" (i.e., primary) functions of a job with or without accommodation. Effective January 1, 2009, the Americans with Disabilities Act (ADA) Amendments Act prohibits consideration of mitigating measures in determining whether an individual has a disability, with the exception of ordinary eyeglasses and contact lenses (Brennan, 2009). A "disability" is a physical or mental impairment that substantially limits one or more major life activities, such as walking, talking, seeing, hearing, or learning. Persons are protected if they currently have an impairment, if they have a record of such an impairment, or if the employer *thinks* they have an impairment (e.g., a person with diabetes under control) (EEOC, 2009c).

Rehabilitated drug and alcohol abusers are protected, but current drug abusers may be fired. The alcoholic, in contrast, is covered and must be reasonably accommodated by being given a firm choice to rehabilitate himself or herself or face career-threatening consequences. The law also protects persons who have tested positive for the AIDS virus (ADA, 1990). At the same time, however, companies don't have to lower work standards, tolerate misconduct, or give someone a make-work job (EEOC, 2009c). Here are five major implications for employers (Janove, 2003; Willman, 2003; Wymer, 1999):

1. Any factory, office, retail store, bank, hotel, or other building open to the public must be made accessible to those with physical disabilities (e.g., by installing ramps, elevators, telephones with amplifiers). "Expensive" is no excuse unless such modifications might lead an employer to suffer an "undue hardship."

2. Employers must make "reasonable accommodations" for job applicants or employees with disabilities (e.g., by restructuring job and training programs, modifying work schedules, or purchasing new equipment that is "user friendly" to blind or deaf people) (Mook, 2007). Qualified job applicants (i.e., individuals with disabilities who can perform the essential functions of a job with or without reasonable accommodation) must be considered for employment. Practices such as the following may facilitate the process (Cascio, 1993c; Wells, 2008):

   • Obtaining a commitment from top management to accommodate workers with disabilities
   • Partnering with public and private disability agencies and community organizations
   • Centralizing recruiting, intake, and monitoring of hiring decisions
   • Using technology to redesign jobs. For example, Walgreens replaced keyboards with touch screens based on large pictures and icons, not words, making it easier for people with cognitive disabilities to learn and complete tasks
   • Developing an orientation process for workers with disabilities, supervisors, and coworkers
   • Publicizing successful accommodation experiences within the organization and among outside organizations
   • Providing in-service training to all employees and managers about the firm's "equal-access" policy and how to distinguish "essential" from "marginal" job functions

3. Preemployment physicals are permissible only if all employees are subject to them, and they cannot be given until after a conditional offer of employment is made. That is, the employment offer is conditioned on passing the physical examination. Prior to the conditional offer of employment, employers are not permitted to ask about past workers' compensation claims or about a candidate's history of illegal drug use. However, even at the preoffer stage, if an employer describes essential job functions, he or she can ask whether the applicant can perform the job in question (EEOC, 2009c). Here is an example of the difference between these two types of inquiries: "Do you have any back problems?" clearly violates the ADA because it is not job specific. However, the employer could state the following: "This job involves lifting equipment weighing up to 50 pounds at least once every hour of an eight-hour shift. Can you do that?"

4. Medical information on employees must be kept separate from other personal or work-related information about them.

5. Drug-testing rules remain intact. An employer can still prohibit the use of alcohol and illegal drugs at the workplace and can continue to give alcohol and drug tests.

Enforcement

The EEOC enforces the ADA (EEOC, 2009c). In cases of *intentional* discrimination, the Supreme Court has ruled that individuals with disabilities may be awarded both compensatory and punitive damages up to $300,000 if it can be shown that an employer engaged in discriminatory practices "with malice or with reckless indifference" (*Kolstad v. American Dental Association*, 1999).

The Civil Rights Act of 1991

This Act overturned six Supreme Court decisions issued in 1989. Here are some key provisions that are likely to have the greatest impact in the context of employment.

Monetary Damages and Jury Trials

A major effect of this Act is to expand the remedies in discrimination cases. Individuals who feel they are the victims of *intentional discrimination* based on race, gender (including sexual harassment), religion, or disability can ask for compensatory damages for pain and suffering, as well as for punitive damages, and they may demand a jury trial. In the past, only plaintiffs in age-discrimination cases had the right to demand a jury.

Compensatory and punitive damages are available only from nonpublic employers (public employers are still subject to compensatory damages up to $300,000) and not for adverse impact (unintentional discrimination) cases. Moreover, they may not be awarded in an ADA case when an employer has engaged in good-faith efforts to provide a reasonable accommodation. The total amount of damages that can be awarded depends on the size of the employer's workforce.

Number of Employees	Maximum Combined Damages Per Complaint
15 to 100	$50,000
101 to 200	$100,000
201 to 500	$200,000
More than 500	$300,000

As we noted earlier, victims of intentional discrimination by race or national origin may sue under the Civil Rights Act of 1866, in which case there are no limits to compensatory and punitive damages. Note also that since intentional discrimination by reason of disability is a basis for compensatory and punitive damages (unless the employer makes a good-faith effort to provide reasonable accommodation), the 1991 Civil Rights Act provides the sanctions for violations of the Americans with Disabilities Act of 1990.

Adverse Impact (Unintentional Discrimination) Cases

The Act clarifies each party's obligations in such cases. As we noted earlier, when an adverse impact charge is made, the plaintiff must identify a specific employment practice as the cause of discrimination. If the plaintiff is successful in demonstrating adverse impact, the burden of producing evidence shifts to the employer, who must prove that the challenged practice is "job related for the position in question and consistent with business necessity."

Protection in Foreign Countries

Protection from discrimination in employment, under Title VII of the 1964 Civil Rights Act and the ADA is extended to U.S. citizens employed in a foreign facility owned or controlled by a U.S. company. However, the employer does not have to comply with U.S. discrimination law if to do so would violate the law of the foreign country. To be covered under this provision, the U.S. citizen must be employed overseas by a firm controlled by an American employer (Lau, 2008).

Racial Harassment

As we noted earlier, the Act amended the Civil Rights Act of 1866 so that workers are protected from intentional discrimination in all aspects of employment, not just hiring and promotion.

Challenges to Consent Decrees

Once a court order or consent decree is entered to resolve a lawsuit, nonparties to the original suit cannot challenge such enforcement actions.

Mixed-Motive Cases

In a mixed-motive case, an employment decision was based on a combination of job-related factors, as well as unlawful factors such as race, gender, religion, or disability. Under the Civil Rights Act of 1991, an employer is guilty of discrimination if it can be shown that a prohibited consideration was a motivating factor in a decision, even though other factors that are lawful were also used. However, if the employer can show that the same decision would have been reached even without the unlawful considerations, the court may not assess damages or require hiring, reinstatement, or promotion.

Seniority Systems

The Act provides that a seniority system that intentionally discriminates against the members of a protected group can be challenged within 180 days of any of the following three points: (1) when the system is adopted, (2) when an individual becomes subject to the system, or (3) when a person is injured by the system.

Race-Norming and Affirmative Action

The Act makes it unlawful "to adjust the scores of, use different cutoff scores for, or otherwise alter the results of employment-related tests on the basis of race, color, religion, sex, or national origin." Prior to the passage of this Act, within-group percentile scoring (so-called race norming) had been used extensively to adjust minority candidates' test scores to make them more comparable to those of nonminority candidates. When race norming was used, each individual's percentile score on a selection test was computed relative only to others in his or her race/ethnic group, and not relative to the scores of all examinees who took the test. However, a merged list of percentile scores (high to low) was presented to those responsible for hiring decisions.

Extension to U.S. Senate and Appointed Officials

The Act extends protection from discrimination on the basis of race, color, religion, gender, national origin, age, and disability to employees of the U.S. Senate, political appointees of the president, and staff members employed by elected officials at the state level. Employees of the U.S. House of Representatives are covered by a House resolution adopted in 1988.

The Family and Medical Leave Act of 1993

The Family and Medical Leave Act (FMLA) covers all private-sector employers with 50 or more employees, including part-timers, who work 1,250 hours over a 12-month period (an average of 25 hours per week). The law gives workers up to 12 weeks of unpaid leave each year for birth, adoption, or foster care of a child within a year of the child's arrival; care for a spouse, parent, or child with a serious health condition; or the employee's own serious health condition if it prevents him or her from working. The employer is responsible for designating an absence or leave as FMLA leave, on the basis of information provided by the employee (Society for Human Resource Management, 2007).

Employers can require workers to provide medical certification of such serious illnesses and can require a second medical opinion. Employers also can exempt from the FMLA key salaried employees who are among their highest paid 10 percent. However, employers must maintain health insurance benefits for leave takers and give them their previous jobs (or comparable positions) when their leaves are over (Davis, 2003). Enforcement provisions of the FMLA are administered by the U.S. Department of Labor. The overall impact of this law was softened considerably by the exemption of some of its fiercest opponents—companies with fewer than 50 employees, or 95 percent of all businesses.

The FMLA was amended and expanded to include military families in 2008. Businesses are required to offer up to 26 weeks of unpaid leave to employees who provide care to wounded U.S. military personnel. Employers also must provide 12 weeks of FMLA leave to immediate family members (spouses, children, or parents) of soldiers, reservists, and members of the National Guard who have a "qualifying exigency." While the measure does not define that term, examples could include overseas assignments, recalls to active duty, and troop mobilizations (Leonard, 2008).

Many employers already offer more than the law requires. In a recent survey, for example, 44 percent of responding companies said they offer job-protected leave for absences that are not covered under the law. The most common examples include substituting sick/vacation leave for FMLA leave, allowing more than 12 weeks for job-protected leave, and offering such leaves for employees with fewer than 12 months' service (Society for Human Resource Management, 2007).

This completes our discussion of "absolute prohibitions" against discrimination. The following sections discuss nondiscrimination as a basis for eligibility for federal funds.

Executive Orders 11246, 11375, and 11478

Presidential executive orders in the realm of employment and discrimination are aimed specifically at federal agencies, contractors, and subcontractors. They have the force of law even though they are issued unilaterally by the president without congressional approval, and they can be altered unilaterally as well. The requirements of these orders are parallel to those of Title VII.

In 1965, President Johnson issued Executive Order 11246, prohibiting discrimination on the basis of race, color, religion, or national origin as a condition of employment by federal agencies, contractors, and subcontractors with contracts of $10,000 or more. Those covered are required to establish and maintain an affirmative action plan in every facility of 50 or more people. Such plans are to include employment, upgrading, demotion, transfer, recruitment or recruitment advertising, layoff or termination, pay rates, and selection for training. If approved by the Office of Federal Contract Compliance Programs (OFCCP), contractors are now permitted to establish an affirmative action plan based on a business function or line of business (Anguish, 2002). Doing so links affirmative action goals and accomplishments to the unit that is responsible for achieving them, rather than to a geographic location.

In 1967, Executive Order 11375 prohibited discrimination in employment based on sex. Executive Order 11478, issued by President Nixon in 1969, went even further, for it prohibited discrimination in employment based on all of the previous factors, plus political affiliation, marital status, and physical disability.

Enforcement of Executive Orders

Executive Order 11246 provides considerable enforcement power. It is administered by the Department of Labor through its OFCCP. Upon a finding by the OFCCP of noncompliance with the order, the Department of Justice may be advised to institute criminal proceedings, and the secretary of labor may cancel or suspend current contracts, as well as the right to bid on future contracts. Needless to say, noncompliance can be *very* expensive.

The Rehabilitation Act of 1973

This Act requires federal contractors (those receiving more than $2,500 in federal contracts annually) and subcontractors actively to recruit qualified individuals with disabilities and to use their talents to the fullest extent possible. The legal requirements are similar to those of the ADA.

The purpose of this act is to eliminate *systemic discrimination*—that is, any business practice that results in the denial of the EEO. Hence, the Act emphasizes "screening in" applicants, not screening them out. It is enforced by the OFCCP.

The Vietnam Era Veterans Readjustment Act of 1974

Federal contractors and subcontractors are required under this act to take affirmative action to ensure EEO for Vietnam-era veterans (August 5, 1964, to May 7, 1975). The OFCCP enforces it.

Uniformed Services Employment and Reemployment Rights Act of 1994

Regardless of its size, an employer may not deny a person initial employment, reemployment, promotion, or benefits based on that person's membership or potential membership in the uniformed services. Uniformed Services Employment and Reemployment Rights Act (USERRA) requires both public and private employers promptly to reemploy individuals returning from uniformed service (e.g., National Guard or activated reservists) in the position they would have occupied and with the seniority rights they would have enjoyed had they never left. Employers are also required to maintain health benefits for employees while they are away, but they are not required to make up the often significant difference between military and civilian pay (Segal, 2006; Thelen, 2006).

To be protected, the employee must provide advance notice. Employers need not always rehire a returning service member (e.g., if the employee received a dishonorable discharge or if changed circumstances at the workplace, such as bankruptcy or layoffs, make reemployment impossible or unreasonable), but the burden of proof will almost always be on the employer. The Veterans Employment and Training Service of the U.S. Department of Labor administers this law.

ENFORCEMENT OF THE LAWS—REGULATORY AGENCIES

State Fair Employment-Practices Commissions

Most states have nondiscrimination laws that include provisions expressing the public policy of the state, the persons to whom the law applies, and the prescribed activities of various administrative bodies. Moreover, the provisions specify unfair employment practices, procedures, and enforcement powers. Many states vest statutory enforcement powers in a state fair employment-practices commission.

Equal Employment Opportunity Commission

The EEOC is an independent regulatory agency whose five commissioners (one of whom is the chair) are appointed by the President and confirmed by the Senate for terms of five years. No more than three of the commissioners may be from the same political party. Like the OFCCP, the EEOC sets policy and in individual cases determines whether there is "reasonable cause" to believe that unlawful discrimination has occurred. It should be noted, however, that the courts give no legal standing to EEOC rulings on whether or not "reasonable cause" exists; each Title VII case constitutes a new proceeding.

The EEOC is the major regulatory agency charged with enforcing federal civil rights laws, and it is a busy one. In 2008, for example, individuals filed 95,402 complaints with the agency. The average filing is resolved within six months, but 73,951 cases remained unresolved at the end of fiscal year 2008 (EEOC Annual Report, 2009). Race, sex, disability, and age discrimination claims are most common, but claims of retaliation by employers against workers who have complained have nearly tripled in the last decade, to almost 32,700 in 2008. In 2008, the EEOC won more than $274 million for aggrieved parties, not including monetary benefits obtained through litigation (EEOC Annual Report, 2009).

The Complaint Process

Complaints filed with the EEOC first are deferred to a state or local fair employment-practices commission if there is one with statutory enforcement power. After 60 days, EEOC can begin its own investigation of the charges, whether or not the state agency takes action. Of course, the state or local agency may immediately re-defer to the EEOC.

The EEOC follows a three-step approach to resolving complaints: investigation, conciliation, and litigation. Throughout the process, the commission encourages the parties to settle and to consider mediation. Although the percentage of employers agreeing to mediate is considerably lower than the percentage of charging parties agreeing to mediate, in 2008 the EEOC conducted 8,840 successful mediations, securing more than $124 million for complaining parties (EEOC annual report, 2009). If conciliation efforts fail, court action can be taken. If the defendant is a private employer, the case is taken to the appropriate federal district court; if the defendant is a public employer, the case is referred to the Department of Justice.

In addition to processing complaints, the EEOC is responsible for issuing written regulations governing compliance with Title VII. Among those already issued are guidelines on discrimination because of pregnancy, sex, religion, and national origin; guidelines on employee selection procedures (in concert with three other federal agencies—see Appendix A); guidelines on affirmative action programs; and a policy statement on preemployment inquiries. These guidelines are not laws, although the Supreme Court (in *Albemarle Paper Co. v. Moody,* 1975) has indicated that they are entitled to "great deference." While the purposes of the guidelines are more legal than scientific, violations of the guidelines will incur EEOC sanctions and possible court action.

The EEOC has one other major function: information gathering. Each organization with 100 or more employees must file annually with the EEOC an EEO-1 form, detailing the number of women and members of four different minority groups employed in nine different job categories from laborers to managers and officials. The specific minority groups tracked are African Americans; Americans of Cuban, Spanish, Puerto Rican, or Mexican origin; Orientals; and Native Americans (which in Alaska includes Eskimos and Aleuts). Through computerized analysis of EEO-1 forms, the EEOC is better able to uncover broad patterns of discrimination and to attack them through class-action suits.

Office of Federal Contract Compliance Programs

The OFCCP is part of the U.S. Department of Labor's Employment Standards Administration. It is responsible for ensuring that employers doing business with the Federal government comply with the laws and regulations requiring nondiscrimination. This mission is based on the underlying principle that employment opportunities generated by Federal dollars should be available to all Americans on an equitable and fair basis. OFCCP administers and enforces three legal authorities that require EEO: Executive Order 11246, Section 503 of the Rehabilitation Act of 1973, and the Vietnam Era Veterans' Readjustment Assistance Act of 1974. "Contract compliance" means that in addition to meeting the quality, timeliness, and other requirements of federal contract work, contractors and subcontractors must satisfy EEO and affirmative action requirements covering all aspects of employment, including recruitment, hiring, training, pay, seniority, promotion, and even benefits (U.S. Department of Labor, 2009).

Goals and Timetables

Whenever job categories include fewer women or minorities "than would reasonably be expected by their availability," the contractor must establish goals and timetables (subject to OFCCP review) for increasing their representation. Goals are distinguishable from quotas in that quotas are inflexible; goals, on the other hand, are flexible objectives that can be met in a realistic amount of time. In determining representation rates, eight criteria are suggested by the OFCCP, including the population of women and minorities in the labor area surrounding the facility, the general availability of women and minorities having the requisite skills in the immediate labor area or in an area in which the contractor can reasonably recruit, and the degree of training the contractor is reasonably able to undertake as a means of making all job classes available to women and minorities.

How has the agency done? In 2008 OFCCP conducted 4,333 compliance reviews and recovered $67.5 million in back pay and other costs. The number of companies debarred from government contracts varies each year, from none to about eight (Crosby et al., 2003).

EMPLOYMENT CASE LAW—GENERAL PRINCIPLES

While the legislative and executive branches may write the law and provide for its enforcement, it is the responsibility of the judicial branch to interpret the law and to determine how it will be enforced. Since judicial interpretation is fundamentally a matter of legal judgment, this area is constantly changing. Of necessity, laws must be written in general rather than specific form, and, therefore, they cannot possibly cover the contingencies of each particular case. Moreover, in any large body of law, conflicts and inconsistencies will exist as a matter of course. Finally, new scientific findings must be considered along with the letter of the law if justice is to be served.

Legal interpretations define what is called **case law**, which serves as a precedent to guide, but not completely to determine, future legal decisions. A considerable body of case law pertinent to employment relationships has developed. The intent of this section is not to document thoroughly all of it, but merely to highlight some significant developments in certain areas.

Testing

The 1964 Civil Rights Act clearly sanctions the use of "professionally developed" ability tests, but it took several landmark Supreme Court cases to spell out the proper role and use of tests. The first of these was *Griggs v. Duke Power Company*, decided in March 1971 in favor of Griggs.

Duke Power was prohibited from requiring a high school education or the passing of an intelligence test as a condition of employment or job transfer because it could not show that either standard was significantly related to job performance:

> "What Congress has forbidden is giving these devices and mechanisms controlling force unless they are demonstrably a reasonable measure of job performance. . . .
>
> What Congress has commanded is that any tests used must measure the person for the job and not the person in the abstract." (p. 428)

The ruling also included four other general principles:

1. The law prohibits not only open and deliberate discrimination but also practices that are fair in form but discriminatory in operation. That is, Title VII prohibits practices having an adverse impact on protected groups, unless they are job related. This is a landmark pronouncement because it officially established adverse impact as a category of illegal discrimination.

   For example, suppose an organization wants to use prior arrests as a basis for selection. In theory, arrests are a "neutral" practice because all persons are equally subject to arrest if they violate the law. However, if arrests cannot be shown to be job related, and, in addition, if a significantly higher proportion of African Americans than whites are arrested, the use of arrests as a basis for selection is discriminatory in operation.

2. The employer bears the burden of proof that any requirement for employment is related to job performance. As affirmed by the Civil Rights Act of 1991, when a charge of adverse impact is made, the plaintiff must identify a specific employment practice as the cause of the discrimination. If the plaintiff is successful, the burden shifts to the employer.

3. It is not necessary for the plaintiff to prove that the discrimination was intentional; intent is irrelevant. If the standards result in discrimination, they are unlawful.

4. Job-related tests and other employment selection procedures are legal and useful.

As is well known, interviews are commonly used as bases for employment decisions to hire or to promote certain candidates in preference to others. Must such "subjective" assessment procedures satisfy the same standards of job relatedness as more "objective" procedures, such as written tests? If they produce an adverse impact against a protected group, the answer is yes, according to the Supreme Court in *Watson v. Fort Worth Bank & Trust* (1988).

As in its *Griggs* ruling, the Court held that it is not necessary for the plaintiff to prove that the discrimination was intentional. If the interview ratings result in adverse impact, they are presumed to be unlawful, unless the employer can show some relationship between the content of the ratings and the requirements of a given job. This need not involve a formal validation study, although the Court agreed unanimously that it is possible to conduct such studies when subjective assessment devices are used (McPhail, 2007).

The lesson for employers? Be sure that there is a legitimate, job-related reason for every question raised in an employment or promotional interview. Limit questioning to "need to know," rather than "nice to know," information, and monitor interview outcomes for adverse impact. Validate this selection method. It is unwise to wait until the selection system is challenged.

In two later rulings, *Albemarle Paper Co. v. Moody* (1975) and *Washington v. Davis* (1976), the Supreme Court specified in much greater detail what "job relevance" means: adequate job analysis; relevant, reliable, and unbiased job performance measures; and evidence that the tests used forecast job performance equally well for minorities and nonminorities.

To this point, we have assumed that any tests used are job related. But suppose that a written test used as the first hurdle in a selection program is not job related *and* that it produces an adverse impact against African Americans. *Adverse impact refers to a substantially different rate of selection in hiring, promotion, or other employment decisions that works to the disadvantage of members of a race, sex, or ethnic group.* Suppose further that among those who pass the test, proportionately more African Americans than whites are hired, so that the "bottom line" of hires indicates no adverse impact. This thorny issue faced the Supreme Court in *Connecticut v. Teal* (1982).

The Court ruled that Title VII provides rights to *individuals*, not to *groups*. Thus, it is no defense to discriminate unfairly against certain individuals (e.g., African American applicants) and then to "make up" for such treatment by treating other members of the same group favorably (i.e., African Americans who passed the test). In other words, it is no defense to argue that the bottom line indicates no adverse impact if intermediate steps in the hiring or promotion process do produce adverse impact and are not job related.

Decades of research have established that when a job requires cognitive ability, as virtually all jobs do, and tests are used to measures it, employers should expect to observe statistically significant differences in average test scores across racial/ethnic subgroups on standardized measures of knowledge, skill, ability, and achievement (Pyburn, Ployhart, & Kravitz, 2008). Alternatives to traditional tests tend to produce equivalent subgroup differences when the alternatives measure job-relevant constructs that require cognitive ability. What can be done? Begin by identifying clearly the kind of performance one is hoping to predict, and then measure the full range of performance goals and organizational interests, each weighted according to its relevance to the job in question (DeCorte, 1999; DeCorte, Lievens, & Sackett, 2007). That domain may include abilities, as well as personality characteristics, measures of motivation, and documented experience (Cascio, Jacobs, & Silva, 2010; Ployhart & Holz, 2008; Sackett, Schmitt, Ellingson, & Kabin, 2001). Chapter 8 provides a more detailed discussion of the remedies available. The end result may well be a reduction in subgroup differences.

Personal History

Frequently, qualification requirements involve personal background information or employment history, which may include minimum education or experience requirements, past wage garnishments, or previous arrest and conviction records. If such requirements have the effect of denying or restricting EEO, they may violate Title VII.

This is not to imply that education or experience requirements should not be used (Moyer, 2009). On the contrary, a review of 83 court cases indicated that educational requirements are most likely to be upheld when (1) a highly technical job, one that involves risk to the safety of the public, or one that requires advanced knowledge is at issue; (2) adverse impact cannot be established; and (3) evidence of criterion-related validity or an effective affirmative action program is offered as a defense (Meritt-Haston & Wexley, 1983).

Similar findings were reported in a review of 45 cases dealing with experience requirements (Arvey & McGowen, 1982). That is, experience requirements typically are upheld for jobs when there are greater economic and human risks involved with failure to perform adequately (e.g., airline pilots) or for higher-level jobs that are more complex. They typically are not upheld when they perpetuate a racial imbalance or past discrimination or when they are applied differently to different groups. Courts also tend to review experience requirements carefully for evidence of business necessity.

Arrest records, by their very nature, are not valid bases for screening candidates because in our society a person who is arrested is presumed innocent until proven guilty. It might, therefore, appear that conviction records are always permissible bases for applicant screening. In fact, conviction records may not be used in evaluating applicants unless the conviction is directly related to the work to be performed—for example, when a person convicted of embezzlement applies for a job as a bank teller (cf. *Hyland v. Fukada*, 1978). In addition, employers should consider carefully the nature and gravity of the offense, the time that has passed since the conviction and/or completion of the sentence, and the nature of the job held or sought (Erlam, 2005). Despite such constraints, remember that personal history items are not unlawfully discriminatory per se, but their use in each instance requires that job relevance be demonstrated.

Sex Discrimination

Judicial interpretation of Title VII clearly indicates that in the United States both sexes must be given equal opportunity to compete for jobs unless it can be demonstrated that sex is a bona fide occupational qualification for the job (e.g., actor, actress). Sex-discrimination cases have been argued under both theories of unlawful discrimination: disparate treatment (e.g., sexual harassment) as well as adverse impact (e.g., physical-ability tests). Many cases involve allegations of gender stereotyping (unwitting preferences by managers) (Crosby, Stockdale, & Ropp, 2007; Parloff, 2007). Such stereotypes are not a thing of the past, and they will play important roles in future employment-law litigation.

Illegal sex discrimination may manifest itself in several different ways. Consider pregnancy, for example. EEOC's interpretive guidelines for the Pregnancy Discrimination Act state:

> A written or unwritten employment policy or practice which excludes from employment applicants or employees because of pregnancy, childbirth, or related medical conditions is in prima facie violation of title VII. (2006, p. 197)

Under the law, an employer is never *required* to give pregnant employees special treatment. If an organization provides no disability benefits or sick leave to other employees, it is not required to provide them to pregnant employees (Pregnancy Discrimination, 2009; Trotter, Zacur, & Greenwood, 1982).

Many of the issues raised in court cases, as well as in complaints to the EEOC itself, were incorporated into the amended Guidelines on Discrimination Because of Sex, revised by the EEOC in 2006. The guidelines state, "the bona fide occupational exception as to sex should be interpreted narrowly." Assumptions about comparative employment characteristics of women in general (e.g., that turnover rates are higher among women than men); sex-role stereotypes; and preferences of employers, clients, or customers do not warrant such an exception. Likewise, the courts have disallowed unvalidated physical requirements—minimum height and weight, lifting strength, or maximum hours that may be worked.

Sexual harassment is a form of illegal sex discrimination prohibited by Title VII. According to the EEOC's guidelines on sexual harassment in the workplace (2006), the term refers to unwelcome sexual advances, requests for sexual favors, and other verbal or physical conduct when submission to the conduct is either explicitly or implicitly a term or condition of an individual's employment; when such submission is used as the basis for employment decisions affecting that individual; or when such conduct creates an intimidating, hostile, or offensive working environment. While many behaviors may constitute sexual harassment, there are two main types:

1. Quid pro quo (you give me this; I'll give you that)
2. Hostile work environment (an intimidating, hostile, or offensive atmosphere)

Quid pro quo harassment exists when the harassment is a *condition of employment*. Hostile-environment harassment was defined by the Supreme Court in its 1986 ruling in *Meritor Savings Bank v. Vinson*. Vinson's boss had abused her verbally, as well as sexually. However, since Vinson was making good career progress, the U.S. District Court ruled that the relationship was a voluntary one having nothing to do with her continued employment or advancement. The Supreme Court disagreed, ruling that whether the relationship was "voluntary" is irrelevant. The key question is whether the sexual advances from the supervisor are "unwelcome." If so, and if they are sufficiently severe or pervasive to be abusive, then they are illegal. This case was groundbreaking because it expanded the definition of harassment to include verbal or physical conduct that creates an intimidating, hostile, or offensive work environment or interferes with an employee's job performance.

The U.S. Supreme Court has gone even further. In two key rulings in 1998, *Burlington Industries, Inc. v. Ellerth* and *Faragher v. City of Boca Raton*, the Court held that an employer always is potentially liable for a supervisor's sexual misconduct toward an employee, even if the employer knew nothing about that supervisor's conduct. However, in some cases, an employer can defend itself by showing that it took reasonable steps to prevent harassment on the job.

More recently, in *Pennsylvania State Police v. Suders* (2004), the Supreme Court emphasized that an employer has no defense when a supervisor harasses an employee and an adverse employment action results. In hostile-environment cases, however, the employer may avoid liability if it can prove that (1) it exercised reasonable care to prevent and promptly correct any sexually harassing behavior, and (2) the plaintiff failed to use any preventive or corrective methods provided by the employer. The key is to establish and follow a thorough antiharassment program in the workplace (Jacobs, 2004).

Take special care when handling a complaint of sexual harassment. As we noted earlier, the Civil Rights Act of 1991 permits victims of sexual harassment—who previously could be awarded only missed wages—to collect a wide range of punitive damages from employers who mishandled a complaint.

Preventive Actions by Employers

What can an employer do to escape liability for the sexually harassing acts of its managers or workers? An effective policy should include the following features:

- A statement from the chief executive officer that states firmly that sexual harassment will not be tolerated.
- A workable definition of sexual harassment that is publicized via staff meetings, bulletin boards, handbooks, and in new-employee orientation programs. It should also include concrete examples of inappropriate behaviors (e.g., derogatory comments, demeaning jokes, visual messages, nicknames that refer to a person's membership in any protected group).
- Create an effective complaint procedure that includes multiple ways to file complaints (supervisor, high-level manager, senior manager, HR representative, or hotline), because the more choices employees have, the less reasonable will be their failure to complain. Every employee must sign a written acknowledgment of receipt of the policy.
- A clear statement of sanctions for violators and protection for those who make charges.
- A prompt, confidential investigation of every claim of harassment, no matter how trivial [Recognize, however, that investigators' knowledge of a prior history of a dissolved workplace romance is likely to affect their responses to an ensuing sexual harassment complaint (Pierce, Aguinis, & Adams, 2000; Pierce, Broberg, McClure, & Aguinis, 2004). Given this potential bias, consider developing an integrated policy that addresses both workplace romance and sexual harassment in the same document or training materials (Pierce & Aguinis, 2001)].
- Preservation of all investigative information, with records of all such complaints kept in a central location.
- Training of all managers and supervisors to recognize and respond to complaints, giving them written materials outlining their responsibilities and obligations when a complaint is made.
- Follow-up to determine if harassment has stopped (Casellas & Hill, 1998; Lublin, 2006; Proskauer Rose LLP, 2002).

Age Discrimination

To discriminate fairly against employees over 40 years old, an employer must be able to demonstrate a "business necessity" for doing so. That is, the employer must be able to show that age is a factor directly related to the safe and efficient operation of its business. It was not always so. When the ADEA was enacted in 1967, 45 percent of the job announcements included a maximum-age listing, saying that people between the ages of 30 and 35 need not apply (McCann, in Grossman, 2003, p. 42). Today, age discrimination is usually more subtle, but it still happens (Levitz & Shishkin, 2009). In a survey by ExecuNet.com, a whopping 84 percent of executives and recruiters surveyed said it starts about age 50 (Fisher, 2002).

To establish a *prima facie* case (i.e., a body of facts presumed to be true until proven otherwise) of age discrimination, an aggrieved individual must show that

1. He or she is within the protected age group (over 40 years of age).
2. He or she is doing satisfactory work.
3. He or she was discharged despite satisfactory work performance.
4. A younger person filled the position (*Schwager v. Sun Oil Co. of Pa.* 1979).

If a case gets to a jury, aggrieved employees have a 78 percent success rate in both state and local jury trials. In federal district courts, the median age discrimination verdict is almost $300,000, tops for all types of discrimination (Grossman, 2003). Here is an example.

When a beer distributor discharged a 60-year-old general sales manager, he filed suit, claiming discrimination because of his age. Cash Distributing Company argued that it fired James Neely for legitimate, business-related reasons. It claimed that he was a poor employee who did not follow instructions, failed to perform required evaluations and weekly reports, did not do daily sales calls, and refused to follow orders. Neely countered that the real reason for his discharge was his age, and he presented evidence that other younger employees who had similar infractions received less severe discipline. A jury agreed with Neely, and so did the Mississippi Court of Appeals, awarding him nearly $200,000 (Smith, 2007).

Aside from termination, age-discrimination complaints are likely to arise following reductions in force, or employment decisions that involve discipline, selection, or promotion. They can be brought under disparate treatment or adverse impact theories of discrimination. Employers can still fire unproductive workers, but the key is to base employment decisions on ability, not on age (Lauricella, 2007; Coy, 2005).

"English Only" Rules—National Origin Discrimination?

Rules that require employees to speak only English in the workplace have come under fire in recent years. Employees who speak a language other than English claim that such rules are not related to the ability to do a job and have a harsh impact on them because of their national origin. The EEOC and many courts agree that blanket English-only rules that lack business justification amount to unlawful national-origin discrimination (Clark, 2002; Jordan, 2005).

Employers should be careful when instituting such a rule. While it is not necessarily illegal to make fluency in English a job requirement or to discipline an employee for violating an "English-only" rule, an employer must be able to show there is a legitimate business need for it. For example, it's a safety issue when medical workers or firefighters do not understand or cannot make themselves understood (Holland, 2008; Prengaman, 2003). Avoid requiring the use of English at all times and in all areas of the workplace. Inform employees in advance of the circumstances where speaking only in English is required and of the consequences of violating the rule. Otherwise, the employer may be subject to discrimination complaints on the basis of national origin. At the same time, many employers would be delighted to have a worker who can speak the language of a non–English-speaking customer.

Seniority

Seniority is a term that connotes length of employment. A seniority system is a scheme that, alone or in tandem with "non-seniority" criteria, allots to employees ever-improving employment rights and benefits as their relative lengths of pertinent employment increase (*California Brewers Association v. Bryant*, 1982).

Various features of seniority systems have been challenged in the courts for many years (Gordon & Johnson, 1982). However, one of the most nettlesome issues is the impact of established seniority systems on programs designed to ensure EEO. Employers often work hard to hire and promote members of protected groups. If layoffs become necessary, however, those individuals may be lost because of their low seniority. As a result, the employer takes a step backward in terms of workforce diversity. What is the employer to do when seniority conflicts with EEO?

The courts have been quite clear in their rulings on this issue. In two landmark decisions, *Firefighters Local Union No. 1784 v. Stotts* (1984) (decided under Title VII) and *Wygant v. Jackson Board of Education* (1986) (decided under the equal protection clause of the Fourteenth Amendment), the Supreme Court ruled that an employer may not protect the jobs of recently hired African American employees at the expense of whites who have more seniority (Greenhouse, 1984).

Voluntary modifications of seniority policies for affirmative action purposes remain proper, but where a collective-bargaining agreement exists, the consent of the union is required. Moreover, in the unionized setting, courts have made it clear that the union must be a party to any decree that modifies a bona fide seniority system (Britt, 1984).

What about seniority systems and the ADA? In *US Airways v. Barnett* (2002), the Supreme Court ruled that that an employer is not required to grant an employee with a disability a job in place of an employee with more seniority—if a seniority system normally is used as a fundamental factor in such decisions. The Court emphasized that seniority does not always trump the ADA, and that such a question must be resolved on a case-by-case basis (Barrier, 2002).

Preferential Selection

An unfortunate side effect of affirmative action programs designed to help minorities and women is that they may, in so doing, place qualified white males at a competitive disadvantage. However, social policy as embodied in Title VII emphasizes that so-called reverse discrimination (discrimination against whites and in favor of members of protected groups) is just as unacceptable as is discrimination by whites against members of protected groups (*McDonald v. Santa Fe Transportation Co.*, 1976).

This is the riddle that has perplexed courts and the public since the dawn of affirmative action 40 years ago: How do you make things fair for oppressed groups while continuing to treat people as equal individuals (Von Drehle, 2003)? Court cases, together with the Civil Rights Act of 1991, have clarified a number of issues in this area:

1. Courts may order, and employers voluntarily may establish, affirmative action plans, including goals and timetables, to address problems of underutilization of women and minorities. Individuals who were not parties to the original suit may not reopen court-approved affirmative action settlements.
2. The plans need not be directed solely to identified victims of discrimination, but may include general classwide relief.
3. While the courts will almost never approve a plan that would result in whites *losing* their jobs through layoffs, they may sanction plans that impose limited burdens on whites in hiring and promotions (i.e., plans that postpone them).

What about numerically based preferential programs? The U.S. Supreme Court issued two landmark rulings in 2003 that clarified this issue. Both cases represented challenges to admissions policies at the University of Michigan, one involving undergraduate admissions (*Gratz v. Bollinger*, 2003) and the other involving law school admissions (*Grutter v. Bollinger*, 2003). The undergraduate admissions policy was struck down because it was too mechanistic. It awarded 20 points of the 150 needed for admission (and eight points more than is earned for a perfect SAT score) to any member of an officially recognized minority group. Such a disguised quota system denied other applicants the equal protection of the law guaranteed by the Fourteenth Amendment to the U.S. Constitution, and, thus, it was ruled illegal.

However, the Court also was mindful of arguments from leading businesses, educational institutions, and former military officials that a culturally diverse, well-educated workforce is vital to the competitiveness of the U.S. economy and that an integrated officer corps produced by diverse military academies and Reserve Officer Training Corps (ROTC) programs is vital to national security. The Court upheld the law school's approach to enrolling a "critical mass" of African Americans, Latinos, and Native Americans, under which the school considers each applicant individually and sets no explicit quota. To be consistent with the constitutional guarantee of equal treatment for all under the law, race-conscious admissions must be limited in time. Thus, the Court noted, "We expect that 25 years from now the use of racial preferences will no longer be necessary."

The Court emphasized that diversity is a "compelling state interest," but that universities may not use quotas for members of racial or ethnic groups or put them on separate admissions tracks. The law school's admissions policy satisfied these principles by ensuring that applicants are evaluated individually. Under that approach, the Court noted, a nonminority student with a particularly interesting contribution to make to the law school's academic climate may sometimes be preferred over a minority student with better grades and test scores.

The net effect of the two rulings is to permit public and private universities to continue to use race as a "plus factor" in evaluating potential students—provided they take sufficient care to evaluate individually each applicant's ability to contribute to a diverse student body ("Court Preserves," 2003; Lane, 2003). The Court made clear that its rationale for considering race was not to compensate for past discrimination, but to obtain educational benefits from a diverse student body. Corporate hiring policies also will have to reflect the Court's double message: Diversity efforts are acceptable, but quotas aren't (Kronholz, Tomsho, & Forelle, 2003).

In Part I, we have examined the legal and social environments within which organizations and individuals function. In order for both to function effectively, however, competent HRM is essential. In the next chapter, therefore, we shall present fundamental tools (systems analysis and decision theory) that will enable the HR professional to develop a conceptual framework for viewing employment decisions and methods for assessing the outcomes of such decisions.

Evidence-Based Implications for Practice

- The intent of the civil rights laws is to "level the playing field" by providing equal opportunities in all aspects of employment for individuals without regard to characteristics such as race, sex, age, national origin, or disability status.
- Know and understand the regulations and guidance provided by federal civil-rights enforcement agencies, the Equal Employment Opportunity Commission, and the Office of Federal Contract Compliance Programs.
- With regard to tests and interviews, be sure that there is a legitimate, job-related reason for every question. Limit questioning to "need to know," rather than "nice to know," information, and monitor outcomes for adverse impact. Validate all selection methods.
- Be prepared to demonstrate the job relevance of all personal-history items (e.g., conviction records).
- Sexual harassment (quid pro quo or hostile environment) is a form of illegal sex discrimination under Title VII. To avoid legal liability, take proactive steps to ensure that all employees and supervisors know how to recognize it, and receive training on company policies, complaint procedures, and sanctions for violators.
- With regard to age discrimination, recognize that employers can still fire unproductive workers, but the key is to base employment decisions on ability, not on age.
- To avoid charges of national-origin discrimination, do not require the use of English at all times and in all areas of the workplace. Inform employees in advance of the circumstances where speaking only in English is required and of the consequences of violating the rule.
- Legitimate seniority systems generally take precedence over affirmative action considerations and disability accommodation, but that could change in light of particular circumstances.
- Diversity efforts are OK, but quotas aren't.

Discussion Questions

1. What advice would you offer to an employer that is considering an "English-only" rule in the workplace?
2. Prepare a brief outline for the senior management of your company that illustrates the requirements and expected impact of the Family and Medical Leave Act.
3. What specific steps would you recommend to a firm in order to ensure fair treatment of persons with disabilities?
4. Prepare a brief outline of an organizational policy on sexual harassment. Be sure to include grievance, counseling, and enforcement procedures.
5. What guidance would you give to an employer who asks about rights and responsibilities in administering a testing program?

People, Decisions, and the Systems Approach

At a Glance

Organizations and individuals frequently are confronted with alternative courses of action, and decisions are made when one alternative is chosen in preference to others. Since different cost consequences frequently are associated with various alternatives, principles are needed that will assist decision makers in choosing the most beneficial or most profitable alternatives. Utility theory, by forcing the decision maker to consider the costs, consequences, and anticipated payoffs of all available courses of action, provides such a vehicle.

Since the anticipated consequences of decisions must be viewed in terms of their implications for the organization as a whole, an integrative framework is needed that will afford a broad macro-perspective. Open-systems theory is one such approach. Organizations are open systems, importing inputs (energy and information) from the environment, transforming inputs into outputs of goods and services, and finally exporting these back into the environment, which then provides feedback on the overall process. The topical areas of personnel psychology also can be cast into an open-systems model. Thus, job analysis and evaluation, workforce planning (WP), recruitment, initial screening, selection, training, performance management, and organizational exit are seen as a network of sequential, interdependent decisions, with feedback loops interconnecting all phases in the process. The costs, consequences, and anticipated payoffs of alternative decision strategies can then be assessed in terms of their systemwide ramifications.

UTILITY THEORY—A WAY OF THINKING

Decisions, decisions—which applicants should be hired, who should be promoted, how much money should be allocated to research and development? Any time a person or an organization is confronted with alternative courses of action, there is a decision problem. For managers and HR professionals, such problems occur daily in their work. Decisions to hire, not to hire, or to place on a waiting list are characteristic outcomes of the employment process, but how does one arrive at sound decisions that will ultimately spell success for the individual or organization affected? Principles are needed that will assist managers and individuals in making the most profitable or most beneficial choices among products, investments, jobs, curricula, etc. The aim in this chapter is not to present a detailed, mathematically sophisticated exposition of decision or utility theory (cf. Boudreau, 1991; Cabrera & Raju, 2001; Cascio & Boudreau, 2008; Cronbach & Gleser, 1965), but merely to arouse and to sensitize the reader to a provocative way of thinking.

Utility theory is engaging, for it insists that costs and expected consequences of decisions always be taken into account (Boudreau & Ramstad, 2003; Cascio & Boudreau, 2008). It stimulates the decision maker to formulate what he or she is after, as well as to anticipate the expected consequences of alternative courses of action. The ultimate goal is to enhance decisions, and the best way to do that is to identify the linkages between employment practices and the ability to achieve the strategic objectives of an organization. For example, the management of a professional football team must make a number of personnel decisions each year in the annual draft of the top college players. Size and speed are two common selection criteria; present ability and future potential are two others. In all cases, the decision maker must state clearly his or her overall objectives prior to actually making the decision, and then he or she must attempt to anticipate the expected consequences of alternative choices in terms of the strategic objectives of the organization.

It should serve as some comfort to know that all employment decision processes can be characterized identically (Cronbach & Gleser, 1965). In the first place, there is an individual about whom a decision is required. Based on certain information about the individual (e.g., aptitude or diagnostic test results), the decision maker may elect to pursue various alternative courses of action. Let us consider a simple example. After an individual is hired for a certain job with an electronics firm, he or she may be assigned to one of three training classes. Class A is for fast learners who already have some familiarity with electronics. Those assigned to class B are slower learners who also possess a basic grasp of the subject matter. Class C individuals are those whose skills are either nonexistent (e.g., the hard-core unemployed) or so rusty as to require some remedial work before entering class B training.

The firm administers an aptitude test to each individual and then processes this diagnostic information according to some strategy or rule for arriving at decisions. For example, assuming a maximum score of 100 points on the aptitude test, the decision maker may choose the following strategy:

Test Score	Assignment
90–100	Class A
70–89	Class B
Below 70	Class C

In any given situation, some strategies are better than others. Strategies are better (or worse) when evaluated against possible outcomes or consequences of decisions (payoffs). Although sometimes it is extremely difficult to assign quantitative values to outcomes, this is less of a problem in business settings, since many outcomes can be expressed in economic (dollar) terms. Once this is accomplished, it becomes possible to compare particular decisions or general strategies, as Cronbach and Gleser (1965) noted:

> The unique feature of decision theory or utility theory is that it specifies evaluations by means of a payoff matrix or by conversion of the criterion to utility units. The values are thus plainly revealed and open to criticism. This is an asset rather than a defect of this system, as compared with systems where value judgments are embedded and often pass unrecognized. (p. 121)

In the previous example, individuals were assigned to training classes according to ability and experience. Alternatively, however, all individuals could have been assigned to a single training class regardless of ability or experience. Before choosing one of these strategies, let us compare them in terms of some possible outcomes.

If the trainees are assigned to different classes based on learning speed, the overall cost of the training program will be higher because additional staff and facilities are required to conduct the different classes. In all likelihood, however, this increased cost may be offset by the percentage of successful training graduates. For strategy I (differential assignment), therefore, assume an $80,000 total training cost and a 75 percent success rate among trainees. Alternatively, the overall cost of strategy II (single training class) would be lower, but the percentage of successful graduates may also be lower. For strategy II, therefore, assume that the total training cost is $65,000 and that 50 percent of the trainees successfully complete the training program. Payoffs from the two strategies may now be compared:

	Total Training Cost	Percentage of Successful Grads
Strategy I—differential assignment	$80,000	75
Strategy II—single training	$65,000	50
Program strategy II—total payoff	+ $15,000	−25

At first glance, strategy II may appear cost effective. Yet, in addition to producing 25 percent fewer graduates, this approach has hidden costs. In attempting to train all new hires at the same rate, the faster-than-average learners will be penalized because the training is not challenging enough for them, while the slower-than-average learners will be penalized in trying to keep up with what they perceive to be a demanding pace. The organization itself also may suffer in that the fast learners may quit (thereby increasing recruitment and selection costs), regarding the lack of challenge in training as symptomatic of the lack of challenge in full-time jobs with the organization.

In summary, utility theory provides a framework for making decisions by forcing the decision maker to define clearly his or her goal, to enumerate the expected consequences or possible outcomes of the decision, and to attach differing utilities or values to each. Such an approach has merit, since resulting decisions are likely to rest on a foundation of sound reasoning and conscious forethought. As we shall see in Chapters 9 through 16, utility theory is an extremely useful tool for the I/O psychologist or HR professional. Another useful tool, one that forces the decision maker to think in terms of multiple causes and multiple effects, is systems analysis.

Organizations as Systems

In recent years, much attention has been devoted to the concept of "systems" and the use of "systems thinking" to frame and solve complex scientific and technological problems. The approach is particularly relevant to the social sciences, and it also provides an integrative framework for organization theory and management practice.

What is a system? One view holds that a system is a collection of interrelated parts, unified by design and created to attain one or more objectives. The objective is to be aware of the variables involved in executing managerial functions so that decisions will be made in light of the overall effect on the organization and its objectives. These decisions must consider not only the organization itself but also the larger systems (e.g., industry and environment) in which the organization operates (Whitten & Bentley, 2006). Classical management theories viewed organizations as closed or self-contained systems whose problems could be divided into their component parts and solved. The closed-system approach concentrated primarily on the internal operation of the organization (i.e., within its own boundary) and tended to ignore the outside environment.

This approach was criticized on several grounds. In concentrating solely on conditions inside the firm, management became sluggish in its response to the demands of the marketplace. An example of this is IBM. As it moved into the 1990s, the company underestimated the popularity of personal computers and workstations. It assumed that businesses would prefer mainframe computers and that domestic and foreign-made "clones" of the IBM PC would not capture much market share. Such a miscalculation led to disastrous results for the company, as it shed assets and more than 100,000 employees. Fortunately the company was able to turn itself around and survive (Garr, 2000). Obviously the closed-system approach does not describe organizational reality. In contrast, a systemic perspective requires managers to integrate inputs from multiple perspectives and environments and to coordinate the various components.

The modern view of organizations, therefore, is that of open systems in continual interaction with multiple, dynamic environments, providing for a continuous import of inputs (in the form of people, capital, raw material, and information) and a transformation of these into outputs, which are then exported back into these various environments to be consumed by clients or customers (see Figure 3-1).

Subsequently, the environments (economic, legal, social, and political) provide feedback on the overall process (Hitt, Ireland, & Hoskisson, 2009; Schein, 1980). Senge (1990) has described the process well:

> Systems thinking is a discipline for seeing wholes. It is a framework for seeing interrelationships rather than things, for seeing patterns of change rather than "snapshots." It is a set of general principles—distilled over the course of the twentieth century, spanning fields as diverse as the physical and social sciences, engineering, and management. It is also a specific set of tools and techniques . . . during the last thirty years these tools have been applied to understand a wide range of corporate, urban, regional, economic, political, ecological, and even physiological systems. And systems thinking is a sensibility for the subtle interconnectedness that gives living systems their unique character. (pp. 68–69)

The hierarchy of systems should be emphasized as well. A system comprises subsystems of a lower order and is also part of a supersystem. However, what constitutes a system or a subsystem is purely relative and largely depends on the level of abstraction or complexity on which one is focusing the analysis. As members of organizations, people are organized into groups, groups are organized into departments, departments are organized into divisions, divisions are organized into companies, and companies are part of an industry and an economy. There seems to be a need for this inclusive, almost concentric mode of organizing subsystems into larger systems and supersystems in order to coordinate activities and processes. It provides

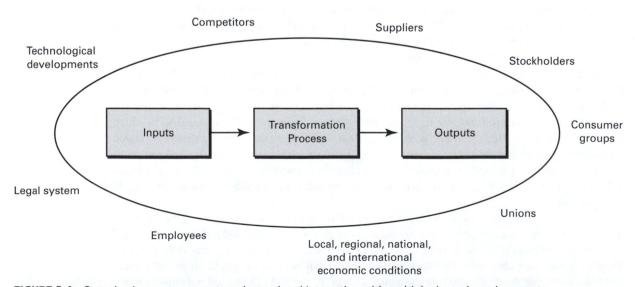

FIGURE 3-1 Organizations are open systems in continual interaction with multiple dynamic environments.

the macro-view from which to visualize events or actions in one system and their effects on other related systems or on the organization as a whole (Katz & Kahn, 1978).

In summary, systems theory has taken us to the edge of a new awareness—that everything is one big system with infinite, interconnected, interdependent subsystems. What we are now discovering is that managers need to *understand* systems theory, but they should resist the rational mind's instinctive desire to use it to predict and control organizational events. Organizational reality will not conform to any logical, systemic thought pattern (Jones, 2009; Senge, 1999). Having said that, it is important to emphasize the implications that systems thinking has for organizational practice—specifically, the importance of the following:

- The ability to scan and sense changes in the outside environment,
- The ability to bridge and manage critical boundaries and areas of interdependence, and
- The ability to develop appropriate strategic responses.

Much of the widespread interest in corporate strategy is a product of the realization that organizations must be sensitive to what is occurring in the world beyond (Jones, 2009).

A SYSTEMS VIEW OF THE EMPLOYMENT PROCESS

In order to appreciate more fully the relevance of applied psychology to organizational effectiveness, it is useful to view the employment process as a network or system of sequential, interdependent decisions (Cascio & Boudreau, in press; Cronbach & Gleser, 1965).

Each decision is an attempt to discover what should be done with one or more individuals, and these decisions typically form a long chain. Sometimes the decision is whom to hire and whom to reject, or whom to train and whom not to train, or for which job a new hire is best suited. While the decision to reject a job applicant is usually considered final, the decision to accept an individual is really a decision to investigate him or her further. The strategy is, therefore, sequential, since information gathered at one point in the overall procedure determines what, if any, information will be gathered next. This open-system, decision-theoretic model is shown graphically in Figure 3-2.

Although we will describe each link in the model more fully in later sections, it is important to point out two general features: (1) Different recruitment, selection, and training strategies are used for different jobs; and (2) the various phases in the process are highly interdependent, as the feedback loops indicate. Consider one such feedback loop—from performance management to job analysis. Suppose both supervisors and job incumbents determine that the task and personal requirements of a particular job have changed considerably from those originally determined in job analysis. Obviously the original job analysis must be updated to reflect the newer requirements, but this may also affect the wage paid on that job. In addition, WP strategies may have to be modified in order to ensure a continuous flow of qualified persons for the changed job, different recruiting strategies may be called for in order to attract new candidates for the job, new kinds of information may be needed in order to select or promote qualified individuals, and, finally, the content of training programs for the job may have to be altered. In short, changes in one part of the system have a "reverberating" effect on all other parts of the system. Now let us examine each link in the model in greater detail.

Job Analysis and Job Evaluation

Job analysis is the fundamental building block on which all later decisions in the employment process must rest. The process of matching the individual and the job typically begins with a detailed specification by the organization of the work to be performed, the skills needed, and the training required by the individual jobholder in order to perform the job satisfactorily.[1]

---

[1] One question that has taken on added significance, especially with the increase in mechanization (the replacement of a human skill by a machine) and in automation (not only replacement of a human skill by a machine, but also automatic control and integration of a process), is whether, in fact, people should be in the system at all (Attewell & Rule, 1984).

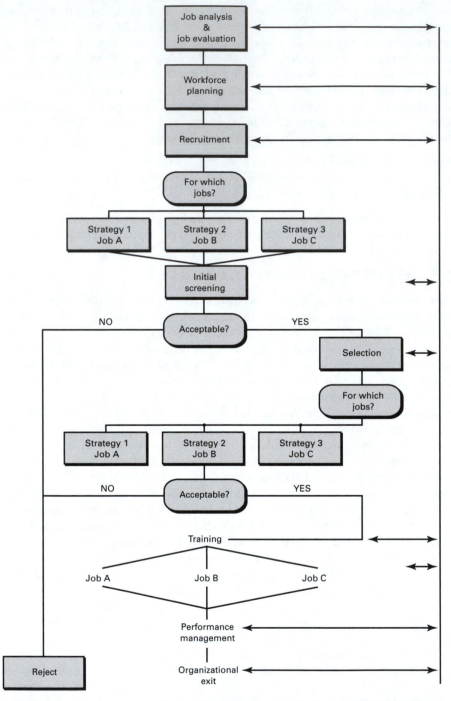

FIGURE 3-2　An open-system, decision-theoretic view of the employment process.

Job analysis supports many organizational activities, but one of the most basic is job evaluation. Organizations must make value judgments on the relative importance or worth of each job to the organization as a whole—that is, in terms of dollars. Divisional managers are paid higher salaries than secretaries. Why is this? We may begin to answer this question by enumerating certain factors or dimensions along which the jobs differ. Responsibility for other employees is one differentiating characteristic, for example; skill requirements is another.

No doubt the reader can think of many other dimensions along which the two jobs differ. When these differences are compounded across all jobs in the organization, the job-evaluation process becomes a rather formidable task requiring detailed methods and replicable procedures that can be applied to all jobs. Alternative methods of job evaluation are currently available, but whichever method is adopted must be acceptable, as well as understandable, to employees, boards of directors, and other concerned groups.

Theoretically, both job analysis and job evaluation are performed independently of the particular individuals who currently happen to be performing the jobs. In theory at least, jobs and wages remain the same even though people come and go. Later on we will see that this is a rather naive assumption, but, for the present, such a conception is useful.

Workforce Planning

WP is concerned with anticipating future staffing requirements and formulating action plans to ensure that enough qualified individuals are available to meet specific staffing needs at some future time. In order to do WP adequately, however, four conditions must be met. First, the organization must devise an inventory of available knowledge, abilities, skills, and experiences of present employees. Second, forecasts of the internal and external human resource supply and demand must be undertaken. This requires a thorough understanding of strategic business plans (Dess, Lumpkin, & Eisner, 2007; Wright, 2008); hence, human resource professionals must become full partners with those responsible for strategic business planning. Third, on the basis of information derived from the talent inventory and human resource supply and demand forecasts, various action plans and programs can be formulated in order to meet predicted staffing needs; such programs may include training, transfers, promotions, or recruitment. Finally, control and evaluation procedures are necessary in order to provide feedback on the adequacy of the WP effort. Adequate and accurate WP is essential if organizations are to cope effectively with the radical economic, demographic, and technological changes that are occurring in the twenty-first century. By examining the systemwide ramifications of all human resource activities, we can plan effectively, lending both direction and scope to subsequent phases in the employment process.

Recruitment

Equipped with the information derived from job analysis, job evaluation, and WP, we can proceed to the next phase in the process—attracting potentially acceptable candidates to apply for the various jobs. The recruitment machinery is typically set into motion by the receipt by the HR office of a staffing requisition from a particular department. Questions such as the following often arise in recruitment: How and where should we recruit? What media or other information sources should we use? Assuming the recruiting will not be done in person, what type and how much information should we include in our advertisements? How much money should we spend in order to attract qualified or qualifiable applicants?

Two basic decisions that the organization must make at this point involve the *cost of recruiting* and the *selection ratio* (Landy & Conte, 2009; Riggio, 2008). For example, the cost of recruiting a design engineer is likely to be high and may involve a nationwide effort. Furthermore, the demanding qualifications and skills required for the job imply that there will be few qualified applicants. In other words, the selection ratio (the number hired relative to the number that apply) will be high or unfavorable from the organization's point of view. On the other hand, a majority of workers probably can perform a job involving small-parts assembly. Therefore, a narrower search effort is required to attract applicants; perhaps an online ad or one in the local newspaper will do. Given a relatively loose labor market, the probabilities are high that many potentially qualified applicants will be available. That is, because the selection ratio will be low or favorable, the organization can afford to be more selective.

Recruitment is critically important in the overall selection–placement process. The impression left on an applicant by company representatives or by media and Internet advertisements can significantly influence the future courses of action both of the applicant and of the organization (Dineen & Soltis, in press; Rynes & Cable, 2003). For example, Cisco's successful approach to attracting technical talent included low-key recruitment efforts at home and garden shows, microbrewery festivals, and bookstores—precisely the places that focus groups suggested were most likely to yield desirable prospects.

Initial Screening

Given relatively favorable selection ratios and acceptable recruiting costs, the resulting applications are then subjected to an initial screening process that is more or less intensive depending on the screening policy or strategy adopted by the organization.

As an illustration, let us consider two extreme strategies for the small-parts assembly job and the design engineer's job described earlier. Strategy I requires the setting of minimally acceptable standards. For example, no educational requirements may be set for the small-parts assembly job; only a minimum passing score on a validated aptitude test of finger dexterity is necessary. This strategy is acceptable in cases where an individual need not have developed or perfected a particular skill at the time of hiring because the skill is expected to develop with training and practice. Such a policy may also be viewed as eminently fair by persons with disabilities (e.g., the blind worker who can probably perform small-parts assembly quickly and accurately as a result of his or her finely developed sense of touch), and by minority and other disadvantaged groups.

Strategy II, on the other hand, may require the setting of very demanding qualifications initially, since it is relatively more expensive to pass an applicant along to the next phase. The design-engineer's job, for example, may require an advanced engineering degree plus several years' experience, as well as demonstrated research competence. The job demands a relatively intense initial-screening process.

Because each stage in the employment process involves a cost to the organization and because the investment becomes larger and larger with each successive stage, it is important to consider the likely consequence of decision errors at each stage. Decision errors may be of two types: erroneous acceptances and erroneous rejections. An *erroneous acceptance* is an individual who is passed on from a preceding stage, but who fails at the following stage. An *erroneous rejection*, on the other hand, is an individual who is rejected at one stage, but who can succeed at the following stage if allowed to continue.

Different costs are attached to each of these errors, but the costs of an erroneous acceptance are immediately apparent. If the organization has invested $20,000 in an applicant who subsequently fails, that $20,000 is also gone. The costs of erroneous rejections are much less obvious and, in many cases, are not regarded as "costly" at all to the employing organization—unless the rejected applicants go to work for competitors and become smashing successes for them!

Selection

This is the central phase in the process of matching individual and job. During this phase, information is collected judgmentally (e.g., by interviews), mechanically (e.g., by written tests), or in both ways. Scorable application forms, written or performance tests, interviews, personality inventories, and background and reference checks are several examples of useful data-gathering techniques. These data, however collected, must then be combined judgmentally, mechanically, or via some mixture of both methods. The resulting combination is the basis for hiring, rejecting, or placing on a waiting list every applicant who reaches the selection phase. During the selection phase, considerations of utility and cost should guide the decision maker in his or her choice of information sources and the method of combining data. For example, the interviewers' salaries, the time lost from production or supervision, and, finally, the very low predictive ability of the informal interview make it a rather expensive selection device. Tests, physical examinations, and credit and background investigations also are expensive, and it is imperative that decision makers weigh the costs of such instruments and procedures against their potential utility.

We will point out the key considerations in determining utility in Chapter 13, but it is important at this point to stress that there is not a systematic or a one-to-one relationship between the cost of a selection procedure and its subsequent utility. That is, it is not universally true that if a selection procedure costs more, it is a more accurate predictor of later job performance. Many well-intentioned operating managers commonly are misled by this assumption. Procedures add genuine utility to the employment process to the extent that they enable an organization to improve its current hit rate in predicting success (at an acceptable cost), however success happens to be defined in that organization. Hence, the organization must assess its present success rate, the favorableness of the selection ratio for the jobs under consideration, the predictive ability of proposed selection procedures, and the cost of adding additional predictive information; then it must weigh the alternatives and make a decision.

Applicants who accept offers are now company employees who will begin drawing paychecks. After orienting the new employees and exposing them to company policies and procedures, the organization faces another critical decision. On which jobs should these employees be placed? In many, if not most, instances, individuals are hired to fill specific jobs (so-called one-shot, selection-testing programs). In a few cases, such as the military or some very large organizations, the decision to hire is made first, and the placement decision follows at a later time. Since the latter situations are relatively rare, however, we will assume that new employees move directly from orientation to training for a specific job or assignment.

Training and Development

HR professionals can increase significantly the effectiveness of the workers and managers of an organization by employing a wide range of training and development techniques. Payoffs will be significant, however, only when training techniques accurately match individual and organizational needs (Goldstein & Ford, 2002; Kraiger, 2003; Noe, 2008). Most individuals have a need to feel competent (Deci, 1972; Lawler, 1969; White, 1959)—that is, to make use of their valued abilities, to realize their capabilities and potential. In fact, competency models often drive training curricula. A *competency* is a cluster of interrelated knowledge, abilities, skills, attitudes, or personal characteristics that are presumed to be important for successful performance on a job (Noe, 2008). Training programs designed to modify or to develop competencies range from basic skill training and development for individuals, to team training, supervisory training, executive-development programs, and cross-cultural training for employees who will work in other countries.

Personnel selection and placement strategies relate closely to training and development strategies. Trade-offs are likely. For example, if the organization selects individuals with minimal qualifications and skill development, then the onus of developing capable, competent employees moves to training. On the other hand, if the organization selects only those individuals who already possess the necessary abilities and skills required to perform their jobs, then the burden of further skill development is minimal. Given a choice between selection and training, however, the best strategy is to choose selection. If high-caliber employees are selected, these individuals will be able to learn more and to learn faster from subsequent training programs than will lower-caliber employees.

Earlier we emphasized the need to match training objectives accurately to job requirements. In lower-level jobs, training objectives can be specified rather rigidly and defined carefully. The situation changes markedly, however, when training programs must be designed for jobs that permit considerable individual initiative and freedom (e.g., selling, research and development, and equipment design) or jobs that require incumbents to meet and deal effectively with a variety of types and modes of information, situations, or unforeseen developments (e.g., managers, detectives, engineers, and astronauts). The emphasis in these jobs is on developing a broad range of skills and competencies in several areas in order to cope effectively with erratic job demands. Because training programs for these jobs are expensive and lengthy, initial qualifications and selection criteria are likely to be especially demanding.

Performance Management

In selecting and training an individual for a specific job, an organization is essentially taking a risk in the face of uncertainty. Although most of us like to pride ourselves on being logical and rational decision makers, the fact is that we are often quite fallible. Equipped with incomplete, partial information about present or past behavior, we attempt to predict future job behavior. Unfortunately, it is only after employees have been performing their jobs for a reasonable length of time that we can evaluate their performance and our predictions.

In observing, evaluating, and documenting on-the-job behavior and providing timely feedback about it to individuals or teams, we are evaluating the degree of success of the individual or team in reaching organizational objectives. While success in some jobs can be assessed partially by objective indices (e.g., dollar volume of sales, number of errors), in most cases, judgments about performance play a significant role.

Promotions, compensation decisions, transfers, disciplinary actions—in short, individuals' livelihoods—are extraordinarily dependent on performance management. Performance management, however, is not the same as performance appraisal. The latter is typically done once or twice a year to identify and discuss the job-relevant strengths and weaknesses of individuals or teams. The objective of performance management, on the other hand, is to focus on improving performance at the level of the individual or team every day. This requires a willingness and commitment on the part of managers to provide timely feedback about performance while constantly focusing attention on the ultimate objective (e.g., world-class customer service).

To be sure, performance appraisals are of signal importance to the ultimate success and survival of a reward system based on merit. It is, therefore, ethically and morally imperative that each individual get a fair shake. If supervisory ratings are used to evaluate employee performance and if the rating instruments themselves are poorly designed, are prone to bias and error, or focus on elements irrelevant or unimportant to effective job performance, or if the raters themselves are uncooperative or untrained, then our ideal of fairness will never be realized. Fortunately these problems can be minimized through careful attention to the development and implementation of appraisal systems and to the thorough training of those who will use them. We will have more to say about these issues in our treatment of performance management in Chapter 5, but, for the present, note the important feedback loops to and from performance management in Figure 3-2. All prior phases in the employment process affect and are affected by the performance-management process. For example, if individuals or teams lack important, job-related competencies—for example, skill in troubleshooting problems—then job analyses may have to be revised, along with recruitment, selection, and training strategies. This is the essence of open-systems thinking.

Organizational Exit

Eventually everyone who joins an organization must leave it. For some, the process is involuntary, as in the case of a termination for cause or a forced layoff. The timing of these events is at the discretion of the organization. For others, the process is voluntary, as in the case of a retirement after many years of service or a voluntary buyout in the context of employment downsizing. In these situations, the employee typically has control over the timing of his or her departure.

The topic of organizational exit may be addressed in terms of processes or outcomes at the level of the individual or organization. Consider involuntary terminations, for example. Psychological processes at the level of the individual include anticipatory job loss; shock, relief, and relaxation; concerted effort; vacillation, self-doubt, and anger; and resignation and withdrawal. Organizational processes relevant to involuntary termination are communication, participation, control, planning, and support (Collarelli & Beehr, 1993; De Meuse, Marks, & Dai, in press). At the level of the individual, involuntary job loss tends to be associated with depression, hostility, anxiety, and loss of self-esteem.

A key outcome at the level of the organization is the reactions of survivors to layoffs. They experience stress in response to uncertainty about their ability to do much about the situation and uncertainty over performance and reward outcomes (Buono, 2003; Kiviat, 2009). At the level of society, massive layoffs may contribute to high levels of cynicism within a nation's workforce. Layoffs signal a lack of commitment from employers. As a result, employees are less likely to trust them, are less likely to commit fully to their organizations, and work to maximize their own outcomes (Cascio, 2002a; De Meuse et al., in press).

Retirement is also a form of organizational exit, but it is likely to have far fewer adverse effects than layoffs or firings, especially when the process is truly voluntary, individuals perceive the financial terms to be fair, and individuals control the timing of their departures. Each of these processes includes personal control; due process, personal control, and procedural justice are key variables that influence reactions to organizational exit (Clarke, 2003; Colquitt, Conlon, Wesson, Porter, & Ng, 2001).

As shown in Figure 3-2, organizational exit influences, and is influenced by, prior phases in the employment process. For example, large-scale layoffs may affect the content, design, and pay of remaining jobs; the recruitment, selection, and training of new employees with strategically relevant skills; and changes in performance-management processes to reflect work reorganization and new skill requirements.

In writing this book, we have attempted to frame our ultimate objectives realistically, for it would be foolish to pretend that a single volume holds the final solution to any of these nagging employment problems. Solutions are found in concerned people—those who apply what books can only preach. Nevertheless, by urging you to consider both costs and anticipated consequences in making decisions, we hope that you will feel challenged to make better decisions and thereby to improve considerably the caliber of human resource management practice. Nowhere is systems thinking more relevant than in the HRM systems of organizations. As we noted earlier, the very concept of a system implies a design to attain one or more objectives. This involves a consideration of desired outcomes. In our next three chapters, we will consider the special problems associated with developing reliable success criteria—that is, outcomes of the HRM process.

Evidence-Based Implications for Practice

Employment decisions always include costs and consequences. Utility theory makes those considerations explicit, and in doing so, makes it possible to compare alternative decisions or strategies. Such a framework demands that decision makers define their goals clearly, enumerate expected consequences of alternative courses of action, and attach different values to each one. This is a useful way of thinking. Here are two other useful frameworks.

- Open-systems theory, which regards organizations as interacting continually with multiple, dynamic environments—economic, legal, political, and social.
- The employment process as a network of sequential, interdependent decisions, in which recruitment, staffing, training, performance management, and organizational exit are underpinned and reinforced by job analysis and workforce planning.

Discussion Questions

1. How is utility theory useful as a framework for making decisions? Why must considerations of utility always be tied to the overall strategy of an organization?

2. Describe three examples of open systems. Can you think of a closed system? Why are organizations open systems?

3. Why is it useful to view the employment process as a network of sequential, interdependent decisions?

4. What is the difference between an erroneous acceptance and an erroneous rejection? Describe situations where one or the other is more serious.

5. Suppose you had to choose between "making" competent employees through training, or "buying" them through selection. Which would you choose? Why?

4

Criteria: Concepts, Measurement, and Evaluation

At a Glance

Adequate and accurate criterion measurement is a fundamental problem in HRM. Criteria are operational statements of goals or desired outcomes. Although criteria are sometimes used for predictive purposes and sometimes for evaluative purposes, in both cases they represent that which is important or desirable.

Before we can study human performance and understand it better, we must confront the fact that criteria do not exist in a vacuum, and that they are multidimensional and dynamic. Also, we must address the challenge of potential unreliability of performance, performance observation, and the various situational factors that affect performance. In addition, in evaluating operational criteria, we must minimize the impact of certain contaminants, such as biasing factors in ratings. Finally, we must be sure that operational criterion measures are relevant, reliable, sensitive, and practical.

In general, applied psychologists are guided by two principal objectives: (1) to demonstrate the utility of their procedures and programs and (2) to enhance their understanding of the determinants of job success. In attempting to achieve these twin objectives, sometimes composite criteria are used and sometimes multiple criteria are used. Although there has been an enduring controversy over the relative merits of each approach, the two positions have been shown to differ in terms of underlying assumptions and ultimate goals. Thus, one or both may be appropriate in a given set of circumstances. In a concluding section of this chapter, several promising research designs are presented that should prove useful in resolving the criterion dilemma and thus in advancing the field.

The development of criteria that are adequate and appropriate is at once a stumbling block and a challenge to the HR specialist. Behavioral scientists have bemoaned the "criterion problem" through the years. The term refers to the difficulties involved in the process of conceptualizing and measuring performance constructs that are multidimensional, dynamic, and appropriate for different purposes (Austin & Villanova, 1992). Yet the effectiveness and future progress of knowledge with respect to most HR interventions depend fundamentally on our ability to resolve this baffling question.

The challenge is to develop theories, concepts, and measurements that will achieve the twin objectives of enhancing the utility of available procedures and programs and deepening our understanding of the psychological and behavioral processes involved in job performance. Ultimately, we must strive to develop a comprehensive theory of the behavior of men and women at work (Viswesvaran & Ones, 2000).

In the early days of applied psychology, according to Jenkins (1946), most psychologists tended to accept the tacit assumption that criteria were either given by God or just to be found lying about. It is regrettable that, even today, we often resort to the most readily available or most expedient criteria when, with a little more effort and thought, we could probably develop better ones. Nevertheless, progress has been made as the field has come to recognize that criterion measures are samples of a larger performance universe, and that as much effort should be devoted to understanding and validating criteria as is devoted to identifying predictors (Campbell, McHenry, & Wise, 1990). Wallace (1965) expressed the matter aptly when he said that the answer to the question "Criteria for what?" must certainly include "for understanding" (p. 417). Let us begin by defining our terms.

DEFINITION

Criteria have been defined from more than one point of view. From one perspective, criteria are standards that can be used as yardsticks for measuring employees' degree of success on the job (Bass & Barrett, 1981; Guion, 1965; Landy & Conte, 2007). This definition is quite adequate within the context of personnel selection, placement, and performance management. It is useful when prediction is involved—that is, in the establishment of a functional relationship between one variable, the predictor, and another variable, the criterion. However, there are times when we simply wish to evaluate without necessarily predicting. Suppose, for example, that the HR department is concerned with evaluating the effectiveness of a recruitment campaign aimed at attracting minority applicants. Various criteria must be used to evaluate the program adequately. The goal in this case is not prediction, but rather evaluation. One distinction between predictors and criteria is time (Mullins & Ratliff, 1979). For example, if evaluative standards such as written or performance tests are administered *before* an employment decision is made (i.e., to hire or to promote), the standards are predictors. If evaluative standards are administered *after* an employment decision has been made (i.e., to evaluate performance effectiveness), the standards are criteria.

The above discussion leads to the conclusion that a more comprehensive definition is required, regardless of whether we are predicting or evaluating. As such, a more general definition is that a criterion represents something important or desirable. It is an operational statement of the goals or desired outcomes of the program under study (Astin, 1964). It is an **evaluative standard** that can be used to measure a person's performance, attitude, motivation, and so forth (Blum & Naylor, 1968). Examples of some possible criteria are presented in Table 4-1, which has been modified from those given by Dunnette and Kirchner (1965) and Guion (1965). While many of these measures often would fall short as adequate criteria, each of them deserves careful study in order to develop a comprehensive sampling of job or program performance. There are several other requirements of criteria in addition to desirability and importance, but, before examining them, we must first consider the use of job performance as a criterion.

TABLE 4-1 Possible Criteria

Output measures

Units produced

Number of items sold

Dollar volume of sales

Number of letters typed

Commission earnings

Number of candidates attracted (recruitment program)

Readership of an advertisement

Quality measures

Number of errors (coding, filing, bookkeeping, typing, diagnosing)

Number of errors detected (inspector, troubleshooter, service person)

Number of policy renewals (insurance sales)

Number of complaints and dissatisfied persons (clients, customers, subordinates, colleagues)

Rate of scrap, reworks, or breakage

Cost of spoiled or rejected work

Lost time

Number of occasions (or days) absent

Number of times tardy

Length and frequency of unauthorized pauses

Employee turnover

Number of discharges for cause

Number of voluntary quits

Number of transfers due to unsatisfactory performance

Length of service

Employability, trainability, and promotability

Time to reach standard performance

Level of proficiency reached in a given time

Rate of salary increase

Number of promotions in a specified time period

Number of times considered for promotion

Length of time between promotions

Ratings of performance

Ratings of personal traits or characteristics

Ratings of behavioral expectations

Ratings of performance in work samples

Ratings of performance in simulations and role-playing exercises

Ratings of skills

Counterproductive behaviors

Abuse toward others

Disciplinary transgressions

Military desertion

Property damage

Personal aggression

Political deviance

Sabotage

Substance abuse

Theft

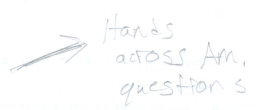

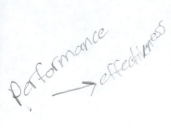

JOB PERFORMANCE AS A CRITERION

Performance may be defined as observable things people do that are relevant for the goals of the organization (Campbell et al., 1990). Job performance itself is multidimensional, and the behaviors that constitute performance can be scaled in terms of the level of performance they represent. It is also important to distinguish *performance* from the outcomes or results of performance, which constitute *effectiveness* (Aguinis, 2009a).

The term **ultimate criterion** (Thorndike, 1949) describes the full domain of performance and includes everything that ultimately defines success on the job. Such a criterion is ultimate in the sense that one cannot look beyond it for any further standard by which to judge the outcomes of performance.

The ultimate criterion of a salesperson's performance must include, for example, total sales volume over the individual's entire tenure with the company; total number of new accounts brought in during the individual's career; amount of customer loyalty built up by the salesperson during his or her career; total amount of his or her influence on the morale or sales records of other company salespersons; and overall effectiveness in planning activities and calls, controlling expenses, and handling necessary reports and records. In short, the ultimate criterion is a concept that is strictly conceptual and, therefore, cannot be measured or observed; it embodies the notion of "true," "total," "long-term," or "ultimate worth" to the employing organization.

Although the ultimate criterion is stated in broad terms that often are not susceptible to quantitative evaluation, it is an important construct because the relevance of any operational criterion measure and the factors underlying its selection are better understood if the conceptual stage is clearly and thoroughly documented (Astin, 1964).

DIMENSIONALITY OF CRITERIA

Operational measures of the conceptual criterion may vary along several dimensions. In a classic article, Ghiselli (1956) identified three different types of criterion dimensionality: static, dynamic, and individual dimensionality. We examine each of these three types of dimensionality next.

Static Dimensionality

If we observe the usual job performance criterion at any single point in time, we find that it is multidimensional in nature (Campbell, 1990). This type of multidimensionality refers to two issues: (1) the fact that individuals may be high on one performance facet and simultaneously low on another and (2) the distinction between maximum and typical performance.

Regarding the various performance facets, Rush (1953) found that a number of relatively independent skills are involved in selling. Thus, a salesperson's learning aptitude (as measured by sales school grades and technical knowledge) is unrelated to objective measures of his or her achievement (such as average monthly volume of sales or percentage of quota achieved), which, in turn, is independent of the salesperson's general reputation (e.g., planning of work, rated potential value to the firm), which, in turn, is independent of his or her sales techniques (sales approaches, interest and enthusiasm, etc.).

In broader terms, we can consider two general facets of performance: task performance and contextual performance (Borman & Motowidlo, 1997). Contextual performance has also been labeled "pro-social behaviors" or "organizational citizenship performance" (Borman, Penner, Allen, & Motowidlo, 2001). An important point to consider is that task performance and contextual performance do not necessarily go hand in hand (Bergman, Donovan, Drasgow, Overton, & Henning, 2008). An employee can be highly proficient at her task, but be an underperformer with regard to contextual performance (Bergeron, 2007). Task performance is defined as (1) activities that transform raw materials into the goods and services that are produced by the organization and (2) activities that help with the transformation process by replenishing the supply of raw materials; distributing its finished products; or providing important planning, coordination, supervising, or staff functions that enable it to function effectively and efficiently (Cascio & Aguinis, 2001). Contextual performance is defined as those behaviors that contribute to the organization's effectiveness by providing a good environment in which task performance can occur. Contextual performance includes behaviors such as the following:

- Persisting with enthusiasm and exerting extra effort as necessary to complete one's own task activities successfully (e.g., being punctual and rarely absent, expending extra effort on the job);
- Volunteering to carry out task activities that are not formally part of the job (e.g., suggesting organizational improvements, making constructive suggestions);
- Helping and cooperating with others (e.g., assisting and helping coworkers and customers);
- Following organizational rules and procedures (e.g., following orders and regulations, respecting authority, complying with organizational values and policies); and
- Endorsing, supporting, and defending organizational objectives (e.g., exhibiting organizational loyalty, representing the organization favorably to outsiders).

Applied psychologists have recently become interested in the "dark side" of contextual performance, often labeled "workplace deviance" or "counterproductive behaviors" (O'Brien & Allen, 2008; Spector, Fox, & Penney, 2006). Although contextual performance and workplace deviance are seemingly at the opposite ends of the same continuum, there is evidence suggesting that they are distinct from each other (Judge, LePine, & Rich, 2006; Kelloway, Loughlin, Barling, & Nault, 2002). In general, workplace deviance is defined as voluntary behavior that violates organizational norms and thus threatens the well-being of the organization, its members, or both (Robinson & Bennett, 1995). Vardi and Weitz (2004) identified over 100 such "organizational misbehaviors" (e.g., alcohol/drug abuse, belittling opinions, breach of confidentiality), and several scales are available to measure workplace deviance based on both self- and other reports (Bennett & Robinson, 2000; Blau & Andersson, 2005; Hakstian, Farrell, & Tweed, 2002; Kelloway et al., 2002; Marcus, Schuler, Quell, & Hümpfner, 2002; Spector et al., 2006; Stewart, Bing, Davison, Woehr, & McIntyre, 2009). Some of the self-reported deviant behaviors measured by these scales are the following:

- Exaggerating hours worked
- Falsifying a receipt to get reimbursed for more money than was spent on business expenses
- Starting negative rumors about the company
- Gossiping about coworkers
- Covering up one's mistakes
- Competing with coworkers in an unproductive way
- Gossiping about one's supervisor
- Staying out of sight to avoid work
- Taking company equipment or merchandise
- Blaming one's coworkers for one's mistakes
- Intentionally working slowly or carelessly
- Being intoxicated during working hours
- Seeking revenge on coworkers
- Presenting colleagues' ideas as if they were one's own

Regarding the typical-maximum performance distinction, typical performance refers to the average level of an employee's performance, whereas maximum performance refers to the peak level of performance an employee can achieve (DuBois, Sackett, Zedeck, & Fogli, 1993; Sackett, Zedeck, & Fogli, 1988). Employees are more likely to perform at maximum levels when they understand they are being evaluated, when they accept instructions to maximize performance on the task, and when the task is of short duration. In addition, measures of maximum performance (i.e., what employees *can* do) correlate only slightly with measures of typical performance (i.e., what employees *will* do). For example, correlations between typical and maximum performance measures were about .20 for objective measures of grocery store checkout clerks' performance (i.e., speed and accuracy; Sackett et al., 1988) and about .40 for subjective measures of military recruits' performance (i.e., performance ratings based on assessment exercises; Ployhart, Lim, & Chan, 2001). Moreover, general mental abilities predicted maximum performance but not typical performance in a study involving samples of 96 programmers and 181 cash-vault employees (Witt & Spitzmuller 2007). In addition, individuals' motivation (i.e., direction, level, and persistence of effort exerted) is more strongly related to maximum than typical performance (Klehe & Anderson, 2007).

Unfortunately, research on criteria frequently ignores the fact that job performance often includes many facets that are relatively independent, such as task and contextual performance and the important distinction between typical and maximum performance. Because of this, employee performance is often not captured and described adequately. To capture the performance domain in a more exhaustive manner, attention should also be paid to the temporal dimensionality of criteria.

Dynamic or Temporal Dimensionality

Once we have defined clearly our conceptual criterion, we must then specify and refine operational measures of criterion performance (i.e., the measures actually to be used). Regardless of the operational form of the criterion measure, it must be taken at some point in time. When is the best time for criterion measurement? Optimum times vary greatly from situation to situation, and conclusions therefore need to be couched in terms of when criterion measurements were taken. Far different results may occur depending on when criterion measurements were taken (Weitz, 1961), and failure to consider the temporal dimension may lead to misinterpretations.

In predicting the short- and long-term success and survival of life insurance agents, for example, ability as measured by standardized tests is significant in determining early sales success, but interests and personality factors play a more important role later on (Ferguson, 1960). The same is true for accountants (Bass & Barrett, 1981). Thus, after two years as a staff accountant with one of the major accounting firms, interpersonal skills with colleagues and clients are more important than pure technical expertise for continued success. In short, criterion measurements are not independent of time.

Earlier, we noted that ultimate criteria embody the idea of long-term effectiveness. Ultimate criteria are not practical for day-to-day decision making or evaluation, however, because researchers and managers usually cannot afford the luxury of the time needed to gather the necessary data. Therefore, substitute criteria, immediate or intermediate, must be used (see Figure 4-1). To be sure, all immediate and intermediate criteria are *partial*, since at best they give only an approximation of the ultimate criterion (Thorndike, 1949).

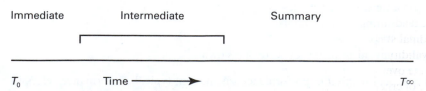

FIGURE 4-1   The temporal dimension of criterion measurement.

Figure 4-1 lacks precision in that there is a great deal of leeway in determining when immediate criteria become intermediate criteria. Immediate criteria are near-term measures, such as test scores on the final day of training class or measurement of the rookie quarterback's performance in his first game. Intermediate criteria are obtained at a later time, usually about six months after initial measurement (i.e., supervisory ratings of performance, work sample performance tests, or peer ratings of effectiveness). Summary criteria are expressed in terms of longer-term averages or totals. Summary criteria are often useful because they avoid or balance out short-term effects or trends and errors of observation and measurement. Thus, a trainee's average performance on weekly tests during six months of training or a student's cumulative college grade-point average is taken as the best estimate of his or her overall performance. Summary criteria may range from measurements taken after three months' performance, to those taken after three to four years' performance, or even longer.

Temporal dimensionality is a broad concept, and criteria may be "dynamic" in three distinct ways: (1) changes over time in average levels of group performance, (2) changes over time in validity coefficients, and (3) changes over time in the rank ordering of scores on the criterion (Barrett, Caldwell, & Alexander, 1985).

Regarding changes in group performance over time, Ghiselli and Haire (1960) followed the progress of a group of investment salespeople for 10 years. During this period, they found a 650 percent improvement in average productivity, and still there was no evidence of leveling off! However, this increase was based only on those salespeople who survived on the job for the full 10 years; it was not true of *all* of the salespeople in the original sample. To be able to compare the productivity of the salespeople, their experience must be the same, or else it must be equalized in some manner (Ghiselli & Brown, 1955). Indeed, a considerable amount of other research evidence cited by Barrett et al. (1985) does not indicate that average productivity improves significantly over lengthy time spans.

Criteria also might be dynamic if the relationship between predictor (e.g., preemployment test scores) and criterion scores (e.g., supervisory ratings) fluctuates over time (e.g., Jansen & Vinkenburg, 2006). About half a century ago, Bass (1962) found this to be the case in a 42-month investigation of salespeople's rated performance. He collected scores on three ability tests, as well as peer ratings on three dimensions, for a sample of 99 salespeople. Semiannual supervisory merit ratings served as criteria. The results showed patterns of validity coefficients for both the tests and the peer ratings that *appeared* to fluctuate erratically over time. However, he reached a much different conclusion when he tested the validity coefficients statistically. He found no significant differences for the validities of the ability tests, and when peer ratings were used as predictors, only 16 out of 84 pairs of validity coefficients (roughly 20 percent) showed a statistically significant difference (Barrett et al., 1985).

Researchers have suggested two hypotheses to explain why validities might change over time. One, the **changing task model**, suggests that while the relative amounts of ability possessed by individuals remain stable over time, criteria for effective performance might change in importance. Hence, the validity of predictors of performance also might change. The second model, known as the **changing subjects model**, suggests that while specific abilities required for effective performance remain constant over time, each individual's level of ability changes over time, and that is why validities might fluctuate (Henry & Hulin, 1987). Neither of the above models has received unqualified support. Indeed, proponents of the view that validity tends to decrease over time (Henry & Hulin, 1987, 1989) and proponents of the view that validity remains stable over time (Ackerman, 1989; Barrett & Alexander, 1989) agree on only one point: Initial performance tends to show some decay in its correlation with later performance. However, when only longitudinal studies are examined, it appears that validity decrements are much more common than are validity increments (Henry & Hulin, 1989). This tends to support the view that validities do fluctuate over time.

The third type of criteria dynamism addresses possible changes in the rank ordering of scores on the criterion over time. This form of dynamic criteria has attracted substantial attention (e.g.,

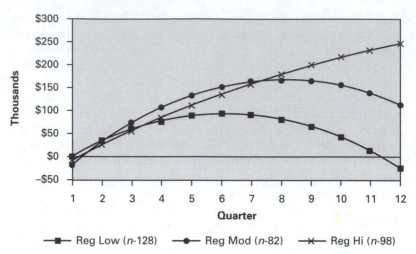

FIGURE 4-2 Regression lines for three ordinary least squares clusters of insurance agents—low, moderate, and high performers—over three years. *Source:* Hoffman, D. A., Jacobs, R., & Baratta, J. E. Dynamic criteria and the measurement of change. *Journal of Applied Psychology, 78,* 194–204. © 1993 American Psych. Assoc.

Hoffmann, Jacobs, & Baratta, 1993; Hulin, Henry, & Noon, 1990) because of the implications for the conduct of validation studies and personnel selection in general. If the rank ordering of individuals on a criterion changes over time, future performance becomes a moving target. Under those circumstances, it becomes progressively more difficult to predict performance accurately the farther out in time from the original assessment. Do performance levels show systematic fluctuations across individuals? The answer seems to be in the affirmative because the preponderance of evidence suggests that prediction deteriorates over time (Keil & Cortina, 2001). Overall, correlations among performance measures collected over time show what is called a "simplex" pattern of higher correlations among adjacent pairs and lower correlations among measures taken at greater time intervals (e.g., the correlation between month 1 and month 2 is greater than the correlation between month 1 and month 5) (Steele-Johnson, Osburn, & Pieper, 2000).

Deadrick and Madigan (1990) collected weekly performance data from three samples of sewing machine operators (i.e., a routine job in a stable work environment). Results showed the simplex pattern such that correlations between performance measures over time were smaller when the time lags increased. Deadrick and Madigan concluded that relative performance is not stable over time. A similar conclusion was reached by Hulin et al. (1990), Hoffmann et al. (1993), and Keil and Cortina (2001): Individuals seem to change their rank order of performance over time (see Figure 4-2). In other words, there are meaningful differences in intraindividual patterns of changes in performance across individuals, and these differences are also likely to be reflected in how individuals evaluate the performance of others (Reb & Cropanzano, 2007). HR professionals interested in predicting performance at distant points in the future face the challenge of identifying factors that affect differences in intraindividual performance trajectories over time.

Individual Dimensionality

It is possible that individuals performing the same job may be considered equally good; yet the nature of their contributions to the organization may be quite different. Thus, different criterion dimensions should be used to evaluate them. Kingsbury (1933) recognized this problem almost 80 years ago when he wrote:

> Some executives are successful because they are good planners, although not successful directors. Others are splendid at coordinating and directing, but their plans

and programs are defective. Few executives are equally competent in both directions. Failure to recognize and provide, in both testing and rating, for this obvious distinction is, I believe, one major reason for the unsatisfactory results of most attempts to study, rate, and test executives. Good tests of one kind of executive ability are not good tests of the other kind. (p. 123)

While in the managerial context described by Kingsbury there is only one job, it might plausibly be argued that in reality there are two (i.e., directing and planning). The two jobs are qualitatively different only in a psychological sense. In fact, the study of individual criterion dimensionality is a useful means of determining whether the same job, as performed by different people, is psychologically the same or different.

CHALLENGES IN CRITERION DEVELOPMENT

Competent criterion research is one of the most pressing needs of personnel psychology today—as it has been in the past. About 70 years ago, Stuit and Wilson (1946) demonstrated that continuing attention to the development of better performance measures results in better predictions of performance. The validity of these results has not been dulled by time (Viswesvaran & Ones, 2000). In this section, therefore, we will consider three types of challenges faced in the development of criteria, point out potential pitfalls in criterion research, and sketch a logical scheme for criterion development.

At the outset, it is important to set certain "chronological priorities." First, criteria must be developed and analyzed, for only then can predictors be constructed or selected to predict relevant criteria. Far too often, unfortunately, predictors are selected carefully, followed by a hasty search for "predictable criteria." To be sure, if we switch criteria, the validities of the predictors will change, but the reverse is hardly true. Pushing the argument to its logical extreme, if we use predictors with no criteria, we will never know whether or not we are selecting those individuals who are most likely to succeed. Observe the chronological priorities! At least in this process we know that the chicken comes first and then the egg follows.

Before human performance can be studied and better understood, four basic challenges must be addressed (Ronan & Prien, 1966, 1971). These are the issues of (un)reliability of performance, reliability of performance observation, dimensionality of performance, and modification of performance by situational characteristics. Let us consider the first three in turn; the fourth is the focus of a later section.

Challenge #1: Job Performance (Un)Reliability

Job performance reliability is a fundamental consideration in HR research, and its assumption is implicit in all predictive studies. Reliability in this context refers to the consistency or stability of job performance over time. Are the best (or worst) performers at time 1 also the best (or worst) performers at time 2? As noted in the previous section, the rank order of individuals based on job performance scores does not necessarily remain constant over time.

What factors account for such performance variability? Thorndike (1949) identified two types of unreliability—intrinsic and extrinsic—that may serve to shed some light on the problem. Intrinsic unreliability is due to personal inconsistency in performance, while extrinsic unreliability is due to sources of variability that are external to job demands or individual behavior. Examples of the latter include variations in weather conditions (e.g., for outside construction work); unreliability due to machine downtime; and, in the case of interdependent tasks, delays in supplies, assemblies, or information. Much extrinsic unreliability is due to careless observation or poor control.

Faced with all of these potential confounding factors, what can be done? One solution is to *aggregate* (average) behavior over situations or occasions, thereby canceling out the effects of incidental, uncontrollable factors. To illustrate this, Epstein (1979, 1980) conducted four studies, each of which sampled behavior on repeated occasions over a period of weeks. Data in the four studies consisted of self-ratings, ratings by others, objectively measured behaviors, responses to personality inventories, and psychophysiological measures such as heart rate. The results provided unequivocal support for the hypothesis that stability can be demonstrated over a wide range of variables so long as the behavior in question is averaged over a sufficient number of occurrences. Once adequate performance reliability was obtained, evidence for validity emerged in the form of statistically significant relationships among variables. Similarly, Martocchio, Harrison, and Berkson (2000) found that increasing aggregation time enhanced the size of the validity coefficient between the predictor, employee lower-back pain, and the criterion, absenteeism.

Two further points bear emphasis. One, there is no shortcut for aggregating over occasions or people. In both cases, it is necessary to sample adequately the domain over which one wishes to generalize. Two, whether aggregation is carried out within a single study or over a sample of studies, it is not a panacea. Certain systematic effects, such as sex, race, or attitudes of raters, may bias an entire group of studies (Rosenthal & Rosnow, 1991). Examining large samples of studies through the techniques of meta-analysis (see Chapter 8; Aguinis & Pierce, 1998b) is one way of detecting the existence of such variables.

It also seems logical to expect that broader levels of aggregation might be necessary in some situations, but not in others. Specifically, Rambo, Chomiak, and Price (1983) examined what Thorndike (1949) labeled extrinsic unreliability and showed that the reliability of performance data is a function both of task complexity and of the constancy of the work environment. These factors, along with the general effectiveness of an incentive system (if one exists), interact to create the conditions that determine the extent to which performance is consistent over time. Rambo et al. (1983) obtained weekly production data over a three-and-a-half-year period from a group of women who were sewing machine operators and a group of women in folding and packaging jobs. Both groups of operators worked under a piece-rate payment plan. Median correlations in week-to-week (not day-to-day) output rates were: sewing = .94; nonsewing = .98. Among weeks separated by one year, they were: sewing = .69; nonsewing = .86. Finally, when output in week 1 was correlated with output in week 178, the correlations obtained were still high: sewing = .59; nonsewing = .80. These are extraordinary levels of consistency, indicating that the presence of a production-linked wage incentive, coupled with stable, narrowly routinized work tasks, can result in high levels of consistency in worker productivity. Those individuals who produced much (little) initially also tended to produce much (little) at a later time. More recent results for a sample of foundry chippers and grinders paid under an individual incentive plan over a six-year period were generally consistent with those of the Rambo et al. (1983) study (Vinchur, Schippmann, Smalley, & Rothe, 1991), although there may be considerable variation in long-term reliability as a function of job content.

In short, the rank order of individuals based on performance scores is likely to fluctuate over time. Several factors explain this phenomenon. Ways to address this challenge include aggregating scores over time and paying more careful attention to factors that produce this phenomenon (e.g., intrinsic and extrinsic factors such as stability of work environment). A better understanding of these factors is likely to allow HR professionals to understand better the extent to which specific operational criteria will be consistent over time.

Challenge #2: Job Performance Observation

This issue is crucial in prediction because all evaluations of performance depend ultimately on observation of one sort or another; but different methods of observing performance may lead to markedly different conclusions, as was shown by Bray and Campbell (1968). In attempting to validate assessment center predictions of future sales potential, 78 men were hired as salespeople, regardless of their performance at the assessment center (we discuss the topic of the assessment center in detail in Chapter 13). Predictions then were related to field performance six months later. Field performance was assessed in two ways. In the first method, a trained independent auditor accompanied each man in the field on as many visits as were necessary to determine whether he did or did not meet accepted standards in conducting his sales activities. The field reviewer was unaware of any judgments made of the candidates at the assessment center. In the second method, each individual was rated by his sales supervisor and his trainer from sales training school. Both the supervisor and the trainer also were unaware of the assessment center predictions.

While assessment center predictions correlated .51 with field performance ratings by the auditor, there were no significant relationships between assessment center predictions and either supervisors' ratings or trainers' ratings. Additionally, there were no significant relationships between the field performance ratings and the supervisors' or trainers' ratings! The lesson to be drawn from this study is obvious: The study of reliability of performance becomes possible only when the reliability of judging performance is adequate (Ryans & Fredericksen, 1951). Unfortunately, while we know that the problem exists, there is no silver bullet that will improve the reliability of judging performance (Borman & Hallam, 1991). We examine this issue in greater detail, including some promising new approaches, in the next chapter.

Challenge #3: Dimensionality of Job Performance

Even the most cursory examination of HR research reveals a great variety of predictors typically in use. In contrast, however, the majority of studies use only a global criterion measure of the job performance. Although ratings may reflect various aspects of job performance, these ratings are frequently combined into a single global score. Lent, Aurbach, and Levin (1971) demonstrated this in their analysis of 406 studies published in *Personnel Psychology*. Of the 1,506 criteria used, "Supervisors' Evaluation" was used in 879 cases. The extent to which the use of a single global criterion is characteristic of unpublished research is a matter of pure speculation, but its incidence is probably far higher than that in published research. Is it meaningful or realistic to reduce performance measurement to a single indicator, given our previous discussion of the multidimensionality of criteria?

Several reviews (Campbell, 1990; Ronan & Prien, 1966, 1971) concluded that the notion of a unidimensional measure of job performance (even for lower-level jobs) is unrealistic. Analyses of even single measures of job performance (e.g., attitude toward the company, absenteeism) have shown that they are much more complex than surface appearance would suggest. Despite the problems associated with global criteria, they seem to "work" quite well in most personnel selection situations. However, to the extent that one needs to solve a specific problem (e.g., too many customer complaints about product quality), a more specific criterion is needed. If there is more than one specific problem, then more than one specific criterion is called for (Guion, 1987).

PERFORMANCE AND SITUATIONAL CHARACTERISTICS

Most people would agree readily that individual levels of performance may be affected by conditions surrounding the performance. Yet most research investigations are conducted without regard for possible effects of variables other than those measured by predictors. In this section, therefore, we will examine six possible extraindividual influences on performance. Taken together, the discussion of these influences is part of what Cascio and Aguinis (2008b) defined as *in situ* performance: "the specification of the broad range of effects—situational, contextual, strategic, and environmental—that may affect individual, team, or organizational performance" (p. 146). A consideration of *in situ* performance involves context—situational opportunities and constraints that affect the occurrence and meaning of behavior in organizations—as well as functional relationships between variables.

Environmental and Organizational Characteristics

Absenteeism and turnover both have been related to a variety of environmental and organizational characteristics (Campion, 1991; Dineen, Noe, Shaw, Duffy, & Wiethoff, 2007; McEvoy & Cascio, 1987; Sun, Aryee, & Law, 2007). These include organizationwide factors (e.g., pay and promotion policies, human resources practices); interpersonal factors (e.g., group cohesiveness, friendship opportunities, satisfaction with peers or supervisors); job-related factors (e.g., role clarity, task repetitiveness, autonomy, and responsibility); and personal factors (e.g., age, tenure, mood, and family size). Shift work is another frequently overlooked variable (Barton, 1994; Staines & Pleck, 1984). Clearly, organizational characteristics can have wide-ranging effects on performance.

Environmental Safety

Injuries and loss of time may also affect job performance (Probst, Brubaker, & Barsotti, 2008). Factors such as a positive safety climate, a high management commitment, and a sound safety communications program that incorporates goal setting and knowledge of results tend to increase safe behavior on the job (Reber & Wallin, 1984) and conservation of scarce resources (cf. Siero, Boon, Kok, & Siero, 1989). These variables can be measured reliably (Zohar, 1980) and can then be related to individual performance.

Lifespace Variables

Lifespace variables measure important conditions that surround the employee both on and off the job. They describe the individual employee's interactions with organizational factors, task demands, supervision, and conditions of the job. Vicino and Bass (1978) used four life-space variables—task challenge on first job assignment, life stability, supervisor–subordinate personality match, and immediate supervisor's success—to improve predictions of management success at Exxon. The four variables accounted for an additional 22 percent of the variance in success on the job over and above Exxon's own prediction system based on aptitude and personality measures. The equivalent of a multiple R of .79 was obtained. Other lifespace variables, such as personal orientation, career confidence, cosmopolitan versus local orientation, and job stress, deserve further study (Cooke & Rousseau, 1983; Edwards & Van Harrison, 1993).

Job and Location

Schneider and Mitchel (1980) developed a comprehensive set of six behavioral job functions for the agency manager's job in the life insurance industry. Using 1,282 managers from 50 companies, they examined the relationship of activity in these functions with five factors: origin of the agency (new versus established), type of agency (independent versus company controlled), number of agents, number of supervisors, and tenure of the agency manager. These five situational variables were chosen as correlates of managerial functions on the basis of their traditionally implied impact on managerial behavior in the life insurance industry. The most variance explained in a job function by a weighted composite of the five situational variables was 8.6 percent (i.e., for the general management function). Thus, over 90 percent of the variance in the six agency-management functions lies in sources other than the five variables used. While situational variables have been found to influence managerial job functions *across* technological boundaries, the results of this study suggest that situational characteristics also may influence managerial job functions *within* a particular technology. Performance thus depends not only on job demands but also on other structural and contextual factors such as the policies and practices of particular companies.

Extraindividual Differences and Sales Performance

Cravens and Woodruff (1973) recognized the need to adjust criterion standards for influences beyond a salesperson's control, and they attempted to determine the degree to which these factors explained variations in territory performance. In a multiple regression analysis using dollar volume of sales as the criterion, a curvilinear model yielded a corrected R^2 of .83, with sales experience, average market share, and performance ratings providing the major portion of explained variation. This study is noteworthy because a purer estimate of individual job performance was generated by combining the effects of extraindividual influences (territory workload, market potential, company market share, and advertising effort) with two individual difference variables (sales experience and rated sales effort).

Leadership

The effects of leadership and situational factors on morale and performance have been well documented (Detert, Treviño, Burris, & Andiappan, 2007; Srivastava, Bartol, & Locke, 2006). These studies, as well as those cited previously, demonstrate that variations in job performance are due to characteristics of individuals (age, sex, job experience, etc.), groups, and organizations (size, structure, management behavior, etc.). Until we can begin to partition the total variability in job performance into intraindividual and extraindividual components, we should not expect predictor variables measuring individual differences to correlate appreciably with measures of performance that are influenced by factors not under an individual's control.

STEPS IN CRITERION DEVELOPMENT

A five-step procedure for criterion development has been outlined by Guion (1961):

1. Analysis of job and/or organizational needs.
2. Development of measures of actual behavior relative to expected behavior as identified in job and need analysis. These measures should supplement objective measures of organizational outcomes such as turnover, absenteeism, and production.
3. Identification of criterion dimensions underlying such measures by factor analysis, cluster analysis, or pattern analysis.
4. Development of reliable measures, each with high construct validity, of the elements so identified.
5. Determination of the predictive validity of each independent variable (predictor) for *each one* of the criterion measures, taking them one at a time.

In step 2, behavior data are distinguished from result-of-behavior data or organizational outcomes, and it is recommended that behavior data supplement result-of-behavior data. In step 4, construct-valid measures are advocated. Construct validity is essentially a judgment that a test or other predictive device does, in fact, measure a specified attribute or construct to a significant degree and that it can be used to promote the understanding or prediction of behavior (Landy & Conte, 2007; Messick, 1995). These two poles, **utility** (i.e., in which the researcher attempts to find the highest and therefore most useful validity coefficient) versus **understanding** (in which the researcher advocates construct validity), have formed part of the basis for an enduring controversy in psychology over the relative merits of the two approaches. We shall examine this in greater detail in the section on composite versus multiple criteria.

EVALUATING CRITERIA

How can we evaluate the usefulness of a given criterion? Let's discuss each of three different yardsticks: relevance, sensitivity or discriminability, and practicality.

Relevance

The principal requirement of any criterion is its judged relevance (i.e., it must be logically related to the performance domain in question). As noted in *Principles for the Validation and Use of Personnel Selection Procedures* (SIOP, 2003), "[A] relevant criterion is one that reflects the relative standing of employees with respect to important work behavior(s) or outcome measure(s)" (p. 14). Hence, it is essential that this domain be described clearly.

Indeed, the American Psychological Association (APA) Task Force on Employment Testing of Minority Groups (1969) specifically emphasized that the most appropriate (i.e., logically relevant) criterion for evaluating tests is a direct measure of the degree of job proficiency developed by an employee after an appropriate period of time on the job (e.g., six months to a year). To be sure, the most relevant criterion measure will not always be the most expedient or the cheapest. A well-designed work sample test or performance management system may require a great deal of ingenuity, effort, and expense to construct (e.g., Jackson, Harris, Ashton, McCarthy, & Tremblay, 2000).

It is important to recognize that objective and subjective measures are not interchangeable, one for the other, as they correlate only about .39 (Bommer, Johnson, Rich, Podsakoff, and Mackenzie, 1995). So, if objective measures are the measures of interest, subjective measures should not be used as proxies. For example, if sales are the desired measure of performance, then organizations should not reward employees based on a supervisor's overall rating of performance. Conversely, if broadly defined performance is the objective, then organizations should not reward employees solely on the basis of gross sales. Nevertheless, regardless of how many criteria are used, if, when considering all the dimensions of job performance, there remains an important aspect that is not being assessed, then an additional criterion measure is required.

Sensitivity or Discriminability

In order to be useful, any criterion measure also must be sensitive—that is, capable of discriminating between effective and ineffective employees. Suppose, for example, that quantity of goods produced is used as a criterion measure in a manufacturing operation. Such a criterion frequently is used inappropriately when, because of machine pacing, everyone doing a given job produces about the same number of goods. Under these circumstances, there is little justification for using quantity of goods produced as a performance criterion, since the most effective workers do not differ appreciably from the least effective workers. Perhaps the amount of scrap or the number of errors made by workers would be a more sensitive indicator of real differences in job performance. Thus, the use of a particular criterion measure is warranted only if it serves to reveal discriminable differences in job performance.

It is important to point out, however, that there is no necessary association between criterion variance and criterion relevance. A criterion element *as measured* may have low variance, but the implications in terms of a different scale of measurement, such as dollars, may be considerable (e.g., the dollar cost of industrial accidents). In other words, the utility to the organization of what a criterion measures may not be reflected in the way that criterion is measured. This highlights the distinction between operational measures and a conceptual formulation of what is important (i.e., has high utility *and* relevance) to the organization (Cascio & Valenzi, 1978).

Practicality

It is important that management be informed thoroughly of the real benefits of using carefully developed criteria. Management may or may not have the expertise to appraise the soundness of a criterion measure or a series of criterion measures, but objections will almost certainly arise if record keeping and data collection for criterion measures become impractical and interfere significantly with ongoing operations. Overzealous HR researchers sometimes view organizations as ongoing laboratories existing solely for their purposes. This should not be construed as an excuse for using inadequate or irrelevant criteria. Clearly a balance must be sought, for the HR department occupies a staff role, assisting through more effective use of human resources those who are concerned directly with achieving the organization's primary goals of profit, growth, and/or service. Keep criterion measurement practical!

CRITERION DEFICIENCY

Criterion measures differ in the extent to which they cover the criterion domain. For example, the job of university professor includes tasks related to teaching, research, and service. If job performance is measured using indicators of teaching and service only, then the measures are deficient because they fail to include an important component of the job. Similarly, if we wish to measure a manager's flexibility, adopting a trait approach only would be deficient because managerial flexibility is a higher-order construct that reflects mastery of specific and opposing behaviors in two domains: social/interpersonal and functional/organizational (Kaiser, Lindberg, & Craig, 2007).

The importance of considering criterion deficiency was highlighted by a study examining the economic utility of companywide training programs addressing managerial and sales/technical skills (Morrow, Jarrett, & Rupinski, 1997). The economic utility of training programs may differ not because of differences in the effectiveness of the programs per se, but because the criterion measures may differ in breadth. In other words, the amount of change observed in an employee's performance after she attends a training program will depend on the percentage of job tasks measured by the evaluation criteria. A measure including only a subset of the tasks learned during training will underestimate the value of the training program.

CRITERION CONTAMINATION

When criterion measures are gathered carelessly with no checks on their worth before use either for research purposes or in the development of HR policies, they are often contaminated. Maier (1988) demonstrated this in an evaluation of the aptitude tests used to make placement decisions about military recruits. The tests were validated against hands-on job performance tests for two Marine Corps jobs: radio repairer and auto mechanic. The job performance tests were administered by sergeants who were experienced in each specialty and who spent most of their time training and supervising junior personnel. The sergeants were not given any training on how to administer and score performance tests. In addition, they received little monitoring during the four months of actual data collection, and only a single administrator was used to evaluate each examinee. The data collected were filled with errors, although subsequent statistical checks and corrections made the data salvageable. Did the "clean" data make a difference in the decisions made? Certainly. The original data yielded validities of 0.09 and 0.17 for the two specialties. However, after the data were "cleaned up," the validities rose to 0.49 and 0.37, thus changing the interpretation of how valid the aptitude tests actually were.

Criterion contamination occurs when the operational or actual criterion includes variance that is unrelated to the ultimate criterion. Contamination itself may be subdivided into two distinct parts, error and bias (Blum & Naylor, 1968). **Error** by definition is random variation (e.g., due to nonstandardized procedures in testing, individual fluctuations in feelings) and cannot correlate with anything except by chance alone. **Bias**, on the other hand, represents systematic criterion contamination, and it can correlate with predictor measures.

Criterion bias is of great concern in HR research because its potential influence is so pervasive. Brogden and Taylor (1950b) offered a concise definition:

> A biasing factor may be defined as any variable, except errors of measurement and sampling error, producing a deviation of obtained criterion scores from a hypothetical "true" criterion score. (p. 161)

It should also be added that because the direction of the deviation from the true criterion score is not specified, biasing factors may serve to increase, decrease, or leave unchanged the obtained validity coefficient. Biasing factors vary widely in their distortive effect, but primarily this distortion is a function of the degree of their correlation with predictors. The magnitude of such effects must be estimated and their influence controlled either experimentally or statistically. Next we discuss three important and likely sources of bias.

Bias Due to Knowledge of Predictor Information

One of the most serious contaminants of criterion data, especially when the data are in the form of ratings, is prior knowledge of or exposure to predictor scores. In the selection of executives, for example, the assessment center method (Chapter 14) is a popular technique. If an individual's immediate superior has access to the prediction of this individual's future potential by the assessment center staff and if at a later date the superior is asked to rate the individual's performance, the supervisor's prior exposure to the assessment center prediction is likely to bias this rating. If the subordinate has been tagged as a "shooting star" by the assessment center staff and the supervisor values that judgment, he or she, too, may rate the subordinate as a "shooting star." If the supervisor views the subordinate as a rival, dislikes him or her for that reason, and wants to impede his or her progress, the assessment center report could serve as a stimulus for a *lower* rating than is deserved. In either case—spuriously high or spuriously low ratings—bias is introduced and gives an unrealistic estimate of the validity of the predictor. Because this type of bias is by definition predictor correlated, it *looks like* the predictor is doing a better job of predicting than it actually is; yet the effect is illusory. The rule of thumb is this: Keep predictor information away from those who must provide criterion data!

Probably the best way to guard against this type of bias is to obtain all criterion data before any predictor data are released. Thus, in attempting to validate assessment center predictions, Bray and Grant (1966) collected data at an experimental assessment center, but these data had no bearing on subsequent promotion decisions. Eight years later the predictions were validated against a criterion of "promoted versus not promoted into middle management." By carefully shielding the predictor information from those who had responsibility for making promotion decisions, a much "cleaner" validity estimate was obtained.

Bias Due to Group Membership

Criterion bias may also result from the fact that individuals belong to certain groups. In fact, sometimes explicit or implicit policies govern the hiring or promotion of these individuals. For example, some organizations tend to hire engineering graduates predominantly (or only) from certain schools. We know of an organization that tends to promote people internally who also receive promotions in their military reserve units!

Studies undertaken thereafter that attempt to relate these biographical characteristics to subsequent career success will necessarily be biased. The same effects also will occur when a group sets artificial limits on how much it will produce.

Bias in Ratings

Supervisory ratings, the most frequently employed criteria (Aguinis, 2009a; Lent et al., 1971; Murphy & Cleveland, 1995), are susceptible to all the sources of bias in objective indices, as well as to others that are peculiar to subjective judgments (Thorndike, 1920). We shall discuss this problem in much greater detail in the next chapter, but, for the present, it is important to emphasize that bias in ratings may be due to spotty or inadequate observation by the rater, unequal opportunity on the part of subordinates to demonstrate proficiency, personal biases or prejudices on the part of the rater, or an inability to distinguish and reliably rate different dimensions of job performance.

CRITERION EQUIVALENCE

If two criteria correlate perfectly (or nearly perfectly) after correcting both for unreliability, then they are equivalent. Criterion equivalence should not be taken lightly or assumed; it is a rarity in HR research. Strictly speaking, if two criteria are equivalent, then they contain exactly the same job elements, are measuring precisely the same individual characteristics, and are occupying exactly the same portion of the conceptual criterion space. Two criteria are equivalent if it doesn't make any difference which one is used.

If the correlation between criteria is less than perfect, however, the two are not equivalent. This has been demonstrated repeatedly in analyses of the relationship between performance in training and performance on the job (Ghiselli, 1966; Hunter & Hunter, 1984), as well as in learning tasks (Weitz, 1961). In analyzing criteria and using them to observe performance, one must, therefore, consider not only the *time* of measurement but also the *type* of measurement— that is, the particular performance measures selected and the reasons for doing so. Finally, one must consider the *level* of performance measurement that represents success or failure (assuming it is necessary to dichotomize criterion performance) and attempt to estimate the effect of the chosen level of performance on the conclusions reached.

For example, suppose we are judging the performance of a group of quality control inspectors on a work sample task (a device with 10 known defects). We set our criterion cutoff at eight—that is, the identification of fewer than eight defects constitutes unsatisfactory performance. The number of "successful" inspectors may increase markedly if the criterion cutoff is lowered to five defects. Our conclusions regarding overall inspector proficiency are likely to change as well. In sum, if we know the rules governing our criterion measures, this alone should give us more insight into the operation of our predictor measures.

The researcher may treat highly correlated criteria in several different ways. He or she may choose to drop one of the criteria, viewing it essentially as redundant information, or to keep the two criterion measures separate, reasoning that the more information collected, the better. A third strategy is to gather data relevant to both criterion measures, to convert all data to standard score form, to compute the individual's average score, and to use this as the best estimate of the individual's standing on the composite dimension. No matter which strategy the researcher adopts, he or she should do so only on the basis of a sound theoretical or practical rationale and should comprehend fully the implications of the chosen strategy.

COMPOSITE CRITERION VERSUS MULTIPLE CRITERIA

Applied psychologists generally agree that job performance is multidimensional in nature and that adequate measurement of job performance requires multidimensional criteria. The next question is what to do about it. Should one combine the various criterion measures into a composite score, or should each criterion measure be treated separately? If the investigator chooses to combine the elements, what rule should he or she use to do so? As with the utility versus understanding issue, both sides have had their share of vigorous proponents over the years. Let us consider some of the arguments.

Composite Criterion

The basic contention of Brogden and Taylor (1950a), Thorndike (1949), Toops (1944), and Nagle (1953), the strongest advocates of the composite criterion, is that the criterion should provide a yardstick or overall measure of "success" or "value to the organization" of each individual. Such a single index is indispensable in decision making and individual comparisons, and even if the criterion dimensions are treated separately in validation, they must somehow be combined into a composite when a decision is required. Although the combination of multiple criteria into a composite is often done subjectively, a quantitative weighting scheme makes objective the importance placed on each of the criteria that was used to form the composite.

If a decision is made to form a composite based on several criterion measures, then the question is whether all measures should be given the same weight or not (Bobko, Roth, & Buster, 2007). Consider the possible combination of two measures reflecting customer service, one collected from external customers (i.e., those purchasing the products offered by the organization) and the other from internal customers (i.e., individuals employed in other units within the same organization). Giving these measures equal weights implies that the organization values both external and internal customer service equally. However, the organization may make the strategic decision to form the composite by giving 70 percent weight to external customer service and 30 percent weight to internal customer service. This strategic decision is likely to affect the validity coefficients between predictors and criteria. Specifically, Murphy and Shiarella (1997) conducted a computer simulation and found that 34 percent of the variance in the validity of a battery of selection tests was explained by the way in which measures of task and contextual performance were combined to form a composite performance score. In short, forming a composite requires a careful consideration of the relative importance of each criterion measure.

Multiple Criteria

Advocates of multiple criteria contend that measures of demonstrably different variables should not be combined. As Cattell (1957) put it, "Ten men and two bottles of beer cannot be added to give the same total as two men and ten bottles of beer" (p. 11). Consider a study of military recruiters (Pulakos, Borman, & Hough, 1988). In measuring the effectiveness of the recruiters, it was found that selling skills, human relations skills, and organizing skills all were important and related to success. It also was found, however, that the three dimensions were unrelated to each other—that is, the recruiter with the best selling skills did not necessarily have the best human relations skills or the best organizing skills. Under these conditions, combining the measures leads to a composite that not only is ambiguous, but also is psychologically nonsensical. Guion (1961) brought the issue clearly into focus:

> The fallacy of the single criterion lies in its assumption that everything that is to be predicted is related to everything else that is to be predicted—that there is a general factor in all criteria accounting for virtually all of the important variance in behavior at work and its various consequences of value. (p. 145)

Schmidt and Kaplan (1971) subsequently pointed out that combining various criterion elements into a composite does imply that there is a single underlying dimension in job performance, but it does not, in and of itself, imply that this single underlying dimension is behavioral or psychological in nature. A composite criterion may well represent an underlying economic dimension, while at the same time being essentially meaningless from a behavioral point of view. Thus, Brogden and Taylor (1950a) argued that when all of the criteria are relevant measures of economic variables (dollars and cents), they can be combined into a composite, regardless of their intercorrelations.

Differing Assumptions

As Schmidt and Kaplan (1971) and Binning and Barrett (1989) have noted, the two positions differ in terms of (1) the nature of the underlying constructs represented by the respective criterion measures and (2) what they regard to be the primary purpose of the validation process itself. Let us consider the first set of assumptions. Underpinning the arguments for the composite criterion is the assumption that the criterion should represent an economic rather than a behavioral construct. The economic orientation is illustrated in Brogden and Taylor's (1950a) "dollar criterion": "The criterion should measure the overall contribution of the individual to the organization" (p. 139). Brogden and Taylor argued that overall efficiency should be measured in dollar terms by applying cost accounting concepts and procedures to the individual job behaviors of the employee. "The criterion problem centers primarily on the quantity, quality, and cost of the finished product" (p. 141).

In contrast, advocates of multiple criteria (Dunnette, 1963a; Pulakos et al., 1988) argued that the criterion should represent a behavioral or psychological construct, one that is behaviorally homogeneous. Pulakos et al. (1988) acknowledged that a composite criterion must be developed when actually making employment decisions, but they also emphasized that such composites are best formed when their components are well understood.

With regard to the goals of the validation process, advocates of the composite criterion assume that the validation process is carried out only for practical and economic reasons, and not to promote greater understanding of the psychological and behavioral processes involved in various jobs. Thus, Brogden and Taylor (1950a) clearly distinguished the end products of a given job (job products) from the job processes that lead to these end products. With regard to job processes, they argued: "Such factors as skill are latent; their effect is realized in the end product. They do not satisfy the logical requirement of an adequate criterion" (p. 141).

In contrast, the advocates of multiple criteria view increased understanding as an important goal of the validation process, along with practical and economic goals: "The goal of the search for understanding is a theory (or theories) of work behavior; theories of human behavior are cast in terms of psychological and behavioral, not economic constructs" (Schmidt & Kaplan, 1971, p. 424).

Resolving the Dilemma

Clearly there are numerous possible uses of job performance and program evaluation criteria. In general, they may be used for research purposes or operationally as an aid in managerial decision making. When criteria are used for research purposes, the emphasis is on the psychological understanding of the relationship between various predictors and separate criterion dimensions, where the dimensions themselves are behavioral in nature. When used for managerial decision-making purposes—such as job assignment, promotion, capital budgeting, or evaluation of the cost effectiveness of recruitment, training, or advertising programs—criterion dimensions must be combined into a composite representing overall (economic) worth to the organization.

The resolution of the composite criterion versus multiple criteria dilemma essentially depends on the objectives of the investigator. Both methods are legitimate for their own purposes. If the goal is increased psychological understanding of predictor-criterion relationships, then the criterion elements are best kept separate. If managerial decision making is the objective, then the criterion elements should be weighted, regardless of their intercorrelations, into a composite representing an economic construct of overall worth to the organization.

Criterion measures with theoretical relevance should not replace those with practical relevance, but rather should supplement or be used along with them. The goal, therefore, is to enhance utility *and* understanding.

RESEARCH DESIGN AND CRITERION THEORY

Traditionally personnel psychologists were guided by a simple prediction model that sought to relate performance on one or more predictors with a composite criterion. Implicit intervening variables usually were neglected.

A more complete criterion model that describes the inferences required for the rigorous development of criteria was presented by Binning and Barrett (1989). The model is shown in Figure 4-3. Managers involved in employment decisions are most concerned about the extent to which assessment information will allow accurate predictions about subsequent job performance (Inference 9 in Figure 4-3). One general approach to justifying Inference 9 would be to generate direct empirical evidence that assessment scores relate to valid measurements of job performance. Inference 5 shows this linkage, which traditionally has been the most pragmatic concern to

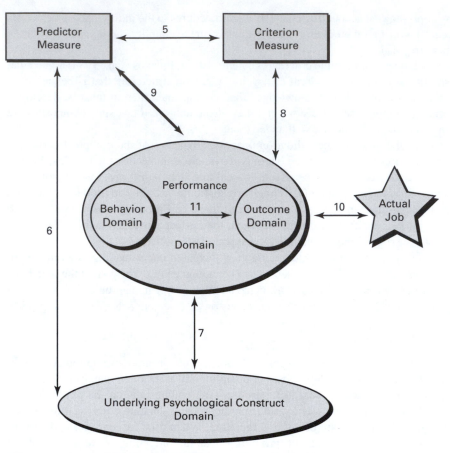

FIGURE 4-3 A modified framework that identifies the inferences for criterion development. *Source:* Linkages in the figure begin with No. 5 because earlier figures in the article used Nos. 1–4 to show critical linkages in the theory-building process. From Binning, J. F., & Barrett, G. V. Validity of personnel decisions: A conceptual analysis of the inferential and evidential bases. *Journal of Applied Psychology, 74,* 478–494. Copyright © 1989 American Psych. Assoc. American Psychological Association. Reprinted with permission.

personnel psychologists. Indeed, the term **criterion related** has been used to denote this type of evidence. However, to have complete confidence in Inference 9, Inferences 5 and 8 *both* must be justified. That is, a predictor should be related to an operational criterion measure (Inference 5), and the operational criterion measure should be related to the performance domain it represents (Inference 8).

Performance domains are comprised of behavior-outcome units (Binning & Barrett, 1989). Outcomes (e.g., dollar volume of sales) are valued by an organization, and behaviors (e.g., selling skills) are the means to these valued ends. Thus, behaviors take on different values, depending on the value of the outcomes. This, in turn, implies that optimal description of the performance domain for a given job requires careful and complete representation of valued outcomes and the behaviors that accompany them. As we noted earlier, composite criterion models focus on outcomes, whereas multiple criteria models focus on behaviors. As Figure 4-3 shows, together they form a performance domain. This is why both are necessary and should continue to be used.

Inference 8 represents the process of criterion development. Usually it is justified by rational evidence (in the form of job analysis data) showing that all major behavioral dimensions or job outcomes have been identified and are represented in the operational criterion measure. In fact, job analysis (see Chapter 9) provides the evidential basis for justifying Inferences 7, 8, 10, and 11.

What personnel psychologists have traditionally implied by the term **construct validity** is tied to Inferences 6 and 7. That is, if it can be shown that a test (e.g., of reading comprehension) measures a specific construct (Inference 6), such as reading comprehension, that has been determined to be critical for job performance (Inference 7), then inferences about job performance from test scores (Inference 9) are, by logical implication, justified. Constructs are simply labels for behavioral regularities that underlie behavior sampled by the predictor, and, in the performance domain, by the criterion.

In the context of understanding and validating criteria, Inferences 7, 8, 10, and 11 are critical. Inference 7 is typically justified by claims, based on job analysis, that the constructs underlying performance have been identified. This process is commonly referred to as **deriving job specifications**. Inference 10, on the other hand, represents the extent to which actual job demands have been analyzed adequately, resulting in a valid description of the performance domain. This process is commonly referred to as developing a **job description**. Finally, Inference 11 represents the extent to which the links between job behaviors and job outcomes have been verified. Again, job analysis is the process used to discover and to specify these links.

The framework shown in Figure 4-3 helps to identify possible locations for what we have referred to as the **criterion problem**. This problem results from a tendency to neglect the development of adequate evidence to support Inferences 7, 8, and 10 and fosters a very shortsighted view of the process of validating criteria. It also leads predictably to two inter-related consequences: (1) the development of criterion measures that are less rigorous psycho-metrically than are predictor measures and (2) the development of performance criteria than are less deeply or richly embedded in the networks of theoretical relationships that are constructs on the predictor side. These consequences are unfortunate, for they limit the development of theories, the validation of constructs, and the generation of evidence to support important inferences about people and their behavior at work (Binning & Barrett, 1989). Conversely, the development of evidence to support the important linkages shown in Figure 4-3 will lead to better-informed staffing decisions, better career development decisions, and, ultimately, more effective organizations.

Evidence-Based Implications for Practice

- The effectiveness and future progress of our knowledge of HR interventions depend fundamentally on careful, accurate criterion measurement.
- It is important to conceptualize the job performance domain broadly and to consider job perform-ance as *in situ* performance (i.e., the specification of the broad range of effects—situational, contextual, strategic, and environmental—that may affect individual, team, or organizational performance)
- Pay close attention to the notion of criterion relevance, which, in turn, requires prior theorizing and development of the dimensions that comprise the domain of performance.
- First formulate clearly your ultimate objectives and then develop appropriate criterion measures that represent economic or behavioral constructs. Criterion measures must pass the tests of relevance, sensitivity, and practicality.
- Attempt continually to determine how dependent your conclusions are likely to be because of (1) the particular criterion measures used, (2) the time of measurement, (3) the conditions outside the control of an individual, and (4) the distortions and biases inherent in the situation or the measuring instrument (human or otherwise).
- There may be many paths to success, and, consequently, we must adopt a broader, richer view of job performance.

Discussion Questions

1. Why do objective measures of performance often tell an incomplete story about performance?

2. Develop some examples of immediate, intermediate, and summary criteria for (a) a student, (b) a judge, and (c) a professional golfer.

3. Discuss the problems that dynamic criteria pose for employment decisions.

4. What are the implications of the typical versus maximum performance distinction for personnel selection?

5. What are the implications for theory and practice of the concept of *in situ* performance?

6. How can the reliability of job performance observation be improved?

7. What are the factors that should be considered in assigning differential weights when creating a composite measure of performance?

8. Describe the performance domain of a university professor. Then propose a criterion measure to be used in making promotion decisions. How would you rate this criterion regarding relevance, sensitivity, and practicality?

5

Performance Management

At a Glance

Performance management is a continuous process of identifying, measuring, and developing the performance of individuals and teams and aligning performance with the strategic goals of the organization. Performance management systems serve both strategic and operational purposes, and because they take place within the social realities of organizations, they should be examined both from both measurement/technical as well as human/emotional points of view.

Performance appraisal, the systematic description of individual or group job-relevant strengths and weaknesses, is a key component of any performance management system. Performance appraisal comprises two processes: observation and judgment, both of which are subject to bias. For this reason, some have suggested that job performance be judged solely on the basis of objective indices such as production data and employment data (e.g., accidents or awards). While such data are intuitively appealing, they often measure not performance, but factors beyond an individual's control; they measure not behavior per se, but rather the outcomes of behavior. Because of these deficiencies, subjective criteria (e.g., supervisory ratings) are often used. However, because ratings depend on human judgment, they are subject to other kinds of biases. Each of the available methods for rating job performance attempts to reduce bias in some way, although no method is completely bias-free. Biases may be associated with raters (e.g., lack of firsthand knowledge of employee performance), ratees (e.g., gender and job tenure), the interaction of raters and ratees (e.g., race and gender), or various situational and organizational characteristics.

Bias can be reduced sharply, however, through training in both the technical and the human aspects of the rating process. Training must also address the potentially incompatible role demands of supervisors (i.e., coach and judge) during performance appraisal interviews. Training must also address how to provide effective performance feedback to rates and set mutually agreeable goals for future performance improvement.

Performance management is a "continuous process of identifying, measuring, and developing the performance of individuals and teams and aligning performance with the strategic goals of the organization" (Aguinis, 2009a, p. 2). It is not a one-time event that takes place during the annual performance-review period. Rather, performance is assessed at regular intervals, and feedback is provided so that performance is improved on an ongoing basis. Performance appraisal, the systematic description of job-relevant strengths and weaknesses within and between employees or groups, is a critical, and perhaps the most delicate, topic in HRM. Researchers are fascinated by this subject; yet their overall inability to resolve definitively the knotty technical and interpersonal problems of performance appraisal has led one reviewer to term it the "Achilles heel" of HRM (Heneman, 1975). This statement, issued in the 1970s, still applies today because supervisors and subordinates who periodically encounter management systems, either as raters or as ratees, are often mistrustful of the uses of such information (Mayer & Davis, 1999). They are intensely aware of the political and practical implications of the ratings and, in many cases, are acutely ill at ease during performance appraisal interviews. Despite these shortcomings, surveys of managers from both large and small organizations consistently show that managers are unwilling to abandon performance management, for they regard it as an important assessment tool (Meyer, 1991; Murphy & Cleveland, 1995).

Many treatments of performance management scarcely contain a hint of the emotional overtones, the human problems, so intimately bound up with it (Aguinis, 2009b). Traditionally, researchers have placed primary emphasis on technical issues—for example, the advantages and disadvantages of various rating systems, sources of error, and problems of unreliability in performance observation and measurement (Aguinis & Pierce, 2008). To be sure, these are vitally important concerns. No less important, however, are the human issues involved, for performance management is not merely a technique—it is a process, a dialogue involving both people and data, and this process also includes social and motivational aspects (Fletcher, 2001). In addition, performance management needs to be placed within the broader context of the organization's vision, mission, and strategic priorities. A performance management system will not be successful if it is not linked explicitly to broader work unit and organizational goals.

In this chapter, we shall focus on both the measurement and the social/motivational aspects of performance management, for judgments about worker proficiency *are* made, whether implicitly or explicitly, whenever people interact in organizational settings. As HR specialists, our task is to make the formal process as meaningful and workable as present research and development will allow.

PURPOSES SERVED

Performance management systems that are designed and implemented well can serve several important purposes:

1. Performance management systems serve a *strategic* purpose because they help link employee activities with the organization's mission and goals. Well-designed performance management systems identify the results and behaviors needed to carry out the organization's strategic priorities and maximize the extent to which employees exhibit the desired behaviors and produce the intended results.

2. Performance management systems serve an important *communication* purpose because they allow employees to know how they are doing and what the organizational expectations are regarding their performance. They convey the aspects of work the supervisor and other organization stakeholders believe are important.

3. Performance management systems can serve as bases for *employment decisions*—to promote outstanding performers; to terminate marginal or low performers; to train, transfer, or discipline others; and to award merit increases (or no increases). In short, information gathered by the performance management system can serve as *predictors* and, consequently, as key input for administering a formal organizational reward and punishment system (Cummings, 1973), including promotional decisions.

4. Data regarding employee performance can serve as *criteria* in HR research (e.g., in test validation).

5. Performance management systems also serve a *developmental* purpose because they can help establish objectives for training programs (when they are expressed in terms of desired behaviors or outcomes rather than global personality characteristics).

6. Performance management systems can provide concrete *feedback* to employees. In order to improve performance in the future, an employee needs to know what his or her weaknesses were in the past and how to correct them in the future. Pointing out strengths and weaknesses is a coaching function for the supervisor; receiving meaningful feedback and acting on it constitute a motivational experience for the subordinate. Thus, performance management systems can serve as vehicles for *personal development*.

7. Performance management systems can facilitate *organizational diagnosis, maintenance, and development*. Proper specification of performance levels, in addition to suggesting training needs across units and indicating necessary skills to be considered when hiring, is important for HR planning and HR evaluation. It also establishes the more general organizational requirement of ability to discriminate effective from ineffective performers. Appraising employee performance, therefore, represents the beginning of a process rather than an end product (Jacobs, Kafry, & Zedeck, 1980).

8. Finally, performance management systems allow organizations to keep proper *records* to document HR decisions and legal requirements.

REALITIES OF PERFORMANCE MANAGEMENT SYSTEMS

Independently of any organizational context, the implementation of performance management systems at work confronts the appraiser with five realities (Ghorpade & Chen, 1995):

1. This activity is inevitable in all organizations, large and small, public and private, and domestic and multinational. Organizations need to know if individuals are performing competently, and, in the current legal climate, appraisals are essential features of an organization's defense against challenges to adverse employment actions, such as terminations or layoffs.

2. Appraisal is fraught with consequences for individuals (rewards/punishments) and organizations (the need to provide appropriate rewards and punishments based on performance).

3. As job complexity increases, it becomes progressively more difficult, even for well-meaning appraisers, to assign accurate, merit-based performance ratings.

4. When sitting in judgment on coworkers, there is an ever-present danger of the parties being influenced by the political consequences of their actions—rewarding allies and punishing enemies or competitors (Longenecker, & Gioia, 1994; Longenecker, Sims, & Gioia, 1987).

5. The implementation of performance management systems takes time and effort, and participants (those who rate performance and those whose performance is rated) must be convinced the system is useful and fair. Otherwise, the system may carry numerous negative consequences (e.g., employees may quit, there may be wasted time and money, and there may be adverse legal consequences).

BARRIERS TO IMPLEMENTING EFFECTIVE PERFORMANCE MANAGEMENT SYSTEMS

Barriers to successful performance management may be organizational, political, or interpersonal. Organizational barriers result when workers are held responsible for errors that may be the result of built-in organizational systems. Political barriers stem from deliberate attempts by raters to enhance or to protect their self-interests when conflicting courses of action are possible. Interpersonal barriers arise from the actual face-to-face encounter between subordinate and superior.

Organizational Barriers

According to Deming (1986), variations in performance within systems may be due to common causes or special causes. Common causes are faults that are built into the system due to prior decisions, defects in materials, flaws in the design of the system, or some other managerial shortcoming. Special causes are those attributable to a particular event, a particular operator, or a subgroup within the system. Deming believes that over 90 percent of the quality problems of American industry are the result of common causes. If this is so, then judging workers according to their output may be unfair.

In spite of the presence of common organizational barriers to performance, individuals or groups may adopt different strategies in dealing with these common problems. And the adoption of these strategies may lead to variations in the resulting levels of performance even when the organizational constraints are held constant. For example, in a study involving 88 construction road crews, some of the crews were able to minimize the impact of performance constraints by maintaining crew cohesion under more frequent and severe contextual problems (Tesluk & Mathieu, 1999). Thus, common causes may not be as significant a determinant of performance as total quality management advocates make them out to be.

Political Barriers

Political considerations are organizational facts of life (Westphal & Clement, 2008). Appraisals take place in an organizational environment that is anything but completely rational, straightforward, or dispassionate. It appears that achieving accuracy in appraisal is less important to managers than motivating and rewarding their subordinates. Many managers will not allow excessively accurate ratings to cause problems for themselves, and they attempt to use the appraisal process to their own advantage (Longenecker et al., 1987).

A study conducted using 979 workers in five separate organizations provided support for the idea that goal congruence between the supervisor and the subordinate helps mitigate the impact of organizational politics (Witt, 1998). Thus, when raters and ratees share the same organizational goals and priorities, the appraisal process may be less affected by political barriers.

Interpersonal Barriers

Interpersonal barriers also may hinder the performance management process. Because of a lack of communication, employees may think they are being judged according to one set of standards when their superiors actually use different ones. Furthermore, supervisors often delay or resist making face-to-face appraisals. Rather than confronting substandard performers with low ratings, negative feedback, and below-average salary increases, supervisors often find it easier to "damn with faint praise" by giving average or above-average ratings to inferior performers (Benedict & Levine, 1988). Finally, some managers complain that formal performance appraisal interviews tend to interfere with the more constructive coaching relationship that should exist between superior and subordinate. They claim that appraisal interviews emphasize the superior position of the supervisor by placing him or her in the role of *judge*, which conflicts with the supervisor's equally important roles of *teacher* and *coach* (Meyer, 1991).

This, then, is the performance appraisal dilemma: Appraisal is widely accepted as a potentially useful tool, but organizational, political, and interpersonal barriers often thwart its successful implementation. Much of the research on appraisals has focused on measurement issues. This is important, but HR professionals may contribute more by improving the attitudinal and interpersonal components of performance appraisal systems, as well as their technical aspects. We will begin by considering the fundamental requirements for all performance management systems.

FUNDAMENTAL REQUIREMENTS OF SUCCESSFUL PERFORMANCE MANAGEMENT SYSTEMS

In order for any performance management system to be used successfully, it must have the following nine characteristics (Aguinis, 2009a):

1. *Congruence with Strategy:* The system should measure and encourage behaviors that will help achieve organizational goals.

2. *Thoroughness:*   All employees should be evaluated, all key job-related responsibilities should be measured, and evaluations should cover performance for the entire time period included in any specific review.

3. *Practicality:*   The system should be available, plausible, acceptable, and easy to use, and its benefits should outweigh its costs.

4. *Meaningfulness:*   Performance measurement should include only matters under the control of the employee; appraisals should occur at regular intervals; the system should provide for continuing skill development of raters and ratees; the results should be used for important HR decisions; and the implementation of the system should be seen as an important part of everyone's job.

5. *Specificity:*   The system should provide specific guidance to both raters and ratees about what is expected of them and also how they can meet these expectations.

6. *Discriminability:*   The system should allow for clear differentiation between effective and ineffective performance and performers.

7. *Reliability and Validity:*   Performance scores should be consistent over time and across raters observing the same behaviors (see Chapter 6) and should not be deficient or contaminated (see Chapter 4).

8. *Inclusiveness:*   Successful systems allow for the active participation of raters and ratees, including in the design of the system (Kleingeld, Van Tuijl, & Algera, 2004). This includes allowing ratees to provide their own performance evaluations and to assume an active role during the appraisal interview, and allowing both raters and ratees an opportunity to provide input in the design of the system.

9. *Fairness and Acceptability:*   Participants should view the process and outcomes of the system as being just and equitable.

Several studies have investigated the above characteristics, which dictate the success of performance management systems (Cascio, 1982). For example, regarding meaningfulness, a study including 176 Australian government workers indicated that the system's meaningfulness (i.e., perceived consequences of implementing the system) was an important predictor of the decision to adopt or reject a system (Langan-Fox, Waycott, Morizzi, & McDonald, 1998). Regarding inclusiveness, a meta-analysis of 27 studies, including 32 individual samples, found that the overall correlation between employee participation and employee reactions to the system (corrected for unreliability) was .61 (Cawley, Keeping, & Levy, 1998). Specifically, the benefits of designing a system in which ratees are given a "voice" included increased satisfaction with the system, increased perceived utility of the system, increased motivation to improve performance, and increased perceived fairness of the system (Cawley et al., 1998).

Taken together, the above nine key requirements indicate that performance appraisal should be embedded in the broader performance management system and that a lack of understanding of the context surrounding the appraisal is likely to result in a failed system. With that in mind, let's consider the behavioral basis for performance appraisal.

BEHAVIORAL BASIS FOR PERFORMANCE APPRAISAL

Performance appraisal involves two distinct processes: (1) observation and (2) judgment. Observation processes are more basic and include the detection, perception, and recall or recognition of specific behavioral events. Judgment processes include the categorization, integration, and evaluation of information (Thornton & Zorich, 1980). In practice, observation and judgment represent the last elements of a three-part sequence:

- *Job analysis*—describes the work and personal requirements of a particular job
- *Performance standards*—translate job requirements into levels of acceptable/unacceptable performance
- *Performance appraisal*—describes the job-relevant strengths and weaknesses of each individual

Job analysis identifies the components of a particular job. Our goal in performance appraisal, however, is not to make distinctions among jobs, but rather to make distinctions among people, especially among people performing the same job. Performance standards provide the critical link in the process. Ultimately it is management's responsibility to establish performance standards: the levels of performance deemed acceptable or unacceptable for each of the job-relevant, critical areas of performance identified through job analysis. For some jobs (e.g., production or maintenance), standards can be set on the basis of engineering studies. For others, such as research, teaching, or administration, the process is considerably more subjective and is frequently a matter of manager and subordinate agreement. An example of one such set of standards is presented in Figure 5-1. Note also that standards are distinct, yet complementary, to goals. Standards are usually constant across individuals in a given job, while goals are often determined individually or by a group (Bobko & Colella, 1994).

Performance standards are essential in all types of goods-producing and service organizations, for they help ensure consistency in supervisory judgments across individuals in the same job. Unfortunately it is often the case that charges of unequal treatment and unfair discrimination arise in jobs where no clear performance standards exist (Cascio & Bernardin, 1981; Martin & Bartol, 1991; Nathan & Cascio, 1986). We cannot overemphasize their importance.

Duty (from Job Description): IMPLEMENT COMPANY EEO AND AFFIRMATIVE ACTION PROGRAM

Task	Output	Performance Standard
Review unit positions and recommend potential upward mobility opportunities	Report with recommendation	*SUPERIOR*—All tasks completed well ahead of time and acceptable to management without change. Actively participates in education programs and provides positive suggestions.
Take part in and promote company program for education of employees in EEO and affirmative action principles	Program participation	Attitude is very positive as exhibited by no discriminatory language or remarks.
Instruct and inform unit employees on EEO and affirmative action programs	Information	*SATISFACTORY*—All tasks completed by deadlines with only minor changes as random occurrences. Participates in education program when asked to do so and counsels employees at their request.
Affirmative action recommendations to management on positions for unit	Recommendation	*UNACCEPTABLE*—Tasks not completed on time with changes usually necessary. Program is accepted but no or little effort to support. Comments sometimes reflect biased language. Employees seek counsel from someone other than supervisor.

FIGURE 5-1   Examples of performance standards.   *Source:* Scott, S. G., & Einstein, W. O. Strategic performance appraisal in team based organizations. . . . *Academy of Management Executive, 15,* 111. © 2001.

Performance appraisal, the last of the three steps in the sequence, is the actual process of gathering information about individuals based on critical job requirements. Gathering job performance information is accomplished by observation. Evaluating the adequacy of individual performance is an exercise of judgment.

WHO SHALL RATE?

In view of the purposes served by performance appraisal, *who* does the rating is important. In addition to being cooperative and trained in the techniques of rating, raters must have direct experience with, or firsthand knowledge of, the individual to be rated. In many jobs, individuals with varying perspectives have such firsthand knowledge. Following are descriptions of five of these perspectives that will help answer the question of who shall rate performance.

Immediate Supervisor

So-called **360-degree feedback** systems, which broaden the base of appraisals by including input from peers, subordinates, and customers, certainly increase the types and amount of information about performance that is available. Ultimately, however, the immediate supervisor is responsible for managing the overall appraisal process (Ghorpade & Chen, 1995).

While input from peers and subordinates is helpful, the supervisor is probably the person best able to evaluate each subordinate's performance in light of the organization's overall objectives. Since the supervisor is probably also responsible for reward (and punishment) decisions such as pay, promotion, and discipline, he or she must be able to tie effective (ineffective) performance to the employment actions taken. Inability to form such linkages between performance and punishment or reward is one of the most serious deficiencies of any performance management system. Not surprisingly, therefore, research has shown that feedback from supervisors is more highly related to performance than that from any other source (Becker & Klimoski, 1989).

However, in jobs such as teaching, law enforcement, or sales, and in self-managed work teams, the supervisor may observe directly his or her subordinate's performance only rarely. In addition, performance ratings provided by the supervisor may reflect not only whether an employee is helping advance organizational objectives but also whether the employee is contributing to goals valued by the supervisor, which may or may not be congruent with organizational goals (Hogan & Shelton, 1998). Moreover, if a supervisor has recently received a positive evaluation regarding his or her own performance, he or she is also likely to provide a positive evaluation regarding his or her subordinates (Latham, Budworth, Yanar, & Whyte, 2008). Fortunately, there are several other perspectives that can be used to provide a fuller picture of the individual's total performance.

Peers

Peer assessment actually refers to three of the more basic methods used by members of a well-defined group in judging each other's job performance. These include **peer nominations**, most useful for identifying persons with extreme high or low levels of KSAOs (knowledge, skills, abilities, and other characteristics); **peer rating**, most useful for providing feedback; and **peer ranking**, best at discriminating various levels of performance from highest to lowest on each dimension.

Reviews of peer assessment methods reached favorable conclusions regarding the reliability, validity, and freedom from biases of this approach (e.g., Kane & Lawler, 1978). However, some problems still remain. First, two characteristics of peer assessments appear to be related significantly and independently to user acceptance (McEvoy & Buller, 1987). Perceived friendship bias is related negatively to user acceptance, and use for developmental purposes is related positively to user acceptance. How do people react upon learning that they have been rated poorly (favorably) by their peers? Research in a controlled setting indicates that such knowledge has predictable effects on group behavior. Negative peer-rating feedback produces significantly lower perceived performance of the group, plus lower cohesiveness, satisfaction, and peer ratings on a subsequent task. Positive peer-rating feedback produces nonsignificantly higher values for these variables on a subsequent task (DeNisi, Randolph, & Blencoe, 1983). One possible solution that might simultaneously increase feedback value and decrease the perception of friendship bias is to specify clearly (e.g., using critical incidents) the performance criteria on which peer assessments are based. Results of the peer assessment may then be used in joint employee–supervisor reviews of each employee's progress, prior to later administrative decisions concerning the employee.

A second problem with peer assessments is that they seem to include more **common method variance** than assessments provided by other sources. Method variance is the variance observed in a performance measure that is not relevant to the behaviors assessed, but instead is due to the method of measurement used (Conway, 2002; Podsakoff, MacKenzie, Lee, & Podsakoff, 2003). For example, Conway (1998a) reanalyzed supervisor, peer, and self-ratings for three performance dimensions (i.e., altruism-local, conscientiousness, and altruism-distant) and found that the proportion of method variance for peers was .38, whereas the proportion of method variance for self-ratings was .22. This finding suggests that relationships among various performance dimensions, as rated by peers, can be inflated substantially due to common method variance (Conway, 1998a).

There are several data-analysis methods available to estimate the amount of method variance present in a peer-assessment measure (Conway, 1998a, 1998b; Scullen, 1999; Williams, Ford, & Nguyen, 2002). At the very least, the assessment of common method variance can provide HR researchers and practitioners with information regarding the extent of the problem. In addition, Podsakoff et al. (2003) proposed two types of remedies to address the common method variance problem:

- *Procedural remedies.*   These include obtaining measures of the predictor and criterion variables from different sources; separating the measurement of the predictor and criterion variables (i.e., temporal, psychological, or methodological separation); protecting respondent anonymity, thereby reducing socially desirable responding; counterbalancing the question order; and improving scale items.
- *Statistical remedies.*   These include utilizing Harman's single-factor test (i.e., to determine whether all items load into one common underlying factor, as opposed to the various factors hypothesized); computing partial correlations (e.g., partialling out social desirability, general affectivity, or a general factor score); controlling for the effects of a directly measured latent methods factor; controlling for the effects of a single, unmeasured, latent method factor; implementing the correlated uniqueness model (i.e., where a researcher identifies the sources of method variance so the appropriate pattern of measurement-error corrections can be estimated); and utilizing the direct-product model (i.e., which models trait-by-method interactions).

The overall recommendation is to follow all the procedural remedies listed above, but the statistical remedies to be implemented depend on the specific characteristics of the research situation one faces (Podsakoff et al., 2003).

Given our discussion thus far, peer assessments are probably best considered as only one element in an appraisal system that includes input from all sources that have unique information or perspectives to offer. Thus, the traits, behaviors, or outcomes to be assessed should be considered in the context of the groups and situations where peer assessments are to be applied. It is impossible to specify, for all situations, the kinds of characteristics that peers are able to rate best.

Subordinates

Subordinates offer a somewhat different perspective on a manager's performance. They know directly the extent to which a manager does or does not delegate, the extent to which he or she plans and organizes, the type of leadership style(s) he or she is most comfortable with, and how well he or she communicates. This is why subordinate ratings often provide information that accounts for variance in performance measures over and above other sources (Conway, Lombardo, & Sanders, 2001). This approach is used regularly by universities (students evaluate faculty) and sometimes by large corporations, where a manager may have many subordinates. In small organizations, however, considerable trust and openness are necessary before subordinate appraisals can pay off.

They can pay off though. For example, in a field study, subordinates rated their managers at two time periods six months apart on a 33-item behavioral observation scale that focused on areas such as the manager's commitment to quality, communications, support of subordinates, and fairness. Based on subordinates' ratings, managers whose initial levels of performance were moderate or low improved modestly over the six-month period, and this improvement could not be attributed solely to regression toward the mean. Further, both managers and their subordinates became more likely over time to indicate that the managers had an opportunity to demonstrate behaviors measured by the upward-feedback instrument (Smither et al., 1995).

Subordinate ratings have been found to be valid predictors of subsequent supervisory ratings over two-, four-, and seven-year periods (McEvoy & Beatty, 1989). One reason for this may have been that multiple ratings on each dimension were made for each manager, and the ratings were averaged to obtain the measure for the subordinate perspective. Averaging has several advantages. First, averaged ratings are more reliable than single ratings. Second, averaging helps to ensure the anonymity of the subordinate raters. Anonymity is important; subordinates may perceive the process to be threatening, since the supervisor can exert administrative controls (salary increases, promotions, etc.). In fact, when the identity of subordinates is disclosed, inflated ratings of managers' performance tend to result (Antonioni, 1994).

Any organization contemplating use of subordinate ratings should pay careful attention to the intended purpose of the ratings. Evidence indicates that ratings used for salary administration or promotion purposes may be more lenient than those used for guided self-development (Zedeck & Cascio, 1982). In general, subordinate ratings are of significantly better quality when used for developmental purposes rather than administrative purposes (Greguras, Robie, Schleicher, & Goff, 2003).

Self

It seems reasonable to have each individual judge his or her own job performance. On the positive side, we can see that the opportunity to participate in performance appraisal, especially if it is combined with goal setting, should improve the individual's motivation and reduce his or her defensiveness during an appraisal interview. Research to be described later in this chapter clearly supports this view. On the other hand, comparisons with appraisals by supervisors, peers, and subordinates suggest that self-appraisals tend to show more leniency, less variability, more bias, and less agreement with the judgments of others (Atkins & Wood, 2002; Harris & Schaubroeck, 1988). This seems to be the norm in Western cultures. In Taiwan, however, modesty bias (self-ratings lower than those of supervisors) has been found (Farh, Dobbins, & Cheng, 1991), although this may not be the norm in all Eastern cultures (Barron & Sackett, 2008).

To some extent, these disagreements may stem from the tendency of raters to base their ratings on different aspects of job performance or to weight facets of job performance differently. Self- and supervisor ratings agree much more closely when both parties have a thorough knowledge of the appraisal system or process (Williams & Levy, 1992). In addition, self-ratings are less lenient when done for self-development purposes rather than for administrative purposes (Meyer, 1991). In addition, self-ratings of contextual performance are more lenient than peer ratings when individuals are high on self-monitoring (i.e., tending to control self-presentational behaviors) and social desirability (i.e., tending to attempt to make oneself look good) (Mersman & Donaldson, 2000). Finally, lack of agreement between sources, as measured using correlation coefficients among sources, may also be due to range restriction

(LeBreton, Burgess, Kaiser, Atchley, & James, 2003). Specifically, correlations decrease when variances in the sample are smaller than variances in the population (Aguinis & Whitehead, 1997), and it is often the case that performance ratings are range restricted. That is, in most cases, distributions are not normal, and, instead, they are negatively skewed. Consistent with the restriction-of-variance hypothesis, LeBreton et al. (2003) found that noncorrelation-based methods of assessing interrater agreement indicated that agreement between sources was about as high as agreement within sources.

The situation is far from hopeless, however. To improve the validity of self-appraisals, consider four research-based suggestions (Campbell & Lee, 1988; Fox & Dinur, 1988; Mabe & West, 1982):

1. Instead of asking individuals to rate themselves on an *absolute* scale (e.g., a scale ranging from "poor" to "average"), provide a *relative* scale that allows them to compare their performance with that of others (e.g., "below average," "average," "above average"). In addition, providing comparative information on the relative performance of coworkers promotes closer agreement between self-appraisal and supervisor rating (Farh & Dobbins, 1989).

2. Provide multiple opportunities for self-appraisal, for the skill being evaluated may well be one that improves with practice.

3. Provide reassurance of confidentiality—that is, that self-appraisals will not be "publicized."

4. Focus on the future—specifically on predicting future behavior.

Until the problems associated with self-appraisals can be resolved, however, they seem more appropriate for counseling and development than for employment decisions.

Clients Served

Another group that may offer a different perspective on individual performance in some situations is that of clients served. In jobs that require a high degree of interaction with the public or with particular individuals (e.g., purchasing managers, suppliers, and sales representatives), appraisal sometimes can be done by the "consumers" of the organization's services. While the clients served cannot be expected to identify completely with the organization's objectives, they can, nevertheless, provide useful information. Such information may affect employment decisions (promotion, transfer, need for training), but it also can be used in HR research (e.g., as a criterion in validation studies or in the measurement of training outcomes on the job) or as a basis for self-development activities.

Appraising Performance: Individual Versus Group Tasks

So far, we have assumed that ratings are given as an individual exercise. That is, each source—be it the supervisor, peer, subordinate, self, or client—makes the performance judgment individually and independently from other individuals. However, in practice, appraising performance is not strictly an individual task. A survey of 135 raters from six different organizations indicated that 98.5 percent of raters reported using at least one secondhand (i.e., indirect) source of performance information (Raymark, Balzer, & De La Torre, 1999). In other words, supervisors often use information from outside sources in making performance judgments. Moreover, supervisors may change their own ratings in the presence of indirect information. For example, a study including participants with at least two years of supervisory experience revealed that supervisors are likely to change their ratings when the ratee's peers provide information perceived as useful (Makiney & Levy, 1998). A follow-up study that included students from a Canadian university revealed that indirect information is perceived to be most useful when it is in agreement with the rater's direct observation of the employee's performance (Uggerslev & Sulsky, 2002). For example, when a supervisor's judgment about a ratee's performance is positive, positive indirect observation produced higher ratings than negative indirect information. In addition, it seems that the presence of indirect information is more likely to change ratings from positive to negative than from negative to positive (Uggerslev & Sulsky, 2002). In sum, although direct observation is the main influence on ratings, the presence of indirect information is likely to affect ratings.

If the process of assigning performance ratings is not entirely an individual task, might it pay off to formalize performance appraisals as a group task? One study found that groups are more effective than individuals at remembering specific behaviors over time, but that groups also demonstrate greater response bias (Martell & Borg, 1993). In a second related study, individuals observed a 14-minute military training videotape of five men attempting to build a bridge of rope and planks in an effort to get themselves and a box across a pool of water. Before observing the tape, study participants were given indirect information in the form of a positive or negative performance cue [i.e., "the group you will observe was judged to be in the top (bottom) quarter of all groups"]. Then ratings were provided individually or in the context of a four-person group (the group task required that the four group members reach consensus). Results showed that ratings provided individually were affected by the performance cue, but that ratings provided by the groups were not (Martell & Leavitt, 2002).

These results suggest that groups can be of help, but they are not a cure-all for the problems of rating accuracy. Groups can be a useful mechanism for improving the accuracy of performance appraisals under two conditions. First, the task needs to have a necessarily correct answer. For example, is the behavior present or not? Second, the magnitude of the performance cue should not be too large. If the performance facet in question is subjective (e.g., "what is the management potential for this employee?") and the magnitude of the performance cue is large, group ratings may actually amplify instead of attenuate individual biases (Martell & Leavitt, 2002).

In summary, there are several sources of appraisal information, and each provides a different perspective, a different piece of the puzzle. The various sources and their potential uses are shown in Table 5-1. Several studies indicate that data from multiple sources (e.g., self, supervisors, peers, subordinates) are desirable because they provide a complete picture of the individual's effect on others (Borman, White, & Dorsey, 1995; Murphy & Cleveland, 1995; Wohlers & London, 1989).

Agreement and Equivalence of Ratings Across Sources

To assess the degree of interrater agreement within rating dimensions (convergent validity) and to assess the ability of raters to make distinctions in performance across dimensions (discriminant validity), a matrix listing dimensions as rows and raters as columns might be prepared (Lawler, 1967). As we noted earlier, however, multiple raters for the same individual may be drawn from different organizational levels, and they probably observe different facets of a ratee's job performance (Bozeman, 1997). This may explain, in part, why the overall correlation between subordinate and self-ratings (corrected for unreliability) is only .14 and the correlation between subordinate and supervisor ratings (also corrected for unreliability) is .22 (Conway & Huffcutt, 1997). Hence, across-organizational-level interrater agreement for ratings on all performance

TABLE 5-1 Sources and Uses of Appraisal Data

	Source				
	Supervisor	Peers	Subordinates	Self	Clients Served
Use					
Employment decisions	X	–	X	–	X
Self-development	X	X	X	X	X
HR research	X	X	–	–	X

dimensions is not only an unduly severe expectation, but may also be erroneous. However, although we should not always expect agreement, we should expect that the construct underlying the measure used should be equivalent across raters. In other words, does the underlying trait measured across sources relate to observed rating scale scores in the same way across sources? In general, it does not make sense to assess the extent of interrater agreement without first establishing **measurement equivalence** (also called **measurement invariance**) because a lack of agreement may be due to a lack of measurement equivalence (Cheung, 1999). A lack of measurement equivalence means that the underlying characteristics being measured are not on the same psychological measurement scale, which, in turn, implies that differences across sources are possibly artifactual, contaminated, or misleading (Maurer, Raju, & Collins, 1998).

Fortunately, there is evidence that measurement equivalence is warranted in many appraisal systems. Specifically, measurement equivalence was found in a measure of managers' team-building skills as assessed by peers and subordinates (Maurer et al., 1998). Equivalence was also found in a measure including 48 behaviorally oriented items designed to measure 10 dimensions of managerial performance as assessed by self, peers, supervisors, and subordinates (Facteau & Craig, 2001) and in a meta-analysis including measures of overall job performance, productivity, effort, job knowledge, quality, and leadership as rated by supervisors and peers (Viswesvaran, Schmidt, & Ones, 2002). However, lack of invariance was found for measures of interpersonal competence, administrative competence, and compliance and acceptance of authority as assessed by supervisors and peers (Viswesvaran et al., 2002). At this point, it is not clear what may account for differential measurement equivalence across studies and constructs, and this is a fruitful avenue for future research. One possibility is that behaviorally based ratings provided for developmental purposes are more likely to be equivalent than those reflecting broader behavioral dimensions (e.g., interpersonal competence) and collected for research purposes (Facteau & Craig, 2001). One conclusion is clear, however. An important implication of this body of research is that measurement equivalence needs to be established before ratings can be assumed to be directly comparable. Several methods exist for this purpose, including those based on confirmatory factor analysis (CFA) and item response theory (Barr & Raju, 2003; Cheung & Rensvold, 1999, 2002; Maurer et al., 1998; Vandenberg, 2002).

Once measurement equivalence has been established, we can assess the extent of agreement across raters. For this purpose, raters may use a hybrid multitrait–multirater analysis (see Figure 5-2), in which raters make evaluations *only* on those dimensions that they are in good position to rate (Borman, 1974) and that reflect measurement equivalence. In the hybrid analysis, within-level interrater agreement is taken as an index of convergent validity. The hybrid matrix provides an improved conceptual fit for analyzing performance ratings, and the probability of obtaining convergent and discriminant validity is probably higher for this method than for the traditional multitrait–multirater analysis.

Another approach for examining performance ratings from more than one source is based on CFA (Williams & Anderson, 1994). Confirmatory factor analysis allows researchers to specify

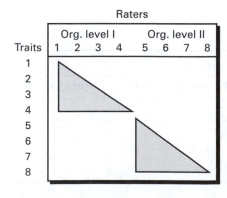

FIGURE 5-2 Example of a hybrid matrix analysis of performance ratings. Level I rates only traits 1–4. Level II rates only traits 5–8.

each performance dimension as a latent factor and assess the extent to which these factors are correlated with each other. In addition, CFA allows for an examination of the relationship between each latent factor and its measures as provided by each source (e.g., supervisor, peer, self). One advantage of using a CFA approach to examine ratings from multiple sources is that it allows for a better understanding of source-specific method variance (i.e., the dimension-rating variance specific to a particular source; Conway, 1998b).

JUDGMENTAL BIASES IN RATING

In the traditional view, judgmental biases result from some systematic measurement error on the part of a rater. As such, they are easier to deal with than errors that are unsystematic or random. However, each type of bias has been defined and measured in different ways in the literature. This may lead to diametrically opposite conclusions, even in the same study (Saal, Downey, & Lahey, 1980). In the minds of many managers, however, these behaviors are not errors at all. For example, in an organization in which there is a team-based culture, can we really say that if peers place more emphasis on contextual than task performance in evaluating others, this is an error that should be minimized or even eliminated (cf. Lievens, Conway, & De Corte, 2008)? Rather, this apparent error is really capturing an important contextual variable in this particular type of organization. With these considerations in mind, let us consider some of the most commonly observed judgmental biases, along with ways of minimizing them.

Leniency and Severity

The use of ratings rests on the assumption that the human observer is capable of some degree of precision and some degree of objectivity (Guilford, 1954). His or her ratings are taken to mean something accurate about certain aspects of the person rated. "Objectivity" is the major hitch in these assumptions, and it is the one most often violated. Raters subscribe to their own sets of assumptions (that may or may not be valid), and most people have encountered raters who seemed either inordinately easy (lenient) or inordinately difficult (severe). Evidence also indicates that leniency is a stable response tendency across raters (Kane, Bernardin, Villanova, & Peyrfitte, 1995). Graphically, the different distributions resulting from leniency and severity are shown in Figure 5-3.

The idea of a normal distribution of job performance appraisals is deeply ingrained in our thinking; yet, in many situations, a lenient distribution may be accurate. Cascio and Valenzi (1977) found this to be the case with lenient ratings of police officer performance. An extensive, valid selection program had succeeded in weeding out most of the poorer applicants prior to appraisals of performance "on the street." Consequently it was more proper to speak of a leniency effect rather than a leniency bias. Even so, senior managers recognize that leniency is not to be taken lightly. Fully 77 percent of sampled Fortune 100 companies reported that lenient appraisals threaten the validity of their appraisal systems (Bretz, Milkovich, & Read, 1990).

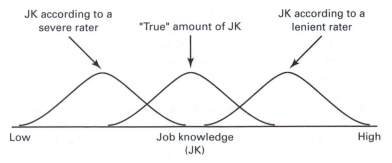

FIGURE 5-3   Distributions of lenient and severe raters.

An important cause for lenient ratings is the perceived purpose served by the performance management system in place. A meta-analysis including 22 studies and a total sample size of over 57,000 individuals concluded that when ratings are to be used for administrative purposes, scores are one-third of a standard deviation larger than those obtained when the main purpose is research (e.g., validation study) or employee development (Jawahar & Williams, 1997). This difference was even larger when ratings were made in field settings (as opposed to lab settings), provided by practicing managers (as opposed to students), and provided for subordinates (as opposed to superiors). In other words, ratings tend to be more lenient when they have *real* consequences in *actual* work environments.

Leniency and severity biases can be controlled or eliminated in several ways: (1) by allocating ratings into a forced distribution, in which ratees are apportioned according to an approximately normal distribution; (2) by requiring supervisors to rank order their subordinates; (3) by encouraging raters to provide feedback on a regular basis, thereby reducing rater and ratee discomfort with the process; and (4) by increasing raters' motivation to be accurate by holding them accountable for their ratings. For example, firms such as IBM, Pratt-Whitney, and Grumman have implemented forced distributions because the extreme leniency in their ratings-based appraisal data hindered their ability to do necessary downsizing based on merit (Kane & Kane, 1993).

Central Tendency

When political considerations predominate, raters may assign all their subordinates ratings that are neither too good nor too bad. They avoid using the high and low extremes of rating scales and tend to cluster all ratings about the center of all scales. "Everybody is average" is one way of expressing the central tendency bias. The unfortunate consequence, as with leniency or severity biases, is that most of the value of systematic performance appraisal is lost. The ratings fail to discriminate either within people over time or between people, and the ratings become virtually useless as managerial decision-making aids, as predictors, as criteria, or as a means of giving feedback.

Central tendency biases can be minimized by specifying clearly what the various anchors mean. In addition, raters must be convinced of the value and potential uses of merit ratings if they are to provide meaningful information.

Halo

Halo is perhaps the most actively researched bias in performance appraisal. A rater who is subject to the halo bias assigns ratings on the basis of a general impression of the ratee. An individual is rated either high or low on specific factors because of the rater's general impression (good–poor) of the ratee's overall performance (Lance, LaPointe, & Stewart, 1994). According to this theory, the rater fails to distinguish among levels of performance on different performance dimensions. Ratings subject to the halo bias show spuriously high positive intercorrelations (Cooper, 1981).

Two critical reviews of research in this area (Balzer & Sulsky, 1992; Murphy, Jako, & Anhalt, 1993) led to the following conclusions: (1) Halo is not as common as believed; (2) the presence of halo does not necessarily detract from the quality of ratings (i.e., halo measures are not strongly interrelated, and they are not related to measures of rating validity or accuracy); (3) it is impossible to separate true from illusory halo in most field settings; and (4) although halo may be a poor measure of rating quality, it may or may not be an important measure of the rating process. So, contrary to assumptions that have guided halo research since the 1920s, it is often difficult to determine whether halo has occurred, why it has occurred (whether it is due to the rater or to contextual factors unrelated to the rater's judgment), or what to do about it. To address this problem, Solomonson and Lance (1997) designed a study in which true halo was actually manipulated as part of an experiment, and, in this way, they were able to examine the relationship between true halo and rater error halo. Results indicated that the effects of rater error halo were homogeneous across a number of distinct performance dimensions, although true halo varied widely. In other words, true halo and rater error halo are, in fact, independent. Therefore, the fact that performance dimensions are sometimes intercorrelated may not mean that there is rater bias but, rather, that there is a common, underlying general performance factor. Further research is needed to explore this potential generalized performance dimension.

As we noted earlier, judgmental biases may stem from a number of factors. One factor that has received considerable attention over the years has been the type of rating scale used. Each type attempts to reduce bias in some way. Although no single method is free of flaws, each has its own particular strengths and weaknesses. In the following section, we shall examine some of the most popular methods of evaluating individual job performance.

TYPES OF PERFORMANCE MEASURES

Objective Measures

Performance measures may be classified into two general types: objective and subjective. **Objective performance** measures include production data (dollar volume of sales, units produced, number of errors, amount of scrap), as well as employment data (accidents, turnover, absences, tardiness). These variables directly define the goals of the organization, but, as we noted in Chapter 4, they often suffer from several glaring weaknesses, the most serious of which are performance unreliability and modification of performance by situational characteristics. For example, dollar volume of sales is influenced by numerous factors beyond a particular salesperson's control—territory location, number of accounts in the territory, nature of the competition, distances between accounts, price and quality of the product, and so forth.

Our objective in performance appraisal, however, is to judge an individual's *performance*, not factors beyond his or her control. Moreover, objective measures focus not on behavior, but rather on the direct outcomes or results of behavior. Admittedly there will be some degree of overlap between behavior and results, but the two are qualitatively different (Ilgen & Favero, 1985). Finally, in many jobs (e.g., those of middle managers), there simply are no good objective indices of performance, and, in the case of employment data (e.g., awards) and deviant behaviors (e.g., covering up one's mistakes), such data are usually present in fewer than 5 percent of the cases examined (Landy & Conte, 2004). Hence, they are often useless as performance criteria.

In short, although objective measures of performance are intuitively attractive, theoretical and practical limitations often make them unsuitable. And, although they can be useful as supplements to supervisory judgments, correlations between objective and subjective measures are often low (Bommer, Johnson, Rich, Podsakoff, & Mackenzie, 1995; Cascio & Valenzi, 1978; Heneman, 1986). Consequently it is often not easy to predict employees' scores on objective measures of performance. For example, general cognitive ability scores predict ratings of sales performance quite well (i.e., $r = .40$), but not objective sales performance (i.e., $r = .04$) (Vinchur, Schippmann, Switzer, & Roth, 1998).

Subjective Measures

The disadvantages of objective measures have led researchers and managers to place major emphasis on **subjective measures** of job performance. However, since subjective measures depend on human judgment, they are prone to the kinds of biases we just discussed. To be useful, they must be based on a careful analysis of the behaviors viewed as necessary and important for effective job performance.

There is enormous variation in the types of subjective performance measures used by organizations. Some organizations use a long list of elaborate rating scales, others use only a few simple scales, and still others require managers to write a paragraph or two concerning the performance of each of their subordinates. In addition, subjective measures of performance may be *relative* (in which comparisons are made among a group of ratees), or *absolute* (in which a ratee is described without reference to others). The following section provides brief descriptions of alternative formats. Interested readers may consult Bernardin and Beatty (1984), Borman (1991), or Murphy and Cleveland (1995) for more detailed information about particular methods.

RATING SYSTEMS: RELATIVE AND ABSOLUTE

We can classify rating systems into two types: relative and absolute. Within this taxonomy, the following methods may be distinguished:

Relative	Absolute
Rank ordering	Essays
Paired comparisons	Behavior checklists
Forced distribution	Critical incidents
—	Graphic rating scales

Results of an experiment in which undergraduate students rated the videotaped performance of a lecturer suggest that no advantages are associated with the absolute methods (Wagner & Goffin, 1997). On the other hand, relative ratings based on various rating dimensions (as opposed to a traditional global performance dimension) seem to be more accurate with respect to differential accuracy (i.e., accuracy in discriminating among ratees within each performance dimension) and stereotype accuracy (i.e., accuracy in discriminating among performance dimensions averaging across ratees). Given the fact that the affective, social, and political factors influencing performance management systems were absent in this experiment conducted in a laboratory setting, view the results with caution. Moreover, a more recent study involving two separate samples found that absolute formats are perceived as fairer than relative formats (Roch, Sternburgh, & Caputo, 2007).

Because both relative and absolute methods are used pervasively in organizations, next we discuss each of these two types of rating systems in detail.

Relative Rating Systems (Employee Comparisons)

Employee comparison methods are easy to explain and are helpful in making employment decisions. (For an example of this, see Siegel, 1982.) They also provide useful criterion data in validation studies, for they effectively control leniency, severity, and central tendency bias. Like other systems, however, they suffer from several weaknesses that should be recognized.

Employees usually are compared only in terms of a single overall suitability category. The rankings, therefore, lack behavioral specificity and may be subject to legal challenge. In addition, employee comparisons yield only ordinal data—data that give no indication of the relative distance between individuals. Moreover, it is often impossible to compare rankings across work groups, departments, or locations. The last two problems can be alleviated, however, by converting the ranks to normalized standard scores that form an approximately normal distribution. An additional problem is related to reliability. Specifically, when asked to rerank all individuals at a later date, the extreme high or low rankings probably will remain stable, but the rankings in the middle of the scale may shift around considerably.

RANK ORDERING   **Simple ranking** requires only that a rater order all ratees from highest to lowest, from "best" employee to "worst" employee. **Alternation ranking** requires that the rater initially list all ratees on a sheet of paper. From this list, the rater first chooses the best ratee (#1), then the worst ratee (#*n*), then the second best (#2), then the second worst (#*n*−1), and so forth, alternating from the top to the bottom of the list until all ratees have been ranked.

PAIRED COMPARISONS   Both simple ranking and alternation ranking implicitly require a rater to compare each ratee with every other ratee, but systematic ratee-to-ratee comparison is not a built-in feature of these methods. For this, we need **paired comparisons**. The number of pairs of ratees to be compared may be calculated from the formula $[n(n-1)]/2$. Hence, if 10 individuals were being compared, $[10(9)]/2$ or 45 comparisons would be required. The rater's task is simply to choose the better of each pair, and each individual's rank is determined by counting the number of times he or she was rated superior.

FORCED DISTRIBUTION   We discussed this employee-comparison method previously. Its primary advantage is that it controls leniency, severity, and central tendency biases rather effectively. It assumes, however, that ratees conform to a normal distribution, and this may introduce a great deal of error if a group of ratees, *as a group*, is either superior or substandard. In short, rather than eliminating error, forced distributions may simply introduce a different kind of error!

Absolute Rating Systems

Absolute rating systems enable a rater to describe a ratee without making direct reference to other ratees.

ESSAY   Perhaps the simplest absolute rating system is the **narrative essay**, in which the rater is asked to describe, in writing, an individual's strengths, weaknesses, and potential, and to make suggestions for improvement. The assumption underlying this approach is that a candid statement from a rater who is knowledgeable of a ratee's performance is just as valid as more formal and more complicated appraisal methods.

The major advantage of narrative essays (when they are done well) is that they can provide detailed feedback to ratees regarding their performance. On the other hand, essays are almost totally unstructured, and they vary widely in length and content. Comparisons across individuals, groups, or departments are virtually impossible, since different essays touch on different aspects of ratee performance or personal qualifications. Finally, essays provide only *qualitative* information; yet, in order for the appraisals to serve as criteria or to be compared objectively and ranked for the purpose of an employment decision, some form of rating that can be *quantified* is essential. Behavioral checklists provide one such scheme.

BEHAVIORAL CHECKLIST   When using a behavioral checklist, the rater is provided with a series of descriptive statements of job-related behavior. His or her task is simply to indicate ("check") statements that describe the ratee in question. In this approach, raters are not so much evaluators as they are reporters of job behavior. Moreover, ratings that are descriptive are likely to be higher in reliability than ratings that are evaluative (Stockford & Bissell, 1949), and they reduce the cognitive demands placed on raters, valuably structuring their information processing (Hennessy, Mabey, & Warr, 1998).

To be sure, some job behaviors are more desirable than others; checklist items can, therefore, be scaled by using attitude-scale construction methods. In one such method, the Likert method of **summated ratings**, a declarative statement (e.g., "she follows through on her sales") is followed by several response categories, such as "always," "very often," "fairly often," "occasionally," and "never." The rater simply checks the response category he or she feels best describes the ratee. Each response category is weighted—for example, from 5 ("always") to 1 ("never") if the statement describes desirable behavior—or vice versa if the statement describes undesirable behavior. An overall numerical rating for each individual then can be derived by summing the weights of the responses that were checked for each item, and scores for each performance dimension can be obtained by using item analysis procedures (cf. Anastasi, 1988).

The selection of response categories for summated rating scales often is made arbitrarily, with equal intervals between scale points simply assumed. Scaled lists of adverbial modifiers of frequency and amount are available, however, together with statistically optimal four- to nine-point scales (Bass, Cascio, & O'Connor, 1974). Scaled values also are available for categories of agreement, evaluation, and frequency (Spector, 1976). A final issue concerns the optimal number of scale points for summated rating scales. For relatively homogeneous items, reliability increases up to five scale points and levels off thereafter (Lissitz & Green, 1975).

Checklists are easy to use and understand, but it is sometimes difficult for a rater to give diagnostic feedback based on checklist ratings, for they are not cast in terms of specific behaviors. On balance, however, the many advantages of checklists probably account for their widespread popularity in organizations today.

FORCED-CHOICE SYSTEM   A special type of behavioral checklist is known as the **forced-choice system**—a technique developed specifically to reduce leniency errors and establish objective standards of comparison between individuals (Sisson, 1948). In order to accomplish this, checklist statements are arranged in groups, from which the rater chooses statements that are most or least descriptive of the ratee. An overall rating (score) for each individual is then derived by applying a special scoring key to the rater descriptions.

Forced-choice scales are constructed according to two statistical properties of the checklist items: (1) **discriminability**, a measure of the degree to which an item differentiates effective from ineffective workers, and (2) **preference**, an index of the degree to which the quality expressed in an item is valued by (i.e., is socially desirable to) people. The rationale of the forced-choice system requires that items be paired so they appear equally attractive (socially desirable) to the rater. Theoretically, then, the selection of any single item in a pair should be based solely on the item's discriminating power, not on its social desirability.

As an example, consider the following pair of items:

1. Separates opinion from fact in written reports.
2. Includes only relevant information in written reports.

Both statements are approximately equal in preference value, but only item 1 was found to discriminate effective from ineffective performers in a police department. This is the defining characteristic of the forced-choice technique: Not all equally attractive behavioral statements are equally valid.

The main advantage claimed for forced-choice scales is that a rater cannot distort a person's ratings higher or lower than is warranted, since he or she has no way of knowing which statements to check in order to do so. Hence, leniency should theoretically be reduced. Their major disadvantage is rater resistance. Since control is removed from the rater, he or she cannot be sure just how the subordinate was rated. Finally, forced-choice forms are of little use (and may even have a negative effect) in performance appraisal interviews, for the rater is unaware of the scale values of the items he or she chooses. Since rater cooperation and acceptability are crucial determinants of the success of any performance management system, forced-choice systems tend to be unpopular choices in many organizations.

CRITICAL INCIDENTS   This performance measurement method has generated a great deal of interest in recent years, and several variations of the basic idea are currently in use. As described by Flanagan (1954a), the critical requirements of a job are those behaviors that make a crucial difference between doing a job effectively and doing it ineffectively. **Critical incidents** are simply reports by knowledgeable observers of things employees did that were especially effective or ineffective in accomplishing parts of their jobs (e.g., Pulakos, Arad, Donovan, & Plamondon, 2000). Supervisors record critical incidents for each employee as they occur. Thus, they provide a behaviorally based starting point for appraising performance. For example, in observing a police officer chasing an armed robbery suspect down a busy street, a supervisor recorded the following:

> June 22, officer Mitchell withheld fire in a situation calling for the use of weapons where gunfire would endanger innocent bystanders.

These little anecdotes force attention on the situational determinants of job behavior and on ways of doing a job successfully that may be unique to the person described (individual dimensionality). The critical incidents method looks like a natural for performance management interviews because supervisors can focus on actual job behavior rather than on vaguely defined traits. Performance, not personality, is being judged. Ratees receive meaningful feedback, and they can see what changes in their job behavior will be necessary in order for them to improve. In addition, when a large number of critical incidents are collected, abstracted, and categorized, they can provide a rich storehouse of information about job and organizational problems in general and are particularly well suited for establishing objectives for training programs (Flanagan & Burns, 1955).

As with other approaches to performance appraisal, the critical incidents method also has drawbacks. First of all, it is time consuming and burdensome for supervisors to record incidents for all of their subordinates on a daily or even weekly basis. Feedback may, therefore, be delayed. Delaying feedback may actually enhance contrast effects between ratees (Maurer, Palmer, & Ashe, 1993). Nevertheless, incidents recorded in diaries allow raters to impose organization on unorganized information (DeNisi, Robbins, & Cafferty, 1989). However, in their narrative form, incidents do not readily lend themselves to quantification, which, as we noted earlier, poses problems in between-individual and between-group comparisons, as well as in statistical analyses.

For these reasons, two variations of the original idea have been suggested. Kirchner and Dunnette (1957), for example, used the method to develop a behavioral checklist (using the method of summated ratings) for rating sales performance. After incidents were abstracted and classified, selected items were assembled into a checklist. For example,

Gives Good Service on Customers' Complaints				
Strongly agree	Agree	Undecided	Disagree	Strongly disagree

A second modification has been the development of behaviorally anchored rating scales, an approach we will consider after we discuss graphic rating scales.

GRAPHIC RATING SCALE   Probably the most widely used method of performance appraisal is the **graphic rating scale**, examples of which are presented in Figure 5-4. In terms of the amount of structure provided, the scales differ in three ways: (1) the degree to which the meaning of the response categories is defined, (2) the degree to which the individual who is interpreting the ratings (e.g., an HR manager or researcher) can tell clearly what response was intended, and (3) the degree to which the performance dimension being rated is defined for the rater.

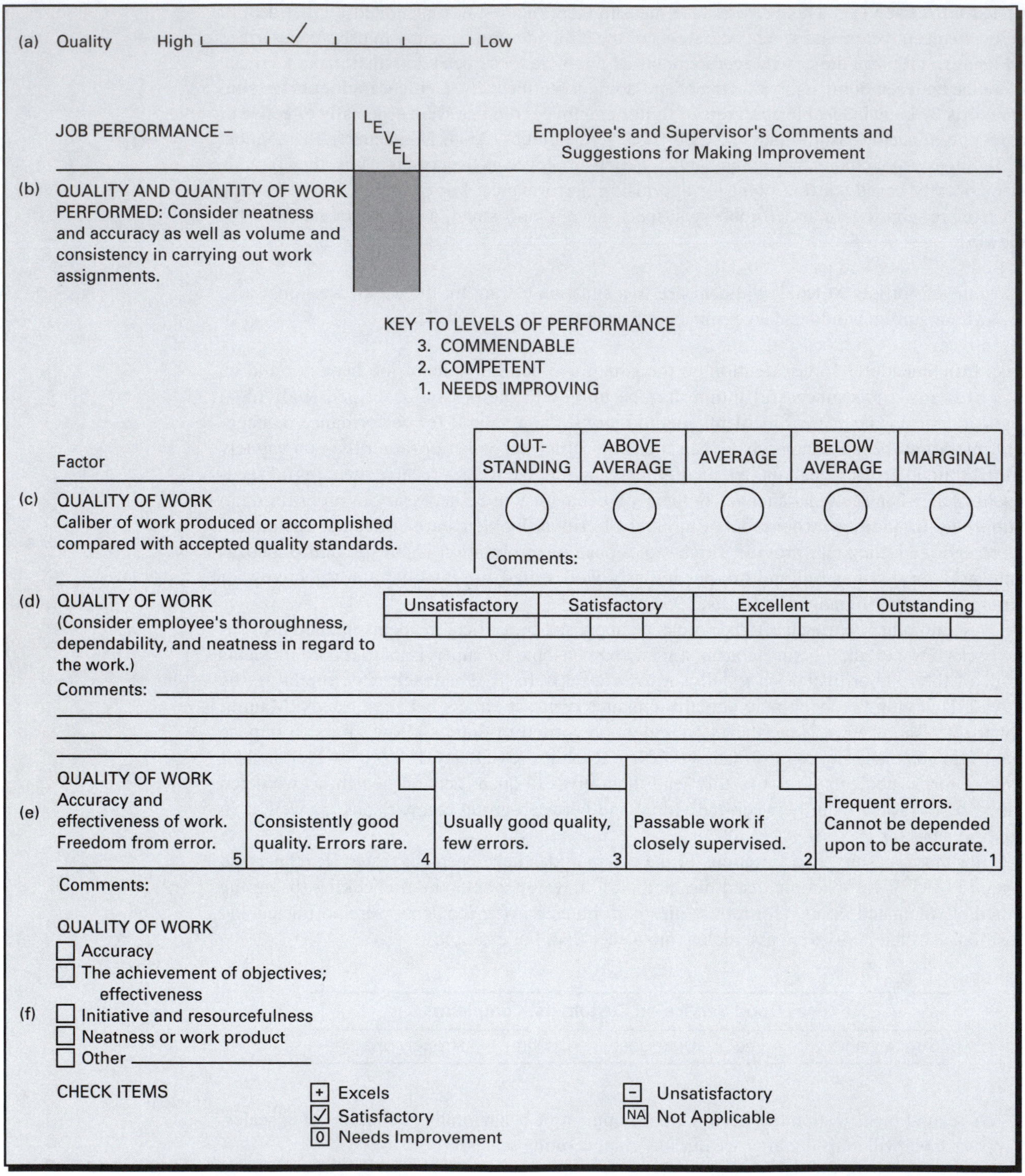

(a) Quality   High └───┬──✓──┬───────┴────┘ Low

JOB PERFORMANCE –   L E V E L   Employee's and Supervisor's Comments and
                                                        Suggestions for Making Improvement

(b) QUALITY AND QUANTITY OF WORK
     PERFORMED: Consider neatness
     and accuracy as well as volume and
     consistency in carrying out work
     assignments.

KEY TO LEVELS OF PERFORMANCE
3. COMMENDABLE
2. COMPETENT
1. NEEDS IMPROVING

Factor	OUT-STANDING	ABOVE AVERAGE	AVERAGE	BELOW AVERAGE	MARGINAL
(c) QUALITY OF WORK Caliber of work produced or accomplished compared with accepted quality standards.	◯	◯	◯	◯	◯

Comments:

(d) QUALITY OF WORK
     (Consider employee's thoroughness,
     dependability, and neatness in regard to
     the work.)

Unsatisfactory	Satisfactory	Excellent	Outstanding

Comments: _____

_____

_____

(e) QUALITY OF WORK Accuracy and effectiveness of work. Freedom from error. 5	Consistently good quality. Errors rare. 4	Usually good quality, few errors. 3	Passable work if closely supervised. 2	Frequent errors. Cannot be depended upon to be accurate. 1

Comments:

QUALITY OF WORK
☐ Accuracy
☐ The achievement of objectives;
      effectiveness
(f) ☐ Initiative and resourcefulness
☐ Neatness or work product
☐ Other _____

CHECK ITEMS   ⊞ Excels   ⊟ Unsatisfactory
                 ☑ Satisfactory   NA Not Applicable
                 ⓪ Needs Improvement

FIGURE 5-4   Examples of graphic rating scales.

On a graphic rating scale, each point is defined on a continuum. Hence, in order to make meaningful distinctions in performance within dimensions, scale points must be defined unambiguously for the rater. This process is called **anchoring**. Scale (a) uses qualitative end anchors only. Scales (b) and (e) include numerical and verbal anchors, while scales (c), (d), and (f) use verbal anchors only. These anchors are almost worthless, however, since what constitutes high and low quality or "outstanding" and "unsatisfactory" is left completely up to the rater. A "commendable" for one rater may be only a "competent" for another. Scale (e) is better, for the numerical anchors are described in terms of what "quality" means in that context.

The scales also differ in terms of the relative ease with which a person interpreting the ratings can tell exactly what response was intended by the rater. In scale (a), for example, the particular value that the rater had in mind is a mystery. Scale (e) is less ambiguous in this respect.

Finally, the scales differ in terms of the clarity of the definition of the performance dimension in question. In terms of Figure 5-4, what does quality mean? Is quality for a nurse the same as quality for a cashier? Scales (a) and (c) offer almost no help in defining quality; scale (b) combines quantity and quality together into a single dimension (although typically they are independent); and scales (d) and (e) define quality in different terms altogether (thoroughness, dependability, and neatness versus accuracy, effectiveness, and freedom from error). Scale (f) is an improvement in the sense that, although quality is taken to represent accuracy, effectiveness, initiative, and neatness (a combination of scale (d) and (e) definitions), at least separate ratings are required for each *aspect* of quality.

An improvement over all the examples in Figure 5-4 is shown below in Figure 5-5. It is part of a graphic rating scale used to rate nurses. The response categories are defined clearly; an individual interpreting the rating can tell what response the rater intended; and the performance dimension is defined in terms that both rater and ratee understand and can agree on.

Graphic rating scales may not yield the depth of information that narrative essays or critical incidents do; but they (1) are less time consuming to develop and administer, (2) permit quantitative results to be determined, (3) promote consideration of more than one performance dimension, and (4) are standardized and, therefore, comparable across individuals. On the other hand, graphic rating scales give maximum control to the rater, thereby exercising no control over leniency, severity, central tendency, or halo. For this reason, they have been criticized. However, when simple graphic rating scales have been compared against more sophisticated forced-choice ratings, the graphic scales consistently proved just as reliable and valid (King, Hunter, & Schmidt, 1980) and were more acceptable to raters (Bernardin & Beatty, 1991).

BEHAVIORALLY ANCHORED RATING SCALE (BARS)   How can graphic rating scales be improved? According to Smith and Kendall (1963):

> Better ratings can be obtained, in our opinion, not by trying to trick the rater (as in forced-choice scales) but by helping him to rate. We should ask him questions which he can honestly answer about behaviors which he can observe. We should reassure him that his answers will not be misinterpreted, and we should provide a basis by which he and others can check his answers. (p. 151)

Their procedure is as follows. At an initial conference, a group of workers and/or supervisors attempts to identify and define all of the important dimensions of effective performance for a particular job. A second group then generates, for each dimension, critical incidents illustrating effective, average, and ineffective performance. A third group is then given a list of dimensions and their definitions, along with a randomized list of the critical incidents generated by the second group. Their task is to sort or locate incidents into the dimensions they best represent.

This procedure is known as **retranslation**, since it resembles the quality control check that is used to ensure the adequacy of translations from one language into another. Material is translated into a foreign language by one translator and then retranslated back into the original by an independent translator. In the context of performance appraisal, this procedure ensures that the meanings of both the job dimensions and the behavioral incidents chosen to illustrate them are specific and clear. Incidents are eliminated if there is not clear agreement among judges (usually 60–80 percent) regarding the dimension to which each incident belongs. Dimensions are eliminated if incidents are not allocated to them. Conversely, dimensions may be added if many incidents are allocated to the "other" category.

Each of the items within the dimensions that survived the retranslation procedure is then presented to a fourth group of judges, whose task is to place a scale value on each incident (e.g., in terms of a seven- or nine-point scale from "highly effective behavior" to "grossly ineffective behavior"). The end product looks like that in Figure 5-5.

As you can see, BARS development is a long, painstaking process that may require many individuals. Moreover, separate BARS must be developed for dissimilar jobs. Consequently this approach may not be practical for many organizations.

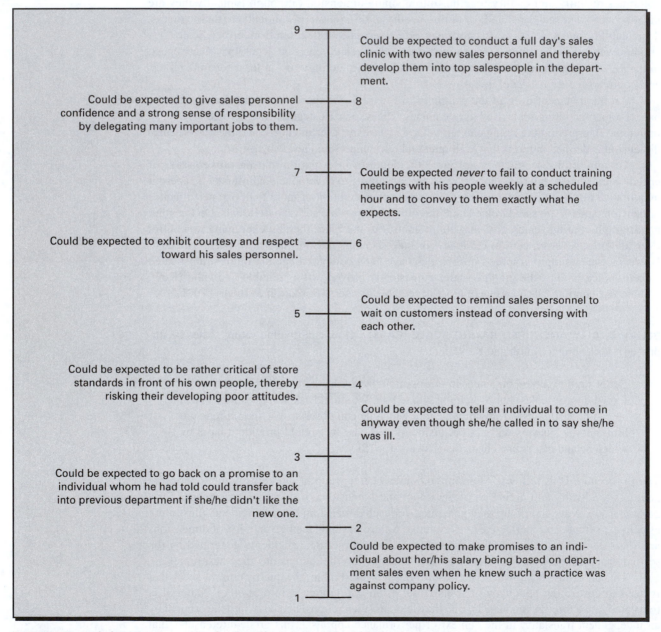

FIGURE 5-5 Scaled expectations rating for the effectiveness with which the department manager supervises his or her sales personnel.   *Source:* Campbell, J. P., Dunnette, M. D., Arvey, R. D., & Hellervik, L. V. The development and evaluation of behaviorally based rating scales. *Journal of Applied Psychology, 57,* 15–22. © 1973 APA.

TABLE 5-2 Known Effects of BARS

Participation
Participation does seem to enhance the validity of ratings, but no more so for BARS than for simple graphic rating scales.

Leniency, central tendency, halo, reliability
BARS not superior to other methods (reliabilities across dimensions in published studies range from about .52 to .76).

External validity
Moderate (R^2s of .21 to .47—Shapira and Shirom, 1980) relative to the upper limits of validity in performance ratings (Borman, 1978; Weekley & Gier, 1989).

Comparisons with other formats
BARS no better or worse than other methods.

Variance in dependent variables associated with differences in rating systems
Less than 5 percent. Rating systems affect neither the level of ratings (Harris and Schaubroeck, 1988), nor subordinates' satisfaction with feedback (Russell and Goode, 1988).

Convergent/discriminant validity
Low convergent validity, extremely low discriminant validity.

Specific content of behavioral anchors
Anchors depicting behaviors observed by rates, but unrepresentative of true performance levels, produce ratings biased in the direction of the anchors (Murphy and Constans, 1987). This is unlikely to have a major impact on ratings collected in the field (Murphy and Pardaffy, 1989).

How have BARS worked in practice? An enormous amount of research on BARS has been and continues to be published (e.g., Maurer, 2002). At the risk of oversimplification, major known effects of BARS are summarized in Table 5-2 (cf. Bernardin & Beatty, 1991). A perusal of this table suggests that there is little empirical evidence to support the superiority of BARS over other performance measurement systems.

SUMMARY COMMENTS ON RATING FORMATS AND RATING PROCESS

For several million workers today, especially those in the insurance, communications, transportation, and banking industries, being monitored on the job by a computer is a fact of life (Kurtzberg, Naquin, & Belkin, 2005; Stanton, 2000). In most jobs, though, human judgment about individual job performance is inevitable, no matter what format is used. This is the major problem with all formats.

Unless observation of ratees is extensive and representative, it is not possible for judgments to represent a ratee's true performance. Since the rater must make *inferences* about performance, the appraisal is subject to all the biases that have been linked to rating scales. Raters are free to distort their appraisals to suit their purposes. This can undo all of the painstaking work that went into scale development and probably explains why no single rating format has been shown to be clearly superior to others.

What can be done? Both Banks and Roberson (1985) and Härtel (1993) suggest two strategies: One, build in as much structure as possible in order to minimize the amount of discretion exercised by a rater. For example, use job analysis to specify what is really relevant to effective job performance, and use critical incidents to specify levels of performance effectiveness in terms of actual job behavior. Two, don't require raters to make judgments that they are not competent to make; don't tax their abilities beyond what they can do accurately. For example, for formats that require judgments of frequency, make sure that raters have had sufficient opportunity to observe ratees so that their judgments are accurate. Above all, recognize that the *process* of performance appraisal, not just the *mechanics*, determines the overall effectiveness of this essential component of all performance management systems.

FACTORS AFFECTING SUBJECTIVE APPRAISALS

As we discussed earlier, performance appraisal is a complex process that may be affected by many factors, including organizational, political, and interpersonal barriers. In fact, idiosyncratic variance (i.e., variance due to the rater) has been found to be a larger component of variance in performance ratings than the variance attributable to actual ratee performance (Greguras & Robie, 1998; Scullen, Mount, & Goff, 2000). For example, rater variance was found to be 1.21 times larger than ratee variance for supervisory ratings, 2.08 times larger for peer ratings, and 1.86 times larger for subordinate ratings (Scullen et al., 2000). Consequently we shall consider individual differences in raters and in ratees (and their interaction) and how these variables affect performance ratings. Findings in each of these areas are summarized in Tables 5-3, 5-4, and 5-5. For each variable listed in the tables, an illustrative reference is provided for those who wish to find more specific information.

TABLE 5-3 Summary of Findings on Rater Characteristics and Performance Ratings

Personal Characteristics

Gender
No general effect (Landy & Farr, 1980).

Race
African American raters rate whites slightly higher than they rate African Americans. White and African American raters differ very little in their ratings of white ratees (Sackett & DuBois, 1991).

Age
No consistent effects (Schwab & Heneman, 1978).

Education level
Statistically significant, but extremely weak effect (Cascio & Valenzi, 1977).

Low self-confidence; increased psychological distance
More critical, negative ratings (Rothaus, Morton, & Hanson, 1965).

Interests, social insight, intelligence
No consistent effect (Zedeck & Kafry, 1977).

Personality characteristics
Raters high on agreeableness are more likely to provide higher ratings, and raters high on conscientiousness are more likely to provide lower ratings (Bernardin, Cooke, & Villanova, 2000), and the positive relationship between agreeableness and ratings is even stronger when a face-to-face meeting is expected (Yun, Donahue, Dudley, & McFarland, 2005). Raters high on self-monitoring are more likely to provide more accurate ratings (Jawahar, 2001). Attitudes toward performance appraisal affect rating behavior more strongly for raters low on conscientiousness (Tziner, Murphy, & Cleveland, 2002).

Job-Related Variables

Accountability
Raters who are accountable for their ratings provide more accurate ratings than those who are not accountable (Mero & Motowidlo, 1995).

Job experience
Statistically significant, but weak positive effect on quality of ratings (Cascio & Valenzi, 1977).

Performance level
Effective performers tend to produce more reliable and valid ratings (Kirchner & Reisberg, 1962).

Leadership style
Supervisors who provide little structure to subordinates' work activities tend to avoid formal appraisals (Fried, Tiegs, & Bellamy, 1992).

Organizational position
(See earlier discussion of "Who Shall Rate?")

Rater knowledge of ratee and job
Relevance of contact to the dimensions rated is critical. Ratings are less accurate when delayed rather than immediate and when observations are based on limited data (Heneman & Wexley, 1983).

Prior expectations and information
Disconfirmation of expectations (higher or lower than expected) lowers ratings (Hogan, 1987). Prior information may bias ratings in the short run. Over time, ratings reflect actual behavior (Hanges, Braverman, & Rentch, 1991).

Stress
Raters under stress rely more heavily on first impressions and make fewer distinctions among performance dimensions (Srinivas & Motowidlo, 1987).

TABLE 5-4 Summary of Findings on Ratee Characteristics and Performance Ratings

Personal Characteristics

Gender
Females tend to receive lower ratings than males when they make up less than 20 percent of a work group, but higher ratings than males when they make up more than 50 percent of a work group (Sackett, DuBois, & Noe, 1991). Female ratees received more accurate ratings than male ratees (Sundvik & Lindeman, 1998). Female employees in line jobs tend to receive lower performance ratings than female employees in staff jobs or men in either line or staff jobs (Lyness & Heilman, 2006).

Race
Race of the ratee accounts for between 1 and 5 percent of the variance in ratings (Borman, White, Pulakos, & Oppler, 1991; Oppler, Campbell, Pulakos, & Borman, 1992).

Age
Older subordinates were rated lower than younger subordinates (Ferris, Yates, Gilmore, & Rowland, 1985) by both black and white raters (Crew, 1984).

Education
No statistically significant effects (Cascio & Valenzi, 1977).

Emotional disability
Workers with emotional disabilities received higher ratings than warranted, but such positive bias disappears when clear standards are used (Czajka & DeNisi, 1988).

Job-Related Variables

Performance level
Actual performance level and ability have the strongest effect on ratings (Borman et al., 1991; Borman et al., 1995; Vance et al., 1983). More weight is given to negative than to positive attributes of ratees (Ganzach, 1995).

Group composition
Ratings tend to be higher for satisfactory workers in groups with a large proportion of unsatisfactory workers (Grey & Kipnis, 1976), but these findings may not generalize to all occupational groups (Ivancevich, 1983).

Tenure
Although age and tenure are highly related, evidence indicates no relationship between ratings and either ratee tenure in general or ratee tenure working for the same supervisor (Ferris et al., 1985).

Job satisfaction
Knowledge of a ratee's job satisfaction may bias ratings in the same direction (+ or −) as the ratee's satisfaction (Smither, Collins, & Buda, 1989).

Personality characteristics
Both peers and supervisors rate dependability highly. However, obnoxiousness affects peer raters much more than supervisors (Borman et al., 1995).

TABLE 5-5 Summary of Findings on Interaction of Rater–Ratee Characteristics and Performance Ratings

---

Gender
In the context of merit pay and promotions, females are rated less favorably and with greater negative bias by raters who hold traditional stereotypes about women (Dobbins, Cardy, & Truxillo, 1988).

Race
Both white and African American raters consistently assign lower ratings to African American ratees than to white ratees. White and African American raters differ very little in their ratings of white ratees (Oppler et al., 1992; Sackett & DuBois, 1991). Race effects may disappear when cognitive ability, education, and experience are taken into account (Waldman & Avolio, 1991).

Actual versus perceived similarity
Actual similarity (agreement between supervisor–subordinate work-related self-descriptions) is a weak predictor of performance ratings (Wexley, Alexander, Greenawalt, & Couch, 1980), but *perceived* similarity is a strong predictor (Turban & Jones, 1988; Wayne & Liden, 1995).

Performance attributions
Age and job performance are generally unrelated (McEvoy & Cascio, 1989).

Citizenship behaviors
Dimension ratings of ratees with high levels of citizenship behaviors show high halo effects (Werner, 1994). Task performance and contextual performance interact in affecting reward decisions (Kiker & Motowidlo, 1999).

Length of relationship
Longer relationships resulted in more accurate ratings (Sundvik & Lindeman, 1998).

Personality characteristics
Similarity regarding conscientiousness increases ratings of contextual work behaviors, but there is no relationship for agreeableness, extraversion, neuroticism, or openness to experience (Antonioni & Park, 2001).

As the tables demonstrate, we now know a great deal about the effects of selected individual differences variables on ratings of job performance. However, there is a great deal more that we do not know. Specifically, we know little about the cognitive processes involved in performance appraisal except that, even when presented with information about how a ratee behaves, raters seem to infer common personality characteristics that go beyond that which is warranted. Such attributions exert an independent effect on appraisals, over and above that which is attributable to actual behaviors (Krzystofiak, Cardy, & Newman, 1988). Later research has found that raters may assign ratings in a manner that is consistent with their previous attitudes toward the ratee (i.e., based on affect) and that they may use affect consistency rather than simply good or bad performance as the criterion for diagnosing performance information (Robbins & DeNisi, 1994). We now know that a rater's affective state interacts with information processing in affecting performance appraisals (Forgas & George, 2001), but the precise mechanisms underlying the affective–cognitive interplay are not yet known. Also, the degree of accountability can lead to improved accuracy in ratings, or to more leniency in ratings, depending on who the audience is (Mero, Guidice, & Brownlee, 2007). More research is needed to understand organizational-level contextual factors that are likely to improve rating accuracy.

This kind of research is needed to help us understand why reliable, systematic changes in ratings occur over time, as well as why ratings are consistent (Vance, Winne, & Wright, 1983). It also will help us understand underlying reasons for bias in ratings and the information-processing strategies used by raters to combine evaluation data (Hobson & Gibson, 1983). In addition, it will help us to identify raters who vary in their ability to provide accurate ratings. Finally, adopting a multilevel approach in which ratees are seen as nested within raters is also a promising avenue for future research (LaHuis & Avis, 2007). Research findings from each of these areas can help to improve the content of rater training programs and, ultimately, the caliber of appraisals in organizations.

EVALUATING THE PERFORMANCE OF TEAMS

Our discussion thus far has focused on the measurement of employees working independently and not in groups. We have been focusing on the assessment and improvement of *individual* performance. However, numerous organizations are structured around teams (LaFasto & Larson, 2001). Team-based organizations do not necessarily outperform organizations that are not structured around teams (Hackman, 1998). However, the interest in, and implementation of, team-based structures does not seem to be subsiding; on the contrary, there seems to be an increased interest in organizing how work is done around teams (Naquin & Tynan, 2003). Therefore, given the popularity of teams, it makes sense for performance management systems to target not only individual performance but also an individual's contribution to the performance of his or her team(s), as well as the performance of teams as a whole.

The assessment of team performance does not imply that individual contributions should be ignored. On the contrary, if individual performance is not assessed and recognized, social loafing may occur (Scott & Einstein, 2001). Even worse, when other team members see there is a "free rider," they are likely to withdraw their effort in support of team performance (Heneman & von Hippel, 1995). So assessing team performance should be seen as complementary to the assessment and recognition of (1) individual performance (as we have discussed thus far), and (2) individuals' behaviors and skills that contribute to team performance (e.g., self-management, communication, decision making, collaboration; Reilly & McGourty, 1998).

Not all teams are created equal, however. Different types of teams require different emphases on performance measurement at the individual and team levels. Depending on the complexity of the task (from routine to nonroutine) and the membership configuration (from static to dynamic), we can identify three different types of teams (Scott & Einstein, 2001):

- *Work or Service Teams*—intact teams engaged in routine tasks (e.g., manufacturing or service tasks)
- *Project Teams*—teams assembled for a specific purpose and expected to disband once their task is complete; their tasks are outside the core production or service of the organization and, therefore, less routine than those of work or service teams
- *Network Teams*—teams whose membership is not constrained by time or space or limited by organizational boundaries (i.e., they are typically geographically dispersed and stay in touch via telecommunications technology); their work is extremely nonroutine

Table 5-6 shows a summary of recommended measurement methods for each of the three types of teams. For example, regarding project teams, the duration of a particular project limits the utility of team outcome–based assessment. Specifically, end-of-project outcome measures may not benefit the team's development because the team is likely to disband once the project is over. Instead, measurements taken during the project can be implemented, so corrective action can be taken, if necessary, before the project is over. This is what Hewlett-Packard uses with its product-development teams (Scott & Einstein, 2001). Irrespective of the type of team that is

TABLE 5-6 Performance Appraisal Methods for Different Types of Teams

Team Type	Who Is Being Rated	Who Provides Rating	What Is Rated?			How Is the Rating Used?		
			Outcome	Behavior	Competency	Development	Evaluation	Self-Regulation
Work or service team	Team member	Manager	✓	✓	✓	✓	✓	—
		Other team members	—	✓	✓	✓	—	—
		Customers	—	✓	—	✓	—	—
		Self	✓	✓	✓	✓	—	✓
	Entire team	Manager	✓	✓	✓	✓	✓	—
		Other teams	—	✓	—	—	—	—
		Customers	—	✓	—	—	—	—
		Self	✓	✓	✓	✓	—	✓
Project team	Team member	Manager	✓	—	✓	✓	✓	—
		Project leaders	—	✓	✓	✓	—	—
		Other team members	—	✓	✓	✓	—	—
		Customers	—	✓	—	—	—	—
		Self	✓	✓	✓	✓	—	✓
	Entire team	Customers	✓	✓	—	—	✓	—
		Self	✓	✓	✓	✓	—	✓
Network team	Team member	Manager	—	✓	✓	✓	✓	—
		Team leaders	—	✓	✓	✓	—	—
		Coworkers	—	✓	✓	✓	—	—
		Other team members	—	✓	✓	✓	—	—
		Customers	—	✓	✓	✓	—	—
		Self	✓	✓	✓	✓	—	✓
	Entire team	Customers	✓	—	—	—	✓	—

Source: Scott, S. G., & Einstein, W. O. (2001). Strategic performance appraisal in team-based organizations: One size does not fit all. *Academy of Management Executive, 15*, 111. Reprinted by permission of ACAD OF MGMT in the format Textbook via Copyright Clearance Center.

evaluated, the interpersonal relationships among the team members play a central role in the resulting ratings (Greguras, Robie, Born, & Koenigs, 2007). For example, self-ratings are related to how one rates and also to how one is rated by others; and, particularly for performance dimensions related to interpersonal issues, team members are likely to reciprocate the type of rating they receive.

Regardless of whether performance is measured at the individual level or at the individual and team levels, raters are likely to make intentional or unintentional mistakes in assigning performance scores (Naquin & Tynan, 2003). They can be trained to minimize such biases, as our next section demonstrates.

RATER TRAINING

The first step in the design of *any* training program is to specify objectives. In the context of rater training, there are three broad objectives: (1) to improve the observational skills of raters by teaching them *what* to attend to, (2) to reduce or eliminate judgmental biases, and (3) to improve the ability of raters to communicate performance information to ratees in an objective and constructive manner.

Traditionally, rater training has focused on teaching raters to eliminate judgmental biases such as leniency, central tendency, and halo effects (Bernardin & Buckley, 1981). This approach assumes that certain rating distributions are more desirable than others (e.g., normal distributions, variability in ratings across dimensions for a single person). While raters may learn a new response set that results in lower average ratings (less leniency) and greater variability in ratings across dimensions (less halo), their accuracy tends to decrease (Hedge & Kavanagh, 1988; Murphy & Balzer, 1989). However, it is important to note that accuracy in appraisal has been defined in different ways by researchers and that relations among different operational definitions of accuracy are generally weak (Sulsky & Balzer, 1988). In addition, rater training programs that attempt to eliminate systematic errors typically have only short-term effects (Fay & Latham, 1982). Regarding unintentional errors, **rater error training (RET)** exposes raters to the different errors and their causes. Although raters may receive training on the various errors that they may make, this awareness does not necessarily lead to the elimination of such errors (London, Mone, & Scott, 2004). Being aware of the unintentional errors does not mean that supervisors will no longer make these errors. Awareness is certainly a good first step, but we need to go further if we want to minimize unintentional errors. One fruitful possibility is the implementation of **frame-of-reference (FOR)** training.

Of the many types of rater training programs available today, meta-analytic evidence has demonstrated reliably that FOR training (Bernardin & Buckley, 1981) is most effective in improving the accuracy of performance appraisals (Woehr & Huffcut, 1994). And the addition of other types of training in combination with FOR training does not seem to improve rating accuracy beyond the effects of FOR training alone (Noonan & Sulsky, 2001). Following procedures developed by Pulakos (1984, 1986), such FOR training proceeds as follows:

1. Participants are told that they will evaluate the performance of three ratees on three separate performance dimensions.
2. They are given rating scales and instructed to read them as the trainer reads the dimension definitions and scale anchors aloud.
3. The trainer then discusses ratee behaviors that illustrate different performance levels for each scale. The goal is to create a common performance theory (frame of reference) among raters such that they will agree on the appropriate performance dimension and effectiveness level for different behaviors.
4. Participants are shown a videotape of a practice vignette and are asked to evaluate the manager using the scales provided.
5. Ratings are then written on a blackboard and discussed by the group of participants. The trainer seeks to identify which behaviors participants used to decide on their assigned ratings and to clarify any discrepancies among the ratings.
6. The trainer provides feedback to participants, explaining why the ratee should receive a certain rating (target score) on a given dimension.

FOR training provides trainees with a "theory of performance" that allows them to understand the various performance dimensions, how to match these performance dimensions to rate behaviors, how to judge the effectiveness of various ratee behaviors, and how to integrate these judgments into an overall rating of performance (Sulsky & Day, 1992). In addition, the provision of rating standards and behavioral examples appears to be responsible for the improvements in rating accuracy. The use of target scores in performance examples and accuracy feedback on practice ratings allows raters to learn, through direct experience, how to use the different rating standards. In essence, the FOR training is a microcosm that includes an efficient model of the process by which performance-dimension standards are acquired (Stamoulis & Hauenstein, 1993).

Nevertheless, the approach described above assumes a single frame of reference for all raters. Research has shown that different sources of performance data (peers, supervisors, subordinates) demonstrate distinctly different FORs and that they disagree about the importance of poor performance incidents (Hauenstein & Foti, 1989). Therefore, training should highlight these differences and focus both on the content of the raters' performance theories and on the process by which judgments are made (Schleicher & Day, 1998). Finally, the training process should identify idiosyncratic raters so their performance in training can be monitored to assess improvement.

Rater training is clearly worth the effort, and the kind of approach advocated here is especially effective in improving the accuracy of ratings for individual ratees on separate performance dimensions (Day & Sulsky, 1995). In addition, trained managers are more effective in formulating development plans for subordinates (Davis & Mount, 1984). The technical and interpersonal problems associated with performance appraisal are neither insurmountable nor inscrutable; they simply require the competent and systematic application of sound psychological principles.

THE SOCIAL AND INTERPERSONAL CONTEXT OF PERFORMANCE MANAGEMENT SYSTEMS

Throughout this chapter, we have emphasized that performance management systems encompass measurement issues, as well as attitudinal and behavioral issues. Traditionally, we have tended to focus our research efforts on measurement issues per se; yet any measurement instrument or rating format probably has only a limited impact on performance appraisal scores (Banks & Roberson, 1985). Broader issues in performance management must be addressed, since appraisal outcomes are likely to represent an interaction among organizational contextual variables, rating formats, and rater and ratee motivation.

Several recent studies have assessed the attitudinal implications of various types of performance management systems (e.g., Kinicki, Prussia, Bin, & McKee-Ryan, 2004). This body of literature focuses on different types of reactions, including satisfaction, fairness, perceived utility, and perceived accuracy (see Keeping & Levy, 2000, for a review of measures used to assess each type of reaction). The reactions of participants to a performance management system are important because they are linked to system acceptance and success (Murphy & Cleveland, 1995). And there is preliminary evidence regarding the existence of an overall multidimensional reaction construct (Keeping & Levy, 2000). So the various types of reactions can be conceptualized as separate, yet related, entities.

As an example of one type of reaction, consider some of the evidence gathered regarding the perceived fairness of the system. Fairness, as conceptualized in terms of due process, includes two types of facets: (1) process facets or interactional justice—interpersonal exchanges between supervisor and employees; and (2) system facets or procedural justice—structure, procedures, and policies of the system (Findley, Giles, & Mossholder, 2000; Masterson, Lewis, Goldman, & Taylor, 2000). Results of a selective set of studies indicate the following:

- Process facets explain variance in contextual performance beyond that accounted for by system facets (Findley et al., 2000).

- Managers who have perceived unfairness in their own most recent performance evaluations are more likely to react favorably to the implementation of a procedurally just system than are those who did not perceive unfairness in their own evaluations (Taylor, Masterson, Renard, & Tracy, 1998).
- Appraisers are more likely to engage in interactionally fair behavior when interacting with an assertive appraisee than with an unassertive appraisee (Korsgaard, Roberson, & Rymph, 1998).

This kind of knowledge illustrates the importance of the social and motivational aspects of performance management systems (Fletcher, 2001). In implementing a system, this type of information is no less important than the knowledge that a new system results in less halo, leniency, and central tendency. Both types of information are meaningful and useful; both must be considered in the wider context of performance management. In support of this view, a review of 295 U.S. Circuit Court decisions rendered from 1980 to 1995 regarding performance appraisal concluded that issues relevant to *fairness* and *due process* were most salient in making the judicial decisions (Werner & Bolino, 1997).

Finally, to reinforce the view that context must be taken into account and that performance management must be tackled from both a technical as well as an interpersonal issue, Aguinis and Pierce (2008) offered the following recommendations regarding issues that should be explored further:

1. *Social power, influence, and leadership.* A supervisor's social power refers to his or her ability, as perceived by others, to influence behaviors and outcomes (Farmer & Aguinis, 2005). If an employee believes that his or her supervisor has the ability to influence important tangible and intangible outcomes (e.g., financial rewards, recognition), then the performance management system is likely to be more meaningful. Thus, future research could attempt to identify the conditions under which supervisors are likely to be perceived as more powerful and the impact of these power perceptions on the meaningfulness and effectiveness of performance management systems.

2. *Trust.* The "collective trust" of all stakeholders in the performance management process is crucial for the system to be effective (Farr & Jacobs, 2006). Given the current business reality of downsizing and restructuring efforts, how can trust be created so that organizations can implement successful performance management systems? Stated differently, future research could attempt to understand conditions under which dyadic, group, and organizational factors are likely to enhance trust and, consequently, enhance the effectiveness of performance management systems.

3. *Social exchange.* The relationship between individuals (and groups) and organizations can be conceptualized within a social exchange framework. Specifically, individuals and groups display behaviors and produce results that are valued by the organization, which in turn provides tangible and intangible outcomes in exchange for those behaviors and results. Thus, future research using a social exchange framework could inform the design of performance management systems by providing a better understanding of the perceived fairness of various types of exchange relationships and the conditions under which these types of relationships are likely to be perceived as being more or less fair.

4. *Group dynamics and close interpersonal relationships.* It is virtually impossible to think of an organization that does not organize its functions at least in part based on teams. Consequently, many organizations include a team component in their performance management system (Aguinis, 2009a). Such systems usually target individual performance and also an individual's contribution to the performance of his or her team(s) and the performance of teams as a whole. Within the context of such performance management systems, future research could investigate how group dynamics affect who measures performance and how performance is measured. Future research could also attempt to understand how close personal relationships, such as supervisor–subordinate workplace romances (Pierce, Aguinis, & Adams, 2000; Pierce, Broberg, McClure, & Aguinis, 2004), which involve conflicts of interest, may affect the successful implementation of performance management systems.

PERFORMANCE FEEDBACK: APPRAISAL
AND GOAL—SETTING INTERVIEWS

One of the central purposes of performance management systems is to serve as a personal development tool. To improve, there must be some feedback regarding present performance. However, the mere presence of performance feedback does not guarantee a positive effect on future performance. In fact, a meta-analysis including 131 studies showed that, overall, feedback has a positive effect on performance (less than one-half of one standard deviation improvement in performance), but that 38 percent of the feedback interventions reviewed had a *negative* effect on performance (Kluger & DeNisi, 1996). Thus, in many cases, feedback does not have a positive effect; in fact, it can actually have a harmful effect on future performance. For instance, if feedback results in an employee's focusing attention on himself or herself instead of the task at hand, then feedback is likely to have a negative effect. Consider the example of a woman who has made many personal sacrifices to reach the top echelons of her organization's hierarchy. She might be devastated to learn she has failed to keep a valued client and then may begin to question her life choices instead of focusing on how to not lose valued clients in the future (DeNisi & Kluger, 2000).

As described earlier in this chapter, information regarding performance is usually gathered from more than one source (Ghorpade, 2000). However, responsibility for communicating such feedback from multiple sources by means of an appraisal interview often rests with the immediate supervisor (Ghorpade & Chen, 1995). A formal system for giving feedback should be implemented because, in the absence of such a system, some employees are more likely to seek and benefit from feedback than others. For example, consider the relationship between **stereotype threat** (i.e., a fear of confirming a negative stereotype about one's group through one's own behavior; Farr, 2003) and the willingness to seek feedback. A study including 166 African American managers in utilities industries found that being the only African American in the workplace was related to stereotype threat and that stereotype threat was negatively related to feedback seeking (Roberson, Deitch, Brief, & Block, 2003). Thus, if no formal performance feedback system is in place, employees who do not perceive a stereotype threat will be more likely to seek feedback from their supervisors and benefit from it. This, combined with the fact that people generally are apprehensive about both receiving and giving performance information, reinforces the notion that the implementation of formal job feedback systems is necessary (London, 2003).

Ideally, a continuous feedback process should exist between superior and subordinate so that both may be guided. This can be facilitated by the fact that in many organizations electronic performance monitoring (EPM) is common practice (e.g., number or duration of phone calls with clients, duration of log-in time). EPM is qualitatively different from more traditional methods of collecting performance data (e.g., direct observation) because it can occur continuously and produces voluminous data on multiple performance dimensions (Stanton, 2000). However, the availability of data resulting from EPM, often stored online and easily retrievable by the employees, does not diminish the need for face-to-face interaction with the supervisor, who is responsible for not only providing the information but also interpreting it and helping guide future performance. In practice, however, supervisors frequently "save up" performance-related information for a formal appraisal interview, the conduct of which is an extremely trying experience for both parties. Most supervisors resist "playing God" (playing the role of judge) and then communicating their judgments to subordinates (McGregor, 1957). Hence, supervisors may avoid confronting uncomfortable issues; but, even if they do, subordinates may only deny or rationalize them in an effort to maintain self-esteem (Larson, 1989). Thus, the process is self-defeating for both groups. Fortunately, this need not always be the case. Based on findings from appraisal interview research, Table 5-7 presents several activities that supervisors should engage in before, during, and after appraisal interviews. Let us briefly consider each of them.

TABLE 5-7 Supervisory Activities Before, During, and After the Appraisal Interview

Before

Communicate frequently with subordinates about their performance.

Get training in performance appraisal.

Judge your own performance first before judging others.

Encourage subordinates to prepare for appraisal interviews.

Be exposed to priming information to help retrieve information from memory.

During

Warm up and encourage subordinate participation.

Judge performance, not personality, mannerisms, or self-concept.

Be specific.

Be an active listener.

Avoid destructive criticism and threats to the employee's ego.

Set mutually agreeable and formal goals for future improvement.

After

Communicate frequently with subordinates about their performance.

Periodically assess progress toward goals.

Make organizational rewards contingent on performance.

Communicate Frequently

Two of the clearest results from research on the appraisal interview are that once-a-year performance appraisals are of questionable value and that coaching should be done much more frequently—particularly for poor performers and with new employees (Cederblom, 1982; Meyer, 1991). Feedback has maximum impact when it is given as close as possible to the action. If a subordinate behaves effectively, tell him or her immediately; if he or she behaves ineffectively, also tell him or her immediately. Do not file these incidents away so that they can be discussed in six to nine months.

Get Training in Appraisal

As we noted earlier, increased emphasis should be placed on training raters to observe behavior more accurately and fairly rather than on providing specific illustrations of "how to" or "how not to" rate. Training managers on how to provide evaluative information and to give feedback should focus on characteristics that are difficult to rate and on characteristics that people think are easy to rate, but that generally result in disagreements. Such factors include risk taking and development (Wohlers & London, 1989).

Judge Your Own Performance First

We often use ourselves as the norm or standard by which to judge others. While this tendency may be difficult to overcome, research findings in the area of interpersonal perception can help us improve the process (Kraiger & Aguinis, 2001). A selective list of such findings includes the following:

1. Self-protection mechanisms like denial, giving up, self-promotion, and fear of failure have a negative influence on self-awareness.
2. Knowing oneself makes it easier to see others accurately and is itself a managerial ability.
3. One's own characteristics affect the characteristics one is likely to see in others.

4. The person who accepts himself or herself is more likely to be able to see favorable aspects of other people.
5. Accuracy in perceiving others is not a single skill (Wohlers & London, 1989; Zalkind & Costello, 1962).

Encourage Subordinate Preparation

Research conducted in a large Midwestern hospital indicated that the more time employees spent prior to appraisal interviews analyzing their job duties and responsibilities, the problems being encountered on the job, and the quality of their performance, the more likely they were to be satisfied with the appraisal process, to be motivated to improve their own performance, and actually to improve their performance (Burke, Weitzel, & Weir, 1978). To foster such preparation, (1) a BARS form could be developed for this purpose, and subordinates could be encouraged or required to use it (Silverman & Wexley, 1984); (2) employees could be provided with the supervisor's review prior to the appraisal interview and encouraged to react to it in specific terms; and (3) employees could be encouraged or required to appraise their own performance on the same criteria or forms their supervisor uses (Farh, Werbel, & Bedeian, 1988).

Self-review has at least four advantages: (1) It enhances the subordinate's dignity and self-respect; (2) it places the manager in the role of counselor, not judge; (3) it is more likely to promote employee commitment to plans or goals formulated during the discussion; and (4) it is likely to be more satisfying and productive for both parties than is the more traditional manager-to-subordinate review (Meyer, 1991).

Use "Priming" Information

A prime is a stimulus given to the rater to trigger information stored in long-term memory. There are numerous ways to help a rater retrieve information about a ratee's performance from memory before the performance-feedback session. For example, an examination of documentation regarding each performance dimension and behaviors associated with each dimension can help improve the effectiveness of the feedback session (cf. Jelley & Goffin, 2001).

Warm Up and Encourage Participation

Research shows generally that the more a subordinate feels he or she participated in the interview by presenting his or her own ideas and feelings, the more likely the subordinate is to feel that the supervisor was helpful and constructive, that some current job problems were cleared up, and that future goals were set. However, these conclusions are true only as long as the appraisal interview represents a low threat to the subordinate; he or she previously has received an appraisal interview from the superior; he or she is accustomed to participating with the superior; and he or she is knowledgeable about issues to be discussed in the interview (Cederblom, 1982).

Judge Performance, Not Personality or Self-Concept

The more a supervisor focuses on the personality and mannerisms of his or her subordinate rather than on aspects of job-related behavior, the lower the satisfaction of both supervisor and subordinate is, and the less likely the subordinate is to be motivated to improve his or her performance (Burke et al., 1978). Also, an emphasis on the employee as a person or on his or her self-concept, as opposed to the task and task performance only, is likely to lead to lower levels of future performance (DeNisi & Kluger, 2000).

Be Specific

Appraisal interviews are more likely to be successful to the extent that supervisors are perceived as constructive and helpful (Russell & Goode, 1988). By being candid and specific, the supervisor offers very clear feedback to the subordinate concerning past actions. He or she also demonstrates knowledge of the subordinate's level of performance and job duties. One should be specific about positive as well as negative behaviors on a job. Data show that the acceptance and perception of accuracy of feedback by a subordinate are strongly affected by the order in which positive or negative information is presented. Begin the appraisal interview with positive feedback associated with minor issues, and then proceed to discuss feedback regarding major issues. Praise concerning minor aspects of behavior should put the individual at ease and reduce the dysfunctional blocking effect associated with criticisms (Stone, Gueutal, & McIntosh, 1984). And it is helpful to maximize information relating to performance improvements and minimize information concerning the relative performance of other employees (DeNisi & Kluger, 2000).

Be an Active Listener

Have you ever seen two people in a heated argument who are so intent on making their own points that each one has no idea what the other person is saying? That is the opposite of "active" listening, where the objective is to empathize, to stand in the other person's shoes and try to see things from her or his point of view.

For example, during an interview with her boss, a member of a project team says: "I don't want to work with Sally anymore. She's lazy and snooty and complains about the rest of us not helping her as much as we should. She thinks she's above this kind of work and too good to work with the rest of us and I'm sick of being around her." The supervisor replies, "Sally's attitude makes the work unpleasant for you."

By reflecting what the woman said, the supervisor is encouraging her to confront her feelings and letting her know that she understands them. Active listeners are attentive to verbal as well as nonverbal cues, and, above all, they accept what the other person is saying without argument or criticism. Listen to and treat each individual with the same amount of dignity and respect that you yourself demand.

Avoid Destructive Criticism and Threats to the Employee's Ego

Destructive criticism is general in nature, is frequently delivered in a biting, sarcastic tone, and often attributes poor performance to internal causes (e.g., lack of motivation or ability). Evidence indicates that employees are strongly predisposed to attribute performance problems to factors beyond their control (e.g., inadequate materials, equipment, instructions, or time) as a mechanism to maintain their self-esteem (Larson, 1989). Not surprisingly, therefore, destructive criticism leads to three predictable consequences: (1) It produces negative feelings among recipients and can initiate or intensify conflict among individuals; (2) it reduces the preference of recipients for handling future disagreements with the giver of the feedback in a conciliatory manner (e.g., compromise, collaboration); and (3) it has negative effects on self-set goals and feelings of self-efficacy (Baron, 1988). Needless to say, this is one type of communication that managers and others would do well to avoid.

Set Mutually Agreeable and Formal Goals

It is important that a formal goal-setting plan be established during the appraisal interview (DeNisi & Kluger, 2000). There are three related reasons why goal setting affects performance. First, it has the effect of providing *direction*—that is, it focuses activity in one particular direction rather than others. Second, given that a goal is accepted, people tend to exert *effort* in proportion to the difficulty of the goal. Third, difficult goals lead to more *persistence* (i.e., directed effort over time) than do easy goals. These three dimensions—direction (choice), effort, and persistence—are central to the motivation/appraisal process (Katzell, 1994).

Research findings from goal-setting programs in organizations can be summed up as follows: Use participation to set specific goals, for they clarify for the individual precisely what is expected. Better yet, use participation to set specific, but difficult goals, for this leads to higher acceptance and performance than setting specific, but easily achievable, goals (Erez, Earley, & Hulin, 1985).

These findings seem to hold across cultures, not just in the United States (Erez & Earley, 1987), and they hold for groups or teams, as well as for individuals (Matsui, Kakuyama, & Onglatco, 1987). It is the future-oriented emphasis in appraisal interviews that seems to have the most beneficial effects on subsequent performance. Top-management commitment is also crucial, as a meta-analysis of management-by-objectives programs revealed. When top-management commitment was high, the average gain in productivity was 56 percent. When such commitment was low, the average gain in productivity was only 6 percent (Rodgers & Hunter, 1991).

As an illustration of the implementation of these principles, Microsoft Corporation has developed a goal-setting system using the label SMART (Shaw, 2004). SMART goals are specific, measurable, achievable, results based, and time specific.

Continue to Communicate and Assess Progress Toward Goals Regularly

When coaching is a day-to-day activity, rather than a once-a-year ritual, the appraisal interview can be put in proper perspective: It merely formalizes a process that should be occurring regularly anyway. Periodic tracking of progress toward goals helps keep the subordinate's behavior on target, provides the subordinate with a better understanding of the reasons why his or her performance is judged to be at a given level, and enhances the subordinate's commitment to effective performance.

Make Organizational Rewards Contingent on Performance

Research results are clear-cut on this issue. Subordinates who see a link between appraisal results and employment decisions are more likely to prepare for appraisal interviews, more likely to take part actively in them, and more likely to be satisfied with the appraisal system (Burke et al., 1978). Managers, in turn, are likely to get more mileage out of their appraisal systems by heeding these results.

Evidence-Based Implications for Practice

- Regardless of the type and size of an organization, its success depends on the performance of individuals and teams. Make sure performance management is more than just performance appraisal, and that it is an ongoing process guided by strategic organizational considerations.
- Performance management has both technical and interpersonal components. Focusing on the measurement and technical issues at the exclusion of interpersonal and emotional ones is likely to lead to a system that does not produce the intended positive results of improving performance and aligning individual and team performance with organizational goals.
- Good performance management systems are congruent with the organization's strategic goals, discriminate between good and poor performance, and are thorough, practical, meaningful, specific, reliable, valid, inclusive, fair, and acceptable.
- Performance can be assessed by means of objective and subjective measures, and also by relative and absolute rating systems. There is no such thing as a "silver bullet" in measuring the complex construct of performance, so consider carefully the advantages and disadvantages of each measurement approach in a given organizational context.
- There are several biases that affect the accuracy of performance ratings. Rater training programs can minimize many of them. Performance feedback does not always lead to positive results and, hence, those giving feedback should receive training so they can give feedback frequently, judge their own performance first, encourage subordinate preparation, evaluate performance and not personality or self-concept, be specific, be active listeners, avoid destructive criticism, and be able to set mutually agreeable goals.

Discussion Questions

1. Why do performance management systems often fail?
2. What is the difference between performance management and performance appraisal?
3. What are the three most important purposes of performance management systems and why?
4. Under what circumstances can performance management systems be said to "work"?
5. What kinds of unique information about performance can each of the following provide: immediate supervisor, peers, self, subordinates, and clients served?
6. What are some of the interpersonal/social interaction dimensions that should be considered in implementing a performance management system?
7. Under what circumstances would you recommend that the measurement of performance be conducted as a group task?
8. What key elements would you design into a rater-training program?
9. Assume an organization is structured around teams. What role, if any, would a performance management system based on individual behaviors and results play with respect to a team-based performance management system?
10. Discuss three "dos" and three "don'ts" with respect to appraisal interviews.

6

Measuring and Interpreting Individual Differences

At a Glance

Measurement of individual differences is the heart of personnel psychology. Individual differences in physical and psychological attributes may be measured on nominal, ordinal, interval, and ratio scales. Although measurements of psychological traits are primarily nominal and ordinal in nature, they may be treated statistically as if they are interval level. Care should be taken in creating scales so that the number and spacing of anchors on each scale item represent the nature of the underlying construct and scale coarseness does not lead to imprecise measurement.

Effective decisions about people demand knowledge of their individuality—knowledge that can be gained only through measurement of individual patterns of abilities, skills, knowledge, and other characteristics. Psychological measurement procedures are known collectively as tests, and HR specialists may choose to use tests that were developed previously or to develop their own. Analysis techniques, including item response theory (IRT) and generalizability theory, allow HR specialists to evaluate the quality of tests, as well as individual items included in tests.

Tests can be classified according to three criteria: content, administration, and scoring. It is crucial, however, that tests be reliable. Reliable measures are dependable, consistent, and relatively free from unsystematic errors of measurement. Since error is present to some degree in all psychological measures, test scores are most usefully considered—not as exact points—but rather as bands or ranges. In addition, intelligent interpretation of individual scores requires information about the relative performance of some comparison group (a norm group) on the same measurement procedures.

Have you ever visited a clothing factory? One of the most striking features of a clothing factory is the vast array of clothing racks, each containing garments of different sizes. Did you ever stop to think of the physical differences among wearers of this clothing? We can visualize some of the obvious ways in which the people who will ultimately wear the clothing differ. We can see large people, skinny people, tall people, short people, old people, young people, and people with long hair, short hair, and every imaginable variant in between.

Psychology's first law is glaringly obvious: "People are different." They differ not only in physical respects, but in a host of other ways as well. Consider wearers of size 42 men's sport coats, for example. Some will be outgoing and gregarious, and others will be shy and retiring; some will be creative, and others will be unimaginative; some will be well adjusted, and some will be maladjusted; some will be honest, and some will be crooks. Physical and psychological variability is all around us. As scientists and practitioners, our goal is to describe this variability and, through laws and theories, to understand it, to explain it, and to predict it. Measurement is one of the tools that enable us to come a little bit closer to these objectives. Once we understand the *why* of measurement, the *how*—that is, measurement techniques—becomes more meaningful (Brown, 1983).

Consider our plight if measurement did not exist. We could not describe, compare, or contrast the phenomena in the world about us. Individuals would not be able to agree on the labels or units to be attached to various physical dimensions (length, width, volume), and interpersonal communication would be hopelessly throttled. Efforts at systematic research would be doomed to failure. Talent would be shamefully wasted, and the process of science would grind to a halt. Fortunately, the state of the scientific world is a bit brighter than this. Measurement does exist, but what is it? We describe this topic next.

WHAT IS MEASUREMENT?

Measurement can be defined concisely. It is the assignment of numerals to objects or events according to rules (Linn & Gronlund, 1995; Stevens, 1951). Measurement answers the question "How much?" Suppose you are asked to judge a fishing contest. As you measure the length of each entry, the rules for assigning numbers are clear. A "ruler" is laid next to each fish, and, in accordance with agreed-on standards (inches, centimeters, feet), the length of each entry is determined rather precisely.

On the other hand, suppose you are asked to judge a sample of job applicants after interviewing each one. You are to rate each applicant's management potential on a scale from 1 to 10. Obviously, the quality and precision of this kind of measurement are not as exact as physical measurement. Yet both procedures satisfy our original definition of measurement. In short, the definition says nothing about the *quality* of the measurement procedure, only that *somehow* numerals are assigned to objects or events. Kerlinger and Lee (2000) expressed the idea well: Measurement is a game we play with objects and numerals. Games have rules. It is, of course, important for other reasons that the rules be "good" rules, but whether the rules are "good" or "bad," the procedure is still measurement (Blanton & Jaccard, 2006).

Thus, the *processes* of physical and psychological measurement are identical. As long as we can define a dimension (e.g., weight) or a trait (e.g., conscientiousness) to be measured, determine the measurement operations, specify the rules, and have a certain scale of units to express the measurement, the measurement of *anything* is theoretically possible.

Psychological measurement is principally concerned with individual differences in psychological **traits**. A trait is simply a descriptive label applied to a group of interrelated behaviors (e.g., dominance, creativity, agreeableness) that may be inherited or acquired. Based on standardized samples of individual behavior (e.g., structured selection interviews, cognitive ability tests), we *infer* the position or standing of the individual on the trait dimension in question. When psychological measurement takes place, we can use one of four types of scales. These four types of scales are not equivalent, and the use of a particular scale places a limit on the types of analyses one can perform on the resulting data.

SCALES OF MEASUREMENT

The first step in any measurement procedure is to specify the dimension or trait to be measured. Then we can develop a series of operations that will permit us to describe individuals in terms of that dimension or trait. Sometimes the variation among individuals is **qualitative**—that is, in terms of kind (sex, hair color); in other instances, it is **quantitative**—that is, in terms of frequency, amount, or degree (Ghiselli, Campbell, & Zedeck, 1981). Qualitative description is classification, whereas quantitative description is measurement.

As we shall see, there are actually four levels of measurement, not just two, and they are hierarchically related—that is, the higher-order scales meet all the assumptions of the lower-order scales plus additional assumptions characteristic of their own particular order. From lower order to higher order, from simpler to more complex, the scales are labeled **nominal**, **ordinal**, **interval**, and **ratio** (Stevens, 1951).

Nominal Scales

This is the lowest level of measurement and represents differences in kind. Individuals are assigned or classified into qualitatively different categories. Numbers may be assigned to objects or persons, but they have no numerical meaning. They cannot be ordered or added. They are merely labels (e.g., telephone numbers; Aguinis, Henle, & Ostroff, 2001).

People frequently make use of nominal scales to systematize or catalog individuals or events. For example, individuals may be classified as for or against a certain political issue, as males or females, or as college educated or not college educated. Athletes frequently wear numbers on their uniforms, but the numbers serve only as labels. In all of these instances, the fundamental operation is **equality**, which can be written in either one of the two ways below, but not both:

$$\text{Either } (a = b) \text{ or } (a \neq b), \text{ but not both} \tag{6-1}$$

All members of one class or group possess some characteristic in common that nonmembers do not possess. In addition, the classes are mutually exclusive—that is, if an individual belongs to group a, he or she cannot at the same time be a member of group b.

Even though nominal measurement provides no indication of magnitude and, therefore, allows no statistical operation except counting, this classifying information, in and of itself, is useful to the HR specialist. Frequency statistics such as χ^2, percentages, and certain kinds of measures of association (contingency coefficients) can be used. In the prediction of tenure using biographical information, for example, we may be interested in the percentages of people in various categories (e.g., classified by educational level or amount of experience—less than one year, 1–2 years, 2–5 years, or more than five years) who stay or leave within some specified period of time. If differences between stayers and leavers can be established, scorable application blanks can be developed, and selection efforts may thereby be improved.

Ordinal Scales

The next level of measurement, the ordinal scale, not only allows classification by category (as in a nominal scale) but also provides an indication of magnitude. The categories are rank ordered according to greater or lesser amounts of some characteristic or dimension. Ordinal scales, therefore, satisfy the requirement of equality (Equation 6-1), as well as **transitivity** or ranking, which may be expressed as

$$\text{If } [(a > b) \text{ and } (b > c)], \text{ then } (a > c) \tag{6-2}$$

or

$$\text{If } [(a = b) \text{ and } (b = c)], \text{ then } (a = c) \tag{6-3}$$

A great deal of physical and psychological measurement satisfies the transitivity requirement. For example, in horse racing, suppose we predict the exact order of finish of three horses. We bet on horse A to win, horse B to place second, and horse C to show third. It is irrelevant whether horse A beats horse B by two inches or two feet and whether horse B beats horse C by *any* amount. If we know that horse A beat horse B and horse B beat horse C, then we know that horse A beat horse C. We are not concerned with the distances between horses A and B or B and C, only with their relative order of finish. In fact, in ordinal measurement, we can substitute many other words besides "is greater than" ($>$) in Equation 6-2. We can substitute "is less than," "is smaller than," "is prettier than," "is more authoritarian than," and so forth.

Simple orders are far less obvious in psychological measurement. For example, this idea of transitivity may not necessarily hold when social psychological variables are considered in isolation from other individual differences and contextual variables. Take the example that worker A may get along quite well with worker B, and worker B with worker C, but workers A and C might fight like cats and dogs. So the question of whether transitivity applies depends on other variables (e.g., whether A and C had a conflict in the past, whether A and C are competing for the same promotion, and so forth).

We can perform some useful statistical operations on ordinal scales. We can compute the *median* (the score that divides the distribution into halves), *percentile ranks* (each of which represents the percentage of individuals scoring below a given individual or score point), *rank-order correlation* such as Spearman's rho and Kendall's *W* (measures of the relationship or extent of agreement between two ordered distributions), and *rank-order analysis of variance*. What we cannot do is say that a difference of a certain magnitude means the same thing at all points along the scale. For that, we need interval-level measurement.

Interval Scales

Interval scales have the properties of (1) equality (Equation 6-1); (2) transitivity, or ranking (Equations 6-2 and 6-3); and (3) **additivity**, or equal-sized units, which can be expressed as

$$(d - a) = (c - a) + (d - c) \tag{6-4}$$

Consider the measurement of length. As shown in the figure below, the distance between *a* (2 inches) and *b* (5 inches) is precisely equal to the distance between *c* (12 inches) and *d* (15 inches)—namely, three inches:

2	5	12	15
a	*b*	*c*	*d*

The scale units (inches) are equivalent at all points along the scale. In terms of Equation 6-4,

$$(15 - 2) = (12 - 2) + (15 - 12) = 13$$

Note that the differences in length between *a* and *c* and between *b* and *d* are also equal. The crucial operation in interval measurement is the establishment of equality of units, which in psychological measurement must be demonstrated empirically. For example, we must be able to demonstrate that a 10-point difference between two job applicants who score 87 and 97 on an aptitude test is equivalent to a 10-point difference between two other applicants who score 57 and 67. In a 100-item test, each carrying a unit weight, we have to establish empirically that, in fact, each item measured an equivalent amount or degree of the aptitude.

On an interval scale, the more commonly used statistical procedures such as indexes of central tendency and variability, the correlation coefficient, and tests of significance can be computed. Interval scales have one other very useful property: Scores can be transformed in any linear manner by adding, subtracting, multiplying, or dividing by a constant, without altering the relationships between the scores. Mathematically these relationships may be expressed as follows:

$$X' = a + bX \tag{6-5}$$

where X' is the transformed score, *a* and *b* are constants, and *X* is the original score. Thus, scores on one scale may be transformed to another scale using different units by (1) adding

TABLE 6-1 Characteristics of Types of Measurement Scales

Scale	Operation	Description
Nominal	Equality	Mutually exclusive categories; objects or events fall into one class only; all members of same class considered equal; categories differ qualitatively not quantitatively.
Ordinal	Equality Ranking	Idea of magnitude enters; object is larger or smaller than another (but not both); any montonic transformation is permissible.
Interval	Equality Ranking	Additivity; all units of equal size; can establish equivalent distances along scale; any linear transformation is permissible.
	Equal-sized units	—
Ratio	Equality Ranking	True or absolute zero point can be defined; meaningful ratios can be derived.
	Equal-sized units	—
	True (absolute) zero	—

Source: Brown, & Frederick G. *Principles of Educational and Psychological Testing.* Copyright © 1970 by The Dryden Press, a division of Holt, Rinehart and Winston. Reprinted by permission of Holt, Rinehart and Winston.

and/or (2) multiplying by a constant. The main advantage to be gained by transforming scores in individual differences measurement is that it allows scores on two or more tests to be compared directly in terms of a common metric.

Ratio Scales

This is the highest level of measurement in science. In addition to equality, transitivity, and additivity, the ratio scale has a natural or **absolute zero point** that has empirical meaning. Height, distance, weight, and the Kelvin temperature scale are all ratio scales. In measuring weight, for example, a kitchen scale has an absolute zero point, which indicates complete absence of the property.

If a scale does not have a true zero point, however, we cannot make statements about the ratio of one individual to another in terms of the amount of the property that he or she possesses or about the proportion one individual has to another. In a track meet, if runner A finishes the mile in four minutes flat while runner B takes six minutes, then we can say that runner A completed the mile in two-thirds the time it took runner B to do so, and runner A ran about 33 percent faster than runner B.

On the other hand, suppose we give a group of clerical applicants a spelling test. It makes no sense to say that a person who spells every word incorrectly cannot spell any word correctly. A different sample of words might elicit some correct responses. Ratios or proportions in situations such as these are not meaningful because the magnitudes of such properties are measured not in terms of "distance" from an absolute zero point, but only in terms of "distance" from an arbitrary zero point (Ghiselli et al., 1981). Differences among the four types of scales are presented graphically in Table 6-1.

SCALES USED IN PSYCHOLOGICAL MEASUREMENT

Psychological measurement scales, for the most part, are nominal- or ordinal-level scales, although many scales and tests commonly used in behavioral measurement and research approximate interval measurement well enough for practical purposes. Strictly speaking, intelligence, aptitude, and personality scales are ordinal-level measures. They indicate not the *amounts* of intelligence, aptitude, or personality traits of individuals, but rather their rank order with respect to the traits in question. Yet, with a considerable degree of confidence, we can often assume an equal interval scale, as Kerlinger and Lee (2000) noted:

> Though most psychological scales are basically ordinal, we can with considerable assurance often assume equality of interval. The argument is evidential. If we have, say, two or three measures of the same variable, and these measures are all substantially and linearly related, then equal intervals can be assumed. This assumption is valid because the more nearly a relation approaches linearity, the more nearly equal are the intervals of the scales. This also applies, at least to some extent, to certain psychological measures like intelligence, achievement, and aptitude tests and scales. A related argument is that many of the methods of analysis we use work quite well with most psychological scales. That is, the results we get from using scales and assuming equal intervals are quite satisfactory. (p. 637)

The argument is a pragmatic one that has been presented elsewhere (Ghiselli et al., 1981). In short, we assume an equal interval scale because this assumption works. If serious doubt exists about the tenability of this assumption, **raw scores** (i.e., scores derived directly from the measurement instrument in use) may be transformed statistically into some form of derived scores on a scale having equal units (Rosnow & Rosenthal, 2002).

Consideration of Social Utility in the Evaluation of Psychological Measurement

Should the value of psychological measures be judged in terms of the same criteria as physical measurement? Physical measurements are evaluated in terms of the degree to which they satisfy the requirements of order, equality, and addition. In behavioral measurement, the operation of addition is undefined, since there seems to be no way physically to add one psychological magnitude to another to get a third, even greater in amount. Yet other, more practical, criteria exist by which psychological measures may be evaluated. Arguably, the most important purpose of psychological measures is decision making. In personnel selection, the decision is whether to accept or reject an applicant; in placement, which alternative course of action to pursue; in diagnosis, which remedial treatment is called for; in hypothesis testing, the accuracy of the theoretical formulation; in hypothesis building, what additional testing or other information is needed; and in evaluation, what score to assign to an individual or procedure (Brown, 1983).

Psychological measures are, therefore, more appropriately evaluated in terms of their social utility. The important question is not whether the psychological measures as used in a particular context are accurate or inaccurate, but, rather, how their predictive efficiency compares with that of other available procedures and techniques.

Frequently, HR specialists are confronted with the tasks of selecting and using psychological measurement procedures, interpreting results, and communicating the results to others. These are important tasks that frequently affect individual careers. It is essential, therefore, that HR specialists be well grounded in applied measurement concepts. Knowledge of these concepts provides the appropriate tools for evaluating the social utility of the various measures under consideration. Hence, the remainder of this chapter, as well as the next two, will be devoted to a consideration of these topics.

SELECTING AND CREATING THE RIGHT MEASURE

Throughout this book, we use the word **test** in the broad sense to include any psychological measurement instrument, technique, or procedure. These include, for example, written, oral, and performance tests; interviews; rating scales; assessment center exercises (i.e., situational tests);

and scorable application forms. For ease of exposition, many of the examples used in the book refer specifically to written tests. In general, a test may be defined as a systematic procedure for measuring a sample of behavior (Brown, 1983). Testing is systematic in three areas: content, administration, and scoring. Item content is chosen systematically from the behavioral domain to be measured (e.g., mechanical aptitude, verbal fluency). Procedures for administration are standardized in that, each time the test is given, directions for taking the test and recording the answers are identical, the same time limits pertain, and, as far as possible, distractions are minimized. Scoring is objective in that rules are specified in advance for evaluating responses. In short, procedures are systematic in order to minimize the effects of unwanted contaminants (i.e., personal and environmental variables) on test scores.

Steps for Selecting and Creating Tests

The results of a comprehensive job analysis should provide clues to the kinds of personal variables that are likely to be related to job success (the topic of job analysis is discussed at length in Chapter 9). Assuming HR specialists have an idea about *what* should be assessed, *where* and *how* do they find what they are looking for? One of the most encyclopedic classification systems may be found in the *Mental Measurements Yearbook*, first published in 1938 and now in its 17th edition (Geisinger, Spies, Carlson, & Plake, 2007). Tests used in education, psychology, and industry are classified into 18 broad content categories. The complete list of tests included from 1985 until the 2007 edition is available at http://www.unl.edu/buros/bimm/html/00testscomplete.html. In total, more than 2,700 commercially published English-language tests are referenced.

In cases where no tests have yet been developed to measure the construct in question, or the tests available lack adequate psychometric properties, HR specialists have the option of creating a new measure. The creation of a new measure involves the following steps (Aguinis, Henle, & Ostroff, 2001):

DETERMINING A MEASURE'S PURPOSE   For example, will the measure be used to conduct research, to predict future performance, to evaluate performance adequacy, to diagnose individual strengths and weaknesses, to evaluate programs, or to give guidance or feedback? The answers to this question will guide decisions, such as how many items to include and how complex to make the resulting measure.

DEFINING THE ATTRIBUTE   If the attribute to be measured is not defined clearly, it will not be possible to develop a high-quality measure. There needs to be a clear statement about the concepts that are included and those that are not, so that there is a clear idea about the domain of content for writing items.

DEVELOPING A MEASURE PLAN   The measure plan is a road map of the content, format, items, and administrative conditions for the measure.

WRITING ITEMS   The definition of the attribute and the measure plan serve as guidelines for writing items. Typically, a sound objective should be to write twice as many items as the final number needed, because many will be revised or even discarded. Since roughly 30 items are needed for a measure to have high reliability (Nunnally & Bernstein, 1994), at least 60 items should be created initially.

CONDUCTING A PILOT STUDY AND TRADITIONAL ITEM ANALYSIS   The next step consists of administering the measure to a sample that is representative of the target population. Also, it is a good idea to gather feedback from participants regarding the clarity of the items.

Once the measure is administered, it is helpful to conduct an **item analysis**. There are several kinds of item analysis. To understand the functioning of each individual item, one can conduct a **distractor analysis** (i.e., evaluate multiple-choice items in terms of the frequency with which incorrect choices are selected), an **item difficulty** analysis (i.e., evaluate how difficult it is to answer each item correctly), and an **item discrimination** analysis (i.e., evaluate whether the response to a particular item is related to responses on the other items included in the measure). Regarding distractor analysis, the frequency of each incorrect response should be approximately equal across all distractors for each item; otherwise, some distractors may be too transparent and should probably be replaced. Regarding item difficulty, one can compute a p value (i.e., number of individuals answering the item correctly divided by the total number of individuals responding to the item); ideally the mean item p value should be about .5. Regarding item discrimination, one can compute a discrimination index d, which compares the number of respondents who answered an item correctly in the high-scoring group with the number who answered it correctly in the low-scoring group (top and bottom groups are usually selected by taking the top and bottom quarters or thirds); items with large and positive d values are good discriminators.

CONDUCTING AN ITEM ANALYSIS USING ITEM RESPONSE THEORY (IRT)   In addition to the above traditional methods, **IRT** can be used to conduct a comprehensive item analysis. IRT explains how individual differences on a particular attribute affect the behavior of an individual when he or she is responding to an item (e.g., Barr & Raju, 2003; Craig & Kaiser, 2003; Stark, Chernyshenko, & Drasgow, 2006). This specific relationship between the latent construct and the response to each item can be assessed graphically through an item-characteristic curve. This curve has three parameters: a difficulty parameter, a discrimination parameter, and a parameter describing the probability of a correct response by examinees with extremely low levels of ability. A test-characteristic curve can be found by averaging all item-characteristic curves.

Figure 6-1 shows hypothetical curves for three items. Items 2 and 3 are easier than item 1 because their curves begin to rise farther to the left of the plot. Item 1 is the one with the highest discrimination, while item 3 is the least discriminating because its curve is relatively flat. Also, item 3 is most susceptible to guessing because its curve begins higher on the y-axis. Once the measure is ready to be used, IRT provides the advantage that one can assess each test taker's ability level quickly and without wasting his or her time on very easy problems or on an embarrassing series of very difficult problems. In view of the obvious desirability of "tailored" tests, we can expect to see much wider application of this approach in the coming years. Also, IRT can be used to assess bias at the item level because it allows a researcher to determine if a given item is more difficult for examinees from one group than for those from another when they all have the same ability. For example, Drasgow (1987) showed that tests of English and mathematics usage provide equivalent measurement for Hispanics and African Americans and for white men and women.

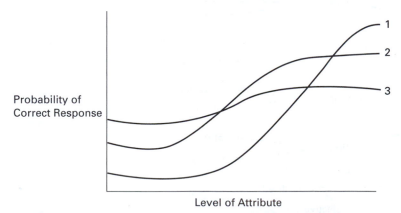

FIGURE 6-1 Item characteristic curves for three hypothetical items. *Source:* Aginis, H., Henle, C. A., & Ostroff, C. (2001). Measurement in work and organizational psychology. In N. Anderson, C. A. Henle, & C. Ostroff (Eds.), *Handbook of industrial, work & organizational psychology* (Vol. 1, p. 32). © Sage.

SELECTING ITEMS   Results of the pilot study and item analysis lead to the selection of the items to be included in the measure. At this stage, it is useful to plot a frequency distribution of scores for each item. A normal distribution is desired because a skewed distribution indicates that items are too hard (positively skewed) or too easy (negatively skewed).

DETERMINING RELIABILITY AND GATHERING EVIDENCE FOR VALIDITY   The next steps involve understanding the extent to which the measure is reliable (i.e., whether the measure is dependable, stable, and/or consistent over time) and the extent to which inferences made from the measure are valid (i.e., whether the measure is assessing the attribute it is supposed to measure and whether decisions based on the measure are correct). The remainder of this chapter and the next provide a more detailed treatment of the key topics of reliability and validity.

REVISING AND UPDATING ITEMS   Once the measure is fully operational, the final step involves continuous revising and updating of items. Some items may change their characteristics over time due to external-contextual factors (e.g., a change in job duties). Thus, it is important that data collected using the measure be monitored on an ongoing basis at both the measure and the item levels.

In sum, specialists can choose to purchase a test from a vendor or develop a new test. Regardless of which choice is made, one is likely to face a bewildering variety and number of tests. Because of this, the need for a fairly detailed test classification system is obvious. We discuss this next.

Selecting an Appropriate Test: Test-Classification Methods

In selecting a test, as opposed to evaluating its technical characteristics, important factors to consider are its content, the ease with which it may be administered, and the method of scoring. One classification scheme is presented in Figure 6-2.

CONTENT   Tests may be classified in terms of the *task* they pose for the examinee. Some tests are composed of verbal content (vocabulary, sentences) or nonverbal content (pictures, puzzles, diagrams). Examinees also may be required to manipulate objects, arrange blocks, or trace a particular pattern. These exercises are known as **performance tests**.

Tests also may be classified in terms of *process*—that is, what the examinee is asked to do. Cognitive tests measure the products of mental ability (intellect) and frequently are subclassified as tests of achievement and aptitude. In general, they require the performance of a task or the giving of

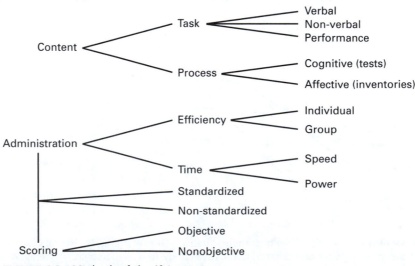

FIGURE 6-2   Methods of classifying tests.

factual information. Aptitude and achievement tests are both measures of ability, but they differ in two important ways: (1) the uniformity of prior experience assumed and (2) the uses made of the tests (AERA, APA, & NCME, 1999). Thus, achievement tests measure the effects of learning that occurred during relatively standardized sets of experiences (e.g., during an apprenticeship program or a course in computer programming). Aptitude tests, on the other hand, measure the effects of learning from cumulative and varied experiences in daily living.

These assumptions help to determine how the tests are used. Achievement tests usually represent a final evaluation of what the individual can do at the completion of training. The focus is on present competence. Aptitude tests, on the other hand, serve to predict subsequent performance, to estimate the extent to which an individual will profit from training, or to forecast the quality of achievement in a new situation. We hasten to add, however, that no distinction between aptitude and achievement tests can be applied rigidly. Both measure the individual's *current* behavior, which inevitably reflects the influence of prior learning.

In contrast to cognitive tests, affective tests are designed to measure aspects of personality (interests, values, motives, attitudes, and temperament traits). Generally they require the reporting of feelings, beliefs, or attitudes ("I think . . .; I feel . . ."). These self-report instruments also are referred to as **inventories**, while aptitude and achievement instruments are called tests. Tests and inventories are different, and much of the popular distrust of testing stems from a confusion of the two. Inventories reflect what the individual says he or she feels; tests measure what he or she knows or can do (Lawshe & Balma, 1966).

ADMINISTRATION   Tests may be classified in terms of the efficiency with which they can be administered or in terms of the time limits they impose on the examinee. Because they must be administered to one examinee at a time, individual tests are less efficient than group tests, which can be administered simultaneously to many examinees, either in paper-and-pencil format or by computer (either locally or remotely, e.g., by using the Internet). In group testing, however, the examiner has much less opportunity to establish rapport, to obtain cooperation, and to maintain the interest of examinees. Moreover, any temporary condition that may interfere with test performance of the individual, such as illness, fatigue, anxiety, or worry, is detected less readily in group testing. These factors may represent a distinct handicap to those unaccustomed to testing.

In test construction, as well as in the interpretation of test scores, time limits play an important role. Pure **speed tests** (e.g., number checking) consist of many easy items, but time limits are very stringent—so stringent, in fact, that no one can finish all the items. A pure **power test**, on the other hand, has a time limit generous enough to permit everyone an opportunity to attempt all the items. The difficulty of the items is steeply graded, however, and the test includes items too difficult for anyone to solve, so that no one can get a perfect score. Note that both speed and power tests are designed to prevent the achievement of perfect scores. In order to allow each person to demonstrate fully what he or she is able to accomplish, the test must have an adequate ceiling, in terms of either number of items or difficulty level. In practice, however, the distinction between speed and power is one of degree, because most tests include both types of characteristics in varying proportions.

STANDARDIZED AND NONSTANDARDIZED TESTS   Standardized tests have fixed directions for administration and scoring. These are necessary in order to compare scores obtained by different individuals. In the process of standardizing a test, it must be administered to a large, representative sample of individuals (usually several hundred), who are similar to those for whom the test ultimately is designed (e.g., children, adults, industrial trainees). This group, termed the **standardization** or **normative sample**, is used to establish **norms** in order to provide a frame of reference for interpreting test scores. Norms indicate not only the average performance but also the relative spread of scores above and below the average. Thus, it is possible to evaluate a test score in terms of the examinee's relative standing within the standardization sample.

Nonstandardized tests are much more common than published, standardized tests. Typically these are classroom tests, usually constructed by a teacher or trainer in an informal manner for a single administration.

SCORING   The method of scoring a test may be objective or nonobjective. Objective scoring is particularly appropriate for employment use because there are fixed, impersonal standards for scoring, and a computer or clerk can score the test (Schmitt, Gilliland, Landis, & Devine, 1993). The amount of error introduced under these conditions is assumed to be negligible. On the other hand, the process of scoring essay tests and certain types of personality inventories (especially those employed in intensive individual examinations) may be quite subjective, and considerable "rater variance" may be introduced. We will discuss this topic more fully in a later section.

Further Considerations in Selecting a Test

In addition to content, administration, standardization, and scoring, several additional factors need to be considered in selecting a test—namely, cost, interpretation, and face validity. Measurement cost is a very practical consideration. Most users operate within a budget and, therefore, must choose a procedure that will satisfy their cost constraints. A complete cost analysis includes direct as well as indirect costs. Direct costs may include the price of software or test booklets (some are reusable), answer sheets, scoring, and reporting services. Indirect costs (which may or may not be of consequence depending on the particular setting) may include time to prepare the test materials, examiner or interviewer time, and time for interpreting and reporting test scores. Users are well advised to make the most realistic cost estimates possible prior to committing themselves to the measurement effort. Sound advance planning can eliminate subsequent "surprises."

Managers frequently assume that since a test can be administered by almost any educated person, it can be interpreted by almost anyone. Not so. In fact, this is one aspect of staffing that frequently is overlooked. Test interpretation includes more than a simple written or verbal reporting of test scores. Adequate interpretation requires thorough awareness of the strengths and limitations of the measurement procedure, the background of the examinee, the situation in which the procedure was applied, and the consequences that the interpretation will have for the examinee. Unquestionably misinterpretation of test results by untrained and incompetent persons is one of the main reasons for the dissatisfaction with psychological testing (and other measurement procedures) felt by many in our society. Fortunately many test vendors now require that potential customers fill out a "user-qualification form" before a test is sold (for an example, see http://psychcorp.pearsonassessments.com/haiweb/Cultures/en-US/Site/ProductsAndServices/HowToOrder/Qualifications.htm). Such forms typically gather information consistent with the suggestions included in the American Psychological Association's *Guidelines for Test User Qualification* (Turner, DeMers, Fox, & Reed, 2001). This includes whether the user has knowledge of psychometric and measurement concepts and, in the context of employment testing, whether the test user has a good understanding of the work setting, the tasks performed as part of the position in question, and the worker characteristics required for the work situation.

A final consideration is **face validity**—that is, whether the measurement procedure *looks like* it is measuring the trait in question (Shotland, Alliger, & Sales, 1998). Face validity does not refer to validity in the technical sense, but is concerned rather with establishing rapport and good public relations. In research settings, face validity may be a relatively minor concern, but when measurement procedures are being used to help make decisions about individuals (e.g., in employment situations), face validity may be an issue of signal importance because it affects the applicants' motivation and reaction to the procedure. If the content of the procedure appears irrelevant, inappropriate, or silly, the result will be poor cooperation, regardless of the technical superiority of the procedure. To be sure, if the examinees' performance is likely to be affected by the content of the procedure, then, if at all possible, select a procedure with high face validity.

RELIABILITY AS CONSISTENCY

As noted earlier in this chapter, the process of creating new tests involves evaluating the technical characteristics of reliability and validity. However, reliability and validity information should be gathered not only for newly created measures but also for *any* measure before it is put to use. In fact, before purchasing a test from a vendor, an educated test user should demand that reliability and validity information about the test be provided. In the absence of such information, it is impossible to determine whether a test will be of any use. In this chapter, we shall discuss the concept of reliability; we shall treat the concept of validity in the next chapter.

Why is reliability so important? As we noted earlier, the main purpose of psychological measurement is to make decisions about individuals. If measurement procedures are to be useful in a practical sense, they must produce dependable scores. The typical selection situation is unlike that at a shooting gallery where the customer gets five shots for a dollar; if he misses his target on the first shot, he still has four tries left. In the case of a job applicant, however, he or she usually gets only one shot. It is important, therefore, to make that shot count, to present the "truest" picture of one's abilities or personal characteristics. Yet potentially there are numerous sources of error—that is, unwanted variation that can distort that "true" picture (Le, Schmidt, & Putka, 2009; Ree & Carretta, 2006; Schmidt & Hunter, 1996). Human behavior tends to fluctuate from time to time and from situation to situation. In addition, the measurement procedure itself contains only a sample of all possible questions and is administered at only one out of many possible times.

Our goal in psychological measurement is to minimize these sources of error—in the particular sampling of items, in the circumstances surrounding the administration of the procedure, and in the applicant—so that the "truest" picture of each applicant's abilities might emerge. In making decisions about individuals, it is imperative from an efficiency standpoint (i.e., minimizing the number of errors), as well as from a moral/ethical standpoint (i.e., being fair to the individuals involved), that our measurement procedures be dependable, consistent, and stable—in short, as reliable as possible.

Reliability of a measurement procedure refers to its freedom from unsystematic errors of measurement. A test taker or employee may perform differently on one occasion than on another for any number of reasons. He or she may try harder, be more fatigued, be more anxious, or simply be more familiar with the content of questions on one test form than on another. For these and other reasons, a person's performance will not be perfectly consistent from one occasion to the next (AERA, APA, & NCME, 1999).

Such differences may be attributable to what are commonly called unsystematic errors of measurement. However, the differences are not attributable to errors of measurement if experience, training, or some other event has made the differences meaningful or if inconsistency of response is relevant to what is being measured (e.g., changes in attitudes from time 1 to time 2). Measurement errors reduce the reliability, and therefore the generalizability, of a person's score from a single measurement.

The critical question is the definition of error. Factors that might be considered irrelevant to the purposes of measurement (and, therefore, error) in one situation might be considered germane in another situation. Each of the different kinds of reliability estimates attempts to identify and measure error in a different way, as we shall see. Theoretically, therefore, there could exist as many varieties of reliability as there are conditions affecting scores, since for any given purpose such conditions might be irrelevant or serve to produce inconsistencies in measurement and thus be classified as error. In practice, however, the types of reliability actually computed are few.

ESTIMATION OF RELIABILITY

Since all types of reliability are concerned with the degree of consistency or agreement between two sets of independently derived scores, the correlation coefficient (in this context termed a **reliability coefficient**) is a particularly appropriate measure of such agreement. Assuming errors of measurement occur randomly, the distribution of differences between pairs of scores for a group of individuals tested twice will be similar to the distribution of the various pairs of scores for the same individual if he or she was tested a large number of times (Brown, 1983). To the extent that each individual measured occupies the same relative position in each of the two sets of measurements, the correlation will be high; it will drop to the extent that there exist random, uncorrelated errors of measurement, which serve to alter relative positions in the two sets of measurements. It can be shown mathematically (Allen & Yen, 1979; Gulliksen, 1950) that the reliability coefficient may be interpreted directly as the percentage of total variance attributable to different sources (i.e., the **coefficient of determination**, r^2). For example, a reliability coefficient of .90 indicates that 90 percent of the variance in test scores is related to systematic variance in the characteristic or trait measured, and only 10 percent is error variance (as error is defined operationally in the method used to compute reliability). The utility of the reliability coefficient in evaluating measurement, therefore, is that it provides an estimate of the proportion of total variance that is systematic or "true" variance.

Reliability as a concept is, therefore, purely theoretical, wholly fashioned out of the assumption that obtained scores are composed of "true" and random error components. In symbols: $X = T + e$, where X is the observed (i.e., raw) score, T is the true (i.e., measurement error–free) score, and e is the error. Yet high reliability is absolutely essential for measurement because it serves as an upper bound for validity. Only systematic variance is predictable, and, theoretically, a test cannot predict a criterion any better than it can predict itself.

In practice, reliability coefficients may serve one or both of two purposes: (1) to estimate the precision of a particular procedure as a measuring instrument, and (2) to estimate the consistency of performance on the procedure by the examinees. Note, however, that the second purpose of reliability includes the first. Logically, it is possible to have unreliable performance by an examinee on a reliable test, but reliable examinee performance on an unreliable instrument is impossible (Wesman, 1952). These purposes can easily be seen in the various methods used to estimate reliability. Each of the methods we shall discuss—test–retest, parallel or alternate forms, internal consistency, stability and equivalence, and interrater reliability—takes into account somewhat different conditions that might produce unsystematic changes in test scores and consequently affect the test's error of measurement.

Test–Retest

The simplest and most direct estimate of reliability is obtained by administering the same form of a test (or other measurement procedure) to the same group of examinees on two different occasions. Scores from both occasions are then correlated to yield a **coefficient of stability**. The experimental procedure is as follows:

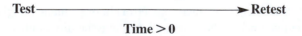

Test ————————————————▶ Retest

Time > 0

In this model, error is attributed to random fluctuations in performance across occasions. Its particular relevance lies in the time interval over which the tests are administered. Since the interval may vary from a day or less to more than several years, different stability coefficients will be obtained depending on the length of the time between administrations. Thus, there is not one, but, theoretically, an infinite number of stability coefficients for any measurement procedure. However, as described in Chapter 4, the magnitude of the correlations tends to show a uniform decrement over time. Consequently, when reported, a stability coefficient always should include information regarding the length of the time interval over which it was computed (e.g., Lubinski, Benbow, & Ryan, 1995).

Since the stability coefficient involves two administrations, any variable that affects the performance of some individuals on one administration and not on the other will introduce random error and, therefore, reduce reliability. Such errors may be associated with differences in administration (poor lighting or loud noises and distractions on one occasion) or with differences in the individual taking the test (e.g., due to mood, fatigue, personal problems). However, because the same test is administered on both occasions, error due to different samples of test items is not reflected in the stability coefficient.

What is the appropriate length of the time interval between administrations, and with what types of measurement procedures should the stability coefficient be used? Retests should not be given immediately, but only rarely should the interval between tests exceed six months (Anastasi, 1988). In general, the retest technique is appropriate if the interval between administrations is long enough to offset the effects of practice. Although the technique is inappropriate for the large majority of psychological measures, it may be used with tests of sensory discrimination (e.g., color vision, hearing), psychomotor tests (e.g., eye–hand coordination), and tests of knowledge that include the entire range of information within a restricted topic. It also is used in criterion measurement—for example, when performance is measured on different occasions.

Parallel (or Alternate) Forms

Because any measurement procedure contains only a sample of the possible items from some content domain, theoretically it is possible to construct a number of parallel forms of the same procedure (each comprising the same number and difficulty of items and each yielding nonsignificant differences in means, variances, and intercorrelations with other variables). For example, Lievens and Sackett (2007) created alternate forms for a situational judgment test adopting three different strategies: random assignment, incident isomorphism, and item isomorphism. The *random assignment* approach consists of creating a large pool of items with the only requirement being that they tap the same domain. Next, these items are randomly assigned to alternate forms. The *incident-isomorphism* approach is a type of cloning procedure in which we change the surface characteristics of items that do not determine item difficulty (also referred to as incidentals), but, at the same time, do not change any structural item features that determine their difficulty. The *item-isomorphism* approach involves creating pairs of items that are designed to reflect the same domain, the same critical incident, but the items differ only regarding wording and grammar. The fact that several samples of items can be drawn from the universe of a domain is shown graphically in Figure 6-3.

With parallel forms, we seek to evaluate the consistency of scores from one form to another (alternate) form of the same procedure. The correlation between the scores obtained on the two

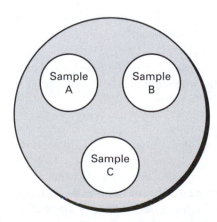

FIGURE 6-3 Measurement procedures as samples from a content domain.

forms (known as the **coefficient of equivalence**) is a reliability estimate. The experimental procedure is as follows:

Form A ⸺⸺⸺⸺⸺⸺⸺⸺⸺⸺⸺⸺⸺➤ **Form B**

Time = 0

Ideally both forms would be administered simultaneously. Since this is often not possible, the two forms are administered as close together in time as is practical—generally within a few days of each other.

In order to guard against order effects, half of the examinees should receive Form A followed by Form B, and the other half, Form B followed by Form A. Since the two forms are administered close together in time, short-term changes in conditions of administration or in individuals cannot be eliminated entirely. Thus, a pure measure of equivalence is impossible to obtain. As with stability estimates, statements of parallel-forms reliability always should include the length of the interval between administrations as well as a description of relevant intervening experiences.

In practice, equivalence is difficult to achieve. The problem is less serious with measures of well-defined traits, such as arithmetic ability or mechanical aptitude, but it becomes a much more exacting task to develop parallel forms for measures of personality or motivation, which may not be as well defined.

In addition to reducing the possibility of cheating, parallel forms are useful in evaluating the effects of some treatment (e.g., training) on a test of achievement. Because parallel forms are merely samples of items from the same content domain, some sampling error is inevitable. This serves to lower the correlation between the forms and, in general, provides a rather conservative estimate of reliability.

Which is the best approach to creating an alternate form? To answer this question, we need to know whether pretesting is possible, if we have a one-dimensional or multidimensional construct, and whether the construct is well understood or not. Figure 6-4 includes a decision tree that can be used to decide which type of development strategy is best for different situations.

Although parallel forms are available for a large number of measurement procedures, they are expensive and frequently quite difficult to construct. For these reasons, other techniques for assessing the effect of different samples of items on reliability were introduced—the methods of internal consistency.

Internal Consistency

Most reliability estimates indicate consistency over time or forms of a test. Techniques that involve analysis of item variances are more appropriately termed measures of internal consistency, since they indicate the degree to which the various items on a test are intercorrelated. The most widely used of these methods were presented by Kuder and Richardson (1937, 1939), although split-half estimates are used as well. We discuss each of these reliability estimates next.

KUDER–RICHARDSON RELIABILITY ESTIMATES   Internal consistency is computed based on a single administration. Of the several formulas derived in the original article, the most useful is their formula 20 (KR-20):

$$r_{tt} = \frac{n}{n-1}\left(\frac{\sigma_t^2 - \Sigma pq}{\sigma_t^2}\right) \qquad \textbf{(6-6)}$$

where r_{tt} is the reliability coefficient of the whole test, n is the number of items in the test, and σ_t^2 is the variance of the total scores on the test. The final term Σpq is found by computing

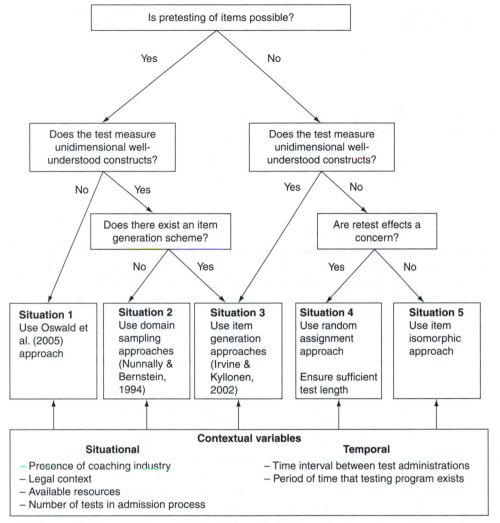

FIGURE 6-4 Decision tree for choosing a parallel form development approach. *Source:* Lievens, F., & Sackett, P. R. (2007). Situational judgment tests in high-stakes settings: Issues and strategies with generating alternate forms. *Journal of Applied Psychology, 92,* 1043–1055.

the proportion of the group who pass (p) and do not pass (q) each item, where $q = 1 - p$. The product of p and q is then computed for each item, and these products are added for all items to yield $\sum pq$. To the degree that test items are unrelated to each other, KR-20 will yield a lower estimate of reliability; to the extent that test items are interrelated (internally consistent), KR-20 will yield a higher estimate of reliability. KR-20 overestimates the reliability of speed tests, however, since values of p and q can be computed only if each item has been attempted by all persons in the group. Therefore, stability or equivalence estimates are more appropriate with speed tests.

The KR-20 formula is appropriate for tests whose items are scored as right or wrong or according to some other all-or-none system. On some measures, however, such as personality inventories, examinees may receive a different numerical score on an item depending on whether they check "Always," "Sometimes," "Occasionally," or "Never." In these cases, a generalized formula for computing internal-consistency reliability has been derived, known as **coefficient alpha** (Cronbach, 1951). The formula differs from KR-20 in only one term: $\sum pq$ is replaced by $\sum \sigma_i^2$, the sum of the variances of item scores. That is, one first finds the variance of all examinees' scores on each item and then adds these variances across all items. The formula for coefficient alpha is, therefore,

$$r_{tt} = \frac{n}{n-1}\left(\frac{\sigma_t^2 - \Sigma\sigma_i^2}{\sigma_t^2}\right) \tag{6-7}$$

Alpha is a sound measure of error variance, but it is affected by the number of items (more items imply higher estimates), item intercorrelations (higher intercorrelations imply higher estimates), and dimensionality (if the scale is measuring more than one underlying construct, alpha will be lower). Although coefficient alpha can be used to assess the consistency of a scale, a high alpha does not necessarily mean that the scale measures a one-dimensional construct (Cortina, 1993).

SPLIT-HALF RELIABILITY ESTIMATES   An estimate of reliability may be derived from a single administration of a test by splitting the test statistically into two equivalent halves after it has been given, thus yielding two scores for each individual. This procedure is conceptually equivalent to the administration of alternate forms on one occasion. If the test is internally consistent, then any one item or set of items should be equivalent to any other item or set of items. Using split-half methods, error variance is attributed primarily to inconsistency in content sampling. In computing split-half reliability, the first problem is how to split the test in order to obtain two halves that are equivalent in content, difficulty, means, and standard deviations. In most instances, it is possible to compute two separate scores for each individual based on his or her responses to odd items and even items. However, such estimates are not really estimates of internal consistency; rather, they yield spuriously high reliability estimates based on equivalence (Guion, 1965).

A preferable approach is to select the items randomly for the two halves. Random selection should balance out errors to provide equivalence for the two halves, as well as varying the number of consecutive items appearing in either half. A correlation coefficient computed on the basis of the two "half" tests will provide a reliability estimate of a test only half as long as the original. For example, if a test contained 60 items, a correlation would be computed between two sets of scores, each of which contains only 30 items. This coefficient underestimates the reliability of the 60-item test, since reliability tends to increase with test length. A longer test (or other measurement procedure) provides a larger sample of the content domain and tends to produce a wider range of scores, both of which have the effect of raising a reliability estimate. However, lengthening a test increases only its consistency, not necessarily its stability over time (Cureton, 1965). And, in some cases, the use of a single-item measure can yield adequate reliability (Wanous & Hudy, 2001). In general, the relationship between reliability and test length may be shown by the Spearman–Brown prophecy formula:

$$r_{nn} = \frac{nr_{11}}{1 + (n-1)r_{11}} \tag{6-8}$$

where r_{nn} is the estimated reliability of a test n times as long as the test available, r_{11} is the obtained reliability coefficient, and n is the number of times the test is increased (or shortened). This formula is used widely to estimate reliability by the split-half method, in which case $n = 2$—that is, the test length is doubled. Under these conditions, the formula simplifies to

$$r_{11} = \frac{2r_{1/2\ 1/2}}{1 + r_{1/2\ 1/2}} \tag{6-9}$$

where r_{11} is the reliability of the test "corrected" to full length and $r_{1/2\ 1/2}$ is the correlation computed between scores on the two half-tests.

For example, if the correlation between total scores on the odd- and even-numbered items is .80, then the estimated reliability of the whole test is

$$r_{11} = \frac{2(.80)}{(1 + .80)} = .89$$

A split-half reliability estimate is interpreted as a **coefficient of equivalence**, but since the two parallel forms (halves) are administered simultaneously, only errors of such a short term that they affect one item will influence reliability. Therefore, since the fewest number of contaminating factors have a chance to operate using this method, corrected split-half correlation generally yields the highest estimate of reliability.

Finally, it should be noted that while there are many possible ways to split a test into halves, Cronbach (1951) has shown that the Kuder–Richardson reliability coefficients are actually the mean of all possible half-splits.

Stability and Equivalence

A combination of the test–retest and equivalence methods can be used to estimate reliability simply by lengthening the time interval between administrations. The correlation between the two sets of scores represents a **coefficient of stability and equivalence** (Schmidt, Le, & Ilies, 2003). The procedure is as follows:

Form A ⸻⸻⸻⸻⸻⸻⸻⸻⸻⸻➤**Form B**

Time > 0

To guard against order effects, half of the examinees should receive Form A followed by Form B, and the other half, Form B followed by Form A. Because all the factors that operate to produce inconsistency in scores in the test–retest design, plus all the factors that operate to produce inconsistency in the parallel forms design, can operate in this design, the coefficient of stability and equivalence will provide the most rigorous test and will give the lower bound of reliability. The main advantage of computing reliability using the stability-and-equivalence estimate is that three different types of errors are taken into consideration (Becker, 2000; Schmidt et al., 2003):

- *Random response errors*, which are caused by momentary variations in attention, mental efficiency, distractions, and so forth within a given occasion
- *Specific factor errors*, which are caused by examinees' idiosyncratic responses to an aspect of the measurement situation (e.g., different interpretations of the wording)
- Transient errors, which are produced by longitudinal variations in examinees' mood or feelings or in the efficiency of the information-processing mechanisms used to answer questionnaires

In summary, the coefficient of equivalence assesses the magnitude of measurement error produced by specific-factor and random-response error, but not transient-error processes. The test–retest estimate assesses the magnitude of transient- and random-response error, but not the impact of specific-factor error. In addition, the coefficient of stability and equivalence assesses the impact of all three types of errors (Schmidt et al., 2003). For example, Schmidt et al. (2003) computed reliability using a coefficient of equivalence (i.e., Cronbach's α) and a coefficient of stability and equivalence for 10 individual-differences variables (e.g., general mental abilities, personality traits such as conscientiousness and extraversion). Results showed that the coefficient of equivalence was, on average, 14.5 percent larger than the coefficient of stability and equivalence.

Interrater Reliability

Thus far, we have considered errors due to instability over time, nonequivalence of the samples of items, and item heterogeneity. These are attributable either to the examinee or to the measurement procedure. Errors also may be attributable to the examiner or rater; this is known as **rater** or **scorer variance**. The problem typically is not serious with objectively scored measures. However, with nonobjective measures (e.g., observational data that involve subtle discriminations), it may be acute. With the latter there is as great a need for interrater reliability as there is for the more usual types of reliability. The reliability of ratings may be defined as the degree to which the ratings are free from unsystematic error variance arising either from the ratee or from the rater (Guion, 1965).

Interrater reliability can be estimated using three methods: (1) interrater agreement, (2) interclass correlation, and (3) intraclass correlation (Aguinis et al., 2001; LeBreton & Senter, 2008). Interrater agreement focuses on exact agreement between raters on their ratings of some dimension. Two popular statistics used are percentage of rater agreement and Cohen's (1960) kappa. When a group of judges rates a single attribute (e.g., overall managerial potential), the degree of rating similarity can be assessed by using James, Demaree, and Wolf's (1993) r_{wg} index. Interclass correlation is used when two raters are rating multiple objects or individuals (e.g., performance ratings). Intraclass correlation estimates how much of the differences among raters is due to differences in individuals on the attribute measured and how much is due to errors of measurement.

All of these indices focus on the extent to which similarly situated raters agree on the level of the rating or make essentially the same ratings. Basically they make the assumption that raters can be considered "alternate forms" of the same measurement instrument, agreements between raters reflect true score variance in ratings, and disagreement between raters is best conceptualized as measurement error (Murphy & DeShon, 2000a). Ideally, to estimate interrater reliability, there is a need to implement a research design in which raters are fully crossed with ratees or ratees are nested within raters. However, this situation is not observed in practice frequently and, instead, it is common to implement "ill-structured" designs in which ratees are neither fully crossed nor nested within raters (Putka, Le, McCloy, & Diaz, 2008). Such designs may lead to less precise estimates of interrater reliability, particularly when there is an increase in the amount of overlap between the sets of raters that rate each ratee and the ratio of rater effect variance to true score variance.

Note that interrater reliability is not a "real" reliability coefficient because it provides no information about the measurement procedure itself. While it does contribute some evidence of reliability (since objectivity of scoring is a factor that contributes to reliability), it simply provides a statement of how much confidence we may have that two scorers (or raters) will arrive at similar scores (or ratings) for a given individual. Also, a distinction is made between interrater consensus (i.e., absolute agreement between raters on some dimension) and interrater consistency (i.e., interrater reliability, or similarity in the ratings based on correlations or similarity in rank order) (Kozlowski & Hattrup, 1992). The lack of agreement between scorers can certainly be due to unsystematic sources of error (e.g., some of the errors discussed in Chapter 5). However, lack of agreement can also indicate that there are systematic rater effects beyond random measurement error (Hoyt, 2000). In general, raters may disagree in their evaluations not only because of unsystematic (i.e., random) measurement error, but also because of systematic differences in (1) what is observed, (2) access to information other than observations of the attribute measured, (3) expertise in interpreting what is observed, and (4) the evaluation of what is observed (Murphy & DeShon, 2000a, 2000b; Scullen, Mount, & Goff, 2000).

Consideration of these issues sheds new light on results regarding the reliability of performance ratings (i.e., ratings from subordinates = .30, ratings from peers = .37, and ratings from supervisors = .50; Conway & Huffcutt, 1997). For example, the average interrater correlation for peers of .37 does not necessarily mean that error accounts for 1−.37 or 63 percent of the variance in performance ratings or that true performance accounts for 37 percent of the variance in ratings. Instead, this result indicates that measurement error does not account for more than 63 percent of the variance in ratings (cf. Murphy & DeShon, 2000a).

TABLE 6-2 Sources of Error in the Different Reliability Estimates

Method of Estimating Reliability	Source of Error
Test–retest	Time sampling
Parallel forms (immediate)	Content sampling
Parallel forms (delayed equivalent)	Time and content sampling
Split-half	Content sampling
Cronbach's α	Content sampling
Kuder–Richardson 20	Content sampling
Interrater agreement	Interrater consensus
Interclass correlation	Interrater consistency
Intraclass correlation	Interrater consistency

Source: H. Aguinis, C. A. Henle, & C. Ostroff, C. (2001). Measurement in work and organizational psychology. In N. Anderson, D. S. Ones, H. K. Sinangil, and C. Viswesvaran (Eds.), Handbook of industrial, work, and organizations psychology (vol. 1), p. 33. London, U.K.: Sage. Reprinted by permission of Sage Publications Inc.

Summary

The different kinds of reliability coefficients and their sources of error variance are presented graphically in Table 6-2.

At this point, it should be obvious that there is no such thing as *the* reliability of a test. Different sources of error are accounted for in the different methods used to estimate reliability. For example, an internal-consistency reliability estimate provides information regarding the extent to which there is consistency across the items chosen for inclusion in the instrument, and generalizations can be made to other items that are also part of the same domain. However, the use of an internal-consistency estimate does not provide information on the extent to which inferences can be extended across time, research settings, contexts, raters, or methods of administration (Baranowski & Anderson, 2005). The *Standards for Educational and Psychological Testing* (AERA, APA, & NCME, 1999) emphasizes this point: "[T]here is no single, preferred approach to quantification of reliability. No single index adequately conveys all of the relevant facts. No one method of investigation is optimal in all situations" (p. 31).

A simple example should serve to illustrate how the various components of total score variance may be partitioned. Suppose we have reliability estimates of equivalence and of stability and equivalence. Assume that the equivalence estimate is .85 and that the stability and equivalence estimate is .75. In addition, suppose a random sample of tests is rescored independently by a second rater, yielding an interrater reliability of .94. The various components of variance now may be partitioned as in Table 6-3.

TABLE 6-3 Sources of Error Variance in Test X

From parallel form (delayed equivalent):	$1 - .75 = .25$ (time and content sampling)
From parallel form (immediate):	$1 - .85 = .15$ (content sampling)
Difference:	.10 (time sampling)
From interrater reliability:	$1 - .94 = .06$ (interrater difference)
Total measured error variance:	$.15 + .10 + .06 = .31$
Systematic or "true" variance:	$1 - .31 = .69$

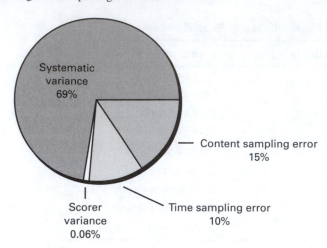

FIGURE 6-5 Proportional distribution of error variance and systematic variance.

Note that, by subtracting the error variance due to content sampling alone (.15) from the error variance due to time and content sampling (.25), 10 percent of the variance can be attributed to time sampling alone. When all three components are added together—that is, the error variance attributable to content sampling (.15), time sampling (.10), and rater (.06)—the total error variance is 31 percent, leaving 69 percent of the total variance attributable to systematic sources. These proportions are presented graphically in Figure 6-5.

INTERPRETATION OF RELIABILITY

Unfortunately, there is no fixed value below which reliability is unacceptable and above which it is satisfactory. It depends on what one plans to do with the scores. Brown (1983) has expressed the matter aptly:

> Reliability is not an end in itself but rather a step on a way to a goal. That is, unless test scores are consistent, they cannot be related to other variables with any degree of confidence. Thus reliability places limits on validity, and the crucial question becomes whether a test's reliability is high enough to allow satisfactory validity. (p. 88)

Hence, the more important the decision to be reached, the greater the need for confidence in the precision of the measurement procedure and the higher the required reliability coefficient. If a procedure is to be used to compare one individual with another, reliability should be above .90. In practice, however, many standard tests with reliabilities as low as .70 prove to be very useful, and measures with reliabilities even lower than that may be useful for research purposes. This statement needs to be tempered by considering some other factors (in addition to speed, test length, and interval between administrations) that may influence the size of an obtained reliability coefficient.

Range of Individual Differences

While the accuracy of measurement may remain unchanged, the size of a reliability estimate will vary with the range of individual differences in the group. That is, as the variability of the scores increases (decreases), the correlation between them also increases (decreases).

This is an important consideration in performance measurement. Frequently the reliability of performance measures is low because of the homogeneous nature of the group in question (e.g., only individuals who are hired and stay long enough to provide performance data are included). Such underestimates serve to reduce or to attenuate correlation coefficients such as interrater reliability coefficients (e.g., correlations between ratings provided by various sources; LeBreton, Burgess, Kaiser, Atchley, & James, 2003) and validity coefficients (e.g., correlations between test scores and performance; Sackett, Laczo, & Arvey, 2002).

Difficulty of the Measurement Procedure

Similar restrictions of the range of variability may result from measures that are too difficult (in which case all examinees do poorly) or too easy (in which case all examinees do extremely well). In order to maximize reliability, the level of difficulty should be such as to produce a wide range of scores, for there can be no correlation without variance.

Size and Representativeness of Sample

Although there is not necessarily a systematic relationship between the size of the sample and the size of the reliability coefficient, a reliability estimate based on a *large* number of cases will have a smaller sampling error than one based on just a *few* cases; in other words, the larger sample provides a more dependable estimate. This is shown easily when one considers the traditional formula for the standard error of r (Aguinis, 2001):

$$\sigma_r = \frac{1 - r^2}{\sqrt{n - 1}} \qquad (6\text{-}10)$$

A reliability estimate of .70 based on a sample size of 26 yields an estimated standard error of .10, but the standard error with a sample of 101 is .05—a value only half as large as the first estimate.

Not only must the sample be large but also it must be representative of the population for which the measurement is to be used. The reliability of a procedure designed to assess trainee performance cannot be determined adequately by administering it to experienced workers. Reliability coefficients become more meaningful the more closely the group on which the coefficient is based resembles the group about whose relative ability we need to decide.

Standard Error of Measurement

The various ways of estimating reliability are important for evaluating measurement procedures, but they do not provide a direct indication of the amount of inconsistency or error to be expected in an individual score. For this, we need the **standard error of measurement**, a statistic expressed in test score (standard deviation) units, but derived directly from the reliability coefficient. It may be expressed as

$$\sigma_{\text{Meas}} = \sigma_x \sqrt{1 - r_{xx}} \qquad (6\text{-}11)$$

where σ_{Meas} is standard error of measurement, σ_x is the standard deviation of the distribution of obtained scores, and r_{xx} is the reliability coefficient. The standard error of measurement provides an estimate of the standard deviation of the normal distribution of scores that an individual would obtain if he or she took the test a large number—in principle, an infinite number—of times. The mean of this hypothetical distribution is the individual's "true" score (Thurstone, 1931). Equation 6-11 demonstrates that the standard error of measurement increases as the reliability decreases. When $r_{xx} = 1.0$, there is no error in estimating an individual's true score from his or her observed score. When $r_{xx} = 0.0$, the error of measurement is a maximum and equal to the standard deviation of the observed scores.

The σ_{Meas} is a useful statistic because it enables us to talk about an individual's true and error scores. Given an observed score, σ_{Meas} enables us to estimate the range of score values that will, with a given probability, include the true score. In other words, we can establish confidence intervals.

The σ_{Meas} may be used similarly to determine the amount of variability to be expected upon retesting. To illustrate, assume the standard deviation of a group of observed scores is 7 and the reliability coefficient is .90. Then $\sigma_{\text{Meas}} = 7\sqrt{1 - .90} = 2.21$. Given an individual's score of 70, we can be 95 percent confident that on retesting the individual's score would be within about four points ($1.96\ \sigma_{\text{Meas}} = 1.96 \times 2.21 = 4.33$) of his original score and that his true score probably lies between ($X +/- 1.96\ \sigma_{\text{Meas}}$) or 65.67 and 74.33. Note that we use negative and positive values for 1.96 because they mark the lower and upper limits of an interval that includes the middle 95 percent of scores in a normal distribution. Different values would be used for different types of confidence intervals (e.g., 90 percent).

In personnel psychology, the standard error of measurement is useful in three ways (Guion, 1965). First, it can be used to determine *whether the measures describing individuals differ significantly* (e.g., assuming a five-point difference between applicants, if the σ_{Meas} for the test is 6, the difference could certainly be attributed to chance). In fact, Gulliksen (1950) showed that the difference between the scores of two individuals on the same test should not be interpreted as significant unless it is equal to at least two standard errors of the difference (SED), where SED $= \sigma_{\text{Meas}}\sqrt{2}$. Second, it may be used to determine *whether an individual measure is significantly different from some hypothetical true score.* For example, assuming a cut score on a test is the true score, chances are two out of three that obtained scores will fall within $+/- 1\sigma_{\text{Meas}}$ of the cut score. Applicants within this range could have true scores above or below the cutting score; thus, the obtained score is "predicted" from a hypothetical true score. A third usage is to determine *whether a test discriminates differently in different groups* (e.g., high versus low ability). Assuming that the distribution of scores approaches normality and that obtained scores do not extend over the entire possible range, then σ_{Meas} will be very nearly equal for high-score levels and for low-score levels (Guilford & Fruchter, 1978). On the other hand, when subscale scores are computed or when the test itself has peculiarities, the test may do a better job of discriminating at one part of the score range than at another. Under these circumstances, it is beneficial to report the σ_{Meas} for score levels at or near the cut score. To do this, it is necessary to develop a scatter diagram that shows the relationship between two forms (or halves) of the same test. The standard deviations of the columns or rows at different score levels will indicate where predictions will have the greatest accuracy.

A final advantage of the σ_{Meas} is that *it forces one to think of test scores not as exact points, but rather as bands or ranges of scores.* Since measurement error is present at least to some extent in all psychological measures, such a view is both sound and proper.

SCALE COARSENESS

Scale coarseness is related to measurement error, but it is a distinct phenomenon that also results in lack of measurement precision (Aguinis, Pierce, & Culpepper, 2009). A measurement scale is coarse when a construct that is continuous in nature is measured using items such that different true scores are collapsed into the same category. In these situations, errors are introduced because continuous constructs are collapsed. Although this fact is seldom acknowledged, personnel-psychology researchers and practitioners use coarse scales every time continuous constructs are measured using Likert-type or ordinal items. We are so accustomed to using these types of items that we seem to have forgotten they are intrinsically coarse. As noted by Blanton and Jaccard (2006), ". . . scales are not strictly continuous in that there is coarseness due to the category widths and the collapsing of individuals with different true scores into the same category. This is common for many psychological measures, and researchers typically assume that the coarseness is not problematic" (p. 28).

Aguinis, Culpepper, and Pierce (2009) provided the following illustration. Consider a typical Likert-type item including five scale points or anchors ranging from 1 = strongly disagree to 5 = strongly agree. When one or more Likert-type items are used to assess continuous constructs such as personality, general mental abilities, and job performance, information is lost because individuals with different true scores are considered to have identical standing regarding the underlying construct. Specifically, all individuals with true scores around 4 are assigned a 4, all those with true scores around 3 are assigned a 3, and so forth. However, differences may exist between these individuals' true scores (e.g., 3.60 versus 4.40 or 3.40 versus 2.60, respectively), but these differences are lost due to the use of coarse scales because respondents are forced to provide scores that are systematically biased downwardly or upwardly. This information loss produces a downward bias in the observed correlation coefficient between a predictor X and a criterion Y. In short, scales that include Likert-type and ordinal items are coarse, imprecise, do not allow individuals to provide data that are sufficiently discriminating, and yet they are used pervasively in personnel psychology to measure constructs that are continuous in nature.

As noted earlier, the random error created by lack of perfect reliability of measurement is different in nature from the systematic error introduced by scale coarseness, so these artifacts are distinct and should be considered separately. As mentioned earlier, $X = T + e$, and e is the error term, which is composed of a random and a systematic (i.e., bias) component (i.e., $e = e_r + e_s$). For example, consider a manager who has a true score of 4.4 on the latent construct "leadership skills," i.e., $X_t = 4.4$). A measure of this construct is not likely to be perfectly reliable, so if we use a multi-item Likert-type scale, X_o is likely to be greater than 4.4 for some of the items and less than 4.4 for some of the other items, given that e_r can be positive or negative due to its random nature. On average, the greater the number of items in the measure, the more likely it is that positive and negative e_r values will cancel out and X_o will be closer to 4.4. So, the greater the number of items for this scale, the less the detrimental impact of random measurement error on the difference between true and observed scores, and this is an important reason why multi-item scales are preferred over single-item scales.

Let's consider the effects of scale coarseness. If we use a scale with only one Likert-type item with, for example, 5 scale points, X_o is systematically biased downwardly because this individual respondent will be forced to choose 4 as his response (i.e., the closest to $X_t = 4.4$), given that 1, 2, 3, 4, or 5 are the only options available. If we add another item and the scale now includes two items instead of only one, the response on each of the two items will be biased systematically by −.4 due to scale coarseness. So, in contrast to the effects of measurement error, the error caused by scale coarseness is systematic and the same for each item. Consequently, increasing the number of items does not lead to a canceling out of error. Similarly, an individual for whom $X_t = 3.7$ will also choose the option "4" on each of the items for this multi-item Likert-type scale (i.e., the closest to the true score, given that 1, 2, 3, 4, and 5 are the only options available). So, regardless of whether the scale includes one or multiple items, information is lost due to scale coarseness, and these two individuals with true scores of 4.4 and 3.7 will appear to have an identical score of 4.0.

What are the consequences of scale coarseness? Although seldom recognized, the lack of precision introduced by coarse scales has a downward biasing effect on the correlation coefficient computed using data collected from such scales for the predictor, the criterion, or both variables. For example, consider the case of a correlation computed based on measures that use items anchored with five scale points. In this case, a population correlation of .50 is attenuated to a value of .44. A difference between correlations of .06 indicates that the correlation is attenuated by about 14 percent.

As is the case with other statistical and methodological artifacts that produce a downward bias in the correlation coefficient, elimination of the methodological artifact via research design and before data are collected is always preferred in comparison to statistical corrections after the data have been collected (Hunter & Schmidt, 2004, p. 98). Thus, one possibility regarding the measurement of continuous constructs is to use a continuous graphic-rating scale (i.e., a line segment without scale points) instead of Likert-type scales. However, this type of data-collection procedure is not practically feasible in most situations unless data are collected electronically (Aguinis, Bommer, & Pierce, 1996). The second-best solution is to use a statistical correction procedure after data are collected. Fortunately, this correction is available and was derived by Peters and van Voorhis (1940, pp. 396–397). The correction is implemented by a computer program available online designed by Aguinis, Pierce, and Culpepper (2009). A screen shot of the program is included in Figure 6-6. This figure shows that, in this particular illustration, the obtained correlation is .25, and this correlation was computed based

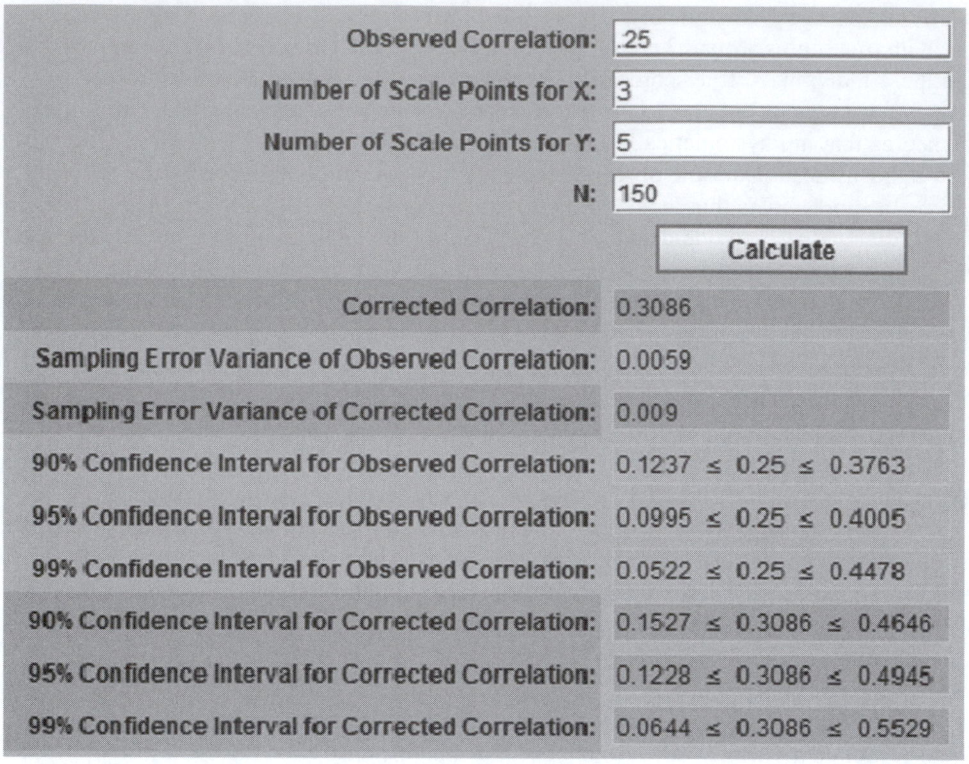

Observed Correlation:	.25
Number of Scale Points for X:	3
Number of Scale Points for Y:	5
N:	150
	Calculate
Corrected Correlation:	0.3086
Sampling Error Variance of Observed Correlation:	0.0059
Sampling Error Variance of Corrected Correlation:	0.009
90% Confidence Interval for Observed Correlation:	0.1237 ≤ 0.25 ≤ 0.3763
95% Confidence Interval for Observed Correlation:	0.0995 ≤ 0.25 ≤ 0.4005
99% Confidence Interval for Observed Correlation:	0.0522 ≤ 0.25 ≤ 0.4478
90% Confidence Interval for Corrected Correlation:	0.1527 ≤ 0.3086 ≤ 0.4646
95% Confidence Interval for Corrected Correlation:	0.1228 ≤ 0.3086 ≤ 0.4945
99% Confidence Interval for Corrected Correlation:	0.0644 ≤ 0.3086 ≤ 0.5529

FIGURE 6-6   Screen shot of program for correcting correlation coefficients for the effect of scale coarseness.   *Source:* Aguinis, H., Pierce, C. A., & Culpepper, S. A. (2009). Scale coarseness as a methodological artifact: Correcting correlation coefficients attenuated from using coarse scales. Organizational Research Methods, Online, Aug 2008; Vol. 0, p. 1094428108318065v1. © 2008 Sage Publications, Inc.

on a predictor (i.e., test) including three anchors and a measure of performance including five anchors. The obtained corrected correlation is .31, which means that the observed correlation was underestimating the construct-level correlation by 24 percent (assuming both predictor and criterion scores are continuous in nature).

In sum, scale coarseness is a pervasive measurement artifact that produces a systematic downward bias in the resulting correlation coefficient. Although distinct from measurement error, the ultimate effect is similar: the relationship between constructs appears weaker than it actually is. Thus, scale coarseness is an artifact that should be considered in designing tests to assess constructs that are continuous in nature.

GENERALIZABILITY THEORY

The discussion of reliability presented thus far is the classical or traditional approach. A more recent statistical approach, termed **generalizability theory**, conceptualizes the reliability of a test score as the precision with which that score, or sample, represents a more generalized universe value of the score (Baranowski & Anderson, 2005; Cronbach, Gleser, Nanda, & Rajaratnam, 1972; Murphy & DeShon, 2000a, 2000b).

In generalizability theory, observations (e.g., examinees' scores on tests) are seen as samples from a universe of **admissible observations**. The universe describes the conditions under which examinees can be observed or tested that produce results that are equivalent to some specified degree. An examinee's **universe score** is defined as the expected value of his or her observed scores over all admissible observations. The universe score is directly analogous to the true score used in classical reliability theory. Generalizability theory emphasizes that different universes exist and makes it the test publisher's responsibility to define carefully his or her universe. This definition is done in terms of **facets** or dimensions.

The use of generalizability theory involves conducting two types of research studies: a generalizability (G) study and a decision (D) study. A G study is done as part of the development of the measurement instrument. The main goal of the G study is to specify the degree to which test results are equivalent when obtained under different testing conditions. In simplified terms, a G study involves collecting data for examinees tested under specified conditions (i.e., at various levels of specified facets), estimating variance components due to these facets and their interactions using analysis of variance, and producing coefficients of generalizability. A coefficient of generalizability is the ratio of universe-score variance to observed-score variance and is the counterpart of the reliability coefficient used in classical reliability theory. A test has not one generalizability coefficient, but many, depending on the facets examined in the G study. The G study also provides information about how to estimate an examinee's universe score most accurately.

In a D study, the measurement instrument produces data to be used in making decisions or reaching conclusions, such as admitting people to programs. The information from the G study is used in interpreting the results of the D study and in reaching sound conclusions. Despite its statistical sophistication, however, generalizability theory has not replaced the classical theory of test reliability (Aiken, 1999).

Several recently published studies illustrate the use of the generalizability-theory approach. As an illustration, Greguras, Robie, Schleicher, and Goff (2003) conducted a field study in which more than 400 managers in a large telecommunications company were rated by their peers and subordinates using an instrument for both developmental and administrative purposes. Results showed that the combined rater and rater-by-ratee interaction effects were substantially larger than the person effect (i.e., the object being rated) for both the peer and the subordinate sources for both the developmental and the administrative conditions. However, the person effect accounted for a greater amount of variance for the subordinate raters when ratings were used for developmental as opposed to administrative purposes, and this result was not found for the peer raters. Thus, the application of generalizability theory revealed that subordinate ratings were of significantly better quality when made for developmental rather than administrative purposes, but the same was not true for peer ratings.

INTERPRETING THE RESULTS OF MEASUREMENT PROCEDURES

In personnel psychology, knowledge of each person's individuality—his or her unique pattern of abilities, values, interests, and personality—is essential in programs designed to use human resources effectively. Such knowledge enables us to make predictions about how individuals are likely to behave in the future. In order to interpret the results of measurement procedures intelligently, however, we need some information about how relevant others have performed on the same procedure. For example, Sarah is applying for admission to an industrial arts program at a local vocational high school. As part of the admissions procedure, she is given a mechanical aptitude test. She obtains a raw score of 48 correct responses out of a possible 68. Is this score average, above average, or below average? In and of itself, the score of 48 is meaningless because psychological measurement is relative rather than absolute. In order to interpret Sarah's score meaningfully, we need to compare her raw score to the distribution of scores of relevant others—that is, persons of approximately the same age, sex, and educational and regional background who were being tested for the same purpose. These persons make up a norm group. Theoretically, there can be as many different norm groups as there are purposes for which a particular test is given and groups with different characteristics. Thus, Sarah's score of 48 may be about average when compared to the scores of her reference group, it might be distinctly above average when compared to the performance of a group of music majors, and it might represent markedly inferior performance in comparison to the performance of a group of instructor mechanics. In short, norms must provide a relevant comparison group for the person being tested.

Immediately after the introduction of a testing or other measurement program, it may be necessary to use norms published in the test manual, but local norms (based on the scores of applicants in a specific organization or geographical area) should be prepared as soon as 100 or more cases become available. These norms should be revised from time to time as additional data accumulate (Ricks, 1971). In employment selection, local norms are especially desirable, since they are more representative and fit specific organizational purposes more precisely. Local norms allow comparisons between the applicant's score and those of his or her immediate competitors.

Up to this point, we have been referring to normative comparisons in terms of "average," "above average," or "below average." Obviously we need a more precise way of expressing each individual's position relative to the norm group. This is accomplished easily by converting raw scores into some relative measure—usually percentile ranks or standard scores. The percentile rank of a given raw score refers to the percentage of persons in the norm group who fall below it. Standard scores may be expressed either as z scores (i.e., the distance of each raw score from the mean in standard deviation units) or as some modification of the z score that eliminates negative numbers and decimal notation. A hypothetical norm table is presented in Table 6-4. The general relationships among percentile ranks, standard scores, and the normal curve for any set of scores are presented graphically in Figure 6-7.

Note that there are no raw scores on the baseline of the curve. The baseline is presented in a generalized form, marked off in standard deviation units. For example, if the mean of a distribution of scores is 30 and if the standard deviation is 8, then $+/- 1\sigma$ corresponds to 38 $(30 + 8)$ and 22 $(30 - 8)$, respectively. Also, since the total area under the curve represents the total distribution of scores, we can mark off subareas of the total corresponding to $+/- 1, 2, 3,$ and 4 standard deviations. The numbers in these subareas are percentages of the total number of people. Thus, in a normal distribution of scores, roughly two-thirds (68.26 percent) of all cases lie between $+/- 1$ standard deviation. This same area also includes scores that lie above the 16th percentile $(- 1\sigma)$ and below the 84th percentile $(+ 1\sigma)$. Based on the scores in Table 6-4, if an individual scores 38, we conclude that this score is $.60\sigma$ above the mean and ranks at the 73rd percentile of persons on whom the test was normed (provided the distribution of scores in the norm group approximates a normal curve).

Percentile ranks, while easy to compute and understand, suffer from two major limitations. First, they are ranks and, therefore, ordinal-level measures; they cannot legitimately be added, subtracted, multiplied, or divided. Second, percentile ranks have a rectangular distribution, while test score distributions generally approximate the normal curve. Therefore, percentile units are not equivalent at all points along the scale. Note that on the percentile equivalents scale in Figure 6-7

TABLE 6-4 Hypothetical Score Distribution, Including Percentile Ranks (rounded to integers) and Standardized Scores

Raw Score	Percentile	z Score
50	93	+1.51
46	89	+1.21
42	82	+0.90
38	73	+0.60
34	62	+0.30
30	50	0.00
26	38	−0.30
22	27	−0.60
18	18	−0.90
14	11	−1.21
10	7	−1.51

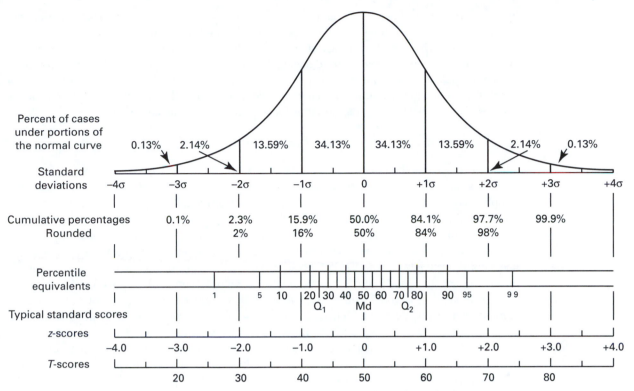

FIGURE 6-7 Normal curve chart showing relationships between percentiles and standard scores.

the percentile distance between percentile ranks 5 and 10 (or 90 and 95) is distinctly greater than the distance between 45 and 50, although the numerical distances are the same. This tendency of percentile units to become progressively smaller toward the center of the scale causes special difficulties in the interpretation of change. Thus, the differences in achievement represented by a shift from 45 to 50 and from 94 to 99 are not equal on the percentile rank scale, since the distance from 45 to 50 is much smaller than that from 94 to 99. In short, if percentiles are used, greater weight should be given to rank differences at the extremes of the scale than to those at the center.

Standard scores, on the other hand, are interval-scale measures (which by definition possess equal-size units) and, therefore, can be subjected to the common arithmetic operations. In addition, they allow direct comparison of an individual's performance on different measures. For example, as part of a selection battery, three measures with the following means and standard deviations (in a sample of applicants) are used:

	Mean	Std. Deviation
Test 1 (scorable application)	30	5
Test 2 (written test)	500	100
Test 3 (interview)	100	10

Applicant A scores 35 on Test 1, 620 on Test 2, and 105 on Test 3. What does this tell us about his or her overall performance? Assuming each of the tests possesses some validity by itself, converting each of these scores to standard score form, we find that applicant A scores $(35 - 30)/5 = +1\sigma$ on Test 1, $(620 - 500)/100 = +1.2\sigma$ on Test 2, and $(105 - 100)/10 = +.5\sigma$ on Test 3. Applicant A appears to be a good bet.

One of the disadvantages of z scores, however, is that they involve decimals and negative numbers. To avoid this, z scores may be transformed to a different scale by adding or multiplying by a constant. However, such a linear transformation does not change the shape of the distribution: the shape of the raw and transformed scores will be similar. If the distribution of the raw scores is skewed, the distribution of the transformed scores also will be skewed. This can be avoided by converting raw scores into normalized standard scores. To compute normalized standard scores, percentile ranks of raw scores are computed first. Then, from a table of areas under the normal curve, the z score corresponding to each percentile rank is located. In order to get rid of decimals and negative numbers, the z scores are transformed into T scores by the formula

$$T = 50 + 10z \qquad\qquad (6\text{-}12)$$

where the mean and the standard deviation are set to equal 50 and 10, respectively.

Normalized standard scores are satisfactory for most purposes, since they serve to smooth out sampling errors, but all distributions should not be normalized as a matter of course. Normalizing transformations should be carried out only when the sample is large and representative and when there is reason to believe that the deviation from normality results from defects in the measurement procedure rather than from characteristics of the sample or from other factors affecting the behavior under consideration (Anastasi, 1988). Of course, when the original distribution of scores is approximately normal, the linearly derived scores and the normalized scores will be quite similar.

Although we devoted extensive attention in this chapter to the concept of reliability, the computation of reliability coefficients is a means to an end. The end is to produce scores that measure attributes consistently across time, forms of a measure, items within a measure, and raters. Consistent scores enable predictions and decisions that are accurate. Making accurate predictions and making correct decisions is particularly significant in employment contexts, where measurement procedures are used as vehicles for forecasting performance. The next chapter addressees the issue of validity, which concerns the accuracy of predictions and decisions based on tests, and is closely connected to the concept of reliability.

Evidence-Based Implications for Practice

- Precise measurement of individual differences (i.e., tests) is essential in HR practice. Tests must be dependable, consistent, and relatively free from unsystematic errors of measurement so they can be used effectively.
- Regardless of whether one chooses to create a new test or to use an existing test, statistical analyse, such as item response theory, and generalizability theory provide information on the quality of the test. In selecting tests, pay careful attention to their content, administration, and scoring.
- Estimation of a test's reliability is crucial because there are several sources of error that affect a test's precision. These include time, item content, and rater idiosyncrasies (when measurement consists of individuals providing ratings). There is no such thing as "the" right reliability coefficient. Different reliability estimates provide information on different sources of error.
- In creating a test to measure constructs that are continuous in nature, the fewer the number of anchors on the items, the less the precision of the test due to scale coarseness. Scale coarseness will attenuate relationships between test scores and other constructs and, thus, it must be prevented in designing tests or corrected for after the data are collected.

Discussion Questions

1. Why are psychological measures considered to be nominal or ordinal in nature?
2. Is it proper to speak of *the* reliability of a test? Why?
3. Which methods of estimating reliability produce the highest and lowest (most conservative) estimates?
4. Is interrater agreement the same as interrater reliability? Why?

5. What type of knowledge can be gathered through the application of item response theory and generalizability theory?
6. What does the standard error of measurement tell us?
7. What is scale coarseness? How can we address scale coarseness before and after data are collected?
8. What do test norms tell us? What do they not tell us?

7

Validation and Use of Individual-Differences Measures

At a Glance

Scores from measures of individual differences derive meaning only insofar as they can be related to other psychologically meaningful characteristics of behavior. The processes of gathering or evaluating the necessary data are called **validation**. So reliability is a necessary, but not a sufficient, property for scores to be useful in HR research and practice.

Two issues are of primary concern in validation: what a test or other procedure measures and how well it measures. Evidence regarding validity can be assessed in several ways: by analyzing the procedure's content (content-related evidence); by relating scores on the procedure to measures of performance on some relevant criterion (predictive and concurrent evidence); or by more thoroughly investigating the extent to which the procedure measures some psychological construct (construct-related evidence). When implementing empirical validation strategies, one needs to consider that group differences, the range restriction, the test's position in the employment process, and the form of the test-predictor relationship can have a dramatic impact on the size of the obtained validity coefficient.

Additional strategies are available when local validation studies are not practically feasible, as in the case of small organizations. These include validity generalization (VG), synthetic validity, and test transportability. These types of evidence are not mutually exclusive. On the contrary, convergence in results gathered using several lines of evidence should be sought and is highly desirable. In fact, new strategies, such as empirical Bayes estimation, allow for the combination of approaches (i.e., meta-analysis and local validation).

Although the validity of individual-differences measures is fundamental to competent and useful HR practice, there is another, perhaps more urgent, reason why both public- and private-sector organizations are concerned about this issue. Legal guidelines on employee selection procedures require comprehensive, documented validity evidence for any procedure used as a basis for an employment decision, if that procedure has an adverse impact on a protected group.

RELATIONSHIP BETWEEN RELIABILITY AND VALIDITY

Theoretically, it would be possible to develop a perfectly reliable measure whose scores were wholly uncorrelated with any other variable. Such a measure would have no practical value, nor could it be interpreted meaningfully, since its scores could be related to nothing other than scores on another administration of the same measure. It would be highly reliable, but would have no validity. For example, in a research project investigating the importance and value of various positions in a police department, three different studies reached the identical conclusion that police officers should be higher than detectives on the pay scale (Milkovich & Newman, 2005). So the studies were reliable in terms of the degree of agreement for the rank ordering of the positions. However, as many popular TV shows demonstrate, in police departments in the United States, the detectives always outrank the uniforms. So the results of the study were reliable (i.e., results were consistent), but not valid (i.e., results were uncorrelated with meaningful variables, and inferences were incorrect). In short, scores from individual-differences measures derive meaning only insofar as they can be related to other psychologically meaningful characteristics of behavior.

High reliability is a necessary, but not a sufficient, condition for high validity. Mathematically it can be shown that (Ghiselli, Campbell, & Zedeck, 1981)

$$r_{xy} \leq \sqrt{r_{xx}} \tag{7-1}$$

where r_{xy} is the obtained validity coefficient (a correlation between scores on procedure X and an external criterion Y) and r_{xx} is the reliability of the procedure. Hence, reliability serves as a limit or ceiling for validity. In other words, validity is reduced by the unreliability in a set of measures. Some degree of unreliability, however, is unavoidably present in criteria as well as in predictors. When the reliability of the criterion is known, it is possible to correct statistically for such unreliability by using the following formula:

$$r_{xt} = \frac{r_{xy}}{\sqrt{r_{yy}}} \tag{7-2}$$

where r_{xt} is the correlation between scores on some procedure and a perfectly reliable criterion (i.e., a "true" score), r_{xy} is the observed validity coefficient, and r_{yy} is the reliability of the criterion. This formula is known as the *correction for attenuation in the criterion variable only*. In personnel psychology, this correction is extremely useful, for it enables us to use as criteria some measures that are highly relevant, yet not perfectly reliable. The formula allows us to evaluate an obtained validity coefficient in terms of how high it is relative to the upper bound imposed by the unreliability of the criterion.

To illustrate, assume we have obtained a validity coefficient of .50 between a test and a criterion. Assume also a criterion reliability of .30. In this case, we have an extremely unreliable measure (i.e., only 30 percent of the variance in the criterion is systematic enough to be predictable, and the other 70 percent is attributable to error sources). Substituting these values into Equation 7-2 yields

$$r_{xt} = \frac{.50}{\sqrt{.30}} = \frac{.50}{.55} = .91$$

The validity coefficient would have been .91 if the criterion had been perfectly reliable. The coefficient of determination (r^2) for this hypothetical correlation is $.91^2 = .83$, which means that 83 percent of the total variance in the criterion Y is explained by the predictor X. Let us now compare this result to the uncorrected value. The obtained validity coefficient ($r_{xy} = .50$) yields a coefficient of determination of $.50^2 = .25$; that is, only 25 percent of the variance in the criterion is associated with variance in the test. So, correcting the validity coefficient for criterion unreliability increased the proportion of variance explained in the criterion by over 300 percent!

Combined knowledge of reliability and validity makes possible practical evaluation of predictors in specific situations. While the effect of the correction for attenuation should never be a consideration when one is deciding how to evaluate a measure as it exists, such information does give the HR specialist a basis for deciding whether there is enough unexplained systematic variance in the criterion to justify a search for more and better predictors. However, if a researcher makes a correction for attenuation in the criterion, he or she should report the corrected *and* the uncorrected coefficients, as well as all statistics used in the correction (AERA, APA, & NCME, 1999).

As was discussed in Chapter 6, there are several ways to estimate reliability. Accordingly, Schmidt and Hunter (1996) described 26 realistic research scenarios to illustrate the use of various reliability estimates in the correction formula based on the research situation at hand. Using different reliability estimates is likely to lead to different conclusions regarding validity. For example, the average internal consistency coefficient alpha for supervisory ratings of overall job performance is .86, whereas the average interrater reliability estimate for supervisory ratings of overall job performance is .52, and the average interrater reliability estimate for peer ratings of overall job performance is .42 (Viswesvaran, Ones, & Schmidt, 1996). If alpha is used as r_{yy} in the example described above, the corrected validity coefficient would be $r_{xt} = \dfrac{.50}{\sqrt{.86}} = .54$, and if interrater reliability for supervisory ratings of performance is used, the corrected validity coefficient would be $r_{xt} = \dfrac{.50}{\sqrt{.52}} = .69$. So, the corresponding coefficients of determination would be $.54^2 = .29$ and $.69^2 = .48$, meaning that the use of interrater reliability produces a corrected coefficient of determination 65 percent larger than does the use of the coefficient alpha. The point is clear: The choice of reliability estimates can have a substantial impact on the magnitude of the validity coefficient (Schmitt, 2007). Accordingly, generalizability theory emphasizes that there is no single number that defines *the* reliability of ratings. Rather, the definition of reliability depends on how the data are collected and the type of generalizations that are made based on the ratings (Murphy & DeShon, 2000b).

In addition to the selection of an appropriate reliability estimate, it is important to consider *how* the coefficient was computed. For example, if the coefficient alpha was computed based on a heterogeneous or multidimensional construct, it is likely that reliability will be underestimated (Rogers, Schmitt, & Mullins, 2002). Note that an underestimation of r_{yy} produces an overestimation of the validity coefficient.

In short, the concepts of reliability and validity are closely interrelated. We cannot understand whether the inferences made based on test scores are correct if our measurement procedures are not consistent. Thus, reliability places a ceiling on validity, and the use of reliability estimates in correcting validity coefficients requires careful thought about the sources of error affecting the measure in question and how the reliability coefficient was computed. Close attention to these issues is likely to lead to useful estimates of probable validity coefficients.

EVIDENCE OF VALIDITY

Traditionally, validity was viewed as the extent to which a measurement procedure actually measures what it is designed to measure. Such a view is inadequate, for it implies that a procedure has only one validity, which is determined by a single study (Guion, 2002). On the contrary, a thorough knowledge of the interrelationships between scores from a particular procedure and other variables typically requires many investigations. The investigative processes of gathering or evaluating the necessary data are called **validation** (AERA, APA, & NCME, 1999). Various methods of validation revolve around two issues: (1) *what* a test or other procedure measures (i.e., the hypothesized underlying trait or construct), and (2) *how well* it measures (i.e., the relationship between scores from the procedure and some external criterion measure). Thus, validity is a not a dichotomous variable (i.e., valid or not valid); rather, it is a matter of degree.

Validity is also a unitary concept (Landy, 1986). There are not different "kinds" of validity, only different kinds of evidence for analyzing validity. Although evidence of validity may be accumulated in many ways, validity always refers to the degree to which the evidence supports inferences that are made from the scores. Validity is neither a single number nor a single argument, but an inference from all of the available evidence (Guion, 2002). It is the *inferences* regarding the specific uses of a test or other measurement procedure that are validated, not the test itself (AERA, APA, & NCME, 1999). Hence, a user first must specify exactly *why* he or she intends to use a selection measure (i.e., what inferences are to be made from it). This suggests a hypothesis about the relationship between measures of human attributes and measures of work behavior, and hypothesis testing is what validation is all about (Landy, 1986).

In short, the user makes a *judgment* about the adequacy of the available evidence of validity in support of a particular instrument when used for a particular purpose. The extent to which score meaning and action implications hold across persons or population groups and across settings or contexts is a persistent empirical question. This is the main reason that validity is an evolving property and validation a continuing process (Messick, 1995).

While there are numerous procedures available for evaluating validity, *Standards for Educational and Psychological Measurement* (AERA, APA, & NCME, 1999) describes three principal strategies: **content-related evidence**, **criterion-related evidence** (predictive and concurrent), and **construct-related evidence**. These strategies for analyzing validity differ in terms of the kinds of inferences that may be drawn. Although we discuss them independently for pedagogical reasons, they are interrelated operationally and logically. In the following sections, we shall consider the basic concepts underlying each of these nonexclusive strategies for gathering validity evidence.

CONTENT-RELATED EVIDENCE

Inferences about validity based on content-related evidence are concerned with whether or not a measurement procedure contains a fair sample of the universe of situations it is supposed to represent. Since this process involves making inferences from a sample to a population, an evaluation of content-related evidence is made in terms of the adequacy of the sampling. Such evaluation is usually a rational, judgmental process.

In employment settings, we are principally concerned with making inferences about a job-performance domain—an identifiable segment or aspect of the job-performance universe that has been defined and about which inferences are to be made (Lawshe, 1975). Three assumptions underlie the use of content-related evidence: (1) The area of concern to the user can be conceived as a meaningful, definable universe of responses; (2) a sample can be drawn from the universe in some purposeful, meaningful fashion; and (3) the sample and the sampling process can be defined with sufficient precision to enable the user to judge how adequately the sample of performance typifies performance in the universe.

In achievement testing, the universe can be identified and defined rigorously, but most jobs have several job-performance domains. Most often, therefore, we identify and define operationally a job-performance domain that is only a segment of the job-performance universe (e.g., a typing test administered to a secretary whose job-performance universe consists of several job-performance domains, only one of which is typing). The behaviors constituting job-performance domains range from those behaviors that are directly observable, to those that are reportable, to those that are highly abstract.

The higher the level of abstraction, the greater the "inferential leap" required to demonstrate validity by other than a criterion-related approach. At the "observation" end of the continuum, sound judgments by job incumbents, supervisors, or other job experts usually can be made. Content-related evidence derived from procedures, such as simple proficiency tests, job knowledge tests, and work sample tests, is most appropriate under these circumstances. At the "abstract" end of the continuum (e.g., inductive reasoning), construct-related evidence is appropriate. "[W]ithin the middle range of the content-construct continuum, the distinction between content and construct should be determined functionally, in relation to the job. If the quality measured is not unduly abstract, and if it constitutes a significant aspect of the job, content validation of the test component used to measure that quality should be permitted" ("Guardians Assn. of N.Y. City Police Dept. v. Civil Service Comm. of City of N.Y.," 1980, p. 47).

It is tempting to conclude from this that, if a selection procedure focuses on work *products* (like typing), then content-related evidence is appropriate. If the focus is on work *processes* (like reasoning ability), then content-related evidence is not appropriate. However, even work products (like typing) are determined by work processes (like producing a sample of typed copy). Typing *ability* implies an inference about an underlying characteristic on which individuals differ. That continuum is not directly observable. Instead, we illuminate the continuum by gathering a sample of behavior that is hypothesized to vary as a function of that underlying attribute. In that sense, typing ability is no different from reasoning ability, or "strength," or memory. None of them can be observed directly (Landy, 1986).

So the question is not *if* constructs are being measured, but what *class* of constructs is being measured. Once that has been determined, procedures can be identified for examining the appropriateness of inferences based on measures of those constructs (Tenopyr, 1977, 1984). Procedures used to support inferences drawn from measures of personality constructs (like emotional stability) differ from procedures used to support inferences from measures of ability constructs (like typing ability). The distinction between a content-related strategy and a construct-related strategy is, therefore, a matter of degree, fundamentally because constructs underlie *all* psychological measurement. Content-related validity evidence can therefore be seen as a precondition for construct-related validity evidence (Schriesheim, Powers, Scandura, Gardiner, & Lankau, 1993).

As an example, consider a content-validation effort that was used to gather evidence regarding tests assessing educational background, experience, and other personal history data, which are usually labeled minimum-qualifications tests (Buster, Roth, & Bobko, 2005). These types of tests, which will be discussed in more detail in Chapter 12, are typically used for initial screening of job applicants. Buster et al. (2005) implemented a content-validity strategy that included the following steps:

Step 1: Conduct a job analysis (for a detailed discussion of this topic, see Chapter 9). The job analysis should capture whether various types of knowledge, skills, abilities, and other characteristics (KSAOs) are important or critical for the position in question and whether they are "needed at entry" (i.e., needed on "Day 1" of the job).

Step 2: Share the list of KSAOs with subject matter experts (SMEs) (usually incumbents or supervisors for the job in question).

Step 3: Remind SMEs and anyone else involved in generating test items that they should think of an individual who is a newly appointed job incumbent. This step helps SMEs frame the item generation process in terms of minimum standards and makes items more defensible in litigation.

Step 4: Remind SMEs and anyone else involved in generating items that they should think about alternative items. For example, could alterative educational experiences (e.g., not-for-credit courses, workshops) be an alternative to an educational degree? Or, could a professional certification (e.g., Aguinis, Michaelis, & Jones, 2005) be used as a proxy for a minimum qualification?

Step 5: Keep minimum qualifications straightforward and express them using the same format. This will make items more reliable and easier to rate.

Step 6: Ask SMEs to rate the list of potential items independently so that one can compute and report statistics on ratings of various potential items.

Step 7: Link each of the potential items or, at least, the final list of items back to the KSAOs identified in Step 1.

Step 8: Group (i.e., bracket) potential items in a thoughtful manner. This grouping provides evidence to substantiate the level of the minimum qualification assessed by the items. For example, the person in charge of the content-validation process could bracket level of education as well as number of years of job experience.

The above eight steps follow best scientific practices and also withstood judicial scrutiny at the federal level (Buster et al., 2005). Thus, it is a very promising approach to content validity that future research could attempt to expand and to apply to other types of tests.

Operationally, content-related evidence may be evaluated in terms of the extent to which members of a *content-evaluation panel* perceive overlap between the test and the job-performance domain (or whichever construct is assessed by the measure in question). Data regarding judgments about each of the items are usually collected using Q-sort procedures (i.e., experts who are not biased are asked to assign each item to its intended construct) or rating scales (i.e., experts rate each item regarding its possible inclusion in the domain of interest). The extent to which scale items belong in the domain of the intended construct can be determined quantitatively by using one of four approaches:

1. *Content-Validity Index (CVI).* Each member of a content-evaluation panel (comprising an equal number of incumbents and supervisors) is presented with a set of test items and asked to independently indicate whether the skill (or knowledge) measured by each item is essential, useful but not essential, or not necessary to the performance of the job (Lawshe, 1975). Responses from all panelists are then pooled, and the number indicating "essential" for each item is determined. A **content-validity ratio (CVR)** is then determined for each item:

$$CVR = \frac{n_e - N/2}{N/2} \tag{7-3}$$

where n_e is the number of panelists indicating "essential" and N is the total number of panelists. Items are eliminated if the CVR fails to meet statistical significance (as determined from a table presented by Lawshe, 1975). The mean CVR value of the retained items (the CVI) is then computed. The CVI represents the extent to which perceived overlap exists between capability to function in a job-performance domain and performance on the test under investigation.

2. *Substantive-Validity Index.* This procedure is an extension of Lawshe's procedure, and it provides information on the extent to which panel members assign an item to its posited construct more than any other construct (Anderson & Gerbing, 1991). Then a binomial test can be implemented to analyze the probability that each item significantly assesses its intended construct.

3. *Content-Adequacy Procedure.* This method does not assess content validity in a strict sense because it does not include an actual CVI, but it allows for the pairing of items with constructs (Schriesheim et al., 1993). Instead of sorting items, panel members are asked to rate each item on a Likert-type scale to indicate the extent to which each item corresponds to each construct definition (of various provided). Results are then analyzed using principal component analysis, extracting the number of factors corresponding to the a priori expectation regarding the number of constructs assessed by the items.

4. *Analysis-of-Variance Approach.* This method builds on the methods proposed by Anderson and Gerbing (1991) and Schriesheim et al. (1993) and asks panel members to rate

each item according to the extent to which it is consistent with a construct definition provided (i.e., from 1 "not at all" to 5 "completely") (Hinkin & Tracey, 1999). A between-subjects design is implemented in which each group of raters is given all items but only one construct definition (although the items provided represent several constructs). The results are analyzed using principal component analysis (as in the Schriesheim et al., 1993, method). Then an ANOVA is used to assess each item's content validity by comparing the item's mean rating on one construct to the item's ratings on the other constructs. A sample size of about 50 panel members seems adequate for this type of analysis.

The procedures described above illustrate that content-related evidence is concerned primarily with inferences about test *construction* rather than with inferences about test *scores*, and, since, by definition, all validity is the accuracy of inferences about test scores, that which has been called "content validity" is really not validity at all (Tenopyr, 1977). Perhaps, instead, we should call it *content-oriented test development* (Guion, 1987). However, this is not intended to minimize its importance.

> Some would say that content validity is inferior to, or less scientifically respectable than, criterion related validity. This view is mistaken in my opinion. Content validity is the only basic foundation for any kind of validity. If the test does not have it, the criterion measures used to validate the test must have it. And one should never apologize for having to exercise judgment in validating a test. Data never substitute for good judgment. (Ebel, 1977, p. 59)

Nevertheless, in employment situations, the use of scores from a procedure developed on the basis of content also has a predictive basis. That is, one measures performance in a domain of job activities that will be performed later. Major concern, then, should be with the *predictive* aspects of tests used for employment decisions rather than with their descriptive aspects. Surely scores from a well-developed typing test can be used to describe a person's skill at manipulating a keyboard, but description is not our primary purpose when we use a typing test to make hiring decisions. We use the typing score to *predict* how successfully someone will perform a job involving typing (Landy, 1986).

Content-related evidence of validity is extremely important in criterion measurement. For example, quantitative indicators (e.g., CVI values or an index of profile similarity between job content and training content) can be applied meaningfully to the evaluation of job knowledge criteria or training program content. Such evidence then permits objective evaluation of the representativeness of the behavioral content of employment programs (Distefano, Pryer, & Craig, 1980; Faley & Sundstrom, 1985).

In summary, although content-related evidence of validity does have its limitations, undeniably it has made a positive contribution by directing attention toward (1) improved domain sampling and job analysis procedures, (2) better behavior measurement, and (3) the role of expert judgment in confirming the fairness of sampling and scoring procedures and in determining the degree of overlap between separately derived content domains (Dunnette & Borman, 1979).

CRITERION-RELATED EVIDENCE

Whenever measures of individual differences are used to *predict* behavior, and it is technically feasible, criterion-related evidence of validity is called for. With this approach, we test the hypothesis that test scores are related to performance on some criterion measure. As we discussed, in the case of content-related evidence, the criterion is expert judgment. In the case of criterion-related evidence, the criterion is a score or a rating that either is available at the time of predictor measurement or will become available at a later time. If the criterion measure is available at the same time as scores on the predictor, then *concurrent* evidence of validity is being assessed. In contrast, if criterion data will not become available until some time after the predictor scores are obtained, then *predictive* evidence of validity is being measured. Both designs involve the same paradigm, in which a relationship is established between predictor and criterion performance:

Predictor performance → Criterion performance (Measure of relationship)

Operationally, predictive and concurrent studies may be distinguished on the basis of time. A **predictive study** is oriented toward the future and involves a time interval during which events take place (e.g., people are trained or gain experience on a job). A **concurrent study** is oriented toward the present and reflects only the status quo at a particular time.

Logically, the distinction is based not on time, but on the objectives of measurement (Anastasi, 1988). Thus, each type of validity strategy is appropriate under different circumstances. A concurrent study is relevant to measures employed for the description of existing status rather than the prediction of future outcomes (e.g., achievement tests, tests for certification). In the employment context, the difference can be illustrated by asking, for example, "Can Laura do the job now?" (concurrent design) and "Is it likely that Laura will be able to do the job?" (predictive design).

The term **criterion-related** calls attention to the fact that the fundamental concern is with the relationship between predictor and criterion scores, not with predictor scores per se. Scores on the predictor function primarily as signs (Wernimont & Campbell, 1968) pointing to something else—criterion performance. In short, the content of the predictor measure is relatively unimportant, for it serves only as a vehicle to predict criterion performance. However, as discussed in Chapter 4, job performance is multidimensional in nature, and, theoretically, there can be as many statements of criterion-related evidence of validity as there are criteria to be predicted.

Predictive Studies

Predictive designs for obtaining evidence of criterion-related validity are the cornerstone of individual differences measurement. When the objective is to forecast behavior on the basis of scores on a predictor measure, there is simply no substitute for it. Predictive studies demonstrate in an objective, statistical manner the actual relationship between predictors and criteria in a particular situation. In this model, a procedure's ability to predict is readily apparent, but, in the concurrent model, predictive ability must be inferred by the decision maker. In conducting a predictive study, the procedure is as follows:

1. Measure candidates for the job.
2. Select candidates without using the results of the measurement procedure.
3. Obtain measurements of criterion performance at some later date.
4. Assess the strength of the relationship between the predictor and the criterion.

In planning validation research, certain issues deserve special consideration. One of these is sample size. Inadequate sample sizes are quite often the result of practical constraints on the number of available individuals, but sometimes they simply reflect a lack of rational research planning. Actually, the issue of sample size is just one aspect of the more basic issue of **statistical power**—that is, the probability of rejecting a null hypothesis when it is, in fact, false. As Cohen (1988) has noted, in this broader perspective, any statistical test of a null hypothesis may be viewed as a complex relationship among four parameters: (1) the power of the test ($1-\beta$, where beta is the probability of making a Type II error); (2) Type I error or α, the region of rejection of the null hypothesis and whether the test is one tailed or two tailed (power increases as α increases); (3) sample size, N (power increases as N increases); and (4) the magnitude of the effect in the population or the degree of departure from the null hypothesis (power increases as the effect size increases). The four parameters are so related that when any three of them are fixed, the fourth is completely determined.

The importance of power analysis as a research planning tool is considerable, for if power turns out to be insufficient, the research plans can be revised (or dropped if revisions are impossible) so that power may be increased (usually by increasing N and sometimes by increasing α). Note that a power analysis should be conducted *before* a study is conducted. Post hoc power analyses, conducted after validation efforts are completed, are of doubtful utility, especially when the observed effect size is used as the effect size one wishes to detect (Aguinis, Beaty, Boik, & Pierce, 2005; Hoenig & Heisey, 2001).

Rational research planning proceeds by specifying α (usually .05 or .01), a desired power (e.g., .80), and an estimated population effect size. Effect size may be estimated by examining the values obtained in related previous work; by positing some minimum population effect that would have either practical or theoretical significance; or by using conventional definitions of "small" (.10), "medium" (.30), or "large" (.50) effects, where the values in parentheses are correlation coefficients. Once α, a power, and an effect size have been specified, required sample size can be determined, and tables (Cohen, 1988) and computer programs that can be executed online (e.g., http://www.StatPages.net) are available for this purpose.

Power analysis would present little difficulty if population effect sizes could be specified easily. In criterion-related validity studies, they frequently are overestimated because of a failure to consider the combined effects of range restriction in both the predictor and the criterion, criterion unreliability, and other artifacts that reduce the observed effect size vis-à-vis population effect sizes (Aguinis, 2004b; Schmidt, Hunter, & Urry, 1976). Thus, the sample sizes necessary to produce adequate power are much larger than typically has been assumed. Hundreds or even several thousand subjects may be necessary, depending on the type of artifacts affecting the validity coefficient. What can be done?

Assuming that multiple predictors are used in a validity study and that each predictor accounts for some unique criterion variance, the effect size of a linear combination of the predictors is likely to be higher than the effect size of any single predictor in the battery. Since effect size is a major determinant of statistical power (and, therefore, of required sample size), more criterion-related validity studies may become technically feasible if researchers base their sample size requirements on unit-weighted linear combinations of predictors rather than on individual predictors (Cascio, Valenzi, & Silbey, 1978, 1980). In short, larger effect sizes mean smaller required sample sizes to achieve adequate statistical power.

Alternatively, when sample size is fixed and effect size cannot be improved, a targeted level of statistical power still can be maintained by manipulating alpha, the probability of a Type I error. To establish the alpha level required to maintain statistical power, all available information (including prior information about effect sizes) should be incorporated into the planning process. Cascio and Zedeck (1983) demonstrated procedures for doing this.

If none of these strategies is feasible, get as many cases as possible, recognize that sample sizes are too small, and continue to collect data even after the initial validation study is completed. Greater confidence, practical and statistical, can be placed in repeated studies that yield the same results than in one single study based on insufficient data.

An additional consideration is the approximate length of the time interval between the taking of the test and the collection of the criterion data. In short, when has an employee been on the job long enough to appraise his or her performance properly? Answer: when there is some evidence that the initial learning period has passed. Certainly the learning period for some jobs is far longer than for others, and training programs vary in length. For many jobs, employee performance can be appraised approximately six months after the completion of training, but there is considerable variability in this figure. On jobs with short training periods and relatively little interpersonal contact, the interval may be much shorter; when the opposite conditions prevail, it may not be possible to gather reliable criterion data until a year or more has passed.

Two further considerations regarding validation samples deserve mention. The sample itself must be representative—that is, made up of individuals of the same age, education, and vocational situation as the persons for whom the predictor measure is recommended. Finally, predictive designs should use individuals who are actual job applicants and who are motivated to perform well. To be sure, motivational conditions are quite different for presently employed individuals who are told that a test is being used only for research purposes than for job applicants for whom poor test performance means the potential loss of a job.

Concurrent Studies

Concurrent designs for obtaining evidence of criterion-related validity are useful to HR researchers in several ways. Concurrent evidence of the validity of criterion measures is particularly important. Criterion measures usually are substitutes for other more important, costly, or complex perform-ance measures. This substitution is valuable only if (1) there is a (judged) close relationship between the more convenient or accessible measure and the more costly or complex measure and (2) the use of the substitute measure, in fact, is more efficient, in terms of time or money, than actu-ally collecting the more complex performance data. Certainly, concurrent evidence of validity is important in the development of performance management systems; yet most often it is either not considered or simply assumed. It is also important in evaluating tests of job knowledge or achieve-ment, trade tests, work samples, or any other measures designed to describe present performance.

With cognitive ability tests, concurrent studies often are used as substitutes for predictive studies. That is, both predictor and criterion data are gathered from present employees, and it is assumed that, if workers who score high (low) on the predictor also are rated as excellent (poor) performers on the job, then the same relationships should hold for job applicants. A review of empirical comparisons of validity estimates of cognitive ability tests using both predictive and concurrent designs indicates that, at least for these measures, the two types of designs do not yield significantly different estimates (Barrett, Phillips, & Alexander, 1981; Schmitt, Gooding, Noe, & Kirsch, 1984). We hasten to add, however, that the concurrent design ignores the effects of motivation and job experience on ability. While the magnitude of these effects may be nonsignificant for cognitive ability tests, this is less likely to be the case with inventories (e.g., measures of attitudes or personality). Jennings (1953), for example, demonstrated empirically that individuals who are secure in their jobs, who realize that their test scores will in no way affect their job standing, and who are participating in a research study are not motivated to the same degree as are applicants for jobs.

Concurrent designs also ignore the effect of *job experience* on the obtained validity coefficient. One of us once observed a group of police officers (whose average on-the-job experience was three years) completing several instruments as part of a concurrent study. One of the instruments was a measure of situational judgment, and a second was a measure of attitudes toward people. It is absurd to think that presently employed police officers who have been trained at a police academy and who have had three years' experience on the street will respond to a test of situational judgment or an inventory of attitudes in the same way as would applicants with no prior experience! People learn things in the course of doing a job, and events occur that may influence markedly their responses to predictor measures. Thus, valid-ity may be enhanced or inhibited, with no way of knowing in advance the direction of such influences.

In summary, for cognitive ability tests, concurrent studies appear to provide useful estimates of empirical validity derived from predictive studies. Although this fact has been demonstrated empirically, additional research is clearly needed to help understand the *reasons* for this equivalence. On both conceptual and practical grounds, the different validity designs are not equivalent or interchangeable across situations (Guion & Cranny, 1982). Without explicit consideration of the influence of uncontrolled variables (e.g., range restriction, differences due to age, motivation, job experience) in a given situation, one cannot simply substitute a concurrent design for a predictive one.

Requirements of Criterion Measures in Predictive and Concurrent Studies

Any predictor measure will be no better than the criterion used to establish its validity. And, as is true for predictors, anything that introduces random error into a set of criterion scores will reduce validity. All too often, unfortunately, it simply is *assumed* that criterion measures are relevant and valid. As Guion (1987) has pointed out, these two terms are different, and it is important to distinguish between them. A job-related construct is one chosen because it represents performance or behavior on the job that is valued by an employing organization. A construct-related criterion is one chosen because of its theoretical relationship, or lack of one, to the construct to be measured. "Does it work?" is a different question from "Does it measure what we wanted to measure?" Both questions are useful, and both call for criterion-related research. For example, a judgment of acceptable construct-related evidence of validity for subjective ratings might be based on high correlations of the ratings with production data or work samples and of independence from seniority or attendance data.

The performance domain must be defined clearly before we proceed to developing tests that will be used to make predictions about future performance. As described in Chapter 4, the concept of *in situ* performance introduced by Cascio and Aguinis (2008) is crucial in this regard. Performance cannot be studied in isolation and disregarding its context. Recall that *in situ* performance involves "the specification of the broad range of effects—situational, contextual, strategic, and environmental—that may affect individual, team, or organizational performance" (Cascio & Aguinis, 2008, p. 146). A more careful mapping of the performance domain will lead to more effective predictor development.

It is also important that criteria be reliable. As discussed in Chapter 6, although unreliability in the criterion can be corrected statistically, unreliability is no trifling matter. If ratings are the criteria and if supervisors are less consistent in rating some employees than in rating others, then criterion-related validity will suffer. Alternatively, if all employees are given identical ratings (e.g., "satisfactory"), then it is a case of trying to predict the unpredictable. A predictor cannot forecast differences in behavior on the job that do not exist according to supervisors!

Finally, we should beware of criterion contamination in criterion-related validity studies. It is absolutely essential that criterion data be gathered independently of predictor data and that no person who is involved in assigning criterion ratings have any knowledge of individuals' predictor scores. Brown (1979) demonstrated that failure to consider such sources of validity distortion can mislead completely researchers who are unfamiliar with the total selection and training process and with the specifics of the validity study in question.

FACTORS AFFECTING THE SIZE OF OBTAINED VALIDITY COEFFICIENTS

Range Enhancement

As we noted earlier, criterion-related evidence of validity varies with the characteristics of the group on whom the test is validated. In general, whenever a predictor is validated on a group that is more heterogeneous than the group for whom the predictor ultimately is intended, estimates of validity will be spuriously high. Suppose a test of spatial relations ability, originally intended as a screening device for engineering applicants, is validated by giving it to applicants for jobs as diverse as machinists, mechanics, tool crib attendants, *and* engineers in a certain firm. This group is considerably more heterogeneous than the group for whom the test was originally intended (engineering applicants only). Consequently, there will be much variance in the test scores (i.e., range enhancement), and it may *look* like the test is discriminating effectively. Comparison of validity coefficients using engineering applicants only with those obtained from the more heterogeneous group will demonstrate empirically the relative amount of overestimation.

Range Restriction

Conversely, because the size of the validity coefficient is a function of two variables, restricting the range (i.e., truncating or censoring) either of the predictor or of the criterion will serve to lower the size of the validity coefficient (see Figure 7-1).

In Figure 7-1, the relationship between the interview scores and the criterion data is linear, follows the elliptical shape of the bivariate normal distribution, and indicates a systematic positive relationship of about .50. Scores are censored neither in the predictor nor in the criterion, and are found in nearly all the possible categories from low to high. The correlation drops considerably, however, when only a limited group is considered, such as those scores falling to the right of line *X*. When such selection occurs, the points assume shapes that are not at all elliptical and indicate much lower correlations between predictors and criteria. It is tempting to conclude from this that selection effects on validity coefficients result from changes in the variance(s) of the variable(s). However, Alexander (1988) showed that such effects are more properly considered as nonrandom sampling that separately influences means, variances, and correlations of the variables.

Range restriction can occur in the predictor when, for example, only applicants who have survived an initial screening are considered or when measures are used for selection *prior* to validation, so that criterion data are unavailable for low scorers who did not get hired. This is known as **direct range restriction** on the predictor. **Indirect** or **incidental range restriction** on the predictor occurs when an experimental predictor is administered to applicants, but is not used as a basis for selection decisions (Aguinis & Whitehead, 1997). Rather, applicants are selected in accordance with the procedure currently in use, which is likely correlated with the new predictor. Incidental range restriction is pervasive in validation research (Aguinis & Whitehead, 1997). Thorndike (1949) recognized this more than 60 years ago when he noted that range restriction "imposed by indirect selection on the basis of some variable other than the ones being compared . . . appears by far the most common and most important one for any personnel selection research program" (p. 175). In both cases, low scorers who are hired may become disenchanted with the job and quit before criterion data can be collected, thus further restricting the range of available scores.

The range of scores also may be narrowed by preselection. Preselection occurs, for example, when a predictive validity study is undertaken *after* a group of individuals has been hired, but *before* criterion data become available for them. Estimates of the validity of the procedure will be lowered, since such employees represent a superior selection of all job applicants, thus curtailing the range of predictor scores and criterion data. In short, selection at the hiring point reduces the range of the predictor variable(s), and selection on the job or during training reduces the range of the criterion variable(s). Either type of restriction has the effect of lowering estimates of validity.

In order to interpret validity coefficients properly, information on the degree of range restriction in either variable should be included. Fortunately, formulas are available that correct

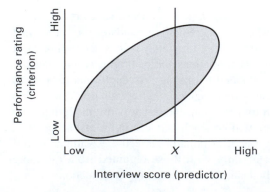

FIGURE 7-1 Effect of range restriction on correlation.

statistically for the various forms of range restriction (Sackett & Yang, 2000; Thorndike, 1949). There are three types of information that can be used to decide which correction formula to implement: (1) whether restriction occurs on the predictor, the criterion, or a third variable correlated with the predictor and/or criterion; (2) whether unrestricted variances for the relevant variables are known; and (3) whether the third variable, if involved, is measured or unmeasured. Sackett and Yang (2000) described 11 different range-restriction scenarios derived from combining these three types of information and presented equations and procedures that can be used for correcting validity coefficients in each situation. However, before implementing a correction, one should be clear about which variables have been subjected to direct and/or indirect selection because the incorrect application of formulas can lead to misleading corrected validity coefficients.

To correct for direct range restriction on the predictor when no third variable is involved, the appropriate formula is as follows (this formula can also be used to correct for direct range restriction on the criterion when no third variable is involved):

$$r_u = \frac{r\dfrac{S}{s}}{\sqrt{1 - r^2 + r^2 \dfrac{S^2}{s^2}}} \tag{7-4}$$

where r_u is the estimated validity coefficient in the unrestricted sample, r is the obtained coefficient in the restricted sample, S is the standard deviation of the unrestricted sample, and s is the standard deviation of the restricted sample.

In practice, all of the information necessary to use Equation 7-4 may not be available. Thus, a second possible scenario is that selection takes place on one variable (either the predictor or the criterion), but the unrestricted variance is not known. For example, this can happen to the criterion due to turnover or transfer before criterion data could be gathered. In this case, the appropriate formula is

$$r_u = \sqrt{1 - \frac{s^2}{S^2}(1 - r^2)} \tag{7-5}$$

where all symbols are defined as above.

In yet a third scenario, if incidental restriction takes place on third variable z and the unrestricted variance on z is known, the formula for the unrestricted correlation between x and y is

$$r_u = \frac{r_{xy} + r_{zx} \cdot r_{zy}(S_z^2/s_z^2 - 1)}{\sqrt{1 - r_{zx}^2(S_z^2/s_z^2 - 1)}\sqrt{1 - r_{zy}^2(S_z^2/s_z^2 - 1)}} \tag{7-6}$$

In practice, there may be range-restriction scenarios that are more difficult to address with corrections. Such scenarios include (1) those where the unrestricted variance on the predictor, the criterion, or the third variable is unknown and (2) those where there is simultaneous or sequential restriction on multiple variables. Fortunately, there are procedures to address each of these types of situations.

Alexander, Alliger, and Hanges (1984) described an approach to address situations where unrestricted variances are not known. For example, assume that the scenario includes direct restriction on the predictor x, but the unrestricted variance on x is unknown. First, one computes

Cohen's (1959) ratio = $s^2/(\bar{x} - k)^2$, where s^2 is the variance in the restricted sample, $\bar{x}$ is the mean of x for the restricted sample, and k is an estimate of the lowest possible x value that could have occurred. Because this ratio has a unique value for any point of selection, it is possible to estimate the proportional reduction in the unrestricted variance (i.e., S_x^2) based on this ratio. Alexander et al. (1984) provided a table that includes various values for Cohen's ratio and the corresponding proportional reduction in variance. Based on the value shown in the table, one can compute an estimate of the unrestricted variance that can be used in Equation 7-4. This procedure can also be used to estimate the (unknown) unrestricted variance for third variable z, and this information can be used in Equation 7-6.

Regarding simultaneous or sequential restriction of multiple variables, Lawley (1943) derived what is called the **multivariate-correction formula**. The multivariate-correction formula can be used when direct restriction (of one or two variables) and incidental restriction take place simultaneously. Also, the equation can be used repeatedly when restriction occurs on a sample that is already restricted. Although the implementation of the multivariate correction is fairly complex, Johnson and Ree (1994) developed the computer program RANGEJ, which makes this correction easy to implement.

In an empirical investigation of the accuracy of such statistical corrections, Lee, Miller, and Graham (1982) compared corrected and uncorrected estimates of validity for the Navy Basic Test Battery to the unrestricted true validity of the test. Groups of sailors were selected according to five different selection ratios. In all cases, the corrected coefficients better estimated the unrestricted true validity of the test. However, later research by Lee and Foley (1986) and Brown, Stout, Dalessio, and Crosby (1988) has shown that corrected correlations tend to fluctuate considerably from test score range to test score range, with higher validity coefficients at higher predictor score ranges. Indeed, if predictor–criterion relationships are actually nonlinear, but a linear relationship is assumed, application of the correction formulas will substantially overestimate the true population correlation. Also, in some instances, the sign of the validity coefficient can change after a correction is applied (Ree, Carretta, Earles, & Albert, 1994).

It is also worth noting that corrected correlations did not have a known sampling distribution until recently. However, Raju and Brand (2003) derived equations for the standard error of correlations corrected for unreliability both in the predictor and the criterion and for range restriction. So, it is now possible to assess the variability of corrected correlations, as well as to conduct tests of statistical significance with correlations subjected to a triple correction.

Although the test of statistical significance for the corrected correlation is robust and Type I error rates are kept at the prespecified level, the ability to consistently reject a false null hypothesis correctly remains questionable under certain conditions (i.e., statistical power does not reach adequate levels). The low power observed may be due to the fact that Raju and Brand's (2003) proposed significance test assumes that the corrected correlations are normally distributed. This assumption may not be tenable in many meta-analytic databases (Steel & Kammeyer-Mueller, 2002). Thus, "there is a definite need for developing new significance tests for correlations corrected for unreliability and range restriction" (Raju & Brand, 2003, p. 66).

As is evident from this section on range restriction, there are several correction procedures available. A review by Van Iddekinge and Ployhart (2008) concluded that using an incorrect procedure can lead to different conclusions regarding validity. For example, if one assumes that a strict top–down selection process has been used when it was not (see Chapter 8 for a more detailed discussion of top–down and test-score banding procedures), then it is likely that corrections will overestimate the impact of range restriction and, therefore, we will believe validity evidence is stronger than it actually is (Yang, Sackett, & Nho, 2004). Also, as noted earlier, if one corrects for direct range restriction only and indirect range restriction was also present, then one would underestimate the effects on the validity coefficient and, hence, conclude that validity evidence is weaker than it actually is (Hunter, Schmidt, & Le, 2006; Schmidt, Oh, & Le, 2006). Similarly, most selection systems include a sequence of tests, what is called a multiple-hurdle process (see Chapter 13). Thus, criterion-related validation efforts focusing on a multiple-hurdle process should consider appropriate corrections that take into account that range restriction, or missing data, takes place after each test is administered (Mendoza, Bard, Mumford, & Ang, 2004).

Finally, we emphasize that corrections are appropriate only when they are justified based on the target population (i.e., the population to which one wishes to generalize the obtained corrected validity coefficient). For example, if one wishes to estimate the validity coefficient for future applicants for a job, but the coefficient was obtained using a sample of current employees (already selected) in a concurrent validity study, then it would be appropriate to use a correction. On the other hand, if one wishes to use the test for promotion purposes in a sample of similarly preselected employees, the correction would not be appropriate. In general, it is recommended that both corrected and uncorrected coefficients be reported, together with information on the type of correction that was implemented (AERA, APA, & NCME, 1999, p. 159). This is particularly important in situations when unmeasured variables play a large role (Sackett & Yang, 2000).

Position in the Employment Process

Estimates of validity based on predictive designs may differ depending on whether a measure of individual differences is used as an initial selection device or as a final hurdle. This is because variance is maximized when the predictor is used as an initial device (i.e., a more heterogeneous group of individuals provides data), and variance is often restricted when the predictor is used later on in the selection process (i.e., a more homogeneous group of individuals provides data).

Form of the Predictor–Criterion Relationship

Scattergrams depicting the nature of the predictor–criterion relationship always should be inspected for extreme departures from the statistical assumptions on which the computed measure of relationship is based. If an assumed type of relationship does not correctly describe the data, validity will be underestimated. The computation of the Pearson product-moment correlation coefficient assumes that both variables are normally distributed, the relationship is linear, and when the bivariate distribution of scores (from low to high) is divided into segments, the column variances are equal. This is called **homoscedasticity**. In less technical terms, this means that the data points are evenly distributed throughout the regression line and the measure predicts as well at high score ranges as at low score ranges (Aguinis, Petersen, & Pierce, 1999; Aguinis & Pierce, 1998). In practice, researchers rarely check for compliance with these assumptions (Weinzimmer, Mone, & Alwan, 1994), and the assumptions often are not met. In one study (Kahneman & Ghiselli, 1962), approximately 40 percent of the validities examined were nonlinear and/or heteroscedastic. Generally, however, when scores on the two variables being related are normally distributed, they also are homoscedastic. Hence, if we can justify the normalizing of scores, we are very likely to have a relationship that is homoscedastic as well (Ghiselli et al., 1981).

CONSTRUCT-RELATED EVIDENCE

Neither content- nor criterion-related validity strategies have as their basic objective the understanding of a trait or construct that a test measures. Content-related evidence is concerned with the extent to which items cover the intended domain, and criterion-related evidence is concerned with the empirical relationship between a predictor and a criterion. Yet, in our quest for improved prediction, some sort of conceptual framework is required to organize and explain our data and to provide direction for further investigation. The conceptual framework specifies the meaning of the construct, distinguishes it from other constructs, and indicates how measures of the construct should relate to other variables (AERA, APA, & NCME, 1999). This is the function of **construct-related evidence of validity**. It provides the evidential basis for the interpretation of scores (Messick, 1995).

Validating inferences about a construct requires a demonstration that a test measures a specific construct that has been shown to be critical for job performance. Once this is accomplished, then inferences about job performance from test scores are, by logical implication, justified (Binning & Barrett, 1989). The focus is on a description of behavior that is broader and more abstract. Construct validation is not accomplished in a single study; it requires an accumulation of evidence derived from many different sources to determine the meaning of the test scores and an appraisal of their social consequences (Messick, 1995). It is, therefore, both a logical and an empirical process.

The process of construct validation begins with the formulation by the investigator of hypotheses about the characteristics of those with high scores on a particular measurement procedure, in contrast to those with low scores. Viewed in their entirety, such hypotheses form a tentative theory about the nature of the construct that the test or other procedure is believed to be measuring. These hypotheses then may be used to predict how people at different score levels on the test will behave on certain other tests or in certain defined situations.

Note that, in this process, the measurement procedure serves as a sign (Wernimont & Campbell, 1968), clarifying the nature of the behavioral domain of interest and, thus, the essential nature of the construct. The construct (e.g., mechanical comprehension, social power) is defined not by an isolated event, but, rather, by a **nomological network**—a system of interrelated concepts, propositions, and laws that relates observable characteristics to either other observables, observables to theoretical constructs, or one theoretical construct to another theoretical construct (Cronbach & Meehl, 1955). For example, for a measure of perceived supervisory social power (i.e., a supervisor's ability to influence a subordinate as perceived by the subordinate; Nesler, Aguinis, Quigley, Lee, & Tedeschi, 1999), one needs to specify the antecedents and the consequents of this construct. The nomological network may include antecedents such as the display of specific nonverbal behaviors—for example, making direct eye contact leading to a female (but not a male) supervisor being perceived as having high coercive power (Aguinis & Henle, 2001a; Aguinis, Simonsen, & Pierce, 1998)—and a resulting dissatisfactory relationship with her subordinate, which, in turn, may adversely affect the subordinate's job performance (Aguinis, Nesler, Quigley, Lee, & Tedeschi, 1996).

Information relevant either to the construct or to the theory surrounding the construct may be gathered from a wide variety of sources. Each can yield hypotheses that enrich the definition of a construct. Among these sources of evidence are the following:

1. Questions asked of test takers about their performance strategies or responses to particular items, or questions asked of raters about the reasons for their ratings (AERA, APA, & NCME, 1999; Messick, 1995).
2. Analyses of the internal consistency of the measurement procedure.
3. Expert judgment that the content or behavioral domain being sampled by the procedure pertains to the construct in question. Sometimes this has led to a confusion between content and construct validities, but, since content validity deals with inferences about test *construction*, while construct validity involves inferences about test *scores*, content validity, at best, is one type of evidence of construct validity (Tenopyr, 1977). Thus, in one study (Schoenfeldt, Schoenfeldt, Acker, & Perlson, 1976), reading behavior was measured directly from actual materials read on the job rather than through an inferential chain from various presumed indicators (e.g., a verbal ability score from an intelligence test). Test tasks and job tasks matched so well that there was little question that common constructs underlay performance on both.
4. Correlations of a new procedure (purportedly a measure of some construct) with established measures of the same construct.
5. Factor analyses of a group of procedures, demonstrating which of them share common variance and, thus, measure the same construct (e.g., Shore & Tetrick, 1991).

6. Structural equation modeling (e.g., using such software packages as AMOS, EQS, or LISREL) that allows the testing of a measurement model that links observed variables to underlying constructs and the testing of a structural model of the relationships among constructs (e.g., Pierce, Aguinis, & Adams, 2000). For example, Vance, Coovert, MacCallum, and Hedge (1989) used this approach to enhance understanding of how alternative predictors (ability, experience, and supervisor support) relate to different types of criteria (e.g., self, supervisor, and peer ratings; work sample performance; and training success) across three categories of tasks (installation of engine parts, inspection of components, and forms completion). Such understanding might profitably be used to develop a generalizable task taxonomy.

7. Ability of the scores derived from a measurement procedure to separate naturally occurring or experimentally contrived groups (group differentiation) or to demonstrate relationships between differences in scores and other variables on which the groups differ.

8. Demonstrations of systematic relationships between scores from a particular procedure and measures of behavior in situations where the construct of interest is thought to be an important variable. For example, a paper-and-pencil instrument designed to measure anxiety can be administered to a group of individuals who subsequently are put through an anxiety-arousing situation, such as a final examination. The paper-and-pencil test scores would then be correlated with the physiological measures of anxiety expression during the exam. A positive relationship from such an experiment would provide evidence that test scores do reflect anxiety tendencies.

9. Convergent and discriminant validation are closely related to the sources of evidence discussed earlier in 3 and 4. Not only should scores that purportedly measure some construct be related to scores on other measures of the same construct (**convergent validation**), but also they should be unrelated to scores on instruments that are not supposed to be measures of that construct (**discriminant validation**).

A systematic experimental procedure for analyzing convergent and discriminant validities has been proposed by Campbell and Fiske (1959). They pointed out that any test (or other measurement procedure) is really a trait-method unit—that is, a test measures a given trait by a single method. Therefore, since we want to know the relative contributions of trait and method variance to test scores, we must study more than one trait (e.g., dominance, affiliation) and use more than one method (e.g., peer ratings, interviews). Such studies are possible using a multitrait–multimethod (MTMM) matrix (see Figure 7-2).

An MTMM matrix is simply a table displaying the correlations among (a) the same trait measured by the same method, (b) different traits measured by the same method, (c) the same trait measured by different methods, and (d) different traits measured by different methods. The procedure can be used to study any number and variety of traits measured by any method. In order to obtain satisfactory evidence for the validity of a construct, the (c) correlations (convergent validities) should be larger than zero and high enough to encourage further study. In addition, the (c) correlations should be higher than the (b) and (d) correlations (i.e., show discriminant validity).

	Traits	Method 1		Method 2	
		A1	B1	A2	B2
Method 1	A1	a			
	B1	b			
Method 2	A2	c			
	B2	d			

FIGURE 7-2   Example of a multitrait–multimethod matrix.

For example, if the correlation between interview (method 1) ratings of two supposedly *different* traits (e.g., assertiveness and emotional stability) is higher than the correlation between interview (method 1) ratings and written test (method 2) scores that supposedly measure the *same* trait (e.g., assertiveness), then the validity of the interview ratings as a measure of the construct "assertiveness" would be seriously questioned.

Note that, in this approach, reliability is estimated by two measures of the same trait using the same method (in Figure 7-2, the (a) correlations), while validity is defined as the extent of agreement between two measures of the same trait using different methods (in Figure 7-2, the (c) correlations). Once again, this shows that the concepts of reliability and validity are intrinsically connected, and a good understanding of both is needed to gather construct-related validity evidence.

Although the logic of this method is intuitively compelling, it does have certain limitations, principally, (1) the lack of quantifiable criteria, (2) the inability to account for differential reliability, and (3) the implicit assumptions underlying the procedure (Schmitt & Stults, 1986). One such assumption is the requirement of maximally dissimilar or uncorrelated methods, since, if the correlation between methods is 0.0, shared method variance cannot affect the assessment of shared trait variance.

When methods are correlated, however, confirmatory factor analysis should be used. Using this method, researchers can define models that propose trait or method factors (or both) a priori and then test the ability of such models to fit the data. The parameter estimates and ability of alternative models to fit the data are used to assess convergent and discriminant validity and method-halo effects. In fact, when methods are correlated, use of confirmatory factor analysis instead of the MTMM approach may actually lead to conclusions that are contrary to those drawn in prior studies (Williams, Cote, & Buckley, 1989).

When analysis begins with multiple indicators of each Trait X Method combination, second-order or hierarchical confirmatory factor analysis (HCFA) should be used (Marsh & Hocevar, 1988). In this approach, first-order factors defined by multiple items or subscales are hypothesized for each scale, and the method and trait factors are proposed as second-order factors.

HCFA supports several important inferences about the latent structure underlying MTMM data beyond those permitted by traditional confirmatory factor analysis (Lance, Teachout, & Donnelly, 1992):

1. A satisfactory first-order factor model establishes that indicators have been assigned correctly to Trait X Method units.
2. Given a satisfactory measurement model, HCFA separates measurement error from unique systematic variance. They remain confounded in traditional confirmatory factor analyses of MTMM data.
3. HCFA permits inferences regarding the extent to which traits and measurement methods are correlated.

Illustration

A construct-validation paradigm designed to study predictor–job performance linkages in the Navy recruiter's job was presented by Borman, Rosse, and Abrahams (1980) and refined and extended by Pulakos, Borman, and Hough (1988). Their approach is described here, since it illustrates nicely interrelationships among the sources of construct-related evidence presented earlier. Factor analyses of personality and vocational interest items that proved valid in a previous Navy recruiter test validation study yielded several factors that were interpreted as underlying constructs (e.g., selling skills, human relations skills), suggesting individual differences potentially important for success on the recruiter job. New items, selected or written to tap these constructs, along with the items found valid in the previous recruiter study, were administered to a separate sample of Navy recruiters. Peer and supervisory performance ratings also were gathered for these recruiters.

Data analyses indicated good convergent and discriminant validities in measuring many of the constructs. For about half the constructs, the addition of new items enhanced validity against the performance criteria. This approach (i.e., attempting to discover, understand, and then confirm individual differences constructs that are important for effectiveness on a job) is a workable strategy for enhancing our understanding of predictor–criterion relationships and an important contribution to personnel selection research.

CROSS-VALIDATION

The prediction of criteria using test scores is often implemented by assuming a linear and additive relationship between the predictors (i.e., various tests) and the criterion. These relationships are typically operationalized using ordinary least squares (OLS) regression, in which weights are assigned to the predictors so that the difference between observed criterion scores and predicted criterion scores is minimized (see Appendix B).

The assumption that regression weights obtained from one sample can be used with other samples with a similar level of predictive effectiveness is not true in most situations. Specifically, the computation of regression weights is affected by idiosyncrasies of the sample on which they are computed, and it capitalizes on chance factors so that prediction is optimized in the sample. Thus, when weights computed in one sample (i.e., current employees) are used with a second sample from the same population (i.e., job applicants), the multiple correlation coefficient is likely to be smaller. This phenomenon has been labeled **shrinkage** (Larson, 1931). Shrinkage is likely to be especially large when (1) initial validation samples are small (and, therefore, have larger sampling errors), (2) a "shotgun" approach is used (i.e., when a miscellaneous set of questions is assembled with little regard to their relevance to criterion behavior and when all items subsequently are retained that yield significant positive or negative correlations with a criterion), and (3) when the number of predictors increases (due to chance factors operating in the validation sample). Shrinkage is likely to be less when items are chosen on the basis of previously formed hypotheses derived from psychological theory or on the basis of past studies showing a clear relationship with the criterion (Anastasi, 1988).

Given the possibility of shrinkage, an important question is the extent to which weights derived from a sample cross-validate (i.e., generalize). **Cross-validity** (i.e., ρ_c) refers to whether the weights derived from one sample can predict outcomes to the same degree in the population as a whole or in other samples drawn from the same population (e.g., Kuncel & Borneman, 2007). If cross-validity is low, the use of assessment tools and prediction systems derived from one sample may not be appropriate in other samples from the same population. Unfortunately, it seems researchers are not aware of this issue. A review of articles published in the *Academy of Management Journal*, *Administrative Science Quarterly*, and *Strategic Management Journal* between January 1990 and December 1995 found that none of the articles reviewed reported empirical or formula-based cross-validation estimates (St. John & Roth, 1999). Fortunately there are procedures available to compute cross-validity. Cascio and Aguinis (2005) provided detailed information on two types of approaches: empirical and statistical.

EMPIRICAL CROSS-VALIDATION   The empirical strategy consists of fitting a regression model in a sample and using the resulting regression weights with a second independent cross-validation sample. The multiple correlation coefficient obtained by applying the weights from the first (i.e., "derivation") sample to the second (i.e., "cross-validation") sample is used as an estimate of ρ_c. Alternatively, only one sample is used, but it is divided into two subsamples, thus creating a derivation subsample and a cross-validation subsample. This is known as a single-sample strategy.

STATISTICAL CROSS-VALIDATION   The statistical strategy consists of adjusting the sample-based multiple correlation coefficient (R) by a function of sample size (N) and the number of predictors (k). Numerous formulas are available to implement the statistical strategy (Raju,

Bilgic, Edwards, & Fleer, 1997). The most commonly implemented formula to estimate cross-validity (i.e., ρ_c) is the following (Browne, 1975):

$$\rho_c^2 = \frac{(N - k - 3)\rho^4 + \rho^2}{(N - 2k - 2)\rho^2 + \rho} \tag{7-7}$$

where ρ is the population multiple correlation. The squared multiple correlation in the population, ρ^2, can be computed as follows:

$$\rho^2 = 1 - \frac{N - 1}{N - k - 1}(1 - R^2). \tag{7-8}$$

Note that Equation 7-8 is what most computer outputs label "adjusted R^2" and is only an *intermediate step* in computing cross-validity (i.e., Equation 7-7). Equation 7-8 does *not* directly address the capitalization on chance in the sample at hand and addresses the issue of shrinkage only partially by adjusting the multiple correlation coefficient based on the sample size and the number of predictors in the regression model (St. John & Roth, 1999). Unfortunately, there is confusion regarding estimators of ρ^2 and ρ_c^2, as documented by Kromrey and Hines (1995, pp. 902–903). The obtained "adjusted R^2" does not address the issue of prediction optimization due to sample idiosyncrasies and, therefore, underestimates the shrinkage. The use of Equation 7-7 *in combination with* Equation 7-8 addresses this issue.

COMPARISON OF EMPIRICAL AND STATISTICAL STRATEGIES   Cascio and Aguinis (2005) reviewed empirical and statistical approaches and concluded that logistical considerations, as well as the cost associated with the conduct of empirical cross-validation studies, can be quite demanding. In addition, there seem to be no advantages to implementing empirical cross-validation strategies. Regarding statistical approaches, the most comprehensive comparison of various formulae available to date was conducted by Raju, Bilgic, Edwards, and Fleer (1999), who investigated 11 cross-validity estimation procedures. The overall conclusion of this body of research is that Equation 7-7 provides accurate results as long as the total sample size is greater than 40.

The lesson should be obvious. Cross-validation, including rescaling and reweighting of items if necessary, should be continual (we recommend it annually), for as values change, jobs change, and people change, so also do the appropriateness and usefulness of inferences made from test scores.

GATHERING VALIDITY EVIDENCE WHEN LOCAL VALIDATION IS NOT FEASIBLE

In many cases, local validation may not be feasible due to logistics or practical constraints, including lack of access to large samples, inability to collect valid and reliable criterion measures, and lack of resources to conduct a comprehensive validity study (Van Iddekinge & Ployhart, 2008). For example, small organizations find it extremely difficult to conduct criterion-related and construct-related validity studies. Only one or, at most, several persons occupy each job in the firm, and, over a period of several years, only a few more may be hired. Obviously, the sample sizes available do not permit adequate predictive studies to be undertaken. Fortunately, there are several strategies available to gather validity evidence in such situations. These include synthetic validity, test transportability, and validity generalization (VG).

Synthetic Validity

Synthetic validity (Balma, 1959) is the process of inferring validity in a specific situation from a systematic analysis of jobs into their elements, a determination of test validity for these elements, and a combination or synthesis of the elemental validities into a whole (Johnson, Carter, Davison, & Oliver, 2001). The procedure has a certain logical appeal. As was pointed out in Chapter 4, criteria are multidimensional and complex, and, if the various dimensions of job performance are independent, each predictor in a battery may be validated against the aspect of job performance it is designed to measure. Such an analysis lends *meaning* to the predictor scores in terms of the multiple dimensions of criterion behavior. Although there are several operationalizations of synthetic validity (Mossholder & Arvey, 1984), all the available procedures are based on the common characteristic of using available information about a job to gather evidence regarding the job relatedness of a test (Hoffman & McPhail, 1998).

For example, the jobs clerk, industrial products salesperson, teamster, and teacher are different, but the teacher and salesperson probably share a basic requirement of verbal fluency; the clerk and teamster, manual dexterity; the teacher and clerk, numerical aptitude; and the salesperson and teamster, mechanical aptitude. Although no one test or other predictor is valid for the total job, tests are available to measure the more basic job aptitudes required. To determine which tests to use in selecting persons for any particular job, however, one first must analyze the job into its elements and specify common behavioral requirements across jobs. Knowing these elements, one then can derive the particular statistical weight attached to each element (the size of the weight is a function of the importance of the element to overall job performance). When the statistical weights are combined with the test element validities, it is possible not only to determine which tests to use but also to estimate the expected predictiveness of the tests for the job in question. Thus, a "synthesized valid battery" of tests may be constructed for each job. The Position Analysis Questionnaire (McCormick, Jeanneret, & Mecham, 1972), a job analysis instrument that includes generalized behaviors required in work situations, routinely makes synthetic validity predictions for each job analyzed. Predictions are based on the General Aptitude Test Battery (12 tests that measure aptitudes in the following areas: intelligence, verbal aptitude, numerical aptitude, spatial aptitude, form perception, clerical perception, motor coordination, finger dexterity, and manual dexterity).

Research to date has demonstrated that synthetic validation is feasible (Steel, Huffcutt, & Kammeyer-Mueller, 2006) and legally acceptable (Trattner, 1982) and that the resulting coefficients are comparable to (albeit slightly lower than) validity coefficients resulting from criterion-related validation research (Hoffman & McPhail, 1998). Moreover, incorporating the O*NET (see Chapter 9) into the synthetic-validity framework makes conducting a synthetic-validity study less onerous and time consuming (Lapolice, Carter, & Johnson, 2008; Scherbaum, 2005).

Test Transportability

Test transportability is another strategy available to gather validity evidence when a local validation study is not feasible. The *Uniform Guidelines on Employee Selection Procedures* (1978) notes that, to be able to use a test that has been used elsewhere locally without the need for a local validation study, evidence must be provided regarding the following (Hoffman & McPhail, 1998):

- The results of a criterion-related validity study conducted at another location
- The results of a test fairness analysis based on a study conducted at another location where technically feasible (test fairness is discussed in detail in Chapter 8)
- The degree of similarity between the job performed by incumbents locally and that performed at the location where the test has been used previously; this can be accomplished by using task- or worker-oriented job analysis data (Hoffman, 1999; job analysis is discussed in detail in Chapter 9)
- The degree of similarity between the applicants in the prior and local settings

Given that data collected in other locations are needed, many situations are likely to preclude gathering validity evidence under the test transportability rubric. On the other hand, the test transportability option is a good possibility when a test publisher has taken the necessary steps to include this option while conducting the original validation research (Hoffman & McPhail, 1998).

Validity Generalization

A meta-analysis is a literature review that is quantitative as opposed to narrative in nature (Hedges & Olkin, 1985; Huffcut, 2002; Hunter & Schmidt, 1990; Rothstein, McDaniel, & Borenstein, 2002). The goals of a meta-analysis are to understand the relationship between two variables across studies and the variability of this relationship across studies (Aguinis & Pierce, 1998; Aguinis, Sturman, & Pierce, 2008). In personnel psychology, meta-analysis has been used extensively to provide a quantitative integration of validity coefficients computed in different samples. The application of meta-analysis to the employment testing literature was seen as necessary, given the considerable variability from study to study in observed validity coefficients and the fact that some coefficients are statistically significant, whereas others are not (Schmidt & Hunter, 1977), even when jobs and tests appear to be similar or essentially identical (Schmidt & Hunter, 2003a). If, in fact, validity coefficients vary from employer to employer, region to region, across time periods, and so forth, the situation specificity hypothesis would be true, local empirical validation would be required in each situation, and it would be impossible to develop general principles and theories that are necessary to take the field beyond a mere technology to the status of a science (Guion, 1976). Meta-analyses conducted with the goal of testing the situational specificity hypothesis have been labeled *psychometric meta-analysis* or VG studies (Schmidt & Hunter, 2003b).

VG studies have been applied to over 500 bodies of research in employment selection, each one representing a different predictor–criterion combination (Schmidt & Hunter, 2003b). Rothstein (2003) reviewed several such studies demonstrating VG for such diverse predictors as grade point average (Roth, BeVier, Switzer, & Schippmann, 1996), biodata (Rothstein, Schmidt, Erwin, Owens, & Sparks, 1990), and job experience (McDaniel, Schmidt, & Hunter, 1988). But note that there is a slight difference between testing whether a validity coefficient generalizes and whether the situation-specificity hypothesis is true (Murphy, 2000, 2003). The VG question is answered by obtaining a mean validity coefficient across studies and comparing it to some standard (e.g., if 90 percent of validity coefficients are greater than .10, then validity generalizes). The situation-specificity question is answered by obtaining a measure of variability (e.g., SD) of the distribution of validity coefficients across studies. Validity may generalize because most coefficients are greater than a preset standard, but there still may be substantial variability in the coefficients across studies (and, in this case, there is a need to search for moderator variables that can explain this variance; Aguinis & Pierce, 1998b; Aguinis, Sturman, & Pierce, 2008).

If a VG study concludes that validity for a specific test–performance relationship generalizes, then this information can be used in lieu of a local validation study. This allows small organizations to implement tests that have been used elsewhere without the need to collect data locally. However, there is still a need to understand the job duties in the local organization. In addition, sole reliance on VG evidence to support test use is probably premature. A review of the legal status of VG (Cascio & Aguinis, 2005) revealed that only three cases that relied on VG have reached the appeals court level, and courts do not always accept VG evidence. For example, in *Bernard v. Gulf Oil Corp.* (1989), the court refused VG evidence by disallowing the argument that validity coefficients from two positions within the same organization indicate that the same selection battery would apply to other jobs within the company without further analysis of the other jobs. Based on this and other evidence, Landy (2003) concluded that "anyone considering the possibility of invoking VG as the sole defense for a test or test type might want to seriously consider including additional defenses (e.g., transportability analyses) and would be well advised to know the essential duties of the job in question, and in its local manifestation, well" (p. 189).

HOW TO CONDUCT A VG STUDY Generally the procedure for conducting a VG study is as follows:

1. Calculate or obtain the validity coefficient for each study included in the review, and compute the mean coefficient across the studies.
2. Calculate the variance of the validity coefficient across studies.
3. Subtract from the result in Step 2 the amount of variance due to sampling error; this yields an estimate of the variance of r in the population.
4. Correct the mean and variance for known statistical artifacts other than sampling error (e.g., measurement unreliability in the criterion, artificial dichotomization of predictor and criterion variables, range variation in the predictor and the criterion, scale coarseness).
5. Compare the corrected standard deviation to the mean to assess the amount of potential variation in results across studies.
6. If large variation still remains (e.g., more than 25 percent), select moderator variables (i.e., variables that can explain this variance; see Chapter 8), and perform meta-analysis on subgroups (Aguinis & Pierce, 1998; Aguinis, Sturman, & Pierce, 2008).

As an example, consider five hypothetical studies that investigated the relationship between an employment test X and job performance:

Study	1	2	3	4	5
Sample size (n)	823	95	72	46	206
Correlation (r)	.147	.155	.278	.329	.20

Step 1. $\bar{\rho} = \dfrac{\sum n_i r_i}{\sum n_i} = .17$

Step 2. $\sigma_r^2 = \dfrac{\sum n_i (r_i - \bar{r}^2)^2}{\sum n_i} = .002$

Step 3. $\sigma_\rho^2 = \sigma_r^2 - \sigma_e^2$ where $\sigma_e^2 = \dfrac{(1 - \bar{r}^2)^2}{k - 1} = .0038$, and therefore

$$\sigma_\rho^2 = .002 - .0038 = -.0018$$

This implies that the variability of validity coefficients across studies, taking into account sampling error, is approximately zero.

Step 4. This step cannot be done based on the data available. Corrections could be implemented, however, by using information about artifacts (e.g., measurement error, range restriction). This information can be used for several purposes: (a) to correct each validity coefficient individually by using information provided in each study (e.g., estimates of reliability for each validity coefficient and degree of range restriction for each criterion variable);

or (b) to correct $\bar{\rho}$ and σ_ρ^2 using artifact information gathered from previous research (i.e., artifact distribution meta-analysis). Because information about artifacts is usually not available from individual studies, about 90 percent of meta-analyses that implement corrections use artifact-distribution methods (Schmidt & Hunter, 2003b).

Step 5. The best estimate of the relationship in the population between the construct measured by test X and performance in this hypothetical example is .17, and all the coefficients are greater than approximately .15. This seems to be a useful level of validity, and, therefore, we conclude that validity generalizes. Also, differences in obtained correlations across studies are due solely to sampling error, and, therefore, there is no support for the situation specificity hypothesis, and there is no need to search for moderators (so Step 6 is not needed).

Given the above results, we could use test X locally without the need for an additional validation study (assuming the jobs where the studies were conducted and the job in the present organization are similar). However, meta-analysis, like any other data analysis technique, is no panacea (Bobko & Stone-Romero, 1998), and the conduct of VG includes technical difficulties that can decrease our level of confidence in the results. Fortunately, several refinements to VG techniques have been offered in recent years. Consider the following selected set of improvements:

1. The estimation of the sampling error variance of the validity coefficient has been improved (e.g., Aguinis, 2001; Aguinis & Whitehead, 1997).
2. The application of Bayesian models allows for the use of previous distributions of validity coefficients and the incorporation of any new studies without the need to rerun the entire VG study (Brannick, 2001; Brannick & Hall, 2003; Steel & Kammeyer-Mueller, 2008).
3. There is an emphasis not just on confidence intervals around the mean validity coefficient but also on credibility intervals (Schmidt & Hunter, 2003a). The lower bound of a credibility interval is used to infer whether validity generalizes, so the emphasis on credibility intervals is likely to help the understanding of differences between VG and situation specificity tests.
4. There is a clearer understanding of differences between random-effects and fixed-effects models (Field, 2001; Hall & Brannick, 2002; Kisamore & Brannick, 2008). Fixed-effects models assume that the same validity coefficient underlies all studies included in the review, whereas random-effects models do not make this assumption and are more appropriate when situation specificity is expected. There is now widespread realization that random-effects models are almost always more appropriate than fixed-effects models (Schmidt & Hunter, 2003a).
5. New methods for estimating $\bar{\rho}$ and σ_ρ^2 are offered on a regular basis. For example, Raju and Drasgow (2003) derived maximum-likelihood procedures for estimating the mean and variance parameters when validity coefficients are corrected for unreliability and range restriction. Nam, Mengersen, and Garthwaite (2003) proposed new methods for conducting so-called multivariate meta-analysis involving more than one criterion.
6. Given the proliferation of methods and approaches, some researchers have advocated taking the best features of each method and combining them into a single meta-analytic approach (Aguinis & Pierce, 1998).
7. Regarding testing for moderating effects, Monte Carlo simulations suggest that the Hunter and Schmidt (2004) procedure produces the most accurate estimate for the moderating effect magnitude, and, therefore, it should be used for point estimation. Second, regarding homogeneity tests, the Hunter and Schmidt (2004) approach provides a slight advantage regarding Type I error rates, and the Aguinis and Pierce (1998) approach provides a slight advantage regarding Type II error rates. Thus, the Hunter and Schmidt (2004) approach is

best for situations when theory development is at the initial stages and there are no strong theory-based hypotheses to be tested (i.e., exploratory or post hoc testing). Alternatively, the Aguinis and Pierce (1998) approach is best when theory development is at more advanced stages (i.e., confirmatory and a priori testing). Third, the Hunter and Schmidt (2004), Hedges and Olkin (1985), and Aguinis and Pierce (1998) approaches yield similar overall Type I and Type II error rates for moderating effect tests, so there are no clear advantages of using one approach over the other. Fourth, the Hunter and Schmidt procedure is the least affected by increasing levels of range restriction and measurement error regarding homogeneity test Type I error rates, and the Aguinis and Pierce (1998) homogeneity test Type II error rates are least affected by these research design conditions (in the case of measurement error, this is particularly true for effect sizes around .2). In short, Aguinis, Sturman, and Pierce (2008) concluded that "the choice of one approach over the other needs to consider the extent to which range restriction and measurement error are research-design issues present in the meta-analytic database to be analyzed" (p. 32).

Despite the above improvements and refinements, there are both conceptual and method-ological challenges in conducting and interpreting meta-analyses that should be recognized. Here is a selective set of challenges:

1. The use of different reliability coefficients can have a profound impact on the resulting corrected validity coefficients (e.g., the use of coefficient alpha versus interrater reliability; see Chapter 6). There is a need to understand clearly what type of measurement error is corrected by using a specific reliability estimate (DeShon, 2003).
2. There are potential construct-validity problems when cumulating validity coefficients. Averaging validity coefficients across studies when those studies used different measures causes a potential "apples and oranges" problem (Bobko & Stone-Romero, 1998). For example, it may not make sense to get an average of validity coefficients that are well estimated in one type of sample (i.e., based on applicant samples) and biased in another (e.g., where undergraduate students pose as potential job applicants for a hypothetical job in a hypothetical organization).
3. The statistical power to detect moderators is quite low; specifically the residual variance (i.e., variance left after subtracting variance due to sampling error and statistical artifacts) may be underestimated (Sackett, 2003). This is ironic, given that advocates of meta-analysis state that one of the chief reasons for implementing the technique is inadequate statistical power of individual validation studies (Schmidt & Hunter, 2003b). In general, the power to detect differences in population validity coefficients of .1 to .2 is low when the number of coefficients cumulated is small (i.e., 10–15) and when sample sizes are about 100 (which is typical in personnel psychology) (Sackett, 2003).
4. The domain of generalization of the predictor is often not sufficiently specified (Sackett, 2003). Take, for example, the result that the relationship between integrity tests and counterproductive behaviors generalizes (Ones, Viswesvaran, & Schmidt, 1993). What is the precise domain for "integrity tests" and "counterproductive behaviors," and what are the jobs and settings for which this relationship generalizes? In the case of the Ones et al. (1993) VG study, about 60 to 70 percent of coefficients come from three tests only (Sackett, 2003). So, given that three tests contributed the majority of validity coefficients, results about the generalizability of all types of integrity tests may not be warranted.
5. The sample of studies cumulated may not represent the population of the studies. For example, published studies tend to report validity coefficients larger than unpublished studies. This is called the file-drawer problem because studies with high validity coefficients, which are also typically statistically significant, are successful in the peer-review process and are published, whereas those with smaller validity coefficients are not (Rosenthal, 1995).

6. Attention needs to be paid to whether there are interrelationships among moderators. For example, Sackett (2003) described a VG study of the integrity testing–counterproductive behaviors literature showing that type of test (of three types included in the review) and type of design (i.e., self-report criteria versus external criteria) were completely confounded. Thus, conclusions about which type of test yielded the highest validity coefficient were, in fact, reflecting different types of designs and not necessarily a difference in validity across types of tests.

7. There is a need to consider carefully the type of design used in the original studies before effect sizes can be cumulated properly. Specifically, effect sizes derived from matched groups or repeated-measures designs for which there exists a correlation between the measures often lead to overestimation of effects (Dunlap, Cortina, Vaslow, & Burke, 1996).

8. When statistical artifacts (e.g., range restriction) are correlated with situational variables (e.g., organizational climate), the implementation of corrections may mask situational variations (James, Demaree, Mulaik, & Ladd, 1992).

9. When statistical artifacts are correlated with each other, corrections may lead to overestimates of validity coefficients.

10. Regarding tests for moderators, authors often fail to provide all the information needed for readers to test for moderators and to interpret results that are highly variable (Cortina, 2003).

11. The choices faced by meta-analysts seem increasingly technical and complex (Schmidt, 2008). The literature on meta-analytic methods has proliferated to such a high rate that meta-analysts face difficult decisions in terms of conducting a meta-analysis, and more often than not, there is no clear research-based guidance regarding which choices are best given a particular situation (i.e., type of predictor and criterion, type of statistical and methodological artifacts, what to correct and how).

Virtually every one of the conceptual and methodological challenges listed above represents a "judgment call" that a researcher needs to make in conducting a VG study (Wanous, Sullivan, & Malinak, 1989). The fact that so many judgment calls are involved may explain why there are meta-analyses reporting divergent results, although they have examined precisely the same domain. For example, three meta-analyses reviewing the relationship between the "Big Five" personality traits and job performance were published at about the same time, and yet their substantive conclusions differ (Barrick & Mount, 1991; Hough, 1992; Tett, Jackson, & Rothstein, 1991).

Inconsistent VG results such as those found in the personality-performance relationship led Landy (2003) to conclude that "one could make the case that there is as much subjectivity and bias in meta-analyses as there is in traditional literature reviews. But, with meta-analysis, at least, there is the appearance of precision" (p. 178). This raises a final point: To be useful, statistical methods must be used thoughtfully. Data analysis is an aid to thought, not a substitute for it. Careful quantitative reviews that adhere to the following criteria can play a useful role in furthering our understanding of organizational phenomena (Bobko & Roth, 2008; Bullock & Svyantek, 1985; Dalton & Dalton, 2008; Rosenthal, 1995):

1. Use a theoretical model as the basis of the meta-analysis research and test hypotheses from that model.

2. Identify precisely the domain within which the hypotheses are to be tested.

3. Include all publicly available studies in the defined content domain (not just published or easily available studies).

4. Avoid screening out studies based on criteria of methodological rigor, age of study, or publication status.

5. Publish or make available the final list of studies used in the analysis.

6. Select and code variables on theoretical grounds rather than convenience.

7. Provide detailed documentation of the coding scheme and the resolution of problems in applying the coding scheme, including estimation procedures used for missing data. A meta-analysis should include sufficient detail regarding data collection and analysis such that it can be replicated by an independent team of researchers.

8. Use multiple raters to apply the coding scheme and provide a rigorous assessment of interrater reliability.

9. Report all variables analyzed in order to avoid problems of capitalizing on chance relationships in a subset of variables.

10. Provide a visual display of the distribution of effect sizes.

11. Conduct a file-drawer analysis (i.e., determine how many additional studies with null effects would be required to obtain an overall validity coefficient that is not different from zero).

12. Publish or make available the data set used in the analysis.

13. Consider alternative explanations for the findings obtained.

14. Limit generalization of results to the domain specified by the research.

15. Report study characteristics to indicate the nature and limits of the domain actually analyzed.

16. Report the entire study in sufficient detail to allow for direct replication.

Empirical Bayes Analysis

Because local validation and VG both have weaknesses, Newman, Jacobs, and Bartram (2007) proposed the use of empirical Bayesian estimation as a way to capitalize on the advantages of both of these approaches. In a nutshell, this approach involves first calculating the average inaccuracy of meta-analysis and a local validity study under a wide variety of conditions and then computing an empirical Bayesian estimate, which is a weighted average of the meta-analytically derived and local study estimates.

Empirical Bayes analysis is a very promising approach because simulation work demonstrated that resulting estimates of validity are more accurate than those obtained using meta-analysis or a local validation study alone. As such, Bayes estimation capitalizes on the strengths of meta-analysis and local validation. However, it is less promising if one considers practical issues, because Bayes analysis requires the conduct of *both* a meta-analysis *and* a local validity study. So, in terms of practical constraints as well as resources needed, Bayes analysis is only feasible when both a meta-analysis and a local validation study are feasible, because Bayes estimation requires meta-analytically derived and local validity estimates as input for the analysis.

Application of Alternative Validation Strategies: Illustration

As in the case of content-, criterion-, and construct-related evidence, the various strategies available to gather validity evidence when the conduct of a local validation study is not possible are not mutually exclusive. In fact, as noted above in the discussion of VG, the use of VG evidence alone is not recommended.

Hoffman, Holden, and Gale (2000) provide an excellent illustration of a validation effort that included a combination of strategies. Although the project was not conducted in a small organization, the study's approach and methodology serve as an excellent illustration regarding the benefits of combining results from various lines of evidence, as is often necessary in small organizations. The goal of this validation project was to gather validity evidence that would support the broader use of cognitive ability tests originally validated in company-research projects. Overall, Hoffman et al. (2000) worked on several lines of evidence including VG research on cognitive ability tests, internal validation studies, and synthetic validity. The combination of these lines of evidence strongly supported the use of cognitive ability tests for predicting training and job performance for nonmanagement jobs.

> **Evidence-Based Implications for Practice**
>
> - Reliability is a necessary, but not sufficient, condition for validity. Other things being equal, the lower the reliability, the lower the validity.
> - Validity, or the accuracy of inferences made based on test scores, is a matter of degree, and inferences can be made by implementing a content-, criterion-, or construct-related validity study. These approaches are not mutually exclusive. On the contrary, the more evidence we have about validity, the more confident we are about the inferences we make about test scores.
> - There are different types of statistical corrections that can be implemented to understand construct-level relationships between predictors and criteria. However, different types of corrections are appropriate in some situations, and not all are appropriate in all situations.
> - There are both empirical and statistical strategies for understanding the extent to which validation evidence from one sample generalizes to another (i.e., cross-validation). Each approach has advantages and disadvantages that must be weighed before implementing them.
> - When local validation is not possible, consider alternatives such as synthetic validity, test transportability, and validity generalization. Bayes estimation is an additional approach to gathering validity evidence, but it requires both a local validation study and a validity generalization study.
> - None of these approaches is likely to serve as a "silver bullet" in a validation effort, and they are not mutually exclusive. Validation is best conceived of as a matter of degree. So the greater the amount of evidence the better.

In the last two chapters, we have examined applied measurement concepts that are essential to sound employment decisions. These are useful tools that will serve the HR specialist well. In the next chapter, we will use these concepts to take a closer look at a topic that is widely debated in contemporary human resource management—fairness in employment decisions.

Discussion Questions

1. What are some of the consequences of using incorrect reliability estimates that lead to over- or underestimation of validity coefficients?
2. Explain why validity is a unitary concept.
3. What are the various strategies to quantify content-related validity?
4. Explain why construct validity is the foundation for all validity.
5. Why is cross-validation necessary? What is the difference between shrinkage and cross-validation?
6. What factors might affect the size of a validity coefficient? What can be done to deal with each of these factors?
7. Provide examples of situations where it would be appropriate and inappropriate to correct a validity coefficient for the effects of range restriction.
8. What are some of the contributions of validity generalization to human resource selection?
9. What are some challenges and unresolved issues in implementing a VG study and using VG evidence?
10. What are some of the similarities and differences in gathering validity evidence in large, as compared to small, organizations?

Fairness in Employment Decisions

At a Glance

Fairness is a social, not a statistical, concept. However, when it is technically feasible, users of selection measures should investigate potential test bias, which involves examining possible differences in prediction systems for racial, ethnic, and gender subgroups. Traditionally, such investigations have considered possible differences in subgroup validity coefficients (differential validity). However, a more complete test bias assessment involves an examination of possible differences in standard errors of estimate and in slopes and intercepts of subgroup regression lines (differential prediction or predictive bias). Theoretically, differential validity and differential prediction can assume numerous forms, but the preponderance of the evidence indicates that both occur infrequently. However, the assessment of differential prediction suffers from weaknesses that often lead to a Type II error (i.e., conclusion that there is no bias when there may be).

If a measure that predicts performance differentially for members of different groups is, nevertheless, used for all applicants, then the measure may discriminate unfairly against the subgroup(s) for whom the measure is less valid. Job performance must be considered along with test performance because unfair discrimination cannot be said to exist if inferior test performance by some subgroup also is associated with inferior job performance by the same group. Even when unfair discrimination does not exist, however, differences in subgroup means can lead to adverse impact (i.e., differential selection ratios across groups), which carries negative legal and societal consequences. Thus, the reduction of adverse impact is an important consideration in using tests. Various forms of test-score banding have been proposed to balance adverse impact and societal considerations. The ultimate resolution of the problem will probably not rest on technical grounds alone; competing values must be considered. Although some errors are inevitable in employment decisions, the crucial question is whether the use of a particular method of assessment results in less organizational and social cost than is now being paid for these errors, considering all other assessment methods.

By nature and by necessity, measures of individual differences are discriminatory. This is as it should be, since in employment settings random acceptance of candidates can only lead to gross misuse of human and economic resources (unless the job is so easy that anyone can do it). To ignore individual differences is to abandon all the potential economic, societal, and personal advantages to be gained by taking into account individual patterns of abilities and varying job requirements. In short, the wisest course of action lies in the accurate matching of people and jobs. Such an approach begins by appraising individual patterns of abilities through various types of selection measures. Such measures are *designed* to discriminate, and, in order to possess adequate validity, they *must* do so. If a selection measure is valid in a particular situation, then legitimately we may attach a different behavioral meaning to high scores than we do to low scores. A valid selection measure accurately discriminates between those with high and those with low probabilities of success on the job. The crux of the matter, however, is whether the measure discriminates *unfairly*. Probably the clearest statement on this issue was made by Guion (1966): "Unfair discrimination exists when persons with equal probabilities of success on the job have unequal probabilities of being hired for the job" (p. 26).

Fairness is defined from social perspectives and includes various definitions. Consequently, there is no consensual and universal definition of fairness. In fact, a study involving 57 human resource practitioners found that their perceptions and definitions of what constitute a fair set of testing practices vary widely (Landon & Arvey, 2007). That fairness is not a consensually agreed-upon concept is highlighted by the fact that 40 participants in this study were alumni and 17 were students in Masters and PhD programs in Human Resources and Industrial Relations from a university in the United States and, hence, they had similar professional background. However, the *Uniform Guidelines on Employee Selection Procedures* (1978), as well as the *Standards for Educational and Psychological Testing* (AERA, APA, & NCME, 1999), recommend that users of selection measures investigate differences in patterns of association between test scores and other variables for groups based on such variables as sex, ethnicity, disability status, and age. Such investigations, labeled *test bias*, *differential prediction*, or *predictive bias* assessment, should be carried out, however, only when it is technically feasible to do so—that is, when sample sizes in each group are sufficient for reliable comparisons among groups and when relevant, unbiased criteria are available. So, although fairness is a socially constructed concept and is defined in different ways, test bias is a psychometric concept and it has been defined quite clearly.

Unfortunately, differential prediction studies are technically feasible far less often than is commonly believed. Samples of several hundred subjects *in each group* are required in order to provide adequate statistical power (Aguinis, 2004b; Aguinis & Stone-Romero, 1997; Drasgow & Kang, 1984). Furthermore, it is often very difficult to verify empirically that a criterion is unbiased.

In the past, investigations of bias have focused on *differential validity* (i.e., differences in validity coefficients across groups) (Boehm, 1977). However, there is a need to go beyond possible differences in validity coefficients across groups and understand that the concept of *differential validity* is distinct from *differential prediction* (Aguinis, 2004b, Bobko & Bartlett, 1978). We need to compare *prediction systems* linking the predictor and the criterion because such analysis has a more direct bearing on issues of bias in selection than do differences in correlations only (Hartigan & Wigdor, 1989; Linn, 1978). As noted in the *Standards* (AERA, APA, & NCME, 1999), "correlation coefficients provide inadequate evidence for or against the differential prediction hypothesis if groups or treatments are found not to be approximately equal with respect to both test and criterion means and variances. Considerations of both regression slopes and intercepts are needed" (p. 82). In other words, equal correlations do not necessarily imply equal standard errors of estimate, nor do they necessarily imply equal slopes or intercepts of group regression equations. With these cautions in mind, we will consider the potential forms of differential validity, then the research evidence on differential validity and differential prediction and their implications.

ASSESSING DIFFERENTIAL VALIDITY

In the familiar bivariate scatterplot of predictor and criterion data, each dot represents a person's score on both the predictor and the criterion (see Figure 8-1). In this figure, the dots tend to cluster in the shape of an ellipse, and, since most of the dots fall in quadrants 1 and 3, with relatively few dots in quadrants 2 and 4, positive validity exists. If the relationship were negative (e.g., the relationship between the predictor "conscientiousness" and the criterion "counterproductive behaviors"), most of the dots would fall in quadrants 2 and 4.

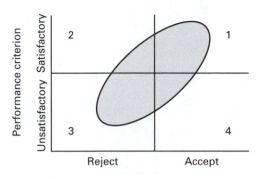

FIGURE 8-1 Positive validity.

Figure 8-1 shows that the relationship is positive and people with high (low) predictor scores also tend to have high (low) criterion scores. In investigating differential validity for groups (e.g., ethnic minority and ethnic nonminority), if the joint distribution of predictor and criterion scores is similar throughout the scatterplot in each group, as in Figure 8-1, no problem exists, and use of the predictor can be continued. On the other hand, if the joint distribution of predictor and criterion scores is similar for each group, but circular, as in Figure 8-2, there is also no differential validity, but the predictor is useless because it supplies no information of a predictive nature. So there is no point in investigating differential validity in the absence of an overall pattern of predictor–criterion scores that allows for the prediction of relevant criteria.

Differential Validity and Adverse Impact

An important consideration in assessing differential validity is whether the test in question produces adverse impact. The *Uniform Guidelines* (1978) state that a "selection rate for any race, sex, or ethnic group which is less than four-fifths (4/5) (or 80 percent) of the rate for the group with the highest rate will generally be regarded by the Federal enforcement agencies as evidence of adverse impact, while a greater than four-fifths rate will generally not be regarded by Federal enforcement agencies as evidence of adverse impact" (p. 123). In other words, adverse impact means that members of one group are selected at substantially greater rates than members of another group. To understand whether this is the case, one compares selection ratios across the groups under consideration. For example, assume that the applicant pool consists of 300 ethnic minorities and 500 nonminorities. Further, assume that 30 minorities are hired, for a selection ratio of $SR_1 = 30/300 = 10$, and that 100 nonminorities are hired, for a selection ratio of $SR_2 = 100/500 = 20$. The adverse impact ratio is $SR_1/SR_2 = .50$, which is substantially smaller than the recommended .80 ratio. Let's consider various

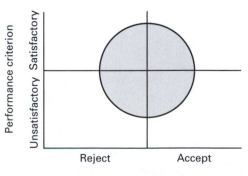

FIGURE 8-2 Zero validity.

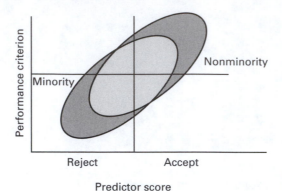

FIGURE 8-3 Valid predictor with adverse impact.

scenarios relating differential validity with adverse impact. The ideas for many of the following diagrams are derived from Barrett (1967) and represent various combinations of the concepts illustrated in Figures 8-1 and 8-2.

Figure 8-3 is an example of a differential predictor–criterion relationship that is legal and appropriate. In this figure, validity for the minority and nonminority groups is equivalent, but the minority group scores lower on the predictor and does poorer on the job (of course, the situation could be reversed). In this instance, the very same factors that depress test scores may also serve to depress job performance scores. Thus, adverse impact is defensible in this case, since minorities do poorer on what the organization considers a relevant and important measure of job success. On the other hand, government regulatory agencies probably would want evidence that the criterion was relevant, important, and not itself subject to bias. Moreover, alternative criteria that result in less adverse impact would have to be considered, along with the possibility that some third factor (e.g., length of service) did not cause the observed difference in job performance (Byham & Spitzer, 1971).

An additional possibility, shown in Figure 8-4, is a predictor that is valid for the combined group, but invalid for each group separately. In fact, there are several situations where the validity coefficient is zero or near zero for each of the groups, but the validity coefficient in both groups combined is moderate or even large (Ree, Carretta, & Earles, 1999). In most cases where no validity exists for either group individually, errors in selection would result from using the predictor without validation or from failing to test for differential validity in the first place. The predictor in this case becomes solely a crude measure of the grouping variable (e.g., ethnicity) (Bartlett & O'Leary, 1969). This is the most clear-cut case of using selection measures to discriminate in terms of race, sex, or any other unlawful basis. Moreover, it is unethical to use a selection device that has not been validated (see Appendix A).

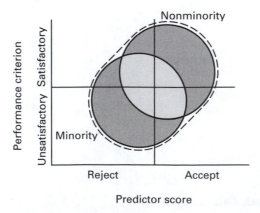

FIGURE 8-4 Valid predictor for entire group; invalid for each group separately.

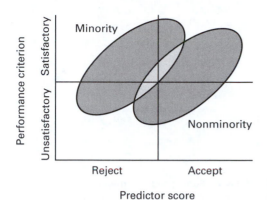

FIGURE 8-5 Equal validity, unequal predictor means.

It also is possible to demonstrate equal validity in the two groups combined with unequal predictor means or criterion means and the presence or absence of adverse impact. These situations, presented in Figures 8-5 and 8-6, highlight the need to examine differential prediction, as well as differential validity.

In Figure 8-5, members of the minority group would not be as likely to be selected, even though the probability of success on the job for the two groups is essentially equal. Under these conditions, an alterative strategy is to use separate cut scores in each group based on predictor performance, while the expectancy of job performance success remains equal. Thus, a Hispanic candidate with a score of 65 on an interview may have a 75 percent chance of success on the job. A white candidate with a score of 75 might have the same 75 percent probability of success on the job. Although this situation might appear disturbing initially, remember that the predictor (e.g., a selection interview) is being used simply as a vehicle to forecast the likelihood of successful job performance. The primary focus is on job performance rather than on predictor performance. Even though interview scores may mean different things for different groups, as long as the expectancy of success on the job is equal for the two (or more) groups, the use of separate cut scores is justified. Indeed, the reporting of an expectancy score for each candidate is one recommendation made by a National Academy of Sciences panel with respect to the interpretation of scores on the General Aptitude Test Battery (Hartigan & Wigdor, 1989). A legal caveat exists, however. In the United States, it is illegal to use different selection rules for identifiable groups in some contexts (Sackett & Wilk, 1994).

Figure 8-6 depicts a situation where, although there is no noticeable difference in predictor scores, nonminority group members tend to perform better on the job than minority group members (or vice versa). If predictions were based on the combined sample, the result would be a systematic

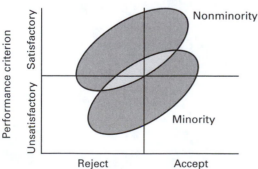

FIGURE 8-6 Equal validity, unequal criterion means.

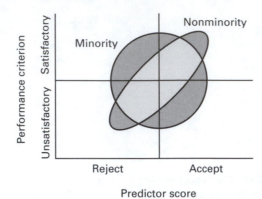

FIGURE 8-7 Equal predictor means, but validity only for the nonminority group.

underprediction for nonminorities and a systematic overprediction for minorities, although there is no adverse impact. Thus, in this situation, the failure to use different selection rules (which would yield more accurate prediction for both groups) may put minority persons in jobs where their probability of success is low and where their resulting performance only provides additional evidence that helps maintain prejudice (Bartlett & O'Leary, 1969). The nonminority individuals also suffer. If a test is used as a placement device, for example, since nonminority performance is systematically underpredicted, these individuals may well be placed in jobs that do not make the fullest use of their talents.

In Figure 8-7, no differences between the groups exist either on predictor or on criterion scores; yet the predictor has validity only for the nonminority group. Hence, if legally admissible, the selection measure should be used only with the nonminority group, since the job performance of minorities cannot be predicted accurately. If the measure were used to select both minority and nonminority applicants, no adverse impact would be found, since approximately the same proportion of applicants would be hired from each group. However, more nonminority members would succeed on the job, thereby reinforcing past stereotypes about minority groups and hindering future attempts at equal employment opportunity (EEO).

In our final example (see Figure 8-8), the two groups differ in mean criterion performance as well as in validity. The predictor might be used to select nonminority applicants, but should not be used to select minority applicants. Moreover, the cut score or decision rule used to select nonminority applicants must be derived solely from the nonminority group, *not* from the combined group. If the minority group (for whom the predictor is not valid) is included, overall validity will be lowered, as will the overall mean criterion score. Predictions will be less accurate because the standard error of estimate will be inflated. As in the previous example, the organization should use the selection measure only for the nonminority group (taking

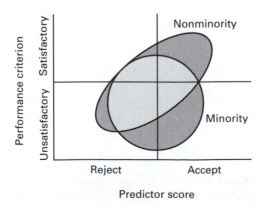

FIGURE 8-8 Unequal criterion means and validity, only for the nonminority group.

into account the caveat above about legal standards) while continuing to search for a predictor that accurately forecasts minority job performance. Recall that the Civil Rights Act of 1991 (see Chapter 2) makes it unlawful to use different cutoff scores on the basis of race, color, religion, sex, or national origin. However, an employer may make test-score adjustments as a consequence of a court-ordered affirmative action plan or where a court approves a conciliation agreement.

In summary, numerous possibilities exist when heterogeneous groups are combined in making predictions. When differential validity exists, the use of a single regression line, cut score, or decision rule can lead to serious errors in prediction. While one legitimately may question the use of race or gender as a variable in selection, the problem is really one of distinguishing between performance on the selection measure and performance on the job (Guion, 1965). If the basis for hiring is expected job performance and if different selection rules are used to improve the prediction of expected job performance rather than to discriminate on the basis of race, gender, and so on, then this procedure appears both legal and appropriate. Nevertheless, the implementation of differential systems is difficult in practice because the fairness of any procedure that uses different standards for different groups is likely to be viewed with suspicion ("More," 1989).

Differential Validity: The Evidence

Let us be clear at the outset that evidence of differential validity provides information only on whether a selection device should be used to make comparisons *within* groups. Evidence of unfair discrimination *between* subgroups cannot be inferred from differences in validity alone; mean job performance also must be considered. In other words, a selection procedure may be fair and yet predict performance inaccurately, or it may discriminate unfairly and yet predict performance within a given subgroup with appreciable accuracy (Kirkpatrick, Ewen, Barrett, & Katzell, 1968).

In discussing differential validity, we must first specify the criteria under which differential validity can be said to exist at all. Thus, Boehm (1972) distinguished between differential and single-group validity. Differential validity exists when (1) there is a significant difference between the validity coefficients obtained for two subgroups (e.g., ethnicity or gender) and (2) the correlations found in one or both of these groups are significantly different from zero. Related to, but different from, differential validity is single-group validity, in which a given predictor exhibits validity significantly different from zero for one group only, and there is no significant difference between the two validity coefficients.

Humphreys (1973) has pointed out that single-group validity is not equivalent to differential validity, nor can it be viewed as a means of assessing differential validity. The logic underlying this distinction is clear: To determine whether two correlations differ from each other, they must be compared directly with each other. In addition, a serious statistical flaw in the single-group validity paradigm is that the sample size is typically smaller for the minority group, which reduces the chances that a statistically significant validity coefficient will be found in this group. Thus, the appropriate statistical test is a test of the null hypothesis of zero difference between the sample-based estimates of the population validity coefficients. However, statistical power is low for such a test, and this makes a Type II error (i.e., not rejecting the null hypothesis when it is false) more likely. Therefore, the researcher who unwisely does not compute statistical power and plans research accordingly is likely to err on the side of *too few* differences. For example, if the true validities in the populations to be compared are .50 and .30, but both are attenuated by a criterion with a reliability of .7, then even without any range restriction at all, one must have 528 persons *in each group* to yield a 90 percent chance of detecting the existing differential validity at alpha = .05 (for more on this, see Trattner & O'Leary, 1980).

The sample sizes typically used in any one study are, therefore, inadequate to provide a meaningful test of the differential validity hypothesis. However, higher statistical power is possible if validity coefficients are cumulated across studies, which can be done using meta-analysis (as discussed in Chapter 7). The bulk of the evidence suggests that statistically significant differential validity is the exception rather than the rule (Schmidt, 1988; Schmidt & Hunter, 1981; Wigdor & Garner, 1982). In a comprehensive review and analysis of 866 black–white employment test validity pairs, Hunter, Schmidt, and Hunter (1979) concluded that findings of apparent differential validity in samples are produced by the operation of chance and a number of statistical artifacts. True differential validity probably does not exist. In addition, no support was found for the suggestion by Boehm (1972) and Bray and Moses (1972) that findings of validity differences by race are associated with the use of subjective criteria (ratings, rankings, etc.) and that validity differences seldom occur when more objective criteria are used.

Similar analyses of 1,337 pairs of validity coefficients from employment and educational tests for Hispanic Americans showed no evidence of differential validity (Schmidt, Pearlman, & Hunter, 1980). Differential validity for males and females also has been examined. Schmitt, Mellon, and Bylenga (1978) examined 6,219 pairs of validity coefficients for males and females (predominantly dealing with educational outcomes) and found that validity coefficients for females were slightly (<.05 correlation units), but significantly larger than coefficients for males. Validities for males exceeded those for females only when predictors were less cognitive in nature, such as high school experience variables. Schmitt et al. (1978) concluded: "The magnitude of the difference between male and female validities is very small and may make only trivial differences in most practical situations" (p. 150).

In summary, available research evidence indicates that the existence of differential validity in well-controlled studies is rare. Adequate controls include large enough sample sizes in each subgroup to achieve statistical power of at least .80; selection of predictors based on their logical relevance to the criterion behavior to be predicted; unbiased, relevant, and reliable criteria; and cross-validation of results.

ASSESSING DIFFERENTIAL PREDICTION AND MODERATOR VARIABLES

The possibility of predictive bias in selection procedures is a central issue in any discussion of fairness and EEO. As we noted earlier, these issues require a consideration of the equivalence of prediction systems for different groups. Analyses of possible differences in slopes or intercepts in subgroup regression lines result in more thorough investigations of predictive bias than does analysis of differential validity alone because the overall regression line determines how a test is used for prediction.

Lack of differential validity, in and of itself, does not assure lack of predictive bias. Specifically the *Standards* (AERA, APA, & NCME, 1999) note: "When empirical studies of differential prediction of a criterion for members of different groups are conducted, they should include regression equations (or an appropriate equivalent) computed separately for each group or treatment under consideration or an analysis in which the group or treatment variables are entered as moderator variables" (Standard 7.6, p. 82). In other words, when there is differential prediction based on a grouping variable such as gender or ethnicity, this grouping variable is called a **moderator**. Similarly, the 1978 *Uniform Guidelines on Employee Selection Procedures* (Ledvinka, 1979) adopt what is known as the Cleary (1968) model of test bias:

> A test is biased for members of a subgroup of the population if, in the prediction of a criterion for which the test was designed, consistent nonzero errors of prediction are made for members of the subgroup. In other words, the test is biased if the criterion score predicted from the common regression line is consistently too high or too low for members of the subgroup. With this definition of bias, there may be a connotation of "unfair," particularly if the use of the test produces a prediction that is too low. If the test is used for selection, members of a subgroup may be rejected when they were capable of adequate performance. (p. 115)

In Figure 8-3, although there are two separate ellipses, one for the minority group and one for the nonminority, a single regression line may be cast for both groups. So this test would demonstrate lack of differential prediction or predictive bias. In Figure 8-6, however, the manner in which the position of the regression line is computed clearly does make a difference. If a single regression line is cast for both groups (assuming they are equal in size), criterion scores for the nonminority group consistently will be *underpredicted*, while those of the minority group consistently will be *overpredicted*. In this situation, there is differential prediction, and the use of a single regression line is inappropriate, but it is the nonminority group that is affected adversely. While the slopes of the two regression lines are parallel, the intercepts are different. Therefore, the same predictor score has a different predictive meaning in the two groups. A third situation is presented in Figure 8-8. Here the slopes are not parallel. As we noted earlier, the predictor clearly is inappropriate for the minority group in this situation. When the regression lines are not parallel, the predicted performance scores differ for individuals with identical test scores. Under these circumstances, once it is determined where the regression lines cross, the amount of over- or underprediction depends on the position of a predictor score in its distribution.

So far, we have discussed the issue of differential prediction graphically. However, a more formal statistical procedure is available. As noted in *Principles for the Validation and Use of Personnel Selection Procedures* (SIOP, 2003), "testing for predictive bias involves using moderated multiple regression, where the criterion measure is regressed on the predictor score, subgroup membership, and an interaction term between the two" (p. 32). In symbols, and assuming differential prediction is tested for two groups (e.g., minority and nonminority), the moderated multiple regression (MMR) model is the following:

$$\hat{Y} = a + b_1X + b_2Z + b_3X \cdot Z \qquad \text{(8-1)}$$

where $\hat{Y}$ is the predicted value for the criterion Y, a is the least-squares estimate of the intercept, b_1 is the least-squares estimate of the population regression coefficient for the predictor X, b_2 is the least-squares estimate of the population regression coefficient for the moderator Z, and b_3 is the least-squares estimate of the population regression coefficient for the product term, which carries information about the moderating effect of Z (Aguinis, 2004b). The moderator Z is a categorical variable that represents the binary subgrouping variable under consideration. MMR can also be used for situations involving more than two groups (e.g., three categories based on ethnicity). To do so, it is necessary to include $k - 2$ Z variables (or code variables) in the model, where k is the number of groups being compared.

Aguinis (2004b) described the MMR procedure in detail, covering such issues as the impact of using dummy coding (e.g., minority: 1, nonminority: 0) versus other types of coding on the interpretation of results. Assuming dummy coding is used, the statistical significance of b_3, which tests the null hypothesis that $\beta_3 = 0$, indicates whether the slope of the criterion on the predictor differs across groups. The statistical significance of b_2, which tests the null hypothesis that $\beta_2 = 0$, tests the null hypothesis that groups differ regarding the intercept. Alternatively, one can test whether the addition of the product term to an equation, including the first-order effects of X and Z, only produces a statistically significant increment in the proportion of variance explained for Y (i.e., R^2).

Lautenschlager and Mendoza (1986) noted a difference between the traditional "step-up" approach, consisting of testing whether the addition of the product term improves the prediction of Y above and beyond the first-order effects of X and Z, and a "step-down" approach. The step-down approach consists of making comparisons between the following models (where all terms are as defined for Equation 8-1 above):

$$1: \hat{Y} = a + b_1X$$
$$2: \hat{Y} = a + b_1X + b_2Z + b_3X \cdot Z$$
$$3: \hat{Y} = a + b_1X + b_3X \cdot Z$$
$$4: \hat{Y} = a + b_1X + b_3X \cdot Z$$

First, one can test the overall hypothesis of differential prediction by comparing R^2s resulting from model 1 versus model 2. If there is a statistically significant difference, we then explore whether differential prediction is due to differences in slopes, intercepts, or both. For testing differences in slopes, we compare model 4 with model 2, and, for differences in intercepts, we compare model 3 with model 2. Lautenschlager and Mendoza (1986) used data from a military training school and found that using a step-up approach led to the conclusion that there was differential prediction based on the slopes only, whereas using a step-down approach led to the conclusion that differential prediction existed based on the presence of both different slopes and different intercepts.

Differential Prediction: The Evidence

When prediction systems are compared, slope-based differences are typically not found, and intercept-based differences, if found, are such that they favor members of the minority group (i.e., overprediction of performance for members of the minority group) (Kuncel & Sackett, 2007; Rotundo & Sackett, 1999; Rushton & Jensen, 2005; Sackett & Wilk, 1994; Schmidt & Hunter, 1998; Sackett, Schmitt, Ellingson, & Kablin, 2001). Aguinis, Culpepper, and Pierce (2010) concluded that the same result has been obtained regarding selection tools used in both work and educational settings to assess a diverse set of constructs ranging from general mental abilities (GMAs) to personality and safety suitability. As they noted: "It is thus no exaggeration to assert that the conclusion that test bias generally does not exist but, when it exists, it involves intercept differences favoring minority group members and not slope differences, is an established fact in I/O psychology and related fields concerned with high-stakes testing." For example, Bartlett, Bobko, Mosier, and Hannan (1978) reported results for differential prediction based on 1,190 comparisons indicating the presence of significant slope differences in about 6 percent and significant intercept differences in about 18 percent of the comparisons. In other words, some type of differential prediction was found in about 24 percent of the tests. Most commonly, the prediction system for the nonminority group slightly overpredicted minority group performance. That is, minorities would tend to do less well on the job than their test scores predict, so there is no apparent unfairness against minority group members.

Similar results have been reported by Hartigan and Wigdor (1989). In 72 studies on the General Ability Test Battery (GATB), developed by the U.S. Department of Labor, where there were at least 50 African American and 50 nonminority employees (average sample sizes of 87 and 166, respectively), slope differences occurred less than 3 percent of the time and intercept differences about 37 percent of the time. However, use of a single prediction equation for the total group of applicants would not provide predictions that were biased against African American applicants, for using a single prediction equation slightly overpredicted performance by African Americans. In 220 tests each of the slope and intercept differences between Hispanics and nonminority group members, about 2 percent of the slope differences and about 8 percent of the intercept differences were significant (Schmidt et al., 1980). The trend in the intercept differences was for the Hispanic intercepts to be lower (i.e., overprediction of Hispanic job performance), but firm support for this conclusion was lacking.

With respect to gender differences in performance on physical ability tests, there were no significant differences in prediction systems for males and females in the prediction of performance on outside telephone-craft jobs (Reilly, Zedeck, & Tenopyr, 1979). However, considerable differences were found on both test and performance variables in the relative performances of men and women on a physical ability test for police officers (Arvey, Landon, Nutting, & Maxwell, 1992). If a common regression line was used for selection purposes, then women's job performance would be systematically overpredicted.

Differential prediction has also been examined for tests measuring constructs other than GMAs. For instance, an investigation of three personality composites from the U.S. Army's instrument to predict five dimensions of job performance across nine military jobs found that differential prediction based on sex occurred in about 30 percent of the cases (Saad & Sackett, 2002). Differential prediction was found based on the intercepts, and not the slopes. Overall, there was overprediction of women's scores (i.e., higher intercepts for men). Thus, the result regarding the overprediction of women's performance parallels that of research investigating differential prediction by race in the GMA domain (i.e., there is an overprediction for women as there is overprediction for ethnic minorities).

Could it be that researchers find lack of differential prediction in part because the criteria themselves are biased? Rotundo and Sackett (1999) examined this issue by testing for differential prediction in the ability-performance relationship (as measured using the GATB) in samples of African American and white employees. The data allowed for between-people and within-people comparisons under two conditions: (1) when a white supervisor rated all employees, and (2) when a supervisor of the same self-reported race as each employee assigned the rating. The assumption was that, if performance data are provided by supervisors of the same ethnicity as the employees being rated, the chances that the criteria are biased are minimized or even eliminated. Analyses including 25,937 individuals yielded no evidence of predictive bias against African Americans.

In sum, the preponderance of the evidence indicates an overall lack of differential prediction based on ethnicity and gender for cognitive abilities and other types of tests (Hunter & Schmidt, 2000). When differential prediction is found, results indicate that differences lie in intercept differences and not slope differences across groups and that the intercept differences are such that the performance of women and ethnic minorities is typically overpredicted, which means that the use of test scores supposedly favors these groups.

Problems in Testing for Differential Prediction

In spite of the consistent findings, Aguinis et al. (2010) argued in favor of revival of differential prediction research because research conclusions based on work conducted over five decades on differential prediction may not be warranted. They provided analytic proof that the finding of intercept-based differences favoring minority-group members may be a statistical artifact. Also, empirical evidence gathered over the past two decades suggests that the slope-based test is typically conducted at low levels of statistical power (Aguinis, 1995, 2004b).

Low power for the slope-based test typically results from the use of small samples, but is also due to the interactive effects of various statistical and methodological artifacts such as unreliability, range restriction, and violation of the assumption that error variances are homogeneous (Aguinis & Pierce, 1998a). The net result is a reduction in the size of observed moderating effects vis-à-vis population effects (Aguinis, Beaty, Boik, & Pierce, 2005). In practical terms, low power affects fairness assessment in that one may conclude *incorrectly* that a selection procedure predicts outcomes equally well for various subgroups based on race or sex—that is, that there is no differential relationship. However, this sample-based conclusion may be incorrect. In fact, the selection procedure actually may predict outcomes differentially across subgroups. Such differential prediction may not be detected, however, because of the low statistical power inherent in test validation research.

Consider the impact of a selected set of factors known to affect the power of MMR. Take, for instance, heterogeneity of sample size across groups. In validation research, it is typically the case that the number of individuals in the minority and female groups is smaller than the number of individuals in the majority and male groups. A Monte Carlo simulation demonstrated that in differential prediction tests that included two groups there was a considerable decrease in power when the size of group 1 was .10 relative to total sample size, *regardless of total sample size* (Stone-Romero, Alliger, & Aguinis, 1994). A proportion of .30, closer to the optimum value of .50, also reduced the statistical power of MMR, but to a lesser extent. Another factor known to affect power is heterogeneity of error variance. MMR assumes that the variance in Y that remains after predicting Y from X is equal across k moderator-based subgroups (see Aguinis & Pierce, 1998a, for a review). Violating the homogeneity-of-error variance assumption has been identified as a factor that can affect the power of MMR to detect test unfairness. In each group, the error variance is estimated by the mean square residual from the regression of Y on X:

$$\sigma_{ei}^2 = \sigma_{Y(i)}(1 - \rho_{XY(i)}^2),\tag{8-2}$$

where $\sigma_{Y(i)}$ and $\rho_{XY(i)}$ are the Y standard deviation and the X-Y correlation in each group, respectively. In the presence of a moderating effect in the population, the X-Y correlations for the two moderator-based subgroups differ, and, thus, the error terms necessarily differ.

Heterogeneous error variances can affect both Type I error (*incorrectly* concluding that the selection procedures are unfair) and statistical power. However, Alexander and DeShon (1994) showed that, when the subgroup with the larger sample size is associated with the larger error variance (i.e., the smaller X-Y correlation), statistical power is lowered markedly. Aguinis and Pierce (1998a) noted that this specific scenario, in which the subgroup with the larger n is paired with the smaller correlation coefficient, is the most typical situation in personnel selection research in a variety of organizational settings. As a follow-up study, Aguinis, Petersen, and Pierce (1999) conducted a review of articles that used MMR during 1987 and 1999 in *Academy of Management Journal*, *Journal of Applied Psychology*, and *Personnel Psychology*. Results revealed that violation of the homogeneity-of-variance assumption occurred in approximately 50 percent of the MMR tests! In an examination of error-variance heterogeneity in tests of differential prediction based on the GATB, Oswald, Saad, and Sackett (2000) concluded that enough heterogeneity was found to urge researchers investigating differential prediction to check for compliance with the assumption and consider the possibility of alternative statistical tests when the assumption is violated.

Can we adopt a meta-analytic approach to address the low-power problem of the differential prediction test? Although, in general, meta-analysis can help mitigate the low-power problem, as it has been used for testing differential validity (albeit imperfectly), conducting a meta-analysis of the differential prediction literature is virtually impossible because regression coefficients are referenced to the specific metrics of the scales used in each study. When different measures are used, it is not possible to cumulate regression coefficients across studies, even if the same construct (e.g., general cognitive abilities) is measured. This is why meta-analysts prefer to cumulate correlation coefficients, as opposed to regression coefficients, across studies (Raju, Pappas, & Williams, 1989). One situation where a meta-analysis of differential prediction tests is possible is where the same test is administered to several samples and the test developer has access to the resulting database.

Regarding the intercept-based test, Aguinis et al. (2010) conducted a Monte Carlo simulation including 3,185,000 unique combinations of a wide range of values for intercept- and slope-based test bias in the population, total sample size, proportion of minority group sample size to total sample size, predictor (i.e., preemployment test scores) and criterion (i.e., job performance) reliability, predictor range restriction, correlation between predictor scores and the dummy-coded grouping variable (e.g., ethnicity, gender), and mean difference between predictor scores across groups. Results based on 15 billion 925 million individual samples of scores suggest that intercept-based differences favoring minority group members are likely to be "found" when they do not exist. And, when they exist in the population, they are likely to be exaggerated in the samples used to assess possible test bias. The simulation results indicate that as differences in test scores between the groups increase and test-score reliability decreases, Type I error rates that indicate intercept-based differences favoring minority-group members also increase. In short, for typical conditions in preemployment testing, researchers are likely to conclude that there is intercept-based bias favoring minority group members when this is actually not true or that differences are larger than they are in actuality.

The established conclusions regarding test bias are convenient for test vendors, users, consultants, and researchers. If tests are not biased, or if they favor minority-group members, then the fact that, on average, minority-group members score lower on GMA tests than those of the majority group is not necessarily a hindrance for the use of such tests. As noted by Kehoe (2002), "a critical part of the dilemma is that GMA-based tests are generally regarded as unbiased" (p. 104). If test bias does not exist against members of ethnic minority groups, then adverse impact against ethnic minorities is a defensible position that has formidable social consequences, and the field will continue to try to solve what seems to be an impossible dilemma between validity and adverse impact (Aguinis, 2004c; Ployhart & Holtz, 2008). A cynical approach to testing would be to perpetuate ethnic-based differences regarding GMA such that minority-group members obtain scores on average lower than majority-group members, to continue to develop tests that are less than perfectly reliable, and to assess potential test bias using the accepted Cleary (1968) regression model. This approach would make "the test 'look good' in the sense that it decreases the likelihood of observing an underprediction for the low-scoring group" (Linn & Werts, 1971, p. 3). Such a cynical approach would guarantee that slope-based differences will not be found and, if intercept-based differences are found, they will appear to favor minority-group members. In other words, there would be no charge that tests are biased against ethnic minority-group members.

In short, Aguinis et al. (2010) challenged conclusions based on 40 years of research on test bias in preemployment testing. Their results indicate that the established and accepted procedure to assess test bias is itself biased: Slope-based bias is likely to go undetected, and intercept-based bias favoring minority-group members is likely to be "found" when, in fact, it does not exist. Preemployment testing is often described as the cradle of the I/O psychology field (e.g., Landy & Conte, 2007). These results open up an important opportunity for I/O psychology researchers to revive the topic of test bias and make contributions with measurable and important implications for organizations and society (cf. Griffore, 2007; Helms, 2006).

Suggestions for Improving the Accuracy of Slope-based Differential Prediction Assessment

Fortunately, there are several remedies for the low-power problem of MMR. Table 8-1 lists several factors that lower the power of MMR, together with recommended strategies to address each of these factors. As shown in this table, there are several strategies available, but they come at a cost. Thus, HR researchers should evaluate the practicality of implementing each strategy. Luckily, there are computer programs available online that can be used to compute power before a study is conducted and that allow a researcher to investigate the pros and cons of implementing various scenarios (Aguinis, Boik, & Pierce, 2001; http://mypage.iu. edu/~haguinis/mmr/index.html). For example, one can compute the power resulting from increasing the sample size by 20 percent as compared to increasing the reliability of the predictor scores by increasing the measure's length by 30 percent. Given the cost associated with an increase in sample size vis-à-vis the improvement in predictor reliability, which of these strategies would be more cost-effective in terms of improving power? One thing is clear, however. If one waits until a validation study is finished to start thinking about statistical power for the differential prediction test, then it is probably too late. Statistical power needs to be considered long before the data are collected.

In summary, although it is reassuring to know that differential prediction does not occur often when subgroups are compared, it has been found often enough to create concern for possible predictive bias when a common regression line is used for selection. In addition, recent research has uncovered the fact that numerous statistical artifacts decrease the ability to detect differential prediction, even when it exists in the population. What's the bottom line? Carefully plan a validation study so that the differential prediction test is technically feasible and the results credible.

TABLE 8-1 Recommended Strategies to Minimize the Adverse Effects of Factors Affecting Power of MMR (adapted from Aguinis, 2004b).

Factor Affecting Power	Strategy to Increase Power
Small total sample size	✓ Plan research design so that sample size is sufficiently large to detect the expected effect size. ✓ Compute power under various sample-size scenarios using programs described by Aguinis (2004b) so that sample size is not unnecessarily large, thereby causing an unnecessary expense in terms of time and money (http://mypage.iu.edu/~haguinis/mmr/index.html). ✓ Implement a synthetic validity approach to the differential prediction test (Johnson, Carter, Davison, & Oliver, 2001).
Low preset Type I error	✓ Do not feel obligated to use the conventional .05 level. Use a preset Type I error based on the judgment of the seriousness of a Type I error vis-à-vis the seriousness of a Type II error.
Small moderating effect size	✓ Use sound theory to make predictions about moderating effects as opposed to going on "fishing expeditions." ✓ Compute the observed effect size using computer programs available online (http://mypage.iu.edu/~haguinis/mmr/index.html).
Predictor variable range restriction (Aguinis & Stone-Romero, 1997)	✓ Draw random samples from the population. ✓ Use an extreme-group design (recognizing that sample variance is increased artificially).
Measurement error	✓ Develop and use reliable measures (see Chapter 6).
Scale coarseness (Aguinis, Bommer, & Pierce, 1996)	✓ Use a continuous criterion scale; this can be done by recording responses on a graphic line segment and then measuring them manually or by using the program CAQ (available at http://mypage.iu.edu/~haguinis/mmr/index.html) or other programs that prompt respondents to indicate their answers by clicking on a graphic line segment displayed on the screen.
Heterogeneous sample size across moderator-based subgroups (Stone-Romero, Alliger, & Aguinis, 1994)	✓ Equalize the sample sizes across subgroups by oversampling from the smaller groups (done at the expense of a resulting nonrepresentative sample). Thus, the significance test will be more accurate, but the effect size will not.
Small validity coefficient	✓ Use sound theory to identify a predictor that is strongly related to the criterion because the validity coefficient (i.e., r_{xy}) is positively related to statistical power.
Heterogeneity of error variance	✓ Check for compliance with assumption, and, if assumption is violated, use alternative statistics. Computer programs are available to perform these tasks (http://mypage.iu.edu/~haguinis/mmr/index.html).

FURTHER CONSIDERATIONS REGARDING ADVERSE IMPACT, DIFFERENTIAL VALIDITY, AND DIFFERENTIAL PREDICTION

As noted above, the *Uniform Guidelines* (1978) recommend the conduct of adverse impact analysis using the "80 percent rule" as a criterion. Assume that the adverse impact ratio is $SR_1/SR_2 = .60$. In this example, we have observed adverse impact in the sample (i.e., .60 is smaller than the recommended .80 ratio). However, the interest is in whether there is adverse impact in the population and whether we can continue to use the test with subsequent applicants. Statistical significance procedures are available to test whether the adverse-impact ratio is different from .80 in the population. Morris and Lobsenz (2000) proposed a new significance test that is based on the same effect size as the 80 percent rule (i.e., a proportion). However, the statistical power for this test, as well as for the frequently used z statistic based on the normal distribution, is low. Accordingly, Collins and Morris (2008) conducted a computer simulation to compare various statistical tools available, including the widely used z-test on the difference between two proportions, a test proposed by Upton (1982), the Fisher Exact Test, and Yates's continuity-corrected chi-square test. Overall, all tests performed poorly in terms of their ability to detect adverse impact in small-sample-size situations; the z-test performed reasonably well, but it also did not perform well when sample size was very small. Given these results, when reporting adverse impact, one should also report a population estimate of the adverse impact ratio along with a confidence interval indicating the degree of precision in the estimate.

The previous section on validity and adverse impact illustrated that a test can be valid and yet yield adverse impact simultaneously. So the presence of adverse impact is not a sufficient basis for a claim of unfair discrimination (Drasgow, 1987). However, apparent, but false nondiscrimination may occur when the measure of job success is itself biased in the same direction as the effects of ethnic background on predictor performance (Green, 1975). Consequently, a selection measure is unfairly discriminatory when some specified group performs less well than a comparison group on the measure, but performs just as well as the comparison group on the job for which the selection measure is a predictor. This is precisely what is meant by differential prediction or predictive bias (i.e., different regression lines across groups based on the intercepts, the slopes, or both).

We hasten to emphasize, however, that the very same factors that depress predictor performance (e.g., verbal ability, spatial relations ability) also may depress job performance. In this case, slopes may be identical across groups, and only intercepts will differ (i.e., there are differences in the mean test scores across groups). Gottfredson (1988) summarized the following problem based on the finding that the mean score in cognitive ability tests is typically lower for African Americans and Hispanics as compared to whites: "The vulnerability of tests is due less to their limitations for measuring important differences than it is to their very success in doing so. . . . The more valid the tests are as measures of general cognitive ability, the larger the average group differences in test scores they produce" (p. 294). Given differences in mean scores for cognitive abilities tests across subgroups, and the consequent adverse impact, does this statement mean that there is an inescapable trade-off between validity and adverse impact?

Fortunately the belief that there is a negative relationship between validity and adverse impact is incorrect in many situations. Specifically, Maxwell and Arvey (1993) demonstrated mathematically that, as long as a test does not demonstrate differential prediction, the most valid selection method will *necessarily* produce the least adverse impact. Hence to minimize adverse impact, HR researchers should strive to produce unbiased, valid tests. However, a problem occurs when, unbeknownst to test users and developers, a test is biased and it is nevertheless put to use. Aguinis and Smith (2007) developed algorithms and a computer program that allow users to enter information on a test, including mean scores for each of the groups (e.g., women and men), mean criterion scores for each of the groups, and means and standard deviations for test and criterion scores. Based on this information, the algorithms estimate whether, and the extent to which, using a test that may be biased is likely to lead to selection errors and adverse impact. Figure 8-9 includes a screen shot of illustrative input and output screens for the program, which is available online at http://mypage.iu.edu/~haguinis/mmr/index.html.

The application of the Aguinis and Smith (2007) integrative framework to tests in actual selection contexts allows test developers and employers to understand selection-decision consequences before a test is put to use. That procedure allows for an estimation of practically meaningful consequences (e.g., expected selection errors and expected adverse impact) of using a particular test *regardless of the results of the test-bias assessment*. Thus, this framework and program allows for an understanding of the practical significance of potential test bias regardless of the statistical significance results that often lead to Type II errors.

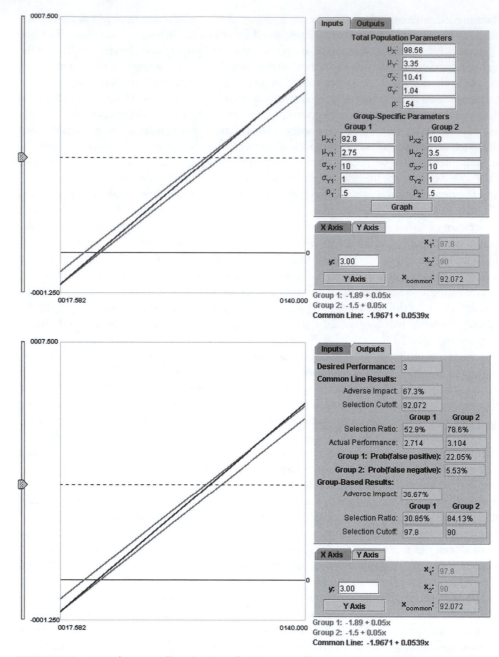

FIGURE 8-9 Input (top panel) and output (bottom panel) screens for computer program that implements all required calculations to estimate resulting prediction errors and adverse impact from using a test that is believed to be unbiased but is actually biased. *Source*: Aguinis, H., & Smith, M. A. (2007). Understanding the impact of test validity and bias on selection errors and adverse impact in human resource selection. *Personnel Psychology*, 60, 165–199. This program is available online at http://mypage.iu.edu/~haguinis/mmr/index.html

It is true that adverse impact based on ethnicity has been found for some types of tests, particularly for tests of cognitive abilities (Outtz, 2002; more information on this issue is included in Chapter 12). Moreover, a similar pattern of differences has been found for other tests, particularly those that have a cognitive component (e.g., Whetzel, McDaniel, & Nguyen, 2008). As noted earlier, this does not mean that these tests are discriminating unfairly. However, using tests with adverse impact can lead to negative organizational and societal consequences and perceptions of test unfairness on the part of important population segments, particularly given that demographic trends indicate that three states (California, Hawaii, and New Mexico) and the District of Columbia now have majority "minority" populations (Hobbs & Stoops, 2002). Such perceptions can damage the image of cognitive abilities testing in particular and personnel psychology in general. Thus, the *Uniform Guidelines* (1978) recommend that, when adverse impact is found, HR specialists strive to use alternative tests with similar levels of validity, but less adverse impact. That is easier said than done. Practically speaking, it would be more efficient to reduce adverse impact by using available testing procedures. How can this be accomplished? The following strategies are available before, during, and after test administration (Hough, Oswald, & Ployhart, 2001; Ployhart & Holtz, 2008; Sackett et al., 2001):

- *Improve the recruiting strategy for minorities.* Adverse impact depends on the selection ratio in each group, and the selection ratio depends on the number of applicants. So the larger the pool of qualified applicants in the minority group, the higher the selection ratio, and the lower the probability of adverse impact. However, attracting qualified minorities may be difficult. For example, in a controlled study including university students, African Americans who viewed a recruitment advertisement were attracted by diversity, but only when it extended to supervisory-level positions. More important, the effect of ethnicity on reactions to diversity in advertisements was contingent on the viewer's openness to racial diversity (other-group orientation) (Avery, 2003). One way to improve recruiting efforts is to implement affirmative action policies. Affirmative action is defined as "any measure, beyond simple termination of a discriminatory practice, adopted to correct or compensate for past or present discrimination or to prevent discrimination from recurring in the future" (United States Commission on Civil Rights, 1977). Note, however, that affirmative action is usually resisted when it is based primarily on giving preference to ethnic minority group members. Also, preferential forms of affirmative action are usually illegal. Thus, the implementation of nonpreferential approaches to affirmative action including targeted recruiting and diversity management programs are more likely to be successful in attracting, selecting, including, and retaining underrepresented group members (Kravitz, 2008).
- *Use cognitive abilities in combination with noncognitive predictors.* The largest differences between ethnic groups in mean scores result from measures of general cognitive abilities. Thus, adverse impact can be reduced by using additional noncognitive predictors such as biodata, personality inventories, and the structured interview as part of a test battery. The use of additional noncognitive predictors may not only reduce adverse impact but also increase the overall validity of the testing process (Schmitt, Rogers, Chan, Sheppard, & Jennings, 1997). Note, however, that in some cases the addition of predictors such as personality inventories may not help mitigate adverse impact by much (Foldes, Duehr, & Ones, 2008; Potosky, Bobko, & Roth, 2005).
- *Use multiple regression and other methods for combining predictors into a composite.* As a follow-up to the previous recommendation, the traditional way to combine predictors into a composite is to use multiple regression. However, De Corte, Lievens, and Sackett (2007, 2008) proposed a new method to determine the set of predictors that will lead to the optimal trade-off between validity and adverse impact issues. The newly proposed approach does not always lead to the same set of predictors that would be selected using the more traditional multiple regression approach. In spite of its promising results, be aware that organizations may wish to include considerations other than validity in the decision making process (Kehoe, 2008). Moreover, the newly proposed approach may not be acceptable because it can be seen as a method that requires that organizations give up some validity to hopefully achieve some reduction in adverse impact (Potosky, Bobko, & Roth, 2008).
- *Use measures of specific, as opposed to only general, cognitive abilities.* Although large mean differences have been found for general cognitive abilities, differences are smaller for specific abilities such as reasoning and quantitative ability. Especially for jobs high on job complexity, one could use more specific types of cognitive abilities as predictors (Lubinski, 2000).

- *Use differential weighting for the various criterion facets,* giving less weight to criterion facets that require more general cognitive abilities. As we discussed in Chapter 4, job performance is a multidimensional construct. Certain criterion dimensions are less general-cognitive-ability-laden than others (e.g., contextual performance may be less cognitive ability laden than certain aspects of task performance). Assigning less weight to the performance facets that are more heavily related to general cognitive abilities, and, therefore, demonstrate the largest between-group differences, is likely to result in a prediction system that produces less adverse impact (Hattrup, Rock, & Scalia, 1997).
- *Use alternate modes of presenting test stimuli.* Subgroup differences result, at least in part, from the verbal and reading components present in paper-and-pencil test administrations. Thus, using formats that do not have heavy reading and verbal requirements, such as video-based tests or noncognitively loaded work samples (i.e., when the subject actually performs a manual task as opposed to describing verbally how he or she would perform it) is likely to lead to less adverse impact (Chan & Schmitt, 1997).
- *Enhance face validity.* Face validity is not a technical term; it is the extent to which applicants believe test scores are valid, regardless of whether they are actually valid. If certain groups have lower perceptions of test validity, their motivation, and subsequent test performance, is likely to be reduced as well (Chan, Schmitt, DeShon, Clause, & Delbridge, 1997; Ryan, 2001). For example, results based on a study including 197 undergraduate students who took a cognitive ability test indicated that (1) pretest reactions affected test performance, and (2) pretest reactions mediated the relationship between belief in tests and test performance (Chan, Schmitt, Sacco, & DeShon, 1998). Under certain conditions, increasing motivation can help reduce adverse impact (Ployhart & Ehrhart, 2002). We will return to issues about perceptions of test fairness and interpersonal issues in employment selection later in this chapter. However, our recommendation is simple: Strive to develop tests that are acceptable to and perceived to be valid by all test takers.
- *Implement test-score banding to select among the applicants.* Tests are never perfectly reliable, and the relationship between test scores and criteria is never perfect. Test-score banding is a decision-making process that is based on these two premises. This method for reducing adverse impact has generated substantial controversy (Campion et al., 2001). In fact, an entire book has been published recently on the topic (Aguinis, 2004c). We discuss test-score banding in detail below.

In closing, adverse impact may occur even when there is no differential validity across groups. However, the presence of adverse impact is likely to be concurrent with the differential prediction test, and specifically with differences in intercepts. HR specialists should make every effort to minimize adverse impact, not only because adverse impact is likely to lead to higher levels of scrutiny from a legal standpoint, but also because the use of tests with adverse impact can have negative consequences for the organization in question, its customers, and society in general.

Minimizing Adverse Impact Through Test-Score Banding

The concept of fairness is not limited to the technical definition of lack of differential prediction. The *Standards* (AERA, APA, & NCME, 1999) expressed it well: "A full consideration of fairness would explore the many functions of testing in relation to its many goals, including the broad goal of achieving equality of opportunity in our society" (p. 73). Test-score banding, a method for referring candidates for selection, addresses this broader goal of test fairness, as well as the appropriateness of the test-based constructs or rules that underlie decision making—that is, distributive justice.

HR specialists are sometimes faced with a paradoxical situation: The use of cognitive abilities and other valid predictors of job performance leads to adverse impact (Schmidt, 1993). If there is a true correlation between test scores and job performance, the use of any strategy other than strict top–down referral results in some expected loss in performance (assuming the out-of-order selection is not based on secondary criteria that are themselves correlated with performance). Thus, choosing predictors that maximize economic utility (as it is typically conceptualized in human resources management and industrial and organizational psychology; Schmidt, 1991) often leads to the exclusion of members of protected groups (Sackett & Wilk, 1994). For some employers that are trying to increase the diversity of their workforces, this may lead to a dilemma: possible loss of some economic utility in order to accomplish broader social objectives.

Cascio, Outtz, Zedeck, and Goldstein (1991) proposed the **sliding-band method** as a way to incorporate both utility and adverse impact considerations in the personnel selection process. It is an attempt to reconcile economic and social objectives within the framework of generally accepted procedures for testing hypotheses about differences in individual test scores. The sliding-band model is one of a class of approaches to test use (banding) in which individuals within a specific score range, or band, are regarded as having equivalent scores. It does not correct for very real differences in test scores that may be observed among groups; it only allows for flexibility in decision making.

The sliding-band model is based on the assumption that no test is perfectly reliable; hence, error is present, to some degree, in all test scores. While the reliability coefficient is an index of the amount of error that is present in the test as a whole, and the standard error of measurement (σ_{Meas} or SEM) allows us to establish limits for the true score of an individual who achieves a given observed score, the standard error of the difference (SED) allows us to determine whether the true scores of two individuals differ from each other.

Based on the reliability estimate of the test, Cascio et al. (1991) proposed the following equation to compute bandwidths:

$$C \cdot \text{SED} = C \cdot \text{SEM} \sqrt{2} = C \cdot s_x \cdot \sqrt{1 - r_{xx}} \sqrt{2} \qquad \text{(8-3)}$$

where C is the standard score indicating the desired level of confidence (e.g., 1.96 indicates a 95 percent confidence interval, and 1.00 indicates a 68 percent confidence interval), s_x is the standard deviation of the test, and r_{xx} is the internal consistency of the test measured on a continuous scale. Substantively, $s_x \cdot \sqrt{1 - r_{xx}}$ is the SEM of the test (computed using sample-based statistics), and $s_x \cdot \sqrt{1 - r_{xx}} \sqrt{2}$ is the SED between two scores on the test. Depending on the relative risk of a Type I or Type II error that an investigator is willing to tolerate, he or she may establish a confidence interval of any desired width (e.g., 95, 90, or 68 percent) by changing the value for C (e.g., 1.96 corresponds to the .05 level of chance) (for more on this, see Zedeck, Cascio, Goldstein, & Outtz, 1996). Banding makes use of this psychometric information to set a cut score. For example, suppose the value of $C \cdot \text{SED} = 7$ points. If the difference between the top score and any observed score is 7 points or fewer, then the scores are considered to be statistically indistinguishable from each other, whereas scores that differ by 8 points or greater are considered distinguishable.

To illustrate, scores of 90 and 83 would not be considered to be different from each other, but scores of 90 and 82 would be. The SED, therefore, serves as an index for testing hypotheses about ability differences among individuals.

The sliding-band procedure works as follows. Beginning with the top score in a band (the score that ordinarily would be chosen first in a top–down selection procedure), a band— say, 1 or 2 SEDs wide—is created. Scores that fall within the band are considered not to differ significantly from the top score in the band, within the limits of measurement error. If the scores are not different from the top score (in effect, they are treated as tied), then secondary criteria (e.g., experience, training, performance, or diversity-based considerations) might be used to break the ties and to determine which candidates should be referred for selection.

When the top scorer within a band is chosen and applicants still need to be selected, then the band slides such that the next highest scorer becomes the referent. A new band is selected by subtracting 7 points from the remaining highest scorer. If the top scorer is not chosen, then the band cannot slide, and any additional selections must be made from within the original band. This is a *minimax* strategy. That is, by proceeding in a top–down fashion, though not selecting in strict rank order, employers can minimize the maximum loss in utility, relative to top–down selection.

Aguinis, Cortina, and Goldberg (1998) proposed an extension of the Cascio et al. (1991) procedure that incorporates not only reliability information for the predictor but also reliability information for the criterion and the explicit relationship between the predictor and criterion scores. This **criterion-referenced banding model** was proposed because Equation 8-3 does not explicitly consider the precise predictor–criterion relationship and operates under the assumption that there is an acceptable level of useful empirical or content validity. Accordingly, based on this "acceptable validity" premise, equivalence regarding predictor scores is equated with equivalence regarding criterion scores. However, few preemployment tests explain more than one-quarter of the variance in a given criterion. Thus, the assumption that two applicants who are indistinguishable (i.e., who fall within the same band) or distinguishable (i.e., who do not fall within the same band) regarding the predictor construct are also indistinguishable or distinguishable regarding the criterion construct may not be tenable (Aguinis, Cortina, & Goldberg, 1998, 2000).

Consider the following illustration provided by Aguinis et al. (1998) regarding a predictor with $r_{xx} = .80$ and $s_x = 5$. Suppose for purposes of illustration that this predictor's correlation with a measure of job performance is zero (i.e., $r_{xy} = 0$). In this case, if $C = 2.00$, the band width computed using Equation 8-2 is 6.32, or 1.26 standard deviation units (SDs). Thus, the applicants within this band would be treated as equivalent, and selection among these "equivalent" people could be made on the basis of other factors (e.g., organizational diversity needs). However, note that in this example the predictor is unrelated to job performance. Thus, the applicants within a particular band are no more likely to perform well on the job than are the applicants outside the band. Hence, the band can be misleading in that it offers a rationale for distinguishing between two groups of applicants (i.e., those within the band and those outside the band) that should be indistinguishable with respect to the variable of ultimate interest—namely, job performance. This is extreme and unrealistic case in which $r_{xy} = 0$, but similar arguments can be made with respect to the more typical predictors with small (but nonzero) validities.

The computation of criterion-referenced bands includes the following three steps. For Step 1, Equation 8-3 is used to compute the width of a band of statistically indistinguishable scores on a *performance* measure:

$$C \cdot s_y \cdot \sqrt{1 - r_{yy}} \sqrt{2} \tag{8-4}$$

Second, for Step 2, the upper and lower limits on the band for Y are determined. The upper limit is determined by obtaining the predicted performance value corresponding to the highest observed predictor score. This can be done by solving $\hat{Y}_{upper} = a + b \cdot X_{max}$, or if the data are standardized, by solving $\hat{Y}_{upper} = r_{xy} \cdot X_{max}$. The lower limit (i.e., $\hat{Y}_{lower}$) is obtained by subtracting the band width from the upper limit.

What remains for Step 3 is the identification of a band of X scores that corresponds to the band of indistinguishable scores on Y identified in Step 2. To do so, the unstandardized regression equation is used to identify the predictor scores that would produce predicted job performance scores equal to the upper and lower limits of the criterion band. Stated differently the regression equation is used to identify the predictor scores that, if entered in the regression equation, would yield predicted values of Y equal to the band limits established in Step 2. Thus, given $\hat{Y}_{upper} = a + b \cdot \hat{X}_{upper}$, we can solve for $\hat{X}_{upper} = (\hat{Y}_{upper} - a)/b$ and similarly, $\hat{X}_{lower} = (\hat{Y}_{lower} - a)/b$.

Aguinis et al. (2000) provided a detailed comparison of predictor-referenced bands (Cascio et al., 1991) and criterion-referenced bands (Aguinis et al., 1998) and highlighted the following differences:

1. *Use of validity evidence.*   There is a difference in the use of validity evidence between the two approaches to banding, and this difference drives differences in the computation of bands.

The criterion-referenced banding procedure allows for the inclusion of criterion-related validity information in the computation of bands when this information is available. However, criterion data may not be available in all situations, and, thus, predictor-referenced bands may be the only option in many situations.

2. **Bandwidth.** Criterion-referenced bands produce wider bands than predictor-referenced bands. Wider bands may decrease the economic utility of the test, but also decrease the number of "false negatives" (i.e., potentially successful applicants that are screened out). As demonstrated empirically by Laczo and Sackett (2004), minority selection is much higher when banding on the criterion than when banding on the predictor. However, predicted job performance is substantially lower. Thus, the usefulness of criterion-referenced bands in increasing minority hiring should be balanced against lower predicted performance (Laczo & Sackett, 2004).

3. **Inclusion of criterion information.** The criterion-referenced procedure makes use of available criterion data, which are likely to be imperfect (e.g., may be deficient). On the other hand, the predictor-referenced method does not include criterion data in computing bandwidth.

4. **Use of reliability information.** As discussed in Chapter 7, the use of various reliability estimates can have profound effects on resulting corrected validity coefficients. Similarly, the use of various reliability estimates can have a profound impact on bandwidth. In the case of predictor-referenced bands, only one reliability coefficient is needed (i.e., that for predictor scores only), whereas in criterion-referenced bands two reliability coefficients (i.e., predictor and criterion) are required. Hence criterion-referenced bands require additional decision making on the part of the HR specialist.

Does banding work? Does it achieve a balance between maximizing test utility and increasing diversity? What are the reactions of individuals who may be seen as receiving "preferential treatment"? Is banding legally acceptable? These are issues of heated debate in the scientific literature, as well as the legal system. In fact, an entire volume has been devoted to technical, societal, and legal issues regarding banding (Aguinis, 2004a). This volume clearly shows that HR practitioners and scholars in favor of and against the use of banding to interpret test scores hold very strong opinions. For example, Schmidt and Hunter (2004) argued that banding is internally logically contradictory and thus scientifically unacceptable. In their view, banding violates scientific and intellectual values, and, therefore, its potential use presents selection specialists with the choice of embracing the "values of science" or "other important values." Guion (2004) offered reasons why the topic of banding is so controversial (e.g., the emotionally charged topic of affirmative action, potential conflict between research and organizational goals), and Cascio, Goldstein, Outtz, and Zedeck (2004) offered counterarguments addressing 18 objections raised against the use of banding, including objections regarding measurement, scientific validity, statistical, and legal issues, among others. Laczo and Sackett (2004) studied expected outcomes (e.g., utility, diversity considerations) resulting from the adoption of different selection rules including eight selection strategies (i.e., top–down and various forms of banding). On a related issue, Schmitt and Oswald (2004) addressed the question of how much importance is being placed on (1) the construct underlying test scores (e.g., general cognitive ability) and on (2) secondary criteria used in banding (e.g., ethnicity) in the selection decision, and examined the outcomes of such decisions.

In the end, as noted by Murphy (2004), whether an organization or individual supports the use of banding is likely to reflect broader conflicts in interests, values, and assumptions about human resource selection. For example, self-interest (i.e., the link between banding and affirmative action and whether the use of banding is likely to improve or diminish one's chances of being selected for a job) has been found to be related to reactions to banding (Truxillo & Bauer, 1999). Another consideration is that, ironically, implementing banding can lead to negative consequences precisely for the individuals that banding is intending to benefit the most (i.e., women, members of ethnic minority groups). For example, Heilman, Simon, and Repper (1987) found that women who believed they were selected for a leadership position primarily on the basis of their gender rather than merit reported negative self-perceptions. More recent research has shown that these deleterious effects may be weakening and may also not apply to members of ethnic minorities (Stewart & Shapiro, 2000).

Based on competing goals and various anticipated outcomes of implementing banding, Murphy (2004) suggested the need to develop methods to help organizations answer questions about the difficult comparison between and relative importance of efficiency and equity. Such a method was offered by Aguinis and Harden (2004), who proposed multiattribute utility analysis as a tool for deciding whether banding or top–down selection may be a better strategy for a specific organization in a specific context. Although time consuming, this method allows for the explicit consideration of competing values and goals in making the decision whether to implement banding.

While adverse impact may still result even when banding is used, characteristics of the applicant pool (the proportion of the applicant pool from the lower-scoring group), differences in subgroup standard deviations and means, and test reliability all combine to determine the impact of the method in any given situation. Nevertheless, in its position paper on banding, the Scientific Affairs Committee of the Society for Industrial and Organizational Psychology (SIOP, 1994) concluded:

> The basic premise behind banding is consistent with psychometric theory. Small differences in test scores might reasonably be due to measurement error, and a case can be made on the basis of classical measurement theory for a selection system that ignores such small differences, or at least does not allow small differences in test scores to trump all other considerations in ranking individuals for hiring. (p. 82)
>
> There is legitimate scientific justification for the position that small differences in test scores might not imply meaningful differences in either the construct measured by the test or in future job performance. (p. 85)

Finally, from a legal standpoint, courts in multiple jurisdictions and at multiple levels have endorsed the concept of banding and the use of secondary criteria, although Barrett and Lueke (2004) argued that these decisions applied to specific circumstances only (e.g., consent decree to remedy past discrimination because banding may reduce adverse impact). For example, a ruling by the Ninth Circuit Court of Appeals ("Officers for Justice v. Civil Service Commission of the City and County of San Francisco," 1993) approved the use of banding in a case where secondary criteria were used. The court concluded:

> The City in concert with the union, minority job applicants, and the court finally devised a selection process which offers a facially neutral way to interpret actual scores and reduce adverse impact on minority candidates while preserving merit as the primary criterion for selection. Today we hold that the banding process is valid as a matter of constitutional and federal law. (p. 9055)

More recently, in a May 2001 ruling, the Seventh Circuit Court of Appeals issued the following decision in *Chicago Firefighters Local 2 v. City of Chicago*:

> If the average black score on a test was 100 and the average white score 110, rescoring the average black tests as 110 would be forbidden race norming; likewise if, regardless of relative means, each black's score was increased by 10 points on account of his race, perhaps because it was believed that a black with a 10-point lower score than a white could perform the job just as well (in other words that blacks are better workers than test takers). What the City actually did was to "band" scores on the various promotional exams that the plaintiffs challenge, and treat scores falling within each band as identical.

So, for example, if 92 and 93 were both in the A band, a black who scored 92 would be deemed to have the same score as a white who scored 93. . . .

We have no doubt that if banding were adopted in order to make lower black scores seem higher, it would indeed be a form of race norming, and therefore forbidden. But it is not race norming per se. In fact it's a universal and normally unquestioned method of simplifying scoring by eliminating meaningless grada- tions. . . . The narrower the range of abilities in a group being tested, the more attractive banding is. If the skill difference between someone who gets 200 questions right and someone else who gets 199 right is trivial to the point of being meaning- less, then giving them different grades is misleading rather than illuminating. . . . Banding in this sense does not discriminate invidiously between a student who would have gotten 85 in a number-grading system and a student who would have gotten 84 in such a system, just because now both get B. (pp. 9–10)

FAIRNESS AND THE INTERPERSONAL CONTEXT OF EMPLOYMENT TESTING

Although thus far we have emphasized mostly technical issues around test fairness, we should not minimize the importance of social and interpersonal processes in test settings. As noted by the *Standards* (AERA, APA, & NCME, 1999), "[t]he interaction of examiner with examinee should be professional, courteous, caring, and respectful. . . . Attention to these aspects of test use and interpretation is no less important than more technical concerns" (p. 73).

An organization's adherence to fairness rules is not required simply because this is part of good professional practice. When applicants and examinees perceive unfairness in the testing procedures, their perceptions of the organization and their perceptions of the testing procedures can be affected negatively (Gilliland, 1993). In addition, perceptions of unfairness (even when testing procedures are technically fair) are likely to motivate test takers to initiate litigation (Goldman, 2001). To understand the fairness and impact of the selection system in place, there- fore, it is necessary not only to conduct technical analyses on the data but also to take into account the perceptions of people who are subjected to the system (Elkins & Phillips, 2000).

From the perspective of applicants and test takers, there are two dimensions of fairness: (1) distributive (i.e., perceptions of fairness of the outcomes) and (2) procedural (i.e., perceptions of fairness of the procedures used to reach a hiring decision). Regarding the distributive aspect, percep- tions are affected based on whether the outcome is seen as favorable. When applicants perceive that their performance on a test has not been adequate or they are not selected for a job, they are likely to perceive that the situation is unfair (Chan, Schmitt, Jennings, Clause, & Delbridge, 1998). Obviously, the impact of this self-serving bias mechanism may be unavoidable in most employment settings in which the goal of the system is precisely to hire some applicants and not others. However, a study including 494 actual applicants for an entry-level state police trooper position found that procedural fairness seems to have a greater impact on individuals' overall fairness perceptions as compared to perceived test performance (Chan et al., 1998). Moreover, applicants' personality profiles are also related to their perceptions of fairness such as those higher on *neuroticism* tend to have more negative perceptions, and those higher on *agreeableness* tend to have more positive perceptions (Truxillo, Bauer, Campion, & Paronto, 2006).

Fortunately, employers do have control of the procedures implemented and can, therefore, improve the perceived fairness of the testing process. For example, Truxillo, Bauer, Campion, and Paronto (2002) conducted a study using police-recruit applicants. Some applicants saw a five-minute videotape and a written flyer before taking the test, whereas others did not. The videotape emphasized that the test was job related (e.g., "it is predictive of how well a person will perform as a police officer"). Those applicants who were exposed to the videotape and written flyer rated the test as being more fair, and they were less likely to rate the process as unfair even *after* they received the test results. Thus, a simple and relatively inexpensive procedural change in the selection process was able to improve applicants' perceptions of fairness.

In summary, although tests may be technically fair and lack predictive bias, the process of implementing testing and making selection decisions can be such that applicants, nevertheless, perceive unfairness. Such perceptions of unfairness are associated with negative outcomes for the organization as well as for the test taker (e.g., lower self-efficacy). In closing, as noted by the *Standards* (AERA, APA, & NCME, 1999), "fair and equitable treatment of test takers involves providing, in advance of testing, information about the nature of the test, the intended use of test scores, and the confidentiality of the results" (p. 85). Such procedures will help mitigate the negative emotions, including perceptions of unfairness, that are held by those individuals who are not offered employment because of insufficient test performance.

FAIR EMPLOYMENT AND PUBLIC POLICY

Social critics often have focused on written tests as the primary vehicles for unfair discrimination in employment, but it is important to stress that no single employment practice (such as testing) can be viewed apart from its role in the total system of employment decisions. Those who do so suffer from social myopia and, by implication, assume that, if only testing can be rooted out, unfair discrimination likewise will disappear—much as the surgeon's scalpel cuts out the tumor that threatens the patient's life.

Yet unfair discrimination is a persistent infirmity that often pervades all aspects of the employment relationship. It shows itself in company recruitment practices (e.g., exhibiting passive nondiscrimination), selection practices (e.g., requiring an advanced degree for a clerical position or using an inordinately difficult or unvalidated test for hiring or promotion), compensation (e.g., paying lower wages to similarly qualified women or minorities than to white men for the same work), placement (e.g., "channeling" members of certain groups into the least desirable jobs), training and orientation (e.g., refusing to provide in-depth job training or orientation for minorities), and performance management (e.g., permitting bias in supervisory ratings or giving less frequent and lower-quality feedback to members of minority groups). In short, unfair discrimination is hardly endemic to employment testing, although testing is certainly a visible target for public attack.

Public interest in measurement embraces three essential functions: (1) diagnosing needs (in order to implement remedial programs), (2) assessing qualifications to *do* (as in employment contexts), and (3) protecting against false credentials. Each of these functions has a long history. A sixteenth-century Spanish document requiring that tests be used to determine admission to specialized courses of study refers to each one (Casteen, 1984).

Over the past three decades, we have moved from naive acceptance of tests (because they are part of the way things are), through a period of intense hostility to tests (because they are said to reflect the way things are to a degree not compatible with our social principles), to a higher acceptance of tests (because we seek salvation in a time of doubt about the quality of our schools, our workers, and, indeed, about ourselves) (Casteen, 1984).

Tests and other selection procedures are useful to society because society must allocate opportunities. Specialized roles must be filled. Through educational classification and employment selection, tests help determine who gains affluence and influence (Cronbach, 1990). Tests serve as instruments of public policy, and public policy must be reevaluated periodically. Indeed, each generation must think carefully about the meaning of the words "equal opportunity." Should especially rich opportunity be given to those whose homes have done least for them? What evidence about individuals should enter into selection decisions? And, once the evidence becomes available, what policies should govern how decisions are made?

To be sure, answers to questions like these are difficult; of necessity, they will vary from generation to generation. But one thing is clear: Sound policy is not *for* tests or *against* tests; what really matters is how tests are *used* (Cronbach, 1990). From a public-policy perspective, the Congress, the Supreme Court, the Equal Employment Opportunity Commission, and the Office of Federal Contract Compliance Programs continuously have reaffirmed the substantial benefits to be derived from the informed and judicious use of staffing procedures within the framework of fair employment practices. (For more on this, see Sharf, 1988.)

Although some errors are inevitable in employment decisions, the crucial question to be asked in regard to each procedure is whether or not its use results in less social cost than is now being paid for these errors, considering all other assessment methods. After carefully reviewing all available evidence on eight alternatives to tests, Reilly and Chao (1982) concluded: "Test fairness research has, with few exceptions, supported the predictability of minority groups even though adverse impact exists. . . . There is no reason to expect alternate predictors to behave differently" (p. 55). As Schmidt (1988) has pointed out, however, "alternatives" are actually misnamed. If they are valid, they should be used in combination with ability measures to maximize overall validity. Thus, they are more appropriately termed "supplements" rather than "alternatives." Indeed, a synthesis of several meta-analytic reviews has suggested just that: The use of cognitive abilities tests in combination with other predictors provides the highest level of accuracy in predicting future performance (Schmidt & Hunter, 1998).

Finally, in reviewing 50 years of public controversy over psychological testing, Cronbach (1975) concluded:

> The spokesmen for tests, then and recently, were convinced that they were improving social efficiency, not making choices about social philosophy. . . . The social scientist is trained to think that he does not know all the answers. The social scientist is not trained to realize that he does not know all the questions. And that is why his social influence is not unfailingly constructive. (p. 13)

As far as the future is concerned, it is our position that staffing procedures will yield better and fairer results when we can specify in detail the linkages between the personal characteristics of individuals and the requirements of jobs for which the procedures are most relevant, taking contextual factors into consideration (i.e., *in situ* performance; Cascio & Aguinis, 2008). The inevitable result can only be a better informed, wiser use of available human resources.

Evidence-Based Implications for Practice

- Fairness is a social concept, but test bias (also labeled differential prediction or predictive bias) is a psychometric concept subject to empirical investigation. When technically feasible, conduct a test-bias analysis to understand whether scores of members of various groups (e.g., based on ethnicity or gender) differ in terms of the relationship between tests and criteria.
- Investigating possible differential validity (i.e., differences between correlation coefficients) is not sufficient to understand whether the relationship between test scores and criteria differs across groups (i.e., differential prediction).
- Investigating for possible differential prediction involves examining both intercept- and slope-based differences. There are several problems with test-bias assessment, and typical situations are likely to lead to incorrect conclusions that there are no slope-based differences and that, if there are intercept-based differences, they favor minority group members.
- Use online algorithms and computer programs to (a) estimate the statistical power of the differential prediction test for slope-based differences, and (b) anticipate consequences in terms of adverse impact and selection errors of using tests that may be biased.
- Take several actions to minimize adverse impact at the recruiting (e.g., targeted recruiting), testing (e.g., use cognitive and noncognitive tests), and posttesting (e.g., use test-score banding) stages.
- Remember that testing is not just a technical issue. It is an issue that has enormous emotional and societal implications.

In the last three chapters, we have examined applied measurement concepts that are essential to sound employment decisions. In the remainder of the book, we shall see how these concepts are applied in practice. Let us begin in Chapter 9 by considering job analysis—a topic that, as a result of legislative and judicial developments, is emerging both in importance and in emphasis.

Discussion Questions

1. Why is the assessment of differential prediction more informative than an assessment of differential validity regarding test bias?
2. Summarize the available evidence on differential validity and its relationship with adverse impact. What advice on this issue would you give to an employer?
3. Discuss some of the difficulties and suggested solutions for conducting a differential prediction analysis.
4. Describe strategies available to reduce adverse impact.
5. When is a measure of individual differences unfairly discriminatory?

6. Provide arguments in favor of and against the use of test-score banding.
7. What are the advantages and disadvantages of implementing a criterion-referenced banding approach as compared to a predictor-referenced approach?
8. What are some strategies available to improve fairness perceptions regarding testing?
9. Discuss some of the public-policy issues that surround testing.

CHAPTER
9

Analyzing Jobs and Work

At a Glance

Despite dramatic changes in the structure of work, individual jobs remain the basic building blocks necessary to achieve broader organizational goals. The objective of job analysis is to define each job in terms of the behaviors necessary to perform it and to develop hypotheses about the personal characteristics necessary to perform those behaviors. Job analyses comprise two major elements: **job descriptions** and **job specifications**. Job descriptions specify the work to be done, while job specifications indicate the personal characteristics necessary to do the work.

Job analyses are used for many different purposes, but no single type of job-analysis data can support all HR activities. Hence, it is critical to align method with purpose and to make strategic choices across the many methods and types of descriptors available.

Competency models focus on identifying broader characteristics of individuals and on using these characteristics to inform HR practices. They differ from job analyses principally in terms of the extent to which they link to an organization's business context and competitive strategy. As such, they are more prescriptive than descriptive. On the other hand, the rigor and documentation of job analyses make them more likely to withstand legal challenge. Both approaches have helped further our understanding of the linkages among workers' personal qualities, the requirements of their jobs, and measures of organizational success.

In the mid-1990s, Bridges (1994a, 1994b) proclaimed "The End of the Job." He argued that the use of jobs as a way of organizing work "is a social artifact that has outlived its usefulness." If organizations expect to be successful, they need to "get rid of jobs" and "redesign to get the best out of the de-jobbed worker." One might ask, if we can no longer expect to hold jobs, can we at least expect to hold a position? Unfortunately, no, because positions may be "too fixed." Roles? Sorry, too unitary, single purposed. Skills and competencies? They will become too obsolete. According to this rationale, postjob workers will likely be self-employed contract workers, hired to work on projects or teams. Just look at Intel or Microsoft, firms that organize work around projects. People will work on 6 to 10 projects, perhaps for different employers at the same time. All of that may come to pass some day, but not yet.

A funny thing happened along the way—the Internet revolution. Go to any company's Web site and discover that it invites applications—for jobs! True, employees may work on 6 to 10 projects at once, but for only one employer. This is not to imply that the concept of work is not changing. Sometimes the changes occur at a dizzying pace as fluid organizations fighting to stay competitive require their people to adapt constantly. They need to adapt to strategic initiatives like empowerment, reengineering, automation, intranet-based self-service HR, the use of self-managed teams that push authority and responsibility down to lower levels, and alternative work arrangements such as virtual teams and telework (Cascio, 2010; Cascio & Aguinis, 2008). Technologies that enhance communications and information management, such as wireless communications, e-mail, and teleconferencing, have made the "anytime, anywhere" workplace a reality (Cascio, 2003c).

Consider just two changes in "traditional" jobs. Librarians who used to recommend and shelve books and provide guidance for research projects now demonstrate how to run computerized searches to sort through an Internet world bursting with information. Automobile assembly plants are replacing retiring workers who were hired right out of high school with people trained to operate computer-based machinery who can work well in teams. Yet, for all the changes, the job as a way to organize and group tasks and responsibilities has not yet disappeared, especially in large organizations (Milkovich & Newman, 2008).

To appreciate why the analysis of jobs and work is relevant and important, consider the following situation. If we were to start a brand-new organization, or a new division of a larger organization, we would be faced immediately with a host of problems, several of which involve decisions about people. What are the broad goals of the new organization or division, and how should it be structured in order to achieve these goals? Since the overall work of the new organization or division is too large for any one individual to handle (e.g., jet aircraft production), how can the work be broken down into pieces (or processes) small enough, yet challenging enough, for individuals or teams? How many positions will we have to staff, and what will be the nature of these positions? What knowledge, abilities, skills, and other characteristics (KSAOs) will be required? How many individuals should we recruit? What factors (personal, social, and technical) should we be concerned with in the selection of these individuals? How should they be trained, and what criteria should we use to measure how well they have performed their jobs? Before any of these decisions can be made, we must first define the jobs in question, specify what employee behaviors are necessary to perform them, and then develop hypotheses about the personal characteristics necessary to perform those work behaviors. This process is known as **job analysis**.

It is difficult to overstate the importance of job or work analysis (Sanchez & Levine, 2001) to employment research and practice. Like Sackett and Laczo (2003), we see the tools and techniques developed under the label "job analysis" as applicable to changing structures of work, and the use of the term *job analysis* is not meant to convey a focus on rigidly prescribed jobs. If thoroughly and competently conducted, job analysis provides a deeper understanding of individual jobs and their behavioral requirements and, therefore, creates a firm basis on which to make employment decisions. As the APA *Standards* (AERA, APA, & NCME, 1999) note: "For selection, classification, and promotion, some form of job . . . analysis provides the primary basis for defining the content domain [of interest]" (pp. 160, 161).

"Such an analysis of work would determine the characteristics workers need to be successful in a specific work setting, or the degree to which the work requirements are similar to requirements for work performed elsewhere" (SIOP, 2003, p. 10). Although some courts insist on extensive job analysis (e.g., as a basis for providing content-related evidence of validity), certain purposes, such as validity generalization, may not require such detail (Guion & Gibson, 1988; Landy, 2003; Schmitt, Cortina, Ingerick, & Wiechmann, 2003). As Figure 9-1 illustrates, there are many uses and purposes for which job analysis information might be collected.

Job analysis can underpin an organization's structure and design by clarifying roles (patterns of expected behavior based on organizational position). Employee responsibilities at all hierarchical levels—from floor sweeper to chairperson of the board—can be specified, thereby avoiding overlap and duplication of effort and promoting efficiency and harmony among individuals and departments. Job analysis is a fundamental tool that can be used in every phase of employment

Organization Design	HR Management	Work and Equipment Design	Additional Uses
Organizing Workforce planning Role definition	Job evaluation Recruitment Selection Placement Orientation Training and development Performance appraisal Promotions and transfers Career-path planning Labor relations	Engineering design Job design Methods improvement Safety	Vocational guidance Rehabilitation counseling Job-classification systems HR research

FIGURE 9-1   Uses of job analysis information.

research and administration; in fact, job analysis is to the HR professional what the wrench is to the plumber.

TERMINOLOGY

HR, like any other specialty area, has its own peculiar jargon, and, although some of the terms are used interchangeably in everyday conversation, technically there are distinct differences among them. These differences will become apparent as we examine job-analysis methods more closely. The definitions that follow generally are consistent with the terminology used by Brannick, Levine, and Morgeson (2007), Gael (1988), McCormick (1979), U.S. Department of Labor (1972, 1982), and Wills (1993).

An **element** is the smallest unit into which work can be divided without analyzing the separate motions, movements, and mental processes involved. Removing a saw from a tool chest prior to sawing wood for a project is an example of a job element.

A **task** is a distinct work activity carried out for a distinct purpose. Running a computer program, typing a letter, and unloading a truckload of freight are examples of tasks.

A **duty** includes a large segment of the work performed by an individual and may include any number of tasks. Examples of job duties include conducting interviews, counseling employees, and providing information to the public.

A **position** consists of one or more duties performed by a given individual in a given firm at a given time, such as clerk typist–level three. There are as many positions as there are workers.

A **job** is a group of positions that are similar in their significant duties, such as two or more mechanics–level two. A job, however, may involve only one position, depending on the size of the organization. For example, the local garage may employ only one mechanic–level two.

A **job family** is a group of two or more jobs that either call for similar worker characteristics or contain parallel work tasks as determined by job analysis.

An **occupation** is a group of similar jobs found in different organizations at different times—for example, electricians and machinists. A **vocation** is similar to an occupation, but the term *vocation* is more likely to be used by a worker than by an employer.

A **career** covers a sequence of positions, jobs, or occupations that one person engages in during his or her working life.

Aligning Method with Purpose

At the outset, it is important to emphasize that there is a wide variety of methods and techniques for collecting information about jobs and work. They vary on a number of dimensions, and such variation creates choices. Job-analysis methods must align with the purpose for which such information was collected. It simply is not true that a single type of job-analysis data can support any HR activity. For example, the kind of information necessary to develop a hierarchy of jobs in a pay structure (job evaluation) is usually not detailed enough to provide useful inputs to a human-factors engineer seeking to redesign a person-machine interface. First, define the purpose of the job analysis (see Figure 9-1), then choose a method that fits that purpose.

Choices

At least eight different choices confront the job analyst (Sackett & Laczo, 2003), although the range of choices can be narrowed once the analyst identifies the specific purpose for collecting work-related information. In brief, these choices include the following:

1. *Activities or attributes?*   Some techniques focus solely on activities or what gets done (tasks), while others focus on how the work gets done [worker attributes, such as knowledge, skills, and abilities (KSAs)]. The former are termed *work oriented*, while the latter are *worker oriented*. Other approaches incorporate separate analyses of activities, as well as attributes, followed by some process for linking the two (determining which attributes contribute to the performance of which activities).
2. *General or specific?*   These choices concern the level of detail needed in the analysis. A brief description of a job for purposes of pay-survey comparisons includes considerably less detail than that needed to develop preemployment assessment procedures based on critical KSAOs.
3. *Qualitative or quantitative?*   The same job can be described in narrative form—that is, qualitatively—or by means of numeric evaluations on a fixed set of scales (time, frequency, importance, or criticality)—that is, quantitatively. Qualitative methods are fine for applications like career planning, but cross-job comparisons require some type of quantitative method.
4. *Taxonomy-based or blank slate?*   The Position Analysis Questionnaire (PAQ) and the Fleishman Ability Requirements Scales, both of which are described later in this chapter, are taxonomy-based approaches in which relatively general work activities apply to a broad range of jobs. Alternatively, trained observers or job incumbents may develop lists of job activities or attributes that apply to specific jobs or job families (Banks, 2009). Subsequently, the activities or attributes are rated on specific scales, as described above. Such blank-slate approaches have the potential for a greater degree of detail than do taxonomy approaches.
5. *Observers or incumbents and supervisors?*   Trained job analysts sometimes observe work directly and then distill their observations into qualitative descriptions or quantitative evaluations of work activities or attributes. Alternatively, information may come from job incumbents and their direct supervisors, who may be asked to identify activities or attributes and then rate them on numeric scales. When a large number of incumbents and supervisors provide such ratings, it becomes possible to assess the consistency of the ratings and to identify clusters of respondents with differing patterns of work activities.
6. *KSAs or KSAOs?*   KSAs are useful in conducting attribute-oriented job analysis, but adding *other personal characteristics* (Os) allows a broader range of attributes to be included in the analysis. These might include personality traits, values, and attitudes. Incorporating the full range of these other characteristics is a defining characteristic of *competency modeling*, and we shall consider it in more detail later in the chapter.
7. *Single job or multiple-job comparison?*   Sometimes the focus is on a specific job, as when developing an entry-level test for the job of bank teller. In other cases, the focus is on documenting similarities and differences across jobs (e.g., to justify using the same selection system with different jobs, to justify using a selection system for the same job in different organizations, or to develop job families and career paths).

8. *Descriptive or prescriptive?* Job analysis typically describes a job as it currently exists. Suppose, however, that a job does not yet exist? Under these circumstances, it is necessary to prescribe activities or attributes for the soon-to-be-created job. Such an approach is termed **strategic job analysis**, and we will discuss it further later on in this chapter.

DEFINING THE JOB

Job analysis, as we have pointed out, consists of defining a job (e.g., in terms of its component tasks), specifying what employee behaviors are necessary to perform them, and then developing hypotheses about the personal characteristics necessary to perform those work behaviors. Two elements stand out in this definition: task requirements and people requirements. In this section, we will consider the task requirements of jobs, and, in the following section, we will consider their behavioral requirements.

In many cases, the characteristics of jobs are "givens" to employees. They include, for example, the equipment used; the arrangement of the work space; the division of labor; and the procedures, methods, and standards of performance of the job. From these data, the analyst produces a **job description** or written statement of what a worker actually does, how he or she does it, and why. This information can then be used to determine what KSAOs are required to perform the job.

Elements of a job description may include

1. *Job title*—for bookkeeping purposes within the firm, as well as to facilitate reporting to government agencies.
2. *Job activities and procedures*—descriptions of the tasks performed, the materials used, the machinery operated, the formal interactions with other workers, and the nature and extent of supervision given or received.
3. *Working conditions and physical environment*—heat, lighting, noise level, indoor/outdoor setting, physical location, hazardous conditions, etc.
4. *Social environment*—for example, information on the number of individuals in the work group and the amount of interpersonal interaction required in order to perform the job.
5. *Conditions of employment*—including, for example, a description of the hours of work, wage structure, method of payment, benefits, place of the job in the formal organization, and opportunities for promotion and transfer. (An example of a job description for architect I is presented in Figure 9-2.)

What we have just described is a traditional, task-based job description. However, some organizations are beginning to develop behavioral job descriptions. These comprise broader abilities that are easier to alter as technologies and customer needs change (Joinson, 2001). For example, instead of focusing on communication skills, such as writing, speaking, and making presentations, behavioral job descriptions incorporate broader behavioral statements, such as "actively listens, builds trust, and adapts his or her style and tactics to fit the audience." These behaviors will not change, even as the means of executing them evolve with technology. Instead of being responsible for simple procedures and predictable tasks, workers are now expected to draw inferences and render diagnoses, judgments, and decisions, often under severe time constraints (Pearlman & Barney, 2000).

JOB SPECIFICATIONS

Job specifications represent the KSAOs deemed necessary to perform a job. For example, keen vision (usually 20/20 uncorrected) is *required* of astronauts and test pilots.

In many jobs, however, job specifications are not rigid and inflexible; they serve only as guidelines for recruitment, selection, and placement. Job specifications depend on the level of performance deemed acceptable and the degree to which some abilities can be substituted for others. For example, in one investigation of power sewing-machine operators, it was thought that good eyesight was necessary to sew sheets until research demonstrated that

---

CITY ARCHITECT I

NATURE OF WORK

This is professional and technical work in the preparation of architectural plans, designs, and specifications for a variety of municipal or public works building projects and facilities.

MINIMUM QUALIFICATIONS

Education and Experience

Graduation from an accredited college or university with a specialization in architecture or architectural engineering or equal.

Knowledges, Abilities, and Skills

Considerable knowledge of the principles and practices of architecture; ability to make structural and related mathematical computations and make recommendations on architectural problems; ability to design moderately difficult architectural projects; ability to interpret local building codes and zoning regulations; ability to secure good working relationships with private contractors and employees; ability to train and supervise the work of technical and other subordinates in a manner conductive to full performance; ability to express ideas clearly and concisely, orally and in writing; skill in the use of architectural instruments and equipment.

ILLUSTRATION OF DUTIES

Prepares or assists in the preparation of architectural plans and designs all types of building projects constructed by the City, including fire stations, park and recreation buildings, office buildings, warehouses, and similar structures; prepares or supervises the preparation of final working drawings including architectural drawings, such as site plans, foundations, floor plans, elevations, section details, diagrams, and schedules rendering general features and scale details; prepares or supervises some of the engineering calculations, drawings and plans for mechanical details, such as plumbing, air-conditioning phases, and lighting features; writes construction standards and project specifications; prepares sketches including plans, elevations, site plans, and renderings and makes reports on feasibility and cost for proposed City work; writes specifications for all aspects of architectural projects including structural, mechanical, electrical, and air-conditioning work; confers with engineering personnel engaged in the preparation of structural plans for a building, making recommendations and suggestions as to materials, construction, and necessary adjustments in architectural designs to fit structural requirements; inspects construction in the field by checking for conformity with plans and material specifications; inspects existing structures to determine need for alterations or improvements and prepares drawings for such changes; performs related work as required.

SUPERVISION RECEIVED

General and specific assignments are received and work is performed according to prescribed methods and procedures with allowance for some independence in judgment in accomplishing the assignments.

SUPERVISION EXERCISED

Usually limited to supervision of technical assistants in any phase.

FIGURE 9-2   A typical job description.

manual dexterity was far more important. The operators could sew sheets just as well with their eyes closed! This illustrates an important point: Some individuals may be restricted from certain jobs because the job specifications are inflexible, artificially high, or invalid. For this reason, job specifications should indicate *minimally acceptable* standards for selection and later performance.

Establishing Minimum Qualifications

Job specifications identify the personal characteristics (e.g., educational background, experience, training) that are valid for screening, selection, and placement. How are these specifications set, and how does one define "minimal qualifications (MQs)"?

Levine, May, Ulm, and Gordon (1997) developed a methodology for determining MQs in the context of a court case that challenged the use of MQs of unknown validity, but high adverse impact. Their methodology is worth describing, since ultimately a court approved it, and it is consistent with sound professional practice.

Working independently with a draft list of tasks and KSAs for a target job, separate groups of subject matter experts (SMEs) rate tasks and KSAs on a set of four scales, as shown in Figure 9-3. Since the ratings are aggregated subsequently in terms of means or percentages, there is no need for consensus among SMEs. Tasks and KSAs meeting the criteria shown in Figure 9-3 are used to form the domains of tasks and KSAs from which MQs are derived. After completing their ratings, the SMEs provide suggested types or amounts of education, work experience, and other data they view as appropriate for MQs. Working with the task and KSA domains, as well as aggregated SME opinions, job analysts prepare a draft set of MQ profiles. Each profile is a statement of education, training, or work experience presumably needed to perform a target job at a satisfactory level. Finally, a new set of SMEs is convened to do three things:

1. Establish a description of a barely acceptable employee;
2. Decide if the list of MQ profiles is complete or if it needs editing; and
3. Rate the finalized profiles on two scales, level and clarity (see Figure 9-4).

Tasks

Perform at Entry: Should a newly hired employee be able to perform this task immediately or after a brief orientation/training period? (Yes/No)

Barely Acceptable: Must even barely acceptable employees be able to perform this task correctly with normal supervision? (Yes/No)

Importance of Correct Performance: How important is it for this task to be done correctly? Think about what happens if an error is made (some delay of service, work must be redone, danger to patients or co-workers, etc.). (1-*Little or no*, to 5-*Extremely important*)

Difficulty: How difficult is it to do this task correctly compared to all other tasks in the job? (1-*Much easier*, to 5-*Much harder*)

Criteria to be in the domain for MQs: Majority rate Yes on both Yes/No scales, score 3 or higher on Correct Performance, 2 or higher on Difficulty.

KSAs

Necessary at Entry: Is it necessary for newly hired employees to possess this KSA upon being hired or after a brief orientation/training period? (Yes/No)

Barely Acceptable: Must even barely acceptable employees possess the level or amount of this KSA to do the job? (Yes/No)

Useful in Hiring: To what extent is this KSA useful in choosing and hiring new employees? (1-*None or very little*, to 5-*To an extremely great extent*)

Unsatisfactory Employees: How well does this KSA distinguish between the barely acceptable and the unsatisfactory employee? (1-*None or very little*, to 5-*To an extremely great extent*)

Criteria to be in the domain for MQs: Majority rate Yes on both Yes/No scales, score 2 or higher on Useful and Unsatisfactory scales; and Useful plus Unsatisfactory Index must equal 5.0 or higher.

FIGURE 9-3   Scales applied to tasks and KSAs and criteria for defining the domains for MQs.
Source: Levine, E. L., May, D. M., Ulm, R. A., & Gordon, T. R. (1997). A methodology for developing and validating minimum qualifications (MQs). *Personnel Psychology, 50,* 1013. © 1997.

Level: To what extent is the profile indicated suitable to identifying the barely acceptable applicant?
    (0-*Not at all*, 1-*Too little to expect*, 2-*About right*, 3-*Too much to expect*)
Clarity: To what extent will this profile be clear to applicants and those who will use the profile
    in screening?
    (0-*Not at all*, 1-*Not too clear*, 2-*Reasonably clear*, 3-*Clear, stands on its own*)

Profiles that meet criteria of majority rating 2 on Level, and 2 or 3 on Clarity, are then compared
    to each task and KSA in the MQ domains with the following scales:

Linkage
Tasks: Does this profile provide an employee with what is needed to perform at a barely acceptable
    level on this task? (Yes/No/Not Sure)
KSAs: Does this profile provide an employee with the level of this KSA needed to perform at a
    barely acceptable level? (Yes/No/Not Sure)

A valid MQ is considered to be one in which the profile is linked to more than half of either
    Tasks or KSAs in the MQ domain, OR is linked to all five of the most important Tasks
    or KSAs.

[1]Profiles are routinely edited before and after rating to ensure that the determination that a profile is invalid is
based on its content and not on clarity of the writing.

FIGURE 9-4   Scales applied to MQ profiles and criteria for defining content-oriented evidence of validity.   *Source:* Levine, E. L., May, D. M., Ulm, R. A., & Gordon, T. R. (1997). A methodology for developing and validating minimum qualifications (MQs). *Personnel Psychology, 50,* 1013. © 1997.

Profiles meeting the criteria on the level and clarity scales are then linked back to the tasks and KSAs (in the domains established earlier) by means of two additional scales, one for tasks and one for KSAs, using the criteria also shown in Figure 9-4. Each profile must meet the linkage criterion in order to demonstrate content-oriented evidence of validity. Six of the nine MQ profiles in Levine et al.'s (1997) study did so.

Subsequently, Buster, Roth, and Bobko (2005) presented a related method for developing content-oriented evidence of validity for education and experience-based MQs that also was approved by a federal court. They offered the following eight recommendations for practice:

1. Begin with a structured job analysis that identifies critical tasks and KSAs, noting which KSAs are needed on day 1 of the job (entry-level KSAs).
2. Distribute a list of tasks and KSAs associated with the job at the first MQ-development meeting.
3. Emphasize that the point of reference for the MQs is an individual who is a newly appointed job incumbent.
4. Instruct individuals who are generating potential MQs to think about alternative MQs (e.g., a professional certification).
5. Use straightforward, targeted MQs because they can be rated more easily and reliably.
6. SMEs should rate the list of MQs independently.
7. Have SMEs link all potential MQs back to KSAs or tasks.
8. Bracket potential MQs with both easier and more difficult statements.

RELIABILITY AND VALIDITY OF JOB-ANALYSIS INFORMATION

A recent meta-analysis of 46 studies and 299 estimates of reliability identified average levels of inter- and intrarater reliability of job-analysis ratings. Interrater reliability refers to the degree to which different raters agree on the components of a target work role or job, or the extent to which their ratings covary. Intrarater reliability is a measure of stability (repeated item and rate–rerate the same job at different times). Data were categorized by specificity (generalized work activity or task data), source (incumbents, analysts, or technical experts), and descriptive scale (frequency, importance, difficulty, or time spent). Across 119 studies, task data demonstrated higher inter- and intrarater reliabilities than generalized work activity data (.77 versus .60, and .72 versus .58, respectively). Analysts showed the highest interrater reliability and incumbents the lowest, regardless of the specificity of the data. Within task data, descriptive scales dealing with perceptions of relative value (importance and difficulty scales) tended to have similar and relatively high interrater-reliability levels, whereas descriptive scales involving temporal judgments (frequency and time-spent scales) displayed similar and relatively low interrater-reliability levels (Dierdorff & Wilson, 2003).

Job descriptions are valid to the extent that they accurately represent job content, environment, and conditions of employment. Job specifications are valid to the extent that persons possessing the personal characteristics believed necessary for successful job performance in fact *do* perform more effectively on their jobs than persons lacking such personal characteristics.

As Morgeson and Campion (1997) have noted, however, many job-analysis processes are based on human judgment, and such judgment is often fallible. Potential sources of inaccuracy in job analysis may be due to two primary sources, social and cognitive. Social sources of inaccuracy apply principally in settings where groups, rather than individuals, make job-analysis judgments. For example, pressures to conform could be a source of inaccuracy if group consensus is required. Cognitive sources, on the other hand, reflect problems that result primarily from our limited ability to process information. For example, demand for large numbers of ratings or for very fine distinctions among job characteristics can cause information overload. In all, Morgeson and Campion (1997) identified 16 potential sources of inaccuracy. Such sources are more likely to affect ratings of subjective and diffuse attributes, such as many KSAOs, than they are ratings of discrete and observable tasks. Thus questions such as, "Do you do this on the job?" require considerably less subjectivity and judgment than do ratings of "criticality."

In a later study, Morgeson, Delaney-Klinger, Mayfield, Ferrara, and Campion (2004) investigated the effect of one particular source of bias: self-presentation—an attempt by some individuals to control the impressions others form of them. Their research showed that self-presentation may be responsible for inflation in ratings, particularly in the case of ability statements.

We also know that the amount of job-descriptive information available to raters significantly affects the accuracy of job analysis. Student raters with more detailed job information were consistently more accurate, relative to the averaged ratings of job incumbents, than were those given only a job title. Moreover, data provided by relatively job-naive raters showed little agreement with data provided by job-content experts (Harvey & Lozada-Larsen, 1988).

In actual organizational settings, however, there is not a readily available standard to assess the accuracy of a job analysis. As Guion (1998) pointed out, job analysis is not science. It always reflects subjective judgment and is best viewed as an information-gathering tool to aid researchers in deciding what to do next. Careful choices and documented decisions about what information to collect and how to collect it are the best assurances of reliable and useful information (Sackett & Laczo, 2003). In our next section, we consider how such information may be obtained.

OBTAINING JOB INFORMATION

Numerous methods exist for describing jobs, although they differ widely in the assumptions they make about jobs, in breadth of coverage, and in precision. Some are work oriented and some are worker oriented, but each method has its own particular set of advantages and disadvantages. For purposes of exposition, we present the various methods separately, but, in practice, several methods should be used to complement each other so the end product represents a valid and comprehensive picture of job duties, responsibilities, and behaviors.

Direct Observation and Job Performance

Observation of job incumbents and actual performance of the job by the analyst are two methods of gathering job information. Data then may be recorded in a narrative format or on some type of checklist or worksheet such as that shown in Figure 9-5. Both methods assume that jobs are relatively static—that is, that they remain constant over time and are not changed appreciably by different job incumbents or different situations. Job observation is appropriate for jobs that require a great deal of manual, standardized, short-cycle activities, and job performance is appropriate for jobs that the job analyst can learn readily.

Observations should include a representative sample of job behaviors. For example, the activity "copes with emergencies" may be crucial to effective nursing performance; yet a continuous eight-hour observation of the activities of a group of staff nurses tending to the needs of a dozen sleepy postoperative patients may reveal little in the way of a valid picture of job requirements.

Furthermore, the job analyst must take care to be unobtrusive in his or her observations, lest the measuring process per se distort what is being measured (Webb, Campbell, Schwartz, Sechrest, & Grove, 1981). This does not imply that the analyst should *hide* from the worker and remain out of sight, but it does imply that the analyst should not get in the way. Consider the following incident, which actually happened: While riding along in a police patrol car as part of a job analysis of police officers, an analyst and an officer were chatting away when a call came over the radio regarding a robbery in progress. Upon arriving at the scene, the analyst and the officer both jumped out of the patrol car, but in the process, the overzealous analyst managed to position himself between the robbers and the police. Although the robbers were apprehended later, they used the analyst as a decoy to make their getaway from the scene of the crime.

JOB ANALYSIS WORKSHEET

NAME OF EMPLOYEE	DATE:
CLASSIFICATION:	ANALYST:
DEPARTMENT:	DIVISION:
LENGTH OF TIME IN JOB:	LENGTH OF TIME WITH ORGANIZATION:

A description of what the classification duties currently are and what is actually needed to do the job. No indications need be made of experiences, abilities, or training acquired after employment.

1. General summary of job (primary duties):
2. Job tasks (tasks with X in front indicate observed duties: use actual examples, indicate frequency, consequences of error (0–10), difficulty (0–10), training received, supervision).
3. How detailed are assignments? Describe the form work comes in decisions that have been made and what still needs to be done with the work.
4. Relation to others in position:
5. Higher positions job prepares one for:
6. Equivalent positions:
7. Tools, machinery, aids:
8. Physical activity: (climbing, lifting, walking, standing, operating heavy equipment, etc.)
9. (Observe) Hazards, or unusual working conditions:
10. (Supervisor-Dept. Head) Qualifications: (competency needed)
11. (Supervisor-Dept. Head) Knowledge, skills, abilities required to do the job:
12. (Supervisor-Dept. Head) Special requirements, licenses, etc.:
13. Clarification of employee written specs, if any:
14. Contacts (inside/outside organization):
15. Supervisory responsibility, if any:

FIGURE 9-5 Job analysis worksheet (condensed).

Observation and job performance are inappropriate for jobs that require a great deal of mental activity and concentration, such as those of lawyer, network analyst, or architect, but there are thousands of jobs for which these methods are perfectly appropriate. A technique known as functional job analysis (FJA) often is used to record observed tasks (Fine, 1989). FJA attempts to identify exactly what the worker *does* in the job, as well as the results of the worker's behavior—that is, *what gets done*. An example of an FJA worksheet summarizing a job analyst's observations of a firefighter performing salvage and overhaul operations in response to an emergency call is shown in Figure 9-6. Let us consider the various sections of the worksheet.

Duties are general areas of responsibility. Tasks describe what gets done. Under *"What?,"* two pieces of information are required: *"Performs What Action?"* (i.e., describe what the worker did, using an action verb) and *"To Whom or to What?"* (i.e., describe the object of the verb). *"Why?"* forces the analyst to consider the purpose of the worker's action (*"To Produce or Achieve What?"*). *"How?"* requires the analyst to describe the tools, equipment, or work aids used to accomplish the task and, in addition, to specify the nature and source of instructions. This section also indicates whether the task is *prescribed* (e.g., by a superior or departmental procedures) or left to the worker's discretion.

Under *"Worker Functions,"* the analyst describes the orientation and level of worker activity with data, people, and things. All jobs involve workers to some extent with information or ideas (data); with clients, coworkers, superiors, and so on (people); and with machines or equipment (things). The percentages listed under *"Data," "People,"* and *"Things"* indicate the relative amount of involvement (orientation) with each of these functions. Numbers indicate the level of complexity according to the following scales, developed by the U.S. Department of Labor:

Data	People	Things
0 Synthesize	0 Mentor	0 Set up
1 Coordinate	1 Negotiate	1 Precision work
2 Analyze	2 Instruct	2 Operate, control
3 Compile	3 Supervise	3 Drive, operate
4 Compute	4 Divert	4 Manipulate
5 Copy	5 Persuade	5 Tend
6 Compare	6 Speak-signal	6 Feed
—	7 Serve	7 Handle
—	8 Take instruction	—

Of course, each of these terms is defined more fully for the analyst, but the important thing to note is that since the level and orientation measures can be applied to all tasks, and therefore to all jobs, the worker-function scales provide a way of comparing all tasks and all jobs on a common basis.

We noted earlier that there are certain work settings where direct, in-person observation is not feasible—for example, restaurants. However, one can, with modern, high-resolution digital cameras, obtain good views of work activity. The video information can then be reviewed and coded offline. Another advantage of digital video is that one can connect the video feed to customized coding software, which enables an analyst to generate data directly from the viewing apparatus. The software permits very simple and intuitive groupings of tasks and viewing logistics. The observer simply watches the video and clicks icons on screen that transfer the observations directly into a data set. The observer then can collect all similarly coded video clips into one place, and view them sequentially, or he or she can compare employees. In addition, with digital-video information, one can create software that directs cameras in whatever way is desired. In this way, one can follow particular employees as they wander through a facility, as if the observer were

Position Series:	Firefighter
Duty:	Response to emergency dispatches
Task Statement:	Performing salvage and overhaul

WHAT?		WHY?	HOW?		WORKER FUNCTIONS Orientation and Level		
Performs What Action? (action verb)	To Whom or to What? (object of verb)	To Produce or Achieve What?	Using What Tools, Equipment, or Work Aids?	Upon What Instructions?	Data	People	Things
1. Piles and covers	Furniture, clothing, and other valuables	In order to protect material from fire and water damage	Salvage covers	Prescribed content: a. Company officer b. Departmental procedure Discretionary content: a. As to the best location for preventing damage to materials	10% 2	10% 8	80% 7
2. Examines	Walls, ceilings, floors, and furniture	In order to locate and extinguish secondary fire sources	Pike pole, charged hose line, portable nozzle, power saw, axe	Prescribed content: a. Company officer b. Departmental procedure Discretionary content: a. As to the area examined for secondary fire sources b. As to the tools used for locating secondary fire sources	50% 2	10% 8	40% 4
3. Carries	Smoldering mattresses and furniture from buildings	In order to reduce fire and smoke damage to buildings and their contents	Crowbar	Prescribed content: a. Company officer b. Departmental procedure Discretionary content: a. As to whether article or material needs to be removed from building	20% 2	10% 8	70% 7

FIGURE 9-6 Behavior observation worksheet in functional job analysis terms.

walking behind them. The coding scheme can be determined after the video observations have been retrieved and can be modified and updated as needed (Saad, 2009).

Interview

The interview is probably the most commonly used technique for establishing the tasks, duties, and behaviors necessary both for standardized or nonstandardized activities and for physical as well as mental work. Because the worker acts as his or her own observer in the interview, he or she can report activities and behaviors that would not often be observed, as well as those activities that occur over long time spans. Moreover, because of his or her thorough knowledge of the job, the worker can report information that might not be available to the analyst from any other source. Viewing the interview as a "conversation with a purpose," however, makes it obvious that the success of this technique depends partly on the skill of the interviewer.

Thorough advance planning and training of the analyst in interview techniques should precede the actual interviewing, and, for reasons of reliability and efficiency, the analyst should follow a structured interview form that covers systematically the material to be gathered during the interview. As a guide, questions used by interviewers may be checked for their appropriateness against the following criteria (McCormick, 1979):

- The question should be related to the purpose of the analysis.
- The wording should be clear and unambiguous.
- The question should not "lead" the respondent; that is, it should not imply that a specific answer is desired.
- The question should not be "loaded" in the sense that one form of response might be considered to be more socially desirable than another.
- The question should not ask for knowledge or information the interviewee doesn't have.
- There should be no personal or intimate material that the interviewee might resent. (p. 36)

Workers often look on interviewers with some suspicion, and they are understandably wary of divulging information about their jobs. For this reason, the analyst should provide a comfortable atmosphere where the worker or team feels free to discuss job duties and responsibilities.

The major stumbling block with the interviewing technique is distortion of information, whether this is due to outright falsification or to honest misunderstanding. For example, if the worker knows (or thinks) that the results of the job analysis may influence wages, he or she may exaggerate certain responsibilities and minimize others. Hence, interviews may require time and a good deal of adroit questioning in order to elicit valid information.

As a check on the information provided by a single job incumbent, it is wise to interview several incumbents, as well as immediate supervisors who know the jobs well. Both high- and low-performing incumbents and supervisors tend to provide similar information (Conley & Sackett, 1987), as do members of different demographic subgroups (Schmitt & Cohen, 1989). However, this may be true only for simple, as opposed to complex, jobs (Mullins & Kimbrough, 1988). Multiple interviews allow analysts to take into account job factors made dynamic by time, people, and situations. This is only a partial solution to the problem, however, for often it is difficult to piece together results from several dissimilar interviews into a comprehensive picture. For this reason, additional information-gathering techniques might well be used to supplement and refine interviewing results.

SME Panels

Panels of 6 to 10 SMEs are often convened for different purposes in job analysis: (1) to develop information on tasks or KSAOs to be used in constructing job-analysis questionnaires, and (2) in test development, to establish linkages between tasks and KSAOs, KSAOs and test items, and tasks and test items. The total group of SMEs usually represents about a 10 to 20 percent sample of job incumbents and supervisors, representative of the race, gender, location, shift, and assignment composition of the entire group of incumbents. Evidence indicates, however, that the most important demographic variable in SME groups is experience (Landy & Vasey, 1991). Failure to include a broad cross-section of experience in a sample of SMEs could lead to distorted ratings. However, representative panels of SMEs provide results very similar to those obtained from broad surveys of respondents in the field (Tannenbaum & Wesley, 1993).

SMEs are encouraged to discuss issues and to resolve disagreements openly. For example, to promote discussion of KSAOs, panel members might be asked questions such as the following:

- Think of workers you know who are better than anyone else at (a particular task). Why do they do so well?
- If you were going to assign a worker to perform (a particular task), what kinds of KSAOs would you want this person to have?
- What do you expect workers to learn in training that would make them effective at the tasks?
- Think of good workers *and* poor workers. What KSAOs distinguish one from the other?

If the task for SMEs is to establish linkages for test-development purposes, quality-control statistics should be computed to ensure that the judgments or work products of the SMEs are meaningful (Hughes & Prien, 1989). For example, questionnaires might include repeat items and "carelessness" items (those that are inappropriate for the job under study). High levels of inter-rater agreement and, for individual SMEs, a near-zero endorsement of "carelessness" items, are important checks on the meaningfulness of the data.

Questionnaires

Questionnaires usually are standardized and require respondents either to check items that apply to a job or to rate items in terms of their relevance to the job in question. In general, they are cheaper and quicker to administer than other job-analysis methods, and sometimes they can be completed at the respondent's leisure, thereby avoiding lost production time. In addition, when there are many workers in each job, questionnaires provide a breadth of coverage that would be exorbitantly expensive and time consuming to obtain by any other method.

There are problems with this method, however. Questionnaires are often time consuming and expensive to develop, and ambiguities or misunderstandings that might have been clarified in an interview are likely to go uncorrected. Similarly, it may be difficult to follow up and augment information obtained in the questionnaires. In addition, the rapport that might have been obtained in the course of face-to-face contact is impossible to achieve with an impersonal instrument. This may have adverse effects on respondent cooperation and motivation. On the other hand, the structured-questionnaire approach probably has the greatest potential for quanti-fying job analysis information, which can then be processed by computer.

Task inventories and checklists are questionnaires that are used to collect information about a particular job or occupation. A job analyst completes a list of tasks or job activities, either by checking or rating each item as it relates to the job in question, in terms of the importance of the item, frequency with which the task is performed, judged difficulty, time to learn, or relation-ship to overall performance. Although these data are adaptable for computer analysis, checklists tend to ignore the sequencing of tasks or their relationships to other jobs. Thus, an overall perspec-tive of the total job is extremely difficult to obtain with checklist information alone.

However, if one purpose of a task inventory is to assess the relative *importance* of each task, then a unit-weighted, additive composite of ratings of task criticality, difficulty of learning the task, and relative time spent may provide the best prediction of average task importance across SMEs (Sanchez & Fraser, 1992).

The Position Analysis Questionnaire

Since task inventories basically are work oriented and make static assumptions about jobs, behavioral implications are difficult to establish. In contrast to this, worker-oriented information describes *how* a job gets done and is more concerned with generalized worker behaviors. One instrument that is based on statistical analyses of primarily worker-oriented job elements and lends itself to quantitative statistical analysis is the Position Analysis Questionnaire (PAQ) (McCormick & Jeanneret, 1988; McCormick, Jeanneret, & Mecham, 1972). The PAQ consists of 194 items or job elements that fall into the following categories: information input (where and how the worker gets the information he or she uses for a job); mental processes (the reasoning, planning, decision making, and so forth, involved in a job); work output (the physical activities performed by the worker and the tools or devices he or she uses); relationships with other persons; and job context (physical and social contexts in which the work is performed). The individual items require the respondent either to check a job element if it applies or to rate it on an appropriate rating scale such as importance, time, or difficulty (see Figure 9-7).

The average item reliability of the PAQ is a very respectable .80. Similar results were obtained with a German form of the PAQ (Frieling, Kannheiser, & Lindberg, 1974). A meta-analysis of 83 studies that used the PAQ revealed an average interrater reliability of .66. The same study revealed an average intrarater reliability of .82 (Dierdorff & Wilson, 2003).

Personal and organizational factors seem to have little impact on PAQ results. In a controlled study, similar profiles resulted, regardless of whether the analyst was male or female, whether the incumbent portrayed his or her job as interesting or uninteresting, or whether a considerable amount of information or less information about a job was presented (Arvey, Davis, McGowen, & Dipboye,

---

RELATIONSHIPS WITH OTHER PERSONS

This section deals with different aspects of interaction between people involved in various kinds of work.

Code	Importance to This Job (1)
DNA	Does not apply
1	Very minor
2	Low
3	Average
4	High
5	Extreme

4.1 Communications

Rate the following in terms of how *important* the activity is to the completion of the job. Some jobs may involve several or all of the items in this section.

4.1.1 Oral (communicating by speaking)

99 | 1 ___ Advising (dealing with individuals in order to counsel and/or guide them with regard to problems that may be resolved by legal, financial, scientific, technical, clinical, spiritual, and/or other professional principles)

100 | 1 ___ Negotiating (dealing with others in order to reach an agreement or solution, for example, labor bargaining, diplomatic relations, etc.)

101 | 1 ___ Persuading (dealing with others in order to influence them toward some action or point of view, for example, selling, political campaigning, etc.)

102 | 1 ___ Instructing (the teaching of knowledge or skills, in either an informal or a formal manner, to others, for example a public school teacher, a journeyman teaching an apprentice, etc.)

103 | 1 ___ Interviewing (conducting interviews directed toward some specific objective, for example, interviewing job applicants, census taking, etc.)

FIGURE 9-7 Sample items from the PAQ. *Source:* McCromick, E. J., Jeanneret, P. R., & Mecham, R. C. Position Analysis Questionnaire, copyright 1969 by Purdue Research Foundation, West Lafayette, Indiana 47907.

1982). However, as has been found using other job-analysis methods, PAQ ratings from expert and job-naive raters are not equivalent (DeNisi, Cornelius, & Blencoe, 1987). There simply are no short-cuts when using the PAQ. For example, one study found near-zero convergence of results based on the rating of each PAQ job dimension as a whole, compared to rating a number of items for each dimension and then combining them (Butler & Harvey, 1988).

McCormick, Jeanneret, and Mecham (1972) believe that structured, worker-oriented job-analysis instruments hold considerable potential for establishing the common denominators that are required to link different jobs. Thus,

> the kinds of common denominators one would seek are those of a worker-oriented nature, since they offer some possibility of serving as bridges or common denomina-tors between and among jobs of very different technologies. One cannot possibly relate butchering, baking, and candlestick-making strictly in these technological terms; their commonalities (if any) might well be revealed if they were analyzed in terms of the more generalized human behaviors involved, that is, in terms of worker-oriented elements. (p. 348)

Despite these claims, research seems to indicate that much of the content of the PAQ is more suited for use with blue-collar manufacturing jobs than it is for professional, managerial, and some technical jobs (Cornelius, DeNisi, & Blencoe, 1984; DeNisi et al., 1987). The PAQ also is subject to two further limitations. First, since no specific work activities are described, *behavioral* simi-larities in jobs may mask genuine *task* differences between them—for example, a police officer's profile is quite similar to a housewife's (according to Arvey & Begalla, 1975) because of the troubleshooting, emergency-handling orientation required in both jobs. A second problem with the PAQ is readability, for a college-graduate reading level is required in order to comprehend the items (Ash & Edgell, 1975). The lesson? Don't administer the PAQ to job incumbents and supervisors unless their jobs require educational levels substantially higher than 10–12 years.

In an effort to make the worker-oriented approach more widely applicable, the Job Element Inventory (JEI) was developed. The JEI is a 153-item, structured questionnaire modeled after the PAQ, but with a much lower reading level (10th grade). Controlled research shows that JEI factors closely parallel those of the PAQ (Harvey & Lozada-Larsen, 1988).

Fleishman Job Analysis Survey (F–JAS)

The F–JAS (Fleishman, 1975, 1992; Fleishman & Reilly, 1992a) is one of the most thoroughly researched approaches to job analysis. Its objective is to describe jobs in terms of the abilities required to perform them. The ability-requirements taxonomy (based on Fleishman & Quaintance, 1984) is intended to reflect the fewest independent ability categories that describe performance in the widest variety of tasks. Areas covered by the taxonomy include 21 cognitive abilities (e.g., oral com-prehension, deductive reasoning, number facility), 10 psychomotor abilities (e.g., reaction time, control precision, finger dexterity), 9 physical abilities (e.g., gross body coordination, static strength, stamina), and 12 sensory/perceptual abilities (e.g., depth perception, visual color discrimination, hearing sensitivity). In addition, 21 social/interpersonal abilities (e.g., persuasion, dependability, social sensitivity) have now been included. The methodology has also been extended to the identifi-cation and definition of 33 types of general occupational knowledge and skill requirements (e.g, customer and personal services, administration and management, building and construction; Costanza, Fleishman, & Marshall-Meis, 1999).

To facilitate a common understanding among raters, rating scales define each ability, distinguish it from related abilities, and provide examples of tasks that require different levels of the ability. An example of one such scale, cognitive ability 10, "Number Facility," is shown in Figure 9-8. Interrater reliabilities for the scales are generally in the mid-.80s, and there is considerable construct and predictive evidence of validity in a variety of studies to support the

10. Number Facility

This ability involves the degree to which adding, subtracting, multiplying, or dividing can be done quickly and correctly. These procedures can be steps in other operations like finding percents and taking square roots.

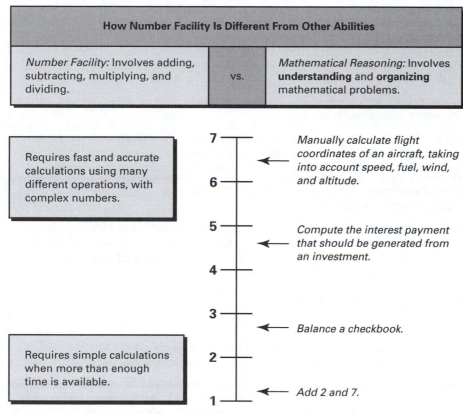

How Number Facility Is Different From Other Abilities

Number Facility: Involves adding, subtracting, multiplying, and dividing.	vs.	Mathematical Reasoning: Involves **understanding** and **organizing** mathematical problems.

Requires fast and accurate calculations using many different operations, with complex numbers.

7 — Manually calculate flight coordinates of an aircraft, taking into account speed, fuel, wind, and altitude.

6

5 — Compute the interest payment that should be generated from an investment.

4

3 — Balance a checkbook.

Requires simple calculations when more than enough time is available.

2

1 — Add 2 and 7.

FIGURE 9-8   Rating scale for "Number Facility," in the Fleishman Job Analysis Survey (F–JAS). *Source:* Fleishman, E. A. (1992). *Fleishman job analysis survey rating scale booklet (F–JAS).* Potomac, MD: Management Research Institute.

meaningfulness of the scales (Fleishman & Reilly, 1992a; Fleishman & Mumford, 1988; 1991). In addition, the *Handbook of Human Abilities: Definitions, Measurements, and Job Task Requirements* (Fleishman & Reilly, 1992b) integrates definitions of the full range of human abilities with information about the kinds of tasks and jobs that require each ability and about published tests that can be used to measure each ability. A portion of the *Handbook* entry for "Number Facility" is shown in Figure 9-9.

Critical Incidents

This is the same method we discussed in connection with performance management (Chapter 5). The critical-incidents approach involves the collection of a series of anecdotes of job behavior (collected from supervisors, employees, or others familiar with the job) that describe especially good or especially poor job performance. The method has value, for typically it yields both static and dynamic dimensions of jobs. Each anecdote describes: (1) what led up to the incident and the context in which it occurred, (2) exactly what the individual did that was so effective or ineffective, (3) the perceived consequences of this behavior, and (4) whether or not such consequences were actually within the control of the employee.

---

10. Number Facility

Definition: Number facility is the ability to add, subtract, multiply, divide, and manipulate numbers quickly and accurately. It is required for steps in other operations, such as finding percentages and taking square roots. This ability does not involve understanding or organizing mathematical problems.

Tasks: Number facility is involved in filling out income tax returns, keeping track of financial accounts, computing interest payments, adding up a restaurant bill, and balancing a checkbook.

Jobs: Jobs that require high levels of number facility include those of an accountant, audit clerk, bookkeeper, cashier, and teller.

Test Examples: Tests of number facility usually require subjects to quickly perform numerical operations such as addition or subtraction. Tests of this type require subjects to either provide the correct answer or choose the correct answer from multiple-choice items.

Guilford-Zimmerman Aptitude Survey: Numerical Operations
Consulting Psychologists Press

This is a paper-pencil, multiple-choice test including simple problems of addition, subtraction, and multiplication. The results yield C-scale, centile, and T-scale norms for college groups. Eight minutes are allowed to complete the test. It has been used with accountants, sales persons, and many types of clerical workers.

Employee Aptitude Survey Test #2—Numerical Ability (EAS #2)
Psychological Services, Inc.

This 75-item, paper-pencil, multiple-choice test assesses addition, subtraction, multiplication, and division skills. Ten minutes are allowed to complete the test. It has been used to select and place executives, supervisors, engineers, accountants, sales, and clerical workers.

FIGURE 9-9 Portion of the *Handbook of Human Abilities* entry for "number facility" in the F–JAS. *Source:* Fleishman, E. A., & Reilly, M. E. (1992b). *Handbook of human abilities: Definitions, measurements, and job task characteristics.* Potomac, MD: Management Research Institute.

Typically, the job analyst gathers a broad sampling of observations of a large number of employees doing their jobs; depending on the nature of the job, hundreds or even thousands of incidents may be required to cover adequately the behavioral domain. Incidents then are categorized according to the job dimensions they represent and assembled into a checklist format. In their entirety, the incidents provide a composite picture of the behavioral requirements of a job.

OTHER SOURCES OF JOB INFORMATION AND JOB-ANALYSIS METHODS

Several other sources of job information are available and may serve as useful supplements to the methods already described. An examination of training materials (such as training manuals, standard operating procedures, or blueprints of equipment used) may reveal what skills, abilities, and behaviors are required for successfully learning to do the work and operating essential equipment. Technical conferences composed of experts selected for their broad knowledge and experience, and diaries in which job incumbents record their work tasks day by day also may prove useful.

The Job Analysis Wizard

The Job Analysis Wizard (JAW) was developed at Lucent Technologies, Inc. (Pearlman & Barney, 2000). Based on the World Wide Web, it capitalizes on advances in computer technology and the availability of sophisticated information search-and-retrieval methods. The JAW incorporates characteristics such as these:

- The use of thousands of different elements organized into broader work- and worker-related dimensions. For example, a first level of the JAW taxonomy includes work requirements. Its second level includes work context, generalized work behaviors, and tools and equipment. Another first-level dimension is worker requirements. Its second level includes abilities, knowledge, skills, education, certifications, languages, and work styles.
- The use of *fuzzy logic* as a decision aid to assist in the placement of new dimensions (e.g., knowledge of new or emerging technologies) into the JAW taxonomy. Fuzzy logic creates a sort of fingerprint by comparing quantitative ratings on a new knowledge (gathered from a confirmatory survey) with the pattern of data for all knowledge elements in the dictionary across every task and tool. If a new programming language, such as Java, is discovered to be important, the system would calculate similarity indices with all other knowledge elements in the database. Then it would recommend a placement near the other programming languages (such as C++) because of the similarity of the patterns they share with related tasks and tools.
- Automation of the entire job-analysis process, coupled with the ability to provide information on products created in the past to support business initiatives.
- Use of electronic surveys that are completed by incumbents, supervisors, and other subject matter experts anywhere in the world, as long as they have access to the internal Lucent Web site.
- The ability to filter data using the JAW's statistical software. The system then creates a series of linkage-matrix surveys designed to link the key work (tasks, tools, equipment) and worker (knowledge, skills) dimensions.
- The use of high-quality graphic reports for ease of data interpretation. When complete, the JAW allows an analyst to upload the results to the common Web site for others to use and immediately to identify preexisting materials (such as tests or interviews) that are relevant to a job of interest.

Incorporating Personality Dimensions into Job Analysis

Personality is the set of characteristics of a person that account for the consistent ways that he or she responds to situations. In recent years, there has been a revival of interest in personality as a determinant of work performance, largely because of the demonstrated positive relationship between some personality characteristics and job performance in some contexts (Ones, Dilchert, Viswesvaran, & Judge, 2007; Tett & Christiansen, 2007). Although there is controversy about the value-added contribution of personality relative to other predictors of performance (Morgeson et al., 2007), some personality traits, such as conscientiousness, can be used as valid predictors for many different types of occupations (Ones et al., 2007).

Personality-based job analysis (PBJA) may be particularly useful for cross-functional and difficult-to-define jobs that cannot be described in terms of simple tasks or discrete KSAs (Brannick et al., 2007). Such jobs are becoming increasingly common in twenty-first-century organizations (Cascio & Aguinis, 2008).

Perhaps the most credible peer-reviewed PBJA tool available in the public domain is the Personality-Related Position Requirements Form (PPRF) (Raymark, Schmit, & Guion, 1997), a worker-oriented job-analysis method that assesses the extent to which each of the "Big Five" personality traits is needed for a particular job. The Big Five is the most established and thoroughly researched personality taxonomy in work settings (Barrick & Mount, 2003; Ones et al., 2007).

It includes the following dimensions: neuroticism, extraversion, openness to experience, agree-ableness, and conscientiousness.

Although we will describe the Big Five model in detail in Chapter 14 in the context of staffing, here we merely define each of its components. **Neuroticism** concerns the degree to which an individual is insecure, anxious, depressed, and emotional versus calm, self-confident, and cool. **Extraversion** concerns the degree to which an individual is gregarious, assertive, and sociable versus reserved, timid, and quiet. **Openness to experience** concerns the degree to which an individual is creative, curious, and cultured versus practical with narrow interests. **Agreeableness** concerns the degree to which an individual is cooperative, warm, and agreeable versus cold, disagreeable, and antagonistic. **Conscientiousness** concerns the degree to which an individual is hard-working, organized, dependable, and persevering versus lazy, disorganized, and unreliable.

The PPRF consists of sets of behavioral indicators associated with the five personality traits. Respondents (typically job incumbents) indicate the extent to which each behavioral indicator is relevant to the job under consideration. Averaged scores across respondents indicate the extent to which each trait (or subdimension of each trait) is relevant.

A recent study (Aguinis, Mazurkiewicz, & Heggestad, 2009) demonstrated that cognitive biases may lead to inflation in correlations between PBJA ratings and raters' own personality characteristics, and that PBJA ratings may be higher than they should be (inflation in mean ratings). They developed a 15-minute, Web-based frame-of-reference training program designed to instill a common mental framework in all raters (see Chapter 5) and demonstrated that it effectively reduced such biases. This should enhance the overall accuracy of PBJA ratings.

Strategic or Future-Oriented Job Analyses

There are times when organizations want information concerning specific skill and ability requirements for jobs or positions that do not yet exist. Examples include jobs related to new technology or hardware that is expected to be in operation three to five years in the future, new plant start-ups with unusual approaches to the organization of work (e.g., Sony's use of manufacturing "cells" of three workers to assemble components), and the reconfiguration of existing jobs into a process-based structure of work (e.g., credit issuance, procurement). Given the dramatic changes that have occurred in the world of work in recent years (Cascio, in press; 2003c), the likelihood of even more change in the future makes strategic job analyses ever more important. Competency models (see below) are future oriented, but standard job-analysis methods can also be adapted for this purpose.

Landis, Fogli, and Goldberg (1998) used standard job-analysis methodology (observations and interviews of SMEs, use of structured questionnaires, linkage of KSAs to task clusters) with an innovative twist. A large insurance company was condensing 11 existing jobs into 3 new ones, and it had hired a consulting team to develop valid selection tests for the new jobs. The consultants recognized that at least three different perspectives on the new jobs existed: those of the organization's steering committee, those of an outside firm responsible for technological changes (e.g., updated computer systems), and those of current members of the organization (e.g., supervisors of and incumbents in similar jobs, experts in system design, training coordinators). To account for these differences, the consultants used SMEs from each of these groups throughout the job-analysis procedure. As a result, changes in technology, job design, and training that could impact the future jobs were identified and addressed early. Scheduled meetings at critical phases of the process provided important feedback and early warning to the organization's steering committee about employee concerns.

A different approach for dealing with such situations was developed by Arvey, Salas, and Gialluca (1992). Using the results of a job-analysis inventory that included assessment of task and skill–ability characteristics, they first developed a matrix of correlations between tasks and skills–abilities. Then, assuming different numbers of tasks might be available to decision makers to describe the requirements of future jobs, Arvey et al. used the set of tasks in a multiple-regression analysis to forecast which skills–abilities would be necessary in the future job. Subsequently they cross-validated these decision outcomes with a different sample of raters.

While such predictions can represent useful forecasting information for decision makers, their validity rests on two assumptions: (1) The covariance relationships among tasks and skills–abilities remain stable over time, and (2) the tasks and skills–abilities included in the database include the same kinds of skills and abilities to be forecasted.

Competency Models

Competency models attempt to identify variables related to overall organizational fit and to identify personality characteristics consistent with the organization's vision (e.g., drive for results, persistence, innovation, flexibility) (Schippmann et al., 2000). As such they are written in terms that operating managers can relate to.

Competency models are a form of job analysis that focuses on broader characteristics of individuals and on using these characteristics to inform HR practices. They focus on the full range of KSAOs (e.g., motives, traits, attitudes and personality characteristics) that are needed for effective performance on the job, and that characterize exceptional performers. Ideally, such a model consists of a set of competencies that have been identified as necessary for successful performance, with behavioral indicators associated with high performance on each competency specified (Goffin & Woychesin, 2006; Mihalevsky, Olson, & Maher, 2007; Sackett & Laczo, 2003).

Unfortunately, there is no consistent definition of the term *competency* (Schippmann et al., 2000). As Pearlman and Barney (2000) note, many competencies that appear in the literature and in competency models (e.g., "visioning") are ill-defined concepts with no clear meaning. Needless to say, such deficiencies transfer to selection tools that make use of those constructs.

How does competency modeling differ from job analysis? A rigorous comparison concluded that competency approaches typically include a fairly substantial effort to understand an organization's business context and competitive strategy and to establish some direct line-of-sight between individual competency requirements and the broader goals of an organization. Job analyses, on the other hand, typically do not make this connection, but their level of rigor and documentation are more likely to enable them to withstand the close scrutiny of a legal challenge. As currently practiced, therefore, competency modeling is not a substitute or replacement for job analysis.

It also is worth noting that the unit of analysis of a competency model can vary from a single job to an entire organization. When the focus is on a single job or job family, differences between competency modeling and traditional job analysis tend to be smaller. The notion of an organization-wide competency model is quite different, however. Specifying a set of attributes valued across the organization may reflect top managers' vision regarding what will be valued and rewarded in the future and is one part of an organizational-change effort. In that sense, competency modeling is more prescriptive, or future oriented, while job analysis is more descriptive in nature (Sackett & Laczo, 2003).

Neither job analysis nor competency modeling is a singular approach to studying work, and there is much variability in the ways they are implemented in actual practice (Schmieder & Frame, 2007). Moreover, no single type of descriptor content (competencies, KSAOs, work activities, performance standards) is appropriate for all purposes, and purpose is a key consideration in choosing any particular approach to the study of work.

INTERRELATIONSHIPS AMONG JOBS, OCCUPATIONAL GROUPS, AND BUSINESS SEGMENTS

The general problem of how to group jobs together for purposes of cooperative validation, validity generalization, and administration of performance appraisal, promotional, and career-planning systems has a long history (Harvey, 1991). Such classification is done to facilitate description, prediction, and understanding. Jobs may be grouped based on the abilities required to do them, task characteristics, behavior description, or behavior requirements (Fleishman & Mumford, 1991).

For example, one can look for *differences* among jobs; this is the analysis of variance or multivariate analysis of variance approach. Alternatively, one can look for *similarities* among jobs; this is the objective of cluster analysis or Q-type factor analysis (Colihan & Burger, 1995; Zedeck & Cascio, 1984). In practice, however, when task and ability-requirement data were used independently to describe 152 jobs in a broad cross-section of occupational fields, each type of indicator yielded similar occupational classifications (Hartman, Mumford, & Mueller, 1992).

To be sure, the practical significance of differences among jobs and among alternative possible job-family configurations is likely to vary according to the objective for which the job-family system has been designed (Harvey, 1986; Pearlman, 1980). Consider one such objective.

In the information-driven organization of today, many firms are using enterprisewide resource planning (ERP) systems offered by vendors such as PeopleSoft, Oracle, and SAP. Such systems require underlying definitions and architectures of work and work requirements in order to build platforms of information that can be used to support a wide range of HR applications. Competency models might provide such information, but rigorous job-analysis techniques should be used to define core competencies. This implies an expansion of the focus of traditional job analysis to place equal emphasis on documenting, analyzing, and displaying what is core or common across jobs, job levels, functions, and business groups in an effort to support integrated systems of HR applications (Schippmann et al., 2000). Occupational information reflects an even broader grouping. To that topic we now turn.

OCCUPATIONAL INFORMATION—FROM THE DICTIONARY OF OCCUPATIONAL TITLES TO THE O*NET

The U.S. Department of Labor published the *Dictionary of Occupational Titles* (DOT) in the 1930s to help deal with the economic crisis of the Great Depression by allowing the new public employment system to link skill supply and skill demand. The last version of the DOT, published by the U.S. Department of Labor in 1991, contains descriptive information on more than 12,000 jobs. However, that information is job specific and does not provide a cross-job organizing structure that would allow comparisons of similarities and differences across jobs. Also, by focusing on tasks, or what gets done, the DOT does not indicate directly what personal characteristics workers must have to perform the job or the context in which the job is performed (Dunnette, 1999).

To deal with these problems, the U.S. Department of Labor sponsored a large-scale research project called the Occupational Informational Network (O*Net). It incorporates information about jobs and work obtained over the 60 years since the DOT was developed. O*Net is a national occupational information system that provides comprehensive descriptions of the attributes of workers and jobs. It is based on four broad design principles: (1) multiple descriptor domains that provide "multiple windows" into the world of work, (2) a common language of work and worker descriptors that covers the entire spectrum of occupations, (3) description of occupations based on a taxonomy from broad to specific, and (4) a comprehensive content model that integrates the previous three principles (LaPolice, Carter, & Johnson, 2008; Peterson et al., 2001).

MULTIPLE WINDOWS These are necessary to allow people to work with the kinds of descriptors that are most useful for the questions they are asking. These descriptors include tasks, abilities, skills, areas of knowledge, and work context. Such organization allows one to ask how specific skills are related to different types of work activities.

COMMON LANGUAGE Since job-specific information can change rapidly, the O*Net uses general descriptors that are more stable. O*Net permits job-specific information, but does so within the organizing structure of broader descriptors, such as generalized work activities (as in the PAQ) like "selling or influencing others" and "assisting or caring for others."

TAXONOMIES AND HIERARCHIES OF OCCUPATIONAL DESCRIPTORS   This approach to occupational classification allows information to be summarized and assigned to fewer categories. Because O*Net is concerned with both positions and occupations, a broad range of descriptors has been developed. For example, some focus on key skills needed to perform specific jobs, while others are concerned with broader organizational and contextual factors, such as organizational climate. Descriptors within each content domain are then arranged in a hierarchy.

THE O*NET CONTENT MODEL   This model incorporated the three design principles—multiple windows, common language, and hierarchical taxonomies—to include the major types of cross-job descriptors and to provide a general descriptive framework of occupational information. Figure 9-10 shows the six major domains of the O*Net content model and the major categories within each one. All of this information is contained in a relational database that is accessible to the general public at http://online.onetcenter.org. The system is quite flexible as well. One can start with a skill or ability profile and find occupations that match it. Conversely, one can start with an occupation and find others with similar characteristics. For more in-depth information about the O*Net system, see Peterson et al. (2001) or Peterson, Mumford, Borman, Jeanneret, and Fleishman (1999).

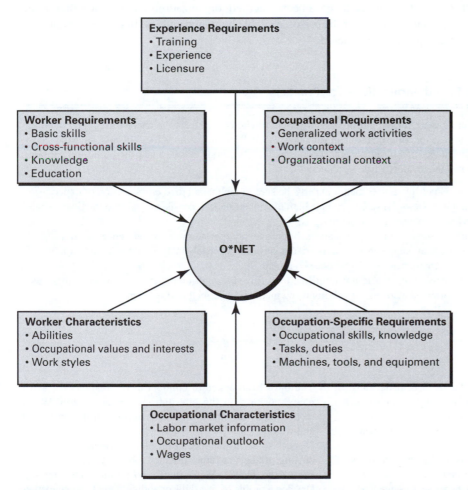

FIGURE 9-10   The O*Net content model.   *Source:* Petersen, N. G., Mumford, M. D., & Borman, W. D. (2001). Understanding work using the occupational information network (O*Net): Implications for practice and research. *Personnel Psychology, 54,* 458. © 2001.

For all of the effort that has gone into it, the O*Net remains a work in progress (Sackett & Laczo, 2003). The basic framework for conceptualizing occupational information is now in place, and future research will enhance the value of the O*Net. One such study identified adult literacy requirements across occupations (LaPolice et al., 2008) using job-component validity, a form of synthetic validity (see Chapter 7). The logic behind that approach is that if one could identify the worker requirements for any given job component, it would be possible to determine the total requirements for a job by knowing all of the components of that job (Scherbaum, 2005).

LaPolice et al. (2008) used both worker-oriented descriptors (KSAs required in a specific occupation) and job-oriented information (generalized work activities required to accomplish major work functions) from the O*Net database of 902 occupations to predict scores on each of three literacy scales. The three scales were *prose* (ability to understand and use information from texts such as editorials, news stories, poems, and fiction); *document* (ability to locate and use information in materials such as job applications, transportation schedules, maps, tables, and graphs); and *quantitative* literacy (ability to apply arithmetic operations, either alone or sequentially, using numbers embedded in printed materials) (Kirsch, Jungeblut, Jenkins, & Kolstad, 2002). Results demonstrated that the three different types of adult literacy were highly predictable (multiple Rs ranged from .79 to .81, corrected for shrinkage) from the O*Net descriptors. In addition to providing construct-oriented evidence of validity for O*Net, these results are useful in vocational guidance and career-counseling settings.

Once behavioral requirements have been specified, organizations can increase their effectiveness if they plan judiciously for the use of available human resources. In the next chapter, we will consider that topic in greater detail.

Evidence-Based Implications for Practice

When collecting work-related information, a variety of choices confront the analyst. Begin by defining clearly the purpose for collecting such information. Since the many methods for collecting such data have offsetting advantages and disadvantages, choose multiple methods that best suit the purpose identified. Here are some other evidence-based guidelines:

- If using panels of subject matter experts, be sure to include a broad cross-section of experience.
- If using interviews, be sure to include both incumbents and supervisors, and take the time to train interviewers in interviewing techniques.
- If using personality-based job analysis, be sure to incorporate frame-of-reference training.
- Recognize that competency models are not substitutes for job analysis. Both include a range of useful information across the practice continuum.
- When establishing minimum qualifications for education or experience, be sure to assess content-oriented evidence of validity using methods described in this chapter.

Discussion Questions

1. Describe some of the choices that need to be made in deciding how to analyze jobs and work. How would you choose an appropriate technique in a given situation?
2. Develop an outline for a job-analysis workshop with a panel of subject matter experts.
3. Your boss asks you to incorporate personality characteristics into job analysis. How would you proceed?
4. What are the similarities and differences between competency modeling and job analysis?
5. You have been asked to conduct a job analysis for astronauts working on the international space station. Which technique(s) might be most appropriate in this situation, and why?
6. Discuss some of the special problems associated with conducting strategic or future-oriented job analyses.
7. Go to the O*Net Web site (http://online.onetcenter.org). Develop a profile of five skills or abilities, and find occupations that match it.

10

Strategic Workforce Planning

At a Glance

People are among any organization's most critical resources; yet systematic approaches to workforce planning (WP), forecasting, and action programs designed to provide trained people to fill needs for particular skills are still evolving.

WP systems include several specific, interrelated activities. **Talent inventories** provide a means of assessing current resources (skills, abilities, promotional potential, assignment histories, etc.). **Forecasts of HR supply and demand** enable planners to predict employment requirements (numbers, skills mix). Together, talent inventories and forecasts help to identify workforce needs that provide operational meaning and direction for **action plans** in many different areas, including recruitment, selection, placement, and performance management, as well as numerous training activities. Finally, **control and evaluation procedures** are required to provide feedback to the WP system and to monitor the degree of attainment of HR goals and objectives.

Ultimate success in WP depends on several factors: the degree of integration of WP with strategic planning activities, the quality of the databases used to produce the talent inventory and forecasts of workforce supply and demand, the caliber of the action programs established, and the organization's ability to implement the programs. The net effect should be a wiser, more efficient use of people at all levels.

The judicious use of human resources is a perpetual problem in society. Specific examples of HR problems that are also top management problems are:

- Finding the specialized technical talent needed to staff specific programs of planned business expansion (e.g., Aston, 2007; Cappelli, 2008; Herbst, 2007).
- Finding seasoned talent to manage new and expanding operations, including people with the capability eventually to assume senior-management positions.
- Developing competent, equitable HR management practices that will ensure compliance with EEO requirements and thus avoid the potentially large settlement costs of discrimination suits.
- Devising alternatives to layoffs or, if layoffs become necessary, implementing equitable and workable layoff policies that acknowledge the needs of all parties.

- Improving productivity, especially among managerial and technical employees.
- Managing career-development opportunities so that an effective pool of talented people can be attracted, motivated, and retained over long periods of time.

To a considerable extent, emphasis on improved HR practice has arisen as a result of recognition by many top managers of the crucial role that talent plays in gaining and sustaining a competitive advantage in a global marketplace. It is the source of innovation and renewal. Despite these encouraging signs, it appears that, while most companies engage in some form of long-range business planning to assess periodically their basic missions and objectives, very few actually are practicing strategic HR management today.

Organizations will not have succeeded in fully using their human resources until they can answer the following questions (Cappelli, 2008; Hirschman, 2007):

1. What talents, abilities, and skills are available within the organization today?
2. Who are the people we can dependably build on for tomorrow?
3. How are we blending the talent available with the organization's needs?
4. What are the qualitative as well as quantitative HR demands of our growth plan?

In this chapter, we shall first describe the WP process, emphasizing its linkage to strategic business planning, and then take a closer look at each element in the process, including the talent inventory, forecasts of HR needs, action plans, and control and evaluation procedures.

WHAT IS WORKFORCE PLANNING?

The purpose of WP is to anticipate and respond to *needs* emerging within and outside the organization, to determine priorities, and to allocate resources where they can do the most good. Although WP means different things to different people, general agreement exists on its ultimate objective—namely, the wisest, most effective use of scarce or abundant talent in the interest of the individual and the organization. Thus, we may define WP broadly as *an effort to anticipate future business and environmental demands on an organization and to meet the HR requirements dictated by these conditions.* This general view of WP suggests several specific, interrelated activities that together comprise a WP system:

1. *Talent inventory*—to assess current resources (skills, abilities, and potential) and analyze current use of employees.
2. *Workforce forecast*—to predict future HR requirements (numbers, skills mix, internal versus external labor supply).
3. *Action plans*—to enlarge the pool of qualified individuals by recruitment, selection, training, placement, transfer, promotion, development, and compensation.
4. *Control and evaluation*—to provide closed-loop feedback to the rest of the system and to monitor the degree of attainment of HR goals and objectives.

Figure 10-1 illustrates such an integrated WP system. Notice how strategic and tactical business plans serve as the basis for HR strategy and how HR strategy interacts with the talent inventory and forecasts of workforce supply and demand to produce net workforce requirements. Note how labor markets also affect the supply of and demand for labor. When labor markets are "loose," the supply of available workers exceeds the demand for them, and unemployment is high. Under these circumstances, turnover tends to decrease, as does employee mobility. Conversely, when labor markets are "tight," demand for workers exceeds supply, and unemployment is low. Under these circumstances, jobs are plentiful, and employee mobility tends to increase.

With a clear understanding of the surpluses or deficits of employees in terms of their numbers, their skills, and their experience that are projected at some future point in time—that is, a statement of net workforce requirements—it is possible to initiate action plans to rectify projected

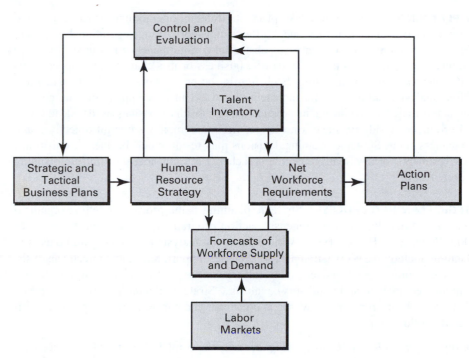

FIGURE 10-1 An integrated workforce-planning system.   *Source:* Cascio, W. F. (2010). Managing human resources: Productivity, quality of work life, profits (8th ed.), p. 175. Burr Ridge, IL: McGraw-Hill/Irwin. Reprinted by permission.

problems. Finally, control and evaluation procedures provide feedback that affects every aspect of the WP process. We will have more to say about each of these processes once we see how they flow from strategic business and HR plans.

Strategic Business and Workforce Plans

Strategies are the means that organizations use to compete, for example, through innovation, quality, speed, or cost leadership. How firms compete with each other and how they attain and sustain competitive advantage are the essence of what is known as strategic management (Dess, Lumpkin, & Eisner, 2007). In order to develop strategies, however, organizations need to plan. Planning is the very heart of management, for it helps managers reduce the uncertainty of the future and thereby do a better job of coping with the future. Hence, a fundamental reason for planning is that *planning leads to success*—not all the time, but studies show consistently that planners outperform nonplanners (MacMillan & Selden, 2008; Miller & Cardinal, 1994; Mitchell, Harman, Lee, & Lee, 2009). A second reason for planning is that it gives managers and organizations a sense of being in control of their fate rather than leaving their fate to chance. Hence, *planning helps organizations do a better job of coping with change*—technological, social, regulatory, and environmental.

   A third reason for planning is that it *requires managers to define the organization's objectives* and thus provides context, meaning, and direction for employees' work. By defining and ensuring that all employees are aware of overall goals—*why* they are doing what they are doing—employers can tie more effectively *what* employees are doing to the organization's overall objectives (Pearce & Robinson, 2009). A great deal of research indicates that the process of defining objectives leads to better employee performance and satisfaction.

   A final reason for planning is that *without objectives effective control is impossible.* "If you don't know where you are going, any road will get you there." Planning may occur, however, over different levels or time frames.

LEVELS OF PLANNING   Planning may take place at strategic, operational, or tactical levels. Strategic planning is long range in nature, and it differs from shorter-range operational or tactical planning. Strategic planning decisions involve substantial commitments of resources, resulting either in a fundamental change in the direction of a business or in a change in the speed of its development along the path it is traveling. Each step in the process may involve considerable data collection, analysis, and iterative management reviews. Thus, a company making components for computers may, after reviewing its product line or subsidiary businesses, decide to divest its chemical-products subsidiary, since it no longer fits the company's overall objectives and long-range business plans. Strategic planning decisions may result in new business acquisitions, new capital investments, or new management approaches. Let's consider the strategic planning process in more detail.

THE STRATEGIC PLANNING PROCESS   Strategic planning is the process of setting organizational objectives and deciding on comprehensive action programs to achieve these objectives (Hamel, 2000; Prahalad & Hamel, 1994). Various business-analysis techniques can be used in strategic planning, including SWOT (strengths, weaknesses, opportunities, and threats) analysis, PEST (political, economic, social, and technological) analysis, or STEER (sociocultural, technological, economic, ecological, and regulatory) analysis ("Strategic Planning," 2009). Based on analyses of the multiple environments in which an organization competes, strategic planning typically includes the following processes:

- *Defining company philosophy by looking at*—why the company exists, what unique contributions it makes, and what business it should be in.
- *Formulating company and divisional statements of identity, purpose, and objectives.*
- *Evaluating the company's strengths, weaknesses, opportunities, and threats*—in order to identify the factors that may enhance or limit the choice of any future courses of action.
- *Determining the organization design*—(structure, processes, interrelationships) appropriate for managing the company's chosen business.
- *Developing appropriate strategies for achieving objectives*—(e.g., time-based points of measurement), including qualitative and quantitative subgoals.
- *Devising programs to implement the strategies.*

An Alternative Approach

The methodology described above is a conventional view of the strategy-development process, and it answers two fundamental questions that are critical for managers: What business are we in? and How shall we compete? While this approach is an exciting intellectual exercise for those crafting the strategy, O'Reilly and Pfeffer (2000) pointed out that it is not particularly engaging to those charged with implementing the strategy. It takes the competitive landscape as a given and devises maneuvers against a given set of competitors, presumed markets, customer tastes, and organizational capabilities. In contrast, O'Reilly and Pfeffer (2000) described a number of companies, including Southwest Airlines, Cisco Systems, The Men's Wearhouse, and AES (which generates electrical power) that took a different tack—namely, they turned the strategy-development process on its head. Figure 10-2 illustrates this alternative approach.

In the alternative, or values-based, approach to developing strategy, organizations begin with a set of fundamental values that are energizing and capable of unlocking the human potential of their people—values such as fun, fairness, challenge, trust, respect, community, and family. They then use these values to develop, or at least to evaluate, management policies and practices that express organizational values in pragmatic ways on a day-to-day basis. For any management practice, from hiring to compensation, the key question is "To what extent is this practice consistent with our core beliefs about people and organizations?"

The management practices that are implemented have effects on people. Consequently, the management practices come to produce core competencies and capabilities at these companies,

A Values-Based View of Strategy

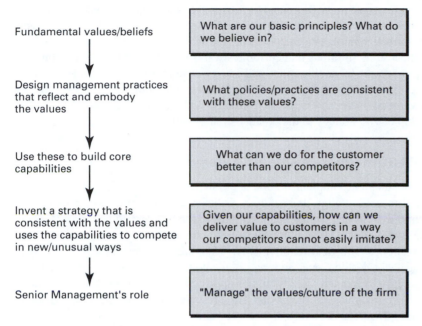

Fundamental values/beliefs → What are our basic principles? What do we believe in?

Design management practices that reflect and embody the values → What policies/practices are consistent with these values?

Use these to build core capabilities → What can we do for the customer better than our competitors?

Invent a strategy that is consistent with the values and uses the capabilities to compete in new/unusual ways → Given our capabilities, how can we deliver value to customers in a way our competitors cannot easily imitate?

Senior Management's role → "Manage" the values/culture of the firm

FIGURE 10-2   A values-based view of strategy.   *Source:* O'Reilly, C. A., and Pfeffer, J. *Hidden value: How great companies achieve extraordinary results with ordinary people,* p. 15. Boston: Harvard Business School Press. Adapted and reprinted by permission of the Harvard Business School Press.

whether it is teamwork, learning, and speed at AES; service and personal development at The Men's Wearhouse; or productivity and quality at Southwest Airlines. In turn, these capabilities and competencies can change the competitive dynamics of the industry. The Men's Wearhouse competes on service, not just on price. Southwest Airlines has productive employees who permit it to save on capital investment and labor costs, while delivering outstanding service at the same time ("Southwest Airlines," 2009). Cisco is able to change technology platforms and to acquire and retain intellectual capital as the industry shifts around it. What these companies can do better than anyone else permits them to develop innovative strategies and approaches that outflank the competition (O'Reilly & Pfeffer, 2000). In his research, Collins (cited in Reingold, 2009) found that the most enduring and successful corporations distinguish their timeless core values and enduring core purpose (which should never change) from their operating practices and business strategies (which should be changing constantly in response to a changing world). In this approach to management, strategy comes last, after the values and practices are aligned and after the company develops capabilities that set it apart.

This is not to imply that strategy is unimportant. Each of the firms described above has a well-developed competitive strategy that helps it make decisions about how and where to compete. Such strategic decisions are secondary, however, to living a set of values and creating the alignment between values and people.

Payoffs from Strategic Planning

The biggest benefit of strategic planning is its emphasis on growth, for it encourages managers to look for new opportunities rather than simply cutting workers to reduce expenses. But the danger of strategic planning—particularly the conventional approach to strategic planning—is that it may lock companies into a particular vision of the future—one that may not come to pass. This poses a dilemma: how to plan for the future when the future changes so quickly. The answer is to make the planning process more democratic. Instead of relegating strategic planning to a separate staff—as in the past—it needs to include a wide range of people, from line managers to customers to suppliers. Top managers must listen and be prepared to shift plans in midstream if conditions demand it. This is exactly the approach that Cisco Systems takes. It is not wedded to any particular technology, for it recognizes that customers are the arbiters of choice. It listens carefully to its customers and then offers solutions that customers want. Sometimes this means acquiring other companies to provide the technology that will satisfy customer demands. Indeed, Cisco acquired 39 companies from 2005 through April 2009 (Cisco Corporation, 2009). This mindset enables Cisco to move in whatever directions that markets and customers dictate. Now let us consider the relationship of HR strategy to the broader strategy of the business.

Relationship of HR Strategy to Business Strategy

HR strategy parallels and facilitates implementation of the strategic business plan. HR strategy is the set of priorities a firm uses to align its resources, policies, and programs with its strategic business plan. It requires a focus on planned major changes in the business and on critical issues such as the following: What are the HR implications of the proposed business strategies? What are the possible external constraints and requirements? What are the implications for management practices, management development, and management succession? What can be done in the short term to prepare for longer-term needs? In this approach to the strategic management of human resources, a firm's business strategy and HR strategy are interdependent (Becker, Huselid, & Ulrich, 2001; Boudreau & Ramstad, 2007; Huselid, Becker, & Beatty, 2005).

Figure 10-3 is a model that shows the relationship of HR strategy to the broader business strategy (based on Boudreau, 1998; Boudreau & Ramstad, 2003). Briefly, the model shows that planning proceeds top–down, while execution proceeds bottom–up. There are four links in the

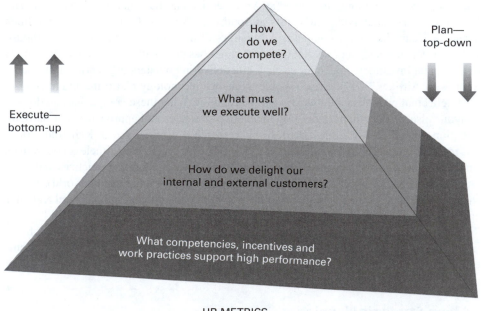

FIGURE 10-3   The relationship of HR strategy to the broader strategy of a business.   *Source: HR in alignment.* DVD produced by the Society for Human Resource Management Foundation, 2004. Alexandria, VA. Used with permission.

model, beginning with the fundamental question "How do we compete?" As we noted earlier, firms may compete on a number of nonindependent dimensions, such as innovation, quality, cost leadership, or speed. From that, it becomes possible to identify business or organizational processes that the firm must execute well in order to compete (e.g., speedy order fulfillment). When processes are executed well, the organization delights its internal and external customers through high performance. This may occur, for example, when an employee presents a timely, cost-effective solution to a customer's problem. To manage and motivate employees to strive for high performance, the right competencies, incentives, and work practices must be in place. Execution proceeds bottom–up, as appropriate competencies, challenging incentives, and work practices inspire high performance, which delights internal and external customers. This, in turn, means that business processes are being executed efficiently, enabling the organization to compete successfully for business in the marketplace.

At a general level, high-performance work practices include the following five features (Paauwe, Williams, & Keegan, 2002):

- Pushing responsibility down to employees operating in flatter organizations
- Increasing the emphasis on line managers as HR managers
- Instilling learning as a priority in all organizational systems
- Decentralizing decision making to autonomous units and employees
- Linking performance measures for employees to financial performance indicators

Workforce plans must flow from, and be consistent with, the overall business and HR strategies. Figure 10-4 shows the relationship between business planning—long range, mid-range, and annual—and parallel processes that occur in WP. As Figure 10-4 shows, WP focuses on firm-level responses to people-related business issues over multiple time horizons. What are some examples of such issues, and how can managers identify them? People-related business concerns, or issues, might include, for example, "What types of skills or competencies will managers need to run the business three to five years from now, and how do we make sure our managers will have them?" At a broader level, issues include the impact of rapid technological change; more complex organizations (in terms of products, locations, customers, and markets); and more frequent responses to external forces such as legislation and litigation, demographic changes, and increasing competition—both domestic and global. In this scenario, changes in the business

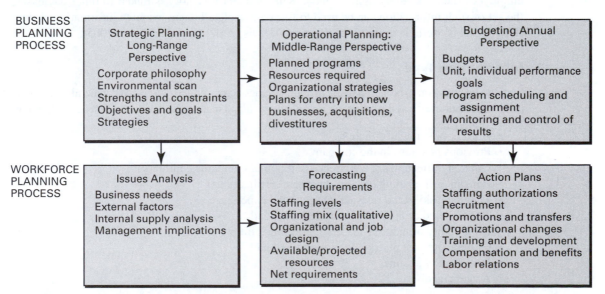

FIGURE 10-4   Impact of three levels of business planning on workforce planning.   *Source:* Cascio, W. F. (2003). *Managing human resources* (6th ed.), p. 177. Burr Ridge, IL: McGraw-Hill/Irwin. Reprinted by permission.

environment drive issues, issues drive actions, and actions include programs and processes to address the business issues identified.

In the remainder of this chapter, we will examine the various components of the WP system, as shown in Figure 10-1. As the figure shows, forecasts and action plans are two key elements of WP. A forecast of net workforce needs is the result of an analysis of the future availability (supply) of labor and future labor requirements (demand), tempered by an analysis of external conditions (e.g., technologies, markets, competition). With respect to the future availability of people with the right skills, an inventory of current talent is essential. We consider that topic next.

TALENT INVENTORY

A talent inventory is a fundamental requirement of an effective WP system. It is an organized database of the existing skills, abilities, career interests, and experience of the current workforce. Prior to actual data collection, however, certain fundamental questions must be addressed:

1. Who should be included in the inventory?
2. What specific information must be included for each individual?
3. How can this information best be obtained?
4. What is the most effective way to record such information?
5. How can inventory results be reported to top management?
6. How often must this information be updated?
7. How can the security of this information be protected?

Answers to these kinds of questions will provide both direction and scope to subsequent efforts. For example, IBM uses a technology-powered staff-deployment tool called "Workforce Management Initiative" (Byrnes, 2005; MacDonald, 2008). It's a sort of in-house version of Monster.com, the online job site. Built on a database of 400,000 résumés, it lets managers search for employees with the precise skills they'll need for particular projects. The initiative cost IBM $100 million to build over three years, but it has already saved more than $500 million, and it has also improved productivity. Its greatest impact, however, may be its ability to help managers analyze what skills staffers possess and how those talents match up to the business outlook. It's part of a broader WP effort that helps managers decide whether to "buy," "make," or "rent" employees (i.e., temporary assignments). When a talent inventory is linked to other databases, the set of such information can be used to form a complete human resource information system (HRIS) that is useful in a variety of situations (Davis, 2007; Geutal & Stone, 2005).

Information Type

Specific information to be stored in the inventory varies across organizations. At a general level, however, information such as the following is typically included in a profile developed for each individual:

- Current position information
- Previous positions in the company
- Other significant work experience (e.g., other companies, military)
- Education (including degrees, licenses, certifications)
- Language skills and relevant international experience
- Training and development programs attended
- Community or industry leadership responsibilities
- Current and past performance appraisal data
- Disciplinary actions
- Awards received

Information provided by individuals may also be included. At Schlumberger, for example, employees add their career goals, information about their families, past assignments, professional affiliations, publications, patents granted, and hobbies. IBM includes the individual's expressed preference for future assignments and locations, including interest in staff or line positions in other IBM locations and divisions (Byrnes, 2005; MacDonald, 2008).

Uses

Although secondary uses of the talent-inventory data may emerge, it is important to specify the primary uses at the concept-development stage. Doing so provides direction and scope regarding who and what kinds of data should be included. Some common uses of a talent inventory include identification of candidates for promotion, succession planning, assignments to special projects, transfer, training, workforce-diversity planning and reporting, compensation planning, career planning, and organizational analysis. Be sure to include a clear statement about employee privacy safeguards and the potential impact on employee privacy of all such in-house systems.

FORECASTING WORKFORCE SUPPLY AND DEMAND

Talent inventories and workforce forecasts must complement each other; an inventory of present talent is not particularly useful for planning purposes unless it can be analyzed in terms of future workforce requirements. On the other hand, a forecast of workforce requirements is useless unless it can be evaluated relative to the current and projected future supply of workers available internally. Only at that time, when we have a clear understanding of the projected surpluses or deficits of employees in terms of their numbers, their skills, and their experience, does it make sense to initiate action plans to rectify projected problems.

Workforce forecasts are attempts to estimate future labor requirements. There are two component processes in this task: anticipating the supply of human resources, both inside and outside the organization, at some future time period; and anticipating organizational demand for various types of employees. Forecasts of labor supply should be considered separately from forecasts of demand because each depends on a different set of variables and assumptions (Cappelli, 2008). Internal supply forecasts tend to relate much more closely to conditions *inside* the organization, such as the age distribution within the workforce, average rates of turnover, retirement, transfer, and new hires within job classes. Demand forecasts depend primarily on the behavior of some business factor (e.g., projected number of retail outlets, sales, and product volume) to which workforce needs can be related. In contrast to forecasts of labor supply, demand forecasts are beset with multiple uncertainties—in consumer behavior, in technology, in the general economic environment, and so forth.

Consider two paradoxes in workforce forecasts: (1) The techniques are basically simple and easy to describe, but applying them successfully may be enormously complex and difficult; and (2) after the forecast has been made, it may prove to be most useful when it proves to be least accurate as a vision of the future.

Here is what the latter paradox implies. Assume that a particular forecast points toward a future HR problem—for example, a surplus of middle managers with comparable skills who were hired at the same time to meet a sudden expansion. The forecast may be most useful if it stimulates action (e.g., appropriate training, transfer, promotion) so that the surplus never actually develops. It is useless only if the surplus develops on schedule as projected. Therein lies the value of workforce forecasts: In themselves, they are little more than academic exercises, but, when integrated into a total planning process, they take on special value because they enable an organization to extend the range of other phases of WP and of planning for other functions.

External Workforce Supply

When an organization plans to expand, recruitment and hiring of new employees may be anticipated. Even when an organization is not growing, the aging of the present workforce, coupled with normal attrition, makes some recruitment and selection a virtual certainty for most firms. It is wise, therefore, to examine forecasts of the external labor market for the kinds of employees that will be needed.

Several agencies regularly make projections of external labor-market conditions and future occupational supply (by occupation), including the Bureau of Labor Statistics of the U.S. Department of Labor, the National Science Foundation, the Department of Education, and the Public Health Service of the Department of Health and Human Services.

For new college and university graduates, the National Association of Colleges and Employers conducts a quarterly salary survey of starting salary offers to new college graduates at the bachelor's-degree level (*www.naceweb.org*), and salary offers reflect supply/demand conditions in the external labor market. Organizations in industries as varied as oil and gas, nuclear power, digital-media advertising, construction, and heavy-equipment service are finding such projections of the external labor market to be helpful in preventing surpluses or deficits of employees (Aston, 2007; Coy & Ewing, 2007; Vranica & Steel, 2006).

It is important to gauge both the future supply of workers in a particular field and the future demand for these workers. Focusing only on the supply side could be seriously misleading. For example, the number of chemical-engineering majors scheduled to graduate from college during the next year may appear large, and certainly adequate to meet next year's hiring needs for chemical engineers for a particular company—until the aggregate demand of all companies for chemical-engineering graduates is compared with the available supply. That comparison may reveal an impending shortage and signal the need for more widespread and sophisticated recruiting efforts. Organizations are finding that they require projections of the external labor market as a starting point for planning, for preventing potential employee shortages from arising, and for dealing effectively with those that are to some extent unavoidable.

Internal Workforce Supply

An organization's current workforce provides a base from which to project the future supply of workers. It is a form of risk management. Thus, when CAN Financial Corporation analyzed the demographics of the incumbents of various mission-critical jobs, it learned that 85 percent of its risk-control safety engineers, who inspect boilers and other machinery in buildings, were eligible for retirement. The company wanted to hold on to their specialized skills, because they were so important to retaining current business. The forecast prompted the company to take action to ensure that projected deficits did not materialize (Hirschman, 2007). Perhaps the most common type of internal supply forecast is the leadership-succession plan.

Leadership-Succession Planning

In a recent international study by the Society for Human Resource Management Foundation, more than 500 senior executives from a variety of functional areas were asked to identify the top human-capital challenges that could derail their firms' ability to achieve key, strategic business objectives in the next three to five years. Fully 75 percent of executives from companies both large and small identified "leadership-succession planning" as their most pressing challenge, followed closely by the need to develop a pipeline of leaders at all levels (SHRM Foundation, 2007).

Succession planning is the one activity that is pervasive, well accepted, and integrated with strategic business planning among firms that do WP (Ogden & Wood, 2008; Welch & Byrne, 2001). In fact, succession planning is considered by many firms to be the sum and substance of WP. The actual mechanics for developing such a plan include steps such as the following: setting a planning horizon, assessing current performance and readiness for promotion, identifying replacement candidates for each key position, identifying career-development needs, and integrating the career goals of individuals with company goals. The overall objective, of course, is to ensure the availability of competent executive talent in the future or, in some cases, immediately (Bower, 2008; Holstein, 2008). Here is an overview of how several companies do it.

Both GE and IBM have had similar processes in place for decades, and many other firms have modeled theirs on these two. The stated objective of both programs is "to assure top quality and ready talent for all executive positions in the corporation worldwide." Responsibility for carrying out this process rests with line executives from division presidents up to the chief executive officer. An executive-resource staff located within the corporate HR function provides staff support.

Each responsible executive makes a formal presentation to a corporate policy committee consisting of the chairman, the vice chairman, and the president. The presentation usually consists of an overall assessment of the strengths and weaknesses of the unit's executive resources, the present performance and potential of key executives and potential replacements (supplemented with pictures of the individuals involved), and the rankings of all incumbents of key positions in terms of present performance and expected potential (Conaty, 2007). Figure 10-5 is an abbreviated example of a typical succession-planning chart for an individual manager.

The policy committee reviews and critiques this information and often provides additional insights to line management on the strengths and weaknesses of both incumbents and their replacements. Sometimes the committee will even direct specific career-development actions to be accomplished before the next review (Conaty, 2007; Welch & Byrne, 2001).

Leadership-succession processes are particularly well developed at 3M Company. With 2008 worldwide sales of $25.3 billion, 64 percent of which came from outside the United States, 3M sells 65,000 products in more than 200 countries, and it employs more than 79,000 people worldwide (3M. Company, 2008). At 3M, a common set of leadership attributes links all management practices with respect to assessment, development, and succession ("Seeing forward," 2008):

- Thinks from outside in
- Drives innovation and growth
- Develops, teaches, and engages others
- Makes courageous decisions
- Leads with energy, passion, and urgency
- Lives 3M values

These leadership attributes describe what leaders need to know, what they need to do, and the personal qualities that they need to display. With respect to *assessment*, managers assess potential as part of the performance-appraisal process. All managers also receive 360-degree feedback as part of leadership classes. Executive hires at the leadership level all go through an

Name:
Title:
Months in Position:

Positive and negative attributes:
+ Global thinker, great coach/mentor, solid technical background
- Still maturing as a leader
Developmental needs:
Needs experience in e-business
Attend company's senior leadership-development program

FIGURE 10-5 A typical chart used for management–succession planning.

extensive psychometric assessment. With respect to *development*, 3M's Leadership Development Institute focuses on "Leaders Teaching Leaders." It is delivered as a key development strategy in the formation of a global leadership pipeline. 3M also uses "Action learning"—training that is focused on developing creative solutions to business-critical problems—as way to learn by doing. Participants present their final recommendations to senior-level executives. Finally, after follow-up coaching and individual-development plans, leaders are assessed in terms of the impact of their growth on the organization strategically.

Succession planning focuses on a few key objectives: to identify top talent, that is, high-potential individuals, both within functions and corporate-wide; to develop pools of talent for critical positions; and to identify development plans for key leaders. 3M's Executive Resources Committee assures consistency both in policy and practice in global succession planning for key management and executive positions—including the process for identifying, developing, and tracking the progress of high-potential individuals ("Seeing forward," 2008).

Chief Executive Officer (CEO) Succession

Recent data indicate that only about half of public and private corporate boards have CEO-succession plans in place. This is the case even at giant global companies that have thousands of employees and spend millions each year to recruit and train talent (Ogden & Wood, 2008; "CEO succession," 2007). Thus, after a combined write-down of more than $15 billion at Citigroup and Merrill Lynch in late 2007, stemming from turmoil in the subprime mortgage market, the chief executives of both firms were forced out, and their respective boards of directors were left to scramble to find replacements.

Is this an anomaly? Hardly. Rather, these were just the latest examples of boards that failed to build solid leadership-succession plans, joining the boards at other firms who had made the same mistake in the past, such as Morgan Stanley, Coca-Cola, Home Depot, AIG, and Hewlett-Packard. These companies stand in stark contrast to such firms as General Electric, ExxonMobil, Goldman Sachs, Johnson & Johnson, Kellogg, United Parcel Service, and Pepsico, which bene-fited enormously from building strong teams of internal leaders, which in turn resulted in seamless transitions in executive leadership. In fact, people development is becoming an important part of the assessment of executive performance. PepsiCo is a good example. Historically it allocated one-third of incentive compensation to the development of people, with the remainder allocated to results. It's now moving to an equal allocation of incentive compensation for people develop-ment and results.

Why weren't the first set of boards grooming internal candidates for the leadership jobs? In part, because at the heart of succession lie personality, ego, power, and, most importantly, mor-tality (George, 2007). Ideally, careful succession planning grooms people internally. Doing so maintains the intellectual capital of an organization, and also motivates senior-level executives to stay and to excel because they might get to lead the company someday.

On the other hand, there are also sound reasons why a company might look to an outside successor. Boards that hire outsiders to be CEOs feel that change is more important than continuity, particularly so in situations where things have not been going well. They expect the outsider to bring about change in a wide variety of organizational dimensions (Finkelstein & Hambrick, 1996). In the case of founders, many simply cannot bring themselves to name successors during their lifetimes. This leads to profound disruption after the founder dies (McBride, 2003). To avoid a future crisis in leadership succession, here are some key steps to take (Bower, 2007; Holstein, 2008): ensure that the sitting CEO understands the importance of this task and makes it a priority; focus on an organization's future needs, not past accomplishments; encourage differ-ences of opinion with respect to management decisions; provide broad exposure to a variety of jobs, changing responsibilities every three to five years; and finally, provide access to the Board, so that managers get a sense of what matters to directors, and directors get to see the talent in the pipeline.

What about small firms, such as family-owned businesses? Unfortunately, only about 30 percent of small, family businesses outlive their founders, usually for lack of planning. Here are some of the ways families are trying to solve the problem:

- 25 percent plan to let the children compete and choose one or more successors with help from the board of directors.
- 35 percent plan to groom one child from an early age to take over.
- 15 percent plan to let the children compete and choose one or more successors, without input from a third party.
- 15 percent plan to form an "executive committee" of two or more children.
- 10 percent plan to let the children choose their own leader, or leaders (Brown, 1988; Hutcheson, 2007; Klein, 2007).

Sometimes family-owned firms look to outsiders, especially for new ideas and technology for the firm. Experts advise firms in that situation to start early, for it may take three to five years for the successor to become fully capable of assuming leadership for the company. Finally, the best successions are those that end with a clean and certain break. In other words, once the firm has a new leader in the driver's seat, the old leader should get off the bus.

One study of 228 CEO successions (Shen & Cannella, 2002) found that it is not the event of CEO succession per se, but rather the succession context, that affects the subsequent performance of the firm. Successors may be outsiders or insiders. Insider successors may be followers who were promoted to CEO positions following the ordinary retirements of their predecessors. Alternatively, they may be contenders who were promoted to CEO positions following the dismissals of their predecessors. However, focusing on the CEO's successor alone, without considering other changes within top management, provides an incomplete picture of the subsequent effect on the financial performance of the firm. Shen and Cannella (2002) showed that turnover among senior executives has a positive effect on a firm's profitability in contender succession, but a negative impact in outsider succession. That is, outsider successors may benefit a firm's operations, but a subsequent loss of senior executives may outweigh any gains that come from the outsider successors themselves.

Furthermore, the tenure of the prior CEO seems to extend to the early years of the successor's tenure. Specifically, the lengthy tenure of the prior CEO leads to inertia, making it difficult for the successor to initiate strategic change. Conversely, if a departing CEO's tenure is too short, the firm may not have recovered sufficiently from the disruption of the previous succession. In other words, there is an inverted U-shaped relationship between departing CEO tenure and post-succession firm performance (Shen & Cannella, 2002).

WORKFORCE DEMAND

Demand forecasts are largely subjective, principally because of multiple uncertainties regarding trends such as changes in technology; consumer attitudes and patterns of buying behavior; local, national, and international economies; number, size, and types of contracts won or lost; and government regulations that might open new markets or close off old ones. Consequently, forecasts of workforce demand are often more subjective than quantitative, although in practice a combination of the two is often used. Begin by identifying pivotal jobs.

Pivotal Jobs

Pivotal jobs drive strategy and revenue, and differentiate an organization in the marketplace (Boudreau & Ramstad, 2007; Cascio & Boudreau, 2008). For example, Valero Energy, a 23,000-employee oil refiner and gas retailer, identified 300 to 500 high-impact positions, and 3,000 to 4,000 mission-critical ones, including engineers and welders employed at the company's 18 oil refineries. The company then linked those specific positions directly to quantifiable revenues, business objectives, and business operations. Corning, Inc., a New York–based technology company that employs 26,000 people worldwide, segmented jobs into four categories—strategic, core, requisite, and noncore. The objective is to deconstruct the business strategy to understand its implications for talent.

Assessing Future Workforce Demand

To develop a reasonable estimate the numbers and skills mix of people needed over some future time period, for example, two to three years, it is important to tap into the collective wisdom of managers who are close to the scene of operations. Consider asking them questions such as the following (Hirschman, 2007):

- What are our key business goals and objectives for the next two years?
- What are the top three priorities we must execute well in order to reach our goals over that time period?
- What are the most critical workforce issues we currently face?
- What are the three to five core capabilities we need to win in our markets?
- What are the required knowledge, skills, and abilities needed to execute the strategy?
- What types of positions will be required? What types will no longer be needed?
- Which types of skills should we have internally versus buy versus rent?
- What actions are necessary to align our resources with priorities?
- How will we know if we are effectively executing our workforce plan and staying on track?

How Accurate Must Demand Forecasts Be?

Accuracy in forecasting the demand for labor varies considerably by firm and by industry type (e.g., utilities versus women's fashions): roughly from a 5 to 35 percent error factor. Factors such as the duration of the planning period, the quality of the data on which forecasts are based, and the degree of integration of WP with strategic business planning all affect accuracy. One study found an overall 30 percent error rate for a one-year forecast (Cappelli, 2008). The degree of accuracy in labor-demand forecasting depends on the degree of flexibility in staffing the workforce. That is, to the extent that people are geographically mobile, multiskilled, and easily hired, there is less need for precise forecasts.

Integrating Supply and Demand Forecasts

If forecasts are to prove genuinely useful to managers, they must result in an end product that is understandable and meaningful. Initial attempts at forecasting may result in voluminous print-outs, but what is really required is a concise statement of projected staffing requirements that integrates supply and demand forecasts (see Figure 10-6). In this figure, net workforce demand at the end of each year of the five-year forecast is compared with net workforce supply for the same year. This yields a "bottom-line" figure that shows an increasing deficit each year during the five-year period. This is the kind of evidence senior managers need in order to make informed decisions regarding the future direction of HR initiatives.

Matching Forecast Results to Action Plans

Workforce demand forecasts affect a firm's programs in many different areas, including recruitment, selection, performance management, training, transfer, and many other types of

Promotion Criteria (cf. Fig 10-6): must be ready now or in less than one year and performing at an excellent level.

	2007	**2008**	**2009**	**2010**	**2011**
Demand					
Beginning in position	213	222	231	240	249
Increases (decreases)	9	9	9	9	10
Total demand (year end)	222	231	240	249	259
Supply (during year)					
Beginning in position	213	222	231	240	249
Minus promotions	(28)	(31)	(31)	(34)	(34)
Minus terminations	(12)	(12)	(13)	(13)	(13)
Minus retirements	(6)	(6)	(6)	(6)	(6)
Minus transfers	(4)	(4)	(4)	(4)	(6)
Subtotal	163	169	177	183	190
Plus promotions in	18	18	18	18	18
Total supply (year end)	181	187	195	201	208
Surplus/deficit (year end)	(41)	(44)	(45)	(48)	(51)

FIGURE 10-6 Integrated workforce supply and demand forecast.

career-enhancement activities. These activities all comprise "action programs." Action programs help organizations adapt to changes in their environments.

Assuming a firm has a choice, however, is it better to *select* workers who already have developed the skills necessary to perform competently, or to select those who do not have the skills immediately, but who can be *trained* to perform competently? This is the same type of "make-or-buy" decision that managers often face in so many other areas of business. As a general principle, to avoid mismatch costs, balance "make" and "buy." Here are some guidelines for determining when "buying" is more effective than "making" (Cappelli, 2008):

- How accurate is your forecast of demand?
  If not accurate, do more buying.
- Do you have the "scale" to develop?
  If not, do more buying.
- Is there a job ladder to pull talent through?
  If not long, do more buying.
- How long will the talent be needed?
  If not long, do more buying.
- Do you want to change culture/direction?
  If yes, do more buying.

Managers have found that it is often more cost-effective to buy rather than to make. This is also true in the context of selection versus training (Schmidt, Hunter, & Pearlman, 1982). Put money and resources into selection. Always strive *first* to develop the most accurate, most valid selection process possible, for it will yield higher-ability workers. *Then* apply those action programs that are most appropriate to increase the performance of your employees further. With high-ability employees, the productivity gain from a training program in, say, financial analysis, might be greater than the gain from the same program with lower-ability employees. Further, even if the training is about equally effective with well-selected, higher-ability employees and poorly selected, lower-ability employees, the *time* required for training may be less for higher-ability employees. Thus, training costs will be reduced, and the net effectiveness of training will be greater when applied along with a highly valid staffing process. This point becomes even more relevant if one views training as a strategy for building sustained competitive advantage. Firms that select high-caliber employees and then continually commit resources to develop them gain a competitive advantage that no other organization can match: a deep reservoir of firm-specific human capital.

CONTROL AND EVALUATION

Control and evaluation are necessary features of any planning system, but organization-wide success in implementing HR strategy will not occur through disjointed efforts. Since WP activities override functional boundaries, broader system controls are necessary to monitor performance. Change is to be expected. The function of control and evaluation is to guide the WP activities through time, identifying deviations from the plan and their causes.

Goals and objectives are fundamental to this process to serve as yardsticks in measuring performance. Qualitative as well as quantitative standards may be necessary in WP, although quantitative standards are preferable, since numbers make the control and evaluation process more objective and deviations from desired performance may be measured more precisely. Such would be the case if a particular HR objective was to reduce the attrition rate of truck drivers in the first year after hire from the present 50 to 20 percent within three years. At the end of the third year, the evaluation process is simplified considerably because the initial objective was stated clearly with respect to the time period of evaluation (three years) and the expected percentage improvement (30 percent).

On the other hand, certain objectives, such as the quality of a diversity-management program or the quality of women and minorities in management, may be harder to quantify. One strategy is to specify subobjectives. For example, a subobjective of a plan to improve the quality of supervision may include participation by each supervisor in a two-week training program. Evaluation at time 2 may include a comparison of the number of employee grievances, requests for transfer, or productivity measures at time 1 with the number at time 2. Although other factors also may account for observed differences, appropriate experimental designs (see Chapter 16) usually can control them. Difficulty in establishing adequate and accurate criteria does not eliminate the responsibility to evaluate programs.

Monitoring Performance

Effective control systems include periodic sampling and measurement of performance. In a space vehicle, for example, computer guidance systems continually track the flight path of the vehicle and provide negative feedback in order to maintain the desired flight path. This is necessary in order to achieve the ultimate objective of the mission. An analogous tracking system should be part of any WP system. In long-range planning efforts, the shorter-run, intermediate objectives must be established and monitored in order to serve as benchmarks on the path to more remote goals. The shorter-run objectives allow the planner to monitor performance through time and to take corrective action before the ultimate success of longer-range goals is jeopardized.

Numerous monitoring procedures are commonly in use: examination of the costs of current practices (e.g., turnover costs, breakeven/payback for new hires); employee and management perceptions of results (e.g., by survey feedback procedures, audits of organizational climate); and measurement and analysis of costs and variations in costs under alternative decisions (e.g., analysis of costs of recruiting versus internal development of current employees).

In the area of performance management, plots of salary and performance progress of individual managers may be compared against organizational norms by age, experience, and job levels. Doing so makes it possible to identify and praise superior performers and to counsel ineffective performers to reverse the trend.

Identifying an Appropriate Strategy for Evaluation

We noted earlier that qualitative and quantitative objectives can both play useful roles in WP. However, the nature of evaluation and control should always match the degree of development of the rest of the WP process. In newly instituted WP systems, for example, evaluation is likely to be more qualitative than quantitative, with little emphasis placed on control. This is because supply-and-demand forecasts are likely to be based more on "hunches" and subjective opinions than on hard data. Under these circumstances, HR professionals should attempt to assess the following (Walker, 1980):

- The extent to which they are tuned in to workforce problems and opportunities, and the extent to which their priorities are sound.
- The quality of their working relationships with line managers who supply data and use WP results. How closely do they work with these managers on a day-to-day basis?
- The extent to which decision makers, from line managers who hire employees to top managers who develop business strategy, are making use of workforce forecasts, action plans, and recommendations.
- The perceived value of WP among decision makers. Do they view the information provided by HR specialists as useful to them in their own jobs?

In more established WP systems, in which objectives and action plans are both underpinned by measured performance standards, key comparisons might include the following (Dyer & Holder, 1988):

- Actual staffing levels against forecast staffing requirements.
- Actual levels of labor productivity against anticipated levels of labor productivity.
- Action programs implemented against action programs planned. (Were there more or fewer? Why?)
- The actual results of the action programs implemented against the expected results (e.g., improved applicant flows, lower quit rates).
- Labor and action-program costs against budgets.
- Ratios of action-program benefits to action-program costs.

An obvious advantage of quantitative information is that it highlights potential problem areas and can provide the basis for constructive discussion of the issues.

Responsibility for Workforce Planning

Responsibility for WP is a basic responsibility of every line manager in the organization. The line manager ultimately is responsible for integrating HR management functions, which include planning, supervision, performance appraisal, and job assignment. The role of the HR professional is to *help* line managers manage effectively by providing tools, information, training, and support. Basic planning assumptions (e.g., sales or volume assumptions for some future time period) may be given to all operating units periodically, but the individual manager must formulate his or her own workforce plans that are consistent with these assumptions. The plans of individual managers then may be reviewed by successively higher organizational units and finally aggregated into an overall workforce plan ("Seeing forward," 2008).

In summary, we plan in order to reduce the uncertainty of the future. We do not have an infinite supply of any resource (people, capital, information, or materials), and it is important not only that we anticipate the future, but also that we actively try to influence it. As George Bernard Shaw said, "the best way to predict the future is to create it." Ultimate success in WP rests on the quality of the action programs established to achieve HR objectives and on the organization's ability to implement these programs. Managing HR problems according to plan can be difficult, but it is a lot easier than trying to manage them with no plan at all.

Evidence-Based Implications for Practice

- Recognize that organizations compete just as fiercely in talent markets as they do in financial and customer markets.
- Plan for people in the context of managing a business strategically, recognizing the tight linkage between HR and business strategies.
- View the four components of a WP system—a talent inventory, forecasts of workforce supply and demand, action plans, and control and evaluation—as an integrated system, not as unrelated activities.
- With respect to leadership succession, recognize that the CEO must drive the talent agenda. It all begins with commitment from the top.
- Identify and communicate a common set of leadership attributes to promote a common set of expectations for everyone in the organization about what is expected of leaders.
- Keep to a regular schedule for performance reviews, broader talent reviews outside one's functional area, and the identification of talent pools for critical positions.
- Link all decisions about talent to the strategy of the organization.

Discussion Questions

1. Contrast the conventional approach to strategic planning with the values-based approach to developing strategy.
2. How are workforce plans related to business and HR strategies?
3. Describe the five features that characterize high-performance work practices.
4. How might the four components of a WP system apply to a hospital setting? What determines specific workforce needs in various areas? What programs might you suggest to meet such needs?
5. Why is WP especially necessary in a downsizing environment?
6. Why are forecasts of workforce demand more uncertain those of workforce supply?
7. The chairperson of the board of directors at your firm asks for advice on leadership succession. What practices or research results might you cite?

Systems thinking and applied measurement concepts, together with job analysis and WP, provide the necessary foundation for sound employment decisions. In the remainder of the book, we shall see how these concepts are applied in practice. Let us begin in Chapter 11 by considering the important process of recruitment.

11

Recruitment

At a Glance

Periodically, organizations recruit in order to add to, maintain, or readjust their workforces. Sound prior planning is critical to the recruiting process. It includes the establishment of workforce plans; the specification of time, cost, and staff requirements; the analysis of sources; the determination of job requirements; and the validation of employment standards. In the operations phase, the Internet is revolutionizing the recruitment process, opening up labor markets and removing geographical constraints. Finally, cost and quality analyses are necessary in order to evaluate the success of the recruitment effort. Such information provides closed-loop feedback that is useful in planning the next round of recruitment.

Whenever human resources must be expanded or replenished, a recruiting system of some kind must be established. Advances in technology, coupled with the growing intensity of competition in domestic and international markets, have made recruitment a top priority as organizations struggle continually to gain competitive advantage through people. Recruitment is a business, and it is big business (Griendling, 2008; Overman, 2008; Society for Human Resource Management, 2007). It demands serious attention from management because any business strategy will falter without the talent to execute it. According to Apple CEO Steve Jobs, "Recruiting is hard. It's finding the needles in the haystack. I've participated in the hiring of maybe 5,000-plus people in my life. I take it very seriously" (Jobs, 2008).

This statement echoes the claims of many recruiters that it is difficult to find good workers and that talent acquisition is becoming more rather than less difficult (Ployhart, 2006). As an example, consider the recent boom in social-networking Web sites designed for domestic and international job seekers, such as linkedin.com and doostang.com (McConnon, 2007; "Online Technologies," 2008). Such sites might be used by recruiters interested in poaching passive job candidates by first developing relationships with them before luring them away from competitors (Cappelli, 2001; Lievens & Harris, 2003). The result? A "leveling of the information playing field" brought about by Web technology. This is just one reason why recruitment is becoming more difficult.

Organizations recruit periodically in order to add to, maintain, or readjust their total work-forces in accordance with HR requirements. As open systems (discussed in Chapter 3), organizations demand this dynamic equilibrium for their own maintenance, survival, and growth. The logic of recruitment calls for sound workforce-planning systems (talent inventories, forecasts of workforce supply and demand, action plans, and control and evaluative procedures) to serve as a base from which to launch recruiting efforts. This will be evident as we begin to examine the operational aspects of the recruitment function.

In this chapter, our objective is to describe how organizations search for prospective employees and influence them to apply for available jobs. Accordingly, we will consider recruitment planning, operations, and evaluation, together with relevant findings from recruitment research, and we will include organizational examples to illustrate current practices. Figure 11-1, from Dineen & Soltis (in press), serves as an overarching framework for the processes described in this chapter. It integrates earlier views of recruitment in terms of sequential stages (Barber, 1998; Breaugh, Macan, & Grambow, 2008), while also integrating contextual/environmental and "key-process" issues (Rynes & Cable, 2003). As shown in Figure 11-1, two key decision points (application and job choice) separate these primary recruitment stages. Within each stage, the framework also identifies important subcategories.

Three contextual/environmental features affect all recruitment efforts, namely, characteristics of the firm (the value of its "brand" and its "personality"; Slaughter, Zickar, Highhouse, & Mohr, 2004); characteristics of the vacancy itself (is it mission critical?); and characteristics of the labor markets in which an organization recruits. Likewise, three sequential stages characterize recruitment efforts: generating a pool of viable candidates, maintaining the status (or interest) of viable candidates, and "getting to yes" after making a job offer (postoffer closure).

Figure 11-1 also identifies key activities that affect each of these three stages. These include strategies for targeting potential candidates and for communicating information to them

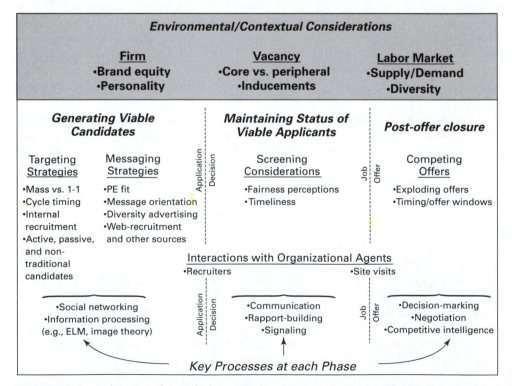

FIGURE 11-1 An integrated model of the recruitment process. *Source:* Dineen, B. R., & Soltis, S. N. (In press). Recruitment: Updating the literature. In S. Zedeck (Ed.), *Handbook of industrial and organizational psychology.* Washington, D. C.: American Psychological Association.

("messaging strategies"); issues related to screening viable candidates and interactions with organizational agents (recruiters, managers, and employees encountered during site visits); and issues related to actual job offers (e.g., timing, "exploding" offers that disappear after specified periods of time). Finally, Figure 11-1 identifies some key processes that affect the outcomes of each stage of the recruitment process, for example, social networking and information processing (seen through the lens of the Elaboration Likelihood Model, Jones, Schultz, & Chapman, 2006) at the candidate-generation stage; communication, rapport building, and signaling to maintain viable candidates; and negotiation, decision making, and competitive intelligence at the postjob-offer stage. Space constraints do not permit us to discuss each of the issues, activities, and processes shown in Figure 11-1, but we present it here because it is rich in implications for advancing both the theory and practice of recruitment. Now let's begin by considering recruitment planning.

RECRUITMENT PLANNING

The process of recruitment planning begins with a clear specification of HR needs (numbers, skills mix, levels) and the time frame within which such requirements must be met. This is particularly relevant to the setting of workforce diversity goals and timetables. Labor-force availability and internal workforce representation of women and minorities are critical factors in this process. The U.S. Census Bureau provides such information based on national census data for specific geographical areas.

Beyond these issues, two other important questions need to be addressed, namely, *whom* to recruit and *where* to recruit (Breaugh, 2008; Ployhart, Schneider, & Schmitt, 2006). With respect to whom to recruit, one strategy is to target executives from poorly performing firms because executives are more apt to search for jobs when their stock options are under water (Dunford, Boudreau, & Boswell, 2005). Answers to both questions, whom and where to recruit, are essential to determining recruitment objectives. For example, a prehire objective might be to attract a certain number of applications for pivotal or mission-critical jobs from passive job candidates—those who are not currently looking for a job. Objectives are also critical to recruitment evaluation, namely, if an employer wishes to compare what it hoped to accomplish with actual recruitment outcomes.

Having established recruitment objectives, an organization should be able to develop a coherent strategy for filling open positions. Among the questions an employer might address in establishing a recruitment strategy are: (1) When to begin recruiting? (2) What message to communicate to potential job applicants? and (3) Whom to use as recruiters? As Breaugh (2008) has noted, answers to these questions should be consistent with the recruitment objectives previously established. In terms of messages, consider the finding that satisfaction with coworkers enhances older-worker engagement (Avery, McKay, & Wilson, 2007). Messages to recruit older workers might therefore be geared toward enhancing perceptions of fit with immediate coworkers (person–group fit). Such messages might also build on the findings of a study by Rau and Adams (2005) that targeted equal employment opportunity statements, the opportunity to transfer knowledge, and flexible schedules, all of which positively influenced attraction of older workers.

With respect to timing, the effective use of "in-house" talent should come first. If external recruitment efforts are undertaken without considering the desires, capabilities, and potential of present employees.

Primed with a comprehensive workforce plan for the various segments of the workforce (e.g., entry level, managerial, professional, and technical), recruitment planning may begin. To do this, three key parameters must be estimated: the time, the money, and the staff necessary to achieve a given hiring rate (Hawk, 1967). The basic statistic needed to estimate these parameters is the *number of leads needed to generate a given number of hires in a given time.* Certainly the easiest way to derive this figure is on the basis of prior recruitment experience. If accurate records were maintained regarding yield ratios and time-lapse data, no problem exists, since

Leads
invites

trends may be determined and reliable predictions generated (assuming labor market conditions are comparable). **Yield ratios** are the ratios of leads to invites, invites to interviews, interviews (and other selection instruments) to offers, and offers to hires obtained over some specified time period (e.g., six months or a year). **Time-lapse data** provide the average intervals between events, such as between the extension of an offer to a candidate and acceptance or between acceptance and addition to the payroll.

If no experience data exist, then it is necessary to use "best guesses" or hypotheses and then to monitor performance as the operational recruitment program unfolds. For the moment, however, suppose ABC Engineering Consultants is contemplating opening two new offices and needs 100 additional engineers in the next six months. Fortunately, ABC has expanded in the past, and, on that basis, it is able to make predictions like this:

Prediction
example
w/ past experience

> With technical candidates, we must extend offers to 2 candidates to gain 1 acceptance, or an offer-to-acceptance ratio of 2:1. If we need 100 engineers, we'll have to extend 200 offers. Further, if the interview-to-offer ratio has been 3:2, then we need to conduct 300 interviews, and, since the invites-to-interview ratio is 4:3, then we must invite as many as 400 candidates. Finally, if contacts or leads required to find suitable candidates to invite are in a 6:1 proportion, then we need to make 2,400 contacts. A recruiting yield pyramid for these data is presented in Figure 11-2.

Actual data from a survey of more than 500 companies revealed the following average yield ratios: 7 percent of incoming résumés were routed to hiring managers (a 14:1 ratio), 26 percent of these were invited to interview, and 40 percent of the interviewees received job offers. Not surprisingly, the nontechnical positions generated twice as many acceptances (82 percent) as technical positions (41 percent) (Lord, 1989).

Additional information, critical to effective recruitment planning, can be derived from time-lapse data. For ABC Engineering Consultants, past experience may show that the interval from receipt of a résumé to invitation averages four days. If the candidate is still available, he or she will be interviewed five days later. Offers are extended, on the average, three days after interviews, and, within a week after that, the candidate either accepts or rejects the offer. If the candidate accepts, he or she reports to work, on the average, three weeks from the date of acceptance. Therefore, if ABC begins today, the best estimate is that it will be 40 days before the first new employee is added to the payroll. With this information, the "length" of the recruitment pipeline can be described and recruiting plans fitted to it. A simple time-lapse chart for these data is presented in Figure 11-3.

			Ratio
Hires	100		
Offers	200	Offers/Hires	2:1
Interviews	300	Interviews/Offers	3:2
Invites	400	Invites/Interviews	4:3
Leads	2400	Leads/Invites	6:1

FIGURE 11-2   Recruiting yield pyramid—engineering candidates, ABC Engineering Consultants.   Adapted by permission of the publisher from Roger H. Hawk, The Recruitment Function. Copyright ©1967 by the American Management Association, Inc.

Average number of days from:	
Résumé to invitation	4
Invitation to interview	5
Interview to offer	3
Offer to acceptance	7
Acceptance to report for work	21

FIGURE 11-3 Time-lapse data for recruitment of engineers.

[handwritten note: Long wait time is frowned upon]

All of this assumes that intervals between events in the pipeline proceed as planned. In fact, longitudinal research indicates that delays in the timing of recruitment events are perceived very negatively by candidates, especially high-quality ones, and often cost job acceptances (Boswell, Roehling, LePine, & Moynihan, 2003; Bretz & Judge, 1998; Chapman, Uggerslev, Carroll, Piasentin, & Jones, 2005; Rynes, Bretz, & Gerhart, 1991; Rynes & Cable, 2003). In addition, time to fill can be misleading, especially if measures of the quality of new hires are ignored (Sullivan, 2008). Here is a simple example: It is one thing to know that a firm's sales openings average 75 days to fill. It's another thing to know that the difference between filling them in 75 versus 50 days costs the firm $30 million revenue, or that a 20 percent improvement in quality of hire will result in an $18 million productivity improvement (Griendling, 2008).

Note, however, that these yield ratios and time-lapse data are appropriate only for ABC's engineers. Other segments of the workforce may respond differently, and widespread use of the Internet by job seekers in all areas may change both yield ratios and time-lapse data. Thus, a study by Recruitsoft/iLogos Research found that across all types and levels of employees posting jobs on the Internet shaves an average of 6 days off a *Fortune 500* company's hiring cycle of 43 days. It saves another four days if the company takes online applications instead of paper ones, and more than a week if the company screens and processes applications electronically (Cappelli, 2001). Of course, the time period also depends on labor-market conditions. A **labor market** is a geographical area within which the forces of supply (people looking for work) interact with the forces of demand (employers looking for people) and thereby determine the price of labor. However, since the geographical areas over which employers extend their recruiting efforts depend partly on the type of job being filled, it is impossible to define the boundaries of a local labor market in any clear-cut manner (Milkovich & Newman, 2008). If the supply of suitable workers in a particular labor market is high relative to available jobs, then the price of labor generally will be cheaper. On the other hand, if the supply is limited (e.g., suppose ABC needs certain types of engineering specialists who are unavailable locally), then the search must be widened and additional labor markets investigated in order to realize required yield ratios.

In traditional internal labor markets, employees are brought into organizations through a small number of entry-level jobs and then are promoted up through a hierarchy of increasingly responsible and lucrative positions. In recent years, however, internal labor markets have weakened, such that high-level jobs have not been restricted to internal candidates, and new employees have been hired from the outside at virtually all levels (Cappelli, 1999; Rynes & Cable, 2003). This has had the predictable effect of weakening employee loyalty and trust in management, and it puts employers at a disadvantage when labor markets tighten.

Staffing Requirements and Cost Analyses

Since experienced professional/technical recruiters can be expected to produce about 50 new hires per year, then approximately four full-time recruiters will be required to meet ABC's staffing requirements for 100 engineers in the next six months. Using the Internet, however, the ratio of recruiters to candidates may go as high as 80:1 (Nakache, 1997).

So far, we have been able to estimate ABC's recruiting time and staffing requirements on the basis of its previous recruiting experience. Several other parameters must be considered before the planning process is complete. The most important of these, as might logically be expected, is cost. Before making cost estimates, however, let us go back and assume that an organization has no prior recruiting experience (or that the necessary data were not recorded). The development of working hypotheses about yield ratios is considerably more complex under these conditions, though far from impossible.

It is important to analyze the external labor market by source, along with analyses of demand for similar types of people by competitors. It is also important to evaluate the entire organizational environment in order to do a "company advantage study." Numerous items must be appraised, including geographic factors (climate, recreation), location of the firm, cost of living, availability of housing, proximity to shopping centers, public and parochial schools, and so forth.

Capitalize on any special factors that are likely to attract candidates, such as organizational image and reputation (Collins, 2007; Collins & Han, 2004; Collins & Stevens, 2002). Image is a strong predictor ($\rho = .48$) of organizational attraction (Allen, Mahto, & Otondo, 2007; Chapman et al., 2005). Such information will prove useful when developing a future recruiting strategy and when gathering baseline data for estimates of recruiting yield.

Rynes and Cable (2003) identified three reasons why a positive organizational image or reputation might influence prospective candidates to apply: (1) People seek to associate themselves with organizations that enhance their self-esteem. Job seekers might pursue high-reputation companies to bask in such organizations' reflected glory or to avoid negative outcomes associated with working for an employer with a poor image (Ashforth & Kreiner, 1999). (2) A positive reputation may signal that an organization is likely to provide other desirable attributes, such as high pay and strong opportunities for career growth and development. (3) A positive reputation may make applicants more receptive to whatever information an organization provides (Barber, 1998).

Yield ratios and time-lapse data are valuable for estimating recruiting staff and time requirements. Recruitment planning is not complete, however, until the costs of alternative recruitment strategies have been estimated. Expenditures by source must be analyzed carefully in advance in order to avoid any subsequent "surprises." In short, analysis of costs is one of the most important considerations in determining where, when, and how to approach the recruiting marketplace.

At the most general level, the gross cost-per-hire figure may be determined by dividing the total cost of recruiting (TCOR) by the number of individuals hired (NH):

$$\text{Gross Cost per Hire } = \text{ TCOR/NH} \tag{11-1}$$

Data from past experience usually provide the inputs to Equation 11-1. For professional employees, this cost can be staggering: 18 months' pay, according to the Hay Group, not including lost sales and productivity (Lavelle, 2003). Although this simple statistic is useful as a first step, it falls far short of the cost information necessary for thorough advance planning and later evaluation of the recruiting effort. In particular, the following cost estimates are essential:

1. *Staff costs*—salaries, benefits, and overtime premiums.
2. *Operational costs*—telephone; recruiting staff travel and living expenses; professional fees and services (agency fees, consultant fees, etc.); advertising expenses (radio and TV, newspapers, technical journals, ads for field trips, etc.); medical expenses for preemployment physical examinations; information services (brochures describing the company and its environment); and supplies, material, and postage.
3. *Overhead*—rental expenses for temporary facilities, office furniture, equipment, etc.

Source Analysis

Analysis of recruiting sources facilitates effective planning. Three types of analyses are typical: cost per hire, time lapse from candidate identification to hire, and source yield. The most expensive sources generally are private employment agencies and executive-search firms, since agency fees may constitute as much as 35 percent of an individual's first-year salary (Maher, 2003a). The next most expensive sources are field trips, for both advertising expenses and recruiters' travel and living expenses are incurred. Less expensive are advertising responses, Internet responses, write-ins, and internal transfers and promotions. Employee referrals, direct applications (mail or Web based), and walk-ins are the cheapest sources of candidates.

Time-lapse studies of recruiting sources are especially useful for planning purposes, since the time from initial contact to report on board varies across sources. In the case of college recruiting, for example, a steady flow of new employees is impossible, since reporting dates typically coincide closely with graduation, regardless of when the initial contact was made.

For those sources capable of producing a steady flow, however, employee referrals and direct applications usually show the shortest delay from initial contact to report. On the other hand, when an organization has an efficient recruiting infrastructure in place, it may be difficult to beat the Internet. Lockheed Martin Corp., which receives more than a million résumés a year and has about 3,000 jobs open at any given time, cut the hiring process from weeks to as little as three days by using résumé-management software and filtering tools (Forster, 2003). Field trips and internal transfers generally produce longer delays, while agency referrals and newspaper ads usually are the slowest sources. As in so many other areas of endeavor, "the organization that hesitates is lost." Competition for top candidates is intense; the organization whose recruiting section functions smoothly and is capable of responding swiftly has the greatest likelihood of landing high-potential people.

The third index of source performance is source yield (i.e., the ratio of the number of candidates generated from a particular source to hires from that source). While no ranking of source yields would have validity across all types of organizations and all labor markets, Breaugh, Greising, Taggart, and Chen (2003) examined the relationship between five recruitment methods (i.e., employee referrals, direct applicants, college placement offices, job fairs, and newspaper ads) and prehire outcomes for applicants for information-technology jobs. No difference was found for level of education or interview score. Not surprisingly, those recruited from college placement offices had less experience than applicants in the other groups. In terms of a job offer, employee referrals and direct applicants were more likely to receive one than those in the other groups. This pattern also held for those who were hired. Thus, although employee referrals and direct applicants did not differ from those in the other groups on two measures of applicant quality, they still were viewed as being more deserving of job offers.

Another study that used job applicants as a sample was conducted by Rafaeli, Hadomi, and Simons (2005). It involved a plant located in Israel and focused on three recruitment methods: employee referrals, geographically focused ads (i.e., the local newspaper), and geographically unfocused ads (i.e., a national newspaper). They found that referrals generated more applicants, more hires, and a higher yield ratio (hires/applicants) than geographically focused ads, which, in turn, outperformed unfocused ads on these three criteria.

Having examined source yield, we are almost ready to begin recruiting operations at this point. Recruiting efficiency can be heightened considerably, however, once employment requirements are defined thoroughly in advance. This is an essential step for both technical and nontechnical jobs. Recruiters must be familiar with the job descriptions of available jobs; they must understand (and, if possible, have direct experience with) the work to be performed. Research has shown clearly that characteristics of organizations and jobs (e.g., location, pay, opportunity to learn, challenging and interesting work) have a greater influence on the likelihood of job acceptance by candidates than do characteristics of the recruiter (Barber & Roehling, 1993; Rynes, 1991; Taylor & Bergmann, 1987).

Nevertheless, at the first stage of recruitment, characteristics of recruiters (personable, trustworthy, informative, competent) do affect the perceptions of candidates (Chapman et al., 2005), particularly with respect to the procedural justice of the process (Chapman & Webster, 2006), but not their intentions to accept job offers (Stevens, 1998). Neither the job function (HR versus line management) nor the gender of the recruiter seems to make much difference to candidates (Chapman et al., 2005). At the same time, there are at least three reasons why recruiters might matter (Breaugh et al., 2008). Different types of recruiters may be important because (1) they vary in the amount of job-related information they possess (and therefore can share), (2) they differ in terms of their credibility in the eyes of recruits, and (3) they signal different things to job candidates. Still, it is likely that applicants rely less on recruiter signals as more information about job and organizational characteristics becomes salient (Dineen & Soltis, in press).

Planning is now complete. HR plans have been established; time, cost, and staff requirements have been specified; sources have been analyzed; and job requirements and employment standards have been determined and validated. Now we are ready to begin recruiting operations.

OPERATIONS

The first step in recruiting operations is to examine internal sources for qualified or qualifiable candidates. This is especially true of large organizations with globally distributed workforces that are likely to maintain comprehensive talent inventories with detailed information on each employee. Such inventories can facilitate global staffing and expatriate assignments (Gong, 2003a, 2003b). Needless to say, periodic updating of the inventory to reflect changes in employee skills, educational and training achievements, job title, and so forth, is essential.

Certainly one of the thorniest issues confronting internal recruitment is the reluctance of managers to grant permission for their subordinates to be interviewed for potential transfer or promotion. To overcome this aversion, promotion-from-within policies must receive strong top-management support, coupled with a company philosophy that permits employees to consider available opportunities within the organization and incentives for managers to release them. At Dell, pay is now determined, in part, by how well a manager does at nurturing people. At 3M, monthly talent reviews by all managers in a particular function (e.g., manufacturing, R&D, sales) help ensure that high-potential employees get noticed (Byrnes, 2005; "Seeing forward," 2008). Actually there is a bright side to "letting go" of valued human capital. It may be beneficial from the standpoint of creating social-network ties to new areas of the business (or to competitors) to which the transferring employee moves (Somaya, Williamson, & Lorinkova, 2008). In many cases, however, organizations turn to external sources to fill entry-level jobs, jobs created by expansion, and jobs whose specifications cannot be met by present employees. To that topic we now turn.

External Sources for Recruiting Applicants

A wide variety of external recruiting sources is available, with the choice of source(s) contingent on specific hiring requirements and source-analysis results. Although we shall not consider each source in detail, available sources include

1. *Advertising*—newspapers (classified and display), the Internet, technical and professional journals, television, radio, and (in some cases) outdoor advertising.
2. *Employment agencies*—federal and state agencies, private agencies, executive search firms, management consulting firms, and agencies specializing in temporary help.
3. *Educational institutions*—technical and trade schools, colleges and universities, co-op work/study programs, and alumni placement offices.
4. *Professional organizations*—technical society meetings and conventions (regional and national) and society placement services.
5. *Military*—out-processing centers and regional and national retired officer associations' placement services.

6. *Labor unions.*
7. *Career fairs.*
8. *Outplacement firms.*
9. *Direct application (walk-ins, write-ins, online applicants)*
10. *Intracompany transfers and company retirees.*
11. *Employee referrals.*

To illustrate how companies try to gain a competitive advantage over their rivals in university recruiting for managerial candidates, consider the following examples.

The sources listed above may be classified as formal (institutionalized search methods such as employment agencies, advertising, search firms) or informal (e.g., walk-ins, write-ins, employee referrals). In terms of the most popular sources used by employers, evidence (Dineen & Soltis, in press; Forster, 2003; Gere, Scarborough, & Collison, 2002; "Online Technologies," 2008) indicates that

- Informal contacts are used widely and effectively at all occupational levels; while social ties are used heavily to fill job vacancies in the start-up phase of a company, there is a shift toward business-network ties in the growth phase (Leung, 2003). Further, Van Hoye and Lievens (2007) found that word-of-mouth information explained incremental variance in attraction and actual application decisions, above recruitment events, publicity, Web sites, or more traditional recruitment messages;
- Use of the public employment service declines as required job skills increase;
- The internal market (job posting on company intranets) is a major recruitment method; and
- Larger firms are the most frequent users of direct applications, the internal market, and rehires of former employees (so-called "boomerangs," White, 2005). Rehires are also less likely to quit than individuals recruited via formal sources (Zottoli & Wanous, 2000).

BOX 11-1

Competing for MBAs: Whirlpool and IBM

Restructurings, downsizings, and layoffs typify the experience of many companies. Hence, campus recruitment is a tough sell these days. To improve their odds, recruiters are visiting business schools earlier and more often, raising starting salaries, and touting their companies' dedication to work-life balance. They are also experimenting with other strategies: mining for résumés online, arranging video interviews, and using instant messaging to cast a wider net and connect more effectively with today's tech-savvy students. Thus, for example, Whirlpool Corporation, of Benton Harbor, Michigan, is experimenting with a technology in which students answer a set of questions via a remote PC-based video camera. The recorded interviews are stored on a secure Web site that only a Whirlpool recruiter can access. Companies are also updating their career Web sites to get more in tune with today's students. Whirlpool, for example, includes a chat feature on its site, assigning employees from different departments to answer questions at designated times. According to the company's recruiting manager, "Today's college graduates want someone right there when they have a question. [They want] to communicate interactively with someone rather than just read someone's observations about the company" (Alsop, 2007).

Among other recruitment tactics, International Business Machines (IBM) is setting up meeting spaces and islands in a virtual community called Second Life, where it plans to hold events such as recruiter question-and-answer sessions, educational lectures, and online interviews. Students can log on, create avatars to represent themselves physically, and visit IBM island. Senior business leaders, engineers, and inventors who often cannot travel to campuses and job fairs because of work demands are able to participate in such virtual events. Says IBM's head of global talent, "Technology is part of the DNA of today's younger generation. They're naturally attracted to things like Second Life and expect IBM as an innovative company to be there" (Alsop, 2007).

- With respect to job advertisements, those that contained more information resulted in a job opening being viewed as more attractive (e.g., Allen et al., 2007) and as more credible (Allen, Van Scotter, & Otondo, 2004) than those that contained less information. Research (Roberson, Collins, & Oreg, 2005) also has shown that advertisements that contain more specific information about a position increase applicant interest in the position and may result in better person–organization fit.

[handwritten note in margin: Informal for Gender?]

However, for recruiting minority workers, a study of more than 20,000 applicants in a major insurance company revealed that female and African American applicants consistently used formal recruitment sources rather than informal ones (Kirnan, Farley, & Geisinger, 1989). Informal sources such as employee referrals can work to the employer's advantage if the workforce is comprised of members from different gender, racial, and ethnic groups. Indeed, evidence indicates that traditional text and picture-based messages about diversity have less impact on outside minority candidates than do video/audio testimonials by present minority employees (Walker, Feild, Giles, Armenakis, & Bernerth, 2008).

Employee referrals are extremely popular today, with about 43 percent of companies using them ("Online Technologies," 2008). While a number of studies have reported that

---

BOX 11-2

Recruiting for Diversity

For organizations that wish to increase the diversity of their workforces, the first (and most difficult) step is to determine their needs, goals, and target populations. Once you know what you want your diversity program to accomplish, you can take steps such as the following (Dineen & Soltis, in press; Kravitz & Klineberg, 2000; Truxillo & Bauer, 1999; Thaler-Carter, 2001):

- Show that you value diversity by communicating values of fairness and inclusion (Avery & McKay, 2006).
- Make initial contacts and gather information from community-support and other external recruitment and training organizations.
- Develop one or more results-oriented programs. What actions will be taken, who will be involved, and how and when will actions be accomplished?
- Invite program representatives to tour your organization, and recognize that they will pay attention to three aspects (Avery & McKay, 2006; McKay & Avery, 2006): the number of minorities at the site, the level of jobs held by minorities, and the types of interactions observed between minority- and majority-group members.
- Select a diversity of organizational contacts and recruiters for outreach and support, including employees outside the HR department.
- Get top-management approval and support. Train managers to value diversity in the workplace.
- Develop procedures for monitoring and follow-up; make revisions as needed to accomplish objectives.
- Think carefully about the messages your organization wishes to transmit concerning its diversity programs; do not leave interpretation to the imagination of the applicant. For example, Cropanzano, Slaughter, and Bachiochi (2005) found that preferential-treatment plans are generally unappealing to prospective minority candidates, who want to ensure that they will be perceived as having been treated fairly and not as receiving preferential treatment.

These are necessary, but not sufficient, conditions for effective diversity recruiting. A WetFeet.com study (Gere et al., 2002) found that, although as many as 44 percent of African American candidates said they eliminated a company from consideration because of a lack of gender or ethnic diversity, three other diversity-related attributes affected their decisions to apply or remain. These were the ready availability of training and career-development programs, the presence of a diverse upper management (Avery, 2003), and the presence of a diverse workforce.

employee referrals are more likely to be hired than nonreferrals, two studies took a more nuanced approach to identify specific effects. Castilla (2005) found that if the employee who did the referring left the organization, the performance trajectory of his/her referral was affected (i.e., did not rise at the rate for referrals whose referrer remained). He suggested this effect was due to the referral no longer feeling "a sense of obligation not to embarrass the referrer" (p. 1249).

A different study (Yakubovich & Lup, 2006) examined independent contractors who worked for a virtual call center. The researchers focused on three groups: those who became aware of jobs via the Internet, those who were referred by current employees who were high performers, and those who were referred by current employees who performed their jobs less well. Yakubovich and Lupp hypothesized that individuals referred by higher-performing employees should be viewed by HR as being of higher quality and should have higher scores on objective selection measures than referrals from lower performers who, in turn, should be viewed more favorably and score higher than Internet recruits. These hypotheses were largely supported. These authors also found that either type of employee referral was more likely to continue in the multistage selection process (i.e., less likely to self-select out) than Internet recruits, but that individuals referred by higher performers had a higher continuation rate.

In practice, companies typically offer cash or a merchandise bonus when a current employee refers a successful candidate. Consider GE Medical Systems, for example. It hires about 500 candidates per year and places heavy emphasis on employee referrals in order to do so. Fully 10 percent of them result in a hire. Nothing else (headhunters, internships) even comes close to that kind of yield. GE doubled the number of employee referrals by doing three simple things. First, the program is simple and rewarding—no complex forms to fill out, just a small gift to the employee for referring a candidate. Second, GE pays the employee $2,000 if the referral is hired and $3,000 if the new hire is a software engineer. Each payment is in lieu of a headhunter's fee of as much as 35 percent of the first-year's salary. Third, GE begins asking new employees for referrals almost from their first day on job. Why? Because three months after hire, the new employee remembers almost everyone from his or her old job. Nine months later the new employee is one of GE's. That's the goal, of course (Useem, 1999).

Which sources yield the highest numbers of qualified candidates? The fact is that most applicants use more than one recruitment source to learn about jobs. Hence, designation of "the" recruitment source they used is misleading and ignores completely the combined effect of multiple sources. In fact, the accumulated evidence on the relationship among recruitment sources, turnover, and job performance suggests that such relationships are quite weak (Williams, Labig, & Stone, 1993). For example, a study of 10 different recruitment sources used by more than 20,000 applicants for the job of insurance agent showed that recruiting source explained 5 percent of the variation in applicant quality, 1 percent of the variation in the survival of new hires, and none of the variation in commissions (Kirnan et al., 1989). In light of these results, what may be more important than the source per se is how much support and information accompany source usage or the extent to which a source embeds prescreening on desired applicant characteristics (Rynes & Cable, 2003). This is especially true with respect to employee referrals, which tend to yield higher numbers of job offers (Breaugh et al., 2003; Rafaeli et al., 2005).

Managing Recruiting Operations

Administratively, recruitment is one of the easiest activities to foul up—with potentially long-term negative publicity for the firm. Traditionally, recruitment was intensively paper based. Today, however, the entire process has been reengineered so that it is computer based. Here is an example of one such system.

With Hiring Gateway from Yahoo! Resumix, automation replaces the entire manual process. Hiring Gateway is a Web-based recruiting and hiring process that takes companies from job requisitions, through matching candidate qualifications, to documented job requirements, then through the interviewing and hiring decision-and-offer process, to finally having new hires

---

BOX 11-3

Internet-Based Recruiting

It is no exaggeration to say that the Internet has revolutionized recruitment practice. For job seekers, there are more than 30,000 job-search sites with literally millions of listings, as well as the ability to research employers and to network (Cohen, 2001). Fully 94 percent of the top 500 U.S. companies recruit via the Internet. Indeed, the only surprise may be that 6 percent aren't (MacMillan, 2007). On a typical Monday, the peak day for job hunts, about four million people search for work on the job board at Monster.com, the leading online talent site. At the same time, thousands of corporate recruiters are scouring Monster's database of more than 70 million employee profiles and résumés, most of which are from people who aren't actively seeking new jobs. In fact, corporate recruiters are increasingly acting like external search firms, hacking into the internal directories of competitors and raiding their employees (Rynes & Cable, 2003).

In short, the Internet is where the action is in recruiting. Despite the allure of commercial job-search sites, evidence indicates that nearly 60 percent of all Internet hires come from a company's own Web site (Forster, 2003). The best ones make it simple for candidates to apply for jobs. They provide a wealth of information about the company, and leave candidates with a favorable impression (Frase-Blunt, 2004). Only about a third as many corporate job openings were listed on corporate Web sites as were posted on the three biggest job boards, Monster.com, HotJobs.com, and Careerbuilder.com (Maher, 2003b; Steel, 2007). For senior executives who earn at least six figures, Forbes.com recommends the following sites: Netshare.com, Flipdog.com, Wetfeet.com, Spencerstuart.com, and Quintcareers.com.

Despite the reach and apparent ease that online searches offer, a surprisingly small proportion of jobs get filled that way. One study found that only 6 percent of hires for management-level jobs currently occur through any Internet site, compared with 61 percent for networking with friends, family, or colleagues (Maher & Silverman, 2002). For that reason, online networking sites—such as LinkedIn, Facebook, Doostang, and Ryze—have become increasingly important to job seekers. Geared toward professional relationships, networking Web sites allow their members to build a web of social and business associates and to interact person-to-person with new contacts ("Job Sites Reviews," 2008; Kadlec, 2007).

What about the traditional belief that 80 percent of job openings are never advertised? Experts call it a myth and note that job seekers can track down 80 to 90 percent of the job openings that exist at a given time by sifting through the career pages on employers' Web sites, in addition to searching other Internet sites and traditional media (Maher, 2003b).

Before we leave this topic, one final issue deserves mention. Are there differences in the types of applicants generated by general job boards (e.g., Monster.com, HotJobs.com) and industry/position-specific job boards? Evidence indicates that the answer is yes. Jattuso and Sinar (2003) reported that applicants generated by industry-specific job boards had better educational qualifications, a higher level of skills, but less work experience than those generated via general job boards.

---

report on board. The software creates a self-service environment that allows hiring managers to create requisitions, permits candidates automatically to upload and edit their résumé information, and allows recruiters to use its "KnowledgeBase" technology to create statements of qualifications that are tied to each individual job as well as to apply screening questions and keyword searches, among other filters (HiringGateway@yahoo-inc.com, 2008).

Hiring Gateway analytics allows recruiters to create many different kinds of reports, such as source effectiveness for different types of jobs and levels, measures of the performance of individual recruiters, measures of the performance of new hires, EEO reporting, and analysis of the database for volume and types of candidates. Developed over the past 15 years, KnowledgeBase search-and-extraction technology draws on more than 20,000 business competencies and 250,000 rules related to various job skills and qualifications. For example, it

- Recognizes the contextual meanings of words within the résumé. Thus, it can distinguish among John Harvard, a candidate; 140 Harvard Street, an address; Harvard University, a

---

BOX 11-4

Using a Hiring Management System (HMS) to Track and Contact Applicants

Application service providers like BrassRing Systems, Icarian, and Recruitsoft enable companies to tap into sophisticated HMSs. Such systems collect applications in a standardized format, screen them, determine where they came from (e.g., job boards or classified ads), monitor the progress of applications, and calculate how long it takes to fill various jobs (in BrassRing's case) or to get a new employee working productively (in Recruitsoft's case). All the application data remain in electronic form, so the systems allow employers to act quickly on the applications—checking references, getting comments from hiring managers, and making e-mail contact with applicants. Union Pacific's HMS allows applicants to check the status of their applications, letting candidates feel more involved in the process and spurring the organization to move things along quickly. Many large companies today use the latest-generation HMS software, and the number is growing rapidly (Cappelli, 2001).

---

school; and Harvard, ID, a town. Simple keyword-based systems are much less efficient, for they will return all résumés containing the word "Harvard." Those résumés will then require subsequent analysis and classification.

- Distinguishes qualitative differences in experience, such as candidates who state they *are* the manager versus those who state that they *report* to the manager.
- Knows when and how to draw logical inferences, such as using "experience managing a fast-growing team" as a proxy for "team-building skills."
- Understands different résumés that contain industry-specific terminology, syntax, and lingo. Using integrated communication tools such as Yahoo! Instant Messenger, online scheduling, and automatic e-mail reminder alerts, Hiring Gateway enables recruiters, hiring managers, and interviewers to collaborate easily and intuitively in real time to pursue their top candidates.

How does the system work in practice? Firms such as Texas Instruments, Disney, Vanguard Group, and United Parcel Service Airlines have found that Resumix6 has cut their cost per hire by up to 50 percent and shortened their hiring cycles by an average of 48 percent (www.HotJobssoftware.com).

MEASUREMENT, EVALUATION, AND CONTROL

If advance recruitment planning has been thorough, later evaluation of the recruitment effort is simplified considerably. Early hypotheses regarding cost and quality can be measured against actual operating results. Critical trade-offs can be made intelligently on the basis of empirical data, not haphazardly on the basis of hunch or intuition. Any number of cost and quality analyses might be performed, but it is critical to choose those that are strategically most relevant to a given organization (Cascio & Boudreau, 2008).

Another consideration is to choose measures of recruiting success that are most relevant to various stages in the recruitment process (See Figure 11-1). An important metric in Stage 1, whose objective is to generate viable candidates, is total résumés received. In Stage 2, maintaining the status of viable applicants, analysis of postvisit and rejection questionnaires is particularly relevant. Finally, in Stage 3, postoffer closure, the acceptance/offer ratio, combined with an analysis of reasons for acceptance and rejection of job offers, are appropriate metrics. Ultimately, however, the success of recruitment efforts depends on the number of successful placements made. Here are some other possible metrics, including those noted above:

- Cost of operations
- Cost per hire
- Cost per hire by source

- Total résumés received
- Résumés by source
- Quality of résumé by source
- Source yield and source efficiency
- Time lapse between recruiting stages by source
- Time lapse between recruiting stages by acceptance versus rejection
- Geographical sources of candidates
- Individual recruiter activity
- Individual recruiter efficiency
- Acceptance/offer ratio
- Offer/interview ratio
- Interview/invitation ratio
- Invitation/résumé input ratio
- Biographical data analyses against acceptance/rejection data
- Analysis of postvisit and rejection questionnaires
- Analysis of reasons for acceptance and rejection of job offers
- Analysis of post–reporting date follow-up interviews
- Placement-test scores of hires versus rejections
- Placement-test scores versus observed performance
- Salary offered—acceptances versus rejections
- Salary versus age, year of first degree, and total work experience

Results of these analyses should be presented graphically for ease of interpretation and communication. Software makes that easy to do. With this information, the individual recruiter can analyze his or her own performance, and senior managers can track cost and hiring trends. In addition, future needs and strategies can be determinexd.

Formal procedures for translating recruitment-related differences in sources and costs into optimum dollar-valued payoffs from recruitment/selection activities are now available (Boudreau & Rynes, 1985; Cascio & Boudreau, 2008; DeCorte, 1999; Law & Myors, 1993; Martin & Raju, 1992). Future research on recruitment effectiveness should incorporate this more meaningful framework.

JOB SEARCH FROM THE APPLICANT'S PERSPECTIVE

How do individuals identify, investigate, and decide among job opportunities? At the outset, it is important to note that research (Breaugh et al., 2008; Rynes & Cable, 2003) has found that many job applicants (1) have an incomplete and/or inaccurate understanding of what a job opening involves, (2) are not sure what they want from a position, (3) do not have a self-insight with regard to their knowledge, skills, and abilities, and (4) cannot accurately predict how they will react to the demands of a new position. At the same time, evidence indicates that the job-choice process is highly social, with friends and relatives playing a large role in the active phase of job search (Barber, Daly, Giannantonio, & Phillips, 1994).

Networking is crucially important (Maher, 2003b; "Online Technologies," 2008; Wanberg, Kanfer, & Banas, 2000; Yang, 2009), because it's often casual contacts that point people to their next jobs. Social-networking sites like LinkedIn, Twitter, or Facebook can facilitate virtual networks, but experts caution that a solid network of 50 people is better than 1,000 acquaintances (Rosato, 2009). Do job seekers tend to follow the same general process? In one study, researchers collected longitudinal data on the actual search behaviors of 186 college and vocational–technical school graduates at three different time periods: (1) early in their search (two to eight months prior to graduation), (2) at graduation, and (3) at three months following graduation for those who remained unemployed. Results showed that individuals tend to follow a sequential model: First, they search broadly to develop a pool of potential jobs (using informal sources and networks of friends and relatives), and then they examine jobs within that pool in detail and reopen the search only if the initial pool does not lead to an acceptable job offer (Barber et al., 1994).

Applicants should exploit the vast capabilities of the Internet, since 94 percent of *Fortune 500* companies now use their corporate sites for recruiting, up from 29 percent in 1998 (Forster, 2003; MacMillan, 2007). They also should use multiple search engines and tools. One such tool is "My Job Search Agent," a tracking device that applicants have access to when they register as members with Monster.com. My Job Search Agent will send an applicant an e-mail, usually within minutes, when a job is posted that matches what he or she has been looking for (Forster, 2003).

Once invited for interviews, candidates sometimes encounter interviews that focus on recruitment per se (i.e., conveying information about the company and about the jobs to be filled). Alternatively, candidates may encounter dual-purpose interviews whose objective is recruitment as well as selection. Which is more effective? It does not seem to matter in terms of organizational attraction (Williamson, Lepak, & King, 2003), but longitudinal research found that applicants acquired and retained more information from recruitment-only interviews. That said, applicants were more likely to persist in pursuing the job when they encountered recruitment–selection interviews (Barber, Hollenbeck, Tower, & Phillips, 1994). A key unresolved issue, however, is when in the recruitment process to provide recruitment-oriented messages and when to provide screening-oriented messages (Dineen & Soltis, in press).

How do organizational characteristics influence applicants' attraction to firms? This is an important question, since many applicants are at least as concerned about picking the right *organization* as with choosing the right *job*. Chapman et al.'s (2005) meta-analytic evidence revealed that work environment ($\rho = .60$) and organizational image ($\rho = .48$) are both strong predictors of organizational attraction. It also revealed that attraction is not directly related to job choice, for it is at least partially mediated by job-pursuit and acceptance intentions.

Allen et al. (2007) found that organizational image, but not mere familiarity, was related to attitudes toward the organization. The most feasible way to improve an organization's recruitment image is to provide more information, not only recruitment information, but also product and service advertisements (Cable, Aiman-Smith, Mulvey, & Edwards, 2000). What about information customized to job seekers? Dineen and Noe (2009) found that the effects of customization tend to encourage poor-fitting job seekers to self-select out, rather than encouraging well-fitting job seekers to self-select in.

With respect to organizational characteristics that are most attractive to applicants, Turban and Keon (1993) found that most applicants preferred decentralized organizations and performance-based pay to centralized organizations and seniority-based pay. However, they also found that preferences for performance-based pay and organizational size varied with subjects' need for achievement.

Realistic Job Previews

One final line of research deserves mention. Given that many employers try to make themselves appear to be a good place to work (Billsberry, 2007), applicant expectations generally are inflated. If hired, individuals possessing inflated job expectations are thought to be more likely to become dissatisfied with their positions and more likely to quit than applicants who have more accurate expectations (Breaugh & Starke, 2000). One way to counter these tendencies is to provide realistic information to job applicants.

Numerous investigations have studied the effect of a realistic job preview (RJP) on withdrawal from the recruitment process, job acceptance, job satisfaction, performance, and turnover. In general, they demonstrate that, when the naive expectations of job applicants are lowered to match organizational reality, there is a small tendency of applicants to withdraw (average correlation of −.03). Job-acceptance rates tend to be lower, and job performance is unaffected, but job survival tends to be higher (average correlation for voluntary turnover of −.09) for those who receive an RJP prior to hire (Phillips, 1998; Premack & Wanous, 1985; Wanous, 1977).

These results might underestimate the actual effects of RJPs on voluntary turnover, as Breaugh (2008) has argued, for two reasons: (1) 59 percent of the studies included in the Phillips (1998) meta-analysis were based on samples of students (not job applicants in a work setting), and (2) more than 50 percent of the studies included RJPs administered *after* hire, and therefore cannot be considered recruitment methods. Beyond that, Phillips did not examine whether RJP effects differed in magnitude based on such things as the visibility of the job in question and applicants' ability to self-select out. Finally, the effect of RJPs on voluntary turnover is moderated by job complexity. Smaller reductions in turnover can be expected in low-complexity jobs than in high-complexity jobs (McEvoy & Cascio, 1985).

BOX 11-5

How Not to Find a New Job

Consider the following scenario, which has happened all too frequently in recent decades (as a result of mergers, restructurings, and downsizings) and is expected to occur often in the future as economic conditions change. You are a midlevel executive, well regarded, well paid, and seemingly well established in your chosen field. Then—whammo!—a change in business strategy or a change in economic conditions results in your layoff from the firm you hoped to retire from. What do you do? How do you go about finding another job? According to management consultants and executive recruiters, the following are some of the key things *not* to do (Dunham, 2002; Rosato, 2009; Yang, 2009):

- ***Don't panic***—a search takes time, even for well-qualified middle- and upper-level managers. People getting hired are not necessarily the most connected, but they are the most creative. Sending out hundreds of résumés is not looking for a job; it's buying a lottery ticket. Target your search.
- ***Don't be bitter***—bitterness makes it harder to begin to search; it also turns off potential employers.
- ***Don't be ashamed***—some executives are embarrassed and don't tell their families or friends what's going on. A better approach, experts say, is to get the word out that you are looking for work, whether it's by phone, e-mail, or online social network. Create a profile on sites like LinkedIn and ZoomInfo. Of the thousands of job sites, these are the two that recruiters say they actually use to find candidates.
- ***Don't drift***—develop a plan, target companies, and go after them relentlessly. Realize that your job is to find a new job.
- ***Don't kid yourself***—do a thorough self-appraisal of your strengths and weaknesses, your likes and dislikes about jobs and organizations. To land an in-person meeting, don't just ask for a job. Offer something in return, like information about the competition. After all, organizations may not have jobs, but they always have problems. If you can help to solve one or more, they are more likely to offer you a job.
- ***Don't be lazy***—Remember, the heart of a good job search is research. Use the Internet or personal contacts to develop a list of target companies. If negotiations get serious, talk to a range of insiders and knowledgeable outsiders to learn about politics and practices. You don't want to wind up in a worse fix than the one you left.
- ***Don't be shy or overeager***—since personal contacts are the most effective means to land a job, you simply must make and maintain them. Find out who will be attending events, show up early, then mix and mingle. Networking is a gradual process of building trust with people. At the same time, resist the temptation to accept the first job that comes along. Unless it's absolutely right for you, the chances of making a mistake are quite high.

- **If sending an e-mail résumé to a recruiter or employer**— recognize that the majority of large companies use software-scanning services to filter résumés. Mimic job-requirement language (e.g., "Marketing Manager") exactly. If following up on an interview, think about what you learned from it, and how it sparked some new ideas about the job. If you've found an article that seems relevant, send it along with some commentary.
- **Don't lie**—experts are unanimous on this point. Don't lie and don't stretch a point— either in résumés or in interviews. Be willing to address failures as well as strengths. More importantly, use the interview to show what you will deliver in the first 30, 60, and 90 days. In today's economic environment, companies don't have time for you to grow into a job.
- **Don't jump the gun on salary**—always let the potential employer bring this subject up first, but, once it surfaces, thoroughly explore all aspects of your future compensation and benefits package.

Those who have been through the trauma of job loss and the challenge of finding a job often describe the entire process as a wrenching, stressful one. Avoiding the mistakes shown above can ensure that finding a new job doesn't take any longer than necessary.

There is a substantial debate about how RJPs work. At the level of the individual job applicant, RJPs are likely to have the greatest impact when the applicant:

1. Can be selective about accepting a job offer;
2. Has unrealistic job expectations; and
3. Would have difficulty coping with job demands without the RJP (Breaugh, 1983, 1992).

Longitudinal research shows that RJPs should be *balanced* in their orientation. That is, they should be conducted to enhance overly pessimistic expectations and to reduce overly optimistic expectations. Doing so helps to bolster the applicant's perceptions of the organization as caring, trustworthy, and honest (Meglino, DeNisi, Youngblood, & Williams, 1988). If the ultimate objective is to develop realistic expectations among job applicants, however, then a multimethod approach to RJPs probably makes the most sense, for the various methods offset each other's shortcomings (Breaugh, 2008). Thus, realistic job information could initially be provided in a job advertisement and on a Web site. This information could be added to during a telephone-screening interview. For people who make it to a site visit, they could take part in a work simulation and a tour of the work site.

Intrinsic rather than extrinsic job factors seem most in need of an RJP. Recruiters find it much easier to communicate factual material than to articulate subtle, intrinsic aspects of organizational climate. Yet intrinsic factors are typically more potent contributors to overall job satisfaction than are extrinsic factors (Kacmar & Ferris, 1989). Those responsible for recruitment training and operations would do well to heed these results.

Thus far we have been discussing RJPs in the context of entry-level hiring, but they can also be quite useful for internal recruitment. For example, a study by Caligiuri and Phillips (2003) described how an employer successfully used an RJP to help current employees make decisions concerning overseas assignments. Similarly, Templer, Tay, and Chandrasekar (2006) documented the effectiveness of an RJP in facilitating cross-cultural adjustment for employees transferred to non-U.S. assignments.

For ease of exposition, we have treated recruitment as if it exists separately, but it is important to emphasize that all components of the recruitment–selection process are interrelated. To illustrate, Ployhart (2006) showed that selection devices that applicants perceive as lacking job relatedness tend to result in recruits being less attracted to an employer. Keep this in mind as you read subsequent chapters in this book.

Evidence-Based Implications for Practice

Recruitment is not a "one-shot" activity. Rather, it is important to recognize three contextual/environmental features that affect all recruitment efforts, namely,

- Characteristics of the firm—the value of its "brand" and its "personality"—make the effort to learn how customers and the public perceive it.
- Characteristics of the vacancy itself (is it mission critical?); this affects not only the resources expended on the search but also the labor markets from which to recruit.
- Characteristics of the labor markets in which an organization recruits (tight versus loose).
- Three sequential stages characterize recruitment efforts: generating a pool of viable candidates, maintaining the status (or interest) of viable candidates, and "getting to yes" after making a job offer (postoffer closure). Devote special attention to each one.
- Recognize that the Internet is where the action is in recruiting. Nearly 60 percent of all Internet hires come from a company's own Web site, and the best ones make it simple for candidates to apply for jobs. They provide a wealth of information about the company, and leave candidates with a favorable impression.
- Finally, provide a realistic job preview to candidates, and ensure that it enhances overly pessimistic expectations, and reduces overly optimistic expectations about the work.

Discussion Questions

1. Describe three key issues to consider in recruitment planning.
2. How do labor-market conditions affect wages and yield ratios?
3. Discuss the advantages and disadvantages of Internet-based recruiting.
4. As a senior manager, what metrics would you find most useful in assessing the effectiveness of recruiting?
5. How would you structure an employee-referral program?
6. How can hiring-management systems enhance the efficiency of recruitment efforts?
7. Outline the components of a diversity-based recruitment effort.
8. Identify five recommendations you would provide to a friend who asks your advice in finding a job.
9. Develop a realistic job preview for a prospective city bus driver.

Selection Methods: Part I

At a Glance

There are many selection methods available. When selection is done sequentially, the earlier stages often are called screening, with the term selection being reserved for the more intensive final stages. Screening also may be used to designate any rapid, rough selection process, even when not followed by further selection procedures. This chapter will focus on some of the most widely used initial screening methods, but it also includes a discussion of selection methods. Additional selection methods, many of which are particularly suited for managerial jobs, are discussed in Chapter 13. This chapter includes a discussion of recommendations and reference checks, personal history data (collected using application blanks or biographical inventories), honesty tests, evaluations of training and experience, drug screening, polygraph testing, and employment interviews. The rationale underlying most of these methods is that past behavior is the best predictor of future behavior.

New technological developments now allow for the collection of information using procedures other than the traditional paper and pencil [e.g., personal computers, videoconferencing, Internet, virtual-reality technology (VRT)]. These new technologies allow for more flexibility regarding data collection, but also present some unique challenges.

RECOMMENDATIONS AND REFERENCE CHECKS

Most initial screening methods are based on the *applicant's* statement of what he or she did in the past. However, recommendations and reference checks rely on the opinions of relevant *others* to help evaluate what and how well the applicant did in the past. Many prospective users ask a very practical question—namely, "Are recommendations and reference checks worth the amount of time and money it costs to process and consider them?" In general, four kinds of information are obtainable: (1) employment and educational history (including confirmation of degree and class standing or grade point average); (2) evaluation of the applicant's character, personality, and interpersonal competence; (3) evaluation of the applicant's job performance ability; and (4) willingness to rehire.

In order for a recommendation to make a meaningful contribution to the screening and selection process, however, certain preconditions must be satisfied. The recommender must have had an adequate opportunity to observe the applicant in job-relevant situations; he or she must be competent to make such evaluations; he or she must be willing to be open and candid; and the evaluations must be expressed so that the potential employer can interpret them in the manner intended (McCormick & Ilgen, 1985). Although the value of recommendations can be impaired by deficiencies in any one or more of the four preconditions, unwillingness to be candid is probably most serious. However, to the extent that the truth of any unfavorable information cannot be demonstrated and it harms the reputation of the individual in question, providers of references may be guilty of defamation in their written (libel) or oral (slander) communications (Ryan & Lasek, 1991).

Written recommendations are considered by some to be of little value. To a certain extent, this opinion is justified, since the research evidence available indicates that the average validity of recommendations is .14 (Reilly & Chao, 1982). One of the biggest problems is that such recommendations rarely include unfavorable information and, therefore, do not discriminate among candidates. In addition, the affective disposition of letter writers has an impact on letter length, which, in turn, has an impact on the favorability of the letter (Judge & Higgins, 1998). In many cases, therefore, the letter may be providing more information about the person who wrote it than about the person described in the letter.

The fact is that decisions *are* made on the basis of letters of recommendation. If such letters are to be meaningful, they should contain the following information (Knouse, 1987):

1. *Degree of writer familiarity with the candidate*—this should include time known and time observed per week.
2. *Degree of writer familiarity with the job in question*—to help the writer make this judgment, the person soliciting the recommendation should supply to the writer a description of the job in question.
3. *Specific examples of performance*—this should cover such aspects as goal achievement, task difficulty, work environment, and extent of cooperation from coworkers.
4. *Individuals or groups to whom the candidate is compared*.

Records and reference checks are the most frequently used methods to screen outside candidates for all types and levels of jobs (Bureau of National Affairs, 1988). Unfortunately, many employers believe that records and reference checks are not permissible under the law. This is not true. In fact, employers may do the following: Seek information about applicants, interpret and use that information during selection, and share the results of reference checking with another employer (Sewell, 1981). In fact, employers may be found guilty of negligent hiring if they *should have known* at the time of hire about the unfitness of an applicant (e.g., prior job-related convictions, propensity for violence) that subsequently causes harm to an individual (Gregory, 1998; Ryan & Lasek, 1991). In other words, failure to check closely enough could lead to legal liability for an employer.

Reference checking is a valuable screening tool. An average validity of .26 was found in a meta-analysis of reference-checking studies (Hunter & Hunter, 1984). To be most useful, however, reference checks should be

- *Consistent*—if an item is grounds for denial of a job to one person, it should be the same for any other person who applies.
- *Relevant*—employers should stick to items of information that really distinguish effective from ineffective employees.
- *Written*—employers should keep written records of the information obtained to support the ultimate hiring decision made.
- *Based on public records, if possible*—such records include court records, workers' compensation, and bankruptcy proceedings (Ryan & Lasek, 1991; Sewell, 1981).

Reference checking can also be done via telephone interviews (Taylor, Pajo, Cheung, & Stringfield, 2004). Implementing a procedure labeled **structured telephone reference check**

BOX 12-1

How to Get Useful Information from a Reference Check

In today's environment of caution, many supervisors are hesitant to provide information about a former employee, especially over the telephone. To encourage them, consider doing the following:

1. Take the supervisor out of the judgmental past and into the role of an evaluator of a candidate's abilities.
2. Remove the perception of potential liability for judging a former subordinate's performance by asking for advice on how best to manage the person to bring out his or her abilities.

Questions such as the following might be helpful (Falcone, 1995):

- We're a mortgage banking firm in an intense growth mode. The phones don't stop ringing, the paperwork is endless, and we're considering Mary for a position in our customer service unit dealing with our most demanding customers. Is that an environment in which she would excel?
- Some people constantly look for ways to reinvent their jobs and assume responsibilities beyond the basic job description. Others adhere strictly to their job duties and "don't do windows," so to speak. Can you tell me where Ed fits on that continuum?

(STRC), a total of 448 telephone reference checks were conducted on 244 applicants for customer-contact jobs (about two referees per applicant) (Taylor et al., 2004). STRCs took place over an eight-month period; they were conducted by recruiters at one of six recruitment consulting firms; and they lasted, on average, 13 minutes. Questions focused on measuring three constructs: conscientiousness, agreeableness, and customer focus. Recruiters asked each referee to rate the applicant compared to others they have known in similar positions, using the following scale: 1 = below average, 2 = average, 3 = somewhat above average, 4 = well above average, and 5 = outstanding. Note that the scale used is a relative, versus absolute, rating scale so as to minimize leniency in ratings. As an additional way to minimize leniency, referees were asked to elaborate on their responses. As a result of the selection process, 191 of the 244 applicants were hired, and data were available regarding the performance of 109 of these employees (i.e., those who were still employed at the end of the first performance appraisal cycle). A multiple-regression model predicting supervisory ratings of overall performance based on the three dimensions assessed by the STRC resulted in $R^2 = .28$, but customer focus was the only one of the three dimensions that predicted supervisory ratings (i.e., standardized regression coefficient of .28).

In closing, although some sources may provide only sketchy information for fear of violating some legal or ethical constraint, recommendations and reference checks can, nevertheless, provide valuable information. Few organizations are willing to abandon altogether the practice of recommendation and reference checking, despite all the shortcomings. One need only listen to a grateful manager thanking the HR department for the good reference checking that "saved" him or her from making a bad offer to understand why. Also, from a practical standpoint, a key issue to consider is the extent to which the constructs assessed by recommendations and reference checks provide unique information above and beyond other data collection methods, such as the employment interview and personality tests.

PERSONAL HISTORY DATA

Selection and placement decisions often can be improved when personal history data (typically found in application forms or biographical inventories) are considered along with other relevant information. We shall discuss these sources in this section.

Undoubtedly one of the most widely used selection procedures is the **application form**. Like tests, application forms can be used to sample past or present behavior briefly, but reliably. Studies of the application forms used by 200 organizations indicated that questions generally focused on information that was job related and necessary for the employment decision (Lowell & DeLoach, 1982; Miller, 1980). However, over 95 percent of the applications included one or more legally indefensible questions. To avoid potential problems, consider omitting any question that

- Might lead to an adverse impact on members of protected groups,
- Does not appear job related or related to a bona fide occupational qualification, or
- Might constitute an invasion of privacy (Miller, 1980).

What can applicants do when confronted by a question that they believe is irrelevant or an invasion of privacy? Some may choose not to respond. However, research indicates that employers tend to view such a nonresponse as an attempt to conceal facts that would reflect poorly on an applicant. Hence, applicants (especially those who have nothing to hide) are ill-advised not to respond (Stone & Stone, 1987).

Psychometric principles can be used to quantify responses or observations, and the resulting numbers can be subjected to reliability and validity analyses in the same manner as scores collected using other types of measures. Statistical analyses of such group data are extremely useful in specifying the personal characteristics indicative of later job success. Furthermore, the scoring of application forms capitalizes on the three hallmarks of progress in selection: standardization, quantification, and understanding (England, 1971).

Weighted Application Blanks (WABs)

A priori, one might suspect that certain aspects of an individual's total background (e.g., years of education, previous experience) should be related to later job success in a specific position. The WAB technique provides a means of identifying *which* of these aspects reliably distinguish groups of effective and ineffective employees. Weights are assigned in accordance with the predictive power of each item, so that a total score can be derived for each individual. A cutoff score then can be established, which, if used in selection, will eliminate the maximum number of potentially unsuccessful candidates. Hence, one use of the WAB is as a rapid screening device, but it may also be used in combination with other data to improve selection and placement decisions. The technique is appropriate in any organization having a relatively large number of employees doing similar kinds of work and for whom adequate records are available. It is particularly valuable for use with positions requiring long and costly training, with positions where turnover is abnormally high, or in employment situations where large numbers of applicants are seeking a few positions (England, 1971).

Weighting procedures are simple and straightforward (Owens, 1976); but, once weights have been developed in this manner, it is *essential* that they be cross-validated. Since WAB procedures represent raw empiricism in the extreme, many of the observed differences in weights may reflect not true differences, but only chance fluctuations. If realistic cost estimates can be assigned to recruitment, the WAB, the ordinary selection procedure, induction, and training, then it is possible to compute an estimate of the payoff, in dollars, that may be expected to result from implementation of the WAB (Sands, 1973).

Biographical Information Blanks (BIBs)

The BIB is closely related to the WAB. Like the WAB, it is a self-report instrument; although items are exclusively in a multiple-choice format, typically a larger sample of items is included, and, frequently, items are included that are not normally covered in a WAB. Glennon, Albright, and Owens (1966) and Mitchell (1994) have published comprehensive catalogs of life history items covering various aspects of the applicant's past (e.g., early life experiences, hobbies, health, social relations), as well as present values, attitudes, interests, opinions, and preferences. Although primary emphasis is on past behavior as a predictor of future behavior, BIBs frequently rely also on present behavior to predict future behavior. Usually BIBs are developed specifically to predict success in a particular type of work. One of the reasons they are so successful is that often they contain all the elements of consequence to the criterion (Asher, 1972). The mechanics of BIB development and item weighting are essentially the same as those used for WABs (Mumford & Owens, 1987; Mumford & Stokes, 1992).

Response Distortion in Application Forms and Biographical Data

Can application forms and biographical data be distorted intentionally by job applicants? The answer is yes. For example, the "sweetening" of résumés is not uncommon, and one study reported that 20 to 25 percent of all résumés and job applications include at least one major fabrication (LoPresto, Mitcham, & Ripley, 1986). The extent of self-reported distortion was found to be even higher when data were collected using the randomized-response technique, which absolutely guarantees response anonymity and, thereby, allows for more honest self-reports (Donovan, Dwight, & Hurtz, 2002).

A study in which participants were instructed to "answer questions in such a way as to make you look as good an applicant as possible" and to "answer questions as honestly as possible" resulted in scores almost two standard deviations higher for the "fake good" condition (McFarland & Ryan, 2000). In fact, the difference between the "fake good" and the "honest" experimental conditions was larger for a biodata inventory than for other measures, including personality traits such as extraversion, openness to experience, and agreeableness. In addition, individuals differed in the extent to which they were able to fake (as measured by the difference between individual's scores in the "fake good" and "honest" conditions). So, if they want to, individuals can distort their responses, but some people are more able than others to do so.

Although individuals have the ability to fake, it does not mean that they do. There are numerous situational and personal characteristics that can influence whether someone is likely to fake. Some of these personal characteristics, which typically are beyond the control of an examiner, include beliefs about faking (which are influenced by individual values, morals, and religion) (McFarland & Ryan, 2000).

Fortunately, there are situational characteristics that an examiner can influence, which, in turn, may make it less likely that job applicants will distort personal history information. One such characteristic is the extent to which information can be verified. More objective and verifiable items are less amenable to distortion (Kluger & Colella, 1993). The concern with being caught seems to be an effective deterrent to faking. Second, option-keyed items are less amenable to distortion (Kluger, Reilly, & Russell, 1991). With this strategy, each item-response option (alternative) is analyzed separately and contributes to the score only if it correlates significantly with the criterion. Third, distortion is less likely if applicants are warned of the presence of a lie scale (Kluger & Colella, 1993) and if biodata are used in a nonevaluative, classification context (Fleishman, 1988). Fourth, a recently tested approach involves asking job applicants to elaborate on their answers. These elaborations require job applicants to describe more fully the manner in which their responses are true or actually to describe incidents to illustrate and support their answers (Schmitt & Kunce, 2002). For example, for the question "How many work groups have you led in the past 5 years?" the elaboration request can be "Briefly describe the work groups and projects you led" (Schmitt & Kunce, 2002, p. 586). The rationale for this approach is that requiring elaboration forces the applicant to remember more accurately and to minimize managing a favorable impression. The use of the elaboration approach led to a reduction in scores of about .6 standard deviation unit in a study including 311 examinees taking a pilot form of a selection instrument for a federal civil service job (Schmitt & Kunce, 2002). Similarly, a study including more than 600 undergraduate students showed that those in the elaboration condition provided responses much lower than those in the nonelaboration condition (Schmitt, Oswald, Gillespie, & Ramsay, 2003). In short, there are several interventions available to reduce distortion on biodata inventories.

Opinions vary regarding exactly what items should be classified as biographical, since biographical items may vary along a number of dimensions—for example, verifiable–unverifiable; historical–futuristic; actual behavior–hypothetical behavior; firsthand–secondhand; external–internal; specific–general; and invasive–noninvasive (see Table 12-1). This is further complicated by the fact that "contemporary biodata questions are now often indistinguishable from personality items in content, response format, and scoring (Schmitt & Kunce, 2002, p. 570). Nevertheless, the core attribute of biodata items is that they pertain to historical events that may have shaped a person's behavior and identity (Mael, 1991).

TABLE 12-1 A Taxonomy of Biographical Items

Historical

How old were you when you got your first paying job?

External

Did you ever get fired from a job?

Objective

How many hours did you study for your real-estate license test?

First hand

How punctual are you about coming to work?

Discrete

At what age did you get your driver's license?

Verifiable

What was your grade point average in college?

Were you ever suspended from your Little League team?

Controllable

How many tries did it take you to pass the CPA exam?

Equal access

Were you ever class president?

Job relevant

How many units of cereal did you sell during the last calendar year?

Noninvasive

Were you on the tennis team in college?

Future or hypothetical

What position do you think you will be holding in 10 years?

What would you do if another person screamed at you in public?

Internal

What is your attitude toward friends who smoke marijuana?

Subjective

Would you describe yourself as shy?

How adventurous are you compared to your coworkers?

Second hand

How would your teachers describe your punctuality?

Summative

How many hours do you study during an average week?

Nonverifiable

How many servings of fresh vegetables do you eat every day?

Noncontrollable

How many brothers and sisters do you have?

Nonequal access

Were you captain of the football team?

Not job relevant

Are you proficient at crossword puzzles?

Invasive

How many young children do you have at home?

Source: Mael, F. A. (1991). Conceptual rationale for the domain and attributes of biodata items. *Personnel Psychology,* *44,* 773. Reprinted by permission of *Personnel Psychology.*

Some have advocated that only historical and verifiable experiences, events, or situations be classified as biographical items. Using this approach, most items on an application blank would be considered biographical (e.g., rank in high school graduating class, work history). On the other hand, if only historical, verifiable items are included on a BIB, then questions such as the following would not be asked: "Did you ever build a model airplane that flew?" Cureton (see Henry, 1965, p. 113) commented that this single item, although it cannot easily be verified for an individual, was almost as good a predictor of success in flight training during World War II as the entire Air Force Battery.

Validity of Application Forms and Biographical Data

Properly cross-validated WABs and BIBs have been developed for many occupations, including life insurance agents; law enforcement officers; service station managers; sales clerks; unskilled, clerical, office, production, and management employees; engineers; architects; research scientists; and Army officers. Criteria include turnover (by far the most common), absenteeism, rate of salary increase, performance ratings, number of publications, success in training, creativity ratings, sales volume, credit risk, and employee theft.

Evidence indicates that the validity of personal history data as a predictor of future work behavior is quite good. For example, Reilly and Chao (1982) reviewed 58 studies that used biographical information as a predictor. Over all criteria and over all occupations, the average validity was .35. A subsequent meta-analysis of 44 such studies revealed an average validity of .37 (Hunter & Hunter, 1984). A later meta-analysis that included results from eight studies of salespeople's performance that used supervisory ratings as the criterion found a mean validity coefficient (corrected for criterion unreliability) of .33 (Vinchur, Schippmann, Switzer, & Roth, 1998).

As a specific illustration of the predictive power of these types of data, consider a study that used a concurrent validity design including more than 300 employees in a clerical job. A rationally selected, empirically keyed, and cross-validated biodata inventory accounted for incremental variance in the criteria over that accounted for by measures of personality and general cognitive abilities (Mount, Witt, & Barrick, 2000). Specifically, biodata accounted for about 6 percent of incremental variance for quantity/quality of work, about 7 percent for interpersonal relationships, and about 9 percent for retention. As a result, we now have empirical support for the following statement made by Owens (1976) over 30 years ago:

> Personal history data also broaden our understanding of what does and does not contribute to effective job performance. An examination of discriminating item responses can tell a great deal about what kinds of employees remain on a job and what kinds do not, what kinds sell much insurance and what kinds sell little, or what kinds are promoted slowly and what kinds are promoted rapidly. Insights obtained in this fashion may serve anyone from the initial interviewer to the manager who formulates employment policy. (p. 612)

A caution is in order, however. Commonly, biodata keys are developed on samples of job incumbents, and it is assumed that the results generalize to applicants. However, a large-scale field study that used more than 2,200 incumbents and 2,700 applicants found that 20 percent or fewer of the items that were valid in the incumbent sample were also valid in the applicant sample. Clearly motivation and job experience differ in the two samples. The implication: Match incumbent and applicant samples as closely as possible, and do not assume that predictive and concurrent validities are similar for the derivation and validation of BIB scoring keys (Stokes, Hogan, & Snell, 1993).

Bias and Adverse Impact

Since the passage of Title VII of the 1964 Civil Rights Act, personal history items have come under intense legal scrutiny. While not unfairly discriminatory per se, such items legitimately may be included in the selection process only if it can be shown that (1) they are job related and (2) do not unfairly discriminate against either minority or nonminority subgroups.

In one study, Cascio (1976b) reported cross-validated validity coefficients of .58 (minorities) and .56 (nonminorities) for female clerical employees against a tenure criterion. When separate expectancy charts were constructed for the two groups, no significant differences in WAB scores for minorities and nonminorities on either predictor or criterion measures were found. Hence, the same scoring key could be used for both groups.

Results from several subsequent studies have concluded that biodata inventories are relatively free of adverse impact, particularly when compared to the degree of adverse impact typically observed in cognitive abilities tests (Reilly & Chao, 1982). However, some differences have been reported. For example, Whitney and Schmitt (1997) used an item response theory (IRT) approach and found that approximately one-quarter of the items from a biodata inventory exhibited differential item functioning between African American and white groups. These differences could not be explained by differences in cultural values across the groups. Unfortunately, when differences exist, we often do not know why. This reinforces the idea of using a rational (as opposed to an entirely empirical) approach to developing biodata inventories, because it has the greatest potential for allowing us to understand the underlying constructs, how they relate to criteria of interest, and how to minimize between-group score differences. As noted by Stokes and Searcy (1999):

> With increasing evidence that one does not necessarily sacrifice validity to use more rational procedures in development and scoring biodata forms, and with concerns for legal issues on the rise, the push for rational methods of developing and scoring biodata forms is likely to become more pronounced. (p. 84)

What Do Biodata Mean?

Criterion-related validity is not the only consideration in establishing job relatedness. Items that bear no rational relationship to the job in question (e.g., "applicant does not wear eyeglasses" as a predictor of credit risk or theft) are unlikely to be acceptable to courts or regulatory agencies, especially if total scores produce adverse impact on a protected group. Nevertheless, external or empirical keying is the most popular scoring procedure and consists of focusing on the prediction of an external criterion using keying procedures at either the item or the item-option level (Stokes & Searcy, 1999). Note, however, that biodata inventories resulting from a purely empirical approach do not help in our understanding of what constructs are measured.

More prudent and reasonable is the rational approach, including job analysis information to deduce hypotheses concerning success on the job under study and to seek from existing, previously researched sources either items or factors that address these hypotheses (Stokes & Cooper, 2001). Essentially we are asking the following questions: "What do biodata mean?" "Why do past behaviors and performance or life events predict nonidentical future behaviors and performance?" (Dean & Russell, 2005). Thus, in a study of recruiters' interpretations of biodata items from résumés and application forms, Brown and Campion (1994) found that recruiters deduced language and math abilities from education-related items, physical ability from sports-related items, and leadership and interpersonal attributes from items that reflected previous experience in positions of authority and participation in activities of a social nature. Nearly all items were thought to tell something about a candidate's motivation. The next step is to identify hypotheses about the relationship of such abilities or attributes to success on the job in question. This rational approach has the advantage of enhancing both the utility of selection procedures and our understanding of how and why they work (cf. Mael & Ashforth, 1995).

Moreover, it is probably the *only* legally defensible approach for the use of personal history data in employment selection.

The rational approach to developing biodata inventories has proven fruitful beyond employment testing contexts. For example, Douthitt, Eby, and Simon (1999) used this approach to develop a biodata inventory to assess people's degree of receptiveness to dissimilar others (i.e., general openness to dissimilar others). As an illustration, for the item "How extensively have you traveled?" the rationale is that travel provides for direct exposure to dissimilar others and those who have traveled to more distant areas have been exposed to more differences than those who have not. Other items include "How racially (ethnically) integrated was your high school?" and "As a child, how often did your parent(s) (guardian(s)) encourage you to explore new situations or discover new experiences for yourself?" Results of a study including undergraduate students indicated that the rational approach paid off because there was strong preliminary evidence in support of the scale's reliability and validity. However, even if the rational approach is used, the validity of biodata items can be affected by the life stage in which the item is anchored (Dean & Russell, 2005). In other words, framing an item around a specific, hypothesized developmental time (i.e., childhood versus past few years) is likely to help applicants provide more accurate responses by giving them a specific context to which to relate their response.

HONESTY TESTS

Paper-and-pencil honesty testing is a multimillion-dollar industry, especially since the use of polygraphs in employment settings has been severely curtailed (we discuss polygraph testing later in this chapter). Written honesty tests (also known as integrity tests) fall into two major categories: **overt integrity tests** and **personality-oriented measures**. Overt integrity tests (e.g., Reid Report and Personnel Selection Inventory, both owned by Pearson Reid London House, http://www.pearsonreidlondonhouse.com/) typically include two types of questions. One assesses attitudes toward theft and other forms of dishonesty (e.g., endorsement of common rationalizations of theft and other forms of dishonesty, beliefs about the frequency and extent of employee theft, punitiveness toward theft, perceived ease of theft). The other deals with admissions of theft and other illegal activities (e.g., dollar amount stolen in the last year, drug use, gambling).

Personality-based measures are not designed as measures of honesty per se, but rather as predictors of a wide variety of counterproductive behaviors, such as substance abuse, insubordination, absenteeism, bogus workers' compensation claims, and various forms of passive aggression. For example, the Reliability Scale of the Hogan Personnel Selection Series (Hogan & Hogan, 1989) is designed to measure a construct called "organizational delinquency." It includes items dealing with hostility toward authority, thrill seeking, conscientiousness, and social insensitivity. Overall, personality-based measures assess broader dispositional traits, such as socialization and conscientiousness. (Conscientiousness is one of the Big Five personality traits; this is discussed in more detail in Chapter 13.) In fact, in spite of the clear differences in content, both overt and personality-based tests seem to have a common latent structure reflecting conscientiousness, agreeableness, and emotional stability (Berry, Sackett, & Wiemann, 2007).

Do honesty tests work? Yes, as several reviews have documented (Ones, Viswesvaran, & Schmidt, 1993; Wanek, 1999). Ones et al. (1993) conducted a meta-analysis of 665 validity coefficients that used 576,460 test takers. The average validity of the tests, when used to predict supervisory ratings of performance, was .41. Results for overt and personality-based tests were similar. However, the average validity of overt tests for predicting theft per se (.13) was much lower. Nevertheless, Bernardin and Cooke (1993) found that scores on two overt integrity tests successfully predicted detected theft (validity = .28) for convenience store employees. For personality-based tests, there were no validity estimates available for the prediction of theft alone. Also, since there was no correlation between race, gender, or age and integrity test scores (Bernardin & Cooke, 1993), such tests might well be used in combination with general mental ability test scores to comprise a general selection procedure. Finally, a study based on 110 job applicants in a Fortune 500 company found that the correlation between a personality-based integrity test and maximal performance was $r = .27$ (Ones & Viswesvaran, 2007).

Despite these encouraging findings, a least four key issues have yet to be resolved. First, as in the case of biodata inventories, there is a need for a greater understanding of the construct validity of integrity tests given that integrity tests are not interchangeable (i.e., scores for the same individuals on different types of integrity tests are not necessarily similar). Some investigations have sought evidence regarding the relationship between integrity tests and some broad personality traits. But there is a need to understand the relationship between integrity tests and individual characteristics more directly related to integrity tests such as object beliefs, negative life themes, and power motives (Mumford, Connelly, Helton, Strange, & Osburn, 2001). Second, women tend to score approximately .16 standard deviation unit higher than men, and job applicants aged 40 years and older tend to score .08 standard deviation unit higher than applicants younger than 40 (Ones & Viswesvaran, 1998). At this point, we do not have a clear reason for these findings. Third, many writers in the field apply the same language and logic to integrity testing as to ability testing. Yet there is an important difference: While it is possible for an individual with poor moral behavior to "go straight," it is certainly less likely that an individual who has demonstrated a lack of intelligence will "go smart." If they are honest about their past, therefore, reformed individuals with a criminal past may be "locked into" low scores on integrity tests (and, therefore, be subject to classification error) (Lilienfeld, Alliger, & Mitchell, 1995). Thus, the broad validation evidence that is often acceptable for cognitive ability tests may not hold up in the public policy domain for integrity tests. And, fourth, there is the real threat of intentional distortion (Alliger, Lilienfeld, & Mitchell, 1996). It is actually quite ironic that job applicants are likely to be dishonest in completing an honesty test. For example, McFarland and Ryan (2000) found that, when study participants who were to complete an honesty test were instructed to "answer questions in such a way as to make you look as good an applicant as possible," scores were 1.78 standard deviation units higher than when they were instructed to "answer questions as honestly as possible." Future research should address the extent to which response distortion has an impact, and the size of this effect, on hiring decisions (Berry et al., 2007).

Given the above challenges and unresolved issues, researchers are exploring alternative ways to assess integrity and other personality-based constructs (e.g., Van Iddekinge, Raymark, & Roth, 2005). One promising approach is **conditional reasoning** (Frost, Chia-Huei, & James, 2007; James et al., 2005). Conditional reasoning testing focuses on how people solve what appear to be traditional inductive-reasoning problems. However, the true intent of the scenarios presented is to determine respondents' solutions based on their implicit biases and preferences. These underlying biases usually operate below the surface of consciousness and are revealed based on the respondents' responses. Another promising approach is to assess integrity as part of a situational-judgment test, in which applicants are given a scenario and they are asked to choose a response that is most closely aligned to what they would do (Becker, 2005). Consider the following example of an item developed by Becker (2005):

> Your work team is in a meeting discussing how to sell a new product. Everyone seems to agree that the product should be offered to customers within the month. Your boss is all for this, and you know he does not like public disagreements. However, you have concerns because a recent report from the research department points to several potential safety problems with the product. Which of the following do you think you would most likely do?
>
> Possible answers:
> **A.** Try to understand why everyone else wants to offer the product to customers this month. Maybe your concerns are misplaced. [−1]
> **B.** Voice your concerns with the product and explain why you believe the safety issues need to be addressed. [1]

C. Go along with what others want to do so that everyone feels good about the team. [−1]

D. Afterwards, talk with several other members of the team to see if they share your concerns. [0]

The scoring for the above item is −1 for answers A and C (i.e., worst-possible score), 0 for answer D (i.e., neutral score), and +1 for item B (i.e., best-possible score). One advantage of using scenario-based integrity tests is that they are intended to capture specific values rather than general integrity-related traits. Thus, these types of tests may be more defensible both scientifically and legally because they are based on a more precise definition of integrity, including specific types of behaviors. A study based on samples of fast-service employees ($n = 81$), production workers ($n = 124$), and engineers ($n = 56$) found that validity coefficients for the integrity test (corrected for criterion unreliability) were .26 for career potential, .18 for leadership, and .24 for in-role performance (all as assessed by managers' ratings) (Becker, 2005).

EVALUATION OF TRAINING AND EXPERIENCE

Judgmental evaluations of the previous work experience and training of job applicants, as presented on résumés and job applications, is a common part of initial screening. Sometimes evaluation is purely subjective and informal, and sometimes it is accomplished in a formal manner according to a standardized method. Evaluating job experience is not as easy as one may think because experience includes both qualitative and quantitative components that interact and accrue over time; hence, work experience is multidimensional and temporally dynamic (Tesluk & Jacobs, 1998). However, using experience as a predictor of future performance can pay off. Specifically, a study including more than 800 U.S. Air Force enlisted personnel indicated that ability and experience seem to have linear and noninteractive effects (Lance & Bennett, 2000). Another study that also used military personnel showed that the use of work experience items predicts performance above and beyond cognitive abilities and personality (Jerry & Borman, 2002). These findings explain why the results of a survey of more than 200 staffing professionals of the National Association of Colleges and Employers revealed that experienced hires were evaluated more highly than new graduates on most characteristics (Rynes, Orlitzky, & Bretz, 1997).

An empirical comparison of four methods for evaluating work experience indicated that the "behavioral consistency" method showed the highest mean validity (.45) (McDaniel, Schmidt, & Hunter, 1988). This method requires applicants to describe their major achievements in several job-related areas. These areas are behavioral dimensions rated by supervisors as showing maximal differences between superior and minimally acceptable performers. The applicant's achievement statements are then evaluated using anchored rating scales. The anchors are achievement descriptors whose values along a behavioral dimension have been determined reliably by subject matter experts.

A similar approach to the evaluation of training and experience, one most appropriate for selecting professionals, is the accomplishment record (AR) method (Hough, 1984). A comment frequently heard from professionals is "My record speaks for itself." The AR is an objective method for evaluating those records. It is a type of biodata/maximum performance/self-report instrument that appears to tap a component of an individual's history that is not measured by typical biographical inventories. It correlates essentially zero with aptitude test scores, honors, grades, and prior activities and interests.

Development of the AR begins with the collection of critical incidents to identify important dimensions of job performance. Then rating principles and scales are developed for rating an individual's set of job-relevant achievements. The method yields (1) complete definitions of the important dimensions of the job, (2) summary principles that highlight key characteristics to look for when determining the level of achievement demonstrated by an accomplishment, (3) actual examples of accomplishments that job experts agree represent various levels of achievement, and (4) numerical equivalents that allow the accomplishments to be translated into quantitative indexes of achievement. When the AR was applied in a sample of 329 attorneys, the reliability of the overall performance ratings was a respectable .82, and the AR demonstrated a validity of .25. Moreover, the method appears to be fair for females, minorities, and white males.

What about academic qualifications? They tend not to affect managers' hiring recommendations, as compared to work experience, and they could have a negative effect. For candidates with poor work experience, having higher academic qualifications seems to reduce their chances of being hired (Singer & Bruhns, 1991). These findings were supported by a national survey of 3,000 employers by the U.S. Census Bureau. The most important characteristics employers said they considered in hiring were attitude, communications skills, and previous work experience. The least important were academic performance (grades), school reputation, and teacher recommendations (Applebome, 1995). Moreover, when grades are used, they tend to have adverse impact on ethnic minority applicants (Roth & Bobko, 2000).

COMPUTER-BASED SCREENING

The rapid development of computer technology over the past few years has resulted in faster microprocessors and more flexible and powerful software that can incorporate graphics and sounds. These technological advances now allow organizations to conduct computer-based screening (CBS). Using the Internet, companies can conduct CBS and administer job-application forms, structured interviews (discussed below), and other types of tests globally, 24 hours a day, 7 days a week (Jones & Dages, 2003).

CBS can be used simply to convert a screening tool from paper to an electronic format that is called an **electronic page turner**. These types of CBS are low on interactivity and do not take full advantage of technology (Olson-Buchanan, 2002). On the other hand, Nike uses interactive voice-response technology to screen applicants over the telephone; the U.S. Air Force uses computer-adaptive testing (CAT) on a regular basis (Ree & Carretta, 1998); and other organizations, such as Home Depot and JCPenney, use a variety of technologies for screening, including CAT (Chapman & Webster, 2003; Overton, Harms, Taylor, & Zickar, 1997).

CAT presents all applicants with a set of items of average difficulty, and, if responses are correct, items with higher levels of difficulty. If responses are incorrect, items with lower levels of difficulty are presented. CAT uses IRT (see Chapter 6) to estimate an applicant's level on the underlying trait based on the relative difficulty of the items answered correctly and incorrectly. The potential value added by computers as screening devices is obvious when one considers that implementation of CAT would be nearly impossible using traditional paper-and-pencil instruments (Olson-Buchanan, 2002).

There are several potential advantages of using CBS (Olson-Buchanan, 2002). First, administration may be easier. For example, standardization is maximized because there are no human proctors who may give different instructions to different applicants (i.e., computers give instructions consistently to all applicants). Also, responses are recorded and stored automatically, which is a practical advantage, but can also help minimize data-entry errors. Second, applicants can access the test from remote locations, thereby increasing the applicant pool. Third, computers can accommodate applicants with disabilities in a number of ways, particularly since tests can be completed from their own (possibly modified) computers. A modified computer can caption audio-based items for applicants with hearing disabilities, or it can allow applicants with limited hand movement to complete a test. Finally, some preliminary evidence suggests that Web-based assessment does not exacerbate adverse impact.

In spite of the increasing availability and potential benefits of CBS, most organizations are not yet taking advantage of it. Approximately 3,000 Society for Human Resource Management (SHRM) members whose primary function is in the employment/recruiting area were asked to complete a survey assessing current and future use of technology in the screening process (Chapman & Webster, 2003). For low- and mid-level positions, participants indicated that manual methods are used most frequently to screen applicants' materials, followed by in-person screening interviews. In the future, respondents expect to see an increase in the use of such technologies as computer-based keyword searches of résumés, computer-based scoring of standardized applications, telephone-based interactive voice-response systems, and videoconferencing. Respondents also expressed several concerns about the implementation of CBS, such as cost and potential cheating. Moreover, some testing experts believe that high-stakes tests, such as those used to make employment decisions, cannot be administered in unproctored Internet settings (Tippins et al., 2006). Additional challenges in implementing CBS include the relative lack of access of low-income individuals to the Internet, or what is called the **digital divide** (Stanton & Rogelberg, 2001).

Consistent with the survey results, Booth (1998) argued that progress in CBS has, in general, not kept pace with such technological progress, and organizations are not taking advantage of available tools. Three reasons were provided for such a conclusion: (1) Technology changes so rapidly that HR professionals simply cannot keep up; (2) CBS is costly; and (3) CBS may have an "image problem" (i.e., low face validity). Olson-Buchanan (2002) reached a similar conclusion that innovations in CBS have not kept pace with the progress in computer technology. This disparity was attributed to three major factors: (1) costs associated with CBS development, (2) lag in scientific guidance for addressing reliability and validity issues raised by CBS, and (3) the concern that investment in CBS may not result in tangible payoffs.

Fortunately, many of the concerns are being addressed by ongoing research on the use, accuracy, equivalence, and efficiency of CBS. For example, Ployhart, Weekley, Holtz, and Kemp (2003) found that proctored, Web-based testing has several benefits compared to the more traditional paper-and-pencil administration. Their study included nearly 5,000 applicants for telephone-service-representative positions who completed, among other measures, a biodata instrument. Results indicated that scores resulting from the Web-based administration had similar or better psychometric characteristics, including distributional properties, lower means, more variance, and higher internal-consistency reliabilities. Another recent study examined reactions to CAT and found that applicants' reactions are positively related to their perceived performance on the test (Tonidandel, Quiñones, & Adams, 2002). Thus, changes in the item-selection algorithm that result in a larger number of items answered correctly have the potential to improve applicants' perceptions of CAT.

In sum, HR specialists now have the opportunity to implement CBS in their organizations. If implemented well, CBS can carry numerous advantages. In fact, the use of computers and the Internet is making testing cheaper and faster, and it may serve as a catalyst for even more widespread use of tests for employment purposes (Tippins et al., 2006). However, the degree of success of implementing CBS will depend not only on the features of the test itself but also on organizational-level variables, such as the culture and climate for technological innovation (Anderson, 2003).

DRUG SCREENING

Drug screening tests began in the military, spread to the sports world, and now are becoming common in employment (Aguinis & Henle, 2005; Tepper, 1994). In fact, about 67 percent of employers use some type of drug screening in the United States (Aguinis & Henle, 2005). Critics charge that such screening violates an individual's right to privacy and that the tests are frequently inaccurate (Morgan, 1989). For example, see the box titled "Practical Application: Cheating on

Drug Tests." These critics do concede, however, that employees in jobs where public safety is crucial—such as nuclear power plant operators—should be screened for drug use. In fact, perceptions of the extent to which different jobs might involve danger to the worker, to coworkers, or to the public are strongly related to the acceptability of drug testing (Murphy, Thornton, & Prue, 1991).

Do the results of such tests forecast certain aspects of later job performance? In perhaps the largest reported study of its kind, the U.S. Postal Service took urine samples from 5,465 job applicants. It never used the results to make hiring decisions and did not tell local managers of the findings. When the data were examined six months to a year later, workers who had tested positively prior to employment were absent 41 percent more often and were fired 38 percent more often. There were no differences in voluntary turnover between those who tested positively and those who did not. These results held up even after adjustment for factors such as age, gender, and race. As a result, the Postal Service is now implementing preemployment drug testing nationwide (Wessel, 1989).

Is such drug screening legal? In two rulings in 1989, the Supreme Court upheld (1) the constitutionality of the government regulations that require railroad crews involved in accidents to submit to prompt urinalysis and blood tests and (2) urine tests for U.S. Customs Service employees seeking drug-enforcement posts. The extent to which such rulings will be limited to safety-sensitive positions has yet to be clarified by the Court. Nevertheless, an employer has a legal right to ensure that employees perform their jobs competently and that no employee endangers the safety of other workers. So, if illegal drug use, on or off the job, may reduce job performance and endanger coworkers, the employer has adequate legal grounds for conducting drug tests.

To avoid legal challenge, consider instituting the following commonsense procedures:

1. Inform all employees and job applicants, in writing, of the company's policy regarding drug use.
2. Include the drug policy and the possibility of testing in all employment contracts.
3. Present the program in a medical and safety context—namely, that drug screening will help to improve the health of employees and also help to ensure a safer workplace.

If drug screening will be used with employees as well as job applicants, tell employees in advance that drug testing will be a routine part of their employment (Angarola, 1985).

BOX 12-2

Practical Application: Cheating on Drug Tests

Employers are increasingly concerned about job applicants and employees cheating on drug tests. The Internet is now a repository of products people can purchase at reasonable prices with the specific goal of cheating on drug tests. Consider the *WHIZZINATOR©*, an easy-to-conceal and easy-to-use urinating device that includes synthetic urine and with an adjustable belt. The price? Just under $150.00.

There are hundreds of similar products offered on the Internet, particularly targeting urine tests. Leo Kadehjian, a Palo Alto–based consultant, noted that "by far the most preferred resource is dilution" (Cadrain, 2003, p. 42). However, a very large number of highly sophisticated products are offered, including the following (Cadrain, 2003):

- Oxidizing agents that alter or destroy drugs and/or their metabolites;
- Nonoxidizing adulterants that change the pH of a urine sample or the ionic strength of the sample; and
- Surfactants, or soaps, which, when added directly to a urine sample, can form microscopic droplets with fatty interiors that trap fatty marijuana metabolites.

To enhance perceptions of fairness, employers should provide advance notice of drug tests, preserve the right to appeal, emphasize that drug testing is a means to enhance workplace safety, attempt to minimize invasiveness, and train supervisors (Konovsky & Cropanzano, 1991; Tepper, 1994). In addition, employers must understand that perceptions of drug testing fairness are affected not only by the actual program's characteristics, but also by employee characteristics. For example, employees who have friends who have failed a drug test are less likely to have positive views of drug testing (Aguinis & Henle, 2005).

POLYGRAPH TESTS

Polygraph instruments are intended to detect deception and are based on the measurement of physiological processes (e.g., heart rate) and changes in those processes. An examiner infers whether a person is telling the truth or lying based on charts of physiological measures in response to the questions posed and observations during the polygraph examination. Although they are often used for event-specific investigations (e.g., after a crime), they are also used (on a limited basis) for both employment and preemployment screening.

The use of polygraph tests has been severely restricted by a federal law passed in 1988. This law, the Employee Polygraph Protection Act, prohibits private employers (except firms providing security services and those manufacturing controlled substances) from requiring or requesting preemployment polygraph exams. Polygraph exams of current employees are permitted only under very restricted circumstances. Nevertheless, many agencies (e.g., U.S. Department of Energy) are using polygraph tests, given the security threats imposed by international terrorism.

Although much of the public debate over the polygraph focuses on ethical problems (Aguinis & Handelsman, 1997a, 1997b), at the heart of the controversy is validity—the relatively simple question of whether physiological measures actually can assess truthfulness and deception (Saxe, Dougherty, & Cross, 1985). The most recent analysis of the scientific evidence on this issue is contained in a report by the National Research Council, which operates under a charter granted by the U.S. Congress. Its Committee to Review the Scientific Evidence on the Polygraph (2003) conducted a quantitative analysis of 57 independent studies investigating the accuracy of the polygraph and concluded the following:

- Polygraph accuracy for screening purposes is almost certainly lower than what can be achieved by specific-incident polygraph tests.
- The physiological indicators measured by the polygraph can be altered by conscious efforts through cognitive or physical means.
- Using the polygraph for security screening yields an unacceptable choice between too many loyal employees falsely judged deceptive and too many major security threats left undetected.

In sum, as concluded by the committee, the polygraph's "accuracy in distinguishing actual or potential security violators from innocent test takers is insufficient to justify reliance on its use in employee security screening in federal agencies" (p. 6). These conclusions are consistent with the views of scholars in relevant disciplines. Responses to a survey completed by members of the Society for Psychophysiological Research and Fellows of the American Psychological Association's Division 1 (General Psychology) indicated that the use of polygraph testing is not theoretically sound, claims of high validity for these procedures cannot be sustained, and polygraph tests can be beaten by countermeasures (Iacono & Lykken, 1997).

In spite of the overall conclusion that polygraph testing is not very accurate, potential alternatives to the polygraph, such as measuring of brain activity through electrical and imaging studies, have not yet been shown to outperform the polygraph (Committee to Review the Scientific Evidence on the Polygraph, 2003). Such alternative techniques do not show any promise of supplanting the polygraph for screening purposes in the near future. Thus, although imperfect, it is likely that the polygraph will continue to be used for employee security screening until other alternatives become available.

EMPLOYMENT INTERVIEWS

Use of the interview in selection today is almost universal (Moscoso, 2000). Perhaps this is so because, in the employment context, the interview serves as much more than just a selection device. The interview is a communication process, whereby the applicant learns more about the job and the organization and begins to develop some realistic expectations about both.

When an applicant is accepted, terms of employment typically are negotiated during an interview. If the applicant is rejected, an important public relations function is performed by the interviewer, for it is essential that the rejected applicant leave with a favorable impression of the organization and its employees. For example, several studies (Kohn & Dipboye, 1998; Schmitt & Coyle, 1979) found that perceptions of the interview process and the interpersonal skills of the interviewer, as well as his or her skills in listening, recruiting, and conveying information about the company and the job the applicant would hold, affected the applicant's evaluations of the interviewer and the company. However, the likelihood of accepting a job, should one be offered, was still mostly unaffected by the interviewer's behavior (Powell, 1991).

As a selection device, the interview performs two vital functions: It can fill information gaps in other selection devices (e.g., regarding incomplete or questionable application blank responses; Tucker & Rowe, 1977), and it can be used to assess factors that can be measured only via face-to-face interaction (e.g., appearance, speech, poise, and interpersonal competence). Is the applicant likely to "fit in" and share values with other organizational members (Cable & Judge, 1997)? Is the applicant likely to get along with others in the organization or be a source of conflict? Where can his or her talents be used most effectively? Interview impressions and perceptions can help to answer these kinds of questions. In fact, well-designed interviews can be helpful because they allow examiners to gather information on constructs that are not typically assessed via other means, such as empathy (Cliffordson, 2002) and personal initiative (Fay & Frese, 2001). For example, a review of 388 characteristics that were rated in 47 actual interview studies revealed that personality traits (e.g., *responsibility*, *dependability*, and *persistence*, which are all related to *conscientiousness*) and applied social skills (e.g., *interpersonal relations*, *social skills*, *team focus*, *ability to work with people*) are rated more often in employment interviews than any other type of construct (Huffcutt, Conway, Roth, & Stone, 2001). In addition, interviews can contribute to the prediction of job performance over and above cognitive abilities and *conscientiousness* (Cortina, Goldstein, Payne, Davison, & Gilliland, 2000), as well as experience (Day & Carroll, 2002).

Since few employers are willing to hire applicants they have never seen, it is imperative that we do all we can to make the interview as effective a selection technique as possible. Next, we will consider some of the research on interviewing and offer suggestions for improving the process.

Response Distortion in the Interview

Distortion of interview information is probable (Weiss & Dawis, 1960; Weiss, England, & Lofquist, 1961), the general tendency being to upgrade rather than downgrade prior work experience. That is, interviewees tend to be affected by social desirability bias, which is a tendency to answer questions in a more socially desirable direction (i.e., to attempt to look good in the eyes of the interviewer). In addition to distorting information, applicants tend to engage in influence tactics to create a positive impression, and they typically do so by displaying self-promotion behaviors (Stevens & Kristof, 1995). The frequency of display of such tactics as conformity and other enhancements are positively related to the applicant's expectancy that he or she will receive a job offer (Stevens, 1997).

But will social desirability distortion be reduced if the interviewer is a computer? According to Martin and Nagao (1989), candidates tend to report their grade point averages and scholastic aptitude test scores more accurately to computers than in face-to-face interviews. Perhaps this is due to the "big brother" effect. That is, because responses are on a computer rather than on paper, they may seem more subject to instant checking and verification through other computer databases. To avoid potential embarrassment, applicants may be more likely to provide truthful responses. However, Martin and Nagao's study also placed an important boundary condition on computer interviews: There was much greater resentment by individuals competing for high-status positions than for low-status positions when they had to respond to a computer rather than a live interviewer.

A more comprehensive study was conducted by Richman, Kiesler, Weisband, and Drasgow (1999). They conducted a meta-analysis synthesizing 61 studies (673 effect sizes), comparing response distortion in computer questionnaires with traditional paper-and-pencil questionnaires and face-to-face interviews. Results revealed that computer-based interviews decreased social-desirability distortion compared to face-to-face interviews, particularly when the interviews addressed highly sensitive personal behavior (e.g., use of illegal drugs). Perhaps this is so because a computer-based interview is more impersonal than the observation of an interviewer and social cues that can arouse an interviewee's evaluation apprehension.

A more subtle way to distort the interview is to engage in **impression-management** behaviors (Lievens & Peeters, 2008; Muir, 2005). For example, applicants who are pleasant and compliment the interviewer are more likely to receive more positive evaluations. Two specific types of impression management, ingratiation and self-promotion, seem to be most effective in influencing interviewers' rating favorably (Higgins & Judge, 2004).

Reliability and Validity

An early meta-analysis of only 10 validity coefficients that were not corrected for range restriction yielded a validity of .14 when the interview was used to predict supervisory ratings (Hunter & Hunter, 1984). Five subsequent meta-analyses that did correct for range restriction and used larger samples of studies reported much more encouraging results. Wiersner and Cronshaw (1988) found a mean corrected validity of .47 across 150 interview validity studies involving all types of criteria. McDaniel, Whetzel, Schmidt, and Maurer (1994) analyzed 245 coefficients derived from 86,311 individuals and found a mean corrected validity of .37 for job performance criteria. However, validities were higher when criteria were collected for research purposes (mean = .47) than for administrative decision making (.36). Marchese and Muchinsky (1993) reported a mean corrected validity of .38 across 31 studies. A fourth study (Huffcutt & Arthur, 1994) analyzed 114 interview validity coefficients from 84 published and unpublished references, exclusively involving entry-level jobs and supervisory rating criteria. When corrected for criterion unreliability and range restriction, the mean validity across all 114 studies was .37. Finally, Schmidt and Rader (1999) meta-analyzed 40 studies of structured telephone interviews and obtained a corrected validity coefficient of .40 using performance ratings as a criterion. The results of these studies agree quite closely.

A different meta-analysis of 111 interrater reliability coefficients and 49 internal consistency reliability estimates (coefficient alphas) derived from employment interviews revealed overall means of .70 for interrater reliability and .39 for internal consistency reliability (Conway, Jako, & Goodman, 1995). These results imply that the upper limits of validity are .67 for highly structured interviews and .34 for unstructured interviews and that the major reason for low validities is not the criteria used, but rather low reliability. Hence, the best way to improve validity is to improve the structure of the interview (discussed later in this chapter).

As Hakel (1989) has noted, interviewing is a difficult cognitive and social task. Managing a smooth social exchange while simultaneously processing information about an applicant makes interviewing uniquely difficult among all managerial tasks. Research continues to focus on cognitive factors (e.g., preinterview impressions) and social factors (e.g., interviewer–interviewee similarity). As a result, we now know a great deal more about what goes on in the interview and about how to improve the process. At the very least, we should expect interviewers to be able to form opinions only about traits and characteristics that are overtly manifest in the interview (or that can be inferred from the applicant's behavior), and not about traits and characteristics that typically would become manifest only over a period of time—traits such as creativity, dependability, and honesty. In the following subsections, we will examine what is known about the interview process and about ways to enhance the effectiveness and utility of the selection interview.

Factors Affecting the Decision-Making Process

A large body of literature attests to the fact that the decision-making process involved in the interview is affected by several factors. Specifically, 278 studies have examined numerous aspects of the interview in the last 10 years or so (Posthuma, Morgeson, & Campion, 2002). Posthuma et al. (2002) provided a useful framework to summarize and describe this large body of research. We will follow this taxonomy in part and consider factors affecting the interview decision-making process in each of the following areas: (1) social/interpersonal factors (e.g., interviewer–applicant similarity), (2) cognitive factors (e.g., preinterview impressions), (3) individual differences (e.g., applicant appearance, interviewer training and experience), (4) structure (i.e., degree of standardization of the interview process and discretion an interviewer is allowed in conducting the interview), and (5) use of alternative media (e.g., videoconferencing).

Social/Interpersonal Factors

As noted above, the interview is fundamentally a social and interpersonal process. As such, it is subject to influences such as interviewer–applicant similarity and verbal and nonverbal cues. We describe each of these factors next.

INTERVIEWER–APPLICANT SIMILARITY Similarity leads to attraction, attraction leads to positive affect, and positive affect can lead to higher interview ratings (Schmitt, Pulakos, Nason, & Whitney, 1996). Moreover, similarity leads to greater expectations about future performance (García, Posthuma, & Colella, 2008). Does similarity between the interviewer and the interviewee regarding race, age, and attitudes affect the interview? Lin, Dobbins, and Farh (1992) reported that ratings of African American and Latino interviewees, but not white interviewees, were higher when the interviewer was the same race as the applicant. However, Lin et al. (1992) found that the inclusion of at least one different-race interviewer in a panel eliminated the effect, and no effect was found for age similarity. Further, when an interviewer feels that an interviewee shares his or her attitudes, ratings of competence and affect are increased (Howard & Ferris, 1996). The similarity effects are not large, however, and they can be reduced or eliminated by using a structured interview and a diverse set of interviewers.

VERBAL AND NONVERBAL CUES As early as 1960, Anderson found that, in those interviews where the interviewer did a lot more of the talking and there was less silence, the applicant was more likely to be hired. Other research has shown that the length of the interview depends much more on the quality of the applicant (interviewers take more time to decide when dealing with a high-quality applicant) and on the expected length of the interview. The longer the expected length of the interview, the longer it takes to reach a decision (Tullar, Mullins, & Caldwell, 1979).

Several studies have also examined the impact of *nonverbal* cues on impression formation and decision making in the interview. Nonverbal cues have been shown to have an impact, albeit small, on interviewer judgments (DeGroot & Motowidlo, 1999). For example, Imada and Hakel (1977) found that positive nonverbal cues (e.g., smiling, attentive posture, smaller interpersonal distance) produced consistently favorable ratings. Most importantly, however, nonverbal behaviors interact with other variables such as gender. Aguinis, Simonsen, and Pierce (1998) found that a man displaying direct eye contact during an interview is rated as more credible than another one not making direct eye contact. However, a follow-up replication using exactly the same experimental conditions revealed that a woman displaying identical direct eye contact behavior was seen as coercive (Aguinis & Henle, 2001a).

Overall, the ability of a candidate to respond concisely, to answer questions fully, to state personal opinions when relevant, and to keep to the subject at hand appears to be more crucial in obtaining a favorable employment decision (Parsons & Liden, 1984; Rasmussen, 1984). High levels of nonverbal behavior tend to have more positive effects than low levels only when the verbal content of the interview is good. When verbal content is poor, high levels of nonverbal behavior may result in lower ratings.

Cognitive Factors

The interviewer's task is not easy because humans are limited information processors and have biases in evaluating others (Kraiger & Aguinis, 2001). However, we have a good understanding of the impact of such factors as preinterview impressions and confirmatory bias, first impressions, stereotypes, contrast effect, and information recall. Let's review major findings regarding the way in which each of these factors affects the interview.

PREINTERVIEW IMPRESSIONS AND CONFIRMATORY BIAS   Dipboye (1982, 1992) specified a model of self-fulfilling prophecy to explain the impact of first preinterview impressions. Both cognitive and behavioral biases mediate the effects of preinterview impressions (based on letters of reference or applications) on the evaluations of applicants. Behavioral biases occur when interviewers behave in ways that confirm their preinterview impressions of applicants (e.g., showing positive or negative regard for applicants). Cognitive biases occur if interviewers distort information to support preinterview impressions or use selective attention and recall of information. This sequence of behavioral and cognitive biases produces a self-fulfilling prophecy.

Consider how one applicant was described by an interviewer given positive information:

Alert, enthusiastic, responsible, well-educated, intelligent, can express himself well, organized, well-rounded, can converse well, hard worker, reliable, fairly experienced, and generally capable of handling himself well.

On the basis of negative preinterview information, the same applicant was described as follows:

Nervous, quick to object to the interviewer's assumptions, and doesn't have enough self-confidence. (Dipboye, Stramler, & Fontanelle, 1984, p. 567)

Content coding of actual employment interviews found that favorable first impressions were followed by the use of confirmatory behavior—such as indicating positive regard for the applicant, "selling" the company, and providing job information to applicants—while gathering less information from them. For their part, applicants behaved more confidently and effectively and developed better rapport with interviewers (Dougherty, Turban, & Callender, 1994). These findings support the existence of the confirmatory bias produced by first impressions.

Another aspect of expectancies concerns test score or biodata score information available prior to the interview. A study of 577 actual candidates for the position of life insurance sales agent found that interview ratings predicted the hiring decision and survival on the job best for applicants with low passing scores on the biodata test and poorest for applicants with high passing scores (Dalessio & Silverhart, 1994). Apparently, interviewers had such faith in the validity of the test scores that, if an applicant scored well, they gave little weight to the interview. When the applicant scored poorly, however, they gave more weight to performance in the interview and made better distinctions among candidates.

FIRST IMPRESSIONS   An early series of studies conducted at McGill University over a 10-year period (Webster, 1964, 1982) found that early interview impressions play a dominant role in final decisions (accept/reject). These early impressions establish a bias in the interviewer (not usually reversed) that colors all subsequent interviewer–applicant interaction. (Early impressions were crystallized after a mean interviewing time of only four minutes!) Moreover, the interview is primarily a search for negative information. For example, just one unfavorable impression was followed by a reject decision 90 percent of the time. Positive information was given much less weight in the final decision (Bolster & Springbett, 1961).

Consider the effect of how the applicant shakes the interviewer's hand (Stewart, Dustin, Barrick, & Darnold, 2008). A study using 98 undergraduate students found that quality of handshake was related to the interviewer's hiring recommendation. It seems that quality of handshake conveys the positive impression that the applicant is extraverted, even when the candidate's physical appearance and dress are held constant. Also, in this particular study women received lower ratings for the handshake compared with men, but they did not, on average, receive lower assessments of employment suitability.

PROTOTYPES AND STEREOTYPES   Returning to the McGill studies, perhaps the most important finding of all was that interviewers tend to develop their own prototype of a good applicant and proceed to accept those who match their prototype (Rowe, 1963; Webster, 1964). Later research has supported these findings. To the extent that the interviewers hold negative stereotypes of a group of applicants, and these stereotypes deviate from the perception of what is needed for the job or translate into different expectations or standards of evaluation for minorities, stereotypes may have the effect of lowering interviewers' evaluations, even when candidates are equally qualified for the job (Arvey, 1979).

Similar considerations apply to gender-based stereotypes. The social psychology literature on gender-based stereotypes indicates that the traits and attributes necessary for managerial success resemble the characteristics, attitudes, and temperaments of the masculine gender role more than the feminine gender role (Aguinis & Adams, 1998). The operation of such stereotypes may explain the conclusion by Arvey and Campion (1982) that female applicants receive lower scores than male applicants.

CONTRAST EFFECTS   Several studies have found that, if an interviewer evaluates a candidate who is just average after evaluating three or four very unfavorable candidates in a row, the average candidate tends to be evaluated very favorably. When interviewers evaluate more than one candidate at a time, they tend to use other candidates as a standard. Whether they rate a candidate favorably, then, is determined partly by others against whom the candidate is compared (Hakel, Ohnesorge, & Dunnette, 1970; Heneman, Schwab, Huett, & Ford, 1975; Landy & Bates, 1973).

These effects are remarkably tenacious. Wexley, Sanders, and Yukl (1973) found that, despite attempts to reduce contrast effects by means of a warning (lecture) and/or an anchoring procedure (comparison of applicants to a preset standard), subjects continued to make this error. Only an intensive workshop (which combined practical observation and rating experience with immediate feedback) led to a significant behavior change. Similar results were reported in a later study by Latham, Wexley, and Pursell (1975). In contrast to subjects in group discussion or control groups, only those who participated in the intensive workshop did not commit contrast, halo, similarity, or first impression errors six months after training.

INFORMATION RECALL A very practical question concerns the ability of interviewers to recall what an applicant said during an interview. Here is how this question was examined in one study (Carlson, Thayer, Mayfield, & Peterson, 1971).

Prior to viewing a 20-minute videotaped selection interview, 40 managers were given an interview guide, pencils, and paper and were told to perform as if *they* were conducting the interview. Following the interview, the managers were given a 20-question test, based on factual information. Some managers missed none, while others missed as many as 15 out of 20 items. The average number was 10 wrong.

After this short interview, half the managers could not report accurately on the information produced during the interview! On the other hand, those managers who had been following the interview guide and taking notes were quite accurate on the test. Those who were least accurate in their recollections assumed the interview was generally favorable and rated the candidate higher in all areas and with less variability. They adopted a halo strategy. Those managers who knew the facts rated the candidate lower and recognized intraindividual differences. Hence, the more accurate interviewers used an individual differences strategy.

None of the managers in this study was given an opportunity to preview an application form prior to the interview. Would that have made a difference? Other research indicates that the answer is no (Dipboye, Fontanelle, & Garner, 1984). When it comes to recalling information *after* the interview, there seems to be no substitute for note taking *during* the interview. However, the act of note taking alone does not necessarily improve the validity of the interview; interviewers need to be trained on how to take notes regarding relevant behaviors (Burnett, Fan, Motowidlo, & DeGroot, 1998). Note taking helps information recall, but it does not in itself improve the judgments based on such information (Middendorf & Macan, 2002). In addition to note taking, other memory aids include mentally reconstructing the context of the interview and retrieving information from different starting points (Mantwill, Kohnken, & Aschermann, 1995).

Individual Differences

A number of individual-difference variables play a role in the interview process. These refer to characteristics of both the applicant and the interviewer. Let's review applicant characteristics first, followed by interviewer characteristics.

APPLICANT APPEARANCE AND OTHER PERSONAL CHARACTERISTICS Findings regarding physical attractiveness indicate that attractiveness is only an advantage in jobs where attractiveness per se is relevant. However, being unattractive appears never to be an advantage (Beehr & Gilmore, 1982). One study found that being perceived as being obese can have a small, although statistically significant, negative effect (Finkelstein, Frautschy Demuth, & Sweeney, 2007). However, another study found that overweight applicants were no more likely to be hired for a position involving minimal public contact than they were for a job requiring extensive public contact (Pingitore, Dugoni, Tindale, & Spring, 1994).

Some of the available evidence indicates that ethnicity may not be a source of bias (Arvey, 1979; McDonald & Hakel, 1985). As noted earlier, there is a small effect for race, but it is related to interviewer–applicant race similarity rather than applicant race. However, a more recent study examining the effects of accent and name as ethnic cues found that these two factors interacted in affecting interviewers' evaluations (Purkiss, Perrewé, Gillespie, Mayes, & Ferris, 2006). Specifically, applicants with an ethnic name who spoke with accent were perceived less positively compared to ethnic-named applicants without an accent and nonethnic-named applicants with and without an accent. These results point to the need to investigate interactions between an interviewee's ethnicity and other variables. In fact, a study involving more than 1,334 police officers found a three-way interaction among interviewer ethnicity, interviewee ethnicity, and panel composition, such that African American interviewers evaluated African

American interviewees more favorably than white applicants only when they were on a pre-dominately African American panel (McFarland, Ryan, Sacco, & Kriska, 2004). Further research is certainly needed regarding these issues, given the demographic and societal trends discussed in Chapters 1 and 2.

Evidence available from studies regarding the impact of disability status is mixed. Some studies show no relationship (Rose & Brief, 1979), whereas others indicate that applicants with disabilities receive more negative ratings (Arvey & Campion, 1982), and yet a third group of studies suggests that applicants with disabilities receive more positive ratings (Hayes & Macan, 1997). The discrepant findings are likely due to the need to include additional variables in the design in addition to disability status. For example, rater empathy can affect whether applicants with a disability receive a higher or lower rating than applicants without a disability (Cesare, Tannenbaum, & Dalessio, 1990).

Applicant personality seems to be related to interview performance. For example, consider a study including a sample of 85 graduating college seniors who completed a personality inventory. At a later time, these graduates reported the strategies they used in the job search and whether these strategies had generated interviews and job offers (Caldwell & Burger, 1998). Results revealed correlations of .38 and .27 for invitations for a follow-up interview and *conscientiousness* and *extraversion*, respectively. And correlations of .34, .27, .23, and −.21 were obtained for relationships between receiving a job offer and *extraversion*, *agreeableness*, *openness to experience*, and *neuroticism*, respectively. In other words, being more conscientious and extraverted enhances the chances of receiving follow-up interviews; being more extraverted, more agreeable, more open to experience, and less neurotic is related to receiving a job offer. Follow-up analyses revealed that, when self-reports of preparation and all personality variables were included in the equation, *conscientiousness* was the only trait related to number of interview invitations received, and *extraversion* and *neuroticism* (negative) were the only traits related to number of job offers. A second study found that applicants' trait negative affectivity had an impact on interview success via the mediating role of job-search self-efficacy and job-search intensity (Crossley & Stanton, 2005). Yet another study found that individuals differ greatly regarding their experienced anxiety during the interview and that levels of interview anxiety are related to interview performance (McCarthy & Goffin, 2004). Taken together, the evidence gathered thus far suggests that an applicant's personality has an effect during and after the interview, and it also affects how applicants prepare *before* the interview.

A final issue regarding personal characteristics is the possible impact of pleasant artificial scents (perfume or cologne) on ratings in an employment interview. Research conducted in a controlled setting found that women assigned higher ratings to applicants when they used artificial scents than when they did not, whereas the opposite was true for men. These results may be due to differences in the ability of men and women to "filter out" irrelevant aspects of applicants' grooming or appearance (Baron, 1983).

APPLICANT PARTICIPATION IN A COACHING PROGRAM   Coaching can include a variety of techniques, including modeling, behavioral rehearsal, role playing, and lecture, among others (Maurer & Solamon, 2007; Tross & Maurer, 2008). Is there a difference in interview performance between applicants who receive coaching on interviewing techniques and those who do not? Two studies (Maurer, Solamon, Andrews, & Troxtel, 2001; Maurer, Solamon, & Troxtel, 1998) suggest so. These studies included police officers and firefighters involved in promotional procedures that required an interview. The coaching program in the Maurer et al. (1998) study included several elements that included: (1) introduction to the interview, including a general description of the process; (2) description of interview-day logistics; (3) description of types of interviews (i.e., structured versus unstructured) and advantages of structured interviews; (4) review of knowledge, abilities, and skills needed for a successful interview; (5) participation in and observation of interview role plays; and (6) interview tips. Participants in the coaching program received higher interview scores than nonparticipants for four different types of jobs (i.e., police sergeant, police lieutenant, fire lieutenant, and fire captain). Differences were found for three of the four jobs when controlling for the effects of applicant precoaching knowledge and motivation to do well on the promotional procedures. In a follow-up study, Maurer et al. (2001) found similar results.

Now let's discuss interviewer characteristics and their effects on the interview.

INTERVIEWER TRAINING AND EXPERIENCE   Some types of interviewer training can be beneficial (Arvey & Campion, 1982), but we do not have sufficient information at this point to specify which programs are best for which criteria (e.g., improvement in reliability, accuracy, etc.). On the other hand, although it has been hypothesized that interviewers with the same amount of experience will evaluate an applicant similarly (Rowe, 1960), empirical results do not support this hypothesis. Carlson (1967) found that, when interviewers with the same experience evaluated the same recruits, they agreed with each other to no greater extent than did interviewers with differing experiences. Apparently interviewers benefit very little from day-to-day interviewing experience, since the conditions necessary for learning (i.e., training and feedback) are not present in the interviewer's everyday job situation. Experienced interviewers who never learn how to conduct good interviews will simply perpetuate their poor skills over time (Jacobs & Baratta, 1989). On the other hand, there may be a positive relationship between experience and improved decision making when experience is accompanied by higher levels of cognitive complexity (Dipboye & Jackson, 1999). In that case, experience is just a proxy for another variable (i.e., complexity) and not the factor improving decision making per se.

INTERVIEWER COGNITIVE COMPLEXITY AND MOOD   Some laboratory studies, mainly using undergraduate students watching videotaped mock interviews, have investigated whether cognitive complexity (i.e., ability to deal with complex social situations) and mood affect the interview. While the evidence is limited, a study by Ferguson and Fletcher (1989) found that cognitive complexity was associated with greater accuracy for female raters, but not for male raters. However, more research is needed before we can conclude that cognitive complexity has a direct effect on interviewer accuracy.

Regarding the effect of mood, Baron (1993) induced 92 undergraduate students to experience positive affect, negative affect, or no shift in current affect. Then students conducted a simulated job interview with an applicant whose qualifications were described as high, ambiguous, or low. This experiment led to the following three findings. First, when the applicant's qualifications were ambiguous, participants in the positive affect condition rated this person higher on several dimensions than did students in the negative affect condition. Second, interviewers' mood had no effect on ratings when the applicant appeared to be highly qualified for the job. Third, interviewers' moods significantly influenced ratings of the applicant when this person appeared to be unqualified for the job, such that participants in the positive affect condition rated the applicant lower than those induced to experience negative affect. In sum, interviewer mood seems to interact with applicant qualifications such that mood plays a role only when applicants are unqualified or when qualifications are ambiguous.

Effects of Structure

Another major category of factors that affect interview decision making refers to the interview structure. Structure is a matter of degree, and there are four dimensions one can consider: (1) questioning consistency, (2) evaluation standardization, (3) question sophistication, and (4) rapport building (Chapman & Zweig, 2005). Overall, structure can be enhanced by basing questions on results of a job analysis, asking the same questions of each candidate, limiting prompting follow-up questioning and elaboration on questions, using better types of questions (e.g., situational questions, which are discussed below), using longer interviews and a larger number of questions, controlling ancillary information (i.e., application forms, résumés, test scores, recommendations), not allowing the applicant to ask questions until after the interview, rating each answer on multiple scales, using detailed anchored rating scales, taking detailed notes, using multiple interviewers, using the same interviewer(s) across all applicants, providing extensive interviewing training, and using statistical rather than clinical prediction (discussed in detail in Chapter 14) (Campion, Palmer, & Campion, 1997).

The impact of structure on several desirable outcomes is clear-cut. First, a review of several meta-analyses reported that structured interviews are more valid (Campion et al., 1997). Specifically, the corrected validities for structured interviews ranged from .35 to .62, whereas those for unstructured interviews ranged from .14 to .33. Second, structure decreases differences between racial groups. A meta-analysis found a mean standardized difference ($\bar{d}$) between white and African American applicants of .32 based on 10 studies with low-structure interviews and $\bar{d} = .23$ based on 21 studies with high-structure interviews (Huffcutt & Roth, 1998). Note, however, that these differences are larger for both types of interviews if one considers the impact of range restriction (Roth, Van Iddekinge, Huffcutt, Eidson, & Bobko, 2002). Third, structured interviews are less likely to be challenged in court based on illegal discrimination as compared to unstructured interviews (Williamson, Campion, Malos, Roehling, & Campion, 1997).

A review of 158 U.S. federal court cases involving hiring discrimination from 1978 to 1997 revealed that unstructured interviews were challenged in court more often than any other type of selection device, including structured interviews (Terpstra, Mohamed, & Kethley, 1999). Specifically, 57 percent of cases involved charges against the use of unstructured interviews, whereas only 6 percent of cases involved charges against the use of structured interviews. Even more important is an examination of the outcomes of such legal challenges. Unstructured interviews were found not to be discriminatory in 59 percent of cases, whereas structured interviews were found not to be discriminatory in 100 percent of cases. Taken together, these findings make a compelling case for the use of the structured interview in spite of HR managers' reluctance to adopt such procedures (van der Zee, Bakker, & Bakker, 2002).

Why are structured interviews qualitatively better than unstructured interviews? Most likely the answer is that unstructured interviews (i.e., the interviewer has no set procedure, but merely follows the applicant's lead) and structured interviews (i.e., the interviewer follows a set procedure) do not measure the same constructs (Huffcutt et al., 2001). Differences in favor of structured interviews compared to unstructured interviews in terms of reliability do not seem to be a sufficient explanation (Schmidt & Zimmerman, 2004). Typically, structured interviews are the result of a job analysis and assess job knowledge and skills, organizational fit, interpersonal and social skills, and applied mental skills (e.g., problem solving). Therefore, constructs assessed in structured interviews tend to have a greater degree of job relatedness as compared to the constructs measured in unstructured interviews. When interviews are structured, interviewers know what to ask for (thereby providing a more consistent sample of behavior across applicants) and what to do with the information they receive (thereby helping them to provide better ratings).

Structured interviews vary based on whether the questions are about past experiences or hypothetical situations. Questions in an experience-based interview are past-oriented; they ask applicants to relate what they did in past jobs or life situations that are relevant to the job in question (Janz, 1982; Motowidlo et al., 1992). The underlying assumption is that the best predictor of future performance is past performance in similar situations. Experience-based questions are of the "Can you tell me about a time when . . . ?" variety.

By contrast, situational questions (Latham, Saari, Pursell, & Campion, 1980; Maurer, 2002) ask job applicants to imagine a set of circumstances and then indicate how they would respond in that situation. Hence, the questions are future-oriented. Situational interview questions are of the "What would you do if . . . ?" variety. Situational interviews have been found to be highly valid and resistant to contrast error and to race or gender bias (Maurer, 2002). Why do they work? Apparently the most influential factor is the use of behaviorally anchored rating scales. Maurer (2002) reached this conclusion based on a study of raters who watched and provided ratings of six situational interview videos for the job of campus police officer. Even without any training, a group of 48 business students showed more accuracy and agreement than job experts (i.e., 48 municipal and campus police officers) who used a structured interview format that did not include situational questions. Subsequent comparison of situational versus nonsituational interview ratings provided by the job experts showed higher levels of agreement and accuracy for the situational type.

Both experience-based and situational questions are based on a job analysis that uses the critical-incidents method (cf. Chapter 9). The incidents then are turned into interview questions. Each answer is rated independently by two or more interviewers on a five-point Likert-type scale. To facilitate objective scoring, job experts develop behavioral statements that are used to illustrate 1, 3, and 5 answers. Table 12-2 illustrates the difference between these two types of questions.

Taylor and Small (2002) conducted a meta-analysis comparing the relative effectiveness of these two approaches. They were able to locate 30 validities derived from situational interviews and 19 validities for experience-based interviews, resulting in a mean corrected validity of .45 for situational interviews and .56 for experience-based interviews. However, a comparison of the studies that used behaviorally anchored rating scales yielded a mean validity of .47 for situational interviews (29 validity coefficients) and .63 for experience-based interviews (11 validity coefficients). In addition, mean interrater reliabilities were .79 for situational interviews and .77 for experience-based interviews. Finally, although some studies have found that the situational interview may be less valid for higher-level positions (Pulakos & Schmitt, 1995) or more complex jobs (Huffcutt, Weekley, Wiesner, DeGroot, & Jones, 2001), the meta-analytic results found no differential validity based on job complexity for either type of interview.

TABLE 12-2 Examples of Experience-Based and Situational Interview Items Designed to Assess Conflict Resolution and Collaborative Problem-Solving Skills

Situational item: Suppose you had an idea for a change in work procedure to enhance quality, but there was a problem in that some members of your work team were against any type of change. What would you do in this situation?

(5) Excellent answer (top third of candidates)—Explain the change and try to show the benefits. Discuss it openly in a meeting.

(3) Good answer (middle third)—Ask them why they are against change. Try to convince them.

(1) Marginal answer (bottom third)—Tell the supervisor.

Experience-based item: What is the biggest difference of opinion you ever had with a coworker? How did it get resolved?

(5) Excellent answer (top third of candidates)—We looked into the situation, found the problem, and resolved the difference. Had an honest conversation with the person.

(3) Good answer (middle third)—Compromised. Resolved the problem by taking turns, or I explained the problem (my side) carefully.

(1) Marginal answer (bottom third)—I got mad and told the coworker off, or we got the supervisor to resolve the problem, or I never have differences with anyone.

Source: Campion, M. A., Campion, J. E., & Hudson, J. P., Jr. (1994). Structured interviewing: A note on incremental validity and alternative question types. *Journal of Applied Psychology*, *79*, 999.

Use of Alternative Media

Technological advances now allow employers to use alternative media as opposed to face-to-face contact in conducting the employment interview. The use of videoconferencing, for example, allows employers to interview distant applicants remotely and inexpensively (Chapman & Rowe, 2002). Telephone interviewing is quite common (Schmidt & Rader, 1999). However, some key differences between face-to-face interviews and interviews using technologies such as the telephone and videoconferencing may affect the process and outcome of the interview (Chapman & Rowe, 2002). In the case of the telephone, an obvious difference is the absence of visual cues (Silvester & Anderson, 2003). On the other hand, the absence of visual cues may reduce some of the interviewer biases based on nonverbal behaviors that were discussed earlier in this chapter. Regarding videoconferencing, the lack of a duplex system that allows for both parties to talk simultaneously may change the dynamics of the interview.

A hybrid way to conduct the interview is to do it face to face, record both audio and video, and then ask additional raters, who were not present in the face-to-face interview, to provide an evaluation (Van Iddekinge, Raymark, Roth, & Payne, 2006). However, a simulation including 113 undergraduate and graduate students provided initial evidence that ratings may not be equivalent. Specifically, face-to-face ratings were significantly higher than those provided based on the videotaped interviews. Thus, further research is needed to establish conditions under which ratings provided in face-to-face and videotaped interviews may be equivalent.

One study compared the equivalence of telephone and face-to-face interviews using a sample of 70 applicants for a job in a large multinational oil corporation (Silvester, Anderson, Haddleton, Cunningham-Snell, & Gibb, 2000). Applicants were randomly assigned to two groups: Group A: a face-to-face interview followed by a telephone interview, and Group B: a telephone interview followed by a face-to-face interview. Results revealed that telephone ratings ($M = 4.30$) were lower than face-to-face ratings ($M = 5.52$), regardless of the interview order. Silvester et al. (2000) provided several possible reasons for this result. During telephone interviews, interviewers may be more focused on content rather than extraneous cues (e.g., nonverbal behavior), in which case the telephone interview may be considered to be more valid than the face-to-face interview. Alternatively, applicants may have considered the telephone interview as less important and could have been less motivated to perform well, or applicants may have had less experience with telephone interviews, which could also explain their lower performance.

Another experimental study compared face-to-face interviews with videoconferencing interviews using a sample of undergraduate students being interviewed for actual jobs (Chapman & Rowe, 2002). Results indicated that applicants in the face-to-face condition were more satisfied with the interviewer's performance and with their own performance during the interview as compared to applicants in the videoconferencing condition (Chapman & Rowe, 2002).

In sum, the limited research thus far evaluating alternative media such as telephone and videoconferencing technology indicates that the use of such media produces different outcomes. Further research is needed to understand more clearly the reason for this lack of equivalence. One thing is clear, however. Although inexpensive on the surface, the use of electronic media in conducting the interview may have some important hidden costs, such as negative applicant reactions and scores that are not as valid as those resulting from face-to-face interviews.

Needed Improvements

Emphasis on employment interview research within a person-perception framework should continue. Also, this research must consider the social and interpersonal dynamics of the interview, including affective reactions on the part of both the applicant and the interviewer. The interviewer's job is to develop accurate perceptions of applicants and to evaluate those perceptions in light of job requirements. Learning more about how those perceptions are formed, what affects their development, and what psychological processes best explain their development are important questions that deserve increased attention. Also, we need to determine whether any of these process variables affect the validity, and ultimately the utility, of the interview (Zedeck & Cascio, 1984). We should begin by building on our present knowledge to make improvements in selection-interview technology. Here are eight research-based suggestions for improving the interview process:

1. Link interview questions tightly to job analysis results, and ensure that behaviors and skills observed in the interview are similar to those required on the job. A variety of types of questions may be used, including situational questions, questions on job knowledge that is important to job performance, job sample or simulation questions, and questions regarding background (e.g., experience, education) and "willingness" (e.g., shift work, travel).

2. Ask the same questions of each candidate because standardizing interview questions has a dramatic effect on the psychometric properties of interview ratings. Consider using the following six steps when conducting a structured interview: (1) Open the interview, explaining its purpose and structure (i.e., that you will be asking a set of questions that pertain to the applicant's past job behavior and what he or she would do in a number of job-relevant situations), and encourage the candidate to ask questions; (2) preview the job; (3) ask questions about minimum qualifications (e.g., for an airline, willingness to work nights and holidays); (4) ask experience-based questions ("Can you tell me about a time when . . . ?"); (5) ask situational questions ("What would you do if . . . ?"); (6) close the interview by giving the applicant an opportunity to ask questions or volunteer information he or she thinks is important, and explain what happens next (and when) in the selection process.

3. Anchor the rating scales for scoring answers with examples and illustrations. Doing so helps to enhance consistency across interviews and objectivity in judging candidates.

4. Whether structured or unstructured, interview panels are no more valid than are individual interviews (McDaniel et al., 1994). In fact, some panel members may see the interview as a political arena and attempt to use the interview and its outcome as a way to advance the agenda of the political network in which they belong (Bozionelos, 2005). As we have seen, however, mixed-race panels may help to reduce the similar-to-me bias that individual interviewers might introduce. Moreover, if a panel is used, letting panel members know that they will engage in a group discussion to achieve rating consensus improves behavioral accuracy (i.e., a rating of whether a particular type of behavior was present or absent) (Roch, 2006).

5. Combine ratings mechanically (e.g., by averaging or summing them) rather than subjectively (Conway et al., 1995).

6. Provide a well-designed and properly evaluated training program to communicate this information to interviewers, along with techniques for structuring the interview (e.g., a structured interview guide, standardized rating forms) to minimize the amount of irrelevant information. As part of their training, give interviewers the opportunity to practice interviewing with minorities or persons with disabilities. This may increase the ability of interviewers to relate.

7. Document the job-analysis and interview-development procedures, candidate responses and scores, evidence of content- or criterion-related validity, and adverse impact analyses in accordance with testing guidelines.

8. Institute a planned system of feedback to interviewers to let them know who succeeds and who fails and to keep them up-to-date on changing job requirements and success patterns.

There are no shortcuts to reliable and valid measurement. Careful attention to detail and careful "mapping" of the interview situation to the job situation are necessary, both legally and ethically, if the interview is to continue to be used for selection purposes.

TOWARD THE FUTURE: VIRTUAL-REALITY SCREENING (VRT)

In previous sections, we described the use of computers, the Internet, and other new technologies, such as videoconferencing. As technology progresses, HR specialists will be able to take advantage of new tools. Aguinis, Henle, and Beaty (2001) suggested that VRT can be one such technological advance that has the potential to alter the way screening is done.

Imagine applicants for truck driver positions stepping into a simulator of a truck to demonstrate their competence. Or imagine applicants for lab technician positions entering a simulated laboratory to demonstrate their ability to handle various chemical substances. VRT has several advantages because it has the potential to create such job-related environments without using real trucks or real chemicals. Thus, users can practice hazardous tasks or simulate rare occurrences in a realistic environment without compromising their safety. VRT also allows examiners to gather valuable information regarding future on-the-job performance. As noted by Aguinis et al. (2001), "[j]ust a few years ago, this would have only been possible in science fiction movies, but today virtual reality technology makes this feasible."

The implementation of VRT presents some challenges, however. For example, VRT environments can lead to sopite syndrome (i.e., eyestrain, blurred vision, headache, balance disturbances, drowsiness; Pierce & Aguinis, 1997). A second potential problem in implementing VRT testing is its cost and lack of commercial availability. However, VRT systems are becoming increasingly affordable. Aguinis et al. (2001) reported that an immersive system, which includes software, data gloves, head-mounted display, PC workstation, and position tracking system, can cost approximately $30,000. A final challenge faced by those contemplating the use of VRT is its technical limitations. In virtual environments, there is a noticeable lag between the user's movement and the change of scenery, and some of the graphics, including the virtual representation of the user, may appear cartoonlike. However, given the frantic pace of technological advances, we should expect that some of the present limitations will soon be overcome.

Evidence-Based Implications for Practice

- There are several methods available to make decisions at the initial stages of the selection process (i.e., screening). None of these methods offers a "silver bullet" solution, so it is best to use them in combination rather than in isolation.
- Recommendations and reference checks are most useful when they are used consistently for all applicants and when the information gathered is relevant for the position in question.
- Personal-history data, collected through application forms or biographical information blanks, are most useful when they are based on a rational approach—questions are developed based on a job analysis and hypotheses about relationships between the constructs underlying items and the job-performance construct.
- Honesty or integrity tests are either overt or personality oriented. Given challenges and unresolved issues with these types of tests, consider using alternative modes of administration to the traditional paper-and-pencil modality, and include situational-judgment and conditional-reasoning tests.
- Evaluations of training and experience qualifications are most useful when they are directly relevant to specific job-related areas.
- For drug screening to be most effective and less liable to legal challenges, it should be presented within a context of safety, and health and as part of a comprehensive policy regarding drug use.
- Polygraph testing is likely to lead to errors, and administrators should be aware that the physiological indicators can be altered by conscious efforts on the part of applicants.
- Employment interviews are used almost universally. Be aware that factors related to social/interpersonal issues, cognitive biases, and individual differences of both interviewers and interviewees, interview structure, and media (i.e., face to face, videotaped) may affect the validity of the employment interview.

Discussion Questions

1. How can the usefulness of recommendations and reference checks be improved?
2. As CEO of a large retailer, you are considering using drug testing to screen new hires. What elements should you include in developing a policy on this issue?
3. What instructions would you give to applicants who are about to complete a biodata instrument so as to minimize response distortion?
4. What is the difference between personality-based and overt honesty tests? Which constructs are measured by each of these types of measures?
5. Are you in favor of or against the use of polygraph testing for screening applicants for security screening positions at airports? Why?
6. In an employment interview, the interviewer asks you a question that you believe is an invasion of privacy. What do you do?
7. Employers today generally assign greater weight to experience than to academic qualifications. Why do you think this is so? Should it be so?
8. Discuss some of the advantages of using computer-based screening (CBS). Given these advantages, why isn't CBS more popular?
9. Your boss asks you to develop a training program for employment interviewers. How will you proceed? What will be the elements of your program, and how will you tell if it is working?
10. Discuss the advantages of using a structured, as opposed to an unstructured, interview. Given these advantages, why do you think HR managers reluctant to conduct structured interviews?
11. Provide examples of constructs and specific jobs for which the use of virtual-reality technology would be an effective alternative compared to more traditional screening methods.

13

Selection Methods: Part II

At a Glance

Managerial selection is a topic that deserves separate treatment because of the unique problems associated with describing the components of managerial effectiveness and developing behaviorally based predictor measures to forecast managerial effectiveness accurately. A wide assortment of data-collection techniques is currently available—cognitive ability tests, objective personality inventories, leadership ability and motivation tests, projective devices, personal history data, and peer ratings—each demonstrating varying degrees of predictive success in particular situations. These are very flexible techniques that can be used to predict job success for a variety of occupations and organizational levels; this chapter addresses each of these techniques, emphasizing their use in the context of managerial selection, but also recognizing that they can be used for some nonmanagerial positions as well.

It seems that, at present, emphasis has shifted to the development of work samples of actual managerial behavior, such as the in-basket, the leaderless group discussion, the business game, and situational judgment tests. Work samples have been well accepted because of their face and content validity, flexibility, and demonstrated ability to forecast success over a variety of managerial levels and in different organizational settings.

Both work samples and paper-and-pencil or Web-administered tests can be integrated into one method—the assessment center (AC). The AC is a behaviorally based selection procedure that incorporates multiple assessments and multiple ratings by trained line managers of various behavioral dimensions that represent the job in question. The method is not free of problems, but it has proved reliable and valid. These qualities probably account for its growing popularity as a managerial selection technique.

HR specialists engaged in managerial selection face special challenges associated with the choice of predictors, criterion measurements, and the many practical difficulties encountered in conducting rigorous research in this area. Results from several studies suggest that *different* knowledge, skills, and abilities are necessary for success at the various levels within management (Fondas, 1992). Therefore, just as success in an entry-level position may reveal little of a predictive nature regarding success as a first-line supervisor (because the job requirements of the two positions are so radically different), success as a first-line supervisor may reveal little about success as a third- or fourth-level manager. In addition, because the organizational pyramid narrows considerably as we go up the managerial ladder, the *sample sizes* required for rigorous research are virtually impossible to obtain at higher managerial levels. Finally, applicant *preselection* poses problems with severe restriction of range. That is, the full range of abilities frequently is not represented because, by the time applicants are considered for managerial positions, they already have been highly screened and, therefore, comprise a rather homogeneous group.

In view of these difficulties, it is appropriate to examine managerial selection in some detail. Hence, we shall first consider the criterion problem for managers; then, we shall examine various instruments of prediction, including cognitive ability tests, personality inventories, leadership-ability tests, projective techniques, motivation to manage, personal history data, and peer and individual assessment; third, we shall consider work samples and the AC in more detail; and finally, we shall discuss the relative merits of combining various instruments of prediction within a selection system. As noted above, although the emphasis of this chapter is managerial selection, many of the instruments of prediction described (most notably cognitive ability tests and personality inventories) are also useful for selecting employees at lower organizational levels. Thus, when appropriate, our discussion also includes a description of the use of these instruments for positions other than managerial positions.

CRITERIA OF MANAGERIAL SUCCESS

Both objective and subjective indicators frequently are used to measure managerial effectiveness. Conceptually, effective management can be defined in terms of organizational outcomes. In particular, Campbell, Dunnette, Lawler, and Weick (1970) view the effective manager as an *optimizer* who uses both internal and external resources (human, material, and financial) in order to sustain, over the long term, the unit for which the manager bears some degree of responsibility. To be a successful optimizer, a manager needs to possess implicit traits, such as business acumen, customer orientation, results orientation, strategic thinking, innovation and risk taking, integrity, and interpersonal maturity (Rucci, 2002).

The primary emphasis in this definition is on managerial *actions or behaviors* judged relevant and important for optimizing resources. This judgment can be rendered only on rational grounds; therefore, informed, expert opinion is needed to specify the full range of managerial behaviors relevant to the conceptual criterion. The process begins with a careful specification of the total domain of the manager's job responsibilities, along with statements of critical behaviors believed necessary for the best use of available resources. The criterion measure itself must encompass a series of observations of the manager's actual job behavior by individuals capable of judging the manager's effectiveness in accomplishing all the things judged necessary, sufficient, and important for doing his or her job (Campbell et al., 1970). The overall aim is to determine psychologically meaningful dimensions of effective executive performance. It is only by knowing these that we can achieve a fuller understanding of the complex web of interrelationships existing between various types of job behaviors and organizational performance or outcome measures (e.g., promotion rates, productivity indexes).

Many managerial prediction studies have used objective, global, or administrative criteria (e.g., Hurley & Sonnenfeld, 1998; Ritchie & Moses, 1983). For example, Hurley and Sonnenfeld (1998) used the criterion "career attainment" operationalized as whether to a manager had been selected for a top management position or whether he or she had remained in a middle-level management position. Because of the widespread use of such global criterion measures, let us pause to examine them critically. First, the good news. Global measures such as supervisory rankings of total managerial effectiveness, salary, and organizational level (statistically corrected for age or length of time in the organization) have several advantages. In the case of ranking, because each supervisor usually ranks no more than about 10 subordinate managers, test–retest and interrater reliabilities tend to be high. In addition, such rankings probably encompass a broad sampling of behaviors over time, and the manager himself or herself probably is being judged rather than organizational factors beyond his or her control. Finally, the manager is compared directly to his or her peers; this standard of comparison is appropriate, because all probably are responsible for optimizing similar amounts of resources.

On the other hand, overall measures or ratings of success include multiple factors (Dunnette, 1963a; Hanser, Arabian, & Wise, 1985). Hence, such measures often serve to obscure more than they reveal about the behavioral bases for managerial success. We cannot know with certainty what portion of a global rating or administrative criterion (such as level changes or salary) is based on actual job behaviors and what portion is due to other factors such as luck, education, "having a guardian angel at the top," political savvy, and so forth. Such measures suffer from both deficiency and contamination—that is, they measure only a small portion of the variance due to individual managerial behavior, and variations in these measures depend on many job-irrelevant factors that are not under the direct control of the manager.

Such global measures may also be contaminated by biases against members of certain groups (e.g., women). For example, there is a large body of literature showing that, due to the operation of gender-based stereotypes, women are often perceived as not "having what it takes" to become top managers (Lyness & Heilman, 2006). Specifically, women are usually expected to behave in a more indirect and unassertive manner as compared to men, which is detrimental to women because directness and assertiveness are traits that people associate with successful managers (Aguinis & Adams, 1998). The incongruence between stereotypes of women's behavior and perceptions of traits of successful managers may explain why women occupy fewer than 5 percent of the most coveted top-management positions in large, publicly traded corporations.

In short, global or administrative criteria tell us where a manager *is* on the "success" continuum, but almost nothing about *how he or she got there.* Because behaviors relevant to managerial success change over time (Korman, 1968), as well as by purpose or function in relationship to the survival of the whole organization (Carroll & Gillen, 1987), the need is great to develop psychologically meaningful dimensions of managerial effectiveness in order to discover the linkages between managerial behavior patterns and managerial success.

What is required, of course, is a behaviorally based performance measure that will permit a systematic recording of observations across the entire domain of desired managerial job behaviors (Campbell et al., 1970). Yet, in practice, these requirements are honored more in the breach than in the observance. Potential sources of error and contamination are rampant (Tsui & Ohlott, 1988). These include inadequate sampling of the job behavior domain, lack of knowledge or lack of cooperation by the raters, differing expectations and perceptions of raters (peers, subordinates, and superiors), changes in the job or job environment, and changes in the manager's behavior (cf. Chapter 5). Fortunately, we now have available the scale-development methods and training methodology to eliminate many of these sources of error; but the translation of such knowledge into everyday organizational practice is a slow, painstaking process.

In summarizing the managerial criterion problem, we hasten to point out that global estimates of managerial success certainly have proven useful in many validation studies (Meyer, 1987). However, they contribute little to our understanding of the wide varieties of job behaviors indicative of managerial effectiveness. While we are not advocating the abandonment of global criteria, employers need to consider supplementing them with systematic observations and recordings of behavior, so that a richer, fuller understanding of the multiple paths to managerial success might emerge. It is also important to note that, from the individual manager's perspective, the variables that lead to objective career success (e.g., pay, number of promotions) often are quite different from those that lead to subjective career success (job and career satisfaction). While ambition and quality and quantity of education predict objective-career success, accomplishments and organization success predict subjective-career success (Judge, Cable, Boudreau, & Bretz, 1995).

The Importance of Context

Management-selection decisions take place in the context of both organizational conditions (e.g., culture, technology, financial health) and environmental conditions (e.g., internal and external labor markets, competition, legal requirements). These factors may explain, in part, why predictors of initial performance (e.g., resource problem-solving skills) are not necessarily as good for predicting subsequent performance as other predictors (e.g., people-oriented skills) (Russell, 2001). Such contextual factors also explain differences in HR practices across organizations (Schuler & Jackson, 1989), and, especially, with respect to the selection of general managers (Guthrie & Olian, 1991). Thus, under unstable industry conditions, knowledge and skills acquired over time in a single organization may be viewed as less relevant than diverse experience outside the organization. Conversely, a cost-leadership strategic orientation is associated with a tendency to recruit insiders who know the business and the organization. For example, consider an organization particularly interested in organizational responsibility, defined as "context-specific organizational actions and policies that take into account stakeholders' expectations and the triple bottom line of economic, social, and environmental performance" (Aguinis, in press). For this organization, criteria of success involve economic-performance indicators such as the maximization of short-term and long-term profit, social-performance indicators such as respecting social customs and cultural heritage, and environmental-performance indicators such as the consumption of fewer natural resources. The criteria for managerial success in an organization that emphasizes the triple bottom line are obviously different from those in an organization that emphasizes only one of these three organizational performance dimensions.

The lesson? A model of executive selection and performance must consider the person as well as situational characteristics (Russell, 2001). There needs to be a fit among the kinds of attributes decision makers pay attention to in selection, the business strategy of the organization, and the environmental conditions in which it operates. Keep this in mind as you read about the many instruments of prediction described in the next section.

INSTRUMENTS OF PREDICTION

Cognitive Ability Tests

At the outset, it is important to distinguish once again between *tests* (which do have correct and incorrect answers) and *inventories* (which do not). In the case of tests, the magnitude of the total score can be interpreted to indicate greater or lesser amounts of ability. In this category, we consider, for example, measures of general intelligence; verbal, nonverbal, numerical, and spatial relations ability; perceptual speed and accuracy; inductive reasoning; and mechanical knowledge and/or comprehension. Rather than review the voluminous studies available, we will summarize the findings of relevant reviews and report only the most relevant studies.

After reviewing hundreds of studies conducted between 1919 and 1972, Ghiselli (1966, 1973) reported that managerial success has been forecast most accurately by tests of general intellectual ability and general perceptual ability. (The correlations range between .25 and .30.) However, when these correlations were corrected statistically for criterion unreliability and range restriction, the validity of tests of general intellectual ability increased to .53 and those for general perceptual ability increased to .43 (Hunter & Hunter, 1984).

The fact is that general cognitive ability is a powerful predictor of job performance (Ree & Carretta, 2002; Sackett, Borneman, & Connelly, 2008; Schmidt, 2002). It has a strong effect on job knowledge, and it contributes to individuals being given the *opportunity* to acquire supervisory experience (Borman, Hanson, Oppler, Pulakos, & White, 1993). General cognitive ability is also a good predictor for jobs with primarily inconsistent tasks (Farrell & McDaniel, 2001) and unforeseen changes (LePine, 2003)—often the case with managerial jobs. In general, most factor-structure studies show that the majority of variance in cognitive ability tests can be attributed to a general factor (Carretta & Ree, 2000). In sum, there is substantial agreement among researchers regarding the validity of cognitive ability tests. For example, results of a survey of 703 members of the Society for Industrial and Organizational Psychology showed that 85 percent of respondents agreed with the statement that "general cognitive ability is measured reasonably well by standardized tests" (Murphy, Cronin, & Tam, 2003). Also, results of a survey including 255 human resources professionals indicated that cognitive ability tests were seen as one of the three most valid types of assessments (Furnham, 2008).

Grimsley and Jarrett (1973, 1975) used a matched-group, concurrent-validity design to determine the extent to which cognitive ability test scores and self-description inventory scores obtained during preemployment assessment distinguished top from middle managers. A matched-group design was used in order to control two moderator variables (age and education), which were presumed to be related both to test performance and to managerial achievement. Hence, each of 50 top managers was paired with one of 50 middle managers, matched by age and field of undergraduate college education. Classification as a top or middle manager (the success criterion) was based on the level of managerial responsibility attained in any company by which the subject had been employed prior to assessment. This design also has another advantage: Contrary to the usual concurrent validity study, these data were gathered not under *research* conditions, but rather under *employment* conditions and from motivated job applicants.

Of the 10 mental-ability measures used (those comprising the Employee Aptitude Survey), eight significantly distinguished the top from the middle manager group: verbal comprehension ($r = .18$), numerical ability ($r = .42$), visual speed and accuracy ($r = .41$), space visualization ($r = .31$), numerical reasoning ($r = .41$), verbal reasoning ($r = .48$), word fluency ($r = .37$), and symbolic reasoning ($r = .31$). In fact, a battery composed of just the verbal reasoning and numerical ability tests yielded a multiple R (statistically corrected for shrinkage) of .52. In comparison to male college students, for example, top and middle managers scored in the 98th and 95th percentiles, respectively, on verbal comprehension and in the 85th and 59th percentiles, respectively, on numerical ability.

In sum, these results support Ghiselli's (1963, 1973) earlier conclusion that differences in intellectual competence are related to the degree of managerial success at high levels of management. Grimsley and Jarrett (1973, 1975) also concluded that differences in test scores between top and middle managers were due to fundamental differences in cognitive ability and personality rather than to the influence of on-the-job experience.

SOME CONTROVERSIAL ISSUES IN THE USE OF COGNITIVE ABILITY TESTS Tests of general mental ability (usually referred to as g) are not without criticism. Although g seems to be the best single predictor of job performance (Murphy, 2002), it is also most likely to lead to adverse impact (e.g., differential selection rates for various ethnic-based groups, cf. Chapter 8). The overall standardized difference (d) between whites and African Americans is about 1.0, and d between whites and Hispanics is about .72, but these values depend on contextual factors such as job complexity and the use of applicant versus incumbent samples (Roth, Bevier, Bobko, Switzer, & Tyler, 2001). There are numerous reasons that may explain such between-group differences. Wiesen (2001) conducted an extensive literature review and identified 105 possible reasons, including physiological factors (e.g., prenatal and postnatal influences such as differential exposure to pollutants and iron deficiency), economic and socioeconomic factors (e.g., differences in health care, criminal justice, education, finances, employment, and housing), psychological factors (e.g., the impact of stereotypes), societal factors (e.g., differences in time spent watching TV), cultural factors (e.g., emphasis of some groups on oral tradition), and test construction and validation factors (e.g., cultural bias).

Regardless of the specific magnitude of d and the relative merits of the various explanations for the existence of differences across groups, the presence of adverse impact has led to a polarization between those individuals who endorse the unique status or paramount importance of g as a predictor of performance and those who do not (Murphy et al., 2003). The position that g should be given a primary role in the selection process has policy implications that may be unpalatable to many people (Schmidt, 2002) because the unique or primary reliance on g could degenerate into a "high-tech and more lavish version of the Indian reservation for the substantial minority of the nation's population, while the rest of America tries to go about its business" (Herrnstein & Murray, 1994, p. 526). Such societal consequences can be seen at a closer and more personal level as well: LePine and Van Dyne (2001) hypothesized that low performers perceived as possessing less general cognitive ability are expected to receive different responses from coworkers and different levels of help. Thus, perceptions of a coworker as having low cognitive ability can become a reinforcer for low performance.

Another criticism is that g represents a limited conceptualization of intelligence because it does not include tacit knowledge (i.e., knowledge gained from everyday experience that has an implicit and unarticulated quality, often referred to as "learning by doing" or "professional intuition") and practical intelligence (i.e., ability to find an optimal fit between oneself and the demands of the environment, often referred to as being "street smart" or having "common sense") (Sternberg, 1997; Sternberg & Hedlund, 2002). Related to this point is the finding that cognitive ability tests are better at predicting maximum as compared to typical performance (Marcus, Goffin, Johnston, & Rothstein, 2007). Moreover, scores on g-loaded tests can improve after retaking the same test several times, as was found in a sample of 4,726 candidates for law-enforcement positions (Hausknecht, Trevor, & Farr, 2002). In other words, the factor underlying retest scores is less saturated with g and more associated with memory than the latent factor underlying initial test scores (Lievens, Reeve, & Heggestad, 2007), and a meta-analysis of 107 samples and 134,436 test takers revealed that the effects are larger when identical forms of the test are used and individuals receive coaching between test administrations (Hausknecht, Halpert, Di Patio, & Moriarty Gerrard, 2007). The inherently imperfect nature of cognitive ability tests has led to the development of test-score banding, which was discussed in detail in Chapter 8 (see Aguinis, 2004c). Finally, others have argued that g should be viewed as a starting point rather than an ending point, meaning that an overemphasis or sole reliance on g in selecting managers and employees is a basis for a flawed selection model (Goldstein, Zedeck, & Goldstein, 2002).

Because of the above criticisms of g, it has been suggested (Outtz, 2002) that tests of general mental ability be combined with other instruments, such as structured interviews, biodata (discussed in Chapter 12) and objective personality inventories, which are described next.

Objective Personality Inventories

Until recently, reviews of results obtained with personality and interest measures in forecasting employee and managerial effectiveness have been mixed at best. However, also until a few years ago, no well-accepted taxonomy existed for classifying personality traits. Today researchers generally agree that there are five robust factors of personality (the "Big Five"), which can serve as a meaningful taxonomy for classifying personality attributes (Barrick, Mount, & Judge, 2001):

- *Extroversion*—being sociable, gregarious, assertive, talkative, and active (the opposite end of extroversion is labeled *introversion*)
- *Neuroticism*—being anxious, depressed, angry, embarrassed, emotional, worried, and insecure (the opposite pole of neuroticism is labeled *emotional stability*)
- *Agreeableness*—being curious, flexible, trusting, good-natured, cooperative, forgiving, softhearted, and tolerant
- *Conscientiousness*—being dependable (i.e., being careful, thorough, responsible, organized, and planful), as well as hardworking, achievement oriented, and persevering
- *Openness to experience*—being imaginative, cultured, curious, original, broad-minded, intelligent, and artistically sensitive

Such a taxonomy makes it possible to determine if there exist consistent, meaningful relationships between particular personality constructs and job performance measures for different occupations. The widespread use of the five-factor model (FFM) of personality is evident, given that Barrick and Mount (2003) reported that at least *16 meta-analytic reviews* have been published using this framework since 1990. There is no other research area in applied psychology or

HR management in which such a large number of meta-analytic reviews have been published in such a short period of time.

Results averaged across meta-analyses revealed the following average corrected correlations for each of the five dimensions (Barrick & Mount, 2003): extroversion (.12), emotional stability (.12), agreeableness (.07), conscientiousness (.22), and openness to experience (.05). Therefore, conscientiousness is the best predictor of job performance across types of jobs. In addition, personality inventories seem to predict performance above and beyond other frequently used predictors such as general cognitive ability. For example, agreeableness and conscientiousness predicted peer ratings of team-member performance above and beyond job-specific skills and general cognitive ability in a sample of over 300 full-time HR representatives at local stores of a wholesale department store organization (Neuman & Wright, 1999).

Barrick et al. (2001) summarized reviews of three meta-analyses that examined the specific relationship between the FFM of personality and managerial performance. The combination of these three meta-analyses included a total of 67 studies and 12,602 individuals. Average corrected correlations across these three meta-analyses were the following: extroversion (.21), emotional stability (.09), agreeableness (.10), conscientiousness (.25), and openness to experience (.10). Thus, conscientiousness and extroversion seem to be the best two predictors of performance for managers.

Judge, Bono, Ilies, and Gerhardt (2002) conducted a related meta-analysis that examined the relationship between the FFM of personality and leadership, a key variable for managerial success. Results indicated the following corrected correlations: extroversion (.31), emotional stability (.24), agreeableness (.08), conscientiousness (.28), and openness to experience (.24). The combination of these meta-analytic results firmly supports the use of personality scales in managerial selection.

Given the encouraging results regarding the predictability of performance using personality traits, there is now a need to understand *why* certain components of the FFM of personality are good predictors of managerial and nonmanagerial performance and its various facets (Murphy & Dzieweczynski, 2005). Some research is starting to shed light on this issue. Barrick, Stewart, and Piotrowski (2002) studied a sample of 164 telemarketing and sales representatives and found that status striving (exerting effort to perform at a higher level than others) and accomplishment striving (exerting effort to complete work assignments) serve as mediators between personality (conscientiousness and extroversion) and job performance. In other words, conscientiousness leads to a motivation to strive for accomplishments, which, in turn, leads to higher levels of performance. Extroversion leads to a motivation for status striving, which, in turn, leads to higher levels of performance. A related meta-analysis found that emotional stability (average validity = .31) and conscientiousness (average validity = .24) were the personality traits most highly correlated with performance motivation (Judge & Ilies, 2002). These results suggest that further research is needed to better understand the relationships among personality, motivation, and performance.

A different approach regarding the understanding of the personality-performance relationship consists of examining contextual variables likely to strengthen or weaken this relationship (Tett & Burnett, 2003). The central concept in this model is **trait activation**, which implies that personality traits are expressed in response to specific situational cues. Tett and Burnett (2003) proposed a model including five types of work situations hypothesized to affect the expression of behaviors consistent with one's personality traits: job demands (i.e., situations allowing for the opportunity to act in a positively valued way), distractors (i.e., situations allowing for the opportunity to act in a way that interferes with performance), constraints (i.e., situations that negate the impact of a trait by restricting cues for its expression), releasers (i.e., situations counteracting constraints), and facilitators (i.e., situations that make trait-relevant information more salient). Tett and Burnett (2003) offered several illustrations for each of the five types of situations. As an example of a distractor, a sociable manager might be distracted from his job-related duties in an organization where most employees are extroverted. In this example, the contextual cue of employees who are extroverted activates the manager's sociability trait, which, in this case, interferes with performance. Future research on each of these situational factors is likely to improve our understanding of when, and to what extent, personality can affect overall performance as well as specific performance dimensions.

Yet another theoretical perspective that has potential to explain why and under which conditions personality predicts performance is socioanalytic theory (Hogan & Holland, 2003). Socioanalytic theory suggests two broad individual motive patterns that translate into behaviors: (1) a "getting along" orientation that underlies such constructs as expressive role, providing consideration, and contextual performance and (2) a "getting ahead" orientation that underlies such constructs as instrumental role, initiating structure, and task performance. Hogan and Holland (2003) defined getting ahead as "behavior that produces results and advances an individual within the group and the group within its competition" (p. 103) and getting along as "behavior that gains the approval of others, enhances cooperation, and serves to build and maintain relationships" (p. 103). Then they conducted a meta-analysis of 43 studies that used the Hogan Personality Inventory (HPI), which is based on the FFM. Prior to analyzing the data, however, subject matter experts (SMEs) with extensive experience in validation research and use of the HPI classified the criteria used in each primary-level study as belonging in the getting-ahead or getting-along category. Subsequently, SMEs were asked to identify the personality trait most closely associated with each performance criterion. Thus, in contrast to previous meta-analyses of the relationship between personality and performance, this study used socioanalytic theory to align specific personality traits with specific job-performance criteria. Then specific predictions were made based on the correspondence between predictors and criteria.

When only criteria deemed directly relevant were used, correlations for each of the Big Five traits were the following: extroversion (.35), emotional stability (.43), agreeableness (.34), conscientiousness (.36), and openness to experience (.34). These correlations, based on congruent predictor–criterion combinations based on socioanalytic theory, are substantially larger than correlations obtained in previous meta-analytic reviews. Thus, this meta-analysis demonstrated the potential of socioanalytic theory to explain why certain personality traits are related to certain types of criteria. This finding reinforces the idea that choosing work-related personality measures on the basis of thorough job and organizational analyses is a fundamental element in the selection process.

Finally, personality testing is not without controversies. Specifically, Morgeson et al. (2007a, 2007b) concluded that response distortion (i.e., faking) on self-report personality tests is virtually impossible to avoid. More importantly, they concluded that a perhaps even more critical issue is that validity coefficients in terms of performance prediction are not very impressive and have not changed much over time, particularly if one examines observed (i.e., uncorrected for statistical artifact) coefficients. Thus, they issued a call for finding alternatives to self-report personality measures. Ones, Dilchert, Viswesvaran, and Judge (2007) and Tett and Christiansen (2007) provided counterarguments in defense of personality testing. These include that personality testing is particularly useful when validation is based on confirmatory research using job analysis and that, taking into account the bidirectionality of trait–performance linkages, the relationship between conscientiousness and performance generalizes across settings and types of jobs. Moreover, personality adds incremental validity to the prediction of job performance above and beyond cognitive ability tests.

To try to solve the question of the extent to which personality testing is useful in predicting performance and managerial performance in particular, theory-driven research is needed on how to improve the validity of personality inventories (Mayer, 2005; Schneider, 2007; Tett & Christiansen, 2007). One promising avenue is to move beyond the Big Five model and focus on compound traits that are broader than the Big Five traits (Viswesvaran, Deller, & Ones, 2007) and also on narrower traits (e.g., components of the Big Five traits) (Dudley, Orvis, Lebiecki, & Cortina, 2006). For example, consider the case of the construct **core self-evaluations** (Judge & Hurst, 2008). Core self-evaluation is a broad, higher-order latent construct indicated by *self-esteem* (i.e., the overall value one places on oneself as a person), *generalized self-efficacy* (i.e., one's evaluation regarding how well one can perform across a variety of situations), *neuroticism* (i.e., one of the Big Five traits as described earlier), and *locus of control* (i.e., one's beliefs about the causes of events in one's life, and where locus is internal when one believes that events are mainly caused by oneself as opposed to external causes) (Johnson, Rosen, & Levy, 2008). Across the four traits that indicate core self-evaluations, the average correlation with performance is .23 (Judge & Bono, 2001). This high correlation, which is comparable to the mean meta-analytically derived corrected correlation between conscientiousness and performance, is presumably due to the effect of core self-evaluations on motivation: Those higher on core self-evaluations have more positive self-views and are more likely to undertake difficult tasks (Bono & Judge, 2003).

RESPONSE DISTORTION IN PERSONALITY INVENTORIES In Chapter 12, we described the evidence regarding the extent to which job applicants can intentionally distort their scores on honesty tests and how to minimize such distortion. Similar concerns exist regarding personality inventories (Komar, Brown, Komar, & Robie, 2008). Specifically, two questions faced by HR specialists willing to use personality inventories are whether intentional response distortion (i.e., faking) affects the validity of such instruments and whether faking affects the quality of decision making (Mueller-Hanson, Heggestad, & Thornton, 2003). Although the preponderance of the evidence shows that criterion-related validity coefficients do not seem to be affected substantially by faking (Barrick & Mount, 1996; Hogan, Barrett, & Hogan, 2007), it is still possible that faking can change the rank order of individuals in the upper portion of the predictor score distribution, and this would obviously affect decision making (Komar et al., 2008; Mueller-Hanson et al. 2003; Rosse, Stecher, Miller, & Levin, 1998). Unless selection ratios are large, decision making is likely to be adversely affected, and organizations are likely to realize lower levels of performance than expected, possibly also resulting in inflated utility estimates.

Fortunately, there are specific strategies that can be used to mitigate distortion. Those strategies described in Chapter 12 to minimize faking in other types of instruments (e.g., biodata, interviews, honesty tests) also apply to the administration of personality inventories. In addition, there are other strategies available specifically to mitigate distortion in personality inventories but could also be used for other types of tests. These involve using forced-choice personality test items and warning against faking (Converse et al, 2008). The use of forced-choice items improved validity in both warning and no-warning conditions. However, the use of warnings against faking did not produce an improvement in the resulting validity coefficient. Note that each of these methods may produce negative reactions on the part of test takers.

There are three additional methods to address response distortion developed specifically for use for personality tests (Hough, 1998; Kuncel & Borneman, 2007). Two are based on the Unlikely Virtues (UV) scale of Tellegen's (in press) Multidimensional Personality Questionnaire to detect intentional distortion. The UV scale consists of nine items using "Yes," "Not sure," and "No" response options. An example of a question that is similar to a question in the UV scale is "Have you ever been grouchy with someone?" (Hough, 1998).

First, one can correct an applicant's score based on that person's score on the UV scale. Specifically, applicants whose scores are inordinately high are "penalized" by a reduction in their scores based on the amount of overly virtuous responding on the UV scale. For example, if an applicant's score is three or more standard deviation units (SDs) above the incumbent UV scale mean, Hough (1998) recommends that his or her score on the personality scale be reduced by 2 SDs (based on incumbent scores). Note that this strategy is different from statistically removing variance due to a social desirability scale because, when a residual score is created on a personality measure using that strategy, substantive variance may also be removed (Ellingson, Sackett, & Hough, 1999).

Second, the UV scale can be used as a selection instrument in itself: Applicants scoring above a specific cut score can be automatically disqualified. Hough (1998) recommended removing applicants whose scores fall within the top 5 percent of the distribution of UV scores.

Hough (1998) illustrated the benefits of the two UV scale–based strategies using samples of job applicants in three different contexts: a telecommunications company, a metropolitan police department, and a state law enforcement agency. The conclusion was that both strategies reduced the effects of intentional distortion without having a detrimental effect on criterion-related validity. However, some caveats are in order (Hough, 1998). First, these strategies can be implemented only in large organizations. Second, these strategies should not be used if UV scores correlate with performance scores. Third, if the personality scale in question is not correlated with the UV scale, then the strategies should not be implemented. Finally, specific contextual circumstances should be taken into account to assess whether the use of UV scale–based corrections would be appropriate in specific settings and for specific job applicants. The importance of taking these caveats into account and the vulnerability of using UV scale–based corrections were confirmed by a study by Hurtz and Alliger (2002), who found that individuals who were coached to "fake good" were able to fake a good impression and also avoid endorsing UV scale items.

The third method recently proposed for specific use in personality testing is based on idiosyncratic item response patterns (Kuncel & Borneman, 2007). This approach is based on scoring items that yield dramatically different response patterns under honest and faking conditions that are not merely an upward shift in scores. An initial study including 215 undergraduates from a large university in the Midwestern United States yielded promising results: Researchers were able to successfully classify between 20 and 37 percent of faked personality measures with only 1 percent false-positive rate in a sample comprising 56 percent honest responses.

An additional method of assessing personality has been proposed that does not rely on descriptive self-reports and consequently may be less subject to faking. We discussed this method in Chapter 12 in the context of personality-based integrity testing. James (1998) proposed the assessment of personality using a **conditional-reasoning** measurement procedure. This procedure is based on the premise that individuals with different standings on a specific personality trait are likely to develop different justification mechanisms to explain their behaviors. Thus, observation of justification mechanisms for various behavioral choices can allow for the deduction of underlying dispositional tendencies. For example, James (1998) provided the case of achievement motivation. One should be able to infer whether the motive to achieve is dominant or subordinate to the motive to avoid failure by assessing which of the following arguments seems more logical to the individual: (1) justifications for approach to achievement-oriented objectives or (2) justifications for avoidance of achievement-oriented objectives. The development of instruments to assess personality traits based on the conditional reasoning paradigm can be quite time consuming. However, initial evidence based on several studies reported by James (1998) suggests that the approach has great promise. We can be confident that research reports on the applicability and usefulness of this approach will be published in the near future, particularly regarding its vulnerability to faking vis-à-vis the more traditional self-report personality inventories (e.g., Bing, LeBreton, Davison, Migetz, & James, 2007; Frost, Chia-Huei, & James, 2007).

Fortunately, personality inventories are rarely the sole instrument used in selecting managers. So the effects of faking are somewhat mitigated. Next we turn to one such additional type of selection instrument: leadership-ability tests.

Leadership-Ability Tests

Logically, one might expect measures of "leadership ability" to be more predictive of managerial success, because such measures should be directly relevant to managerial job requirements. Scales designed to measure two major constructs underlying managerial behavior, *providing consideration* (one type of "getting along" construct) and *initiating structure* (one type of "getting ahead" construct), have been developed and used in many situations (Fleishman, 1973).

Providing consideration involves managerial acts oriented toward developing mutual trust, which reflect respect for subordinates' ideas and consideration of their feelings. High scores on providing consideration denote attitudes and opinions indicating good rapport and good two-way communication, whereas low scores indicate a more impersonal approach to interpersonal relations with group members (Fleishman & Peters, 1962).

Initiating structure reflects the extent to which an individual is likely to define and structure his or her own role and those of his or her subordinates to focus on goal attainment. High scores on initiating structure denote attitudes and opinions indicating highly active direction of group activities, group planning, communication of information, scheduling, willingness to try out new ideas, and so forth.

Instruments designed to measure initiating structure and providing consideration (the Leadership Opinion Questionnaire, the Leader Behavior Description Questionnaire, and the Supervisory Behavior Description Questionnaire) have been in use for many years. However, evidence of their predictive validity has been mixed, so Judge, Piccolo, and Ilies (2004) conducted a meta-analysis of the available literature. These authors were able to synthesize 163 correlations linking providing consideration with leadership outcomes and 159 correlations linking initiating structure with leadership outcomes. Each of the leadership dimensions was related to six different leadership criteria (i.e., follower job satisfaction, follower satisfaction with the leader, follower motivation, leader job performance, group/organization performance, and leader effectiveness). Overall, the corrected correlation between providing consideration and all criteria combined was .48, whereas the overall corrected correlation between initiating structure and all criteria was .29. In addition, results showed that providing consideration was more strongly related to follower job satisfaction, follower motivation, and leader effectiveness, whereas initiating structure was slightly more strongly related to leader job performance and group/organization performance. In spite of these encouraging overall results, substantial variability was found for the correlations even after corrections for sampling error and measurement error were applied. In short, the ability of these two dimensions to predict leadership success varies across studies in noticeable ways.

Our inability to predict the effects of hierarchical leader behaviors consistently might be due to subordinate, task, or organizational characteristics that serve as "neutralizers of" or "substitutes for" hierarchical leader behaviors (Kerr & Jermier, 1978). *Neutralizers* are variables in a leader's environment that effectively eliminate the impact of a leader's behavior on subordinate outcome variables, but do not replace the impact of such behavior with an effect of their own. *Substitutes* are special types of neutralizers that reduce a leader's ability to influence subordinates' attitudes and performance and that effectively replace the impact of a leader's behavior with one of their own. Potential neutralizers or substitutes include subordinate characteristics (e.g., their ability, experience, training, or knowledge), task characteristics (e.g., intrinsically satisfying tasks; routine, invariant tasks; task feedback), and organizational characteristics (e.g., rewards outside the leader's control, rule inflexibility, work group cohesiveness). Reliable, construct-valid measures of such "Substitutes for Leadership Scales" are now available (Podsakoff & MacKenzie, 1994). If it were possible to identify factors that may moderate the effect of leader behaviors on subordinates' attitudes, behaviors, and perceptions, this would explain why some leader behaviors are effective in some situations, but not in others. It is the task of future research to determine whether these sorts of moderating effects really do exist.

Our ability to predict successful managerial behaviors will likely improve if we measure more specific predictors and more specific criteria rather than general abilities as predictors and overall performance as a criterion. For example, a study including 347 managers and supervisors from six different organizational contexts, including a telecommunications company, a university, a printing company, and a hospital, found that conflict-resolution skills, as measured using an interactive video-assessment instrument, predicted ratings of on-the-job performance in managing conflict (Olson-Buchanan et al., 1998). *Specific* skills (e.g., conflict resolution) predicted *specific* criteria that were hypothesized to be directly linked to the predictor (e.g., ratings of on-the-job conflict resolution performance). This is point-to-point correspondence.

Projective Techniques

Let us first define our terms. According to Brown (1983):

> Projection refers to the process by which individuals' personality structure influences the ways in which they perceive, organize, and interpret their environment and experiences. When tasks or situations are highly structured their meaning usually is clear, as is the appropriate way to respond to the situation . . . projection can best be seen and measured when an individual encounters new and/or ambiguous stimuli, tasks, or situations. The implication for test construction is obvious: To study personality, one should present an individual with new and/or ambiguous stimuli and observe how he reacts and structures the situation. From his responses we can then make inferences concerning his personality structure. (p. 419)

Kelly (1958) has expressed the issue concisely: An objective test is a test where the test taker tries to guess what the examiner is thinking, and a projective test is a test where the examiner tries to guess what the test taker is thinking!

In a critical review of the application of projective techniques in personnel psychology since 1940 (e.g., the Rorschach, the Thematic Apperception Test or TAT), Kinslinger (1966) concluded that the need exists "for thorough job specifications in terms of personality traits and extensive use of cross-validation studies before any practical use can be made of projective techniques in personnel psychology" (p. 134).

A later review reached similar conclusions. Across five studies, the average validity for projectives was .18 (Reilly & Chao, 1982). It would be a mistake to conclude from this, however, that projectives should *never* be used, especially when they are scored in terms of dimensions relevant to "motivation to manage."

Motivation to Manage

One projective instrument that has shown potential for forecasting managerial success is the Miner Sentence Completion Scale (MSCS), a measure of motivation to manage.

The MSCS consists of 40 items, 35 of which are scored. The items form seven subscales (authority figures, competitive games, competitive situations, assertive role, imposing wishes, standing out from the group, and routine administrative functions). Definitions of these subscales are shown in Table 13-1. The central hypothesis is that there is a positive relationship between positive affect toward these areas and managerial success. Median MSCS subscale intercorrelations range from .11 to .15, and reliabilities in the .90s have been obtained repeatedly with experienced scorers (Miner, 1978a).

Validity coefficients for the MSCS have ranged as high as .69, and significant results have been reported in over 25 different studies (Miner, 1978a, 1978b; Miner & Smith, 1982). By any criterion used—promotion rates, grade level, choice of managerial career—more-successful managers have tended to obtain higher scores, and managerial groups have scored higher on the MSCS than nonmanagerial groups (Miner & Crane, 1981). Longitudinal data indicate that those with higher initial MSCS scores subsequently are promoted more rapidly in bureaucratic systems and that those with the highest scores (especially on the subscales related to power, such as competing for resources, imposing wishes on others, and respecting authority) are likely to reach top-executive levels (Berman & Miner, 1985). In another study, 59 entrepreneurs completed the MSCS as they launched new business ventures. Five and a half years later, MSCS total scores predicted the performance of their firms (growth in number of employees, dollar volume of sales, and entrepreneurs' yearly income) with validities in the high .40s (Miner, Smith, & Bracker, 1994). The consistency of these results is impressive, and, because measures of intelligence are unrelated to scores on the MSCS, the MSCS can be a useful addition to a battery of management-selection measures.

TABLE 13-1 Subscales of the Miner Sentence Completion Scale and Their Interpretation

Subscale	Interpretation of Positive Responses
Authority figures	A desire to meet managerial role requirements in terms of positive relationships with superior.
Competitive games	A desire to engage in competition with peers involving games or sports and thus meet managerial role requirements in this regard.
Competitive situations	A desire to engage in competition with peers involving occupational or work-related activities and thus meet managerial role requirements in this regard.
Assertive role	A desire to behave in an active and assertive manner involving activities which in this society are often viewed as predominantly masculine, and thus to meet managerial role requirements.
Imposing wishes	A desire to tell others what to do and to use sanctions in influencing others, thus indicating a capacity to fulfill managerial role requirements in relationships with subordinates.
Standing out from group	A desire to assume a distinctive position of a unique and highly visible nature in a manner that is role-congruent for the managerial job.
Routine administrative functions	A desire to meet managerial role requirements regarding activities often associated with managerial work, which are of a day-to-day administrative nature.

Source: Miner, J. B. & Smith, N. R. (1982). Decline and stabilization of managerial motivation over a 20-year period. *Journal of Applied Psychology*, *67*, 298. Copyright 1979 by the American Psychological Association. Reprinted by permission of the author.

Further, because the causal arrow seems to point from motivation to success, companies might be advised to include "motivation to manage" in their definitions of managerial success.

A somewhat different perspective on motivation to manage comes from a longitudinal study of the development of young managers in business. A 3.5-day assessment of young Bell System employees shortly after beginning their careers with the company included (among other assessment procedures) three projectives—two sentence-completion blanks and six cards from the TAT (Grant, Katkovsky, & Bray, 1967).

To determine the relative amount of influence exerted by the projective ratings on staff judgments, the projective ratings were correlated with the assessment staff's overall prediction of each individual's management potential. The higher the correlations, the greater the influence of the projective reports on staff judgments. The ratings also were correlated with an index of salary progress shown by the candidates seven to nine years after the assessment. These results are presented separately for college and noncollege men in Table 13-2.

Although in general the correlations are modest, two points are worthy of note. First, the projective-report variables correlating highest with staff predictions also correlate highest with management progress (i.e., the salary index). Second, motivational variables (e.g., achievement motivation, willingness to accept a leadership role) are related more closely to management progress than are more adjustment-oriented variables (e.g., optimism, general adjustment). In sum, these results suggest that projective techniques may yield useful predictions when they are interpreted according to motivations relevant to management (Grant et al., 1967).

The story does not end here though. TAT responses for 237 managers who were still employed by the company were rescored 16 years later in terms of three motivational constructs: need for power, achievement, and affiliation (hereafter nPow, nAch, and nAff). In earlier work, McClelland and Burnham (1976) found that a distinctive motive pattern, termed the "Leadership Motive Pattern" (LMP)—namely, moderate-to-high nPow, low nAff, and

TABLE 13-2 Correlations of Projective Variables with Staff Judgments and Salary Progress

Projective Variable	College Graduates		Noncollege	
	Staff Prediction (N = 207)	Salary Progress (N = 81)	Staff Prediction (N = 148)	Salary Progress (N = 120)
Optimism–Pessimism	.11	.01	.13	.17
General adjustment	.19	.10	.17	.19
Self-confidence	.24	.11	.29	.21
Affiliation	.07	.06	.15	.07
Work or career orientation	.21	.16	.22	.17
Leadership role	.35	.24	.38	.19
Dependence	.30	.35	.30	.23
Subordinate role	.25	.25	.29	.23
Achievement motivation	.30	.26	.40	.30

Source: Grant, D. L., Katkovsky, W., & Bray, D. W. (1967). Contributions of projective techniques to assessment of management potential. *Journal of Applied Psychology, 51*, 226–231. Copyright 1967 by the American Psychological Association. Reprinted with permission.

high activity inhibition (a constraint on the need to express power)—was related to success in management.

The theoretical explanation for the LMP is as follows. High nPow is important because it means the person is interested in the "influence game," in having an impact on others. Lower nAff is important because it enables a manager to make difficult decisions without worrying unduly about being disliked; and high self-control is important because it means the person is likely to be concerned with maintaining organizational systems and following orderly procedures (McClelland, 1975).

When the rescored TAT responses were related to managerial job level 16 years later, the LMP clearly distinguished senior managers in nontechnical jobs from their less senior colleagues (McClelland & Boyatzis, 1982). In fact, progress in management after 8 and 16 years was highly correlated ($r = .75$), and the estimated correlation between the LMP and management progression was .33. This is impressive, considering all of the other factors (such as ability) that might account for upward progression in a bureaucracy over a 16-year period.

High nAch was associated with success at lower levels of nontechnical management jobs, in which promotion depends more on individual contributions than it does at higher levels. This is consistent with the finding among first-line supervisors that nAff was related to performance and favorable subordinate attitudes, but need for power or the LMP was not (Cornelius & Lane, 1984). At higher levels, in which promotion depends on demonstrated ability to manage others, a high nAch is not associated with success.

Whereas high nAch seems not to be related to managerial success in a bureaucracy, it is strongly related to success as an entrepreneur (Boyatzis, 1982). As for technical managers, the LMP did not predict who was more or less likely to be promoted to higher levels of management in the company, but verbal fluency clearly did. These individuals were probably promoted for their technical competencies, among which was the ability to explain what they know. When these findings are considered, along with those for the MSCS, one conclusion is that both the need for power and the willingness to exert power may be important for managerial success *only* in situations where technical expertise is not critical (Cornelius & Lane, 1984).

Two criticisms of the TAT are that it is subject to social desirability bias (i.e., respondents provide answers that they believe will be received favorably) (Arnold & Feldman, 1981)

In this job, the likelihood that a major portion of your duties will involve
—establishing and maintaining friendly relationships with others is   VERY HIGH (95%)
—influencing the activities or thoughts of a number of individuals is   VERY LOW (5%)
—accomplishing difficult (but feasible) goals later receiving detailed information about your personal performance is   VERY HIGH (95%)

DECISION A. With the factors and associated likelihood levels shown above in mind, indicate the attractiveness of this job to you.

−5	−4	−3	−2	−1	0	+1	+2	+3	+4	+5
Very unattractive										Very attractive

FURTHER INFORMATION ABOUT JOB #1. If you exert a great deal of effort to get this job, the likelihood that you will be successful is MEDIUM (50%)

DECISION B. With both the attractiveness and likelihood information presented above in mind, indicate the level of effort you would exert to get this job.

0		1	2	3	4	5	6	7	8	9	10
Zero effort to get it											Great effort to get it

FIGURE 13-1 Sample item from the job choice exercise. *Source:* From Stahl, M. J. and Harrell, A. M. (1981). Modeling effort decisions with behavioral decision theory: Toward an individual differences version of expectancy theory. *Organizational Behavior and Human Performance, 27,* 303–325. Copyright © 1981 with permission from Elsevier.

and that it requires content analysis of each subject's written responses by a trained scorer. The Job Choice Exercise (JCE) was developed (Harrell & Stahl, 1981; Stahl & Harrell, 1982) to overcome these problems. The JCE requires a subject to make 24 decisions about the attractiveness of hypothetical jobs that are described in terms of criteria for nPow, nAch, and nAff (see Figure 13-1).

Figure 13-1 contains one of the jobs from the JCE. The Further Information and Decision B scales are fillers. To compute a score for each motive—nPow, nAch, and nAff—the Decision A values are regressed on the three criteria. Studies conducted with a variety of samples indicate that the JCE does, in fact, measure nPow, nAch, and nAff; that test–retest and internal consistency reliabilities range from .77 to .89; that these motives do distinguish managers from nonmanagers; that there are no differences between the sexes or races on the JCE; and that the JCE is not subject to social desirability bias. The JCE is self-administered and requires 15–20 minutes to complete. On top of that, it does not correlate significantly with the MSCS (Stahl, 1983; Stahl, Grigsby, & Gulati, 1985). In view of these results, the JCE merits closer attention as a research instrument and as a practical tool for selecting managers.

Another nonprojective approach to assessing motivation to manage has been proposed by Chan and Drasgow (2001). These researchers defined **motivation to lead (MTL)** as an individual differences construct that "affects a leader's or leader-to-be's decisions to assume leadership training, roles, and responsibility and that affects his or her intensity of effort at leading and persistence as a leader" (p. 482). The scale developed to assess MTL includes three components: (1) affective-identity MTL (example item: "I am the type of person who likes to be in charge of others"), (2) noncalculative MTL (example item: "If I agree to lead a group, I would never expect any advantages or special benefits"), and (3) social-normative MTL (example item: "I agree to lead whenever I am asked or nominated by the other members").

Using the MTL in a sample of over 1,300 military recruits in Singapore demonstrated that affective-identity MTL scores ($r = .39$) and noncalculative MTL scores ($r = .20$) were reasonable predictors of multisource behavioral-leadership potential ratings. MTL scores also provided additional explained variance in the criterion (i.e., leadership potential ratings) above and beyond other predictors including general cognitive ability, military attitude, and the Big Five personality factors. These promising results provide HR specialists with an additional tool to predict leadership success.

Personal-History Data

Biographical information has been used widely in managerial selection—capitalizing on the simple fact that one of the best predictors of future behavior is past behavior. Unfortunately, the approach has been characterized more by raw empiricism than by theoretical formulation and rigorous testing of hypotheses. On the positive side, however, the items are usually nonthreatening and, therefore, are probably not as subject to distortion as are typical personality inventories (Cascio, 1975).

One review found that, across seven studies (total $N = 2,284$) where personal-history data were used to forecast success in management, the average validity was a respectable .38. When personal-history data were used to predict sales success, it was .50, and, when used to predict success in science/engineering, it was .41 (Reilly & Chao, 1982). Another study examined the relationship between college experiences and later managerial performance at AT&T (Howard, 1986). The choice of major (humanities, social science, business versus engineering) and extracurricular activities both validly forecast the interpersonal skills that are so critical to managerial behavior.

In conducting a literature review on managerial success, Campbell et al. (1970) concluded:

> What is impressive is that indicators of past successes and accomplishments can be utilized in an objective way to identify persons with differing odds of being successful over the long term in their management career. People who are already intelligent, mature, ambitious, energetic and responsible and who have a record of prior achievement when they enter an organization are in excellent positions to profit from training opportunities and from challenging organizational environments. (p. 196)

Can biodata instruments developed to predict managerial success (e.g., rate of promotional progress) in one organization be similarly valid in other organizations, including organizations in different industries? The answer is yes, but this answer also needs to be qualified by the types of procedures used in developing the instrument. There are four factors believed to influence the generalizability of biodata instruments (Carlson, Scullen, Schmidt, Rothstein, & Erwin, 1999). First, the role of theory is crucial. Specifically, there should be clear reasons why the instrument would generalize to other populations and situations. In the absence of such clear expectations, some predictive relationships may not be observed in the new setting. Second, the criterion measure used for key development should be valid and reliable. When criterion measures are not adequate, there will be little accuracy in identifying meaningful relationships with the biodata items. Third, the validity of *each item* in the inventory should be determined. Doing so reduces the sample dependence of the instrument. Sample dependence increases when items are developed using an empirical as opposed to a theory-based approach (see Chapter 12). Finally, if large samples are used to develop the instrument, results are less likely to be affected as adversely by sampling error, and the chances of generalization increase.

Peer Assessment

In the typical peer-assessment paradigm, raters are asked to predict how well a peer will do if placed in a leadership or managerial role. Such information can be enlightening, for peers typically draw on a different sample of behavioral interactions (i.e., those of an equal, non–supervisor–subordinate nature) in predicting future managerial success. Peer assessment is actually a general term for three more basic methods used by members of a well-defined group in judging each other's performance. **Peer nomination** requires each group member to designate a certain number of group members (excluding himself or herself) as being highest (lowest) on a particular dimension of performance (e.g., handling customers' problems). **Peer rating** requires each group member to rate every other group member on several performance dimensions using, for example, some type of graphic rating scale. A final method, **peer ranking**, requires each group member to rank all the others from best to worst on one or more factors.

Reviews of over 50 studies relevant to all three methods of peer assessment (Kane & Lawler, 1978, 1980; Mumford, 1983; Schmitt, Gooding, Noe, & Kirsch, 1984) found that all the methods showed adequate reliability, validity (average $r =.43$), and freedom from bias. However, the three methods appear to "fit" somewhat different assessment needs. Peer nominations are most effective in discriminating persons with extreme (high or low) levels of knowledge, skills, or abilities from the other members of their groups. For example, peer nomination for top-management responsibility correlated .32 with job advancement 5–10 years later (Shore, Shore, & Thornton, 1992). Peer rating is most effective in providing feedback, while peer ranking is probably best for discriminating throughout the entire performance range from highest to lowest on each dimension.

The reviews noted three other important issues in peer assessment:

1. *The influence of friendship*—It appears from the extensive research evidence available that effective performance probably causes friendship rather than the independent influence of friendship biasing judgments of performance. These results hold up even when peers know that their assessments will affect pay and promotion decisions.
2. *The need for cooperation in planning and design*—Peer assessments implicitly require people to consider privileged information about their peers in making their assessments. Thus, they easily can infringe on areas that either will raise havoc with the group or cause resistance to making the assessments. To minimize any such adverse consequences, it is imperative that groups be intimately involved in the planning and design of the peer-assessment method to be used.
3. *The required length of peer interaction*—It appears that the validity of peer nominations for predicting leadership performance develops very early in the life of a group and reaches a plateau after no more than three weeks for intensive groups. Useful validity develops in only a matter of days. Thus, peer nominations possibly could be used in assessment centers to identify managerial talent if the competitive atmosphere of such a context does not induce excessive bias. We hasten to add, however, that in situations where peers do not interact intensively on a daily basis (e.g., life insurance agents), peer ratings are unlikely to be effective predictors for individuals with less than six months' experience (Mayfield, 1970, 1972).

In summary, peer assessments have considerable potential as effective predictors of managerial success, and Mumford (1983) and Lewin and Zwany (1976) have provided integrative models for future research. To be sure, as Kraut (1975) noted, the use of peer ratings among managers may merely formalize a process in which managers already engage informally.

WORK SAMPLES OF MANAGERIAL PERFORMANCE

Up to this point, we have discussed tests as signs or indicators of predispositions to behave in certain ways rather than as samples of the characteristic behavior of individuals. Wernimont and Campbell (1968) have argued persuasively, however, that prediction efforts are likely to be much more fruitful if we focus on meaningful samples of behavior rather than on signs or predispositions. Because selection measures are really surrogates or substitutes for criteria, we should be trying to obtain measures that are as similar to criteria as possible. Criteria also must be measures of behavior. Hence, it makes little sense to use a behavior sample to predict an administrative criterion (promotion, salary level, etc.), since the individual frequently does not exercise a great deal of control over such organizational outcome variables. In order to understand more fully individual behavior in organizations, work-sample measures must be related to observable job-behavior measures. Only then will we understand exactly how, and to what extent, an individual has influenced his or her success. This argument is not new (cf. Campbell et al., 1970; Dunnette, 1963b; Smith & Kendall, 1963), but it deserves reemphasis.

Particularly with managers, effectiveness is likely to result from an *interaction* of individual and situational or context variables, for, as we noted earlier, the effective manager is an optimizer of all the resources available to him or her. It follows, then, that a work sample whose objective is to assess the ability to do rather than the ability to know should be a more representative measure of the real-life complexity of managerial jobs. In work samples (Flanagan, 1954b):

> Situations are selected to be typical of those in which the individual's performance is to be predicted. . . . [Each] situation is made sufficiently complex that it is very difficult for the persons tested to know which of their reactions are being scored and for what variables. There seems to be much informal evidence (face validity) that the person tested behaves spontaneously and naturally in these situations. . . . It is hoped that the naturalness of the situations results in more valid and typical responses than are obtained from other approaches. (p. 462)

These ideas have been put into theoretical form by Asher (1972), who hypothesized that the greater the degree of point-to-point correspondence between predictor elements and criterion elements, the higher the validity. By this rationale, work sample tests that are miniature replicas of specific criterion behavior should have point-to-point relationships with the criterion. This hypothesis received strong support in a meta-analytic review of the validity of work sample tests (Schmitt et al., 1984). In fact, when work samples are used as a basis for promotion, their average validity is .54 (Hunter & Hunter, 1984). A more recent meta-analysis found an average correlation (corrected for measurement error) of .33 with supervisory ratings of job performance (Roth, Bobko, & McFarland, 2005). High validity and cost-effectiveness (Cascio & Phillips, 1979), high face validity and acceptance (Steiner & Gilliland, 1996), lack of bias based on race and gender (Lance, Johnson, Douthitt, Bennett, & Harville, 2000), and, apparently, substantially reduced adverse impact (Brugnoli, Campion, & Basen, 1979; Schmidt, Greenthal, Hunter, Berner, & Seaton, 1977) make work sampling an especially attractive approach to staffing. In fact, studies conducted in the Netherlands (Anderson & Witvliet, 2008) and in Greece (Nikolaou & Judge, 2007) concluded that, similar to results of past studies conducted in the United States, France, Spain, Portugal, and Singapore, work samples are among the three most accepted selection methods among applicants (Hausknecht, Day, & Thomas, 2004). Although the development of "good" work samples is time consuming and can be quite difficult (cf. Plumlee, 1980), monetary and social payoffs from their use may well justify the effort. Note, however, that further research is needed regarding the conclusion that work samples reduce adverse impact substantially given that a study using incumbent, rather than applicant, samples revealed that range restriction may have caused an underestimation of the degree of adverse impact in past research (Bobko, Roth, & Buster, 2005). In fact, a more recent meta-analysis including samples of job applicants found that the mean score for African Americans is .80 standard deviations lower than the mean score for whites for work-sample test ratings of cognitive and job knowledge skills. This difference was much lower, in the .21 to .27 range, but still favoring white applicants, for ratings of various social skills (Roth, Bobko, McFarland, & Buster, 2008).

In the context of managerial selection, two types of work samples are used. In **group exercises**, participants are placed in a situation in which the successful completion of a task requires interaction among the participants. In **individual exercises**, participants complete a task independently. Both individual and group exercises can be specified further along several continua (Callinan & Robertson, 2000): (1) bandwidth (the extent to which the entire job domain is part of the work sample), (2) fidelity (the extent to which the work sample mirrors actual job conditions),

(3) task specificity (the extent to which tasks are specific to the job in question or more general in nature), (4) necessary experience (the extent to which previous knowledge of the position is needed), (5) task types (e.g., psychomotor, verbal, social), and (6) mode of delivery and response (e.g., behavioral, verbal, or written). Based on these categories, it should be apparent that there are numerous choices regarding the design and implementation of work samples. Next we shall discuss four of the most popular types of work samples: the Leaderless Group Discussion (LGD), the In-Basket Test, the Business Game, and the Situational Judgment Test (SJT).

Leaderless Group Discussion (LGD)

The LGD is a disarmingly simple technique. A group of participants simply is asked to carry on a discussion about some topic for a period of time (Bass, 1954). Of course, face validity is enhanced if the discussion is about a job-related topic. No one is appointed leader. Raters do not participate in the discussion, but remain free to observe and rate the performance of each participant. For example, IBM uses an LGD in which each participant is required to make a five-minute oral presentation of a candidate for promotion and then subsequently defend his or her candidate in a group discussion with five other participants. All roles are well defined and structured. Seven characteristics are rated, each on a five-point scale of effectiveness: aggressiveness, persuasiveness or selling ability, oral communications, self-confidence, resistance to stress, energy level, and interpersonal contact (Wollowick & McNamara, 1969).

RELIABILITY   Interrater reliabilities of the LGD generally are reasonable, averaging .83 (Bass, 1954; Tziner & Dolan, 1982). Test–retest reliabilities of .72 (median of seven studies; Bass, 1954) and .62 (Petty, 1974) have been reported. Reliabilities are likely to be enhanced, however, to the extent that LGD behaviors simply are described rather than evaluated in terms of presumed underlying personality characteristics (Bass, 1954; Flanagan, 1954b).

VALIDITY   In terms of *job performance*, Bass (1954) reported a median correlation of .38 between LGD ratings and performance ratings of student leaders, shipyard foremen, administrative trainees, foreign-service administrators, civil-service administrators, and oil-refinery supervisors. In terms of *training performance*, Tziner and Dolan (1982) reported an LGD validity of .24 for female officer candidates; in terms of ratings of five-year and career *potential*, Turnage and Muchinsky (1984) found LGD validities in the low .20s; and, in terms of changes in position level three years following the LGD, Wollowick and McNamara (1969) reported a predictive validity of .25. Finally, since peer ratings in the LGD correlate close to .90 or higher with observers' ratings (Kaess, Witryol, & Nolan, 1961), it is possible to administer the LGD to a large group of candidates, divide them into small groups, and have them rate each other. Gleason (1957) used such a peer rating procedure with military trainees and found that reliability and validity held up as well as when independent observers were used.

EFFECTS OF TRAINING AND EXPERIENCE   Petty (1974) showed that, although LGD experience did not significantly affect performance ratings, previous training did. Individuals who received a 15-minute briefing on the history, development, rating instruments, and research relative to the LGD were rated significantly higher than untrained individuals. Kurecka, Austin, Johnson, and Mendoza (1982) found similar results and showed that the training effect accounted for as much as 25 percent of criterion variance. To control for this, either all individuals trained in the LGD can be put into the same group(s), or else the effects of training can be held constant statistically. One or both of these strategies are called for in order to interpret results meaningfully and fairly.

The In-Basket Test

This is an individual work sample designed to simulate important aspects of the manager's position. Hence, different types of in-basket tests may be designed, corresponding to the different requirements of various levels of managerial jobs. The first step in in-basket development is to determine what aspects of the managerial job to measure. For example, in assessing candidates for middle-manager positions, IBM determined that the following characteristics are important for middle-management success and should be rated in the in-basket simulation: oral communications, planning and organizing, self-confidence, written communications, decision making, risk taking, and administrative ability (Wollowick & McNamara, 1969). On the basis of this information, problems then are created that encompass the kinds of issues the candidate is likely to face, should he or she be accepted for the job.

In general, an in-basket simulation takes the following form (Fredericksen, 1962):

> It consists of the letters, memoranda, notes of incoming telephone calls, and other materials which have supposedly collected in the in-basket of an administrative officer. The subject who takes the test is given appropriate background information concerning the school, business, military unit, or whatever institution is involved. He is told that he is the new incumbent of the administrative position, and that he is to deal with the material in the in-basket. The background information is sufficiently detailed that the subject can reasonably be expected to take action on many of the problems presented by the in-basket documents. The subject is instructed that he is not to play a role, he is not to pretend to be someone else. He is to bring to the new job his own background of knowledge and experience, his own personality, and he is to deal with the problems as though he were really the incumbent of the administrative position. He is not to say what he would do; he is actually to write letters and memoranda, prepare agendas for meetings, make notes and reminders for himself, as though he were actually on the job. (p. 1)

Although the situation is relatively unstructured for the candidate, each candidate faces exactly the same complex set of problem situations. At the conclusion of the in-basket test, each candidate leaves behind a packet full of notes, memos, letters, and so forth, which constitute the record of his behavior. The test then is scored (by describing, not evaluating, what the candidate did) in terms of the job-relevant characteristics enumerated at the outset. This is the major asset of the in-basket: It permits *direct* observation of individual behavior within the context of a highly job-relevant, yet standardized, problem situation.

In addition to high face validity, the in-basket also discriminates well. For example, in a middle-management training program, AT&T compared the responses of management trainees to those of experienced managers (Lopez, 1966). In contrast to experienced managers, the trainees were wordier; they were less likely to take action on the basis of the importance of the problem; they saw fewer implications for the organization as a whole in the problems; they tended to make final (as opposed to investigatory) decisions and actions more frequently; they tended to resort to complete delegation, whereas experienced executives delegated with some element of control; and they were far less considerate of others than the executives were. The managers' approaches to dealing with in-basket materials later served as the basis for discussing the "appropriate" ways of dealing with such problems.

In-basket performance does predict success in training, with correlations ranging from .18 to .36 (Borman, 1982; Borman, Eaton, Bryan, & Rosse, 1983; Tziner & Dolan, 1982). A crucial question, of course, is that of predictive validity. Does behavior during the in-basket simulation reflect actual job behavior? Results are mixed. Turnage and Muchinsky (1984) found that, while in-basket scores did forecast ratings of five-year and career potential (rs of .19 and .25), they did not predict job performance rankings or appraisals. On the other hand, Wollowick and McNamara (1969) reported a predictive validity coefficient of .32 between in-basket scores and changes in position level for 94 middle managers three years later, and, in a concurrent study, Brass and Oldham (1976) reported significant validities that ranged from .24 to .34 between four in-basket scoring dimensions and a composite measure of supervisory effectiveness. Moreover, since the LGD and the in-basket test share only about 20 percent of variance in common (Tziner & Dolan, 1982), in combination they are potentially powerful predictors of managerial success.

The Business Game

The business game is a "live" case. For example, in the assessment of candidates for jobs as Army recruiters, two exercises required participants to make phone calls to assessors who role-played two different prospective recruits and then to meet for follow-up interviews with these role-playing assessors. One of the cold-call/interview exercises was with a prospective recruit unwilling to consider Army enlistment, and the other was with a prospect more willing to consider joining. These two exercises predicted success in recruiter training with validities of .25 and .26 (Borman et al., 1983). A desirable feature of the business game is that intelligence, as measured by cognitive ability tests, seems to have no effect on the success of players (Dill, 1972).

A variation of the business game focuses on the effects of measuring "cognitive complexity" on managerial performance. Cognitive complexity is concerned with "how" persons think and behave. It is independent of the content of executive thought and action, and it reflects a style that is difficult to assess with paper-and-pencil instruments (Streufert, Pogash, & Piasecki, 1988). Using computer-based simulations, participants assume a managerial role (e.g., county disaster control coordinator, temporary governor of a developing country) for six task periods of one hour each. The simulations present a managerial task environment that is best dealt with via a number of diverse managerial activities, including preventive action, use of strategy, planning, use and timeliness of responsive action, information search, and use of opportunism. Streufert et al. (1988) reported validities as high as .50 to .67 between objective performance measures (computer-scored simulation results) and self-reported indicators of success (a corrected measure of income at age, job level at age, number of persons supervised, and number of promotions during the last 10 years). Although the self-reports may have been subject to some self-enhancing bias, these results are sufficiently promising to warrant further investigation. Because such simulations focus on the structural style of thought and action rather than on content and interpersonal functioning, as in ACs (discussed later in this chapter), the two methods in combination may account for more variance in managerial performance than is currently the case.

Situational Judgment Tests (SJT)

SJTs are considered a low-fidelity (i.e., low correspondence between testing and work situations) work sample. Because they consist of a series of job-related situations presented in written, verbal, or visual form, it can be argued that SJTs are not truly work samples, in that hypothetical behaviors, as opposed to actual behaviors, are assessed. In many SJTs, job applicants are asked to choose an alternative among several choices available. Consider the following illustration from an Army SJT (Northrop, 1989, p. 190):

> A man on a very urgent mission during a battle finds he must cross a stream about 40 feet wide. A blizzard has been blowing and the stream has frozen over. However, because of the snow, he does not know how thick the ice is. He sees two planks about 10 feet long near the point where he wishes to cross. He also knows where there is a bridge about 2 miles downstream. Under the circumstances he should:
>
> **A.** Walk to the bridge and cross it.
> **B.** Run rapidly across the ice.
> **C.** Break a hole in the ice near the edge of the stream to see how deep the stream is.
> **D.** Cross with the aid of the planks, pushing one ahead of the other and walking on them.
> **E.** Creep slowly across the ice.

The following is an illustration of an item from an SJT used for selecting retail associates (Weekley & Jones, 1999, p. 685):

> A customer asks for a specific brand of merchandise the store doesn't carry. How would you respond to the customer?

A. Tell the customer which stores carry that brand, but point out that your brand is similar.

B. Ask the customer more questions so you can suggest something else.

C. Tell the customer that the store carries the highest quality merchandise available.

D. Ask another associate to help.

E. Tell the customer which stores carry that brand.

QUESTIONS FOR PARTICIPANTS

- Which of the options above do you believe is the *best* under the circumstances?
- Which of the options above do you believe is the *worst* under the circumstances?

The above illustrations should remind us of the discussion in Chapter 12 regarding the situational interview. In fact, situational interviews can be considered a special case of SJTs; interviewers present the scenarios verbally and job applicants also respond verbally.

SJTs are inexpensive to develop, administer, and score compared to other types of work samples described in this chapter (Clevenger, Pereira, Wiechmann, Schmitt, & Harvey, 2001). Also, the availability of new technology has made it possible to create and administer video-based SJTs effectively (Weekley & Jones, 1997). Regarding SJT validity, a meta-analysis based on 102 validity coefficients and 10,640 individuals found an average validity of .34 (without correcting for range restriction), and that validity was generalizable (McDaniel, Morgeson, Finnegan, Campion, & Braverman, 2001). Perhaps more important, SJTs have been shown to add incremental validity to the prediction of job performance above and beyond job knowledge, cognitive ability, job experience, the Big Five personality traits, and a composite score including cognitive ability and the Big-Five traits (Clevenger et al., 2001; McDaniel, Hartman, Whetzel, & Grubb, 2007; O'Connell, Hartman, McDaniel, Grubb, & Lawrence, 2007). SJTs also show less adverse impact based on ethnicity than do general cognitive ability tests (McDaniel & Nguyen, 2001). However, there are race-based differences favoring white compared to African American, Latino, and Asian American test takers, particularly when the instructions for taking the judgment test are g loaded (i.e., heavily influenced by general mental abilities) (Whetzel, McDaniel, & Nguyen, 2008). Thus, using a video-based SJT, which is not as heavily g loaded as a written SJT, seems like a very promising alternative given that a study found that the video format had higher predictive and incremental validity for predicting interpersonally oriented criteria than did the written version (Lievens & Sackett, 2006).

In spite of these positive features, there are several challenges in using SJTs (McDaniel & Nguyen, 2001). Most notably, SJTs do not necessarily measure any one particular construct; while SJTs do work, we often do not understand why, and this lack of knowledge may jeopardize the legal defensibility of the test. For example, response instructions affect the underlying psychological constructs assessed by SJTs such that those with knowledge instructions have higher correlations with cognitive ability and those with behavioral-tendency instructions have higher correlations with personality constructs (McDaniel, Hartman, Whetzel, & Grubb, 2007). Nor do we know with certainly why SJTs show less adverse impact than general cognitive ability tests, although it seems that the degree to which an SJT is g loaded plays an important role. Related to this point, it seems that SJTs show less adverse impact when they include a smaller cognitive ability component. This issue deserves future attention (McDaniel & Nguyen, 2001). Finally, choices made in conducting meta-analyses of the validity of SJTs can affect the resulting validity estimates (Bobko & Roth, 2008). Despite these ongoing challenges, cumulative evidence to date documents the validity and usefulness of SJTs.

ASSESSMENT CENTERS (AC)

The AC is a method, not a place. It brings together many of the instruments and techniques of managerial selection that we have been discussing in a piecemeal fashion up to this point. By using multiple assessment techniques, by standardizing methods of making inferences from such techniques, and by pooling the judgments of multiple assessors in rating each candidate's behavior, the likelihood of successfully predicting future performance is enhanced considerably (Taft, 1959). Additional research (Gaugler, Rosenthal, Thornton, & Bentson, 1987; Schmitt et al., 1984) supports this hypothesis. Moreover, ACs have been found successful at predicting long-term career success (i.e., corrected correlation of .39 between AC scores and average salary growth seven years later) (Jansen & Stoop, 2001). In addition, candidate perceptions of AC exercises as highly job related are another advantage, for this enhances legal defensibility and organizational attractiveness (Smither, Reilly, Millsap, Pearlman, & Stoffey, 1993). Reviews of the predominantly successful applications of AC methodology (cf. Klimoski & Brickner, 1987) underscore the flexibility of the method and its potential for evaluating success in many different occupations.

Assessment Center: The Beginnings

Multiple assessment procedures were used first by German military psychologists during World War II. They felt that paper-and-pencil tests took too "atomistic" a view of human nature; therefore, they chose to observe a candidate's behavior in a complex situation to arrive at a "holistic" appraisal of his reactions. Building on this work and that of the War Office Selection Board of the British army in the early 1940s, the U.S. Office of Strategic Services used the method to select spies during World War II. Each candidate had to develop a cover story that would hide his identity during the assessment. Testing for the ability to maintain cover was crucial, and ingenious situational tests were designed to seduce candidates into breaking cover (McKinnon, 1975; OSS, 1948).

The first industrial firm to adopt this approach was AT&T in 1956 in its Management Progress Study. This longitudinal study is likely the largest and most comprehensive investigation of managerial career development ever undertaken. Its purpose was to attempt to understand what characteristics (cognitive, motivational, and attitudinal) were important to the career progress of young employees who move through the Bell System from their first job to middle- and upper-management levels (Bray, Campbell, & Grant, 1974). The original sample ($N = 422$) was composed of 274 college men and 148 noncollege men assessed over several summers from 1956 to 1960. In 1965, 174 of the college men and 145 of the noncollege men still were employed with the company.

Each year (between 1956 and 1965) data were collected from the men's companies (e.g., interviews with departmental colleagues, supervisors, former bosses), as well as from the men themselves (e.g., interviews, questionnaires of attitudes and expectations) to determine their progress. No information about any man's performance during assessment was ever given to company officials. There was no contamination of subsequent criterion data by the assessment results, and staff evaluations had had no influence on the careers of the men being studied.

By July 1965, information was available on the career progress of 125 college men and 144 noncollege men originally assessed. The criterion data included management level achieved and current salary. The predictive validities of the assessment staff's global predictions were .44 for college men and .71 for noncollege men. Of the 38 college men who were promoted to middle-management positions, 31 (82 percent) were identified correctly by the AC staff. Likewise, 15 (75 percent) of the 20 noncollege men who were promoted into middle management were identified correctly. Finally, of the 72 men (both college and noncollege) who were not promoted, the AC staff correctly identified 68 (94 percent).

A second assessment of these men was made eight years after the first one, and the advancement of the participants over the ensuing years was followed (Bray & Howard, 1983). Results of the two sets of predictions in forecasting movement over a 20-year period through the seven-level management hierarchy found in Bell operating companies are shown in Figure 13-2.

These results are impressive—so impressive that operational use of the method has spread rapidly. Currently several thousand business, government, and nonprofit organizations worldwide use the AC method to improve the accuracy of their managerial selection decisions, to help determine individual training and development needs, and to facilitate more accurate workforce planning.

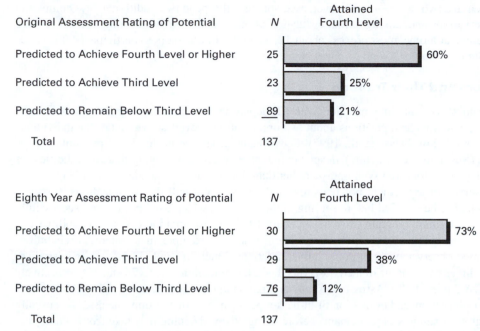

FIGURE 13-2   Ratings at original assessment and eight years later, and management level attained at year 20.   *Source:* Bray, D.W., and Howard, A. (1983). Longitudinal studies of adult psychological development. New York: Guilford.

In view of the tremendous popularity of this approach, we will examine several aspects of AC operation (level and purpose, length, size, staff, etc.), as well as some of the research on reliability and validity.

Level and Purpose of Assessment

Since the pioneering studies by Bray and his associates at AT&T, new applications of the AC method have multiplied almost every year. There is no one best way to structure a center, and the specific design, content, administration, and cost of centers fluctuate with the target group, as well as with the objectives of the center. A survey including 215 organizations revealed that the three most popular reasons for developing an AC are (1) selection, (2) promotion, and (3) development planning (Spychalski, Quiñones, Gaugler, & Pohley, 1997). These goals are not mutually exclusive, however. Some firms combine assessment with training, so that once development needs have been identified through the assessment process, training can be initiated immediately to capitalize on employee motivation.

A major change in the last 15 years is the large number of firms that use AC methodology *solely* to diagnose training needs. In these cases, ACs may change their name to **development centers** (Tillema, 1998). In contrast to situations where assessment is used for selection purposes, not all eligible employees may participate in development-oriented assessments. Although participation is usually based on self-nomination or the recommendation of a supervisor, the final decision usually rests with an HR director (Spychalski et al., 1997).

Duration and Size

The duration of the center typically varies with the level of candidate assessment. Centers for first-level supervisory positions often last only one day, while middle- and higher-management centers may last two or three days. When assessment is combined with training activities, the program may run five or six days.

Even in a two-day center, however, assessors usually spend two additional days comparing their observations and making a final evaluation of each candidate. While some centers process only 6 people at a time, most process about 12. The ratio of assessors to participants also varies from about three-to-one to one-to-one (Gaugler et al., 1987).

Assessors and Their Training

Some organizations mix line managers with HR department or other staff members as assessors. In general, assessors hold positions about two organizational levels above that of the individuals being assessed (Spychalski et al., 1997). Few organizations use professional psychologists as assessors (Spychalski et al., 1997), despite cumulative evidence indicating that AC validities are higher when assessors are psychologists rather than line managers (Gaugler et al., 1987).

A survey of assessment practices revealed that in about half the organizations, surveyed assessors had to be certified before serving in this capacity, which usually involved successfully completing a training program (Spychalski et al., 1997). Substantial increases in reliabilities can be obtained as a result of training observers. In one study, for example, mean interrater reliabilities for untrained observers were .46 on a human relations dimension and .58 on an administrative-technical dimension. For the trained observers, however, reliabilities were .78 and .90, respectively (Richards & Jaffee, 1972). Assessors usually are trained in interviewing and feedback techniques, behavior observation, and evaluation of in-basket performance. In addition, the assessors usually go through the exercises as participants before rating others. Training may take from two days to several weeks, depending on the complexity of the center, the importance of the assessment decision, and the importance management attaches to assessor training.

Training assessors is important because several studies (Gaugler & Rudolph, 1992; Gaugler & Thornton, 1989) have shown that they have a limited capacity to process information and that the more complex the judgment task is, the more they will be prone to cognitive biases such as contrast effects. In addition, untrained assessors seem first to form an overall impression of participants' performance, and these overall impressions then drive more specific dimension ratings (Lance, Foster, Gentry, & Thoresen, 2004).

Because of the known cognitive limitations of assessors, developers of ACs should limit the cognitive demands placed on assessors by implementing one or more of the following suggestions:

- Restrict the number of dimensions that assessors are required to process.
- Have assessors assess broad rather than narrow qualities (e.g., interpersonal skills versus behavior flexibility).
- Use **behavioral coding** to reduce the cognitive demands faced by assessors and also to structure information processing (Hennessy, Mabey, & Warr, 1998). Behavioral coding requires assessors to tally the frequency of important behaviors immediately, as they are observed. Note, however, that not all methods of note taking are beneficial, because taking notes that are too detailed and cumbersome to record can place additional cognitive demands on assessors' information processing (Hennessy et al., 1998).

The *Guidelines and Ethical Considerations for Assessment Center Operations* (Task Force on Assessment Center Guidelines, 1989) suggest that a sound assessor training program should last a minimum of two days for every day of AC exercise and that assessors should gain the following knowledge and skills at the completion of training:

1. Knowledge of the organization and target job
2. Understanding of assessment techniques, dimensions, and typical behavior
3. Understanding of assessment dimensions and their relationship to job performance
4. Knowledge of performance standards
5. Skill in techniques for recording and classifying behavior and in use of the AC forms
6. Understanding of evaluation, rating, and data-integration processes

7. Understanding of assessment policies and practices
8. Understanding of feedback procedures
9. Skill in oral and written feedback techniques (when applicable)
10. Objective and consistent performance in role-play or fact-finding exercises

Chapter 5 described how frame-of-reference (FOR) training can be successful in improving the accuracy of supervisors as they assess the performance of their subordinates in the context of a performance management system. This same type of training method can be used for training assessors. One study including 229 I/O psychology students and 161 managers demonstrated the effectiveness of FOR training for training assessors in ACs (Lievens, 2001). Results showed that not only did FOR training outperform a minimum-training condition, but it also outperformed a data-driven training program that covered the processes of observing, recording, classifying, and evaluating participant behavior. Specifically, interrater reliability and rating accuracy were better for the FOR training condition than for the data-driven training condition. There is additional evidence that implementing FOR training improves both the criterion- and the construct-related validity of ACs (Schleicher, Day, Mayes, & Riggio, 2002). In the end, participating in FOR training produces assessors that are more experienced with the task and rating system. Such experience is known to be an important predictor of assessor accuracy (Kolk, Born, van der Flier, & Olman, 2002).

Performance Feedback

The performance-feedback process is crucial. Most organizations emphasize to candidates that the AC is only one portion of the assessment process. It is simply a supplement to other performance-appraisal information (both supervisory and objective), and each candidate has an opportunity on the job to refute any negative insights gained from assessment. Empirically, this has been demonstrated to be the case (London & Stumpf, 1983).

What about the candidate who does poorly at the center? Organizations are justifiably concerned that turnover rates among the members of this group—many of whom represent substantial investments by the company in experience and technical expertise—will be high. Fortunately, it appears that this is not the case. Kraut and Scott (1972) reviewed the career progress of 1,086 nonmanagement candidates who had been observed at an IBM AC one to six years previously. Analysis of separation rates indicated that the proportions of low- and high-rated employees who left the company did not differ significantly.

Reliability of the Assessment Process

Interrater reliabilities vary across studies from a median of about .60 to over .95 (Adams & Thornton, 1989; Schmitt, 1977). Raters tend to appraise similar aspects of performance in candidates. In terms of temporal stability, an important question concerns the extent to which dimension ratings made by individual assessors change over time (i.e., in the course of a six-month assignment as an assessor). Evidence on this issue was provided by Sackett and Hakel (1979) as a result of a large-scale study of 719 individuals assessed by four assessor teams at AT&T. Mean interrater reliabilities across teams varied from .53 to .86, with an overall mean of .69. In addition to generally high stability, there was no evidence for consistent changes in assessors' or assessor teams' patterns of ratings over time.

In practice, therefore, it makes little difference whether an individual is assessed during the first or sixth month that an assessor team is working together. Despite individual differences among assessors, patterns of information usage were very similar across team consensus ratings. Thus, this study provides empirical support for one of the fundamental underpinnings of the AC method—the use of multiple assessors to offset individual biases, errors of observation or interpretation, and unreliability of individual ratings.

Standardizing an AC program so that each candidate receives relatively the same treatment is essential so that differences in performance can be attributed to differences in candidates' abilities and skills, and not to extraneous factors. Standardization concerns include, for example:

- *Exercise instructions*—provide the same information in the same manner to all candidates.
- *Time limits*—maintain them consistently to equalize opportunities for candidates to perform.
- *Assigned roles*—design and pilot test them to avoid inherently advantageous or disadvantageous positions for candidates.
- *Assessor/candidate acquaintance*—minimize it to keep biases due to previous exposure from affecting evaluations.
- *Assessor consensus discussion session*—conduct it similarly for each candidate.
- *Exercise presentation order*—use the same order so that order effects do not contaminate candidate performance.

Validity

Applicants tend to view ACs as more face valid than cognitive ability tests and, as a result, tend to be more satisfied with the selection process, the job, and the organization (Macan, Avedon, Paese, & Smith, 1994). Reviews of the predictive validity of AC ratings and subsequent promotion and performance generally have been positive. Over all types of criteria and over 50 studies containing 107 validity coefficients, meta-analysis indicates an average validity for ACs of .37, with upper and lower bounds on the 95 percent confidence interval of .11 and .63, respectively (Gaugler et al., 1987). A more recent study examined objective career advancement using a sample of 456 academic graduates over a 13-year period (Jansen & Vinkenburg, 2006). The criterion-related validity for AC ratings measuring interpersonal effectiveness, firmness, and ambition was .35. Yet research indicates also that AC ratings are not equally effective predictors of all types of criteria. For example, Gaugler et al. (1987) found median corrected correlations (corrected for sampling error, range restriction, and criterion unreliability) of .53 for predicting potential, but only .36 for predicting supervisors' ratings of performance.

A meta-analytic integration of the literature on the predictive validity of the AC examined individual AC dimensions as opposed to overall AC scores (Arthur, Day, McNelly, & Edens, 2003). Criteria included any job-related information presented in the original articles (e.g., job performance ratings, promotion, salary). This review included a total of 34 articles, and the authors were able to extract the following AC dimensions: (1) consideration/awareness of others, (2) communication, (3) drive, (4) influencing others, (5) organization and planning, and (6) problem solving. This analysis allowed the authors to examine not method-level data (e.g., overall AC scores) but construct-level data (i.e., specific dimensions). The resulting corrected validity coefficients for the six dimensions were in the .30s except for drive ($r = .25$). The highest validity coefficient was for problem solving (.39), followed by influencing others (38), and organization and planning (.37).

As a follow-up analysis, the criteria were regressed on the six dimensions, yielding $R = .45$, meaning that approximately 20 percent of the criterion variance was explained by the AC dimensions. In this regression analysis, however, neither drive nor consideration/awareness of others was statistically significant, so the 20 percent of variance explained is due to the other four dimensions only. This is a larger R^2 than the result obtained by Gaugler et al. (1987) for overall AC scores (i.e., $R^2 = .14$). In addition, when considered alone, problem solving explained 15 percent of variance in the criterion, with smaller incremental contributions made by influencing others (3 percent), organization and planning (1 percent), and communication (1 percent). These results are encouraging on two fronts. First, they confirm the validity of ACs. Second, given the redundancy found among dimensions, the number of dimensions assessed in ACs could probably be reduced substantially (from the average of approximately 10 reported by Woehr and Arthur, 2003) without a substantial loss in overall validity.

The result showing that problem solving, a type of cognitive ability, is the most valid dimension of those included in the Arthur et al. (2003) meta-analysis may lead to the conclusion that validity of ACs rests solely on the extent to which they include a cognitive ability component. Not true. A study of 633 participants in a managerial AC showed that, when the cognitive ability component was removed from five different types of AC exercises (i.e., in-basket, subordinate meeting, in-basket coaching, project presentation, and team preparation), only the in-basket exercise did not account for significant variance in the scores (Goldstein, Yusko, Braverman, Smith, & Chung, 1998). In short, AC exercises measure more than just cognitive ability, and the additional constructs contribute incremental variance to the prediction of performance. For example, the in-basket-coaching exercise and the project-presentation exercise contributed an additional 12 percent of variance each, and the subordinate-meeting exercise contributed an additional 10 percent of variance. Dayan, Kasten, and Fox (2002) reached a similar conclusion regarding the incremental validity of AC scores above and beyond cognitive ability in a study of 712 applicants for positions in a police department.

One final point concerning AC predictive validity studies deserves reemphasis. Assessment procedures are behaviorally based; yet again and again they are related to organizational outcome variables (e.g., salary growth, promotion) that are all complexly determined. In order to achieve a fuller understanding of the assessment process and of exactly what aspects of managerial job behavior each assessment dimension is capable of predicting, assessment dimensions must be related to behaviorally based multiple criteria. Only then can we develop comprehensive psychological theories of managerial effectiveness.

Fairness and Adverse Impact

Adverse impact is less of a problem in an AC as compared to an aptitude test designed to assess the cognitive abilities that are important for the successful performance of work behaviors in professional occupations (Hoffman & Thornton, 1997). A study including two nonoverlapping samples of employees in a utility company showed that the AC produced adverse impact (i.e., violation of the 80 percent rule) at the 60th percentile, whereas the aptitude test produced adverse impact at the 20th percentile. Although the AC produced a slightly lower validity coefficient ($r = .34$) than the aptitude test ($r = .39$) and cost about 10 times more than the test, the AC produced so much less adverse impact that it was preferred. Also, a more recent meta-analysis found an overall standardized mean difference in scores between African Americans and whites of .52 and an overall mean difference between Latinos and whites of .28 (both favoring whites) (Dean, Roth, & Bobko, 2008). Regarding gender, the meta-analysis found a difference of $d = .19$ favoring women. So, overall, although whites score on average higher than African Americans and Hispanics, the difference is not as large as that found for cognitive ability tests. Moreover, on average, women receive higher AC ratings compared to men.

Assessment Center Utility

In a field study of 600 first-level managers, Cascio and Ramos (1986) compared the utility of AC predictions to those generated from multiple interviews. Using the general utility equation (Equation 14-4, see Chapter 14), they confirmed the findings of an earlier study (Cascio & Silbey, 1979)—namely, that the cost of the procedure is incidental compared to the possible losses associated with promotion of the wrong person into a management job. Given large individual differences in job performance, use of a more valid procedure has a substantial bottom-line impact. Use of the AC instead of the multiple-interview procedure to select managers resulted in an improvement in job performance of about $2,700 per year per manager ($6,654 in 2009 dollars). If the average manager stays at the first level for five years, then the net payoff per manager is more than $13,000 (more than $32,000 in 2009 dollars).

Potential Problems

A growing concern in the use of ACs is that assessment procedures may be applied carelessly or improperly. For example, content-related evidence of validity is frequently used to establish the job relatedness of ACs. Yet, as Sackett (1987) has pointed out, such a demonstration requires more than the careful construction of exercises and identification of dimensions to be rated. *How* the stimulus materials are presented to candidates (including response options) and *how* candidate responses are evaluated are also critical considerations in making judgments about content-related evidence of validity. For example, requiring candidates to write out responses to an exercise would be inappropriate if the job requires verbal responses.

A second potential problem, raised by Klimoski and Strickland (1977), is that a subtle criterion contamination phenomenon may inflate assessment validities when global ratings or other summary measures of effectiveness (e.g. salary, management level reached) are used as criteria. This inflation will occur to the extent that assessors, supervisors, and upper-level managers share similar stereotypes of an effective manager. Hence, it is possible that assessors' ratings on the various dimensions are tied closely to actual performance at the AC, but that ratings of overall potential may include a bias, either implicitly or explicitly, that enters into their judgments. Behavior-based ratings can help to clarify this issue, but it is possible that it will not be resolved definitively until studies are done in which one group from *outside an organization* provides AC ratings, while another provides criterion data, with the latter not allowed access to the predictions of the former (McEvoy & Beatty, 1989).

A third problem for ACs is construct validity (Lance, Foster, Nemeth, Gentry, & Drollinger, 2007; Lance, Woehr, & Meade, 2007). Studies have found consistently that correlations between different dimensions within exercises are higher than correlations between the same dimensions across exercises (Harris, Becker, & Smith, 1993; Kleinman, 1993). Arthur et al. (2003) reported an average corrected intercorrelation across AC dimensions of .56, indicating a low level of interdimension discrimination. Consistent with this finding, when AC ratings are factor analyzed, the solutions usually represent exercise factors, not dimension factors. This suggests that assessors are capturing exercise performance in their ratings, not stable individual differences characteristics (Joyce, Thayer, & Pond, 1994).

Why such weak support for the construct validity of assessment centers? One reason is that different types of exercises may elicit the expression of different behaviors based on the trait-activation model described earlier. For example, Haaland and Christiansen (2002) conducted an AC with 79 law enforcement officers and compared the average within-dimension correlation of ratings from exercises that allowed for more opportunity to observe personality trait-relevant behavior to the average of those from exercises for which there was less opportunity. For each of the Big Five personality traits, ratings from exercises that allowed for the expression of the personality trait displayed stronger convergence ($r = .30$) than ratings from exercises that did not allow for the expression of the trait ($r = .15$). In other words, situations that allowed for the expression of the same personality trait resulted in scores more highly intercorrelated than situations that did not involve the activation of the same trait. Consideration of which trait was activated by each exercise improved the correlations in the expected direction and the resulting conclusion regarding construct validity.

A review of 34 studies, including multitrait–multimethod matrices, also concluded that the variation in how exercises elicit individual differences is one of the reasons for the poor construct validity of ACs (Lievens & Conway, 2001). Although exercise-variance components dominate over dimension-variance components (Lance, Lambert, Gewin, Lievens, & Conway, 2004), a model including both dimensions and exercises as latent variables provided the best fit for the data, even better than a model with only dimensions and a model with only exercises as latent variables. Hence, specific dimensions are the building blocks for ACs, but the various types of exercises used play an important role as well. Nevertheless, some dimensions such as communication, influencing others, organizing and planning, and problem solving seem to be more construct valid than others, such as consideration/awareness of others and drive (Bowler & Woehr, 2006). When providing feedback to participants, therefore, emphasize information about specific dimensions *within a specific context* (i.e., the exercise in question) (Lievens & Conway, 2001).

Other investigations regarding the "construct-validity puzzle" of ACs concluded that the factors that play a role are (1) cross-situational inconsistency in participant performance; (2) poor AC design (i.e., assessors are not experienced or well trained, too many dimensions are assessed); and (3) assessor unreliability (including the theories of performance held by the managers who serve as assessors) (Jones & Born, 2008; Lievens, 2002). While there are both assessor-related and participant-related factors that affect construct validity, what is most relevant in considering the construct validity of ACs is whether the participants perform consistently across exercises. In many situations, participants actually do *not* perform differently across dimensions and do not perform consistently across exercises. Thus, participants' levels of true performance (i.e., performance profiles) seem to be the key determinants of AC construct validity rather than biases on the part of assessors.

Fortunately, there are a number of research-based suggestions that, if implemented, can improve the construct validity of ACs. Lievens (1998) provided the following recommendations:

1. *Definition and selection of dimensions:*
   - Use a small number of dimensions, especially if ACs are used for hiring purposes.
   - Select dimensions that are conceptually unrelated to each other.
   - Provide definitions for each dimension that are clearly job related.
2. *Assessors:*
   - Use psychologists as members of assessor teams.
   - Focus on quality of training (as opposed to length of training).
   - Implement a FOR training program.
3. *Situational exercises:*
   - Use exercises that assess specific dimensions. Avoid "fuzzy" exercises that elicit behaviors potentially relevant to several dimensions.
   - Standardize procedures as much as possible (e.g., train role-players).
   - Use role-players who actively seek to elicit behaviors directly related to the dimensions in question.
   - Let participants know about the dimensions being assessed, particularly in development centers.
4. *Observation, evaluation, and integration procedures:*
   - Provide assessors with observational aids (e.g., behavior checklists).
   - Operationalize each dimension's checklist with at least 6 behaviors, but not more than 12 behaviors.
   - Group checklist behaviors in naturally occurring clusters.

Careful attention to each of these issues will ensure that the AC method is implemented successfully.

COMBINING PREDICTORS

For the most part, we have examined each type of predictor in isolation. Although we have referred to the incremental validity of some predictors vis-à-vis others (especially cognitive abilities), our discussion so far has treated each predictor rather independently of the others. However, as should be obvious by now and organizations use more than one instrument in their managerial and nonmangerial selection processes. For example, an organization may first use a test of cognitive abilities, followed by a personality inventory, an overt honesty test, and a structured interview. For a managerial position, an organization may still use each of these tools and also work samples, all administered within the context of an assessment center. This situation raises the following questions: What is the optimal combination of predictors? What is the relative contribution of each type of tool to the prediction of performance? What are the implications of various predictor combinations for adverse impact?

Although we do not have complete answers for the above questions, some investigations have shed some light on these issues. For example, Schmidt and Hunter (1998) reviewed meta-analytic findings of the predictive validity of several selection procedures and examined the validity of combining general cognitive ability with one other procedure. Results indicated that the highest corrected predictive validity coefficient was for cognitive ability combined with an integrity test ($r = .65$), followed by cognitive ability combined with a work sample test ($r = .63$) and cognitive ability combined with a structured interview ($r = .63$). More detailed information on the average predictive validity of each of the procedures reviewed and the combination of each of the procedures with cognitive ability is shown in Table 13-3.

The results shown in Table 13-3 are incomplete because they include combinations of two predictors only, and one of them is always general cognitive ability. Many organizations typically use more than two procedures, and many organizations do not use cognitive ability tests at all in their selection procedures. The results shown in Table 13-3 also do not take into account the fact that the same combination of predictors may yield different multiple R results for different types of jobs (e.g., managerial versus nonmanagerial). Results that include combinations of more

TABLE 13-3 Summary of Mean Predictive Validity Coefficients for Overall Job Performance for Different Selection Procedures (*r*) and Predictive Validity of Paired Combinations of General Cognitive Ability with Other Procedures (Multiple *R*)

Selection Procedure	*r*	Multiple *R*
General cognitive ability tests	.51	
Work sample tests	.54	.63
Integrity tests	.41	.65
Conscientiousness tests	.31	.60
Employment interviews (structured)	.51	.63
Job knowledge tests	.48	.58
Peer ratings	.49	.58
Training and experience behavioral consistency method	.45	.58
Reference checks	.26	.57
Job experience (years)	.18	.54
Biographical data measures	.35	.52
Assessment centers	.37	.53
Years of education	.10	.52
Graphology	.02	.51
Age	−.01	.51

Source: Adapted from Schmidt, F. L. & Hunter, J. E. (1998). The validity and utility of selection methods in personnel psychology: Practical and theoretical implications of 85 years of research findings. *Psychological Bulletin, 124*, table 1, 265.

than two predictors may be possible in the future, as more data may become available to make such analyses feasible.

In a related literature review of meta-analytic findings, Bobko, Roth, and Potosky (1999) derived a correlation matrix incorporating the relationships among cognitive ability, structured interview, conscientiousness, biodata, and job-performance scores. In contrast to the review by Schmidt and Hunter (1998), correlations were not corrected for various artifacts (e.g., measurement error, range restriction). The overall validity coefficient between cognitive ability and job performance was .30, the same coefficient found for the relationship between structured interview and job performance scores. The correlation between biodata and job performance was found to be .28, and the correlation between conscientiousness and job performance was reported to be .18. Similar to Schmidt and Hunter (1998), Bobko et al. (1999) computed multiple R coefficients derived from regressing performance on various combinations of predictors. The multiple R associated with all four predictors combined was .43, whereas the multiple R associated with all predictors excluding cognitive ability was .38.

In addition, however, Bobko et al. computed average d values associated with each combination of predictors to assess mean group differences in scores (which would potentially lead to adverse impact). Results indicated $d = .76$ for the situation where all four predictors were combined, versus $d = .36$ when all predictors (except cognitive ability) were combined. In each situation, the majority group was predicted to obtain higher scores, but the difference was notably lower for the second scenario, which included a loss in prediction of only $r = .43 - .38 = .05$. This analysis highlights an issue to which we have referred in several places in this book (e.g., Chapter 8): the trade-off between validity and adverse impact. In many situations, a predictor or combination of predictors yielding lower validity may be preferred if this choice leads to less adverse impact.

In short, different combinations of predictors lead to different levels of predictive efficiency, and also to different levels of adverse impact. Both issues deserve serious attention when choosing selection procedures.

Evidence-Based Implications for Practice

- Because managerial performance is a complex construct, consider attempting to predict a combination of objective and subjective criteria of success. In order to improve our understanding of the multiple paths to executive success, we need to do three things: (1) describe the components of executive success in behavioral terms; (2) develop behaviorally based predictor measures to forecast the different aspects of managerial success (e.g., situational tests); and (3) adequately map the interrelationships among individual behaviors, managerial effectiveness (behaviorally defined), and organizational success (objectively defined).
- There are several methods that can be used for selecting individuals for managerial positions, including tests to measure: cognitive ability, personality, leadership ability, motivation to manage, and personal history. Many of these methods can also be used for other types of positions.
- In addition to tests that can be used as signs or indicators of future performance, consider using measures that are surrogates or substitutes for criteria, such as work samples (e.g., leaderless group discussion, in-basket tests, business games, and situational judgment tests).
- Assessment centers bring together many of the instruments and techniques of managerial selection. Given the established criterion-related validity of assessment center ratings, consider using them in most managerial selection contexts. Make sure assessors receive proper training and the dimensions underlying the assessment are defined clearly.
- Given that most selection situations include more than one measurement procedure, establish the collective validity and utility of the selection process by considering all procedures used.

Discussion Questions

1. Why is it difficult to predict success in management?
2. Would you place primary importance on g (i.e., general mental abilities) in selecting for the position of HR director? Why?
3. Would you consider not using a valid cognitive abilities test that produces adverse impact? What factors guided your decision? What are the trade-offs involved?
4. Which personality traits would you use in the selection of managers? How would you minimize the effects of faking?
5. What are the underlying mechanisms for the personality-performance link?
6. What options are available to mitigate response distortion on personality inventories?
7. You are developing a selection process for supervisors of computer programmers. Identify the key dimensions of the job, and then assemble a battery of predictors. How and why will you use each one?
8. What are the advantages of a well-designed training program for assessors in assessment centers? What are the key components of a sound training program?
9. Describe the "construct-validity puzzle" regarding assessment centers. What are the key pieces in this puzzle?
10. What are some advantages and disadvantages of work samples as predictors of success in management?

CHAPTER

14

Decision Making for Selection

At a Glance

Selection of individuals to fill available jobs becomes meaningful only when there are more applicants than jobs. Personnel selection decisions (e.g., accept or reject) are concerned with the assignment of individuals to courses of action whose outcomes are important to the organizations or individuals involved. In the classical validity approach to personnel selection, primary emphasis is placed on measurement accuracy and predictive efficiency. Simple or multiple regression, a statistical technique that enables a decision maker to forecast each individual's criterion status based on predictor information, is the basic prediction model in this approach. This method of combining data (i.e., mechanical or statistical) is superior to a clinical or global method. Multiple regression is compensatory, however, and assumes that low scores on one predictor can be offset by high scores on another. In some situations (e.g., pilot selection), such assumptions are untenable, and, therefore, other selection models, such as multiple cutoff or multiple hurdle, must be used. Various procedures are available to choose appropriate cutoff scores.

The classical validity approach to selection has been criticized sharply, for it ignores certain external parameters of the situation that largely determine the overall worth and usefulness of a selection instrument. In addition, the classical validity approach makes unwarranted utility assumptions and fails to consider the systemic nature of the selection process. Decision theory, a more recent approach to selection, attempts to overcome these deficiencies. Decision theory acknowledges the importance of psychometric criteria in evaluating measurement and prediction, and, in addition, it recognizes that the *outcomes* of prediction are of primary importance to individuals and organizations in our society. These outcomes must, therefore, be evaluated in terms of their consequences for individuals and organizations (i.e., in terms of their utility). In considering the cost consequences of alternative selection strategies, the impact of selection on recruitment, induction, and training also must be considered.

Fortunately decision-oriented, systemic selection models are now available that enable the decision maker to evaluate the payoff—in dollars—expected to result from the implementation of a proposed selection program. Some such models go beyond an examination of the size of the validity coefficient and instead consider a host of issues, such as capital budgeting and strategic outcomes at the group and organizational levels.

PERSONNEL SELECTION IN PERSPECTIVE

If variability in physical and psychological characteristics were not so pervasive a phenomenon, there would be little need for selection of people to fill various jobs. Without variability among individuals in abilities, aptitudes, interests, and personality traits, we would forecast identical levels of job performance for all job applicants. Likewise, if there were 10 job openings available and only 10 suitably qualified applicants, selection would not be a significant issue, since all 10 applicants must be hired. Selection becomes a relevant concern only when there are more qualified applicants than there are positions to be filled, for selection implies choice and choice means exclusion.

In personnel selection, decisions are made about individuals. Such decisions are concerned with the assignment of individuals to courses of action (e.g., accept/reject) whose outcomes are important to the institutions or individuals involved (Cronbach & Gleser, 1965). Since decision makers cannot know in advance with absolute certainty the outcomes of any assignment, outcomes must be *predicted* in advance on the basis of available information. This is a two-step procedure: *measurement* (i.e., *collecting* data using tests or other assessment procedures that are relevant to job performance) and *prediction* (i.e., *combining* these data in such a way as to enable the decision maker to minimize predictive error in forecasting job performance) (Wiggins, 1973). Methods of data collection were described in detail in Chapters 12 and 13. In this chapter, we address the issue of prediction.

Traditionally, personnel-selection programs have attempted to maximize the accuracy of measurement and the efficiency of prediction, issues we considered in Chapters 6 and 7. Decision theory, while not downgrading the importance of psychometric criteria in evaluating measurement and prediction, recognizes that the *outcomes* of predictions are of primary importance to individuals and organizations in our society. From this perspective, then, measurement and prediction are simply technical components of a system designed to make *decisions* about the assignment of individuals to jobs (Boudreau, 1991; Cascio & Boudreau, 2008). Decision outcomes must, therefore, be evaluated in terms of their consequences for individuals and organizations (i.e., in terms of their utility). In short, traditional selection programs emphasize measurement accuracy and predictive efficiency as final goals. In the contemporary view, these conditions merely set the stage for the decision problem.

In this chapter, we will consider first the traditional, or classical, validity approach to personnel selection. Then we will consider decision theory and utility analysis and present alternative models that use this approach to formulate optimal recruiting-selection strategies. Our overall aim is to arouse and sensitize the reader to thinking in terms of *utility* and the broader organizational context of selection decision making (Cascio & Aguinis, 2008). Such a perspective is useful for dealing with a wide range of employment decisions and for viewing organizations as open systems.

CLASSICAL APPROACH TO PERSONNEL SELECTION

As we noted earlier, individual differences provide the basic rationale for selection. To be sure, the goal of the selection process is to capitalize on individual differences in order to select those persons who possess the greatest amount of particular characteristics judged important for job success.

Figure 14-1 illustrates the selection model underlying this approach. Since we described the elements of the model in previous chapters, we will present them only in outline form here. Note that job analysis is the cornerstone of the entire selection process. On the basis of this information, one or more sensitive, relevant, and reliable criteria are selected. At the same time, one or more predictors (e.g., measures of aptitude, ability, personality) are selected that presumably bear some relationship to the criterion or criteria to be predicted. Educated guesses notwithstanding, predictors should be chosen on the basis of competent job analysis information, for such information provides clues about the type(s) of predictor(s) most likely to forecast criterion performance accurately. In the case of a predictive criterion-related validation study, once predictor measures have been selected, they are then administered to all job applicants. Such measures are *not* used in making selection decisions at this time, however; results simply are filed away and applicants are selected on the basis of whatever procedures or methods are currently being used.

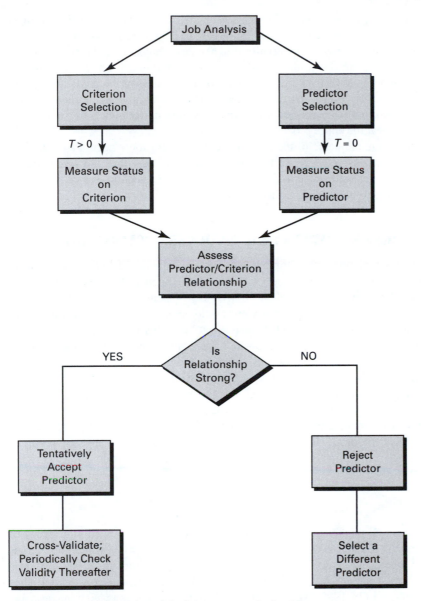

FIGURE 14-1 Traditional model of the personnel selection process.

The rationale for not using the scores on the new predictor immediately is unequivocal from a scientific point of view. Yet management, concerned with the costs of developing and administering predictor measures, often understandably wants to use the scores without delay as a basis for selection. However, if the scores are used immediately, the organization will never know how those individuals who were not selected would have performed on the job. That is, if we simply *presume* that all persons with high (low) predictor scores will perform well (poorly) on the job without evidence to support this presumption and, if we subsequently select only those with high predictor scores, we will never be able to assess the job performance of those with low scores. It is entirely possible that the unselected group might have been superior performers relative to the selected group—an outcome we could not know for sure unless we gave these individuals the chance.

Hence, criterion status is measured at some later time ($T > 0$ in Figure 14-1)—the familiar predictive-validity paradigm. Once criterion and predictor measures are available, the form and strength of their relationship may be assessed. To be sure, job-success prediction is not possible unless a systematic relationship can be established between predictor and criterion. The stronger the relationship, the more accurate the prediction. If a predictor cannot be shown to be job related, it must be discarded; but, if a significant relationship can be demonstrated, then the predictor is accepted *tentatively*, pending the computation of cross-validation estimates (empirical or formula based). It is important to recheck the validity or job relatedness of the predictor periodically (e.g., annually) thereafter. Subsequently, if a once-valid predictor no longer relates to a job performance criterion (assuming the criterion itself remains valid), discontinue using it and seek a new predictor. Then repeat the entire procedure.

In personnel selection, the name of the game is prediction, for more accurate predictions result in greater cost savings (monetary as well as social). Linear models often are used to develop predictions, and they seem well suited to this purpose. In the next section, we shall examine various types of linear models and highlight their extraordinary flexibility.

EFFICIENCY OF LINEAR MODELS IN JOB-SUCCESS PREDICTION

The statistical techniques of simple and multiple linear regression are based on the general linear model (for the case of one predictor, predicted $y = a + bx$) (cf. Appendix B). Linear models are extremely robust, and decision makers use them in a variety of contexts. Consider the typical interview situation, for example. Here the interviewer selectively reacts to various pieces of information (cues) elicited from the applicant. In arriving at his or her decision, the interviewer subjectively weights the various cues into a composite in order to forecast job success. Multiple linear regression encompasses the same process, albeit in more formal mathematical terms. Linear models range from those that use least-squares regression procedures to derive optimal weights, to those that use subjective or intuitive weights, to those that apply unit weights.

In a comprehensive review of linear models in decision making, Dawes and Corrigan (1974) concluded that a wide range of decision-making contexts have structural characteristics that make linear models appropriate. In fact, in some contexts, linear models are so appropriate that those with randomly chosen weights outperform expert judges! Consider unit weighting schemes, for example.

Unit Weighting

Unit weighting (in which all predictors are weighted by 1.0) does extremely well in a variety of contexts (Bobko, Roth, & Buster, 2007). Unit weighting also is appropriate when populations change from time to time (Lawshe & Schucker, 1959) and when predictors are combined into a composite to boost effect size (and, therefore, statistical power) in criterion-related validity studies (Cascio, Valenzi, & Silbey, 1978, 1980). These studies all demonstrate that unit weighting does just as well as optimal weighting when the weights are applied to a new sample. Furthermore, Schmidt (1971) has shown that, when the ratio of subjects to predictors is below a critical sample size, the use of regression weights rather than unit weights could result in a reduction in the size of obtained correlations. In general, unit weights perform well compared to weights derived from simple or multiple regression when sample size is small (i.e., below 75; Bobko et al., 2007).

Critical sample sizes vary with the number of predictors. In the absence of suppressor variables (discussed next), a sample of 40 individuals is required to ensure no loss of predictive power from the use of regression techniques when just two predictors are used. With 6 predictors, this figure increases to 105, and, if 10 predictors are used, a sample of about 194 is required before regression weights become superior to unit weights. This conclusion holds even when cross-validation is performed on samples from the same (theoretical) population. Einhorn and Hogarth (1975) have noted several other advantages of unit-weighting schemes: (1) they are not estimated from the data and, therefore, do not "consume" degrees of freedom; (2) they are "estimated" without error (i.e., they have no standard errors); and (3) they cannot reverse the "true" relative weights of the variables.

Nevertheless, if it is technically feasible to use regression weights, the loss in predictive accuracy from the use of equal weights may be considerable. For example, if an interview (average validity of .14) is given equal weight with an ability composite (average validity of .53) instead of its regression weight, the validity of the combination (at most .47; Hunter & Hunter, 1984) will be lower than the validity of the best single predictor!

Suppressor Variables

Suppressor variables can affect a given predictor–criterion relationship, even though such variables bear little or no direct relationship to the criterion itself. However, they *do* bear a significant relationship to the predictor. In order to appreciate how suppressor variables function, we need to reconsider our basic prediction model—multiple regression. As we note in Appendix B, the prediction of criterion status is likely to be high when each of the predictor variables $(X_1, X_2, \ldots X_n)$ is highly related to the criterion, yet unrelated to the other predictor variables in the regression equation (e.g., $r_{x_1 x_2} \to 0$). Under these conditions, each predictor is validly predicting a unique portion of criterion variance with a minimum of overlap with the other predictors (see Figure B-5).

In practice, this laudable goal is seldom realized with more than four or five predictors. Horst (1941) was the first to point out that variables that have exactly the *opposite* characteristics of conventional predictors may act to produce marked increments in the size of multiple *R*. He called such variables **suppressor variables**, for they are characterized by a lack of association with the criterion (e.g., $r_{x_1 y} = 0$) and a high intercorrelation with one or more other predictors (e.g., $r_{x_1 x_2} \to 1$) (see Figure 14-2). In computing regression weights (w) for X_1 and X_2 using least-squares procedures, the suppressor variable (X_2) receives a *negative* weight (i.e., $\hat{Y} = w_1 X_1 - w_2 X_2$); hence, the irrelevant variance in X_2 is "suppressed" by literally subtracting its effects out of the regression equation.

As an example, consider a strategy proposed to identify and eliminate halo from performance ratings (Henik & Tzelgov, 1985). Assume that p is a rating scale of some specific performance and g is a rating scale of general effectiveness designed to capture halo error. Both are used to predict a specific criterion c (e.g., score on a job-knowledge test). In terms of a multiple-regression model, the prediction of c is given by

$$\hat{c} = w_p p + w_g g$$

The ws are the optimal least-squares weights of the two predictors, p and g. When g is a classical suppressor—that is, when it has no correlation with the criterion c and a positive correlation with the other predictor, p—then g will contribute to the prediction of c only through the subtraction of the irrelevant (halo) variance from the specific performance variable, p.

In practice, suppression effects of modest magnitude are sometimes found in complex models, particularly those that include aggregate data, where the variables are sums or averages

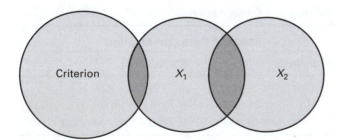

FIGURE 14-2   Operation of a suppressor variable.

of many observations. Under these conditions, where small error variance exists, Rs can approach 1.0 (Cohen, Cohen, West, & Aiken, 2003).

However, since the only function suppressor variables serve is to remove redundancy in measurement (Tenopyr, 1977), comparable predictive gain often can be achieved by using a more conventional variable as an additional predictor. Consequently, the utility of suppressor variables in prediction remains to be demonstrated.

DATA-COMBINATION STRATEGIES

Following a taxonomy developed by Meehl (1954), we shall distinguish between strategies for combining data and various types of instruments used. Data-combination strategies are *mechanical* (or statistical) if individuals are assessed on some instrument(s), if they are assigned scores based on that assessment, and if the scores subsequently are correlated with a criterion measure. Most ability tests, objective personality inventories, biographical data forms, and certain types of interviews (e.g., structured interviews) permit the assignment of scores for predictive purposes. Alternatively, predictions are *judgmental* or clinical if a set of scores or impressions must be combined subjectively in order to forecast criterion status. Assessment interviews and observations of behavior clearly fall within this category.

However, the dichotomy between judgmental and mechanical data combination does not tell the whole story. Data *collection* also may be judgmental (i.e., the data collected differ from applicant to applicant at the discretion of the collector) or mechanical (i.e., rules are prespecified so that no subjective judgment need be involved). This leads to six different prediction strategies (see Table 14-1). It is important to maintain this additional distinction in order to ensure more informed or complete comparisons between judgmental and mechanical modes of measurement *and* prediction (Sawyer, 1966).

In the **pure clinical strategy**, data are collected *and* combined judgmentally. For example, predictions of success may be based solely on an interview conducted without using any objective information. Subsequently, the interviewer may write down his or her impressions and prediction in an open-ended fashion. Alternatively, data may be collected judgmentally (e.g., via interview or observation). However, in combining the data, the decision maker summarizes his or her impressions on a standardized rating form according to prespecified categories of behavior. This is **behavior**, or **trait**, **rating**.

Even if data are collected mechanically, however, they still may be combined judgmentally. For example, a candidate is given an objective personality inventory (e.g., the California Psychological Inventory), which, when scored, yields a pattern or "profile" of scores. Subsequently, a decision maker interprets the candidate's profile without ever having interviewed or observed him or her. This strategy is termed **profile interpretation**.

On the other hand, data may be collected *and* combined mechanically (e.g., by using statistical equations or scoring systems). This **pure statistical strategy** frequently is used in the collection and interpretation of biographical information blanks, BIBs, or test batteries.

TABLE 14-1 Strategies of Data Collection and Combination

Mode of Data Collection	Mode of Data Combination	
	Judgmental	Mechanical
Judgmental	1. Pure clinical	2. Behavior rating
Mechanical	3. Profile interpretation	4. Pure statistical
Both	5. Clinical composite	6. Mechanical composite

Source: Adapted from Sawyer, J. Measurement and prediction, clinical and statistical. (1966). *Psychological Bulletin, 66,* 178–200. Copyright 1966 by the American Psychological Association. Reprinted by permission.

In the **clinical-composite strategy**, data are collected *both* judgmentally (e.g., through interviews and observations) and mechanically (e.g., through tests and BIBs), but combined judgmentally. This is perhaps the most common strategy, in which all information is integrated by either one or several decision makers to develop a composite picture and behavioral prediction of a candidate. Finally, data may be collected judgmentally and mechanically, but combined in a mechanical fashion (i.e., according to prespecified rules, such as a multiple-regression equation) to derive behavioral predictions from all available data. This is a **mechanical composite**.

Effectiveness of Alternative Data-Combination Strategies

Sawyer (1966) uncovered 49 comparisons in 45 studies of the relative efficiency of two or more of the different methods of combining assessments. He then compared the predictive accuracies (expressed either as the percentage of correct classifications or as a correlation coefficient) yielded by the two strategies involved in each comparison. Two strategies were called equal when they failed to show an accuracy difference significant at the .05 level or better. As can be seen in Table 14-2, the pure clinical method was never superior to other methods with which it was compared, while the pure statistical and mechanical composite were never inferior to other methods. A more recent review of 50 years of research reached a similar conclusion (Westen & Weinberger, 2004). In short, the mechanical methods of combining predictors were superior to the judgmental methods, *regardless* of the method used to collect predictor information.

There are several plausible reasons for the relative superiority of mechanical prediction strategies (Bass & Barrett, 1981; Hitt & Barr, 1989). First, accuracy of prediction may depend on appropriate weighting of predictors (which is virtually impossible to judge accurately). Second, mechanical methods can continue to incorporate additional evidence on candidates and thereby improve predictive accuracy. However, an interviewer is likely to reach a plateau beyond which he or she will be unable to continue to make modifications in judgments as new evidence accumulates. Finally, in contrast to more objective methods, an interviewer or judge needs to guard against his or her own needs, response set, and wishes, lest they contaminate the accuracy of his or her subjective combination of information about the applicant.

What, then, is the proper role for subjective judgment? Sawyer's (1966) results suggest that judgmental methods should be used to complement mechanical methods (since they do provide rich samples of behavioral information) in *collecting* information about job applicants, but that mechanical procedures should be used to formulate optimal ways of combining the data and producing prediction rules. This is consistent with Einhorn's (1972) conclusion that experts should be used for measurement and mechanical methods for data combination.

TABLE 14-2 Comparisons Among Methods of Combining Data

Method	Number of Comparisons	Percentage of Comparisons in Which Method Was		
		Superior	Equal	Inferior
Pure clinical	8	0	50	50
Behavior rating	12	8	76	16
Profile interpretation	12	0	75	25
Pure statistical	32	31	69	0
Clinical composite	24	0	63	37
Mechanical composite	10	60	40	0

Source: Sawyer, J. Measurement and prediction, clinical and statistical. (1966). *Psychological Bulletin, 66,* 178–200. Copyright 1966 by the American Psychological Association, Reprinted by permission of the author.

Ganzach, Kluger, and Klayman (2000) illustrated the superiority of the "expert-measurement and mechanical-combination" approach over a purely clinical (i.e., "global") expert judgment. Their study included 116 interviewers who had completed a three-month training course before interviewing 26,197 prospects for military service in the Israeli army. Each interviewer interviewed between 41 and 697 prospects using a structured interview that assessed six traits: activity, pride in service, sociability, responsibility, independence, and promptness. Interviewers were trained to rate each dimension independently of the other dimensions. Also, as part of the interview, interviewers provided an overall rating of their assessment of the expected success of each prospect. The number of performance deficiencies (i.e., disciplinary transgressions such as desertion) was measured during the soldiers' subsequent three-year compulsory military service. Then correlations were obtained between the criterion, number of deficiencies, and the two sets of predictors: (1) linear combination of the ratings for each of the six traits and (2) global rating. Results showed the superiority of the mechanical combination (i.e., $R = .276$) over the global judgment ($r = .230$). However, the difference was not very large. This is probably due to the fact that interviewers provided their global ratings after rating each of the individual dimensions. Thus, global ratings were likely influenced by scores provided on the individual dimensions.

In short, as can be seen in Table 14-2, the best strategy of all (in that it always has proved to be either equal to or better than competing strategies) is the mechanical composite, in which information is collected *both* by mechanical and by judgmental methods, but is combined mechanically.

ALTERNATIVE PREDICTION MODELS

Although the multiple-regression approach constitutes the basic prediction model, its use in any particular situation requires that its assumptions, advantages, and disadvantages be weighed against those of alternative models. Different employment decisions might well result, depending on the particular strategy chosen. In this section, therefore, we will first summarize the advantages and disadvantages of the **multiple-regression** model and then compare and contrast two alternative models—**multiple cutoff** and **multiple hurdle**. Although still other prediction strategies exist (e.g., profile matching, actuarial prediction), space constraints preclude their elaboration here.

Multiple-Regression Approach

Beyond the statistical assumptions necessary for the appropriate use of the multiple-regression model, one additional assumption is required. Given predictors $X_1, X_2, X_3, \ldots X_n$, the particular values of these predictors will vary widely across individuals, although the statistical weightings of each of the predictors will remain constant. Hence, it is possible for individuals with widely different configurations of predictor scores to obtain identical predicted criterion scores. The model is, therefore, *compensatory* and assumes that high scores on one predictor can substitute or compensate for low scores on another predictor. All individuals in the sample then may be rank ordered according to their predicted criterion scores.

If it is reasonable to assume linearity, trait additivity, and compensatory interaction among predictors in a given situation and if the sample size is large enough, then the advantages of the multiple-regression model are considerable. In addition to minimizing errors in prediction, the model combines the predictors optimally so as to yield the most efficient estimate of criterion status. Moreover, the model is extremely flexible in two ways. Mathematically (although such embellishments are beyond the scope of this chapter) the regression model can be modified to handle nominal data, nonlinear relationships, and both linear and nonlinear interactions (see Aguinis, 2004b). Moreover, regression equations for each of a number of jobs can be generated using either the same predictors (weighted differently) or different predictors. However, when the assumptions of multiple regression are untenable, then a different strategy is called for—such as a multiple-cutoff approach.

Multiple-Cutoff Approach

In some selection situations, proficiency on one predictor *cannot* compensate for deficiency on another. Consider the prediction of pilot success, for example. Regardless of his or her standing on any other characteristics important for pilot success, if the applicant is functionally blind, he or she cannot be selected. In short, when some *minimal* level of proficiency on one or more variables is crucial for job success and when no substitution is allowed, a simple or multiple-cutoff approach is appropriate. Selection then is made from the group of applicants who meet or exceed the required cutoffs on all predictors. Failure on any one predictor disqualifies the applicant from further consideration.

Since the multiple-cutoff approach is *noncompensatory* by definition, it assumes curvilinearity in predictor–criterion relationships. Although a minimal level of visual acuity is necessary for pilot success, increasing levels of visual acuity do not necessarily mean that the individual will be a correspondingly better pilot. Curvilinear relationships can be handled within a multiple-regression framework, but, in practice, the multiple-cutoff and multiple-regression approaches frequently lead to different decisions even when approximately equal proportions of applicants are selected by each method (see Figure 14-3).

In Figure 14-3, predictors X_1 and X_2 intercorrelate about .40. Both are independent variables, used jointly to predict a criterion, Y, which is not shown. Note that the multiple-regression cutoff is *not* the same as the regression line. It simply represents the minimum score necessary to qualify for selection. First, let us look at the similar decisions resulting from the two procedures. Regardless of which procedure is chosen, all individuals in area A always will be accepted, and all individuals in area R always will be rejected. Those who will be treated differently depending on the particular model chosen are in areas B, C, and D. If multiple regression is used, then those individuals in areas C and D will be accepted, and those in area B will be rejected. Exactly the opposite decisions will be made if the multiple-cutoff model is used: Those in areas C and D will be rejected, and those in area B will be accepted.

In practice, the issue essentially boils down to the relative desirability of the individuals in areas B, C, and D. Psychometrically, Lord (1962) has shown that the solution is primarily a function of the reliabilities of the predictors X_1 and X_2. To be sure, the multiple-cutoff model easily could be made less conservative by lowering the cutoff scores. But what rationale guides the selection of an appropriate cutoff score?

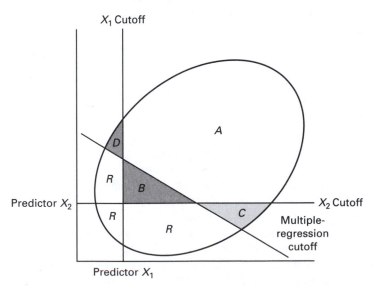

FIGURE 14-3 Geometric comparison of decisions made by multiple-regression and multiple-cutoff models when approximately equal proportions are selected by either method.

SETTING A CUTOFF   In general, no satisfactory solution has yet been developed for setting optimal cutoff scores in a multiple-cutoff model. In a simple cutoff system (one predictor), either the Angoff method (Angoff, 1971) or the expectancy chart approach is often used (both discussed below). With the latter strategy, given a knowledge of the number of positions available during some future time period (say, six months), the number of applicants to be expected during that time, and the expected distribution of their predictor scores (based on reliable local norms), a cutoff score may be set. For example, if a firm will need 50 secretaries in the next year and anticipates about 250 secretarial applicants during that time, then the selection ratio (SR) (50/250) is equal to .20.

Note that, in this example, the term *selection ratio* refers to a population parameter representing the proportion of successful applicants. More specifically, it represents the proportion of individuals in the population scoring above some cutoff score. It is equivalent to the hiring rate (a sample description) only to the extent that examinees can be considered a random sample from the applicant population and only when the sample counts infinitely many candidates (Alexander, Barrett, & Doverspike, 1983).

To continue with our original example, if the hiring rate does equal the SR, then approximately 80 percent of the applicants will be rejected. If an aptitude test is given as part of the selection procedure, then a score at the 80th percentile on the local norms plus or minus one standard error of measurement should suffice as an acceptable cutoff score.

As the *Principles for the Validation and Use of Personnel Selection Procedures* (SIOP, 2003) note:

> There is no single method for establishing cutoff scores. If based on valid predictors demonstrating linearity or monotonicity throughout the range of prediction, cutoff scores may be set as high or as low as needed to meet the requirements of the organization. . . . Professional judgment is necessary in setting any cutoff score and typically is based on a rationale that may include such factors as estimated cost-benefit ratio, number of vacancies and selection ratio, expectancy of success versus failure, the consequences of failure on the job, performance and diversity goals of the organization, or judgments as to the knowledge, skill, ability, and other characteristics required by the work. (pp. 46–47)

Based on a summary of various reviews of the legal and psychometric literatures on cutoff scores (Cascio & Aguinis, 2001, 2005; Cascio, Alexander, & Barrett, 1988; Truxillo, Donahue, & Sulzer, 1996), we offer the following guidelines:

- Determine if it is necessary to set a cutoff score at all; legal and professional guidelines do not demand their use in all situations.
- It is unrealistic to expect that there is a single "best" method of setting cutoff scores for all situations.
- Begin with a job analysis that identifies relative levels of proficiency on critical knowledge, skills, abilities, and other characteristics.
- Follow Standard 4.19 (AERA, APA, & NCME, 1999), which notes the need to include a description and documentation of the method used, the selection and training of judges, and an assessment of their variability. These recommendations are sound no matter which specific method of setting cutoff scores decision makers use.
- The validity and job relatedness of the assessment procedure are critical considerations.
- If a cutoff score is to be used as an indicator of minimum proficiency, relating it to what is necessary on the job is essential. Normative methods of establishing a cutoff score (in which a cutoff score is set based on the relative performance of examinees) do not indicate what is necessary on the job.
- When using judgmental methods, sample a sufficient number of subject matter experts (SMEs). That number usually represents about a 10 to 20 percent sample of job incumbents

and supervisors, representative of the race, gender, location, shift, and assignment composition of the entire group of incumbents. However, the most important demographic variable in SME groups is experience (Landy & Vasey, 1991). Failure to include a broad cross-section of experience in a sample of SMEs could lead to distorted ratings.

- Consider errors of measurement and adverse impact when setting a cutoff score. Thus if the performance of incumbents is used as a basis for setting a cutoff score that will be applied to a sample of applicants, it is reasonable to set the cutoff score one standard error of measurement below the mean score achieved by incumbents.
- Set cutoff scores high enough to ensure that minimum standards of performance are met. The Angoff procedure (described next) can help to determine what those minimum standards should be.

Angoff Method In this approach, expert judges rate each item in terms of the probability that a barely or minimally competent person would answer the item correctly. The probabilities (or proportions) are then averaged for each item across judges to yield item cutoff scores, which are summed to yield a test cutoff score. The method is easy to administer, is as reliable as other judgmental methods for setting cutoff scores, and has intuitive appeal because expert judges (rather than a consultant) use their knowledge and experience to help determine minimum performance standards. Not surprisingly, therefore, the Angoff method has become the favored judgmental method for setting cutoff scores on employment tests (Cascio et al., 1988; Maurer & Alexander, 1992). If the method used is to produce optimal results, however, judges should be chosen carefully based on their knowledge of the job and of the knowledge, skills, abilities, and other characteristics needed to perform it. Then they should be trained to develop a common conceptual framework of a minimally competent person (Maurer & Alexander, 1992; Maurer, Alexander, Callahan, Bailey, & Dambrot, 1991).

EXPECTANCY CHARTS   Such charts are frequently used to illustrate visually the impact of cutoff scores on future hiring decisions. **Expectancy charts** depict the likelihood of successful criterion performance for any given level of predictor scores. Figure 14-4 depicts one such chart, an *institutional* expectancy chart.

In essence, the chart provides an answer to the question "Given a selection ratio of .20, .40, .60, etc., what proportion of successful employees can be expected, if the future is like the past?" Such an approach is useful in attempting to set cutoff scores for future hiring programs. Likewise, we can draw *individual* expectancy charts that illustrate the likelihood of successful criterion performance for an individual whose score falls within a specified range on the predictor distribution.

Expectancy charts are computed directly from raw data and need not be limited to the one-variable or composite-variable case (cf. Wesman, 1966) or to discontinuous predictors

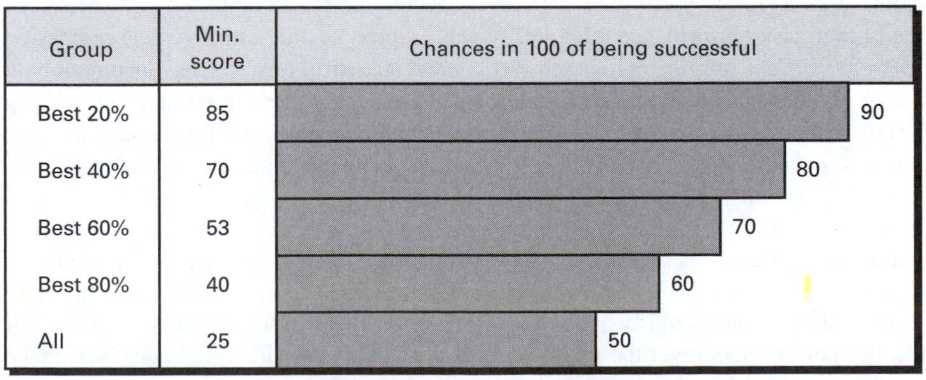

Group	Min. score	Chances in 100 of being successful
Best 20%	85	90
Best 40%	70	80
Best 60%	53	70
Best 80%	40	60
All	25	50

FIGURE 14-4 Institutional expectancy chart illustrating the likelihood of successful criterion performance at different levels of predictor scores.

(Lawshe & Bolda, 1958; Lawshe, Bolda, Brune, & Auclair, 1958). Computational procedures for developing empirical expectancies are straightforward, and theoretical expectancy charts are also available (Lawshe & Balma, 1966). In fact, when the correlation coefficient is used to summarize the degree of predictor–criterion relationship, expectancy charts are a useful way of illustrating the effect of the validity coefficient on future hiring decisions. When a test has only modest validity for predicting job performance, score differences that appear large will correspond to modest scores on the expectancy distribution, reflecting the modest predictability of job performance from test score (Hartigan & Wigdor, 1989).

Is there one best way to proceed in the multiple predictor situation? Perhaps a combination of the multiple-regression and multiple-cutoff approaches is optimal. Multiple-cutoff methods might be used initially to select individuals on those variables where certain minimum levels of ability are mandatory. Following this, multiple-regression methods then may be used with the remaining predictors to forecast criterion status. What we have just described is a multiple-hurdle or sequential approach to selection, and we shall consider it further in the next section.

Multiple-Hurdle Approach

Thus far, we have been treating the multiple-regression and multiple-cutoff models as single-stage (nonsequential) decision strategies in which terminal or final assignments of individuals to groups are made (e.g., accept/reject), regardless of their future performance. In multiple hurdle, or sequential, decision strategies, cutoff scores on some predictor may be used to make investigatory decisions. Applicants then are provisionally accepted and assessed further to determine whether or not they should be accepted permanently. The investigatory decisions may continue through several additional stages of subsequent testing before final decisions are made regarding all applicants (Cronbach & Gleser, 1965). Such an approach is particularly appropriate when subsequent training is long, complex, and expensive (Reilly & Manese, 1979).

Hanisch and Hulin (1994) used a two-stage, sequential selection procedure in a complex experimental simulation that was developed to conduct research on the tasks and job of an air traffic controller. The procedure is shown in Figure 14-5. Assessments of ability occur in stage 1 because this information is relatively inexpensive to obtain. Applicants who reach the cutoff score on the ability measures progress to Stage 2; the others are rejected. Final selection decisions are then based on Stage 1 and Stage 2 information. Stage 2 information would normally be more expensive than ability measures to obtain, but the information is obtained from a smaller, prescreened group, thereby reducing the cost relative to obtaining Stage 2 information from all applicants.

Hanisch and Hulin (1994) examined the validity of training as second-stage information *beyond* ability in the prediction of task performance. Across 12 blocks of trials, the training performance measure added an average of an additional 13 percent to the variance accounted for by the ability measures. Training performance measures accounted for an additional 32 percent of the variance in total task performance after ability was entered first in a hierarchical regression analysis. These results are significant in both practical and statistical terms. They document both the importance of ability in predicting performance and the even greater importance of training performance on similar tasks. However, in order to evaluate the *utility* of training as second-stage information in sequential selection decisions, it is necessary to compute the incremental costs and the incremental validity of training (Hanisch & Hulin, 1994).

Although it is certainly in the organization's (as well as the individual's) best interest to reach a final decision as early as possible, such decisions must be as accurate as available information will permit. Often we must pay a price (such as the cost of training) for more accurate decisions. Optimal decisions could be made by selecting on the criterion itself (e.g., actual air traffic controller performance); yet the time, expense, and safety considerations involved make such an approach impossible to implement.

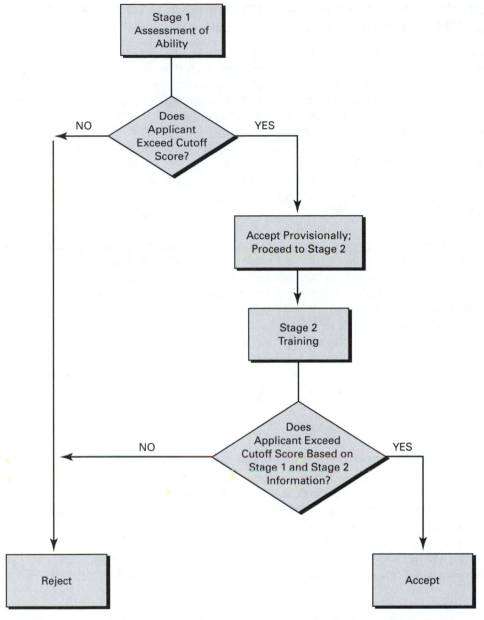

FIGURE 14-5   Two-stage sequential selection procedure used by Hanisch and Hulin (1994).

Finally, note that implementing a multiple-hurdle approach has important implications for the estimation of criterion-related validity (Mendoza, Bard, Mumford, & Ang, 2004). Specifically, when a multiple-hurdle approach is implemented, predictor scores are restricted after each stage in the selection process and, as a result, the observed validity coefficient is smaller than its population counterpart. This happens because data become increasingly restricted as applicants go through the multiple-selection stages (i.e., application forms, personality tests, cognitive ability tests, and so forth). Mendoza et al. (2004) proposed an approach, based on procedures for dealing with missing data, that allows for the estimation of what the population-level validity would be if a multiple-hurdle approach had not been used, including a confidence interval for the corrected coefficient.

EXTENDING THE CLASSICAL VALIDITY APPROACH TO SELECTION DECISIONS: DECISION-THEORY APPROACH

The general objective of the classical validity approach can be expressed concisely: The best selection battery is the one that yields the highest multiple R (the square of which denotes the proportion of variance explained in the criterion). This will minimize selection errors. Total emphasis is, therefore, placed on measurement and prediction. This approach has been criticized sharply, for it ignores certain external parameters of the situation that largely determine the overall worth of a selection instrument. Overall, there is a need to consider broader organizational issues so that decision making is not simply legal-centric and validity-centric but **organizationally sensible** (Pierce & Aguinis, 2009; Roehling & Wright, 2006). For example, in developing a new certification exam for HR professionals, we need to know not only about validity but also about its utility for individuals, organizations, and the profession as a whole (Aguinis, Michaelis, & Jones, 2005).

Taylor and Russell (1939) pointed out that utility depends not only on the validity of a selection measure but also on two other parameters: the **selection ratio (SR)** (the ratio of the number of available job openings to the total number of available applicants) and the **base rate (BR)** (the proportion of persons judged successful using current selection procedures). They published a series of tables illustrating how the interaction among these three parameters affects the **success ratio** (the proportion of selected applicants who subsequently are judged successful). The success ratio, then, serves as an operational measure of the value or utility of the selection measure. In addition to ignoring the effects of the SR and the BR, the classical validity approach makes unwarranted utility assumptions and also fails to consider the systemic nature of the selection process. On the other hand, a **decision-theory** approach considers not only validity, but also SR, BR, and other contextual and organizational issues that are discussed next.

The Selection Ratio

Whenever a quota exists on the total number of applicants that may be accepted, the SR becomes a major concern. As the SR approaches 1.0 (all applicants must be selected), it becomes *high* or unfavorable from the organization's perspective. Conversely, as the SR approaches zero, it becomes *low* or favorable, and, therefore, the organization can afford to be selective. The wide-ranging effect the SR may exert on a predictor with a given validity is illustrated in Figure 14-6 (these figures and those that follow are derived from tables developed by Taylor and Russell, 1939). In each case, C_x represents a cutoff score on the predictor. As can be seen in Figure 14-6, even predictors with very low validities can be useful if the SR is low and if an organization needs to choose only the "cream of the crop." For example, given an SR of .10, a validity of .15, and a BR of .50, the success ratio is .61. If the validity

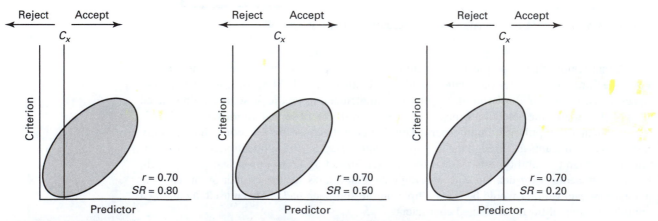

FIGURE 14-6 Effect of varying selection ratios on a predictor with a given validity.

in this situation is .30, then the success ratio jumps to .71; if the validity is .60, then the success ratio becomes .90—a 40 percent improvement over the base rate! Conversely, given high SRs, a predictor must possess substantial validity before the success ratio increases significantly. For example, given a BR of .50 and an SR of .90, the maximum possible success ratio (with a validity of 1.0) is only .56.

It might, thus, appear that, given a particular validity and BR, it is always best to decrease the SR (i.e., be more selective). However, the optimal strategy is not this simple (Law & Myors, 1993). When the HR manager must achieve a certain quota of satisfactory individuals, lowering the SR means that more recruiting is necessary. This strategy may or may not be cost-effective. If staffing requirements are *not* fixed or if the recruiting effort can be expanded, then the SR itself becomes flexible. Under these conditions, the problem becomes one of determining an **optimal cutoff score** on the predictor battery that will yield the desired distribution of outcomes of prediction. This is precisely what the expectancy chart method does.

When predictor scores are plotted against criterion scores, the result is frequently a scatter-gram similar to the one in Figure 14-7. Raising the cutoff score (c_x) decreases the probability of erroneous acceptances, but it simultaneously increases the probability of erroneous rejections. Lowering the cutoff score has exactly the opposite effect. Several authors (Cronbach & Gleser, 1965; Ghiselli, Campbell, & Zedeck, 1981; Gordon & Leighty, 1988) have developed a simple procedure for setting a cutoff score when the objective is to minimize both kinds of errors. If the frequency distributions of the two groups are plotted separately along the same baseline, the optimum cutoff score for distinguishing between the two groups will occur at the point where the two distributions intersect (see Figure 14-8).

However, as we have seen, to set a cutoff score based on the *level* of job performance deemed minimally acceptable, the Angoff method is most popular. Procedures using utility concepts and Bayesian decision theory also have been suggested (Chuang, Chen, & Novick, 1981), but we do not consider them here, since, in most practical situations, decision makers are not free to vary SRs.

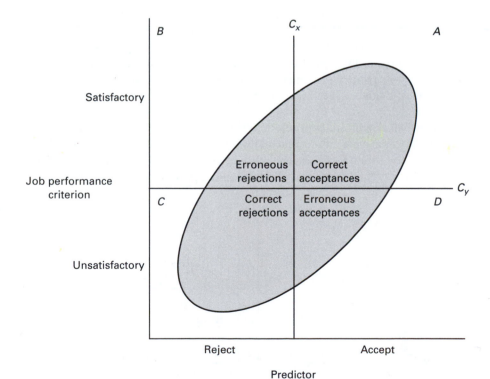

FIGURE 14-7   Selection decision–outcome combinations.

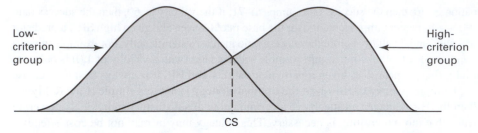

FIGURE 14-8 Procedure for setting an optimal cutoff score (CS) when the objective is to minimize both erroneous acceptances and erroneous rejections.

The Base Rate

In a classic article, Meehl and Rosen (1955) pointed out the importance of base rates in evaluating the worth of a selection measure. In order to be of any use in selection, the measure must demonstrate *incremental* validity (Murphy, 1987) by improving on the BR. That is, the selection measure must result in more correct decisions than could be made without using it. As Figure 14-9 demonstrates, the higher the BR is, the more difficult it is for a selection measure to improve on it.

In each case, c_y represents the minimum criterion standard (criterion cutoff score) necessary for success. Obviously, the BR in a selection situation can be changed by raising or lowering this minimum standard on the criterion. Figure 14-9 illustrates that, given a BR of .80, it would be difficult for *any* selection measure to improve on this figure. In fact, when the BR is .80, a validity of .45 is required in order to produce an improvement of even 10 percent over BR prediction. This is also true at very low BRs, where the objective is to predict failure (as would be the case, e.g., in the psychiatric screening of job applicants). Given a BR of .20 and a validity of .45, the success ratio is .30—once again representing only a 10 percent increment in correct decisions.

Selection measures are most useful, however, when BRs are about .50. This is because the variance of a dichotomous variable is equal to p times q, where p and q are the proportions of successes and failures, respectively. The variance is a maximum when $p = q = 0.50$. Other things being equal, the greater the variance, the greater the potential relationship with the predictor. As the BR departs radically in either direction from .50, the benefit of an additional predictor becomes questionable, especially in view of the costs involved in gathering the additional information.

The lesson is obvious: Applications of selection measures to situations with markedly different SRs or BRs can result in quite different predictive outcomes and cost-benefit ratios. When it is not possible to gain significant incremental validity by adding a predictor, then the predictor should not be used, since it cannot improve on classification of persons by the base rate.

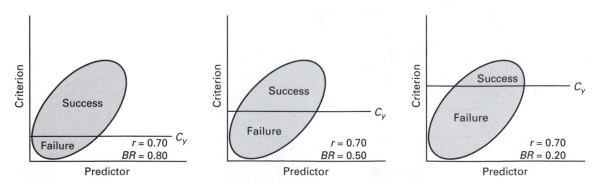

FIGURE 14-9 Effect of varying base rates on a predictor with a given validity.

Utility Considerations

Consider the four decision-outcome combinations in Figure 14-7. The classical validity approach, in attempting to maximize multiple R (and thereby minimize the number of erroneous acceptances and rejections), does not specifically take into account the varying utilities to the organization of each of the four possible outcomes. Implicitly, the classical validity approach treats both kinds of decision errors as equally costly; yet, in most practical selection situations, organizations attach different utilities to these outcomes. For example, it is much more serious to accept an airline pilot erroneously than it is to reject one erroneously. Most organizations are not even concerned with erroneous rejections, except as it costs money to process applications, administer tests, and so forth. On the other hand, many professional athletic teams spend lavish amounts of money on recruiting, coaching, and evaluating prospective players so as "not to let a good one get away."

The classical validity approach is deficient to the extent that it emphasizes measurement and prediction rather than the outcomes of decisions. Clearly the task of the decision maker in selection is to combine a priori predictions with the values placed on alternative outcomes in such a way as to maximize the purpose of the sponsoring organization.

Evaluation of the Decision-Theory Approach

By focusing only on selection, the classical validity approach neglects the implications of selection decisions for the rest of the HR system (Cascio & Boudreau, 2008). Such an observation is not new. On the contrary, over four decades ago, several authors (Dudek, 1963; Dunnette, 1962) noted that an optimal selection strategy may not be optimal for other employment functions, such as recruiting and training. In addition, other factors such as the cost of the selection procedure, the loss resulting from error, the implications for the organization's workforce diversity, and the organization's ability to evaluate success must be considered. When an organization focuses solely on selection, to the exclusion of other related functions, the performance effectiveness of the overall HR system may suffer considerably.

In short, any selection procedure must be evaluated in terms of its total benefits to the organization. Thus, Boudreau and Berger (1985) developed a utility model that can be used to assess the interactions among employee acquisitions and employee separations. Such a model provides an important link between staffing utility and traditional research on employee separations and turnover.

The main advantage of the decision-theory approach to selection is that it addresses the SR and BR parameters and compels the decision maker to consider explicitly the kinds of judgments he or she has to make. For example, if erroneous acceptances are a major concern, then the predictor cutoff score may be raised. Of course, this means that a larger number of erroneous rejections will result and the SR must be made more favorable, but the mechanics of this approach thrusts such awareness on the decision maker. While the validity coefficient provides an index of predictor–criterion association throughout the entire range of scores, the decision-theory approach is more concerned with the effectiveness of a chosen cutoff score in making a certain type of decision. The model is straightforward (see Figure 14-7), requiring only that the decision recommended by the predictor be classified into two or more mutually exclusive categories, that the criterion data be classified similarly, and that the two sets of data be compared.

One index of decision-making accuracy is the proportion of total decisions made that are correct decisions. In terms of Figure 14-7, such a proportion may be computed as follows:

$$\text{PC}_{\text{TOT}} = \frac{A + C}{A + B + C + D} \tag{14-1}$$

where PC_{TOT} is the proportion of total decisions that are correct and A, B, C, and D are the numbers of individuals in each cell of Figure 14-7. Note that Equation 14-1 takes into account all decisions that are made. In this sense, it is comparable to a predictive validity coefficient wherein all applicants are considered. In addition, observe that cells B and D (erroneous rejections and erroneous acceptances) are both weighted equally. In practice, as we noted earlier, some differential weighting of these categories (e.g., in terms of dollar costs) usually occurs. We will address this issue further in our discussion of utility.

In many selection situations, erroneous acceptances are viewed as far more serious than erroneous rejections. The HR manager generally is more concerned about the success or failure of those persons who are hired than about those who are not. In short, the organization derives no benefit from rejected applicants. Therefore, a more appropriate index of decision-making accuracy is the proportion of "accept" decisions that are correct decisions:

$$\text{PC}_{\text{ACC}} = \frac{A}{A + D} \qquad\qquad (14\text{-}2)$$

where PC_{ACC} is the proportion of those accepted who later turn out to be satisfactory and A and D represent the total number accepted who are satisfactory and unsatisfactory, respectively. When the goal of selection is to maximize the proportion of individuals selected who will be successful, Equation 14-2 applies.

The above discussion indicates that, from a practical perspective, numbers of correct and incorrect decisions are far more meaningful and more useful in evaluating predictive accuracy than are correlational results. In addition, the decision-theory paradigm is simple to apply, to communicate, and to understand.

In spite of its several advantages over the classical validity approach, the decision-theory approach has been criticized because errors of measurement are not considered in setting cutoff scores. Therefore, some people will be treated unjustly—especially those whose scores fall just below the cutoff score. This criticism is really directed at the way the cutoffs are used (i.e., the decision strategy) rather than at the decision-theory approach per se. As we noted earlier, the proper role of selection measures is as tools in the decision-making process. Cutoff scores need not (and should not) be regarded as absolute. Rather, they should be considered in a relative sense (with the standard error of measurement providing bands or confidence limits around the cutoff), to be weighted along with other information in order to reach a final decision. In short, we are advocating a sequential decision strategy in selection, where feasible.

Despite its advantages, tabulation of the number of "hits" and "misses" is appropriate only if we are predicting *attributes* (e.g., stayers versus leavers, successes versus failures in a training program), not *measurements* (such as performance ratings or sales). When we are predicting measurements, we must work in terms of *by how much*, on the average, we have missed the mark. How much better are our predictions? How much have we reduced the errors that would have been observed had we not used the information available? We compare the average deviation between fact and prediction with the average of the errors we would make without using such knowledge as a basis for prediction (Guilford & Fruchter, 1978). The **standard error of estimate** (see Appendix B) is the statistic that tells us this. However, even knowing the relative frequency of occurrence of various outcomes does not enable the decision maker to evaluate the worth of the predictor unless the utilities associated with each of the various outcomes can be specified.

SPEAKING THE LANGUAGE OF BUSINESS: UTILITY ANALYSIS

Operating executives justifiably demand estimates of expected costs and benefits of HR programs. Unfortunately, few HR programs actually are evaluated in these terms, although techniques for doing so have been available for years (Brogden, 1949; Cascio & Boudreau, 2008; Cronbach & Gleser, 1965; Sands, 1973). More often selection or promotion systems are evaluated solely in correlational terms—that is, in terms of a validity coefficient. Despite the fact that the validity coefficient alone has been shown to be an incomplete index of the value of a selection device as other parameters in the situation change, few published studies incorporate more accurate estimates of expected payoffs. However, as HR costs continue to consume larger and larger proportions of the cost of doing business, we may expect to see increased pressure on HR executives to justify new or continuing programs of employee selection. This involves a consideration of the relative utilities to the organization of alternative selection strategies.

The utility of a selection device is the *degree to which its use improves the quality of the individuals selected beyond what would have occurred had that device not been used* (Blum & Naylor, 1968). Quality, in turn, may be defined in terms of (1) the proportion of individuals in the selected group who are considered "successful," (2) the average standard score on the criterion for the selected group, or (3) the dollar payoff to the organization resulting from the use of a particular selection procedure. Earlier, we described briefly the Taylor–Russell (1939) utility model. Now, we summarize and critique two additional utility models, the Naylor and Shine (1965) model and the Brogden (1946, 1949) and Cronbach and Gleser (1965) model, together with appropriate uses of each. In addition, we address more recent developments in selection utility research, such as the integration of utility models with capital budgeting models, the perceived usefulness of utility-analysis results, multiattribute utility analysis, and the relationship between utility analysis and strategic business objectives.

The Naylor–Shine Model

In contrast to the Taylor–Russell utility model, the Naylor–Shine (1965) approach assumes a linear relationship between validity and utility. This relationship holds at all SRs. That is, given any arbitrarily defined cutoff on a selection measure, the higher the validity, the greater the increase in average criterion score for the selected group over that observed for the total group (mean criterion score of selectees minus mean criterion score of total group). Thus, the Naylor–Shine index of utility is defined in terms of the increase in average criterion score to be expected from the use of a selection measure with a given validity and SR. Like Taylor and Russell, Naylor and Shine assume that the new predictor will simply be added to the current selection battery. Under these circumstances, the validity coefficient should be based on the concurrent validity model. Unlike the Taylor–Russell model, however, the Naylor–Shine model does not require that employees be dichotomized into "satisfactory" and "unsatisfactory" groups by specifying an arbitrary cutoff on the criterion dimension that represents "minimally acceptable performance." Thus, less information is required in order to use this utility model.

The basic equation underlying the Naylor–Shine model is

$$\overline{Z}_{y_i} = r_{xy}\frac{\lambda_i}{\phi_i} \tag{14-3}$$

where $\overline{Z}_{y_i}$ is the mean criterion score (in standard score units) of all cases above the predictor cutoff; r_{xy} is the validity coefficient; λ_i is the ordinate or height of the normal distribution at the predictor cutoff, $\overline{Z}_{x_i}$ (expressed in standard score units); and ϕ_i is the SR. Equation 14-3 applies whether r_{xy} is a zero-order correlation coefficient or a multiple-regression coefficient linking the criterion with more than one predictor (i.e., R).

Using Equation 14-3 as a basic building block, Naylor and Shine (1965) present a series of tables that specify, for each SR, the standard (predictor) score corresponding to that SR, the ordinate of the normal curve at that point, and the quotient $\frac{\lambda_i}{\phi_i}$. The table can be used to answer several important questions: (1) Given a specified SR, what will be the average performance level of those selected? (2) Given a desired SR, what will $\overline{Z}_{y_i}$ be? (3) Given a desired improvement in the average criterion score of those selected, what SR and/or predictor cutoff value (in standard score units) should be used?

This model is most appropriate when differences in criterion performance cannot be expressed in dollar terms, but it can be assumed that the function relating payoff (i.e., performance under some treatment) to predictor score is linear. For example, in the prediction of labor turnover (expressed as a percentage) based on scores from a predictor that demonstrates some validity (e.g., a weighted application blank), if percentages are expressed as standard scores, then the expected decrease in the percentage of turnover can be assessed as a function of variation in the SR (the predictor cutoff score). If appropriate cost-accounting procedures are used to calculate actual turnover costs (cf. Cascio & Boudreau, 2008), expected savings resulting from reduced turnover can be estimated.

The Naylor–Shine utility index appears more applicable in general than the Taylor–Russell index because in many, if not most, cases, given valid selection procedures, an increase in average criterion performance would be expected as the organization becomes more selective in deciding whom to accept. However, neither of these models formally integrates the concept of cost of selection or dollars gained or lost into the utility index. Both simply imply that larger differences in the percentage of successful employees (Taylor–Russell) or larger increases in the average criterion score (Naylor–Shine) will yield larger benefits to the employer in terms of dollars saved.

The Brogden–Cronbach–Gleser Model

Both Brogden (1946, 1949) and Cronbach and Gleser (1965) arrived at the same conclusions regarding the effects of the validity coefficient, the SR, the cost of selection, and the variability in criterion scores on utility in fixed treatment selection. The only assumption required to use this model is that the relationship between test scores and job performance is linear—that is, the higher the test score, the higher the job performance, and vice versa. This assumption is justified in almost all circumstances (Cesare, Blankenship, & Giannetto, 1994; Coward & Sackett, 1990). If we assume further that test scores are normally distributed, then the average test score of those selected ($\overline{Z}_x$) is λ/SR, where SR is the selection ratio and λ is the height of the standard normal curve at the point of cutoff value corresponding to the SR.

When these assumptions are met, both Brogden (1949) and Cronbach and Gleser (1965) have shown that the net gain in utility from selecting N individuals is as follows:

$$\Delta U = (N)(T)(SD_y)(r_{xy})(\overline{Z}_x) - (N)(C) \tag{14-4}$$

where

ΔU = the increase in average dollar-valued payoff resulting from use of a test or other selection procedure (x) instead of selecting randomly;

T = the expected tenure of the selected group;

r_{xy} = the correlation of the selection procedure with the job performance measure (scaled in dollars) in the group of all applicants that have been screened by any procedure that is presently in use and will continue to be used;

SD_y = the standard deviation of dollar-valued job performance in the (prescreened) applicant group;

$\overline{Z}_x$ = the average standard predictor score of the selected group; and

C = the cost of testing one applicant.

Note that in this expression (SD_y) (r_{xy}) is the slope of the payoff function relating expected payoff to score. An increase in validity leads to an increase in slope, but, as Equation 14-4 demonstrates, slope also depends on the dispersion of criterion scores. For any one treatment, SD_y is constant and indicates both the magnitude and the practical significance of individual differences in payoff. Thus, a selection procedure with r_{xy} = .25 and SD_y = \$10,000 for one selection decision is just as

TABLE 14-3 Summary of the Utility Indexes, Data Requirements, and Assumptions of the Taylor–Russell, Naylor–Shine, and Brogden–Cronbach–Gleser Utility Models

Model	Utility Index	Data Requirements	Distinctive Assumptions
Taylor–Russell (1939)	Increase in percentage successful in selected group	Validity, base rate, selection ratio	All selectees classified either as successful or unsuccessful.
Naylor–Shine (1965)	Increase in mean criterion score of selected group	Validity, selection ratio	Equal criterion performance by all members of each group: cost of selection = $0.
Brogden–Cronbach–Gleser (1965)	Increase in dollar payoff of selected group	Validity, selection ratio, criterion standard deviation in dollars	Validity linearly related to utility: cost of selection = $0.

Note: All three models assume a validity coefficient based on present employees (concurrent validity).

Source: Cascio, W. F. (1980). Responding to the demand for accountability: A critical analysis of three utility models. *Organizational Behavior and Human Performance, 25*, 32–45. Copyright © 1980 with permission from Elsevier.

useful as a procedure with $r_{xy} = .50$ and SDy = $5,000 for some other decision (holding other parameters constant). Even procedures with low validity can still be useful when SDy is large. A summary of these three models is presented in Table 14-3.

Further Developments of the Brogden–Cronbach–Gleser Model

There have been technical modifications of the model (Raju, Burke, & Maurer, 1995), including the ability to treat recruitment and selection costs separately (Law & Myors, 1993; Martin & Raju, 1992). However, here we discuss three other key developments in this model: (1) development of alternative methods for estimating SDy, (2) integration of this selection-utility model with capital-budgeting models, and (3) assessments of the relative gain or loss in utility resulting from alternative selection strategies. Briefly, let's consider each of these.

ALTERNATIVE METHODS OF ESTIMATING SDy   A major stumbling block to wider use of this model has been the determination of the standard deviation of job performance in monetary terms. At least four procedures are now available for estimating this parameter, which we summarize here, along with references that interested readers may consult for more detailed information.

- *Percentile method:*   Supervisors are asked to estimate the monetary value (based on the quality and quantity of output) of an employee who performs at the 15th, 50th, and 85th percentiles. SDy is computed as the average of the differences between the 15th and 50th percentile estimates and between the 50th and 85th percentile estimates (Schmidt, Hunter, McKenzie, & Muldrow, 1979). Further refinements can be found in Burke and Frederick (1984, 1986).
- *Average-salary method:*   Because most estimates of SDy seem to fluctuate between 40 and 70 percent of mean salary, 40 percent of mean salary can be used as a low (i.e., conservative) estimate for SDy, and 70 percent of mean salary can be used as a high (i.e., liberal) estimate (Schmidt & Hunter, 1983). Subsequent work by Hunter, Schmidt, and Judiesch (1990) demonstrated that these figures are not fixed, and, instead, they covary with job complexity (the information-processing requirements of jobs).

- *Cascio–Ramos estimate of performance in dollars (CREPID):*   This method involves decomposing a job into its key tasks, weighting these tasks by importance, and computing the "relative worth" of each task by multiplying the weights by average salary (Cascio & Ramos, 1986). Then performance data from each employee are used to multiply the rating obtained for each task by the relative worth of that task. Finally, these numbers are added together to produce the "total worth" of each employee, and the distribution of all the total-worth scores is used to obtain SDy. Refinements of this procedure have also been proposed (Edwards, Frederick, & Burke, 1988; Orr, Sackett, & Mercer, 1989).
- *Superior equivalents and system effectiveness techniques:*   These methods consider the changes in the numbers and performance levels of system units that lead to increased aggregate performance (Eaton, Wing, & Mitchell, 1985). The superior equivalents technique consists of estimating how many superior (85th percentile) performers would be needed to produce the output of a fixed number of average (50th percentile) performers. The system effectiveness technique is based on the premise that, for systems including many units (e.g., employees in a department), total aggregate performance may be improved by increasing the number of employees or improving the performance of each employee. The aggregate performance improvement value is estimated by the cost of the increased number of units required to yield comparable increases in aggregate system performance (Eaton et al., 1985).

More than a dozen studies have compared results using alternative methods for estimating SDy (for a review, see Cascio & Boudreau, 2008). However, in the absence of a meaningful external criterion, one is left with little basis for choosing one method over another (Greer & Cascio, 1987). A recent review of the utility literature concluded that, when the percentile method is used, there is substantial variation among the percentile estimates provided by supervisors (Cabrera & Raju, 2001). On the other hand, results using the 40 percent of average method and the CREPID approach tend to produce similar estimates (Cabrera & Raju, 2001). In addition, when they exist, resulting differences among SDy estimates using different methods are often less than 50 percent and may be less than $5,000 in many cases (Boudreau, 1991).

It is possible that all subjective methods underestimate the true value of SDy. Using a unique set of field data, Becker and Huselid (1992) estimated SDy directly. SDy values ranged from 74 to 100 percent of mean salary—considerably greater than the 40 to 70 percent found in subjective estimates. One reason for this is that, when subjective methods are used, supervisors interpret the dollar value of output in terms of wages or salaries rather than in terms of sales revenue. However, supervisory estimates of the variability of output as a percentage of mean output (SDp) are more accurate (Judiesch, Schmidt, & Mount, 1992).

Due to the problems associated with the estimation of SDy, Raju, Burke, and Normand (1990) proposed a method that does not use this variable and instead incorporates total compensation (TC) (i.e., salary, bonuses, etc.), and SDR (i.e., standard deviation of job-performance ratings). Further research is needed to compare the accuracy of utility estimates using SDy to those using TC and SDR.

While it is tempting to call for more research on SDy measurement, another stream of research concerned with **break-even analysis** suggests that this may not be fruitful. Break-even values are those at which the HRM program's benefits equal ("are even with") the program's costs. Any parameter values that exceed the break-even value will produce positive utility. Boudreau (1991) computed break-even values for 42 studies that had estimated SDy. Without exception, the break-even values fell at or below 60 percent of the estimated value of SDy. In many cases, the break-even value was less than 1 percent of the estimated value of SDy. However, as Weekley, Frank, O'Connor, and Peters (1985) noted, even though the break-even value might be low when comparing implementing versus not implementing an HRM program, comparing HRM programs to other organizational investments might produce decision situations where differences in SDy estimates do affect the ultimate decision. Research that incorporates those kinds of contextual variables (as well as others described below) might be beneficial.

INTEGRATION OF SELECTION UTILITY WITH CAPITAL-BUDGETING MODELS   It can be shown that selection-utility models are remarkably similar to capital-budgeting models that are well established in the field of finance (Cronshaw & Alexander, 1985). In both cases, a projected stream of future returns is estimated, and the costs associated with the selection program are subtracted from this stream of returns to yield expected net returns on utility. That is:

$$\text{Utility} = \text{Returns} - \text{Costs}.$$

However, while HR professionals consider the net dollar returns from a selection process to represent the end product of the evaluation process, capital-budgeting theory considers the forecasting of dollar benefits and costs to be only the first step in the estimation of the project's utility or usefulness. What this implies is that a high net dollar return on a selection program may not produce maximum benefits for the firm. From the firm's perspective, only those projects should be undertaken that increase the market value of the firm even if the projects do not yield the highest absolute dollar returns (Brealey & Myers, 2003).

In general, there are three limitations that constrain the effectiveness of the Brogden–Cronbach–Gleser utility model in representing the benefits of selection programs within the larger firm and that lead to overly optimistic estimates of payoffs (Cronshaw & Alexander, 1985):

1. It does not take into account the time value of money—that is, the discount rate.
2. It ignores the concept of risk.
3. It ignores the impact of taxation on payoffs. That is, any incremental income generated as a result of a selection program may be taxed at prevailing corporate tax rates. This is why after-tax cash returns to an investment are often used for purposes of capital budgeting. Selection-utility estimates that ignore the effect of taxation may produce overly optimistic estimates of the benefits accruing to a selection program.

Although the application of capital-budgeting methods to HR programs has not been endorsed universally (cf. Hunter, Schmidt, & Coggin, 1988), there is a theory-driven rationale for using such methods. They facilitate the comparison of competing proposals for the use of an organization's resources, whether the proposal is to construct a new plant or to train new employees. To make a valid comparison, both proposals must be presented in the same terms—terms that measure the benefit of the program for the organization as a whole—and in terms of the basic objectives of the organization (Cascio & Morris, 1990; Cronshaw & Alexander, 1991).

HR researchers have not totally ignored these considerations. For example, Boudreau (1983a, 1983b) developed modifications of Equation 14-4 that consider these economic factors, as well as the implications of applying selection programs for more than one year for successive groups of applicants. Returns from valid selection, therefore, accrue to overlapping applicant groups with varying tenure in the organization.

To be sure, the accuracy of the output from utility equations depends on the (admittedly fallible) input data. Nevertheless, the important lesson to be learned from this analysis is that it is more advantageous and more realistic from the HR manager's perspective to consider a cash outlay for a human resource intervention as a long-term *investment*, not just as a short-term operating cost.

Application of the Brogden–Cronbach–Gleser Model and the Need to Scrutinize Utility Estimates

Utility has been expressed in a variety of metrics, including productivity increases, reductions in labor costs, reductions in the numbers of employees needed to perform at a given level of output, and levels of financial return. For example, Schmidt et al. (1979) used Equation 14-4 to estimate the impact of a valid test (the Programmer Aptitude Test) on productivity if it was used to select new computer programmers for one year in the federal government. Estimated productivity increases were presented for a variety of SRs and differences in validity between the new test and a previous procedure. For example, given an SR of .20, a difference of .46 in validity between the old and new selection procedures, 618 new hires annually, a per-person cost of testing of $10, and an average tenure of 9.69 years for computer programmers, Schmidt et al. (1979) showed that the average gain in productivity *per selectee* is $64,725 spread out over the 9.69 years. In short, millions of dollars in lost productivity can be saved by using valid selection procedures just in this one occupation.

Other studies investigated the impact of assessment centers (discussed in Chapter 13) on management performance (Cascio & Ramos, 1986; Cascio & Silbey, 1979). In the latter study, the payoff associated with first-level management assessment, given that 1,116 managers were selected and that their average tenure at the first level was 4.4 years, was over $13 million. This represents about $12,000 in improved performance per manager over 4.4 years, or about $2,700 per year in improved job performance.

In another study, Hunter and Hunter (1984) concluded that, in the case of federal entry-level jobs, the substitution of a less valid predictor for the most valid ones (ability and work sample test) would result in productivity losses costing from $3.12 billion (job tryout) to $15.89 billion (age) per year. Hiring on the basis of ability alone had a utility of $15.61 billion per year, but it affected minority groups adversely.

At this point, one might be tempted to conclude that, if top–down hiring is used, the dollar gains in performance will almost always be as high as predicted, and this would help establish the credibility (and funding) of a selection system. Is this realistic? Probably not. Here is why.

TOP SCORERS MAY TURN THE OFFER DOWN   The utility estimates described above assume that selection is accomplished in a top–down fashion, beginning with the highest-scoring applicant. In practice, some offers are declined, and lower-scoring candidates must be accepted in place of higher-scoring candidates who decline initial offers. Hence, the average ability of those *actually* selected almost always will be lower than that of those who receive the initial offers. Consequently, the actual increase in utility associated with valid selection generally will be lower than that which would be obtained if all offers were accepted.

Murphy (1986) presented formulas for calculating the average ability of those actually selected when the proportion of initial offers accepted is less than 100 percent. He showed that under realistic circumstances utility formulas currently used could overestimate gains by 30 to 80 percent. Tight versus loose labor markets provide one explanation for variability in the quality of applicants who accept job offers (Becker, 1989).

THERE IS A DISCREPANCY BETWEEN EXPECTED AND ACTUAL PERFORMANCE SCORES
When all applicants scoring above a particular cutoff point are selected, which is a common situation, the expected average predictor score of the selected applicants will decrease as the number of applicants decreases (DeCorte, 1999). Consequently, actual performance scores will also be smaller than expected performance scores as the number of applicants decreases, which is likely to reduce the economic payoff of the selection system (cf. Equation 14-3).

This is the case even if the sample of applicants is a random sample of the population because the SR will not be the same as the hiring rate (DeCorte, 1999). Consider the following example. Assume top–down selection is used and there are 10 applicants under consideration. Assume the best-scoring applicant has a score of 95, the second highest 92, and the third highest 90. Given a hiring rate of .2, the predictor cutoff can be equated either to 92 or to any value between 92 and 90, because all these choices result in the same number of selectees (i.e., 2). DeCorte (1999) provided equations for a more precise estimate of mean expected performance when samples are finite, which is the usual situation in personnel selection. The use of these equations is less likely to yield overestimates of economic payoff.

ECONOMIC FACTORS AFFECT UTILITY ESTIMATES   None of the studies described earlier incorporated adjustments for the economic factors of discounting, variable costs, and taxes. Doing so may have produced estimates of net payoffs that were as much as 70 percent smaller (Boudreau, 1988; 1991). However, in examining the payoffs derived from the validity of clerical selection procedures, where the validities were derived from alternative validity generalization methods, Burke and Doran (1989) did incorporate adjustments for economic factors. They found that, regardless of the validity generalization estimation method used, the change in utility associated with moving from the organization's current selection procedure to an alternative procedure was still sizable.

In fact, a number of factors might affect the estimated payoffs from selection programs (Cascio, 1993a). Table 14-4 is a summary of them. Incorporating such factors into the decision-making process should make utility estimates more realistic.

MANAGERS MAY NOT BELIEVE THE RESULTS   As described above, utility estimates expressed in dollar value can be very large. Do these figures help HR practitioners receive top management support for their selection programs? Recent research demonstrates that the answer is not always in the affirmative. For example, a study by Latham and Whyte (1994) supported a possible "futility of utility analysis" in some cases. In this study, 143 participants in an executive MBA program were presented with a written description of a proposed selection system in a hypothetical corporation. Results showed that managers were *less* likely to accept the proposed system and commit resources to it when presented with utility information than when presented with validity information. In other words, utility analysis *reduced* the support of managers for implementing a valid selection procedure, even though the analysis indicated that the net benefits from the new procedure were substantial. In a follow-up study, 41 managers were randomly assigned to one of the three following conditions (Whyte & Latham, 1997):

- *Group 1:*   these managers were exposed to written advice to adopt new selection procedures from a hypothetical psychologist that included an explanation of validation procedures.
- *Group 2:*   these managers were exposed to the same information as group 1 plus written support of that advice from a hypothetical trusted adviser.

TABLE 14-4 Some Key Factors that Affect Economic Payoffs from Selection Programs

Generally Increase Payoffs	Generally Decrease Payoffs	May Increase or Decrease Payoffs
Low selection ratios	High selection ratios	Changes in the definition of the criterion construct
Multiple employee cohorts	Discounting	—
Start-up costs[a]	Variable costs (materials + wages)	Changes in validity
Employee tenure	Taxes	Changes in the variability of job performance
Loose labor markets	Tight labor markets	—
	Time lags to fully competent performance	—
	Unreliability in performance across time periods	—
	Recruitment costs	—

[a]Start-up costs decrease payoffs in the period incurred, but they act to increase payoffs thereafter, because only recurring costs remain.

Source: Cascio, W. F. (1993). Assessing the utility of selection decisions: Theoretical and practical considerations. In Schmitt, N. & Borman, W. C. (Eds.), *Personnel selection in organizations* (p. 330). San Francisco: Jossey-Bass. Used by permission of John Wiley & Sons, Inc.

• *Group 3:*   these managers were exposed to the same information as group 1 plus a written explanation of utility analysis, an actual utility analysis showing that large financial benefits would flow from using the proposed procedures, and a videotaped presentation from an expert on utility analysis in which the logic underlying utility analysis and its benefits were explained.

Once again, results were not encouraging regarding the expected positive impact of utility information. On the contrary, results showed that the presentation of a positive utility analysis *reduced* support for implementing the selection procedure, in spite of the fact that the logic and merits of utility analysis were thoroughly described by a recognized expert. These results are also consistent with the view of other practicing HR specialists who have seen negative effects of using utility information in their organizations. For example, Tenopyr (2002) noted that she "simply stopped doing the analyses because of the criticism of high utility estimates" (p. 116).

Steven Cronshaw was the individual who served as the expert in the Whyte and Latham (1997) study and provided an alternative explanation for the results. Cronshaw (1997) argued that the hypothesis tested in the Whyte and Latham (1997) study was not the informational hypothesis that utility information would affect decisions regarding the selection system, but instead a persuasional hypothesis. That is, Cronshaw offered the explanation that his videotaped presentation "went even beyond coercion, into intimidating the subjects in the utility condition" (p. 613). Thus, the expert was seen as attempting to sell the selection system as opposed to serving in an advisory role. Managers resisted such attempts and reacted negatively to the utility information. So Cronshaw (1997) concluded that "using conventional dollar-based utility analysis is perilous under *some* conditions" (p. 614). One such condition seems to be when managers perceive HR specialists as trying to sell their product (internally or externally) as opposed to using utility information as an aid in making an investment decision.

Carson, Becker, and Henderson (1998) examined another boundary condition for the effectiveness of utility information in gaining management support for a selection system. They conducted two studies, the first one including 145 managers attending an executive MBA program at three different universities and the second one including 186 students (in MBA and executive MBA programs) from six universities. The first noteworthy finding is that results did not replicate those found by Latham and Whyte (1994), although the exact same scenarios were used. Unfortunately, it is not clear why results differed. Second, when information was presented in a way that was easier to understand, the addition of utility information *improved* the acceptability of the selection procedures. In short, a second boundary condition for the effectiveness of utility information is the manner in which such information is presented. When information is presented in a user-friendly manner (i.e., when the presentation is made shorter and easier to comprehend by minimizing technical jargon and computational details), utility information can have a positive effect. The same conclusion was reached by a separate study in which managers were more accepting of utility results involving the computation of SD_y based on the simpler 40 percent of average salary procedure as opposed to the more involved CREPID method (Hazer & Highhouse, 1997). To be sure, more research is needed on the impact of how, and how much, utility information is presented on management decisions and acceptability of selection systems.

UTILITY AND USEFULNESS   Aguinis and Harden (2004) noted that conducting a traditional utility analysis does not answer the key question of whether the use of banding decreases the usefulness of a selection instrument. Even if the result of the Brogden–Cronbach–Gleser model is adjusted by using some of the factors described earlier, this utility model continues to focus on a single central factor: the correlation coefficient between test scores and job performance (i.e., criterion-related validity coefficient). It is a "single-attribute" utility analysis, and focuses exclusively on quantitative data and ignores qualitative data (cf. Jereb, Rajkovic, & Rajkovic, 2005).

Instead, as described in Chapter 8 briefly, multiattribute utility analysis (Aguinis & Harden, 2004; Roth & Bobko, 1997) can be a better tool to assess a selection system's usefulness to an organization. A multiattribute utility analysis includes not only the Brogden–Cronbach–Gleser result but also information on other desired outcomes such as increased diversity, cost reduction in minority recruitment, organizational flexibility, and an organization's public image. Thus, a multiattribute utility analysis incorporates the traditional single-attribute utility estimate, but goes beyond this and also considers key strategic business variables at the group and organizational levels. Also, such an approach combines quantitative and qualitative data (Jereb et al., 2005). This can be particularly useful when organizations need to choose between two selection systems or two types of assessments. For example, Hoffman and Thornton (1997) faced a situation in which an assessment center produced a slightly lower validity and cost about 10 times as much per candidate as using an aptitude test, but the assessment center produced less adverse impact. Multiattribute utility analysis can help make the decision of whether the use of the assessment center may, nevertheless, be more useful than the aptitude test.

Another advantage of multiattribute utility analysis is that it involves the participation of various stakeholders in the process. Participation on the part of management in the estimation of utility provides a sense of ownership of the data, but, more often than not, management is presented with a final result that is not easy to understand (Rauschenberger & Schmidt, 1987). The mere presentation of a final (usually very large) dollar figure may not convince top management to adopt a new selection system (or other HR initiative, such as training). On the other hand, multiattribute analysis includes the various organizational constituents likely to be affected by a new selection system, such as top management, HR, and in-house counsel, who, for example, may have a different appreciation for a system that, in spite of its large utility value expressed in dollars, produces adverse impact. For more on this approach, see Aguinis and Harden (2004).

THE STRATEGIC CONTEXT OF PERSONNEL SELECTION

While certain generic economic objectives (profit maximization, cost minimization) are common to all private-sector firms, strategic opportunities are not, and they do not occur within firms in a uniform, predictable way (Ansoff, 1988). As strategic objectives (e.g., economic survival, growth in market share) vary, so also must the "alignment" of labor, capital, and equipment resources. As strategic goals change over time, assessment of the relative contribution of a selection system is likely also to change. The Brogden–Cronbach–Gleser approach is deficient to the extent that it ignores the strategic context of selection decisions; and it assumes that validity and SDy are constant over time, when, in fact, they probably vary (Russell, Colella, & Bobko, 1993). As Becker and Huselid (1992) noted, even if the effect of employee performance on organizational output is relatively stable over time, product market changes that are beyond the control of employees will affect the economic value of their contribution to the organization.

To be more useful to decision makers, therefore, utility models should be able to provide answers to the following questions (Russell et al., 1993):

- Given all other factors besides the selection system (e.g., capitalization, availability of raw materials), what is the expected level of performance generated by a manager (ΔU per selectee)?
- How much of a gain in performance can we expect from a new performance system (ΔU for a single cohort)?
- Are the levels of performance expected with or without the selection system adequate to meet the firm's strategic needs (ΔU computed over existing cohorts and also expected new cohorts of employees)?
- Is the incremental increase in performance expected from selection instrument A greater than that expected from instrument B?

Russell et al. (1993) presented modifications of the traditional utility equation (Equation 14-4) to reflect changing contributions of the selection system over time (validity and *SDy*) and changes in what is important to strategic HR decision makers (strategic needs).

Such modifications yield a more realistic view of how firms benefit from personnel selection. They may also overcome some of the skepticism that operating managers understandably express toward "raw" (unmodified) estimates of the economic value of valid selection procedures (Latham & Whyte, 1994).

Evidence-Based Implications for Practice

- The classical validity approach to employee selection emphasizes measurement accuracy and predictive efficiency. Within this framework, use multiple regression to forecast job success. In some situations, however, compensatory models are inappropriate, and, thus, use noncompensatory models (such as multiple cutoff or multiple hurdle).
- The classical validity approach is incomplete, for it ignores the effects of the selection ratio and base rate, makes unwarranted utility assumptions, and fails to consider the systemic nature of the selection process. Thus, use decision theory, which forces the decision maker to consider the utility of alternative selection strategies, as a more suitable alternative.
- The Taylor–Russell, Naylor–Shine, and Brogden–Cronbach–Gleser utility models can provide useful planning information to help managers make better informed and wiser HR decisions. However, the consideration of single-attribute utility analysis, which focuses mainly on the validity coefficient, may not be sufficient to convince top management regarding the value added of a proposed selection system. Consider strategic business issues by conducting a multiattribute utility analysis.

The last few chapters focused on "buying talent" through selection. The next two chapters address the issue of "building talent" internally through the training and development of employees who have already been hired. A sensible balance between buying and building talent is likely to result in a successful workforce.

Discussion Questions

1. Critique the classical validity approach to employee selection.
2. What happens to our prediction models in the presence of a suppressor variable?
3. Describe the circumstances under which sequential selection strategies might be superior to single-stage strategies.
4. Why are clinical decision-making processes not as accurate as mechanical processes?
5. What is the role of human judgment in selection decisions?
6. How might an expectancy chart be useful to a decision maker?
7. Cite two examples to illustrate how the selection ratio and base rate affect judgments about the usefulness of a predictor.
8. Why, and under what conditions, can utility estimates be detrimental to the implementation of a new selection system?
9. What are the main differences between single-attribute and multiattribute utility analyses? What are the relative advantages and disadvantages of each method?
10. Provide examples of strategic business outcomes that can be included in a multiattribute utility analysis.

15

Training and Development: Considerations in Design

At a Glance

Training and development imply changes—changes in skill, knowledge, attitude, or social behavior. Although there are numerous strategies for effecting changes, training and development are common and important ones.

Training and development activities are planned programs of organizational improvement, and it is important that they be planned as thoroughly as possible, for their ultimate objective is to link training content to desired job behaviors. This is a five-step process. First, conduct a comprehensive analysis of the training and development system, including its interaction with other organizational systems. Then determine training needs and specify training objectives clearly and unambiguously. The third step is to create an optimal environment for training, decomposing the learning task into its structural components, and the fourth is to determine an optimum sequencing of the components. Finally, consider alternative ways of learning. Careful attention to these five steps helps to determine what is to be learned and what the substantive content of training and development should be.

Various theoretical models can help guide training and development efforts. These include the individual differences model, principles of learning and transfer, motivation theory, goal setting, and behavior modeling. Each offers a systematic approach to training and development, and each emphasizes a different aspect of the training process. Any single model, or a combination of models, can yield maximum payoff, however, only when programs are designed to match accurately targeted training needs.

Change, growth, and development are bald facts of organizational life. Consider downsizing as an example. In 2008 alone, France, Russia, Britain, Japan, India, and China shed more than 21 million jobs (Thornton, 2009). In the United States, more than 3.2 million people lost their jobs from December, 2007 through March, 2009 (Da Costa, 2009). At the same time as firms are firing some people, however, they are hiring others, presumably people with the skills to execute new strategies. As companies lose workers in one department, they are adding people with different skills in another, continually tailoring their workforces to fit the available work and adjusting quickly to swings in demand for products and services (Cascio, 2002a; Goodman & Healy, 2009). In addition to incessant change, modern organizations face other major challenges (2008 HR Trend Book; "Developing Business Leaders for 2010," 2003; Noe, 2008; Tannenbaum, 2002):

- *Hypercompetition*—such competition, both domestic and international, is largely due to trade agreements and technology (most notably, the Internet). As a result, senior executives will be required to lead an almost constant reinvention of business strategies/models and organizational structures.

- *A power shift to the customer*—customers who use the Internet have easy access to data-bases that allow them to compare prices and examine product reviews; hence, there are ongoing needs to meet the product and service needs of customers.
- *Collaboration across organizational and geographic boundaries*—in some cases, suppliers are collocated with manufacturers and share access to inventory levels. Outsourcing, the geographical dispersion of work, and strategic international alliances often lead to new organizational forms that involve multinational teams. Organizations must therefore address cultural and language issues, along with new approaches to collaboration (Cascio, 2008).
- *The need to maintain high levels of talent*—since products and services can be copied, the ability of a workforce to innovate, refine processes, solve problems, and form relationships becomes an organization's only sustainable advantage. Attracting, retaining, and develop-ing people with critical competencies is vital for success.
- *Changes in the workforce*—unskilled and undereducated youth will be needed for entry-level jobs, and currently underutilized groups of racial and ethnic minorities, women, and older workers will need training. At the same time, as the members of the baby boom gen-eration retire, the transfer of knowledge to those who remain will become a priority.
- *Changes in technology*—increasingly sophisticated technological systems impose train-ing and retraining requirements on the existing workforce.
- *Teams*—as more firms move to employee involvement and teams in the workplace, team members need to learn such behaviors as asking for ideas, offering help without being asked, listening and providing feedback, and recognizing and considering the ideas of others (Salas & Cannon-Bowers, 2001; Salas, Burke, & Cannon-Bowers, 2002).

Indeed, as the demands of the information age spread, companies are coming to regard training expenses as no less a part of their capital costs than plants and equipment (Mattioli, 2009). The American Society for Training and Development estimates that U.S. organizations spend $126 billion annually on employee training and development (Paradise, 2007). At the level of the individual firm, Google, rated by *Fortune* magazine as the #1 best employer to work for in America in 2008 and #4 in 2009, is exemplary. It offers each employee 100 hours of professional training per year (Levering & Moskowitz, 2008, 2009). What's the bottom line in all of this? Organizations that provide superior opportunities for learning and growth have a distinct advan-tage when competing for talented employees (Buckingham & Coffman, 1999; O'Brien, 2009).

These trends suggest a dual responsibility: The organization is responsible for providing an atmosphere that will support and encourage change, and the individual is responsible for deriving maximum benefit from the learning opportunities provided. This may involve the acquisition of new information, skills, attitudes, or patterns of social behavior through training and development.

Change can, of course, be effected through a variety of other methods as well: replacement of poor performers; imposition of controls (e.g., budgets, sign-off procedures, or close supervision); reorganization of individual job assignments; use of participative decision making; bargaining; or outright coercion, either social or physical. In short, training is not necessarily the *only* alternative available for enhancing the person/job organization match, and it is narrow-minded to view it as an elixir for all performance problems. Training and development are important managerial tools, but there are limits to what they can accomplish.

In view of the considerable amount of time, money, and effort devoted to these activities by organizations, we shall consider some important issues in training and development in this and the following chapter. Primarily we will emphasize the *design* of training and development pro-grams, the *measurement* of the outcomes of these efforts, and the *interaction* of training outcomes with other organizational subsystems. We place substantially less emphasis on specific training methods and techniques.

Both training and development entail the following general properties and characteristics (Goldstein & Ford, 2002; Kraiger, 2003; Noe, 2008):

1. Training and development are learning experiences.
2. They are planned by the organization.
3. They occur after the individual has joined the organization.
4. They are intended to further the organization's goals.

Training and development activities are, therefore, planned programs of organizational improvement undertaken to bring about a relatively permanent change in employee knowledge, skills, attitudes, or social behavior. The term *training* generally refers to activities directed toward the acquisition of knowledge, skills, and attitudes for which there is an immediate or near-term application (e.g., introduction of a new process). The term *development*, on the other hand, refers to the acquisition of attributes or competencies for which there may be no immediate use.

We include the phrase "relatively permanent" in the definition of training and development to distinguish learning from performance. The distinction is principally a temporal one. Learning is a relatively permanent change in behavior that occurs as a result of practice or experience (not simple maturation). Learning is the ability to perform; it is available over a long period of time. Performance, on the other hand, refers to the *demonstration* of learning—it is observable, measurable behavior from which we *infer* learning. Performance is often a function of the individual's physical or mental state. For example, if an individual is fatigued, temporarily unmotivated, or distracted because of some environmental condition—noise, commotion, anxiety—he or she may not perform well in a given situation. The person is, therefore, unable to demonstrate all that he or she has *learned*. These conditions are more likely to affect short-run performance than long-term learning.

To be sure, a great deal of learning takes place in organizations—from peers, superiors, and subordinates. Some of this learning is planned and formally sanctioned by the organization, but much of it is serendipitous, unplanned, and informal (e.g., learning from someone who has the "inside track"). In fact, a study by the Center for Workforce Development of 1,000 employees in various organizations reported that up to 70 percent of workplace learning is informal (Pfeffer & Sutton, 2000; see also McCall, 2004). The critical aspect of our definition of training and development is that it implies that training results must be defined in terms of measurable change either in individual states (knowledge, attitudes) or in individual performance (skills, social behavior). The definition is necessarily broad and includes simple programs of skill training, as well as complex, systemwide programs of organizational development.

TRAINING DESIGN

We begin this section by examining organizational and individual characteristics related to effective training. Then we consider fundamental requirements of sound training practice: defining what is to be learned and the interaction of training and development with the broader organizational environment, determining training needs, specifying training objectives, and creating an optimal environment for training.

Characteristics of Effective Training

If done well, training and development lead to sustained changes that can benefit individuals, teams, organizations, and society (Aguinis & Kraiger, 2009). Surveys of corporate training and development practices have found consistently that four characteristics seemed to distinguish companies with the most effective training practices (2008 HR Trend Book; "Developing Business Leaders for 2010," 2003):

• Top management is committed to training and development; training is part of the corporate culture. This is especially true of leading big companies, such as Google, Disney,

Accenture, and Marriott, and also of leading small- and medium-sized companies, like Kyphon and Triage Consulting (Grossman, 2006).

* Training is tied to business strategy and objectives and is linked to bottom-line results.
* Organizational environments are "feedback rich"; they stress continuous improvement, promote risk taking, and afford opportunities to learn from the successes and failures of one's decisions.
* There is commitment to invest the necessary resources, to provide sufficient time and money for training.

Does top management commitment really matter? Absolutely. For example, meta-analysis indicates that, when management-by-objectives is implemented with high commitment from top management, productivity gains are five times higher than when commitment is low (Rodgers & Hunter, 1991). A subsequent meta-analysis found that job satisfaction increases about a third of a standard deviation when top management commitment is high—and little or not at all when top management commitment is low or moderate (Rodgers, Hunter, & Rogers, 1993).

Additional Determinants of Effective Training

Evidence indicates that training success is determined not only by the quality of training, but also by the interpersonal, social, and structural characteristics that reflect the relationship of the trainee and the training program to the broader organizational context. Variables such as organizational support, as well as an individual's readiness for training, can enhance or detract from the direct impact of training itself (Aguinis & Kraiger, 2009; Colquitt, LePine, & Noe, 2000). Figure 15-1 shows a model of training effectiveness developed by Noe and Colquitt (2002). The model shows that individual characteristics (including trainability—that is, the ability to learn the content of the training—personality, age, and attitudes) influence motivation, learning, transfer of training back to the job, and job performance. Features of the work environment (climate, opportunity to perform trained tasks, manager support, organizational justice, and individual versus team context) also affect each stage of the training process. The model, therefore, illustrates that characteristics of the individual, as well as of the work environment, are critical factors before training (by affecting motivation), during training (by affecting learning), and after training (by influencing transfer and job performance).

Admittedly, some of the individual characteristics, such as trainability and personality, are difficult, if not impossible, for organizations to influence through policies and practices. The organization clearly can influence others, however. These include, for example, job or career attitudes, pretraining self-efficacy (a person's belief that he or she can learn the content of the training successfully), the valence of training (the attractiveness of training outcomes), and the work environment itself (Quiñones, 1997; Switzer, Nagy, & Mullins, 2005).

Fundamental Requirements of Sound Training Practice

As an instrument for change, the potential of the training and development enterprise is awesome. To reach that potential, however, it is important to resist the temptation to emphasize technology and techniques; instead, define first what is to be learned and what the substantive content of training and development should be (Campbell, 1971, 1988). One way to do this is to view training and development as a network of interrelated components. After all, training is an activity that is embedded within a larger organizational context (Aguinis & Kraiger, 2009; Quiñones, 1995, 1997). Figure 15-2 shows such a model.

Program development comprises three major phrases, each of which is essential for success: a needs assessment or *planning* phase, a training and development or *implementation* phase, and an *evaluation* phase. In brief, the needs-assessment phase serves as the foundation for the entire program, for, as Figure 15-2 shows, subsequent phases depend on inputs from it.

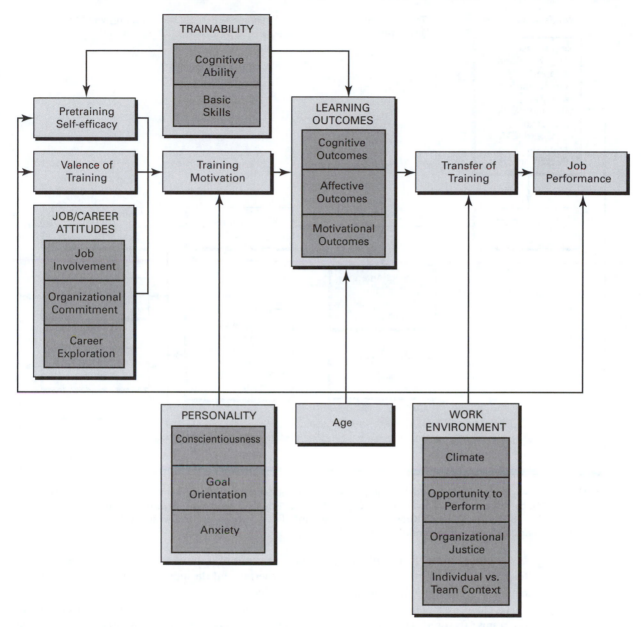

FIGURE 15-1 A model of individual and work environment characteristics influencing learning and transfer of training. *Source:* Noe, R. A. and Colquitt, J. A. (2002). Planning for training impact: Principles of training effectiveness. In Kraiger, K. (Ed.), *Creating, implementing, and managing effective training and development* (pp. 60–61). San Francisco: Jossey-Bass. Used by permission of John Wiley & Sons, Inc.

If needs assessment is incomplete, the training that actually is implemented may be far out of tune with what an organization really needs.

Having specified instructional objectives, the next task is to design the training environment in order to achieve the objectives. This is the purpose of the training and development phase—"a delicate process that requires a blend of learning principles and media selection, based on the tasks that the trainee is eventually expected to perform" (Goldstein & Ford, 2002, p. 28). We will have more to say on this topic later in the chapter. If assessment and implementation have been done carefully, the evaluation should be straightforward. Evaluation (Chapter 16)

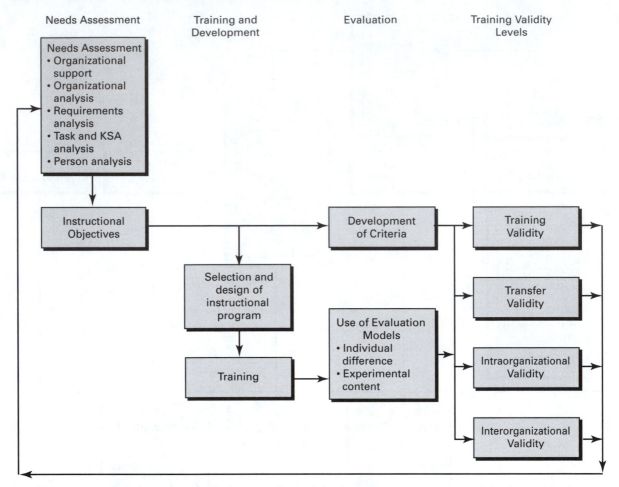

Needs Assessment

Training and Development

Evaluation

Training Validity Levels

FIGURE 15-2 A general systems model of the training and development process. From Training in organizations (4th ed., p. 24), by Goldstein, I. L. and Ford, J. K. Copyright © 2001 by Wadsworth Inc. Reprinted by permission of Brooks/Cole Publishing Co., Pacific Grove, CA 93950. Reprinted with permission from Wadsworth, a division of Thomson Learning: www.thomsonrights.com Fax 800 730 2215

is a twofold process that involves establishing measures of training and job-performance success (criteria), and using experimental and quasi-experimental designs to determine what changes have occurred during the training and transfer process.

There are a number of different designs that can be used to assess the outcomes of training programs. To some extent, the choice of design(s) depends on the questions to be asked and the constraints operating in any given situation. The last column of Figure 15-2 lists a number of possible training goals:

1. *Training validity.* Did trainees learn anything during training?
2. *Transfer validity.* To what extent did the knowledge, skills, abilities, or other characteristics (KSAOs) learned in training lead to improved performance on the job?
3. *Intraorganizational validity.* Is the performance of a new group of trainees in the same organization that developed the training program similar to the performance of the original training group?
4. *Interorganizational validity.* Can a training program that "works" in one organization be used successfully in another organization?

These questions often result in different evaluation models or, at the very least, different forms of the same evaluation model (Kraiger, 2002; Mattson, 2003; Wang & Wilcox, 2006). Evaluation, therefore, should provide continuous closed-loop feedback that can be used to reassess instructional needs, thereby creating input for the next stage of development. The purpose of Figure 15-2 is to provide a model that can help to organize the material in Chapters 15 and 16. Let us begin by defining what is to be learned.

Defining What Is to Be Learned

There are six steps in defining what is to be learned and what the substantive content of training and development should be:

1. Analyze the training and development subsystem and its interaction with other systems.
2. Determine the training needs.
3. Specify the training objectives.
4. Decompose the learning task into its structural components.
5. Determine an optimal sequencing of the components.
6. Consider alternative ways of learning.

Our overall goal—and we must never lose sight of it—is to link training content to desired job behaviors. This is consistent with the modern view of the role of the trainer, which represents a change from focusing on training per se to focusing on performance improvement (Tannenbaum, 2002; Tyler, 2008).

The Training and Development Subsystem

Training and development operate in a complex organizational milieu. Failure to consider the broader organizational environment often contributes to programs that either result in no observable changes in attitudes or behavior or, worse yet, produce negative results that do more harm than good. As an example, consider what appears at first glance to be a simple question—namely, "Whom do we train?"

Traditionally, the pool of potential trainees was composed of an organization's own employees. Today, however, organizational boundaries are blurring, such that the border between customers, suppliers, and even competitors is becoming fuzzier. As a result, *any* individual or group that has a need to acquire specific capabilities to ensure an organization's success is a potential candidate for training (Cascio, in press).

If a company relies on its suppliers to ensure customer satisfaction and the supplier fails to fulfill its obligations, everyone suffers. For this reason, some organizations now train their suppliers in quality-management techniques. To appreciate the importance and relevance of this approach, consider how Dell Computer operates.

BOX 15-1

Dell Computer—Integrator Extraordinaire

Dell prospers by remaining perfectly clear about what it is and what it does. "We are a really superb product integrator. We're a tremendously good sales-and-logistics company. We're not the developer of innovative technology" (Topfer, in Morris, 2000, p. 98). Dell sells IBM-compatible personal computers in competition with HP–Compaq, Apple, and Sony. While others rely primarily on computer stores or dealers, Dell sells directly to consumers, who read about the products on the company's Web page, in newspaper ads, or in catalogs. A buyer either orders online or calls a toll-free number and places an order with a staff of well-trained salespeople.

Dell doesn't build a zillion identical computers, flood them out to retailers, and hope you like what you see. Instead, it waits until it has your custom order (and your money), and then it orders components from suppliers and assembles the parts. At its OptiPlex factory in Austin, Texas, 84 percent of orders are built, customized, and shipped within eight hours. Some components, like the monitor or speakers, may be sent directly from the supplier to your home (never passing through Dell) and arrive on your doorstep at the same time as everything else (O'Reilly, 2000).

This same logic may also extend to individual customers. Providing them with information about how to use products and services most effectively increases the chances that they will get the best value from the product and builds their trust and loyalty. Technology-delivered instruction (via Web, PDA, or MP3 player) provides easier access for customers and suppliers (Welsh, Wanberg, Brown, & Simmering, 2003). It has made training economically feasible to provide to individuals outside an organization's own employees.

Unfortunately, training does not always lead to effective behaviors and enhanced organizational results. One reason for this is lack of alignment between training and an organization's strategic direction—that is, a failure to recognize that training and development are part of broader organizational systems ("Developing Business Leaders for 2010," 2003). To promote better alignment, organizations should do three things (Tannenbaum, 2002): (1) For any important change or organizational initiative, it is important to identify what new capabilities will be needed, how they compare to current capabilities, and what steps are necessary to bridge the gap. (2) Leaders should periodically seek to identify key strategic capabilities that will be needed as the organization goes forward. (3) Training organizations should compare their current programs and services against the organization's strategic needs.

Recognition of the interaction of training with other organizational processes is necessary, but not sufficient, for training and development efforts to succeed. Three other conditions must be present: The individual must be capable of learning new material ("can do"), he or she must be motivated to learn it ("will do"), and those individuals who exert influence over him or her must support the development effort. A key element of any such effort is the careful identification of training needs.

Assessing Training Needs

It has been said often that, if you don't know where you are going, any road will get you there; *but,* if you do know where you are going, you will get there sooner. This is especially true of training and development efforts. The purpose of needs assessment is to determine if training is necessary *before* expending resources on it.

Kraiger (2003) noted three important points about needs assessment. First, across multiple disciplines, it is perceived as an essential starting point in virtually all instructional-design models. Second, despite its assumed importance, in practice, many training programs do not use it. A recent, large-scale meta-analysis of training effectiveness found that only 6 percent of the studies analyzed reported any needs assessment prior to training implementation (Arthur, Bennett, Edens, & Bell, 2003). Third, in contrast to other areas of training, there is very little ongoing research or theory with respect to needs assessment.

Having said that, we noted earlier that pretraining motivation is an important determinant of training success. Motivation increases as adults perceive the training as relevant to their daily activities, and a thorough needs assessment that includes experienced subject-matter experts should be able to demonstrate the value of training before it actually begins, lower trainees' anxiety about training, and enhance organizational support for transfer of training back to the job (Goldstein & Ford, 2002; Klein, Noe, & Wang, 2006).

Many methods have been proposed for uncovering specific training needs—that is, the components of job performance that are relevant to the organization's goals and the enhancement of which through training would benefit the organization (Campbell, 1988; Goldstein & Ford, 2002). In general, they may be subsumed under the three-facet approach described in McGehee and Thayer's (1961) classic text on training. These are *organization analysis* (identification of where training is needed within the organization), *operations analysis* (identification of the content of the training), and *person analysis* (identification of who needs training and of what kind is needed). Each of these facets contributes *something*, but, to be most fruitful, all three must be conducted in a continuing, ongoing manner and at all three levels: at the organization level, with managers who set its goals; at the operations level, with managers who specify how the organization's goals are going to be achieved; and at the individual level, with managers and workers who do the work and achieve those goals.

These three managerial levels are but three possible populations of individuals. In fact, needs analysis done at the policy level based on different populations is called *demographic analysis* (Latham, 1988), and it should be added to the traditional trichotomy of organization, job, and person analyses. This broader schema is shown in Figure 15-3. We now describe various portions of Figure 15-3 in greater detail.

As Figure 15-3 demonstrates, an important consideration in the needs-assessment process is the external environment, and especially the economic and legal constraints, such as environmental requirements or new laws that may affect the objectives of training programs. The next step is organization analysis.

Organization Analysis

The purpose of organization analysis is to link strategic workforce-planning considerations (see Chapter 10) with training needs-assessment results. Another objective is to pinpoint inefficient organizational units to determine whether training is the appropriate antidote to performance problems. The important question is "Will training produce changes in employee behavior that will contribute to the organization's goals?" If that connection cannot be made, then the training is probably not necessary. A final objective is to estimate the extent of organizational support for the application of what is learned in training to actual performance on the job—that is, transfer of training.

Demographic Analysis

Demographic analysis can be helpful in determining the special needs of a particular group, such as workers over 40, women on expatriate assignments, or managers at different levels. Those needs may be specified at the organizational level, at the business-unit level, or at the individual level (Goldstein & Ford, 2002). With respect to managers, for example, level, function, and attitudes toward the usefulness of training have small, but significant, effects on the self-reported training needs of managers (Ford & Noe, 1987).

Demographic analysis deserves treatment in its own right because the information it provides may transcend particular jobs, and even divisions of an organization. Taking this information into account lends additional perspective to the job and person analyses to follow.

Operations Analysis

Operations analysis requires a careful examination of the work to be performed after training. It involves (1) a systematic collection of information that describes how work is done, (2) determination of standards of performance for that work, (3) how tasks are to be performed to meet the standards; and (4) the competencies necessary for effective task performance. To ensure the collection of valid data, seek the opinions of managers and subordinates close to the scene of operations (Aguinis & Kraiger, 2009). After all, they know the jobs best. In addition, their involvement helps build *commitment* to the training effort. It is important to ensure, however, that all raters have the experience and self-confidence to provide meaningful data (Ford, Smith, Sego, & Quiñones, 1993).

For jobs that are complex, are dynamic, and have high-stakes outcomes (e.g., pilots, accident investigation teams), cognitive task analysis (CTA) may be appropriate (Dubois, 2002). CTA differs from traditional task analysis in that it focuses explicitly on identifying the mental aspects of performance—activities such as decision making, problem solving, pattern recognition, and situational assessment—that are not directly observable. Conventional task analysis seeks to identify what gets done, while CTA focuses on the details of how it gets done—cues, decisions, strategies, and goals. CTA can be a useful supplement to traditional methods to identify cognitive tasks and knowledge requirements that are difficult to describe using standard procedures.

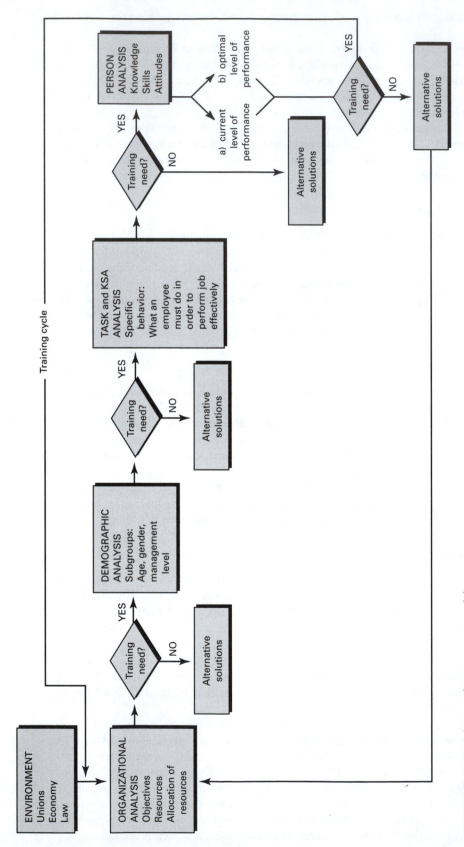

FIGURE 15-3 Training needs-assessment model.

An emerging trend is the use of competency models to drive training curricula. A competency is a cluster of interrelated knowledge, skills, values, attitudes, or personal characteristics that are presumed to be important for successful performance on the job (Noe, 2008). Once validated, an organization-specific competency model may be used for a variety of purposes: to design training programs or personal-development plans, 360-degree performance appraisals, long-term staffing plans, or screening-and-selection tools (Kraiger, 2003).

Person Analysis

Having identified the kinds of characteristics required to perform effectively on the job, emphasis shifts to assessing how well each employee actually performs his or her job, relative to standards required by the job. This is the purpose of person analysis (Goldstein & Ford, 2002). In the rapidly changing environments that many organizations face today, along with demands for "better, cheaper, faster" products and services, performance standards also change. An important aspect of person analysis, therefore, is to determine whether training can fill that gap or whether other interventions, such as new hiring strategies, job redesign, or some combination of strategies, should be used.

One procedure that links individual or team behavior directly to performance standards is that of critical incidents (see Chapter 5). Critical incidents are recorded on the job as they happen, usually by the immediate supervisor. For example, Foley (1969) determined the effective behaviors of retail sales employees by collecting critical incidents from customers. He collected more than 2,000 incidents, categorized them, and made them the basis for training in customer service. When 360-degree feedback is used in performance appraisal (cf. Chapter 5) or when developmental assessment information is fed back to candidates, they serve the same purpose—namely, they are vehicles for identifying training needs and linking them directly to individual or team behavior.

Individual Development Plans (IDPs)

One especially fruitful approach to the identification of individual training needs is to combine behaviorally based performance-management systems with IDPs derived from self-analysis. IDPs provide a road map for self-development, and should include

1. *Statements of aims*—desired changes in knowledge, skills, attitudes, values, or relationships with others.
2. *Definitions*—descriptions of areas of study, search, reflection, or testing, including lists of activities, experiences, or questions that can help achieve these aims.
3. *Ideas about priorities*—feelings of preference or urgency about what should be learned first.

Individuals often construct their own IDPs, with assistance, in career-planning workshops, through structured exercises, in the practice of management by objectives, or in assessment centers. They provide a blueprint for self-development.

As a result of needs assessment, it should be possible to determine what workers do, what behaviors are essential to do what they do effectively, what type of learning is necessary to acquire those behaviors, and what type of instructional content is most likely to accomplish that type of learning (Goldstein, 1989; Goldstein & Ford, 2002). This kind of information should guide all future choices about training methods and evaluation strategies.

Training Objectives

Specification of training objectives (i.e., what is to be learned) becomes possible once training and development needs have been identified. This is *the* fundamental step in training design (Blanchard & Thacker, 2007; Campbell, 1988). Such objectives define what the learner should be able to do after finishing the program that he or she could not do before it. Objectives are stated either in behavioral or in operational terms. Behavioral objectives refer to actions, movements, or behaviors that are observable and measurable. Each objective should describe (1) the desired behavior, (2) the conditions under which the behavior should occur, and (3) the standards by which the trainee's behavior is to be judged (Mager, 1984). For example, consider a behavioral objective for a training program for civil engineering students:

> In a two-hour test following the last week of training [conditions under which behavior should occur], the student will be able to list the sequence of steps involved in building an on-ramp to a highway, specifying the standards for completion of each step [desired behavior]. All steps must be included in the correct order, and the standards for completion must match those in the textbook [success criteria].

Objectives also may be stated in operational or end-result terms. For example, it is one thing to have an objective to "lower production costs." It is quite another thing to have an objective to "lower the costs of producing Model 600 lawn sprinklers 15 percent by April 30, by having one operator execute all operations using computer-controlled machinery." The latter is a much more specific statement of what the objective actually is and how it will be reached. In addition, the more precise the statement is, the easier it is to assess its contribution to successful operations. "To lower costs 15%" makes it possible to determine what changes in price or increases in profits can be anticipated as a result of the introduction of computer-controlled machinery. The end result of training, of course, is the successful execution of all operations by a single operator.

It is important to understand the "action" component of objectives, and what it implies. Many of the crucial mediating factors of management performance are attitudes; yet it is difficult to demonstrate the link between attitudes and job performance (Cascio & Boudreau, 2008). This also is true of improvements in decision-making skills—another prime focus of management training ("Needed," 2003). Operationally, we are interested in the characteristics of the end results or behaviors that permit us to *infer* the type of mental activity that produced them. Hence, we emphasize observable actions. If trainers were not concerned with bringing about changes in individuals or groups, they would not have to bother looking at behavior—but they do bear that responsibility, and cannot shirk it.

Creating an Optimal Environment for Training and Learning

Having specified training objectives, the next task is to design the training environment in order to achieve the objectives. Summarizing existing research, Noe and Colquitt (2002) identified seven features of the learning environment that facilitate learning and transfer:

- Trainees understand the objectives of the training program—the purpose and outcomes expected.
- Training content is meaningful. Examples, exercises, assignments, concepts, and terms used in training are relevant.
- Trainees are given cues that help them learn and recall training content, such as diagrams, models, key behaviors, and advanced organizers.
- Trainees have opportunities to practice.
- Trainees receive feedback on their learning from trainers, observers, video, or the task itself.
- Trainees have the opportunity to observe and interact with other trainees.
- The training program is properly coordinated and arranged.

In terms of coordination, a classic paper by Gagné (1962) offered three psychological principles that are useful in training design:

1. Any human task may be analyzed into a set of component tasks that are quite distinct from each other in terms of the operations needed to produce them.

2. These task components are mediators of the final task performance; that is, their presence ensures positive transfer to a final performance, and their absence reduces such transfer to near zero.

3. The basic principles of training design consist of (a) identifying the component tasks of a final performance, (b) ensuring that each of these component tasks is fully achieved, and (c) arranging the total learning situation in a sequence that will ensure optimal mediational effect from one component to another (p. 88).

In this framework, "what is to be learned" is of signal importance. Successful final performance on a task depends on first attaining competence on the various subtasks that compose it. In short, it appears that there is a *more efficient* and a *less efficient* sequence that can be arranged for the learning of a procedural task (i.e., a task composed of at least two component tasks), and this sequence involves learning each subtask before undertaking the total task. Gagné's ideas were based on a great deal of research on skill learning in the military. Subsequent reviews of the empirical evidence lend considerable support to the validity of these principles (Gagné, 1967, 1977; Gagné & Briggs, 1979; Gagné & Rohwer, 1969). A similar approach may be used to design training programs that attempt to change knowledge or attitudes.

Gagné recognized that these principles are necessary, but not sufficient, conditions for learning. As noted earlier, a variety of individual and work-environment characteristics affect learning and transfer (Noe & Colquitt, 2002). Here is an illustration. Tracey, Hinkin, Tannenbaum, and Mathieu (2001) collected data from 420 hotel managers who attended a two-and-a-half-day managerial knowledge and skills training program. Results showed that managers' job involvement, organizational commitment, and perceptions of the work environment (i.e., perceived support and recognition) predicted pretraining self-efficacy, which, in turn, was related to pretraining motivation. Pretraining motivation was related to posttraining measures of utility reactions, affective reactions, declarative-knowledge scores, and procedural-knowledge scores.

Computer-based training offers another opportunity to illustrate the effects of individual differences. With computer-based training, the learner typically has more control than in traditional, instructor-led training. The learner makes choices about the level and focus of effort to exert, and specifically regarding the amount of practice to engage in, the amount of time to spend on task, and the level of attention to devote to the learning opportunity.

Based on a study of 78 employees taking a training course delivered by an intranet, Brown (2001) found considerable variability among trainees in their level of practice and time on task, both of which predicted knowledge gain. Learners who elected to skip materials or to move quickly reduced their knowledge gain. Thus, employees who learn most from this type of training environment are those who complete more of the practice opportunities made available to them and who take more time to complete the experience.

The answer to the question "Why do employees learn?" is that they invest effort and time in the learning opportunity (Brown, 2001). Regardless of the instructional features embedded in a program, it will work only through deliberate cognitive processing by the learner. Accordingly, computer-based training should be designed to promote active learning by trainees. Trainees demonstrating active learning are motivated, mastery-oriented, and mindful (Brown & Ford, 2002; Hira, 2007). The specification of objectives and the creation of an optimal environment for training are essential features of sound training design. So also is careful attention to the determinants of effective team performance, assuming teams are relevant to a given situation.

This concludes our treatment of training design. Before we consider theoretical models to guide training and development efforts, however, we pause to examine a topic of special and growing importance—team training.

Team Training

As part of the changing nature of work, there has been an increasing emphasis on team performance (Sundstrom, McIntyre, Halfhill, & Richards, 2000). More than 80 percent of U.S.

corporations use teams of one sort or another (Vella, 2008). A *team* is a group of individuals who are working together toward a common goal (Blum & Naylor, 1968). It is this common goal that really defines a team, and, if two team members have opposite or conflicting goals, the efficiency of the total unit is likely to suffer. For example, consider the effects on a baseball team when one of the players *always* tries to hit home runs, regardless of the team's situation.

Clearly, individual training cannot do the whole job; we need to address interactions among team members. These interactions make team training unique—it always uses some form of simulation or real-life practice and always focuses on the interactions of team members, equipment, and work procedures (Bass, 1980; Colvin, 2006). While the notion of team-based work is attractive, we hasten to add that simply placing a task (e.g., monitoring air traffic or command and control) within a team context may not improve overall performance (Hollenbeck, Ilgen, Tuttle, & Sego, 1995). Nevertheless, there are many situations where teams are appropriate and where their special training can make an important difference in performance.

Researchers (Cannon-Bowers, Tannenbaum, Salas, & Volpe, 1995; Salas et al., 2002; Salas & Cannon-Bowers, 2000) have developed a systematic approach to team training that includes four steps.

1. ***Conduct a team-training needs analysis.*** Such an analysis has two objectives: (a) to identify interdependencies among team members and the skills required to master coordination of team tasks and (b) to identify the cognitive skills and knowledge needed to interact as a team (e.g., knowledge of team member roles and responsibilities).
2. ***Develop training objectives that address both taskwork and teamwork skills.*** In general, a core set of skills characterizes effective teamwork. These include adaptability, shared awareness of situations, performance monitoring and feedback, leadership/team management, interpersonal skills, coordination, communication, and decision-making skills. Attitudinal skills that characterize effective teamwork include belief in the importance of teamwork skills, belief in placing the team's goals above those of individual members, mutual trust, and shared vision (Cannon-Bowers et al., 1995). Sequence the training so that trainees can master taskwork skills before learning teamwork skills (Salas et al., 2002).
3. ***Design exercises and training events based on the objectives from Step 2.*** As with individual training, opportunities for guided practice and constructive feedback are particularly important for team training (Salas et al., 2002). Strategies for doing this include the following:
   • Team-coordination training (focusing on teamwork skills that facilitate information exchange, cooperation, and coordination of job-related behaviors),
   • Cross-training (providing exposure to and practice with other teammates' tasks, roles, and responsibilities in an effort to increase shared understanding and knowledge among team members), and
   • Guided team self-correction (providing guidance to team members in reviewing team events, identifying errors and exchanging feedback, and developing plans for the future).
4. ***Design measures of team effectiveness based on the objectives set at Step 2, evaluate the effectiveness of the team training, and use this information to guide future team training.*** Important constructs to evaluate include collective efficacy, shared knowledge structures, team situational awareness, and shared mental models (Kraiger, 2003).

A popular intervention that uses these principles is Crew Resource Management (CRM) training, usually conducted using sophisticated flight simulators. Its purpose is to improve team communication and team effectiveness, and therefore aviation safety, among aircrews. Evidence across more than 50 studies shows positive benefits in terms of improved communication and performance (Aguinis & Kraiger, 2009), but CRM seems to be more effective in aviation settings than in health care settings, where its application is more recent (Salas, Wilson, & Burke, 2006).

A second important finding is that managers of effective work groups tend to monitor the performance of their team members regularly, and they provide frequent feedback to them (Jose, 2001; Komaki, Desselles, & Bowman, 1989). In fact, as much as 35 percent of the variability in team performance can be explained by the frequency of use of monitors and consequences. Incorporating these findings into the training of team members and their managers should lead to better overall team performance.

THEORETICAL MODELS TO GUIDE TRAINING AND DEVELOPMENT EFFORTS

Once we have specified behavioral objectives, created an optimal environment for training, and determined the optimum sequencing for learning subtasks, there remains one additional problem: how to acquire the appropriate responses. This is an important question to consider because different people have their own favorite ways of learning. For example, suppose Susan wants to learn a new skill, such as photography. She might begin by checking out three books on the topic from her local library. Alternately, Nancy might sign up for a photography class at a local school because she wants to experience it, not just to read about it. Finally, Nicole might just begin to take pictures, experimenting in a trial-and-error fashion until she gets the result she is looking for.

Susan, Nancy, and Nicole each prefer different learning methods. Susan prefers verbal learning, Nancy opts for kinesthetic (hands-on) learning, and Nicole chooses trial-and-error experiential learning. These are not the only methods; other people learn best from visual material (pictures, charts, graphs) or from vicarious experience (watching others).

The growing popularity of various forms of technology-delivered instruction offers the opportunity to tailor learning environments to individuals (Brown & Ford, 2002; Kraiger & Jerden, 2007). It also transfers more control to learners about what and how to learn, but that may have a negative effect, especially among low-ability or inexperienced learners (DeRouin, Fritzsche, & Salas, 2004). One promising technique to counter that effect is to supplement learner control with adaptive guidance. Specifically, Bell and Kozlowski (2002) concluded that providing adaptive guidance in a computer-based training environment substantively improved trainees' study and practice effort, knowledge acquired, and performance. Findings such as these are extremely useful, for they help guide the training through the implementation phase. Let us begin by considering a model of learning based on individual differences.

Trainability and Individual Differences

Individual differences in abilities, interests, and personality play a central role in applied psychology. Variables such as prior achievement and initial skill level ("can do" factors), along with training expectations ("will do" factors), should be effective predictors of training performance. Available evidence indicates that they are (Gordon & Cohen, 1973; Robertson & Downs, 1979, 1989). In fact, general mental ability alone predicts success in training in a wide variety of jobs (Colquitt et al., 2000; Ree & Earles, 1991). So also does trainability.

Trainability refers to a person's ability to acquire the skills, knowledge, or behavior necessary to perform a job at a given level and to achieve these outcomes in a given time (Robertson & Downs, 1979). It is a combination of an individual's ability and motivation levels. Meta-analyses based on independent samples and using different predictor–criterion pairs (sample sizes of 2,542 and 2,772) showed that in most situations work-sample trainability tests are valid predictors of training performance, more so than for job performance (Robertson & Downs, 1989).

In order to study more precisely the behavioral transitions that occur in learning or training, however, we need to establish a behavioral baseline for each individual. Behavioral baselines result from each individual's prior history. The major advantage of this approach is that each individual's initial state serves as his or her own control. Bass, Cascio, McPherson, and Tragash (1976) used this procedure in a training program designed to cope with problems of race in the working environment. In order to assess changes in attitude *after* training, a behavioral baseline first was established for each of more than 2,000 subjects by having them complete a statistically derived attitude questionnaire *prior* to training. Unfortunately, however, a great deal of training research ignores the concept of the behavioral baseline and the measurement of initial state.

Adaptive training is a logical extension of this idea (Cronbach & Snow, 1977). In adaptive training, methods are varied to suit the abilities and characteristics of the trainees. In terms of training design, this suggests that we should measure the existing achievement levels of potential trainees and then tailor training content accordingly. Adaptive training is as appropriate for human relations training as it is for skill training.

Training-effectiveness research has renewed interest in individual aptitudes, attitudes, and personality characteristics as determinants of training outcomes (Aguinis & Kraiger, 2009; Baldwin & Magjuka, 1997; Colquitt & Simmering, 1998; Martocchio & Judge, 1997). If trainee attitudes and personal characteristics predict main effects in training, it seems logical to explore the interactions of these factors with specific instructional methods (Kraiger, 2003). Regardless of the medium used to deliver training, however, and regardless of its specific content, if the program is to be successful, trainers must pay careful attention to how trainees learn. Application of the classic principles of learning is essential.

PRINCIPLES THAT ENHANCE LEARNING

If training and development are to have any long-term benefit, then efficient learning, long-term retention, and positive transfer to the job situation are essential. Hence, it is not surprising that the principal theoretical basis for training in organizations has been the "learning principles" developed over the past century. The principles do not stand alone, but rather must be integrated with other considerations, such as the factors identified in the training-effectiveness model (Figure 15-1), thorough task and competency analyses, and optimum sequencing, to make the overall training experience effective. In view of their importance, we shall highlight several learning principles, paying special attention to their practical implementation.

Knowledge of Results (Feedback)

Information about one's attempts to improve is essential for learning to occur. Knowledge of results (KR) provides information that enables the learner to correct mistakes (as long as the learner is told *why* he or she is wrong and *how* he or she can correct the behavior in the future) and reinforcement (which makes the task more intrinsically interesting, thereby motivating the learner). KR may be intrinsic (i.e., stemming directly from the performance of the task itself) or extrinsic (i.e., administered by an outside individual). It may be qualitative ("that new ad is quite pleasing to the eye"), quantitative ("move the lever two inches down"), informative ("that new machine just arrived"), or evaluative ("you did a good job on that report—it was clear and brief").

As we noted in Chapter 5, findings generally show that the presence of KR improves performance (Ilgen, Fisher, & Taylor, 1979; Martocchio & Webster, 1992; Stajkovic & Luthans, 2003), but managers often misperceive its effects. Thus, Greller (1980) found that supervisors consistently underestimated the importance subordinates attach to feedback from the task itself, comparisons to the work of others, and coworkers' comments. They overestimated the importance of formal rewards, informal assignments, and comments from the boss.

Consider eight important research findings in this area:

1. KR often results from the performers themselves proactively seeking, interpreting, and generating information (Herold & Parsons, 1985). This is more likely to occur when employees suspect the existence of a problem in their work that challenges their self-image as good, competent performers (Larson, 1989).

2. When managers attribute poor performance to lack of effort by a subordinate, they are likely to use a problem-solving approach in communicating performance feedback (two-way communication). However, when managers attribute poor performance to the subordinate's lack of ability, they are more likely to use a "tell-and-sell" approach (one-way communication). Only the problem-solving approach leads to changes in behavior (Dugan, 1989).

3. More KR may not always be better. A 10-month field study of the behavioral safety performance of factory employees found that providing KR once every two weeks was about as effective as providing it once a week (Chhokar & Wallin, 1984). In addition, the level of specificity of feedback should vary (Goodman & Wood, 2004). Increasing the specificity of feedback benefits the learning of responses for good performance, but it may be detrimental to the learning of responses for poor performance.

4. Immediate feedback may not be appropriate for all learners. Withholding feedback from more experienced learners can help them think more critically about their own performance, and, as a result, improve retention and generalization. In short, provide immediate feedback to novices and less frequent feedback to experienced learners (Brown & Ford, 2002; Schmidt & Bjork, 1992).

5. The impact of KR on performance is not always positive; it depends on the *type* of KR involved. Only KR that attributes prior performance to causes within the trainee's control and that explains *why* performance was effective/ineffective and what specifically needs to be done to improve performance will be useful (Jacoby, Mazursky, Troutman, & Kuss, 1984; Martocchio & Dulebohn, 1994).

6. To be accepted by performers as accurate, KR should include positive information first, followed by negative information (not vice versa) (Stone, Gueutal, & McIntosh, 1984). When providing performance feedback on more than one dimension, allow employees the freedom to choose feedback on each dimension to reduce the possibility of redundancy and to minimize the amount of time they need to receive and evaluate feedback (Ilgen & Moore, 1987).

7. KR can help improve performance over and above the level achieved with *only* training and goal setting. In other words, to bring about genuine improvements in performance, present training, goal setting, and feedback as a package (Chhokar & Wallin, 1984).

8. Feedback affects group, as well as individual, performance. For example, application of performance-based feedback in a small fast-food store over a one-year period led to a 15 percent decrease in food costs and to a 193 percent increase in profits (Florin-Thuma & Boudreau, 1987). Another study, conducted in five organizational units at an Air Force base, applied feedback for five months, then goal setting for five months, and finally incentives for five months (all in an additive fashion). Results indicated that group-level feedback increased productivity an average of 50 percent over baseline, group goal setting increased it 75 percent over baseline, and group incentives increased it 76 percent over baseline. Control-group data showed no or only a slight increase over the same time period, and the level of employees either stayed the same or decreased. Work attitudes were as good or better following the interventions (Pritchard, Jones, Roth, Stuebing, & Ekeberg, 1988).

The trainee's immediate supervisor is likely to provide the most powerful KR. If he or she does not reinforce what is learned in training, however, the results of training will transfer ineffectively to the job, if at all.

Transfer of Training

To a great extent, the usefulness of organizational training programs depends on the effective transfer of training—the application of behaviors learned in training to the job itself. Transfer may be positive (i.e., improve job performance), negative (i.e., hamper job performance), or neutral. It probably is the single most important consideration in training and development programs

(Baldwin & Ford, 1988). At the same time, a recent meta-analysis of 107 evaluations of management training revealed that there were substantial effects in the size of training-transfer effects across rating sources (Taylor, Russ-Eft, & Taylor, 2009). In particular, the sole use of trainees' self-ratings in an evaluation of training transfer may lead to an overly optimistic assessment of transfer, whereas the sole use of subordinate ratings may lead to an overly pessimistic view of the impact of training on managers' job behavior. The use of multiple rating sources with different perspectives (supervisors, peers, subordinates, and self-ratings) is necessary to provide a more realistic assessment of transfer effects.

To maximize positive transfer, while recognizing that transfer environments are probably unique to each training application (Holton, Chen, & Naquin, 2003), designers of training programs should consider doing the following before, during, and after training (Machin, 2002):

1. Ensure that the transfer climate and work environment are positive—that is, situations and actions convey the support of supervisors and peers for the transfer of training, as well as the value the organization places on training (Kontoghiorghes, 2004). The influence of workplace support on transfer is moderated, however, by the extent to which trainees identify with the groups providing support (Pidd, 2004).
2. Maximize the similarity between the training situation and the job situation.
3. Provide trainees as much experience as possible with the tasks, concepts, or skills being taught so that they can deal with situations that do not fit textbook examples exactly. This is adaptive expertise (Ford & Weissbein, 1997; Hesketh, 1997a).
4. Ensure that trainees thoroughly understand the principles being taught, particularly in jobs that require the *application* of principles to solve problems, such as those of engineers, investment analysts, or systems analysts.
5. Provide a strong link between training content and job content ("What you learn in training today, you'll use on the job tomorrow").
6. In the context of team-based training (e.g., in employee involvement), transfer is maximized when teams have open, unrestricted access to information; when the membership includes diverse job functions and administrative backgrounds; and when a team has sufficient members to draw on to accomplish its activities. In one study, over half the variance in participant and supervisor ratings of team effectiveness could be attributed to those three design elements (Magjuka & Baldwin, 1991).
7. Ensure that what is learned in training is used and rewarded on the job. Supervisors and peers are key gatekeepers in this process (Ford, Quiñones, Sego, & Sorra, 1992; Pidd, 2004). If immediate supervisors or peers, by their words or by their example, do not support what was learned in training, don't expect the training to have much of an impact on job performance (Tannenbaum, 2002; Tracey, Tannenbaum, & Kavanagh, 1995; Wexley & Latham, 2002).

The attitudes of trainees may also affect transfer (Noe, 1986, 2008; Switzer et al., 2005). Transfer is likely to be higher when trainees (1) are confident in using their newly learned skills, (2) are aware of work situations where they can demonstrate their new skills, (3) perceive that both job and organizational performance will improve if they use the new skills, and (4) believe that the knowledge and skills emphasized in training are helpful in solving work-related problems. Such attitudes help employees generalize KSAOs learned in one training context (e.g., employee-involvement training) to other contexts (e.g., regular job duties) (Tesluk, Farr, Mathieu, & Vance, 1995).

Self-Regulation to Maintain Changes in Behavior

Self-regulation is a novel approach to the maintenance of newly trained behaviors (Schmidt & Ford, 2003). Although it was developed originally in the context of addictive behaviors (Marx, 1982; Witkiewitz & Marlatt, 2004), it has implications for maintaining newly trained behaviors as well. Self-regulation refers to the extent to which executive-level cognitive systems in the learner monitor and exert control on the learner's attention and active engagement of training content (Vancouver & Day 2005).

Training programs usually stress the positive results for participants; they usually do not make participants aware of how the training process itself is vulnerable to breakdown. In this model, trainees are asked to pinpoint situations that are likely to sabotage their attempts to maintain new learning (Marx, 1982). For example, in a study designed to control the abuse of sick leave (Frayne & Latham, 1987), employees listed family problems, incompatibility with supervisor or coworkers, and transportation problems as the most frequent reasons for using sick leave. Then employees were taught to self-monitor their behavior, for example, by recording (1) their own attendance, (2) the reason for missing a day of work, and (3) steps followed subsequently to get to work. Employees did this using charts and diaries.

Trainees also identified their own reinforcers (e.g., self-praise, purchasing a gift) and punishers (a disliked activity, easily self-administered, such as cleaning one's garage) to administer as a result of achieving or failing to achieve their near-term goals. Application of this system of self-regulation increased the self-efficacy of trainees, and their attendance was significantly higher than that of a control group. This effect held over a 12-month follow-up period (Latham & Frayne, 1989). In fact, self-regulation training may provide trainees who are low in self-efficacy with a skill-development-and-maintenance program that they would not otherwise undertake due to low self-confidence (Gist, Stevens, & Bavetta, 1991). Despite its demonstrated effectiveness (Chen, Thomas, & Wallace, 2005), other studies (Gaudine & Saks, 2004; Huint & Saks, 2003) suggest that transfer climate and peer and supervisor support are more powerful determinants of transfer than self-regulation in maintaining desired behaviors after training.

Adaptive Guidance

Related to self-management, adaptive guidance is designed to provide trainees with information about future directions they should take in sequencing study and practice in order to improve their performance (Bell & Kozlowski, 2002). It is particularly relevant to technology-based learning. For example, in Web-based training, individuals can use hyperlinks and menus to customize the material to which they attend, determine the sequence by which they learn, and control the amount of time they spend on a particular topic. In distance-learning applications, individuals can participate in learning at their convenience and with little or no supervision. Such learner control may be associated with a number of negative outcomes, such as less time spent on task and poor learning strategies (Brown, 2001).

In a laboratory study, Bell and Kozlowski (2002) adapted the guidance presented to trainees based on their performance in a training situation (below the 50th percentile, between the 50th and 85th percentiles, and above the 85th percentile). The guidance included evaluative information to help each trainee judge his or her progress and individualized suggestions about what the trainee should study and practice to improve.

Adaptive guidance had substantial impacts on self-regulation process indicators and on the sequence of trainees' study and practice. It yielded significant improvements in the acquisition of basic knowledge and performance capabilities early in training, in the acquisition of strategic knowledge and performance skills later in training, and in the capacity to retain and adapt skills in a more difficult and complex generalization situation. Adaptive guidance holds promise as an effective training strategy and also as a means for guiding individuals through advanced-technology training applications (Bell & Kozlowski, 2002).

Reinforcement

In order for behavior to be acquired, modified, and sustained, it must be rewarded (reinforced). The principle of reinforcement also states that punishment results in only a temporary suppression of behavior and is a relatively ineffective influence on learning. Reward says to the learner, "Good, repeat what you have done" and punishment says, "Stop, you made the wrong response."

Mild punishment may serve as a warning for the learner that he is getting off the track, but, unless it is followed immediately by corrective feedback, punishment can be intensely frustrating.

In practice, it is difficult to apply this principle, especially the specification *prior* to training of what will function as a reward. Will it be praise from the trainer, a future promotion or salary increase, supervisory or peer commendation, or heightened feelings of self-determination and personal worth? Clearly there are numerous sources from which rewards may originate, but, as we have seen, the most powerful rewards may be those provided by the trainee's immediate supervisor and peers (Pidd, 2004). If they do not reinforce what is learned in training, then the training itself will be "encapsulated" (Haire, 1964), and transfer will be minimal or negative.

Practice

For anyone learning a new skill or acquiring factual information, there must be an opportunity to practice what is being learned. Practice refers to the active use of training content. It has three aspects: active practice, overlearning, and the length of the practice session.

Active Practice

Particularly during skills learning (e.g., learning to operate a machine), it simply is not enough for a trainee to verbalize or to read what he or she is expected to do. Only active practice provides the internal cues that regulate motor performance. As their practice continues and as they are given appropriate feedback, trainees discard inefficient motions and retain the internal cues associated with smooth and precise performance. This is a traditional approach that focuses on teaching correct methods and avoiding errors. Error-management training, however, is an alternative approach (Keith & Frese, 2005) whose objective is to encourage trainees to make errors and then to engage in reflection to understand their causes and to identify strategies to avoid making them in the future. Meta-analysis (Keith & Frese, 2008) reported that overall, error-management training was superior both to error-avoidant training and to exploratory training without error encouragement ($d = .44$). Effect sizes were greater, however, for posttransfer measures and for tasks that were not similar to those encountered in training. Error training might therefore facilitate a deeper understanding of tasks that facilitates transfer to novel tasks (Aguinis & Kraiger, 2009).

Overlearning

If trainees are given the opportunity to practice far beyond the point where they perform a task correctly several times, the task becomes "second nature"—they have overlearned it. For some tasks, such as those that must be performed infrequently and under great stress (e.g., CPR performed by a nurse to save a patient's life), overlearning is critical. It is less important in jobs where workers practice their skills on a daily basis, such as auto mechanics, technicians, and assemblers. Overlearning has several advantages (Driskell, Willis, & Copper, 1992):

- It increases the length of time that trained material will be retained. The greater the degree of overlearning, the greater the retention.
- It makes learning more "reflexive," so tasks become automatic with continued practice.
- It is effective for cognitive as well as physical tasks, but the effect is stronger for cognitive tasks.

However, without refresher training, the increase in retention due to overlearning is likely to dissipate to zero after five to six weeks (Driskell et al., 1992).

Length of the Practice Session

Practice may be *distributed*, involving rest intervals between sessions, or *massed*, in which practice sessions are crowded together. Although there are exceptions, most of the research evidence indicates that for the same amount of practice, learning is better when practice is distributed rather than massed (Goldstein & Ford, 2002). Here are two reasons why:

1. Continuous practice is fatiguing, so that individuals cannot show all that they have learned. Thus, their performance is poorer than it would be if they were rested.
2. During a practice session, people usually learn both the correct performance and some irrelevant performances that interfere with it. But the irrelevant performances are likely to be less well practiced and so may be forgotten more rapidly between practice sessions. Performance should, therefore, improve if there are rest periods between practice sessions.

In fact, Holladay and Quiñones (2003) showed that adding variability to practice trials resulted in better long-term retention, presumably because trainees had to exert greater effort during skill acquisition. One exception to the superiority of massed over distributed practice, however, is when people need to learn difficult conceptual material or other "thought problems." There seems to be an advantage to staying with the problem for a few massed practice sessions at first rather than spending a day or more between sessions.

Motivation

In order actually to learn, one first must *want* to learn (Noe & Wilk, 1993). In practice, however, more attention usually is paid to trainees' ability to learn than to their motivation to learn or to the interaction of ability and motivation. This is a mistake, since meta-analytic and path-analytic evidence indicates that motivation to learn explains significant variance in learning outcomes, over and above cognitive ability per se (Colquitt et al., 2000). But what factors explain high motivation?

Motivation is a force that energizes, directs, and maintains behavior (Steers & Porter, 1975). In the context of training, this force influences enthusiasm for the training (*energizer*), keeps attention focused on training per se (*director*), and reinforces what is learned in training, even in the face of pressure back on the job to discard what has just been learned (*maintainer*).

Figure 15-1 shows that trainees bring a number of characteristics with them that predict motivation to learn (Colquitt et al., 2000; Noe & Colquitt, 2002):

- *Pretraining self-efficacy*—the belief that an individual can learn the content successfully (Bandura, 1997; Eden & Aviram, 1993; Gist et al., 1991; Mathieu, Martineau, & Tannenbaum, 1993; Quiñones, 1995; Saks, 1995; Switzer et al., 2005);
- *Valence of training*—the attractiveness of training outcomes (Colquitt & Simmering, 1998); framing the context of training as an *opportunity* can enhance this belief (Martocchio, 1992);
- *Job involvement*—the degree to which employees identify psychologically with their jobs and the importance of their work to their self-image (Brown, 1996);
- *Organizational commitment*—both affective (belief in the organization's goals and values) and behavioral (willingness to exert effort for the organization) (Facteau, Dobbins, Russell, Ladd, & Kudisch, 1995; Mowday, Porter, & Steers, 1982);
- *Career exploration*—thorough self-assessment and search for information from peers, friends, managers, and family members (Facteau et al., 1995; Noe & Wilk, 1993). In addition, three personality characteristics predict motivation to learn:
- *Conscientiousness*—being dependable, organized, persevering, and achievement oriented (Martocchio & Judge, 1997);
- *Goal orientation*—focusing on the mastery of new skills or experiences (Fisher & Ford, 1998; Klein et al., 2006; Phillips & Gully, 1997; Steele-Johnson, Beauregard, Hoover, & Schmidt, 2000); and
- *Anxiety*—having an acquired or learned fear, negatively related to motivation to learn, because it can disrupt cognitive functioning and attention (Colquitt et al., 2000).

While the factors shown in Figure 15-1 clearly affect trainees' motivation, so also do the *expectations* of the trainer. In fact, expectations have a way of becoming self-fulfilling prophecies, so that the higher the expectations are, the better the trainees perform (and vice versa). This phenomenon of the self-fulfilling prophecy is known as the *Pygmalion effect*. It was demonstrated in one study over a 15-week combat command course with adult trainees (Eden & Shani, 1982). Where instructors had been induced to expect better performance from the group of trainees, the trainees scored significantly higher on objective achievement tests, showed more positive attitudes, and perceived more positive leader behavior. The Pygmalion effect has been confirmed in many studies using both male and female trainees (Begley, 2003). However, it does not appear to hold in situations where women are led (or instructed) by women (Dvir, Eden, & Banjo, 1995).

Goal Setting

A person who wants to develop herself or himself will do so; a person who wants to be developed rarely is. This statement illustrates the role that motivation plays in training—to learn, you must want to learn. One of the most effective ways to raise a trainee's motivation is by setting goals. Goal setting has a proven track record of success in improving employee performance in a variety of settings (Latham, 2007; Locke & Latham, 1990, 2002, 2009; Locke, Shaw, Saari, & Latham, 1981). Goal setting is founded on the premise that an individual's conscious goals or intentions regulate his or her behavior (Locke, 1968). Research findings are clear-cut with respect to six issues:

1. Reviews of the literature show that goal-setting theory is among the most scientifically valid and useful theories in organizational science (Locke & Latham, 2009). Goal-setting effects are strongest for easy tasks and weakest for more complex tasks (Wood, Mento, & Locke, 1987).
2. Commitment to goals by employees is a necessary condition for goal setting to work (Locke, Latham, & Erez, 1988). Self-efficacy (a judgment about one's capability to perform a task) affects commitment to goals, such as improving attendance (Frayne & Latham, 1987). It can be enhanced through practice, modeling, and persuasion (Bandura, 1986).
3. When tasks are complex, participation in goal setting seems to enhance goal acceptance, particularly when employees are presented with a goal that they reject initially because it appears to be unreasonable or too difficult (Erez, Earley, & Hulin, 1985; Erez & Zidon, 1984). However, when tasks are simple, assigned goals may enhance goal acceptance, task performance, and intrinsic motivation (Shalley, Oldham, & Porac, 1987).
4. When given a choice, employees tend to choose more difficult goals if their previous goals were easy to attain and to choose easier goals if their previous goals were difficult to attain. Thus, past experience with goal setting affects the level of goals employees choose in the future (Locke, Frederick, Buckner, & Bobko, 1984).
5. Once an employee accepts a goal, specific, difficult goals result in higher levels of performance than do easy goals or even a generalized goal such as "do your best" (Locke & Latham, 2006; Eden, 1988). However, this effect seems to disappear or to reverse for novel tasks that allow multiple alternative strategies (Earley, Connolly, & Ekegren, 1989).
6. The effects of goal setting on performance can be enhanced further by providing information to performers about how to work on a task and by providing a rationale about why the goal and task are important (Earley, 1985).

Goal setting is not risk free, and possible side effects, such as excessive risk taking, ignoring non-goal dimensions of performance, pressures to cheat, feelings of failure, and increases in stress, do exist but can be controlled (Latham & Locke, 2006; Locke & Latham, 2009; Ordóñez, Schweitzer, Galinsky, & Bazerman, 2009).

That said, the results of research on goal setting are exciting. They have three important implications for motivating trainees:

1. Make the objectives of the training program clear at the outset.
2. Set goals that are challenging and difficult enough that the trainees can derive personal satisfaction from achieving them, but not so difficult that they are perceived as impossible to reach.
3. Supplement the ultimate goal of finishing the program with subgoals during training, such as trainer evaluations, work-sample tests, and periodic quizzes. As trainees clear each hurdle successfully, their confidence about attaining the ultimate goal increases.

Behavior Modeling

Behavior modeling is based on social-learning theory (Bandura, 1977, 1986, 1991). In simple terms, social-learning theory holds that we learn by observing others. The learning process per se requires attention, retention, the ability to reproduce what was learned, and motivation.

These principles might profitably be incorporated into a four-step "applied learning" approach to behavior modeling (Goldstein & Sorcher, 1974):

1. *Modeling,* in which trainees watch video of model persons behaving effectively in a problem situation.
2. *Role-playing,* which gives trainees the opportunity to practice and rehearse the effective behaviors demonstrated by the models.
3. *Social reinforcement,* which the trainer provides to trainees in the form of praise and constructive feedback.
4. *Transfer of training,* which enables the behavior learned in training to be used effectively on the job.

Stated simply, the objective is to have people observe a model, remember what the model did, do what the model did, and finally use what they learned when they are on the job (Baldwin, 1992). Such training affects the learning of skills through a change in trainees' knowledge structures or mental models (Davis & Yi, 2004), and this is true both at the level of the individual and the team (Marks, Sabella, Burke, & Zacarro, 2002).

Sometimes the goal of behavior modeling is to enable the trainee to *reproduce* the modeled behaviors (e.g., a golf swing). However, the objective of most interpersonal- and supervisory-skills training (e.g., in problem solving, conflict resolution) is to develop *generalizable* rules or concepts. If the goal is reproducibility, then only show positive (correct) examples of behavior. If the goal is generalization, then mix positive and negative examples (Baldwin, 1992).

Various types of retention aids can enhance modeling (Decker & Nathan, 1985; Mann & Decker, 1984): reviewing written descriptions of key behaviors (so-called learning points), mentally rehearsing the behaviors, and rewriting the learning points. Encourage trainees to write their own list of learning points if they wish to do so (Hogan, Hakel, & Decker, 1986; Marks et al., 2002). This leads to the development of cognitive "scripts" that serve as links between cognition and behavior (Cellar & Wade, 1988).

Research also suggests that the most effective way to practice skills in a behavior-modeling program is to include a videotape replay of each rehearsal attempt, and to do so in a small group with two role-players and only one or two observers (Decker, 1983). As a result of research done since the mid-1970s, the formula for behavior modeling training now includes five components: modeling, retention processes, role-playing (or behavioral rehearsal), social reinforcement, and transfer of training (Decker & Nathan, 1985).

Meta-analytic research demonstrates the effectiveness of behavior modeling (Taylor, Russ-Eft, & Chan, 2005). Their analysis of 117 behavior-modeling training studies revealed that the largest effects were for declarative and procedural knowledge (*d*s of about 1.0, resulting from comparing training versus a no-training or pretest condition). Declarative knowledge is knowledge about "what" (e.g., facts, meaning of terms), whereas procedural knowledge is knowledge about "how" (i.e., how to perform skilled behavior). The overall mean effect on changes in job behavior was $d = 0.27$. However, Taylor et al. (2005) reported substantial variance in the distribution of effect sizes, indicating the need to investigate moderators of the relationship between behavior-modeling training and outcomes, that is, variables that might explain the conditions under which an effect or relationship is likely to be present and likely to be stronger (Aguinis, 2004b).

Despite these encouraging results, behavior modeling may not be suitable for everyone. Different training methods may be needed for persons with high and low self-efficacy. For example, in a study involving the use of computer software, Gist, Schwoerer, and Rosen (1989) found that modeling increased performance for people whose pretest self-efficacy was in the range of moderate to high. However, for those with low self-efficacy, a one-on-one tutorial was more effective.

Another potential problem surfaces when the impact of behavior modeling is evaluated in terms of its ability to produce actual behavior change back on the job (i.e., transfer). Why? In some studies (e.g., Russell, Wexley, & Hunter, 1984), trainees were encouraged to use their newly acquired skills, but no formal evaluations were made, and no sanctions were levied on those who failed to comply. The result: There was no long-term behavior change. In other studies (e.g., Latham & Saari, 1979), trainees were directed and encouraged by their managers to use the new skills, and, in two cases, supervisors who refused to use them were removed from their positions. Not surprisingly, behavior changed back on the job. Conclusion: Although behavior modeling does produce positive trainee reactions and learning, more than modeling is needed to produce sustained changes in behavior and performance on the job (May & Kahnweiler, 2000). Here are three strategies suggested by research findings (Russell et al., 1984):

1. Show supervisors why their new behaviors are more effective than their current behaviors.
2. Encourage each trainee to practice the new behavior mentally until it becomes consistent with the trainee's self-image. Then try the new behavior on the job.
3. To facilitate positive transfer, follow the training by goal setting and reinforcement in the work setting.

Why does behavior-modeling training work? To a large extent because it overcomes one of the shortcomings of earlier approaches to training: telling instead of showing.

Evidence-Based Implications for Practice

Perhaps the most important practical lesson from this chapter is to resist the temptation to emphasize technology and techniques in training; instead, take the time to do a thorough needs analysis that will reveal what is to be learned at the individual or team levels and what the substantive content of training and development should be. In addition:

- Recognize that organizational boundaries are blurring, such that the border between customers, suppliers, and even competitors is becoming fuzzier. As a result, *any* individual or group that has a need to acquire specific capabilities to ensure an organization's success is a potential candidate for training.
- Create an optimal environment for learning to occur—ensure that the objectives are clear, material is meaningful and relevant, incorporate opportunities for practice and feedback, and ensure that the broader organization supports the content of the training.
- Incorporate principles of learning, goal setting, motivation, and behavior modeling into training.
- The most fundamental objective of well-designed training is positive transfer back to the job. To provide a realistic assessment of transfer effects, use multiple rating sources with different perspectives (supervisors, peers, subordinates, and self-ratings).

The design of a training and development program is critical to its eventual success. No less critical, though, are implementation of the program and the measurement of outcomes resulting from it. We will consider both of these important issues in Chapter 16.

Discussion Questions

1. Your boss asks you to identify some key characteristics of organizations and individuals that are related to effective training. What would you say?
2. Transfer of training is important. What would you do to maximize it?
3. Outline a needs-assessment process to identify training needs for supermarket checkers.
4. What should individual development plans include?
5. What would an optimal environment for training and learning look like?
6. Describe the components of an integrated approach to the design of team-based training.
7. How might behavior modeling be useful in team-based training?
8. How do behavioral baselines help researchers to assess behavioral transitions in training?
9. Top management asks you to present a briefing on the potential effects of goal setting and feedback. What would you say?

16

Training and Development: Implementation and the Measurement of Outcomes

At a Glance

The literature on training and development techniques is massive. In general, however, it falls into three categories: information-presentation techniques, simulation methods, and on-the-job training. Selection of a particular technique is likely to yield maximal payoff when designers of training follow a two-step sequence—*first*, specify clearly what is to be learned; *only then* choose a specific method or technique that accurately matches training requirements.

In measuring the outcomes of training and development, use multiple criteria (varying in time, type, and level), and map out and understand the interrelationships among the criteria and with other organizational variables. In addition, impose enough experimental or quasi-experimental control to allow unambiguous inferences regarding training effects.

Finally, in measuring training and development outcomes, be sure to include (1) provision for saying something about the practical and theoretical significance of the results, (2) a logical analysis of the process and content of the training, and (3) some effort to deal with the "systems" aspects of training impact. The ultimate objective is to assess the individual and organizational utility of training efforts.

Once we define what trainees should learn and what the substantive content of training and development should be, the critical question then becomes "How should we teach the content and who should do it?"

The literature on training and development techniques is massive. However, while many choices exist, evidence indicates that, among U.S. companies that conduct training, few make any systematic effort to assess their training needs before choosing training methods (Arthur, Bennett, Edens, & Bell, 2003; Saari, Johnson, McLaughlin, & Zimmerle, 1988). This implies that firms view hardware, software, and techniques as more important than outcomes. They view (mistakenly) the identification of what trainees should learn as secondary to the choice of technique.

New training methods appear every year. Some of them are deeply rooted in theoretical models of learning and behavior change (e.g., behavior modeling, team-coordination training), others seem to be the result of trial and error, and still others (e.g., interactive multimedia, computer-based business games) seem to be more the result of technological than of theoretical developments. We will make no attempt to review specific training methods that are or have been in use. Other sources are available for this purpose (Goldstein & Ford, 2002;

Noe, 2008; Wexley & Latham, 2002). We will only highlight some of the more popular techniques, with special attention to computer-based training, and then present a set of criteria for judging the adequacy of training methods.

Training and development techniques fall into three categories (Campbell, Dunnette, Lawler, & Weick, 1970): information-presentation techniques, simulation methods, and on-the-job training.

Information-presentation techniques include

1. Lectures.
2. Conference methods.
3. Correspondence courses.
4. Videos/compact disks (CDs).
5. Reading lists.
6. Interactive multimedia (CDs, DVDs, video).
7. Intranet and Internet.
8. Systematic observation (closely akin to modeling).
9. Organization development—systematic, long-range programs of organizational improvement through action research, which includes (a) preliminary diagnosis, (b) data gathering from the client group, (c) data feedback to the client group, (d) data exploration by the client group, (e) action planning, and (f) action; the cycle then begins again.

While action research may assume many forms (Austin & Bartunek, 2003), one of the most popular is *survey feedback* (Church, Waclawski, & Kraut, 2001; Czaja & Blair, 2005). The process begins with a comprehensive assessment of the way the organization is currently functioning—typically via the administration of anonymous questionnaires to all employees. Researchers tabulate responses at the level of individual work groups and for the organization as a whole. Each manager receives a summary of this information, based on the responses of his or her immediate subordinates. Then a change agent (i.e., a person skilled in the methods of applied behavioral science) meets privately with the manager recipient to maximize his or her understanding of the survey results. Following this, the change agent attends a meeting (face to face or virtual) of the manager and subordinates, the purpose of which is to examine the survey findings and to discuss implications for corrective action. The role of the change agent is to help group members to better understand the survey results, to set goals, and to formulate action plans for the change effort.

Simulation methods include the following:

1. The case method, in which representative organizational situations are presented on paper, usually to groups of trainees who subsequently identify problems and offer solutions. Individuals learn from each other and receive feedback on their own performances.
2. The incident method is similar to the case method, except that trainees receive only a sketchy outline of a particular incident. They have to question the trainer, and, when they think they have enough information, they attempt a solution. At the end of the session, the trainer reveals all the information he or she has, and trainees compare their solution to the one based on complete information.
3. Role-playing includes multiple role-playing, in which a large group breaks down into smaller groups and role-plays the same problem within each group without a trainer. All players then reassemble and discuss with the trainer what happened in their groups.
4. Experiential exercises are simulations of experiences relevant to organizational psychology. This is a hybrid technique that may incorporate elements of the case method, multiple role-playing, and team-coordination training. Trainees examine their responses first as individuals, then with the members of their own groups or teams, and finally with the larger group and with the trainer.
5. The task model has trainees construct a complex, but easily built physical object, and a group of trainees must then duplicate it, given the proper materials. Trainees use alternative

communication arrangements, and only certain trainees may view the object. Trainees discuss communication problems as they arise, and they reach solutions through group discussion.

6. The in-basket technique.
7. Business games.
8. Assessment centers.
9. Behavior or competency modeling.

On-the-job training methods are especially popular—both in basic skills training and in management training and development (Tyler, 2008). Broadly conceived, they include

1. Orientation training.
2. Apprenticeships.
3. On-the-job training.
4. Near-the-job training, which duplicates exactly the materials and equipment used on the job, but takes place in an area away from the actual job situation. The focus is exclusively on training.
5. Job rotation.
6. Understudy assignments, in which an understudy relieves a senior executive of selected responsibilities, thereby allowing him or her to learn certain aspects of the executive's job. Firms use such assignments for purposes of succession planning and professional development. Benefits for the trainee depend on the quality of his or her relationship with the executive, as well as on the executive's ability to teach effectively through verbal communication and competency modeling.
7. Executive coaching is used by organizations for a wide range of leadership-development activities, to address both individual and organizationwide issues (Hollenbeck, 2002; Underhill, McAnally, & Koriath, 2008). Focusing specifically on executives and their performance, it draws heavily on well-established principles of consulting, industrial and organizational psychology, and change management. The process usually proceeds through several stages: contracting and problem definition, assessment, feedback, action planning, implementation, and follow-up. At any stage in the process, however, new data may result in looping back to an earlier stage.
8. Performance management (see Chapter 5).

Computer-Based Training

As Brown and Ford (2002) have noted, "computer-based training, in its many forms, is the future of training—and the future has arrived" (p. 192). In view of the growing shift away from instructor-led, classroom training toward learner-centered, technology-delivered training, this topic deserves special attention. Computer-based training (CBT) is the presentation of text, graphics, video, audio, or animation via computer for the purpose of building job-relevant knowledge and skill (Kraiger, 2003). CBT is a form of technology-delivered instruction, a topic we addressed in the previous chapter. Here we focus on CBT design, implementation, and evaluation of its effects.

Common forms of CBT include multimedia learning environments (CDs, DVDs, desktop systems), intranet- and Web-based instruction, e-learning, intelligent tutoring systems, full-scale simulations, and virtual reality training (Steele-Johnson & Hyde, 1997). Two features that characterize most forms of CBT are *customization* (in which programs can be adapted based on characteristics of the learner) and *learner control* (in which learners may modify the learning environment to suit their own purposes) (Brown & Ford, 2002). CBT, therefore, represents adaptive learning, and its flexibility, adaptability, and potential cost savings suggest strongly that its popularity will only increase over time.

Is CBT more effective than instructor-led training? Two meta-analyses have found no significant differences in the formats, especially when both are used to teach the same type of knowledge, declarative or procedural (Sitzmann, Kraiger, Stewart, & Wisher, 2006; Zhao, Lei, Lai, & Tan, 2005). What we do know, however, is that training that is designed poorly will not stimulate and support learning, regardless of the extent to which appealing or expensive technology is used to deliver it (Brown & Ford, 2002; Kozlowski & Bell, 2003). Hence, if learner-centered instructional technologies are to be maximally effective, they must be designed to encourage active learning in participants. To do so, consider incorporating the following four principles into CBT design (Brown & Ford, 2002):

1. Design the information structure and presentation to reflect both meaningful organization (or chunking) of material and ease of use,
2. Balance the need for learner control with guidance to help learners make better choices about content and process,
3. Provide opportunities for practice and constructive feedback, and
4. Facilitate meta-cognitive monitoring and control to encourage learners to be mindful of their cognitive processing and in control of their learning processes.

Selection of Technique

A training method can be effective only if it is used appropriately. Appropriate use, in this context, means rigid adherence to a two-step sequence: *first*, define what trainees are to learn, and *only then* choose a particular method that best fits these requirements. Far too often, unfortunately, trainers choose methods first and then force them to fit particular needs. This "retrofit" approach not only is wrong but also is often extremely wasteful of organizational resources—time, people, and money. It should be banished.

In order to select a particular technique, the following checklist may prove useful. A technique is adequate to the extent that it provides the minimal conditions for effective learning to take place. To do this, a technique should

1. Motivate the trainee to improve his or her performance,
2. Clearly illustrate desired skills,
3. Provide for the learner's active participation,
4. Provide an opportunity to practice,
5. Provide feedback on performance while the trainee learns,
6. Provide some means to reinforce the trainee while learning,
7. Be structured from simple to complex tasks,
8. Be adaptable to specific problems, and
9. Enable the trainee to transfer what is learned in training to other situations.

Designers of training can apply this checklist to all proposed training techniques. If a particular technique appears to fit training requirements, yet is deficient in one or more checklist areas, then either modify it to eliminate the deficiency or bolster it with another technique. The next step is to conduct the training. Although a checklist of the many logistical details involved is not appropriate here, actual implementation should not be a major stumbling block if prior planning and design have been thorough. The final step, of course, is to measure the effects of training and their interaction with other organizational subsystems. To this topic we now turn.

MEASURING TRAINING AND DEVELOPMENT OUTCOMES

"Evaluation" of a training program implies a dichotomous outcome (i.e., either a program has value or it does not). In practice, matters are rarely so simple, for outcomes are usually a matter of degree. To assess outcomes, we need to document systematically how trainees actually behave back on their jobs and the relevance of their behavior to the objectives of the organization (Machin, 2002; Snyder,

Raben, & Farr, 1980). Beyond that, it is important to consider the intended purpose of the evaluation, as well as the needs and sophistication of the intended audience (Aguinis & Kraiger, 2009).

Why Measure Training Outcomes?

Evidence indicates that few companies assess the outcomes of training activities with any procedure more rigorous than participant reactions following the completion of training programs (Brown, 2005; Sugrue & Rivera, 2005; Twitchell, Holton, & Trott, 2001). This is unfortunate because there are at least four reasons to evaluate training (Sackett & Mullen, 1993):

1. To make decisions about the future use of a training program or technique (e.g., continue, modify, eliminate),
2. To make decisions about individual trainees (e.g., certify as competent, provide additional training),
3. To contribute to a scientific understanding of the training process, and
4. To further political or public relations purposes (e.g., to increase the credibility and visibility of the training function by documenting success).

At a broader level, these reasons may be summarized as decision making, feedback, and marketing (Kraiger, 2002). Beyond these basic issues, we also would like to know whether the techniques used are more efficient or more cost-effective than other available training methods. Finally, we would like to be able to compare training with other approaches to developing workforce capability, such as improving selection procedures and redesigning jobs. To do any of this, certain elements are essential.

ESSENTIAL ELEMENTS FOR MEASURING TRAINING OUTCOMES

At the most basic level, the task of evaluation is counting—counting new customers, counting interactions, counting dollars, counting hours, and so forth. The most difficult tasks of evaluation are deciding *what* things to count and developing routine *methods* for counting them. As Albert Einstein famously said, "Not everything that counts can be counted, and not everything that can be counted counts." In the context of training, here is what counts (Campbell et al., 1970):

1. Use of multiple criteria, not just for the sake of numbers, but also for the purpose of more adequately reflecting the multiple contributions of managers to the organization's goals.
2. Some attempt to study the criteria themselves—that is, their relationships with each other and with other variables. The relationship between internal and external criteria is especially important.
3. Enough experimental control to enable the causal arrow to be pointed at the training program. How much is enough will depend on the possibility of an interactive effect with the criterion measure and the susceptibility of the training program to the Hawthorne effect.
4. Provision for saying something about the practical and theoretical significance of the results.
5. A thorough, logical analysis of the process and content of the training.
6. Some effort to deal with the "systems" aspects of training impact—that is, how training effects are altered by interaction with other organizational subsystems. For example: Are KSAOs learned in training strengthened or weakened by reward practices (formal or informal) in the work setting? Is the nature of the job situation such that trainees can use the skills they have learned, or are other organizational changes required? Will the new skills that trainees have learned hinder or facilitate the functioning of other organizational subunits?

Trainers must address these issues before they can conduct any truly meaningful evaluation of training's impact. The remainder of this chapter will treat each of these points more fully and provide practical illustrations of their use.

Criteria

As with any other HR program, the first step in judging the value of training is to specify multiple criteria. Although we covered the criterion problem already in Chapter 4, it is important to emphasize that the assessment of training outcomes requires multiple criteria because training is usually directed at specific components of performance. Organizations deal with multiple objectives, and training outcomes are multidimensional. Training may contribute to movement toward some objectives and away from others at the same time (Bass, 1983). Let us examine criteria according to time, type, and level.

TIME   The important question here is "When, relative to the actual conduct of the training, should we obtain criterion data?" We could do so prior to, during, immediately after, or much later after the conclusion of training. To be sure, the timing of criterion measurement can make a great deal of difference in the interpretation of training's effects (Sprangers & Hoogstraten, 1989). Thus a study of 181 Korean workers (Lim & Morris, 2006) found that the relationship between perceived applicability (utility of training) and perceived application to the job (transfer) decreased as the time between training and measurement increased.

   Conclusions drawn from an analysis of changes in trainees from before to immediately after training may differ drastically from conclusions based on the same criterion measures 6 to 12 months after training (Freeberg, 1976; Keil & Cortina, 2001; Steele-Johnson, Osburn, & Pieper, 2000). Yet both measurements are important. One review of 59 studies found, for example, that the time span of measurement (the time between the first and last observations) was one year or less for 26 studies, one to three years for 27 studies, and more than three years for only 6 studies (Nicholas & Katz, 1985). Comparisons of short- versus long-term training effects may yield valuable information concerning the interaction of training effects with other organizational processes (e.g., norms, values, leadership styles). Finally, it is not the absolute level of behavior (e.g., number of grievances per month, number of accidents) that is crucial, but rather the *change* in behavior from the beginning of training to some time after its conclusion.

TYPES OF CRITERIA   It is important to distinguish internal from external criteria. Internal criteria are those that are linked directly to performance in the training situation. Examples of internal criteria are attitude scales and objective achievement examinations designed specifically to measure what the training program is designed to teach. External criteria, on the other hand, are measures designed to assess actual changes in job behavior. For example, an organization may conduct a two-day training program in EEO law and its implications for HR management. A written exam at the conclusion of training (designed to assess mastery of the program's content) would be an internal criterion. On the other hand, ratings by subordinates, peers, or supervisors and documented evidence regarding the trainees' on-the-job application of EEO principles constitute external criteria. Both internal and external criteria are necessary to evaluate the relative payoffs of training and development programs, and researchers need to understand the relationships among them in order to draw meaningful conclusions about training's effects.

   Criteria also may be qualitative or quantitative. Qualitative criteria are attitudinal and perceptual measures that usually are obtained by interviewing or observing of employees or by administering written instruments. Quantitative criteria include measures of the outcomes of job behavior and system performance, which are often contained in employment, accounting, production, and sales records. These outcomes include turnover, absenteeism, dollar volume of sales, accident rates, and controllable rejects.

   Both qualitative and quantitative criteria are important for a thorough understanding of training effects. Traditionally, researchers have preferred quantitative measures, except in organization development research (Austin & Bartunek, 2003; Nicholas, 1982; Nicholas & Katz, 1985). This may be a mistake, since there is much more to interpreting the outcomes of training than quantitative measures alone. By ignoring qualitative (process) measures, we may miss the richness of detail concerning *how* events occurred. In fact, Goldstein (1978), Goldstein and Ford (2002), and Jick (1979) described studies where data would have been misinterpreted if the researchers had been unaware of the events that took place during training.

LEVELS OF CRITERIA   "Levels" of criteria may refer either to the organizational levels from which we collect criterion data or to the relative level of rigor we adopt in measuring training outcomes. With respect to organizational levels, information from trainers, trainees, subordinates, peers, supervisors, and the organization's policy makers (i.e., the training program's sponsors) can be extremely useful. In addition to individual sources, group sources (e.g., work units, teams, squads) can provide aggregate data regarding morale, turnover, grievances, and various cost, error, and/or profit measures that can be helpful in assessing training's effects.

Kirkpatrick (1977, 1983, 1994) identified four levels of rigor in the evaluation of training and development programs: reaction, learning, behavior, and results. However, it is important to note that these levels provide only a vocabulary and a rough taxonomy for criteria. Higher levels do not necessarily provide more information than lower levels do, and the levels need not be causally linked or positively intercorrelated (Alliger & Janak, 1989). In general, there are four important concerns with Kirkpatrick's framework (Alliger, Tannenbaum, Bennett, Traver, & Shortland, 1997; Holton, 1996; Kraiger, 2002; Spitzer, 2005):

1. The framework is largely atheoretical; to the extent that it may be theory-based, it is founded on a 1950s behavioral perspective that ignores modern, cognitively based theories of learning.
2. It is overly simplistic in that it treats constructs such as trainee reactions and learning as unidimensional when, in fact, they are multidimensional (Alliger et al., 1997; Brown, 2005; Kraiger, Ford, & Salas, 1993; Morgan & Casper, 2001; Warr & Bunce, 1995). For example, reactions include affect toward the training as well as its perceived utility.
3. The framework makes assumptions about relationships between training outcomes that either are not supported by research (Bretz & Thompsett, 1992) or do not make sense intuitively. For example, Kirkpatrick argued that trainees cannot learn if they do not have positive reactions to the training. Yet a meta-analysis by Alliger et al. (1997) found an overall average correlation of only .07 between reactions of any type and immediate learning. In short, reactions to training should not be used blindly as a surrogate for the assessment of learning of training content.
4. Finally, the approach does not take into account the purposes for evaluation—decision making, feedback, and marketing (Kraiger, 2002).

Figure 16-1 presents an alternative measurement model developed by Kraiger (2002), which attempts to overcome the deficiencies of Kirkpatrick's (1994) four-level model. It clearly distinguishes evaluation targets (training content and design, changes in learners, and organizational payoffs) from data-collection methods (e.g., with respect to organizational payoffs, cost-benefit analyses, ratings, and surveys). Targets and methods are linked through the options available for measurement—that is, its focus (e.g., with respect to changes in learners, the focus might be cognitive, affective, or behavioral changes). Finally, targets, focus, and methods are linked to evaluation purpose—feedback (to trainers or learners), decision making, and marketing. Kraiger (2002) also provided sample indicators for each of the three targets in Figure 16-1. For example, with respect to organizational payoffs, the focus might be on transfer of training (e.g., transfer climate, opportunity to perform, on-the-job behavior change), on results (performance effectiveness or tangible outcomes to a work

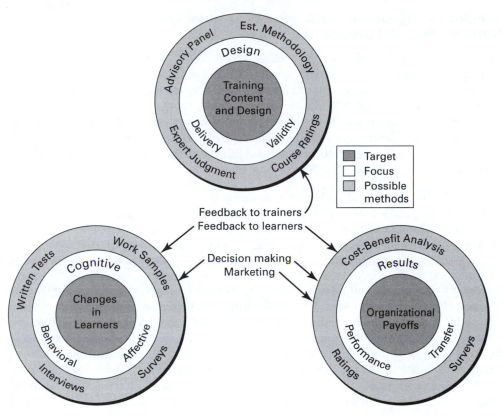

FIGURE 16-1   An integrative model of training evaluation.   *Source*: Kraiger, K. (2002). Decision-based evaluation. In K. Kraiger (Ed.), Creating, implementing, and managing effective training and development (p. 343). San Francisco: Jossey-Bass. This material is used by permission of John Wiley & Sons, Inc.

group or organization), or on financial performance as a result of the training [e.g., through measures of return on investment (ROI) or utility analysis].

Additional Considerations in Measuring the Outcomes of Training

Regardless of the measures used, our goal is to be able to make meaningful inferences and to rule out alternative explanations for results. To do so, it is important to administer the measures according to some logical plan or procedure (experimental design) (e.g., before and after training, as well as to a comparable control group). Numerous experimental designs are available for this purpose, and we shall consider them in a later section.

In assessing on-the-job behavioral changes, allow a reasonable period of time (e.g., at least three months) after the completion of training before taking measures. This is especially important for development programs that are designed to improve decision-making skills or to change attitudes or leadership styles. Such programs require *at least* three months before their effects manifest themselves in measurable behavioral changes. A large-scale meta-analysis reported an average interval of 133 days (almost 4.5 months) for the collection of outcome measures in behavioral terms (Arthur et al., 2003). To detect the changes, we need carefully developed techniques for systematic observation and measurement. Examples include scripted, job-related scenarios that use empirically derived scoring weights (Ostroff, 1991), BARS, self-reports (supplemented by reports of subordinates, peers, and supervisors), critical incidents, or comparisons of trained behaviors with behaviors that were not trained (Frese, Beimel, & Schoenborn, 2003).

Strategies for Measuring the Outcomes of Training in Terms of Financial Impact

As Aguinis and Kraiger (2009) noted, there continue to be calls for establishing the ROI for training, particularly as training activities continue to be outsourced and as new forms of technology-delivered instruction are marketed as cost effective. At the same time, there are few published studies on ROI. Let us begin by examining what ROI is.

ROI relates program profits to invested capital. It does so in terms of a ratio in which the numerator expresses some measure of profit related to a project, and the denominator represents the initial investment in a program (Cascio & Boudreau, 2008). More specifically, ROI includes the following (Boudreau & Ramstad, 2006):

1. The inflow of returns produced by an investment.
2. The offsetting outflows of resources required to make the investment.
3. How the inflows and outflows occur in each future time period.
4. How much what occurs in future time periods should be "discounted" to reflect greater risk and price inflation.

ROI has both advantages and disadvantages. Its major advantage is that it is simple and widely accepted. It blends in one number all the major ingredients of profitability, and it can be compared with other investment opportunities. On the other hand, it suffers from two major disadvantages. One, although the logic of ROI analysis appears straightforward, there is much subjectivity in items 1, 3, and 4 above. Two, typical ROI calculations focus on one HR investment at a time and fail to consider how those investments work together as a portfolio (Boudreau & Ramstad, 2007). Training may produce value beyond its cost, but would that value be even higher if it were combined with proper investments in individual incentives related to the training outcomes?

Alternatively, financial outcomes may be assessed in terms of utility analysis (see Chapter 13). Such measurement is not easy, but the technology to do it is available and well developed. In fact, the basic formula for assessing the outcomes of training in dollar terms (Schmidt, Hunter, & Pearlman, 1982) builds directly on the general utility formula for assessing the payoff from selection programs (Equation 13-5):

$$\Delta U = T \times N \times d_t \times SD_y - N \times C \tag{16-1}$$

where

ΔU = dollar value of the training program

T = number of years' duration of the training effect on performance

N = number of persons trained

d_t = true difference in job performance between the average trained worker and the average untrained worker in standard z-score units (see Equation 16-2)

SD_y = variability (standard deviation) of job performance in dollars of the untrained group

C = the per-person cost of the training

Note the following:

1. If the training is not held during working hours, then C should include only direct training costs. If training is held during working hours, then C should include, in addition to direct costs, all costs associated with having employees away from their jobs during the training.
2. The term d_t is called the *effect size*. We begin with the assumption that there is no difference in job performance between trained workers (those in the experimental group) and untrained

workers (those in the control group). The effect size tells us (a) if there is a difference between the two groups and (b) how large it is. The formula for effect size is

$$d_t = \frac{\overline{X}_e - \overline{X}_c}{SD\sqrt{r_{yy}}} \qquad \text{(16-2)}$$

$\overline{X}_e$ = average job performance of the trained workers (those in the experimental group)

$\overline{X}_c$ = average job performance of the untrained workers (those in the control group)

SD = standard deviation of the job performance measure in the untrained group

r_{yy} = reliability of the job performance measure (e.g., the degree of interrater agreement expressed as a correlation coefficient)

Equation 16-2 expresses effect size in standard-deviation units. To express it as a percentage change in performance (X), the formula is:

$$\% \text{ change in X} = d_t \times 100 \times SD_{pretest}/Mean_{pretest} \qquad \text{(16-3)}$$

where $100 \times SD_{pretest}/Mean_{pretest}$ (the coefficient of variation) is the ratio of the SD of pretest performance to its mean, multiplied by 100, where performance is measured on a ratio scale. Thus, to change d_t into a change-in-output measure, multiply d_t by the coefficient of variation for the job in question (Sackett, 1991).

When several studies are available, or when d_t must be estimated for a proposed human resource development (HRD) program, d_t is best estimated by the cumulated results of all available studies, using the methods of meta-analysis. Such studies are available in the literature (Arthur et al., 2003; Burke & Day, 1986; Guzzo, Jette, & Katzell, 1985; Morrow, Jarrett, & Rupinski, 1997). As they accumulate, managers will be able to rely on cumulative knowledge of the expected effect sizes associated with proposed HRD programs. Such a "menu" of effect sizes for HRD programs will allow HR professionals to compute the expected utilities of proposed HRD programs before the decision is made to allocate resources to such programs.

ILLUSTRATION   To illustrate the computation of the utility of training, suppose we wish to estimate the net payoff from a training program in supervisory skills. We develop the following information: $T = 2$ years; $N = 100$; $d_t = .31$ (Mathieu & Leonard, 1987); $SD_y = \$30,000$ (calculated by any of the methods we discussed in Chapter 13); $C = \$4,000$ per person. According to Equation 16-1, the net payoff from the training program is

$$\Delta U = 2 \times 100 \times .31 \times \$30,000 - (100)(\$4,000)$$

$$\Delta U = \$1,460,000 \text{ over two years}$$

Yet this figure is illusory because it fails to consider both economic and noneconomic factors that affect payoffs. For example, it fails to consider the fact that $1,460,000 received in two years is only worth $1,103,970 today (using the discount rate of 15 percent reported by Mathieu & Leonard, 1987). It also fails to consider the effects of variable costs and taxes (Boudreau, 1988). Finally, it looks only at a single cohort; but, if training is effective, managers want to apply it to multiple cohorts. Payoffs over subsequent time periods also must consider the effects of attrition of trained employees, as well as decay in the strength of the training effect over time (Cascio, 1989; Cascio & Boudreau, 2008). Even after taking all of these considerations into account, the monetary payoff from training and development efforts still may be substantial and well worth demonstrating.

As an example, consider the results of a four-year investigation by a large, U.S.-based multinational firm of the effect and utility of 18 managerial and sales/technical training programs. The study is noteworthy, for it adopted a strategic focus by comparing the payoffs from different types of training in order to assist decision makers in allocating training budgets and specifying the types of employees to be trained (Morrow et al., 1997).

Over all 18 programs, assuming a normal distribution of performance on the job, the average improvement was about 17 percent (.54 of an SD). However, for technical/sales training, it was higher (.64 SD), and, for managerial training, it was lower (.31 SD). Thus, training in general was effective.

The mean ROI was 45 percent for the managerial training programs and 418 percent for the sales/technical training programs. However, one inexpensive time-management program developed in-house had an ROI of nearly 2,000 percent. When the economic utility of that program was removed, the overall average ROI of the remaining training programs was 84 percent, and the ROI of sales/technical training was 156 percent.

WHY NOT HOLD ALL TRAINING PROGRAMS ACCOUNTABLE STRICTLY IN ECONOMIC TERMS? In practice, this is a rather narrow view of the problem, for economic indexes derived from the performance of operating units often are subject to bias (e.g., turnover, market fluctuations). Measures such as unit costs are not always under the exclusive control of the manager, and the biasing influences that are present are not always obvious enough to be compensated for.

This is not to imply that measures of results or financial impact should not be used to demonstrate a training program's worth; on the contrary, every effort should be made to do so. However, those responsible for assessing training outcomes should be well aware of the difficulties and limitations of measures of results or financial impact. They also must consider the utility of information-gathering efforts (i.e., if the costs of trying to decide whether the program was beneficial outweigh any possible benefits, then why make the effort?). On the other hand, given the high payoff of effective management performance, the likelihood of such an occurrence is rather small. In short, don't ignore measures of results or financial impact. Thorough evaluation efforts consider measures of training content and design, measures of changes in learners, and organizational payoffs. Why? Because together they address each of the purposes of evaluation: to provide feedback to trainers and learners, to provide data on which to base decisions about programs, and to provide data to market them.

Influencing Managerial Decisions with Program-Evaluation Data

The real payoff from program-evaluation data is when the data lead to organizational decisions that are strategically important. To do that, it is important to embed measures per se in a broader framework that drives strategic change. One such framework is known as LAMP—logic, analytics, measures, and process (Boudreau & Ramstad, 2007; Cascio & Boudreau, 2008). Logic provides the "story" that connects numbers with effects and outcomes. Analytics is about drawing the right conclusions from data; it transforms logic and measures into rigorous, relevant insights. To do that, it uses statistics and research design, and then goes beyond them to include skill in identifying and articulating key issues, gathering and using appropriate data, and setting the appropriate balance between statistical rigor and practical relevance. Measures are the numbers that populate the formulas and research design. Finally, effective measurement systems must fit within a change-management process that reflects principles of learning and knowledge transfer. Hence measures and the logic that supports them are part of a broader influence process.

Mattson (2003) demonstrated convincingly that training-program evaluations that are expressed in terms of results do influence the decisions of operating managers to modify, eliminate, continue, or expand such programs. He showed that variables such as organizational cultural values (shared norms about important organizational values), the complexity of the information presented to decision makers, the credibility of that information, and the degree of its abstractness/concreteness affect managers' perceptions of the usefulness and ease of use of the evaluative information.

Other research has shed additional light on the best ways to present evaluation results to operating managers. To enhance managerial acceptance in the Morrow et al. (1997) study described earlier, the researchers presented the utility model and the procedures that they proposed to use to the CEO, as well as to senior strategic planning and HR managers, *before* conducting their research. They presented the model and procedures as fallible, but reasonable, estimates. As Morrow et al. (1997) noted, senior management's approval *prior* to actual application and consideration of utility results in a decision-making context is particularly important when one considers that nearly any field application of utility analysis will rely on an effect size calculated with an imperfect quasi-experimental design.

Mattson (2003) also recognized the importance of emphasizing the same things that managers of operating departments were paying attention to. Thus, in presenting results to managers of a business unit charged with sales and service, he emphasized outcomes attributed to the training program in terms that were important to those managers (volume of sales, employee-retention figures, and improvement in customer-service levels). Clearly the "framing" of the message is critical and has a direct effect on its ultimate acceptability.

CLASSICAL EXPERIMENTAL DESIGN

An experimental design is a plan, an outline for conceptualizing the relations among the variables of a research study. It also implies how to control the research situation and how to analyze the data (Kerlinger & Lee, 2000; Mitchell & Jolley, 2010).

Experimental designs can be used with either internal or external criteria. For example, researchers can collect "before" measures on the job before training and collect "after" measures at the conclusion of training, as well as back on the job at some time after training. Researchers use experimental designs so that they can make causal inferences. That is, by ruling out alternative plausible explanations for observed changes in the outcome of interest, researchers want to be able to say that training *caused* the changes.

Unfortunately, most experimental designs and most training studies do not permit the causal arrow to point unequivocally toward training (x) as *the* explanation for observed results (y). To do that, there are three necessary conditions (see Shadish, Cook & Campbell, 2002 for more on this). The first requirement is that y did not occur until after x; the second is that x and y are actually shown to be related; and the third (and most difficult) is that other explanations of the relationship between x and y can be eliminated as plausible rival hypotheses.

To illustrate, consider a study by Batt (2002). The study examined the relationship among HR practices, employee quit rates, and organizational performance in the service sector. Quit rates were lower in establishments that emphasized high-involvement work systems. Batt (2002) showed that a range of HR practices was beneficial. Does that mean that the investments in training per se "caused" the changes in the quit rates and sales growth? No, but Batt (2002) did not claim that they did. Rather, she concluded that the entire set of HR practices *contributed* to the positive outcomes. It was impossible to identify the unique contribution of training alone. In fact, Shadish et al. (2002) suggest numerous potential contaminants or threats to valid interpretations of findings from field research. The threats may affect the following:

1. *Statistical-conclusion validity*—the validity of inferences about the correlation (covariation) between treatment (e.g., training) and outcome;
2. *Internal validity*—the validity of inferences about whether changes in one variable caused changes in another;
3. *Construct validity*—the validity of inferences from the persons, settings, and cause-and-effect operations sampled within a study to the constructs these samples represent; or
4. *External validity*—the validity of inferences about the extent to which results can be generalized across populations, settings, and times.

In the context of training, let us consider 12 of these threats:

1. *History*—specific events occurring between the "before" and "after" measurements in addition to training.
2. *Maturation*—ongoing processes within the individual, such as growing older or gaining job experience, which are a function of the passage of time.
3. *Testing*—the effect of a pretest on posttest performance.
4. *Instrumentation*—the degree to which an instrument may measure different attributes of an individual at two different points in time (e.g., parallel forms of an attitude questionnaire administered before and after training, or different raters rating behavior before and after training).
5. *Statistical regression*—changes in criterion scores resulting from selecting extreme groups on a pretest.
6. *Differential selection*—using different procedures to select individuals for experimental and control groups.
7. *Attrition*—differential loss of respondents from various groups.
8. *Interaction of differential selection and maturation*—that is, assuming experimental and control groups were different to begin with, the disparity between groups is compounded further by maturational changes occurring during the training period.
9. *Interaction of pretest with the experimental variable*—during the course of training, something reacts with the pretest in such a way that the pretest has a greater effect on the trained group than on the untrained group.
10. *Interaction of differential selection with training*—when more than one group is trained, differential selection implies that the groups are not equivalent on the criterion variable (e.g., skill in using a computer) to begin with; therefore, they may react differently to the training.
11. *Reactive effects of the research situation*—that is, the research design itself so changes the trainees' expectations and reactions that one cannot generalize results to future applications of the training.
12. *Multiple-treatment interference*—residual effects of previous training experiences affect trainees differently (e.g., finance managers and HR managers might not react comparably to a human relations training program because of differences in their previous training).

Table 16-1 presents examples of several experimental designs. These designs are by no means exhaustive; they merely illustrate the different kinds of inferences that researchers may draw and, therefore, underline the importance of considering experimental designs *before* training.

TABLE 16-1 Experimental Designs Assessing Training and Development Outcomes

	A		B	C		D			
	After-Only (One Control Group)		Before-After (No Control Group)	Before-After (One Control Group)		Solomon Four-Group Design Before-After (Three Control Groups)			
	E	C	E	E	C	E	C_1	C_2	C_3
Pretest	No	No	Yes	Yes	Yes	Yes	Yes	No	No
Training	Yes	No	Yes	Yes	No	Yes	No	Yes	No
Posttest	Yes	Yes	Yes	Yes	Yes	Yes	Yes	Yes	Yes

Note: E refers to the experimental group. C refers to the control group.

Design A

Design A, in which neither the experimental nor the control group receives a pretest, has not been used widely in training research. This is because the concept of the pretest is deeply ingrained in the thinking of researchers, although it is not actually essential to true experimental designs (Campbell & Stanley, 1963). We hesitate to give up "knowing for sure" that experimental and control groups were, in fact, "equal" before training, despite the fact that the most adequate all-purpose assurance of lack of initial biases between groups is randomization. Within the limits of confidence stated by tests of significance, randomization can suffice without the pretest (Campbell & Stanley, 1963, p. 25).

Design A controls for testing as main effect and interaction, but it does not actually measure them. While such measurement is tangential to the real question of whether training did or did not produce an effect, the lack of pretest scores limits the ability to generalize, since it is impossible to examine the possible interaction of training with pretest ability level. In most organizational settings, however, variables such as job experience, age, or job performance are available either to use as covariates or to "block" subjects—that is, to group them in pairs matched on those variable(s) and then randomly to assign one member of each pair to the experimental group and the other to the control group. Both of these strategies increase statistical precision and make posttest differences more meaningful. In short, the main advantage of Design A is that it avoids pretest bias and the "give-away" repetition of identical or highly similar material (as in attitude-change studies), but this advantage is not without costs. For example, it does not prevent subjects from maturing or regressing; nor does it prevent events other than treatment (such as history) from occurring after the study begins (Shadish et al., 2002).

Design B

The defining characteristic of Design B is that it compares a group with itself. In theory, there is no better comparison, since all possible variables associated with characteristics of the subjects are controlled. In practice, however, when the objective is to measure change, Design B is fraught with difficulties, for there are numerous plausible rival hypotheses that might explain changes in outcomes. History is one. If researchers administer pre- and posttests on different days, then events in between may have caused any difference in outcomes. While the history effect is trivial if researchers administer pre- and posttests within a one- or two-hour period, it becomes more and more plausible as an alternative explanation for change as the time between pre- and posttests lengthens.

Aside from specific external events, various biological or psychological processes that vary systematically with time (i.e., maturation) also may account for observed differences. Hence, between pre- and posttests, trainees may have grown hungrier, more fatigued, or bored. "Changes" in outcomes simply may reflect these differences.

Moreover, the pretest itself may change that which is being measured. Hence, just the administration of an attitude questionnaire may change an individual's attitude; a manager who knows that his sales-meeting conduct is being observed and rated may change the way he behaves. In general, expect this reactive effect whenever the testing process is itself a stimulus to change rather than a passive record of behavior. The lesson is obvious: Use nonreactive measures whenever possible (cf. Rosnow & Rosenthal, 2008; Webb, Campbell, Schwartz, & Sechrest, 2000).

Instrumentation is yet a fourth uncontrolled rival hypothesis in Design B. If different raters do pre- and posttraining observation and rating, this could account for observed differences.

A fifth potential contaminant is statistical regression (i.e., less-than-perfect pretest–posttest correlations) (Furby, 1973; Kerlinger & Lee, 2000). This is a possibility whenever a researcher selects a group for training *because* of its extremity (e.g., all low scorers or all high scorers). Statistical regression has misled many a researcher time and again. The way it works is that lower scores on the pretest tend to be higher on the posttest and higher scores tend to be lower on the posttest when, in fact, no real change has taken place. This can deceive a researcher into concluding erroneously that a training program is effective (or ineffective). In fact, the higher and lower scores of the two groups may be due to the regression effect.

A control group allows one to "control" for the regression effect, since both the experimental and the control groups have pretest and posttest scores. If the training program has had a "real" effect, then it should be apparent over and above the regression effect. That is, both groups should be affected by the same regression and other influences, other things equal. So if the groups differ in the posttest, it should be due to the training program (Kerlinger & Lee, 2000). The interaction effects (selection and maturation, testing and training, and selection and training) are likewise uncontrolled in Design B.

Despite all of the problems associated with Design B, it is still better to use it to assess change (together with a careful investigation into the plausibility of various threats), if that is the best one can do, than to do no evaluation. After all, organizations will make decisions about future training efforts with or without evaluation data (Kraiger, McLinden, & Casper, 2004; Sackett & Mullen, 1993). Moreover, if the objective is to measure individual achievement (a targeted level of performance), Design B can address that.

Design C

Design C (before-after measurement with a single control group) is adequate for most purposes, assuming that the experimental and control sessions are run simultaneously. The design controls history, maturation, and testing insofar as events that might produce a pretest–posttest difference for the experimental group should produce similar effects in the control group. We can control instrumentation either by assigning observers randomly to single sessions (when the number of observers is large) or by using each observer for both experimental and control sessions and ensuring that they do not know which subjects are receiving which treatments. Random assignment of individuals to treatments serves as an adequate control for regression or selection effects. Moreover, the data available for Design C enable a researcher to tell whether experimental mortality is a plausible explanation for pretest–posttest gain.

Information concerning interaction effects (involving training and some other variable) is important because, when present, interactions limit the ability to generalize results—for example, the effects of the training program may be specific only to those who have been "sensitized" by the pretest. In fact, when highly unusual test procedures (e.g., certain attitude questionnaires or personality measures) are used or when the testing procedure involves deception, surprise, stress, and the like, designs having groups that do not receive a pretest (e.g., Design A) are highly desirable, if not essential (Campbell & Stanley, 1963; Rosnow & Rosenthal, 2008). In general, however, *successful replication* of pretest–posttest changes at different times and in different settings increases our ability to generalize by making interactions of training with selection, maturation, instrumentation, history, and so forth less likely.

To compare experimental and control group results in Design C, either use analysis of covariance with pretest scores as the covariate, or analyze "change" scores for each group (Cascio & Kurtines, 1977; Cronbach & Furby, 1970; Edwards, 2002).

Design D

The most elegant of experimental designs, the Solomon (1949) four-group design (Design D), parallels Design C except that it includes two additional control groups (lacking the pretest). C_2 receives training plus a posttest; C_3 receives only a posttest. In this way, one can determine both the main effect of testing and the interaction of testing with training. The four-group design allows substantial increases in the ability to generalize, and, when training does produce changes in criterion performance, this effect is replicated in four different ways:

1. For the experimental group, posttest scores should be greater than pretest scores.
2. For the experimental group, posttest scores should be greater than C_1 posttest scores.

3. C_2 posttest scores should be greater than C_3 posttest scores.

4. C_2 posttest scores should be greater than C_1 pretest scores.

If data analysis confirms these directional hypotheses, this increases substantially the strength of inferences that can be drawn on the basis of this design. Moreover, by comparing C_3 posttest scores with experimental-group pretest scores and C_1 pretest scores, one can evaluate the combined effect of history and maturation.

Statistical analysis of the Solomon four-group design is not straightforward, since there is no one statistical procedure that makes use of all the data for all four groups simultaneously.

Since all groups do not receive a pretest, the use of analysis of variance of gain scores (gain = posttest − pretest) is out of the question. Instead, consider a simple 2×2 analysis of variance of posttest scores (Solomon, 1949):

	No Training	Training
Pretested	C_1	E
Not Pretested	C_3	C_2

Estimate training main effects from column means, estimate pretesting main effects from row means, and estimate interactions of testing with training from cell means.

LIMITATIONS OF THE SOLOMON FOUR-GROUP DESIGN Despite its apparent advantages, the Solomon four-group design is not without theoretical and practical problems (Bond, 1973; Kerlinger & Lee, 2000). For example, it assumes that the simple passage of time and training experiences affect all posttest scores independently. However, some interaction between these two factors is inevitable, thus jeopardizing the significance of comparisons between posttest scores for C_3 and pretest scores for E and C_1.

Serious practical problems also may emerge. The design requires large numbers of persons in order to represent each group adequately and to generate adequate statistical power. For example, in order to have 30 individuals in each group, the design requires 120. This may be impractical or unrealistic in many settings.

Here is a practical example of these constraints (Sprangers & Hoogstraten, 1989). In two field studies of the impact of pretesting on posttest responses, they used nonrandom assignment of 37 and 58 subjects in a Solomon four-group design. Their trade-off of low statistical power for greater experimental rigor illustrates the extreme difficulty of applying this design in field settings.

A final difficulty lies in the application of the four-group design. Solomon (1949) has suggested that, after the value of the training is established using the four groups, the two control groups that did not receive training then could be trained, and two new groups could be selected to act as controls. In effect, this would replicate the entire study—but would it? Sound experimentation requires that conditions remain constant, but it is quite possible that the first training program may have changed the organization in some way, so that those who enter the second training session already have been influenced.

Cascio (1976a) showed this empirically in an investigation of the stability of factor structures in the measurement of attitudes. The factor structure of a survey instrument designed to provide a baseline measure of managerial attitudes toward African Americans in the working environment did not remain constant when compared across three different samples of managers from the same company at three different time periods. During the two-year period that the training program ran, increased societal awareness of EEO, top management emphasis of it, and the fact that over 2,200 managers completed the training program probably altered participants' attitudes and expectations even before the training began.

Despite its limitations, when it is possible to apply the Solomon four-group design realistically, to assign subjects randomly to the four groups, and to maintain proper controls, this design controls most of the sources of invalidity that it is possible to control in one experimental design. Table 16-2 presents a summary of the sources of invalidity for Designs A through D.

TABLE 16-2 Sources of Invalidity for Experimental Designs A Through D

Design	History	Maturation	Testing	Instrumentation	Regression	Selection	Mortality	Interaction of Selection and Maturation	Interaction of Testing and Training	Interaction of Selection and Training	Reactive Arrangements	Multiple-Treatment Interference
A. After-Only (one control)	+	+	+	+	+	+	+	+	+	?	?	
B. Before-After (no control)	−	−	−	−	?	+	+	−	−	−	?	
C. Before-After (one control)	+	+	+	+	+	+	+	+	+	?	?	
D. Before-After (three controls) Solomon Four-Group Design		+	+	+	+	+	+	+	+	+	?	?

Note: A "+" indicates that the factor is controlled, a "−" indicates that the factor is not controlled, a "?" indicates possible source of concern, and a blank indicates that the factor is not relevant. See text for appropriate qualifications regarding each design.

Limitations of Experimental Designs

Having illustrated some of the nuances of experimental design, let us pause for a moment to place design in its proper perspective. First of all, exclusive emphasis on the design aspects of measuring training outcomes is rather narrow in scope. An experiment usually settles on a single criterion dimension, and the whole effort depends on observations of that dimension (Newstrom, 1978; Weiss & Rein, 1970). Hence, experimental designs are quite limited in the amount of information they can provide. There is no logical reason why investigators cannot consider several criterion dimensions, but unfortunately this usually is not the case. Ideally, an experiment should be part of a continuous feedback process rather than just an isolated event or demonstration (Shadish et al., 2002; Snyder et al., 1980).

Second, meta-analytic reviews have demonstrated that effect sizes obtained from single-group pretest–posttest designs (Design B) are systematically higher than those obtained from control or comparison-group designs (Carlson & Schmidt, 1999; Lipsey & Wilson, 1993). Type of experimental design therefore moderates conclusions about the effectiveness of training programs. Fortunately, corrections to mean effect sizes for data subgrouped by type of dependent variable (differences are most pronounced when the dependent variable is knowledge assessment) and type of experimental design can account for most such biasing effects (Carlson & Schmidt, 1999).

Third, it is important to ensure that any attempt to measure training outcomes through the use of an experimental design has adequate statistical power. Power is the probability of correctly rejecting a null hypothesis when it is false (Murphy & Myors, 2003). Research indicates that the power of training-evaluation designs is a complex issue, for it depends on the effect size obtained, the reliability of the dependent measure, the correlation between pre- and posttest scores, the sample size, and the type of design used (Arvey, Cole, Hazucha, & Hartanto, 1985). Software that enables straightforward computation of statistical power and confidence intervals (*Power & Precision*, 2000) should make power analysis a routine component of training-evaluation efforts.

Finally, experiments often fail to focus on the real goals of an organization. For example, experimental results may indicate that job performance after treatment A is superior to performance after treatment B or C. The really important question, however, may not be whether treatment A is more effective, but rather what levels of performance we can expect from almost all trainees at an acceptable cost and the extent to which improved performance through training "fits" the broader strategic thrust of an organization.

QUASI-EXPERIMENTAL DESIGNS

In field settings, there often are major obstacles to conducting true experiments. True experiments require the manipulation of at least one independent variable, the random assignment of participants to groups, and the random assignment of treatments to groups (Kerlinger & Lee, 2000). Managers may disapprove of the random assignment of people to conditions. Line managers do not see their subordinates as interchangeable, like pawns on a chessboard, and they often distrust randomness in experimental design. Beyond that, some managers see training evaluation as disruptive and expensive (Frese et al., 2003).

Despite calls for more rigor in training-evaluation designs (Littrell, Salas, Hess, Paley, & Riedel, 2006; Wang, 2002), some less-complete (i.e., quasi-experimental) designs can provide useful data even though a true experiment is not possible. Shadish et al. (2002) offered a number of quasi-experimental designs with the following rationale: The central purpose of an experiment is to eliminate alternative hypotheses that also might explain results. If a quasi-experimental design can help eliminate some of these rival hypotheses, then it may be worth the effort.

Because full experimental control is lacking in quasi-experiments, it is important to know which specific variables are uncontrolled in a particular design (cf. Tables 16-2 and 16-3). Investigators should, of course, design the very best experiment possible, given their circumstances, but where full control is not possible, they should use the most rigorous design that *is* possible. For these reasons, we present four quasi-experimental designs, together with their respective sources of invalidity, in Table 16-3.

TABLE 16-3 Sources of Invalidity for Four Quasi-Experimental Designs

Design \ Sources	History	Maturation	Testing	Instrumentation	Regression	Selection	Mortality	Interaction of Selection and Maturation	Interaction of Testing and Training	Interaction of Selection and Training	Reactive Arrangements	Multiple-Treatment Interference
E. Time-series design												
Measure (M) M (Train) MMM	−	+	+	?	+	+	+	+	−		?	?
F. Nonequivalent control-group design												
I. M train M												
II. M no train M	+	+	+	+	?	+	+	−	−		?	?
G. Nonequivalent dependent variable design												
M (experimental and control variables) train	−	−	+	?	−	+	+	+	+		+	+
M (experimental and control variables)												
H. Institutional-cycle design												
Time 1 2 3	+	−	+	+	?	−	?		+		?	+
I. M (train) M (no train) M												
II. M (no train) M (train) M												

Note: A "+" indicates that the factor is controlled, a "−" indicates that the factor is not controlled, a "?" indicates a possible source of concern, and blank indicates that the factor is not relevant.

Design E

The *time series design* is especially relevant for assessing the outcomes of training and development programs. It uses a single group of individuals and requires that criterion data be collected at several points in time, both before and after training. Criterion measures obtained before the introduction of the training experience then are compared to those obtained after training. A curve relating criterion scores to time periods may be plotted, and, in order for an effect to be demonstrated, there should be a discontinuity or change in the series of measures, corresponding to the training program, that does not occur at any other point. This discontinuity may represent an abrupt change either in the slope or in the intercept of the curve. Of course, the more observations pre- and posttraining, the better, for more observations decrease uncertainty about whether training per se caused the outcome(s) of interest (Shadish et al., 2002).

Although Design E bears a superficial resemblance to Design B (both lack control groups and both use before–after measures), it is much stronger in that it provides a great deal more data on which to base conclusions about training's effects. Its most telling weakness is its failure to control for history—that is, perhaps the discontinuity in the curve was produced not by training, but rather by some more or less simultaneous organizational event. Indeed, if one cannot rule out history as an alternative plausible hypothesis, then the entire experiment loses credibility. To do so, either arrange the observational series to hold known cycles constant (e.g., weekly work cycles, seasonal variations in performance, or communication patterns) or else make it long enough to include several such cycles completely (Shadish et al., 2002).

BOX 16-1

Practical Illustration: A True Field Experiment with a Surprise Ending

The command teams of 18 logistics units in the Israel Defense Forces were assigned randomly to experimental and control conditions. Each command team included the commanding officer of the unit plus subordinate officers, both commissioned and noncommissioned. The command teams of the nine experimental units underwent an intensive three-day team-development workshop. The null hypothesis was that the workshops had no effect on team or organizational functioning (Eden, 1985).

The experimental design provided for three different tests of the hypothesis, in ascending order of rigor. First, a Workshop Evaluation Questionnaire was administered to team members after the workshop to evaluate their subjective *reactions* to its effectiveness.

Second, Eden (1985) assessed the before-and-after perceptions of command team members in both the experimental and the control groups by means of a Team Development Questionnaire, which included ratings of the team leader, subordinates, team functioning, and team efficiency. This is a true experimental design (Design C), but its major weakness is that the outcomes of interest were assessed in terms of responses from team members who personally had participated in the workshops. This might well lead to positive biases in the responses.

To overcome this problem, Eden used a third design. He selected at random about 50 subordinates representing each experimental and control unit to complete the Survey of Organizations both before and after the team-development workshops. This instrument measures organizational functioning in terms of general management, leadership, coordination, three-way communications, peer relations, and satisfaction. Since subordinates had no knowledge of the team-development workshops and therefore no ego involvement in them, this design represents the most internally valid test of the hypothesis. Moreover, since an average of 86 percent of the subordinates drawn from the experimental-group units completed the posttraining questionnaires, as did an average of 81 percent of those representing control groups, Eden could rule out the effect of attrition as a threat to the internal validity of the experiment. Rejection of the null hypothesis would imply that the effects of the team-development effort really did affect the rest of the organization.

To summarize: Comparison of the command team's before-and-after perceptions tests whether the workshop influenced the team; comparison of the subordinates' before-and-after perceptions tests whether team development affected the organization. In all, 147 command-team members and 600 subordinates completed usable questionnaires.

Results

Here's the surprise: Only the weakest test of the hypothesis, the postworkshop reactions of participants, indicated that the training was effective. Neither of the two before-and-after comparisons detected any effects, either on the team or on the organization. Eden concluded:

> The safest conclusion is that the intervention had no impact. This disconfirmation by the true experimental designs bares the frivolity of self-reported after-only perceptions of change. Rosy testimonials by [trainees] may be self-serving, and their validity is therefore suspect. (1985, p. 98)

Design F

Another makeshift experimental design, Design F, is the *nonequivalent control-group design.* Although Design F appears identical to Design C (before-after measurement with one control group), there is a critical difference: In Design F, individuals from a common population are not assigned randomly to the experimental and control groups. This design is common in applied settings where naturally occurring groups must be used (e.g., work group A and work group B). Design F is especially appropriate when Designs A and C are impossible because even the addition of a nonequivalent control group makes interpretation of the results much less ambiguous than in Design B, the single-group pretest–posttest design. Needless to say, the nonequivalent control group becomes much more effective as an experimental control as the similarity between experimental and control-group pretest scores increases.

BOX 16-2

Practical Illustration: The Hazards of Nonequivalent Designs

This is illustrated neatly in the evaluations of a training program designed to improve the quality of group decisions by increasing the decision-making capabilities of its members. A study by Bottger and Yetton (1987) that demonstrated the effectiveness of this approach used experimental and control groups whose pretest scores differed significantly. When Ganster, Williams, and Poppler (1991) replicated the study using a true experimental design (Design C) with random assignment of subjects to groups, the effect disappeared.

The major sources of invalidity in this design are the selection-maturation interaction and the testing-training interaction. For example, if the experimental group happens to consist of young, inexperienced workers and the control group consists of older, highly experienced workers who are tested and retested, a gain in criterion scores that appears specific to the experimental group might well be attributed to the effects of training when, in fact, the gain would have occurred even without training.

Regression effects pose a further threat to unambiguous inferences in Design F. This is certainly the case when experimental and control groups are "matched" (which is no substitute for randomization), yet the pretest means of the two groups differ substantially. When this happens, changes in criterion scores from pretest to posttest may well be due to regression effects, not training. Despite these potential contaminants, we encourage increased use of

Design F, especially in applied settings. However, be aware of potential contaminants that might make results equivocal, and attempt to control them as much as possible.

Design G

We noted earlier that many managers reject the notion of random assignment of participants to training and no-training (control) groups. A type of design that those managers may find useful is the nonequivalent dependent variable design (Shadish et al., 2002) or "internal-referencing" strategy (Haccoun & Hamtieux, 1994). The design is based on a single treatment group and compares two sets of dependent variables—one that training should affect (experimental variables), and the other that training should not affect (control variables). Design G can be used whenever the evaluation is based on some kind of performance test.

Perhaps the major advantage of this design is that it effectively controls two important threats to internal validity: testing and the Hawthorne effect (i.e., simply reflecting on one's behavior as a result of participating in training could produce changes in behavior). Another advantage, especially over a nonequivalent control-group design (Design F), is that there is no danger that an unmeasured variable that differentiates the nonequivalent control group from the trained group might interact with the training. For example, it is possible that self-efficacy might be higher in the nonequivalent control group because volunteers for such a control group may perceive that they do not need the training in question (Frese et al., 2003).

Design G does not control for history, maturation, and regression effects, but its most serious potential disadvantage is that the researcher is able to control how difficult or easy it is to generate significant differences between the experimental and control variables. The researcher can do this by choosing variables that are very different from/similar to those that are trained.

To avoid this problem, choose control variables that are conceptually similar to, but distinct from, those that are trained. For example, in a program designed to teach inspirational communication of a vision as part of training in charismatic leadership, Frese et al. (2003) included the following as part of set of experimental (trained) items: variation of speed, variation of loudness, and use of "we." Control (untrained) items included, among others, the following: combines serious/factual information with witty and comical examples from practice, and good organization, such as a, b, and c. The control items were taken from descriptions of two training seminars on presentation techniques. A different group of researchers independently coded them for similarity to inspirational speech, and the researchers chose items coded to be least similar.

Before-after coding of behavioral data indicated that participants improved much more on the trained variables than on the untrained variables (effect sizes of about 1.0 versus 0.3). This suggests that training worked to improve the targeted behaviors, but did not systematically influence the untargeted behaviors. At the same time, we do not know if there were long-term, objective effects of the training on organizational performance or on the commitment of subordinates.

Design H

A final quasi-experimental design, appropriate for cyclical training programs, is known as the *recurrent institutional cycle design*. It is Design H in Table 16-3. For example, a large sales organization presented a management-development program, known as the State Manager Program, every two months to small groups (12–15) of middle managers (state managers). The one-week program focused on all aspects of retail sales (new product development, production, distribution, marketing, merchandising, etc.). The program was scheduled so that all state managers (approximately 110) could be trained over an 18-month period. This is precisely the type of situation for which Design H is appropriate—that is, a large number of persons will be trained, but not all at the same time. Different *cohorts* are involved. Design H is actually a combination of two (or more) before-after studies that occur at different points in time. Group I receives a pretest at time 1, then training, and then a posttest at time 2. At the same chronological time (time 2), Group II receives a pretest, training, and then a posttest at time 3. At time 2, therefore, an experimental and a control group have, in effect, been created. One can obtain even more information (and with quasi-experimental designs, it is *always* wise to collect as much data as possible or to demonstrate the effect of training in several different ways) if it is possible to measure Group I again at time 3 and to give Group II a pretest at time 1. This controls the effects of history. Moreover, the time 3 data for Groups I and II and the posttests for all groups trained subsequently provide information as to how the training program is interacting with other organizational events to produce changes in the criterion measure.

Several cross-sectional comparisons are possible with the "cycle" design:

- Group I posttest scores at time 2 can be compared with Group II pretest scores at time 2,
- Gains made in training for Group I (time 2 posttest scores) can be compared with gains in training for Group II (time 3 posttest scores), and
- Group II posttest scores at time 3 can be compared with Group I posttest scores at time 3 [i.e., gains in training versus gains (or no gains) during the no-training period].

This design controls history and test–retest effects, but not differences in selection. One way to control for possible differences in selection, however, is to split one of the groups (assuming it is large enough) into two equated samples, one measured both before and after training and the other measured only after training:

	Time 2	Time 3	Time 4
Group II$_a$	Measure	Train	Measure
Group II$_b$	—	Train	Measure

Comparison of the posttest scores of two carefully equated groups (Groups II$_a$ and II$_b$) is more precise than a similar comparison of posttest scores of two unequated groups (Groups I and II).

A final deficiency in the "cycle" design is the lack of adequate control for the effects of maturation. This is not a serious limitation if the training program is teaching specialized skills or competencies, but it is a plausible rival hypothesis when the objective of the training program is to change attitudes.

Campbell and Stanley (1963) expressed aptly the logic of these makeshift designs:

[O]ne starts out with an inadequate design and then adds specific features to control for one or another of the recurrent sources of invalidity. The result is often an inelegant accumulation of precautionary checks, which lacks the intrinsic symmetry of the "true" experimental designs, but nonetheless approaches experimentation. (p. 57)

Other quasi-experimental designs (cf. Kerlinger & Lee, 2000; Shadish et al., 2002) are appropriate in specialized situations, but the ones we have discussed seem well suited to the types of problems that applied researchers are likely to encounter.

STATISTICAL, PRACTICAL, AND THEORETICAL SIGNIFICANCE

As in selection, the problem of *statistical* versus *practical* significance is relevant for the assessment of training outcomes. Demonstrations of statistically significant change scores may mean little in a practical sense. From the practical perspective, researchers must show that the effects of training *do* make a difference to organizational goals—in terms of lowered production costs, increased sales, fewer grievances, and so on. In short, external criteria are important.

A related issue concerns the relationship between practical and theoretical significance. Training researchers frequently are content to demonstrate only that a particular program "works"—the prime concern being to sell the idea to top management or to legitimize an existing (perhaps substantial) investment in a particular development program. This is only half the story. The real test is whether the new training program is superior to previous or existing methods for accomplishing the same objectives. To show this, firms need systematic research to evaluate the effects of independent variables that are likely to affect training outcomes—for example, different training methods, different depths of training, or different types of media for presenting training.

If researchers adopt this two-pronged approach to measuring training outcomes and if they can map the effects of relevant independent variables across different populations of trainees and across different criteria, then the assessment takes on theoretical significance. For example, using meta-analysis, Arthur et al. (2003) found medium-to-large effect sizes for organizational training (sample-weighted average effect sizes of .60 for reaction criteria, .63 for measures of learning, and .62 for measures of behavior or results). Other organizations and other investigators may use this knowledge to advantage in planning their own programs. The concept of statistical significance, while not trivial, in no sense guarantees practical or theoretical significance—the major issues in outcome measurement.

Logical Analysis

Experimental control is but one strategy for responding to criticisms of the internal or statistical conclusion validity of a research design (Cascio & Boudreau, 2008; McLinden, 1995; Sackett & Mullen, 1993). A logical analysis of the process and content of training programs can further enhance our understanding of *why* we obtained the results we did. As we noted earlier, both qualitative and quantitative criteria are important for a thorough understanding of training's effects. Here are some qualitative issues to consider:

1. Were the goals of the training clear both to the organization and to the trainees?
2. Were the methods and content of the training really relevant to the goals?
3. Were the proposed methods actually used and the proposed content actually taught?
4. Did it appear that learning really was taking place?
5. Does the training program conflict with any other program in the organization?
6. What kinds of criteria should really be expected to show change as a result of the training? (Korb, 1956)

For every one of these questions, supplement the subjective opinions of experts with objective data. For example, to provide broader information regarding question 2, document the linkage between training content and job content. A quantitative method is available for doing this (Bownas, Bosshardt, & Donnelly, 1985). It generates a list of tasks that receive undue emphasis in training, those that are not being trained, and those that instructors intend to train, but that graduates report being unable to perform. It proceeds as follows:

1. Identify curriculum elements in the training program.
2. Identify tasks performed on the job.
3. Obtain ratings of the emphasis given to each task in training, of how well it was learned, and of its corresponding importance on the job.
4. Correlate the two sets of ratings—training emphasis and job requirements—to arrive at an overall index of fit between training and job content.
5. Use the ratings of training effectiveness to identify tasks that appear to be over- or under-emphasized in training.

Confront these kinds of questions during program planning *and* evaluation. When integrated with answers to the other issues presented earlier in this chapter, especially the "systems" aspects of training impact, then training outcomes become much more meaningful. This is the ultimate payoff of the measurement effort.

Evidence-Based Implications for Practice

Numerous training methods and techniques are available, but each one can be effective only if it is used appropriately. To do that, first define what trainees are to learn, and only then choose a particular method that best fits these requirements.

- In evaluating training outcomes, be clear about your purpose. Three general purposes are to provide feedback to trainers and learners, to provide data on which to base decisions about programs, and to provide data to market them.
- Use quantitative as well as qualitative measures of training outcomes. Each provides useful information.
- Regardless of the measures used, the overall goal is to be able to make meaningful inferences and to rule out alternative explanations for results. To do that, it is important to administer the measures according to some logical plan or procedure (experimental or quasi-experimental design). Be clear about what threats to valid inference your design controls for and fails to control for.
- No less important is a logical analysis of the process and content of training programs, for it can enhance understanding of *why* we obtained the results we did.

In our next chapter, we shall carry our presentation one step further by examining emerging international issues in applied psychology. We shall begin by considering the growth of HR management issues across borders.

Discussion Questions

1. Discuss the advantages and disadvantages of interactive multimedia training.
2. Your boss asks you to design a study to evaluate the effects of a training class in stress reduction. How will you proceed?
3. Describe some of the key differences between experimental and quasi-experimental designs.
4. Your firm decides to train its entire population of employees and managers (500) to provide "legendary customer service." Suggest a design for evaluating the impact of such a massive training effort.
5. What additional information might a logical analysis of training outcomes provide that an experimental or quasi-experimental design does not?

17

International Dimensions of Applied Psychology

At a Glance

Globalization is a fact of modern organizational life. Globalization refers to commerce without borders, along with the interdependence of business operations in different locations (Cascio, 2010). Consider semiconductor manufacturer Intel Corporation, for example. The company is truly global, earning almost 80 percent of its revenues outside of the United States (Intel Corp., 2008). Cross-cultural exposure, if not actual interaction, has become the norm. Applied psychologists have made valuable contributions to facilitate understanding and effective interactions across cultures, and there is great opportunity for future contributions. In this chapter, we make no effort to be comprehensive in examining this body of work. Rather, after considering the concept of culture, we emphasize five main areas—namely, identification of potential for international management, selection for international assignments, cross-cultural training and development, performance management, and repatriation.

Although the behavioral implications of globalization can be addressed from a wide variety of perspectives, we have chosen to focus only on five of them, as noted above: identification of potential for international management, selection for international assignments, cross-cultural training (CCT) and development, performance management, and repatriation. We recognize that there are many other worthy issues to explore, such as work motivation across cultures (Gelfand, Erez, & Aycan, 2007), leadership (House, Hanges, Javidan, Dorfman, & Gupta, 2004), decision making in multinational teams (Yuki, Maddux, Brewer, & Takemura, 2005), and international career development (Peiperl & Jonsen, 2007), but space constraints limit our ability to address them here. Let us begin our treatment by considering some factors that are driving globalization. Then we shall address the central role that the concept of culture plays in interactions among people from different parts of the world.

Globalization, Culture, and Psychological Measurement

The demise of communism, the fall of trade barriers, and the rise of networked information have unleashed a revolution in business. Market capitalism guides every major country on earth. Goods and services flow across borders more freely than ever; vast information networks instantly link nations, companies, and people; and foreign direct investment now totals at least US$9 trillion, with approximately 65 percent coming from and going to developed countries.

The result—twenty-first-century capitalism (Briscoe, Schuler, & Claus, 2009).

Many factors are driving change, but none is more important than the rise of Internet technologies (Friedman, 2005, 2008). The Internet, as it continues to develop, has certainly changed the ways that people live and work. At the same time, mass collaboration through file sharing, blogs, and social-networking services is making leaps in creativity possible, and it is changing the ways companies in a variety of industries do business (Hof, 2005). Here are some examples.

- *Research and Development.*   Procter & Gamble makes use of outside scientific networks to generate 35 percent of new products from outside the company, up from 20 percent three years ago. That has helped boost sales per R&D person by 40 percent.
- *Software Development.*   By coordinating their efforts online, programmers worldwide volunteer on more than 100,000 open-source projects, such as Linux, thereby challenging traditional software.
- *Telecommunications.*   More than 41 million people use Skype software to share computer-processing power and bandwidth, allowing them to call each other for free over the Internet. That has cut revenues sharply at traditional telecom providers.
- *Retail.*   With 61 million active members, eBay has created a self-sustaining alternative to retail stores.

Globalization and Culture

As every advanced economy becomes global, a nation's most important competitive asset becomes the skills and cumulative learning of its workforce. Globalization, almost by definition, makes this true. Virtually all developed countries can design, produce, and distribute goods and services equally well and equally fast. Every factor of production other than workforce skills can be duplicated anywhere in the world. Capital moves freely across international boundaries, seeking the lowest costs. State-of-the-art factories can be erected anywhere. The latest technologies move from computers in one nation, up to satellites parked in space, and back down to computers in another nation—all at the speed of electronic impulses. It is all fungible—capital, technology, raw materials, information—all except for one thing, the most critical part, the one element that is unique about a nation or a company: its workforce.

Does this imply that cultural nuances in different countries and regions of the world will become less important? Hardly. To put this issue into perspective, let us consider the concept of culture.

Triandis (1998; 2002) emphasizes that culture provides implicit theories of social behavior that act like a "computer program," controlling the actions of individuals. He notes that cultures include unstated assumptions, the way the world is. These assumptions influence thinking, emotions, and actions without people noticing that they do. Members of cultures believe that their ways of thinking are obviously correct and need not be discussed. Individuals and companies that seek to do business in countries outside their own ignore these alternative ways of thinking and acting at their peril. Scholars define the term "culture" in many different ways, and it operates on multiple levels—individual, organizational, national (Gelfand, Erez, & Aycan, 2007; Gelfand, Leslie, & Fehr, 2008; House et al., 2004). For ease of exposition, we focus on national-level culture in what follows. To understand what cultural differences imply, consider one typology, the theory of vertical and horizontal individualism and collectivism.

VERTICAL AND HORIZONTAL INDIVIDUALISM AND COLLECTIVISM   Triandis (1998) notes that vertical cultures accept hierarchy as a given, whereas horizontal cultures accept equality as a given. Individualistic cultures emerge in societies that are complex (many subgroups with different attitudes and beliefs) and loose (relatively few rules and norms about what is correct behavior in different types of situations). Collectivism emerges in societies that are simple (individuals agree on beliefs and attitudes) and tight (many rules and norms about what is correct behavior in different types of situations).

Triandis argues that these syndromes (shared patterns of attitudes, beliefs, norms, and values organized around a theme) constitute the parameters of any general theory about the way culture influences people. Crossing the cultural syndromes of individualism and collectivism with the cultural syndromes of vertical and horizontal relationships yields a typology of four kinds of cultures.

Additional culture-specific attributes define different kinds of individualism or collectivism. According to Triandis, the following four may be the universal dimensions of these constructs:

1. *Definition of the self*—autonomous and independent from groups (individualists) versus interdependent with others (collectivists).
2. *Structure of goals*—priority given to personal goals (individualists) versus priority given to in-group goals (collectivists).
3. *Emphasis on norms versus attitudes*—attitudes, personal needs, perceived rights, and contracts as determinants of social behavior (individualists) versus norms, duties, and obligations as determinants of social behavior (collectivists).
4. *Emphasis on relatedness versus rationality*—collectivists emphasize relatedness (giving priority to relationships and taking into account the needs of others), whereas individualists emphasize rationality (carefully computing the costs and benefits of relationships).

Culture determines the uniqueness of a human group in the same way that personality determines the uniqueness of an individual (Gelfand et al., 2008; Hofstede, 2001). There are many implications and patterns of variation of these important differences with respect to organizational issues and globalization. Two of them are goal-setting and reward systems (individual versus team- or organizationwide) and communications (gestures, eye contact, and body language in high-context cultures versus precision with words in low-context cultures). Two others are performance feedback and assessment practices. With respect to performance feedback, the characteristics of the culture (vertical/horizontal or individual/collectivist) interact with the objectives, style, frequency, and inherent assumptions of the performance-feedback process (Varela & Premaux, 2008). With respect to assessment practices, different cultures prefer different approaches, and there is the possibility of variation in validity across cultures.

Finally, there are implications for training and development. These include, for example, language training for expatriates, along with training to avoid the culture shock that results from repeated disorientation experienced by individuals in a foreign land whose customs and culture differ from one's own (Cascio, 1998, 2010; Triandis, 1994). In short, culture affects the ways we think, feel, and act.

Country-Level Cultural Differences

Geert Hofstede, a Dutch researcher, identified five dimensions of cultural variation in values in more than 50 countries and 3 regions (East Africa, West Africa, and Arab countries). Initially, he relied on a database of surveys covering, among other things, the values of employees of subsidiaries of IBM in 72 countries (Hofstede, 2001; Hofstede & Hofstede, 2005). He analyzed 116,000 questionnaires, completed in 20 languages, matching respondents by occupation, gender, and age at different time periods (1968 and 1972). Over the next several decades, he collected additional data from other populations, unrelated to IBM, but matched across countries. Hofstede's five dimensions reflect basic problems that any society has to cope with, but for which solutions differ. They are power distance, uncertainty avoidance, individualism, masculinity, and long-term versus short-term orientation (see Figure 17-1). These five dimensions were verified empirically, and each country could be positioned somewhere between their poles. The dimensions are statistically independent and occur in all possible combinations. Other researchers generally have confirmed these dimensions (Barkema & Vermuelen, 1997; Gerhart & Fang, 2005; Sondergaard, 1994; Triandis, 2004).

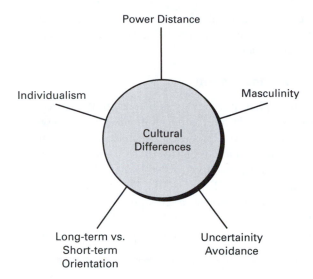

FIGURE 17-1 The five dimensions that Hofstede (2001) identified in assessing cultural differences across countries.

Power distance refers to the extent that members of an organization accept inequality and to whether they perceive much distance between those with power (e.g., top management) and those with little power (e.g., rank-and-file workers). Hofstede found the top power-distance countries to be Malaysia, Guatemala, and the Philippines; the bottom ones were Austria, Israel, and Denmark.

Uncertainty avoidance is the extent to which a culture programs its members to feel either comfortable or uncomfortable in unstructured situations (those that are novel, unknown, surprising, different from usual). Countries that score high on this dimension (e.g., Greece, Portugal, Belgium, and Japan) tend to rely more on rules and rituals to make the future more predictable. Those that score low (e.g., Singapore, Denmark, Sweden, and Hong Kong) tend to be more pragmatic. The United States scores low on this dimension.

Individualism reflects the extent to which people emphasize personal or group goals. If they live in nuclear families that allow them to "do their own thing," individualism flourishes. However, if they live with extended families or tribes that control their behavior, collectivism—the essence of which is giving preference to in-group over individual goals—is more likely (Triandis, 1998). The most individualistic countries are the United States and the other English-speaking countries. The most collectivist countries are Guatemala, Ecuador, and Panama.

Hofstede's fourth dimension, **masculinity**, is found in societies that differentiate very strongly by gender. Femininity is characteristic of cultures where sex-role distinctions are minimal. Masculine cultures tend to emphasize ego goals—the centrality of work, careers, and money. Feminine cultures, on the other hand, tend to emphasize social goals—quality of life, helping others, and relationships. Hofstede found the most masculine cultures to be Japan, Austria, and Venezuela, while the most feminine were Sweden, Norway, and the Netherlands.

Finally **long-term versus short-term orientation** refers to the extent to which a culture programs its members to accept delayed gratification of their material, social, and emotional needs. Countries scoring highest in long-term orientation include China, Hong Kong, and Taiwan; Pakistan, Nigeria, and the Philippines score at the opposite end. Americans tend to be relatively short-term oriented.

There have been a number of critiques of Hofstede's work (Ailon, 2008; Baskerville, 2003; Eckhardt, 2002; Kitayama, 2002), yet his typology remains remarkably influential (Bhagat, 2002; Kirkman, Lowe, & Gibson, 2006), both in science (Oyserman, Coon, & Kemelmeier, 2002; Schmimmack, Oishi, & Diener, 2005) as well as in practice (Bing, 2004). Hofstede's work is valuable because it provides the standard against which new work on cultural differences is validated (Triandis, 2004). It also helps us to understand and place into perspective current theories of motivation, leadership, and organizational behavior. Now let us consider an emerging topic—the globalization of psychological measurement.

The Globalization of Psychological Measurement

Psychological measurement and research in applied psychology is increasing in importance worldwide, as a 44-year review of published articles in the *Journal of Applied Psychology* and *Personnel Psychology* revealed (Cascio & Aguinis, 2008). A similar conclusion emerged in an earlier review of all articles written by authors with affiliations outside of the United States in the journals *Educational and Psychological Measurement* and *Applied Psychological Measurement* from January 1995 to December 1999 (Aguinis, Henle, & Ostroff, 2001). The latter review found that many studies described the construction and validation of a variety of measures, and also the reliability of existing measures. Many of the topics discussed in this book, such as computerized adaptive testing, item-response theory, item analysis, generalizability theory, and the multitrait–multimethod matrix, are currently being studied in several countries.

Transporting Psychological Measures across Cultures

Psychological measures are often developed in one country and then transported to another. Guidelines for doing this—*International Guidelines for Adapting Educational and Psychological Tests* (Hambleton, 1994; Hambleton & Kanjee, 1995)—are available. From a measurement perspective, the problem is that each culture views life in a unique fashion depending on the norms, values, attitudes, and experiences particular to that specific culture. Thus, the comparability of any phenomenon can pose a major methodological problem in international research that uses, for example, surveys, questionnaires, or interviews (Harpaz, 1996).

The first step in transferring a measure to another culture is to establish translation equivalence (Aguinis et al., 2001). Blind back-translation assesses the equivalence of the wording of a measure that has been translated into a different language. The process begins when an individual translates the measure from the original language to another. Then a second individual, who has not seen the original measure, translates it back to the original language. Finally, the second version of the measure is compared with the original, and discrepancies are discussed and resolved.

Translation equivalence is a necessary, but not a sufficient, condition for ensuring transferability to another culture. The measure must also demonstrate two other types of equivalence. The first is conceptual equivalence—that is, the attribute being measured has a similar meaning across cultures (Brett, Tinsley, Janssens, Barsness, & Lytle, 1997). Measures must produce the same conceptual frame of reference in different cultures, which means that different cultures are defining an attribute in the same way (Riordan & Vandenberg, 1994). The construct of leadership offers an example of nonequivalence, for it tends to refer to organizational leadership in the United States and to political leadership in Asian cultures (House, Wright, & Aditya, 1997). As another example, consider that the Western notion of "truth" is irrelevant in Confucian thinking (Adler, Campbell, & Laurent, 1989). Respondents also must interpret response options in the same way (Riordan & Vandenberg, 1994). For example, "neither disagree nor agree" may be interpreted as indifference in one culture and as slight agreement in another (Aguinis et al., 2001).

Finally, metric equivalence requires that statistical associations among dependent and independent variables remain relatively stable, regardless of whether a measure is used domestically or internationally (see Chapter 5). Correlation matrices and factor structures should also remain similar (Harpaz, 1996; Salgado, Viswesvaran, & Ones, 2001). This was the approach taken by Tsaousis and Nikolaou (2001) in demonstrating the conceptual and metric equivalence of a measure of the five-factor model (FFM) of personality in the Greek language. With respect to integrity tests, Berry, Sackett, and Wiemann (2007) reported no major differences in scale means, standard deviations, criterion-related validities, or admissions of counterproductive work behaviors across five countries.

In summary, before measures developed in one culture can be used in another, it is important to establish translation, conceptual, and metric equivalence. Doing so will enhance the ability of a study to provide a meaningful understanding of cross-cultural similarities and differences.

Terminology

Before proceeding further, let us introduce four terms that we shall use in subsequent sections of the chapter:

- An **expatriate** or *foreign-service employee* is a generic term applied to anyone working outside her or his home country with a planned return to that or a third country.
- **Home country** is the expatriate's country of residence.
- **Host country** is the country in which the expatriate is working.
- A **third-country national** is an expatriate who has transferred to an additional country while working abroad. A German working for a U.S. firm in Spain is a third-country national.

Thousands of firms have operations in countries around the globe. Expatriates staff many, if not most, such overseas operations. An important challenge, therefore, is to identify individuals early on in their careers who have potential for international management. This is the subject of our next section.

IDENTIFICATION OF POTENTIAL FOR INTERNATIONAL MANAGEMENT

In today's global economy, it is no exaggeration to say that the work of the executive is becoming more international in orientation. An international executive is one who is in a job with some international scope, whether in an expatriate assignment or in a job dealing with international issues more generally (Spreitzer, McCall, & Mahoney, 1997). Given the current competitive climate and the trends suggesting ever more interdependent global operations in the future, early identification of individuals with potential for international management is extremely important to a growing number of organizations.

On the basis of a careful literature review that identified both executive competencies and the ability to learn from experience, Spreitzer et al. (1997) developed a 116-item questionnaire, termed Prospector, for rating the potential of aspiring international executives. Executive competencies include characteristics such as cognitive or analytic ability, business knowledge, interpersonal skills, commitment, courage to take action, and ease in dealing with cross-cultural issues. In addition, there is a long history of research confirming that the ability to learn from experience, coupled with appropriate developmental job experiences, is likely to be important in developing executive potential (Keys & Wolfe, 1988; McCall, 2004; McCall, Lombardo, & Morrison, 1988; Wexley & Baldwin, 1986). Four themes seem to underlie the ability to learn from experience: (1) taking a proactive approach to learning by seeking out opportunities to learn, (2) seeing mistakes as an opportunity to learn and improve, (3) exhibiting flexibility and adaptability, and (4) seeking and using feedback.

Spreitzer et al. (1997) developed the Prospector questionnaire to measure both the executive competencies and the ability to learn from experience. A sample of 838 lower-, middle-, and senior-level managers from 6 international firms and 21 countries completed Prospector. The sample included both managers who had high potential and managers who were solid performers, but not likely to advance. Eight factor-analytically derived dimensions appeared consistent with the executive competencies identified in the literature review: Is Insightful (assesses aspects of cognitive and analytic ability), Has Broad Business Knowledge, Brings Out the Best in People (assesses interpersonal skills), Acts with Integrity, Has the Courage to Take a Stand, Takes Risks, Is Committed to Making a Difference, and Is Sensitive to Cultural Differences. Six of the dimensions appeared more consistent with the learning themes identified in the literature review: Seeks Opportunities to Learn, Seeks Feedback, Uses Feedback, Is Culturally Adventurous, Is Open to Criticism, and Is Flexible.

In terms of validity, all 14 dimensions were correlated strongly with the boss's general rating of current performance in two samples—a validation sample and a cross-validation sample. In 72 percent of the cases, the 14 dimensions also successfully distinguished managers identified by their companies as high potential from those identified as solid-performing managers. Notably, bosses rated the high-potential managers significantly higher than the solid-performing managers on all 14 dimensions.

Two dimensions—Is Insightful and Seeks Opportunities to Learn—were related significantly to a measure of learning job content, in both the validation and the cross-validation samples. In terms of learning behavioral skills, Is Open to Criticism was significant in both the validation and the cross-validation samples. It is particularly important in learning new ways of interacting effectively with people in getting one's job done.

The dimension Is Culturally Adventurous was significantly correlated with three international criteria—archival data on previous expatriate experience, archival data on multiple languages spoken, and the boss's perception that the individual could manage international issues successfully—in both the validation and the cross-validation samples. The dimension Is Sensitive to Cultural Differences was correlated significantly with two of the international criteria: expatriate experience and the boss's perception that the individual could manage international issues successfully.

What do these results imply for the development of future international executives? Spreitzer et al. (1997) speculated that the 14 Prospector dimensions operate through four broad processes to facilitate the development of future international executives. These processes are

1. *Gets organizational attention and investment.*   Individuals who have a propensity for risk taking, a passion for or commitment to seeing the organization succeed, the courage to go against the grain, and a keen mind are likely to stand out in the organization. Five Prospector dimensions seem to reflect such basic qualities: Is Committed to Making a Difference, Is Insightful, Has the Courage to Take a Stand, Has Broad Business Knowledge, and Takes Risks.
2. *Takes or makes more opportunities to learn.*   Three of the dimensions appear to reflect the sense of adventure required to break with the status quo: Seeks Opportunities to Learn, Is Culturally Adventurous, and Seeks Feedback. High scores on these dimensions indicate curiosity and enjoyment of novelty and new challenges—essential characteristics of successful international managers.
3. *Is receptive to learning opportunities.*   This is reflected in the following dimensions: Acts with Integrity (that is, taking responsibility for one's own actions is a prerequisite for learning from them); Brings Out the Best in People; Is Sensitive to Cultural Differences; and Is Open to Criticism (i.e., receptiveness and lack of defensiveness are essential in order to hear the feedback that others are willing to share).
4. *Changes as a result of experience.*   That is, the successful international executive recognizes the need to retain current competencies, but also to incorporate the competencies required for the future business environment. High ratings on the dimensions Is Flexible and Uses Feedback may pinpoint hardiness and resiliency, both of which are important in being able to start over after a setback.

These four processes may provide a starting point for the creation of a theoretical framework that specifies how current executive competencies, coupled with the ability to learn from experience and the right kind of developmental experiences, may facilitate the development of successful international executives (Spreitzer et al., 1997). Having identified those with potential for international management, the next step is to institute a selection process for international assignments. We consider this topic next.

SELECTION FOR INTERNATIONAL ASSIGNMENTS

As Chapters 13 and 14 demonstrate, there is a large and well-developed literature on selection instruments for domestic assignments. However, as Hough and Oswald (2000) noted, "validities of domestic selection instruments may not generalize to international sites, because different predictor and criterion constructs may be relevant, or, if the constructs are the same, the behavioral indicators may differ" (p. 649).

Unfortunately, recent reviews indicate that the selection process for international managers is, with few exceptions (e.g., Lievens, Harris, Van Keer, & Bisqueret, 2003), largely intuitive and unsystematic (Caligiuri & Tarique, 2006; Deller, 1997; Sinangil & Ones, 2001). A major problem is that the selection of people for overseas assignments often is based *solely* on their technical competence and job knowledge (Aryee, 1997; Schmit & Chan, 1998).

Highly developed technical skills, of course, are the basic rationale for selecting a person to work overseas. A problem arises, however, when technical skills are the *only* criterion for selection. This is so because technical competence per se has nothing to do with one's ability to adapt to a new environment, to deal effectively with foreign coworkers, or to perceive and, if necessary, imitate foreign behavioral norms (Collings & Scullion, 2006; Mendenhall & Oddou, 1995). Keep this in mind as you consider various factors that determine success in an international assignment. Let us begin with general mental ability.

General Mental Ability

Given the increasingly global scope of the science and practice of industrial and organizational psychology, it is important to determine if research findings from the United States generalize to other continents, countries, and cultures. One such construct is that of general mental ability (GMA), which may be defined broadly as the ability to learn. It includes any measure that combines two, three, or more specific aptitudes or any measure that includes a variety of items that measure specific abilities (e.g., verbal, numerical, spatial relations) (Schmidt, 2002). Thus, GMA may be measured using an omnibus test (e.g., the Wonderlic Personnel Test, Ravens Progressive Matrices) or using different specific tests combined into a battery (e.g., the General Aptitude Test Battery, Differential Aptitude Test).

The validity of GMA as a predictor of job performance, as well as performance in training, is well established in the United States on the basis of meta-analyses of hundreds of studies (Hunter & Hunter, 1984; Schmidt & Hunter, 1998). The estimated validity of GMA for predicting supervisory ratings of job performance is .57 for high-complexity jobs (17 percent of U.S. jobs), .51 for medium-complexity jobs (63 percent of U.S. jobs), and .38 for low-complexity jobs (20 percent of U.S. jobs). The estimated validity of GMA as a predictor of training success is .63. Validity may be somewhat higher or lower for different jobs or occupational groups.

Among organizations in the European Community, tests of GMA are used more frequently than in the United States (Salgado & Anderson, 2002). The same study also found that the majority of European companies are medium or small (fewer than 500 employees), that there are only small differences among the majority of the European countries in the popularity of tests of GMA, that the perceptions of applicants in the European Community are very similar, and that there are initiatives to harmonize the legislative structures and testing standards in Europe. Is GMA as robust a predictor of job performance and training in Europe as it is in the United States?

The answer is yes. On the basis of a meta-analysis of 85 independent samples with job performance as the criterion and 89 independent samples with training success as the criterion, the validity of GMA as a predictor of job-performance, as well as performance in training, across 12 occupational categories has been established in the European Community (Salgado et al., 2003). For predicting job-performance ratings, validities were as follows: .67 (managers), .66 (sales), .63 (engineers), .61 (information and message-distribution clerks), .55 (skilled workers), .54 (electricians), typing and filing occupations (.45), drivers (.45), and police (.24).

These results are similar or somewhat larger than the U.S. findings for similar occupational groups. GMA measures are, therefore, valid predictors for all occupational categories, and their validity generalized across samples and countries of the European Community. Similar results have been reported in meta-analyses of GMA as a predictor of job performance in the United Kingdom (operational validities of .5 to .6) (Bertua, Anderson, & Salgado, 2005), and also in Germany (Hülsheger, Maier, & Stumpp, 2007) (mean operational validity of .534).

With respect to the training criterion, GMA measures validly predicted success for 10 occupational groups analyzed. They showed operational validities in excess of .50 for 5 of the 10 occupations (the largest being .74 for engineers and .72 for chemists) and moderately large validities (.40, .40, and .49) for three additional groups (mechanics, drivers, and apprentices, respectively). Overall, these results are similar, though slightly lower, than the operational validity estimates found in U.S. meta-analyses for the same occupational groups. Again, similar findings with respect to the prediction of success in training were reported in the United Kingdom (Bertua et al., 2005) and Germany (Hülsheger et al., 2007) (mean operational validity of .467).

In terms of job complexity, Salgado et al. (2003) found results similar to those reported in the United States for job performance (.64 for high-complexity jobs, .53 for medium complexity, and .51 for low complexity) and training (.74 for high-complexity jobs, .53 for medium complexity, and .36 for low complexity). Comparable results were reported by Bertua et al. (2005) in the United Kingdom. Such results demonstrate a linearly positive relationship between GMA and job complexity and show that job complexity is a powerful moderator of the validity of GMA.

In Germany, however, with respect to the prediction of training success, Hülsheger et al. (2007) reported the opposite result, namely, the lower the skill level, the higher the operational validity. They attributed such results to the stratification of the German educational system. That is, people who receive higher education, and thereby qualification for highly complex jobs, are clearly a preselected group. As a result, range restriction is stronger and validities are lower for jobs of higher complexity than they are for jobs of lower complexity.

In summary, these results indicate that there is international validity generalization for GMA as a predictor of performance in training and on the job in the United States and in the European Community. GMA tests are, therefore, robust predictors for expatriate assignments across these two continents, although the same findings have not yet been demonstrated elsewhere. Beyond GMA, other factors are important determinants of success in an overseas assignment. A key consideration is the personality of the candidate.

Personality

As we noted in Chapter 13, recent studies have found promising results for the validity of the FFM of personality—that is, the "Big Five"—as a predictor of job performance (Barrick, Mount, & Judge, 2001). Summarizing cumulative knowledge that has accrued over the past century about the relationship between personality and performance, Barrick et al. (2001) analyzed 15 prior meta-analyses that have investigated the relationship between the FFM and job performance. With the exception of Salgado (1997), all of these meta-analyses used samples from the United States and Canada. Salgado's meta-analysis of personality-performance relations used 36 studies from the European Community, none of which overlapped with studies included in any other meta-analyses. His results showed that the validity of both conscientiousness and emotional stability generalized across all occupations and criterion types studied. The validity of the other dimensions differed by occupation or criterion type.

Barrick et al. (2001) found almost identical results. They conducted analyses across a number of performance criteria, including overall work performance, supervisory ratings, objective indicators (productivity data, turnover, promotions, and salary measures), training, and teamwork. They also conducted analyses across specific occupational groups (managers, salespersons, professionals, police, skilled labor, and semiskilled labor).

Conscientiousness is a valid predictor of performance across all criterion types and all occupational groups (validities ranged from .23 to .31). Its validity is the highest overall and underscores its importance as a fundamental individual-difference variable that has numerous implications for work outcomes. Results for the remaining personality dimensions show that each predicts at least some criteria for some jobs. Emotional stability was the only other Big Five dimension to show nonzero, true-score correlations with overall work performance (.13).

The remaining three dimensions—extroversion, agreeableness, and openness to experience—predicted some aspects of performance in some occupations. None predicted consistently across criterion types. For example, extroversion and openness to experience predicted training performance especially well (with an upper-bound credibility value of .41 for both dimensions). Emotional stability and agreeableness (in addition to conscientiousness) predicted teamwork moderately well (.22 and .34, respectively). Overall, it appears that conscientiousness and emotional stability are valid predictors of performance in the United States, Canada, and the European Community.

DEVELOPING A GLOBAL MEASURE OF PERSONALITY   One difficulty of the transportability approach is that, even though personality may not be different across cultures, the way it is expressed is highly likely to differ (Schmit, Kihm, & Robie, 2000). Moreover, instruments are likely to be changed substantively when they are transported to different countries, making cross-cultural comparisons difficult. To overcome these problems, Schmit et al. (2000) developed a Global Personality Inventory (GPI) using both an emic approach, in which a culture is observed from within, and an etic approach, which examines many cultures from a perspective outside those cultural systems for purposes of comparison.

Ten international teams from the United States, the United Kingdom, Sweden, France, Belgium, Germany, Spain, Japan, Korea, Singapore, Argentina, and Columbia collaborated in the development of the GPI. The FFM was used as the organizing structure, and sophisticated psychometric procedures (e.g., item-response theory, differential item functioning, factor analyses) were used when translating the GPI into languages other than English. Evidence of the construct-oriented and criterion-related validity of the GPI is encouraging (see, e.g., Benson & Campbell, 2007), although development of the instrument is ongoing.

PERSONALITY DIMENSIONS RELATED TO EXPATRIATE SUCCESS   If an organization defines success in terms of the completion of the expatriate assignment and the supervisory ratings of performance on the assignment, statistical evidence indicates that three personality characteristics are related to ability to complete the assignment. These are extroversion and agreeableness (which facilitate interacting and making social alliances with host nationals and other expatriates) and emotional stability. Conscientiousness is a general work ethic that supervisors "see" in their subordinates, and this affects their performance ratings. Expatriate assignments require a great deal of persistence, thoroughness, and responsibility—all of which conscientious people possess and use (Caligiuri, 2000).

An important qualifier, however, is the type of assignment in question. For example, the necessary level of openness and extroversion would be much higher for an executive in a networking role than it would be for a technician working predominately with a system or machine (Caligiuri & Tarique, 2006).

As Caligiuri noted, since personality characteristics are relatively immutable, organizations should think of selection (on the basis of personality) as the precursor to cross-cultural training. First, identify expatriate candidates with the requisite personality characteristics, and then offer CCT to those identified. This sequence is reasonable, since CCT may be effective only when trainees are predisposed to success in the first place.

Other Characteristics Related to Success in International Assignments

Lievens et al. (2003) examined the validity of a broad set of predictors for selecting European managers for a CCT program in Japan. The selection procedure assessed cognitive ability, personality (using the FFM), and dimensions measured by an assessment center and a behavior-description interview. Two assessment-center exercises, an analysis-presentation exercise and a group-discussion exercise, were designed to measure the personal characteristics related to performance in an international context. The analysis-presentation exercise assessed the following:

- *Tenacity–resilience*—keeps difficulties in perspective, stays positive despite disappointments and setbacks
- *Communication*—communicates clearly, fluently, and to the point; talks at a pace and level that hold people's attention, both in group and in individual situations
- *Adaptability*—adapts readily to new situations and ways of working, is receptive to new ideas, is willing and able to adjust to changing demands and objectives
- *Organizational and commercial awareness*—is alert to changing organizational dynamics, is knowledgeable about financial and commercial issues, focuses on markets and business opportunities that yield the largest returns

In addition to the dimensions of communication, adaptability, and organizational and commercial awareness, the group-discussion exercise assessed the following:

- *Teamwork*—cooperates and works well with others in the pursuit of team goals, shares information, develops supportive relationships with colleagues, and creates a sense of team spirit

Finally, in addition to tenacity–resilience and teamwork, the behavior-description interview was designed to assess

- *Self-discipline*—is committed, consistent, and dependable, can be relied on to deliver what has been agreed to, is punctual and conscientious
- *Cross-cultural awareness*—is able to see issues from the perspective of people from other cultures

Results indicated that cognitive ability was significantly correlated with the test measuring language acquisition (corrected correlation of .27), but was not significantly correlated with instructors' ratings of CCT performance. Openness was significantly related to instructors' ratings of CCT performance (corrected correlation of .33), yet neither extroversion nor conscientiousness was. Agreeableness correlated significantly negatively with instructors' ratings of CCT performance (corrected correlation of −.26). As Caligiuri (2000) noted, although agreeableness may be universally positive for forming social relationships, individuals who are too agreeable may be seen as pushovers in some cultures. Hence, agreeableness may be culturally bound in terms of perceptions of professional competence.

Finally, emotional stability correlated significantly negatively with the language-proficiency test (corrected correlation of −.29). All dimensions measured in the group-discussion exercise were significantly correlated with instructor ratings (corrected correlations ranged from .31 to .40) and with the language-proficiency test (corrected correlations ranged from .33 to .44). None of the dimensions assessed either with the analysis-presentation exercise or with the behavior-description interview was significantly correlated with the criteria in the study.

Three dimensions measured by the group-discussion exercise accounted for a significant amount of additional variance in CCT performance. Teamwork explained significant additional variance in training performance beyond cognitive ability and agreeableness. Communication accounted for significant additional variance in training performance beyond cognitive ability and extroversion. Adaptability added a significant amount of variance over cognitive ability and openness.

Like Caligiuri (2000), Lievens et al. (2003) used a process of selecting people into cross-cultural training, providing the training to those selected, and then sending abroad those who passed the training. Performance in the CCT significantly predicted executives' performance in the Japanese companies (correlations of .38 for instructors' ratings and .45 for Japanese language proficiency). An important advantage of this process is that it may reduce the costs of international assignees because only people who pass the selection process and who, therefore, are predisposed for expatriate success are sent to the training and then abroad. Now let us consider CCT itself.

CROSS-CULTURAL TRAINING

Many organizations send their employees to other countries to conduct business. To maximize their effectiveness, the companies often provide opportunities for CCT prior to departure. Indeed, a 2008 Global Relocation Trends survey revealed that 84 percent of multinationals provide cross-cultural preparation of at least one day's duration, and all family members are eligible to participate. Unfortunately, however, fully 77 percent make it optional (GMAC Global Relocation Services, 2008). *Cross-cultural training* (CCT) refers to formal programs designed to prepare persons of one culture to interact effectively in another culture or to interact more effectively with persons from different cultures (Aguinis & Kraiger, 2009; Bhawuk & Brislin, 2000). Such programs typically focus on cognitive, affective, and behavioral competencies (Littrell, Salas, Hess, Paley, & Riedel, 2006).

To survive, cope, and succeed, expatriates need training in three areas: the culture, the language, and practical day-to-day matters (Dowling, Festing, & Engle, 2009). Female expatriates need training on the norms, values, and traditions that host nationals possess about women and also on how to deal with challenging situations they may face as women (Caligiuri & Cascio, 2000; Harris, 2006; Napier & Taylor, 2002). Females accounted for 20 percent of expatriates in 2008, compared with 10 percent in 1994 (GMAC Global Relocation Services, 2008).

A key characteristic of successful international managers is adaptability. Empirical research has revealed eight different dimensions of adaptability: handling emergencies or crisis situations; handling work stress; solving problems creatively; dealing with uncertain and unpredictable work situations; learning work tasks, technologies, and procedures; demonstrating interpersonal adaptability; demonstrating cultural adaptability; and demonstrating physically oriented adaptability (Pulakos, Arad, Donovan, & Plamondon, 2000). This implies that an effective way to train employees to adapt is to expose them to situations like they will encounter in their assignments that require adaptation. Such a strategy has two benefits: (1) It enhances transfer of training, and (2) it is consistent with the idea that adaptive performance is enhanced by gaining experience in similar situations.

As is true of any training program, needs assessment should precede actual training in order to incorporate the three key elements of CCT: the needs of the expatriate, the customization of design and content, and overall program quality (Littrell et al. 2006). To identfy the needs of the expatriate, assess strenghts and weaknesses with respect to interpersonl, cogntive, and self-maintenance skills, along with spousal and family needs. Customization can then proceed to meet the needs identified. In addition, CCT should be designed and delivered by individuals regarded as experts on the destination country as well as on the expatriation process (Bennett, Aston, & Colquhoun, 2000; Littrell et al., 2006). Finally, build in an evaluation component that addresses both performance in the overseas assignment, as well as a critique of training in preparing the expatriate and his or her family for their foreign assignment.

CCT usually includes several components. The first is awareness or orientation—helping trainees to become aware of their own cultural values, frameworks, and customs. A second is behavioral—providing opportunities for trainees to learn and practice behaviors that are appropriate to the culture in question (Brislin & Bhawuk, 1999; Landis & Bhagat, 1996). Within this framework, the cross-cultural assimilator method has emerged as one of the most valid tools for CCT (Triandis, 1994).

The cultural assimilator is a programmed learning technique that was developed by Fiedler, Mitchell, and Triandis (1971). It uses 35–100 critical incidents that focus on cultural differences. Trainees are then presented with alternative behavioral options, and they must select one of them. Depending on the response chosen, the text directs trainees to a specific page and provides an explanation of why the choice was correct or incorrect. If their response was incorrect, trainees must reread the material and choose again.

Harrison (1992) compared the effectiveness of a Japanese culture assimilator, behavior-modeling training, a combination of the two methods, and no training at all in a field experiment involving 65 U.S. government employees. Participants receiving the combination of methods displayed significantly higher performance on a role-play task (evaluated in terms of behavior) than the no-training control group, and significantly higher gains in learning than either those who received a single method or those in the no-training control group. These results suggest the need for both a cognitive- and an experiential-based program in cross-cultural management training, although it would be valuable to replicate them using a larger sample of trainees.

While most applications of the cultural assimilator focus on a specific culture—for example, Greece, Iran, Thailand, Honduras, or Turkey (e.g., Gazur, 1994)—it is also possible to provide general culture training in a culture-assimilator format. Such training applies to any culture (Triandis, Kurowski, & Gelfand, 1994). For example, Cushner and Brislin (1996) developed more than 100 critical incidents based on a general model of competencies valuable in cross-cultural interactions. Initial research supports the efficacy of this type of training (Kraiger, 2003).

Quantitative as well as qualitative reviews of research on CCT have found that it has a positive impact on an individual's development of skills, on his or her adjustment to the cross-cultural situation, and on his or her managerial effectiveness. Thus Morris & Robie (2001) conducted a meta-analysis of the effects of CCT on expatriate performance and adjustment. They included 16 studies that investigated adjustment and 25 studies that investigated job performance as the focal dependent variable. The mean correlation for the relationship between training and adjustment was 0.12 ($p < 0.05$), and the correlation for the relationship between training and performance was 0.23 ($p < 0.05$). However, there was substantial variability in the distribution of effect sizes, suggesting that potential moderators existed.

More recently, Littrell et al. (2006) conducted a qualitative review of 25 years (1980–2005) of research addressing the effectiveness of CCT in preparing managers for an international assignment. The researchers examined 29 prior conceptual reviews and 16 empirical studies. Overall, they concluded that CCT is effective at enhancing the expatriate's success on overseas assignments. They also identified many variables that moderate the effects of training, including its timing (e.g., predeparture, while on assignment, and postassignment), family issues (e.g., spouse's adjustment), attributes of the job (e.g., job discretion), and cultural differences between the home country and the assignment country.

In another study, Lievens et al. (2003) reported correlations of .38 and .45, respectively, between CCT and both supervisor ratings and language proficiency. Evidence also indicates that training should take place prior to departure (information about local living conditions and the cross-cultural adjustment process), as well as after arrival in the new location (learning how to learn in the new environment) (Littrell et al., 2006). Formal mentoring for expatriates by host-country nationals also shows organizational support, and it can help to improve both language skills and the ability to interact effectively (Kraimer, Wayne, & Jaworski, 2001). Indeed, a multilevel, cross-cultural study of mentoring (Gentry, Weber, & Sadri, 2008) found that managers who are rated by their direct reports as engaging in career-related mentoring behaviors are perceived as better performers by their bosses. However, the societal-culture dimension of Performance Orientation was a significant cross-level moderator of the career-related mentoring–performance relationship. Performance Orientation refers to the extent to which a society or culture encourages and rewards group members for performance improvement and excellence (House et al., 2004).

With respect to language training, experts note that even easier languages, such as Spanish, require 150 classroom hours to reach a minimal level of proficiency. Minimal proficiency means being able to exchange greetings, get directions, shop, and order food in a restaurant, for example. That level of proficiency in a difficult language, such as Chinese, requires 350 classroom hours (Tyler, 2004).

One final issue deserves mention, namely, the relationship between the stage of global-ization of a firm and CCT rigor and breadth. Firms tend to evolve from domestic (exporters) to international (or multidomestic) to multinational to global, and, in some cases, to transnational (Dowling et al., 2009). In general, the more a firm moves away from the export stage of development, the more rigorous the training should be, including its breadth of content. At the multinational and global stages, managers need to be able to socialize host-country managers into the firm's corporate culture and other firm-specific practices. This added managerial responsibility intensifies the need for rigorous training.

Performance Management

Performance management is just as important in the international context as it is in domestic operations. The major difference is that *implementation* is much more difficult in the interna-tional arena (Briscoe et al., 2009). Although we covered this topic extensively in Chapter 5, the special considerations associated with international assignments require that we address it here as well. At its most basic level, performance management in the international context refers to the evaluation and continuous improvement of individual or team performance (Cascio, 2006). It includes goals, appraisal, and feedback.

Consider four broad constraints on the achievement of goals in the international context (Dowling et al., 2009). One, from the perspective of home-country executives, differences in local accounting rules or labor laws may make it difficult to compare the relative performance of managers of subsidiaries in different countries. Two, in turbulent international environments, long-term objectives need to be flexible. Three, separation by time and distance may make it dif-ficult for performance management systems to take account of country-specific factors. Four, market development in foreign subsidiaries is generally slower and more difficult than at home. Hence, expatriates need more time to achieve results.

At the same time, a number of factors affect the actual level of job performance of expatri-ate managers (Davis, 1998; Engle, Dowling, & Festing, 2008; Oddou & Mendenhall, 2000). These include technical knowledge (95 percent of expatriates believe it to be crucial for job success), personal (and family) adjustment to the culture, and environmental factors (political and labor-force stability, currency fluctuations, and cultural distance from one's home culture). While technical knowledge is important, the expatriate who is an expert in his or her field but who ignores cultural variables such as procedures and customs that are important to job perform-ance will likely be ineffective. This was the case with an expatriate of a construction firm who was sent to India. Unintentionally, he ignored local work customs and became an object of hatred and distrust. The project was delayed more than six months because of his behavior (Oddou & Mendenhall, 2000).

The degree of support from headquarters (benefits and services, including job-search help for the spouse and financial support for his or her children's education) also affects an expatriate's job performance ("For dual-career expats," 2009). Finally, characteristics of the host-country environment have a powerful impact—its stage of economic development, its physical demands on the expatriate (heat, humidity, cold), and the type of business operation (e.g., international joint venture versus wholly owned subsidiary). Figure 17-2 presents a sum-mary of these factors.

Performance Criteria

A thorough review of research in this area led Sinangil and Ones (2001) to propose the following working model of the dimensions of expatriate job performance:

- **Establishment and maintenance of business contacts**—identification, development and use of such contacts to achieve goals
- **Technical performance**—that is, task performance

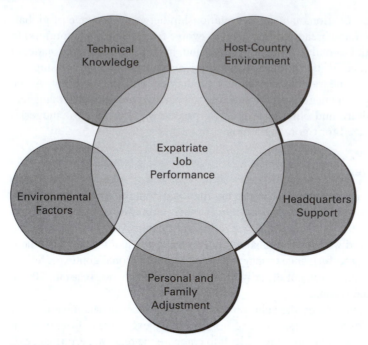

FIGURE 17-2   Some factors that affect the performance of expatriates.

- **Productivity**—volume of work the expatriate produces
- **Ability to work with others**—proficiency in working with and assisting others in the organization
- **Communication and persuasion**—oral and written proficiency in gathering and transmitting information; persuading others
- **Effort and initiative**—dedication to one's job; amount of effort expended in striving to do a good job
- **Personal discipline**—avoidance of counterproductive behaviors at work
- **Interpersonal relations**—the degree to which the expatriate facilitates team performance and supports others in the organization and unit
- **Management and supervision**—proficiency in the coordination of different roles in the organization
- **Overall job performance**—composite of all dimensions of expatriate job performance described above

This list reflects intangibles that are often difficult to measure—and usually are not measured—using typical performance appraisal methods. It also suggests that performance criteria for expatriates fall into three broad categories (Davis, 1998; Dowling et al., 2009): objective criteria, subjective criteria, and contextual criteria.

Objective criteria include such measures as gross revenues, market share, and return on investment. There are several potential problems with such measures. First, all financial figures generally are subject to the problem of currency conversion, and currency fluctuations may make accurate assessment of financial contribution difficult. Second, host governments may place restrictions on the repatriation of profits and also on currency conversion. Third, financial measures ignore the ways that results are obtained. That is, they ignore the behaviors used to generate the results. Especially when political or work environments are unstable (e.g., frequent strikes), such behaviors are critical. These shortcomings suggest that additional criteria should be used to provide a deeper, fuller understanding of expatriate performance. Such criteria include subjective and contextual criteria.

Subjective criteria include judgments, usually by local executives, of factors such as the expatriate's leadership style and interpersonal skills. While local management tends to appraise the expatriate's performance from its own cultural frame of reference, such an evaluation is usually perceived as more accurate than that from the home office (Oddou & Mendenhall, 2000). Janssens (1994) suggests that performance appraisals of managers of subsidiaries using objective criteria are often supplemented by frequent visits by staff from headquarters and meetings with executives from the parent company. Subjective criteria can be used to complement objective criteria and take into account areas that are difficult to quantify, such as integrity, customer orientation, and teamwork.

Contextual criteria take into consideration factors that result from the situation in which performance occurs. They include organizational citizenship behaviors (helping and cooperating with others, working with enthusiasm, volunteering for activities, being flexible and open to change), as well as indicators of cross-cultural skill development (e.g., language, host culture, communication, networking) (Davis, 1998; Piekkari, 2006).

When implementing performance appraisal internationally, therefore, first determine the purpose of the appraisal (professional development versus administrative decision making). Second, whenever possible, set standards of performance against quantifiable assignments, tasks, or objectives. Third, allow more time to achieve results abroad than is customary in the domestic market. Fourth, keep the objectives flexible and responsive to potential market and environmental conditions (Engle et al., 2008).

WHO SHOULD DO APPRAISALS?   Earlier we noted that host-country managers can take contextual criteria into account in assessing an expatriate's job performance, but they may have culture-bound biases that prevent them from putting the expatriate's performance into a broader organizational context. The reverse is true of home-country managers. They may not be able to take contextual criteria into account, but they can put the expatriate's performance into a broader organizational context. What about the expatriate's own self-evaluation? It is important to take his or her insights into account in order to provide a balanced perspective and to give him or her credit for relevant insights into the interdependencies among domestic and foreign operations.

How does the process actually work in practice? A recent study found that 36 percent of multinational enterprises used host-country performance reviews, and 35 percent used both home- and host-country reviews (GMAC Relocation Services, 2008). As in the domestic environment, be sure that whoever does the appraisal is knowledgeable of the employee's performance and is well trained.

PERFORMANCE FEEDBACK   In individualistic cultures, such as the United States, Great Britain, and Australia, a popular topic in first-level supervisory training programs is how to conduct appraisal interviews. Indeed, the ability to conduct performance appraisal interviews well and the ability to communicate "bad news" are considered key skills for a successful manager in such cultures. By contrast, in collectivist societies, such as Korea, Guatemala, and Taiwan, discussing a person's performance openly with him or her is likely to clash head-on with the society's norm of harmony, and the subordinate may view it as an unacceptable loss of face. Such societies have more subtle, indirect ways of communicating feedback, as by withdrawing a normal favor or communicating concerns verbally via a mutually trusted intermediary (Hofstede, 2001; Hofstede & Hofstede, 2005).

We covered the process of delivering feedback in the domestic context in Chapter 5. The important point here is that it is crucial to be sensitive to local customs with respect to the process used to communicate feedback (Cascio, 2006). As with domestic assignments, ongoing coaching and feedback are hallmarks of effective performance-management systems (Aguinis, 2009a).

Upon the expatriate's return from an overseas assignment, have a formal debriefing with him or her. Key topics to address are ways to improve the overall selection, training, appraisal, compensation, and expatriate-management process. This is the first step in repatriation, the topic we discuss next.

REPATRIATION

The problems of repatriation, for those who succeed abroad as well as for those who do not, have been well documented. All repatriates experience some degree of anxiety in three areas: personal finances, reacclimation to the home-country lifestyle, and readjustment to the corporate structure (Black & Gregersen, 1991; McClenahen, 1997). Fully 68 percent of U. S. expatriates do not know what their jobs will be when they return home, and only 5 percent believe their companies value overseas experience (Milkovich & Newman, 2008). Precisely the same issues have been found in studies of Japanese and Finnish expatriates (Black, Gregersen, & Mendenhall, 1992; Gregersen & Black, 1996).

Financially, repatriates face the loss of foreign-service premiums (e.g., for children's education, maid service, clubs) and the effect of inflation on home purchases. Having become accustomed to foreign ways, upon reentry they often find home-country customs strange and, at the extreme, annoying. Such "reverse culture shock" may be more challenging than the culture shock experienced when going overseas (Gregersen, 1992)! Possible solutions to these problems fall into three areas: planning, career management, and compensation.

Planning

Both the expatriation assignment and the repatriation move should be examined as parts of an integrated whole—not as unrelated events in an individual's career (Briscoe et al., 2009). Unfortunately, this occurs less than half the time (48 percent). For the remainder of expatriates, 55 percent held repatriation discussions fewer than six months before the completion of their assignments (GMAC Global Relocation services, 2008). To improve this process, it is necessary to define a clear strategic purpose for the move. Prior to the assignment, the firm should define one or more of the three primary purposes for sending a particular expatriate abroad: executive development, coordination and control between headquarters and foreign operations, and transfer of information and technology. Research shows that, unless there is a planned purpose in repatriation, the investment of as much as $1 million to send an expatriate overseas is likely to be squandered completely (Black et al., 1992; Roberts, Kossek, & Ozeki, 1998).

Increasingly, multinational corporations are seeking to improve their HR planning and also to implement it on a worldwide basis. Careful inclusion of expatriation and repatriation moves in this planning will help reduce uncertainty and the fear that accompanies it. Here's how Monsanto does it.

BOX 17-1

Company Example: Repatriation at Monsanto

Monsanto is an agricultural, chemical, and pharmaceutical company with many suppliers, customers, and operations outside the United States. Periodically, it sends U.S. employees to work with large customers or suppliers overseas (Postovit, 2002). Preparation for repatriation begins before the employee actually leaves the United States. The employee, together with both the sending and the receiving managers, prepares an agreement that specifies mutual understandings of the assignment and how it fits into the company's business objectives. It also specifies expectations and how the employee will use the knowledge gained upon his or her return. In an effort to help educate home-country colleagues about different business and cultural issues, all returning expatriates share their experiences with peers, subordinates, and higher-level managers. Finally, the returning expatriate debriefs with a trained counselor, who discusses all of the important aspects of the repatriation and helps the employee understand what he or she is experiencing.

Career Management

The attrition rate for repatriated workers is among the highest in corporate life, as data from a large 2008 survey revealed. Fully 25 percent of expatriates left their companies during their assignments, 27 percent within one year of returning, 25 percent between the first and second year, and 23 percent after two years. That's compared to 13 percent average annual turnover in the United States for all employees (GMAC Global Relocation services, 2008). Two-thirds of respondents in the same survey said that "opportunities to use international experience" was the best method to reduce expatriate turnover. Research with 111 expatriates from 23 countries who returned to their home countries within the previous year suggested that happens infrequently. Compared to their expatriate job assignments, 16 percent of the repatriates were in a job that they considered a demotion, 57 percent were in a job considered a lateral move, and 27 percent were in a job considered a promotion. Receiving a promotion upon repatriation, however, signaled that the organization values international experience, and it contributed to repatriates' beliefs that the organization met their expectations regarding training and career development. These two perceptions, in turn, related positively to career satisfaction and to intentions to stay (Kraimer, Shaffer, Harrison, & Ren, 2007).

Compensation

The loss of a monthly premium to which the expatriate has been accustomed is a severe shock financially, whatever the rationale. To overcome this problem, some firms have replaced the monthly foreign-service premium with a onetime "mobility premium" (e.g., six months' pay) for each move—overseas, back home, or to another overseas assignment. A few firms also provide low-cost loans or other financial assistance so that expatriates can get back into their hometown housing markets at a level at least equivalent to what they left. Finally, there is a strong need for financial counseling for repatriates. Such counseling has the psychological advantage of demonstrating to repatriates that the company is willing to help with the financial problems that they may encounter in uprooting their families once again to bring them home (Thompson, 1998; Woodward, 2007).

Evidence-Based Implications for Practice

Globalization and the rise of the Internet are perhaps the most important developments in our time. While societies are becoming more interconnected than ever before, this does not imply that cultural nuances in different countries and regions of the world will become less important. They change at a glacial pace. Here are some other key implications:

- The study of country- or regional-level differences in behavior is important because it allows us to put current theories of motivation, leadership, and organizational behavior into perspective.
- Early identification of potential for international management will become more critical, as the world becomes more interconnected. Sound measurement of key executive competencies is important in this context, and well-developed psychological measures, like Prospector, are available for that purpose.
- Research has demonstrated the international validity generalization of GMA and personality dimensions in the prediction of job and training success, as well as in predicting the adjustment and job performance of expatriates.
- Expatriates need training in three areas: the culture, the language, and practical day-to-day matters. A variety of cross-cultural training methods have proven effective, but as is true of any training program, needs assessment should precede actual training in order to incorporate three key elements: the needs of the expatriate, the customization of design and content, and overall program quality.

> • When implementing performance appraisal internationally, first determine the purpose of the appraisal; set standards of performance against quantifiable assignments, tasks, or objectives; allow more time to achieve results abroad than is customary in the domestic market; and keep the objectives flexible and responsive to potential market and environmental conditions.
> • Finally, treat expatriation and repatriation as parts of an integrated whole—not as unrelated events in an individual's career.

In our next and last chapter, we shall consider emerging ethical issues in applied psychology. We shall begin by considering the nature of ethics, employee privacy, and fair information-practice policies in the information age.

Discussion Questions

1. How does the theory of vertical and horizontal individualism and collectivism help to deepen our understanding of cultural differences?
2. Explain Hofstede's five dimensions that describe differences across countries. Identify countries that are high (low) on each dimension.
3. Four broad processes seem to facilitate the development of future international executives. Explain why each is relevant.
4. You have been asked to develop a selection program for expatriates to Vietnam. Based on research results in the applied psychology literature, what would you propose?

5. What might an effective performance-management program for expatriates look like?
6. Adaptability is a key feature of successful international managers. How does adaptability manifest itself, and how would you train prospective expatriates to be more adaptable?
7. Your boss asks you for advice on how to reduce the attrition rate of repatriates. How would you respond?

Organizational Responsibility and Ethical Issues in Human Resource Management

At a Glance

Organizational responsibility (OR) is defined as context-specific organizational actions and policies that take into account stakeholders' expectations and the triple bottom line of economic, social, and environmental performance (Aguinis, in press). OR subsumes the concept of ethics because voluntary actions or patterns of behavior that have the potential to harm or alter the welfare of others are considered unethical. By taking into account stakeholders' expectations, the chances of causing harm are reduced and, therefore, OR leads to more ethical actions and policies. Although largely unrecognized, HRM researchers and practitioners can play a central role in OR research and practice. Thus, OR provides a unique and valuable opportunity for HRM researchers and practitioners to make contributions that are consistent with the field's dual mission of enhancing human well-being and maximizing organizational performance, and that have the potential to elevate the field in the eyes of society at large.

Regarding both OR and ethics, one cannot prescribe them by inflexible rules. Rather, OR and ethical behavior adapt and change in response to social norms and in response to the needs and interests of those stakeholders served by a profession. In the context of HRM, three areas in particular deserve special emphasis: employee privacy, testing and evaluation, and organizational research. Regarding employee privacy, some key concerns are the use and disclosure of employee records and the monitoring of computer files and e-mail communications. Public concern for ethical behavior in testing and evaluation centers around obligations of HR experts to their profession, to job applicants and employees, and to their employers. Finally, researchers in organizational settings frequently encounter ethical dilemmas arising from role ambiguity, role conflict, and ambiguous or conflicting norms. Such dilemmas are likely to be present at each of the stages of the research process, beginning with research planning and ending with the reporting of results. Strategies are available for resolving these dilemmas so that an acceptable consensus among interested parties regarding an ethical course of action can be reached.

The challenge of being responsible and ethical in managing people does not lie in the mechanical application of moral prescriptions. It is found in the process of creating and maintaining genuine relationships from which to address ethical dilemmas that cannot be covered by prescription. One's personal values play an important part in this process.

Organizational responsibility (OR) is defined as context-specific organizational actions and policies that take into account stakeholders' expectations and the triple bottom line of economic, social, and environmental performance (Aguinis, in press). OR subsumes the concept of ethics because voluntary actions or patterns of behavior that have the potential to harm or alter the welfare of others are considered unethical. By taking into account stakeholders' expectations, the chances of causing harm are reduced and, therefore, OR leads to more ethical actions and policies. To be ethical is to conform to moral standards or to conform to the standards of conduct of a given group (Webster's New World Dictionary, 2009). Ethical behavior is not governed by hard-and-fast rules; it adapts and changes in response to social norms and in response to the needs and interests of those served by a profession. It represents a "continuous adjustment of interests" (Brady, 1985, p. 569). This is very obvious in HRM. What was considered responsible and ethical in the 1950s and the 1960s (deep-probing selection interviews; management prescriptions of standards of dress, ideology, and lifestyle; refusal to let employees examine their own employment files) would be considered improper today. Increased accountability and concern for human rights has placed HR policies, procedures, and research practices in the public domain (Aguinis, in press). Civil rights laws, discrimination suits, and union agreements have been effective instruments of social change. The resulting emphasis on freedom of information and concern for individual privacy are sensitizing both employees and employers to ethical concerns.

Our intention in this chapter is not to offer as truth a set of principles for OR and ethical behavior in HRM. Rather, our intent is to highlight emerging ethical concerns in several important areas. We make no attempt to be comprehensive, and, in fact, we will limit discussion to three areas: employee privacy, testing and evaluation, and organizational research. Although we cannot prescribe the *content* of responsible and ethical behavior across all conceivable situations, we can prescribe *processes* that can lead to an acceptable (and temporary) consensus among interested parties regarding an ethical course of action. Where relevant, we will not hesitate to do so.

Let us begin by defining some important terms:

- *Privacy:* The interest that employees have in controlling the use that is made of their personal information and in being able to engage in behavior free from regulation or surveillance (Piller, 1993b).
- *Confidentiality:* The treatment of information provided with the expectation that it will not be disclosed to others. Confidentiality may be established by law, by institutional rules, or by professional or scientific relationships (American Psychological Association, 2002).
- *Ethics and morality:* Behaviors about which society holds certain values (Reese & Fremouw, 1984).
- *Ethical choice:* Considered choice among alternative courses of action where the interests of all parties have been clarified and the risks and gains have been evaluated openly and mutually (Mirvis & Seashore, 1979).
- *Ethical decisions about behavior:* Those that take account not only of one's own interests but also equally of the interests of those affected by the decision (Cullen, Victor, & Stephens, 1989).
- *Validity:* In this context, the overall degree of justification for the interpretation and use of an assessment procedure (Messick, 1980, 1995).

ORGANIZATIONAL RESPONSIBILITY: DEFINITION AND GENERAL FRAMEWORK

Following Aguinis (in press), we use the more encompassing term "organizational" instead of the narrower term "corporate" to emphasize that responsibility refers to any type of organization (e.g., publicly traded, privately owned, governmental, nongovernmental, entrepreneurial). In addition, although initially seen as the exclusive realm of large corporations, we see OR as not only possible but also necessary for start-ups and small and medium-sized organizations if they want to be successful in today's globalized and hypercompetitive economy. Finally, we use the broader term "responsibility" instead of the narrower phrase "social responsibility" to highlight that responsibility refers to several types of stakeholders, including employees and suppliers, and issues that subsume but also go beyond topics defined as being in the social realm (e.g., the natural environment). Note that the issues we discuss in this chapter, which have traditionally been the focus of HRM research and practice, refer also to international stakeholders (e.g., employees, participants in a research study).

This definition includes several important components. First, as noted earlier, the definition refers to all types of organizations regardless of ownership structure, mission, and size. For example, although their focus is not on economic performance, even governmental and nongovernmental organizations (NGOs) need to be managed in financially sound ways to survive. Second, this definition goes beyond a more passive underlying value position of "not doing harm," to a more proactive position of "doing the right thing." Third, as noted earlier, this definition subsumes the concept of ethics because voluntary actions or patterns of behavior that have the potential to harm or alter the welfare of others are considered unethical. By taking into account stakeholders' expectations, the chances of causing harm are reduced. Accordingly, OR leads to more ethical actions and policies. Fourth, also related to stakeholders, an important component of this definition is that their expectations are taken into account. Stakeholders are the groups and individuals who affect or can be affected by the achievement of the organization's objectives (Freeman, 1984). Thus, stakeholders can include owners and investors, employees, external contractors, suppliers, customers, partners in various collaborations, and the surrounding community. Considering their expectations means going from stakeholder analysis or stakeholder management to stakeholder engagement. Although HRM researchers and practitioners typically think about employees and other internal issues (Moir, 2007), considering stakeholders' expectations more broadly forces the HRM field to think about external stakeholders as well. Because there are both internal and external stakeholders, OR is driven both internally and externally, and OR initiatives do not take place only reactively as a consequence of external forces, but also proactively as a consequence of internal and external stakeholders' expectations. Responsible organizations go beyond merely disseminating organizational information and, instead, communicate with stakeholders in an ongoing two-way process (Burchell & Cook, 2006). Unless there is stakeholder engagement, OR risks becoming an inconsequential statement posted on an organization's Web site.

The definition of OR refers to the triple bottom line of economic, social, and environmental performance. Unfortunately, the traditional view is that these performance dimensions are negatively correlated. For example, there is the view that a mining company may not be highly profitable if it adheres to strict environmental codes and respects the wishes of the surrounding communities (Alexandrescu, 2007). As a second example, there is the view that a cloth manufacturer may not be able to maximize profits and also provide fair wages and good working conditions to employees in its sweatshops abroad (Varley, 1998).

The skepticism regarding the simultaneous maximization of economic, social, and environmental performance also stems from critics who argue that OR is a ploy of corporations to "look" good, a mere public relations campaign to protect organizations' reputations and profit margins. The potential incompatibility between economic and social goals and values is a recurring theme in the history of the field of HRM (e.g., Baritz, 1960). As noted rather forcefully by Hersey (1932), "The psychologist . . . who goes into an industrial establishment for the sole purpose of increasing production, rather than bettering the adjustment of the individual members of the concern . . . is a traitor to his calling. . . ." (p. 304). The skepticism about the simultaneous maximization of what seem to be incompatible goals is reflected well in the following quote attributed to Groucho Marx: "What you need to succeed in business is honesty. Fake that and you've got it made."

In spite of the skepticism surrounding OR, there are two factors that now serve as important catalysts for OR: changes in twenty-first-century organizations and accountability. Regarding twenty-first-century organizational changes, a critical one has been caused by the use of the Internet. The Internet allows individuals inside and outside of the organization to access a mind-boggling array of information instantaneously and almost from anywhere. In contrast to just a few years ago, information about organizations and their policies and actions can now be accessed around the globe almost without delay. For example, companies such as Nike and Gap have made important efforts to reduce the abuse of workers in their contract factories in Indonesia and El Salvador, respectively, given intense public scrutiny led by activist groups who used the Internet to disseminate information (Varley, 1998). Web sites such as youtube.com have been used to show clips of executives from Enron, WorldCom, and ImClone being led away in handcuffs with great fanfare (Greenfield, 2004). There are numerous examples of organizations such as BP, Shell, ExxonMobil, and Starbucks that have adopted more responsible practices due, in part, to how the Internet has allowed people to share information quickly and inexpensively (see Aguinis, in press).

Another important consequence of the Internet is that the twenty-first-century organization looks like a web instead of a pyramid because it connects various stakeholders, such as partners, employees, external contractors, suppliers, and customers in various collaborations (Cascio & Aguinis, 2008b). The twenty-first-century organization is boundaryless and global because it uses talent and resources wherever they are available around the globe, just as it sells products and offers its services wherever demand exists around the globe. As noted by Cascio and Aguinis (2008b), "The new global organization might be based in the United States but does its software programming in Sri Lanka, its engineering in Germany, and its manufacturing in China. Every outpost will be connected seamlessly by the Net, so that far-flung employees and freelancers can work together in real time" (pp. 135–136). Regardless of the extent to which an organization engages in OR initiatives, one important implication is that the various stakeholders are becoming increasingly interdependent and, given the flow of information and work, it is difficult to distinguish employees from nonemployees and internal from external stakeholders.

The availability of information and increased stakeholder engagement has led to a wave of accountability that permeates organizations ranging from universities to governmental organizations and NGOs, up to multinational corporations. For example, universities in the United States control about $400 billion in capital and have been under pressure for several decades to invest their endowments in ways that prevent or correct social injury (i.e., activities that violate rules of domestic or international law intended to protect individuals from deprivation of health, safety, or basic freedoms) (The Responsible Endowment Coalition, 2009). In addition, many governmental organizations now implement performance management systems that hold managers and employees, and their organizational units, accountable for how they spend taxpayer money and for initiatives that are perceived to be important in their communities (Aguinis, 2009a).

In short, twenty-first-century organizations find it increasingly difficult to hide information about their policies and actions. In addition, the twenty-first-century organization is increasingly dependent on a global network of stakeholders who have expectations about the organization's policies and actions. These two factors have led to increased accountability, which is an important motivator for organizations for acting responsibly.

ORGANIZATIONAL RESPONSIBILITY: BENEFITS

The preponderance of the empirical evidence accumulated thus far suggests that pursuing social and environmental goals is related to positive economic results (Aguinis, in press). In other words, there are clear benefits for organizations that choose to pursue the triple bottom line instead of economic performance exclusively and organizations can both do good and well. Although some refer to an antagonistic relationship between organizational profit and productivity objectives on the one hand versus societal goals and considerations on the other, this seems a false dichotomy (Haigh & Jones, 2007). Organizations are successful in the long run only if they do both: please shareholders and also please other stakeholders. The challenge is "how to ensure that the firm pays wider attention to the needs of multiple stakeholders whilst at the same time delivering shareholder value" (Moir, Kennerley, & Ferguson, 2007, p. 388).

Consider the following selective evidence (Aguinis, in press):

- Capriotti and Moreno (2007) described a consumer study conducted in Spain and found that 75 percent of consumers have penalized or were willing to penalize companies they perceived as not being socially responsible. A separate consumer study conducted in the United Kingdom found that more than 75 percent of consumers consider that an organization's level of social responsibility is important and about 90 percent of employees believe their organizations should be socially responsible.

• From an organizational-strategy perspective, results from a 2002 survey by Pricewater-houseCoopers, including 1,200 CEOs from 33 countries (Simms, 2002; Verschoor, 2003), found that about 70 percent of global chief executives think that corporate social responsibility is vital to their companies, even during an economic downturn. In fact, some argue that OR is even more crucial during difficult economic times. Specifically, "The financial crisis and the subsequent economic downturn represent a significant upheaval in the evolution of markets and the private sector. Restoring trust and confidence, and shifting to a long-term paradigm of economic value creation in the spirit of universal values should therefore be viewed as the central imperatives . . ." (The Global Economic Downturn, 2009).

• A study of 602 companies in the Morgan Stanley Capital International World Index that have been included in the Oekom's Corporate Responsibility Ratings showed that the 186 companies that received the highest responsibility ratings outperformed the 416 companies that received the lowest ratings by 23.4 percent between January 2000 and October 2003 (Hollender, 2004).

• A meta-analysis of 52 independent studies demonstrated that there is a positive relationship between social/environmental performance and financial performance (Orlitzky, Schmidt, & Rynes, 2003). This meta-analysis found an average correlation between corporate social/environmental performance and corporate financial performance of $\rho = .36$. This correlation was obtained after correcting for sampling error and measurement error in the predictor and criterion measures and was based on 388 separate correlations and a total sample size of 33,878. The average relationship between corporate social/environmental performance and financial performance was still positive when it excluded correlations computed using reputation measures for social/environmental performance and surveys for financial performance (i.e., $\rho = .15$).

• A separate meta-analysis (using part of the same database) found that that relationship does not depend on firm size (Orlitzky, 2001). It is also noteworthy that the average correlation between social performance and financial performance was $\rho = .47$, whereas the average correlation between environmental performance and financial performance was $\rho = .13$.

• Ambec and Lanoie (2008) conducted an extensive qualitative literature review focusing exclusively on the benefits of environmentally responsible practices. The overall conclusion is that benefits of such practices are related to both increased revenues as well as cost reduction through separate mechanisms. Specifically, better environmental performance is related to increased revenues due to better access to certain markets, better product differentiation, and better pollution-control technology. Also, better environmental performance is related to a reduction in cost due to better risk management and relations with external stakeholders, lower cost of material, energy, and services, lower cost of capital, and lower cost of labor.

• Numerous organizations are very much aware of the benefits of being responsible. This is why many create a position of "Corporate Responsibility Officer" (Marshall & Heffes, 2007). However, although this specific title exists, more common titles are vice president or director of corporate social responsibility. Regardless of the title, which can also be chief compliance officer, chief ethics officer, or investor relations officer (Marshall & Heffes, 2007), the point is that OR is seen as an important ingredient of business strategy. Job announcements for such positions include a variety of responsibilities addressing both strategic and operational issues, such as working collaboratively with internal business partners, developing industry relationships to benchmark best practices, creating a unified innovative approach to green and community impact initiatives, adopting operating policies that exceed compliance with social and environmental laws, and conducting training for corporate social responsibility monitoring firms, suppliers and brand names and providing support to internal and external training programs.

In sum, the survey, qualitative, and meta-analytic evidence gathered thus far indicates that there is an overall positive relationship between social and environmental performance and financial performance, but the strength of this positive relationship varies depending on how one operationalizes social and/or environmental performance and financial performance.

ORGANIZATIONAL RESPONSIBILITY: IMPLEMENTATION AND THE ROLE OF HRM RESEARCH AND PRACTICE

Aguinis (in press) proposed the new concept of strategic responsibility management (SRM). SRM is a process that allows organizations to approach responsibility actions in a systematic and strategic manner. It involves the following steps (see Figure 18-1):

Step 1: Creating a vision and values related to responsibility

Step 2: Identifying expectations through dialogue with stakeholders and prioritizing them

Step 3: Developing initiatives that are integrated with corporate strategy

Step 4: Raising internal awareness through employee training

Step 5: Institutionalizing SRM as a way of doing business on an ongoing basis by measuring and rewarding processes and results

Step 6: Reporting on the status of the dialogue and the initiatives through a yearly OR report that is made available internally and externally

HRM researchers and practitioners are in a unique position to create and disseminate knowledge on how best to implement SRM. First, there is a need to create a shared vision and set of values about responsibility. Organizations cannot go down the OR path without considering management's personal values. Like any other organizationwide intervention, OR requires sponsorship from senior management and organizationwide ownership. Second, stakeholder engagement is crucial, but we need to define how and to what extent and in what capacity stakeholders are engaged (Greenwood, 2007). We also need to define how various OR polices and actions are directly related to each stakeholder group. These are areas to which HRM can clearly contribute

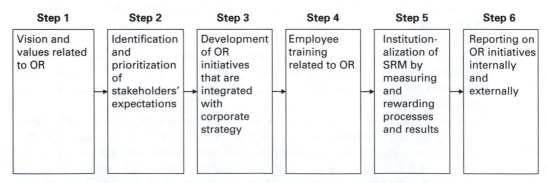

FIGURE 18-1 Sequence of steps involved in strategic responsibility management (SRM).
Source: Aguinis, H. (in press). Organizational responsibility: Doing good and doing well. In S. Zedeck (Ed.), *APA Handbook of industrial and organizational psychology (Vol. 1)*. Washington, DC: American Psychological Association.

Note: OR: Organizational responsibility.

given the vast literature on employee engagement (e.g., Maslach & Leiter, 2008). In terms of the identification of stakeholders, they can be mapped on a chart to indicate their relative importance, and management can prioritize OR issues based on how likely they are to affect the business (Hillenbrand & Money, 2007). The fourth step includes training of all organizational members all the way up to top management about OR and responsibility management. This training can include how SRM works, what is expected of employees, and how employees will benefit from SRM. In terms of specific content, at a minimum, training should provide answers to the following questions (Aguinis, 2009a):

- What is strategic responsibility management? Answering this question involves providing general information about SRM, how SRM is implemented in other organizations, and the general goals of SRM.
- How does SRM fit in our strategy? To answer this question, training should include information on the relationship between SRM and strategic planning. Specifically, information is provided on how SRM is directly related to the organization's strategic goals.
- What's in it for me? A good training program describes the benefits of implementing SRM for all those involved.

The fifth step addresses the consequences associated with OR. This includes creating indicators of success and describing how each indicator will be assessed, together with the clear consequences based on the results. For example, an indicator of stakeholder engagement is the extent to which the communication between staff members as well as with customers and other stakeholders is honest and complete (Hollender, 2004). Thus, the organization's performance management system must measure and reward OR policies and actions. Many organizations are already doing so. For example, data on 90 publicly traded companies in Canada show that long-term compensation of CEOs is related to OR actions related to products (Mahoney & Thorne, 2005). Finally, the last step involves reporting organizational activities related to OR. This reporting can include corporate financial reporting, corporate governance, OR, and reporting stakeholder value creation. This is also consistent with integrating OR within the organization's overall strategy.

The topic of OR is not on the mainstream HRM research agenda (Aguinis, in press). Possible reasons for the lack of attention to OR in the HRM literature include a general science–practice gap in the field; an emphasis on employees and internal organizational processes, usually at the individual level of analysis, versus other external stakeholders; external processes; and organizational-level phenomena. Nevertheless, HRM research has made important contributions to understanding certain aspects of OR. For example, consider the areas of test-score banding discussed in Chapter 8. The traditional approach to staffing decision making is to use a strict top–down procedure in which selection is made based on who obtained the highest test score(s). However, those involved in staffing decisions face a paradoxical situation because using general cognitive abilities and other valid predictors of job performance leads to adverse impact (Aguinis & Smith, 2007). Consequently, users of selection instruments face what seems to be a catch-22: choosing to use general cognitive abilities tests and risk decreasing the diversity of an organization's workforce, or choosing to use predictors that will not diminish diversity, but are not as valid as cognitive abilities tests. Based on this description, the situation seems the classical "win–lose" scenario of pitting social versus economic performance in a mutually exclusive manner. As discussed in Chapter 8, test-score banding was proposed as a method to solve this apparent dilemma because it is an alternative to the strict top–down selection strategy that often leads to adverse impact. Banding is based on the premise that an observed difference in the scores of two job applicants may be the result of measurement error instead of actual differences in the construct that is measured. Consequently, if it cannot be determined with a reasonable amount of certainty that two applicants differ on the construct underlying a predictor or criterion score, then there may be little reason to believe that they differ with respect to job performance. In other words, banding groups applicants who have "indistinguishable" scores. Consequently, job applicants who fall within the same band are considered equally qualified for the job in question. Therefore, choices can then be made among these "equivalent" applicants based on criteria other than test scores, such as diversity considerations. The case of test-score banding, although not labeled as such in the HRM literature, is an example of SRM in which the organization considers both economic and social interests.

Looking toward the future, there are many additional areas related to OR to which HRM researchers and practitioners can make important contributions (Aguinis, in press). Consider the following selected set of issues:

- The implementation of SRM can benefit from research design, measurement, and data-analytic tools that are routinely reported in HRM psychology research (e.g., Aguinis, Pierce, Bosco, & Muslin, 2009). For example, what are appropriate procedures for data collection from various stakeholder groups? Can HRM researchers and practitioners develop valid and standardized measures to assess the economic, social, and environmental performance dimensions? How can data from various stakeholders be combined or aggregated? What qualitative and quantitative research methods can be used separately or in combination to measure OR processes and outcomes? What types of research design can be implemented to gather convincing evidence regarding the causal effects of OR on various outcomes?

- Like any other organizational-change intervention, implementing SRM must be accompanied with a change in performance measurement and the reward structure. There is an important HRM psychology literature on the design and implementation of performance management systems, and motivation theories, that can help with the implementation of OR initiatives (Aguinis, 2009a). For example, performance management systems that include the measurement of both behaviors and results can be used to assess the relative effectiveness of OR initiatives.

- OR is intrinsically a multilevel phenomenon. The measurement and reporting of OR efforts can benefit from the HRM literature on multilevel issues (e.g., Aguinis et al., 2009). Specifically, multilevel data-analytic techniques can be particularly useful for assessing the effects of OR initiatives on individuals, groups, organizations, and society in general, as well as for assessing potential same-level and cross-level moderating effects.

- Issues such as commitment, engagement, dysfunctional and functional turnover, training, and employability are discussed in the OR literature but are typically absent from balance sheets or corporate reports. HRM practitioners can help make the business case for OR by extrapolating, adapting, and using measurement and psychometric techniques developed in other areas (e.g., training evaluation, performance management).

- Business schools are being criticized for not being responsible and are even blamed for training executives deficiently. Moreover, this training deficiency is, to some extent, seen as the culprit for some of the recent corporate scandals (Bendell, 2007). Should the field of HRM rethink its education and training programs so that OR takes on a more prominent role?

- HRM research tends to emphasize the individual level of analysis, and this type of approach can be beneficial for future research directions. For example, in terms of decision-making processes, are there individual-level variables (e.g., attitudes, personality) that explain why some individuals and, in turn, organizations are more likely to engage in organizational-level responsible initiatives compared to others? What is the role of culture (both at the organizational and national level), and how does it affect approaches to OR? Related to these questions, what are some of the underlying psychological processes that connect OR initiatives with individual-level attitudes and behaviors (Aguilera, Rupp, Williams, & Ganapathi, 2007)? For example, what is the relationship between OR and organizational attractiveness, job satisfaction, organizational commitment, citizenship behavior, and job performance (cf. Rupp, Ganapathi, Aguilera, & Williams, 2006)?

- The analysis of jobs and work has a long history in the field of HRM. However, a search on the O*NET (http://online.onetcenter.org/) revealed that there is no information on occupations related to OR. Thus, future applied research can investigate what are the knowledge, skills, and abilities required for OR officers in various types of industries. Such work would also inform the field regarding the extent to which HRM practitioners may be sufficiently equipped to occupy these positions.

In sum, since its inception, the field of HRM has walked a tightrope trying to balance employee well-being with maximization of organizational performance and profits. This dual role is a source of tension, as is reflected in the test-score banding literature and the staffing decision making literature in general. OR is a concept consistent with HRM's mission as well as the scientist-practitioner model. However, there is still concern and skepticism on the part of some that OR is more rhetoric and public relations than a reality. For example, Soares (2003) noted that "in the 'game' of corporations, moral responsibility is a word without meaning" (p. 143). HRM psychology researchers and practitioners can help address these concerns by designing and implementing SRM systems that induce organizations to act in responsible ways. HRM researchers and practitioners can also help make the business case for SRM and demonstrate that it is a win-win approach to management and not philanthropy that hurts the organization's "real" bottom line. Thus, OR provides a unique opportunity for HRM researchers and practitioners to make contributions consistent with the field's mission and that have the potential to elevate the field in the eyes of society at large.

There are some additional specific areas directly or indirectly related to OR to which HRM research has made important contributions. These include employee privacy, testing and evaluation, and organizational research. The next sections of the chapter address each of these issues.

EMPLOYEE PRIVACY

In the specific case of the United States, the U.S. Constitution, along with numerous federal and state laws and executive orders, defines legally acceptable behavior in the public and private sectors of the economy. Note, however, that, while illegal behaviors are by definition unethical, meeting minimal legal standards does not necessarily imply conformity to accepted guidelines of the community (Hegarty & Sims, 1979). Such legal standards have affected HR research and practice in at least three ways:

- EEO legislation, together with the interpretive guidelines of federal regulatory agencies, has emphasized the meaning and extent of unfair discrimination (e.g., with respect to racial or sexual harassment) and how it can be avoided.
- Both professional standards and federal guidelines illustrate appropriate procedures for developing and validating assessment procedures (see Appendix A). The values implied by these standards are that high-quality information should be used to make decisions about people and that HR professionals are responsible for developing procedures that result in the most accurate decisions possible.
- Twin concerns for individual privacy and freedom of information are raising new research questions and challenges. For example, does an employer have the right to search an employee's computer files or review the employee's e-mail and voice mail? How can confidentiality of information be guaranteed and invasion of privacy avoided while providing information to those who make employment decisions?

Employees clearly are more aware of these issues, and they are willing to take legal action when they believe that their privacy rights have been violated by their employers. See Box 18-1 for some examples.

Attention in this area centers on three main issues: the kind of information retained about individuals, how that information is used, and the extent to which that information can be

---

BOX 18-1

Practical Application: Do Employees Have a Right to Electronic Privacy?

When Alana Shoars arrived for work at Epson America, Inc., one morning, she discovered her supervisor reading and printing out electronic mail messages between other employees. Ms. Shoars was appalled. When she had trained employees to use the computerized system, she had told them their mail was private. Now a company manager was violating that trust.

When she questioned the practice, Ms. Shoars says she was told to mind her own business. A day later, she was fired for insubordination. Then she filed a $1 million lawsuit for wrongful termination. Although she soon found a job as e-mail administrator at another firm, she still bristles about Epson: "You don't read other people's mail, just as you don't listen to their phone conversations. Right is right, and wrong is wrong."

Michael Simmons, chief information officer at the Bank of Boston, disagrees completely. "If the corporation owns the equipment and pays for the network, that asset belongs to the company, and it has a right to look and see if people are using it for purposes other than running the business." The court agreed with this logic. Ms. Shoars lost. In another case, a supervisor at a Nissan subsidiary in California discovered e-mail between two female subordinates poking fun at his sexual prowess. When he fired them, the women sued and lost. The judge ruled (as in the Epson case) that the company had the right to read the e-mail because it owned and operated the equipment (McMorris, 1995).

---

disclosed to others. Unfortunately, many companies are failing to safeguard the privacy of their employees. Thus, a study of 126 *Fortune 500* companies employing 3.7 million people found the following (Solomon, 1989):

- While 87 percent of the companies allow employees to look at their personnel files, only 27 percent give them access to supervisors' files, which often contain more subjective information.
- Fifty-seven percent use private investigative agencies to collect or verify information about employees, and 42 percent collect information without telling the employee.
- Thirty-eight percent have no policy covering release of data to the government; of those that do, 38 percent don't require a subpoena.
- Eighty percent of companies will give information to an employee's potential creditor without a subpoena, and 58 percent will give information to landlords.

The results of a survey of top corporate managers of 301 businesses of all sizes and in a wide range of industries revealed another unsettling fact: Fewer than one in five had a written policy regarding electronic privacy—that is, privacy of employee computer files, voice mail, e-mail, and other networking communications. With respect to employee records contained in an HR information system, 66 percent of HR managers reported that they have unlimited access to such information, while 52 percent of executives do (Piller, 1993a). The apparent lack of attention to policies regarding information stored electronically is particularly troubling because employees are likely to feel safer when reporting personal information via a computer as compared to face to face (Richman, Kiesler, Weisband, & Dragow, 1999). Moreover, privacy concerns affect job applicants' test-taking motivation, organizational attraction, and organizational intentions (Bauer et al., 2006). Thus, because employees are likely to provide personal information electronically that they would not provide in person, organizations should take extra care in handling information gathered electronically.

Safeguarding Employee Privacy

Since September 11, 2001, workplace security and employees' expectation of privacy have changed in the United States. The USA Patriot Act of 2001 (available online at www.epic.org/privacy/terrorism/hr3162.html) grants broad powers to the government to track individuals' use of the Internet and requires that employers report any imminent threats to the government (with certain immunities for employers making the reports) (Obdyke, 2002). Because of these changes, it is particularly important for employers to establish a privacy-protection policy. Here are some general recommendations:

1. Set up guidelines and policies on requests for various types of data, on methods of obtaining the data, on retention and dissemination of information, on employee or third-party access to information, on the release of information about former employees, and on the mishandling of information.
2. Inform employees of these information-handling policies.
3. Become thoroughly familiar with state and federal laws regarding privacy.
4. Establish a policy that states specifically that employees or prospective employees cannot waive their rights to privacy.
5. Establish a policy that states that any manager or nonmanager who violates these privacy principles will be subject to discipline or termination ("A Model," 1993).
6. Permit employees to authorize disclosure of personal information and maintain personal information within the organization (Eddy, Stone, & Stone-Romero, 1999).

Fair Information Practice in the Information Age

The Electronic Communications Privacy Act of 1986 prohibits "outside" interception of e-mail by a third party—the government, the police, or an individual—without proper authorization (such as a search warrant). Information sent on public networks, such as Yahoo! and GMail, to which individuals and companies subscribe, is therefore protected. However, the law does not cover "inside" interception, and, in fact, no absolute privacy exists in a computer system, even for bosses. They may view employees on closed-circuit TV; tap their phones, e-mail, and network communications; and rummage through their computer files with or without employee knowledge or consent 24 hours a day (Elmer-Dewitt, 1993). In fact, a survey including over 1,000 HR managers showed that 78 percent of participants reported that their organizations monitor employees electronically in some respect: 47 percent monitor employees' e-mail, and 63 percent monitor employees' use of the Web (American Management Association, 2001). These results indicate that safeguards to protect personal privacy are more important than ever. Here are some suggestions.

First, *employers should periodically and systematically review their HR recordkeeping practices.* This review should consider the following:

- The number and types of records an organization maintains on employees, former employees, and applicants
- The items maintained in each record
- The uses made of information in each type of record
- The uses of information within the organization
- The disclosures made to parties outside the organization
- The extent to which individuals are aware and informed of the uses and disclosures of information about them in the records department

Indeed, research has shown that an individual's perceived control over the uses of information after its disclosure is the single most important variable affecting perceptions of invasion of privacy (Fusilier & Hoyer, 1980).

After reviewing their current practices, *employers should articulate, communicate, and implement fair information-practice policies* by the following means:

- Limit the collection of information about individuals to that which is relevant to specific decisions.
- Inform individuals of the uses to be made of such information.

- Inform individuals as to the types of information being maintained about them.
- Adopt reasonable procedures for ensuring accuracy, timeliness, and completeness of information about individuals. The objective is to preserve the integrity of the information collected (Mitsch, 1983).
- Permit individuals to see, copy, correct, or amend records about themselves.
- Limit the internal use of records, for example, by implementing security measures such as physical security, system audit trails, passwords, read/write authentication routines, or encryption of data (Mitsch, 1983).
- Limit external disclosures of information, particularly those made without the individual's authorization.
- Provide for regular reviews of compliance with articulated fair information-practice policies.

Particularly since the corporate wrongdoings of Enron, Andersen, Adelphia, Tyco, WorldCom, and other organizations, the public in general, as well as peers and subordinates, tends to give executives low marks for honesty and ethical behavior (e.g., Alsop, 2004). However, companies that have taken the kinds of measures described above, such as IBM, Bank of America, AT&T, Cummins Engine, Avis, and TRW, report that they have not been overly costly, produced burdensome traffic in access demands, or reduced the general quality of their HR decisions. Furthermore, they receive strong employee approval for their policies when they ask about them on company attitude surveys.

To illustrate the consequences of implementing sound information practices, consider an experiment that included 206 undergraduate students recruited to perform work at an on-campus satellite office (Alge, 2001). The students were assigned randomly to conditions that varied as to whether performance monitoring would be focused on job-relevant information (e.g., number of Web sites verified, which was part of their job duties) and participation in the monitoring procedure (i.e., whether students were able to provide input into the monitoring and evaluation procedure). Students' perceptions of invasion of privacy was measured using 13 items, two examples of which are the following: "I feel that the information being collected is none of anybody's business but my own" and "I felt like the manner in which I was evaluated was an invasion of my privacy" (Alge, 2001, p. 800). Both relevance and participation had a negative impact on perceptions of invasion of privacy, with relevance having the strongest effect ($\eta^2 = .25$, or 25 percent of variance in perceptions of invasion of privacy was explained by the job-relevance manipulation). Employees are therefore less likely to perceive their privacy has been invaded when the information collected is job related and they have input regarding the procedures used in gathering information.

Employee Searches and Other Workplace Investigations

Thus far, we have been dealing with *information* privacy, but the *physical* privacy of employees is no less important. The issue of employee searches in the workplace involves a careful balancing of the employer's right to manage its business and to implement reasonable work rules and standards against the privacy rights and interests of employees. Reviews of precedents in constitutional law and tort law and of labor statutes suggest the following guidelines for employers (Nobile, 1985; Segal, 2002):

- Base the search and seizure policy on legitimate employer interests, such as the prevention of theft, drinking on company property, and use, possession, or sale of illegal drugs on company property. Most employees view reasons such as these as reasonable.
- Conduct searches only when you have a reason to believe you will find the specific object of the search. Avoid random searches, which are likely to result in employee anger and resentment.
- Include all types of searches (personal office, locker, etc.). Advise employees that the offices and lockers are the property of the company issued for the convenience of

employees, that the company has a master key, and that these areas may be inspected at any time. This will help to preclude an employee's claim of discriminatory treatment or invasion of privacy. Such searches (without a warrant) are permissible, according to a federal court, if they are work related and reasonable under the circumstances (Rich, 1995).

- Provide adequate notice to employees (and labor unions, if appropriate) before implementing the policy.
- Instruct those responsible for conducting the actual searches to not touch any employee or, if this is not possible, to limit touching to effects and pockets. This will provide a defense against an employee's claim of civil harassment or even a criminal charge of assault and battery.
- It is a good idea to have a witness to all searches who can testify regarding what took place and what did not take place. It is also a good idea to choose a witness who is the same gender as the person being searched and to use a union shop steward as a witness if the employee being searched is a bargaining-unit employee.
- When an employee is suspected of theft, conduct the search away from other employees and on company time.
- Whenever searches are conducted, ensure that they are performed in a dignified and reasonable manner, with due regard for each employee's rights to due process.

Workplace investigations often involve the observation of an employee. There are only five means that an employer can use to do this legally: electronic (photographic or video images), stationary (e.g., an investigator in a van watching an exit door), moving (following an employee on foot or in a vehicle), undercover operatives, and investigative interviews (Vigneau, 1995). Each carries risks.

For example, tape recording and photography are off limits in areas where there is a reasonable expectation of privacy, such as a restroom or a home. To do otherwise is to violate privacy rights. Use undercover operatives as a last resort (e.g., at an open construction site or an open loading dock). Employees will probably react extremely negatively if they discover a "spy" in the workplace.

Investigative interviews should be voluntary. To be effective, make the employee comfortable, provide access to a phone, and allow the employee to take a break on request. Offer the employee the opportunity to call or be represented by an attorney, and be willing to conduct the interview with one present. The outcome should be a sworn statement that is written as well as recorded in the presence of a company representative. The employee's written statement should include an explanation of what happened and how he or she was treated. The recording preserves the true nature of the interview and its integrity (Vigneau, 1995). Now let's consider some ethical issues associated with testing and evaluation.

TESTING AND EVALUATION

HR decisions to select, to promote, to train, or to transfer are often major events in individuals' careers. Frequently these decisions are made with the aid of tests, interviews, situational exercises, performance appraisals, and other techniques developed by HR experts, often I/O psychologists. The experts, or psychologists, must be concerned with questions of fairness, propriety, and individual rights, as well as with other ethical issues. In fact, as London and Bray (1980) have pointed out, HR experts and psychologists have obligations to their profession, to job applicants and employees, and to their employers. Employers also have ethical obligations. We will consider each of these sets of obligations shortly, but first let us describe existing standards of ethical practice.

Among the social and behavioral science disciplines, psychologists have the most richly developed and documented ethical guidelines, as well as institutionalized agencies for surveillance of practice and resolution of public complaints. These include *Ethical Principles of*

Psychologists and Code of Conduct (American Psychological Association, 2002), *Ethical Conflicts in Psychology* (Bersoff, 2003), *Standards for Educational and Psychological Testing* (AERA, APA, & NCMEA, 1999), and *Principles for the Validation and Use of Employment Selection Procedures* (SIOP, 2003—see Appendix A).

Another document, developed by a task force of researchers and practitioners of assessment-center methodology, is *Guidelines and Ethical Considerations for Assessment Center Operations* (Task Force, 1989). As described in Chapter 13, these standards specify minimally acceptable practices in training assessors, informing participants about what to expect, and using assessment center data. Other ethical issues deal with the relevance of assessment center exercises to what is being predicted, how individuals are selected to attend a center, and the rights of participants. Finally, the Academy of Management (1995) has published a code of ethical conduct for its members. It covers five major areas: student relationships, the advancement of managerial knowledge, the Academy of Management and the larger professional environment, managers and the practice of management, and the world community.

While the details of any particular set of standards are beyond the scope of this chapter, let us consider briefly the ethical obligations we noted earlier. Many of the ideas in this section come from Aguinis and Henle (2002), London and Bray (1980), Messick (1995), and the sets of guidelines and standards listed above.

Obligations to One's Profession

Psychologists are expected to abide by the standards and principles for ethical practice set forth by the American Psychological Association (APA). HR experts who are not psychologists often belong to professional organizations (e.g., the Society for Human Resource Management, the Academy of Management) and are expected to follow many of the same standards. Such standards generally include keeping informed of advances in the field, reporting unethical practices, and increasing colleagues' sensitivity to ethical issues.

Keeping up with advances implies continuing one's education, being open to new procedures, and remaining abreast of federal, state, and local regulations relevant to research and practice. Specifically, for example, the APA's *Guidelines for Test User Qualifications* (Turner, DeMers, Fox, & Reed, 2001) specify that test users should possess psychometric and measurement knowledge (e.g., descriptive statistics, reliability, validity) and that, in the context of employment testing, test users should have "an understanding of the work setting, the work itself, and the worker characteristics required for the work situation" (p. 1104).

The type of knowledge included in the APA *Guidelines* becomes particularly relevant in playing the role of an expert witness in litigation. The *Daubert* standards guide courts in accepting expert testimony (Barrett & Lueke, 2004). The *Daubert* standards were set forth in *Daubert v. Merrell Dow Pharmaceuticals* (1993) and clarified through subsequent federal district, appeals, and Supreme Court cases. The criteria used in determining admissibility of scientific evidence include whether the reasoning or underlying methodology is scientifically valid (and not mere speculation on the part of the expert witness) and whether it can be properly applied to the specific issue in the court case. Having adequate knowledge and keeping up with scientific advances is a key component of the *Daubert* standards.

Perhaps the only positive outcome of the recent corporate scandals is that an increasing number of universities, particularly business programs, are now including ethics components in their curricula. Such components may include the following (Dahringer, 2003):

- A required course in "Ethics and Social Responsibility"
- Full integration of ethical consideration throughout the curriculum
- A required Live Case Study program that enlists the business expertise of students on behalf of nonprofit organizations in the community
- Retreats such as one entitled "Putting Values into Action" that can conclude a graduate program

Such educational initiatives may help HR professionals identify unethical behavior more easily and help them move from the question "Is it legal?" to the question "Is it right?" (Dahringer, 2003). However, identifying unethical behavior when a fellow professional is involved poses especially knotty problems. The *Ethical Principles of Psychologists* (American Psychological Association, 2002) advises that efforts be made to rectify the unethical conduct directly and initially informally with the individual in question. Failing that, the next step is to bring the unethical activities to the attention of appropriate authorities, such as state licensing boards or APA ethics committees. Members, as well as nonmembers, can file complaints with the APA's Ethics Committee, or the committee may decide to initiate a complaint (i.e., sua sponte complaint). Complaints by APA members must be filed within one year of the violation or its discovery, while nonmembers have up to five years to file a complaint. The *Ethical Principles* include a specific standard (# 1.08) that prohibits any unfair discrimination against people filing or responding to a complaint. While the peer review process for all professions has been criticized as being lax and ineffective, at the very least, peer review makes accountability to one's colleagues a continuing presence in professional practice (Theaman, 1984). Increasing colleagues' sensitivity to ethical practices may diminish unethical behavior and increase the likelihood that it will be reported.

Obligations to Those Who Are Evaluated

In the making of career decisions about individuals, issues of accuracy and equality of opportunity are critical. Beyond these, ethical principles include the following:

- Guarding against invasion of privacy
- Guaranteeing confidentiality
- Obtaining employees' and applicants' informed consent before evaluation
- Respecting employees' right to know
- Imposing time limitations on data
- Minimizing erroneous acceptance and rejection decisions
- Treating employees with respect and consideration

Since we already have examined the employee privacy issue in some detail, we will focus only on areas not yet considered. Let us begin with the issue of test accuracy. If validity is the overall degree of justification for test interpretation and use, and because human and social values affect interpretation as well as use, then test validity should consider those value implications in the overall judgment. One of the key questions is "Should the test be used for that purpose?" There are few prescriptions for how to proceed here, but one recommendation is to contrast the potential social consequences of the proposed testing with the potential social consequences of alternative procedures and even of procedures antagonistic to testing (such as not testing at all). Such a strategy draws attention to vulnerabilities in the proposed use and exposes its value assumptions to open debate.

Should individuals be denied access to a test because prior knowledge of test items may decrease the test's validity? Yes, if the results are used in making decisions about them; no, if the results do not affect them in any way. "Truth in testing" legislation in New York and California requires that college and graduate school entrance tests and correct answers be made public within 30 days after the results are distributed. It also requires testing services to provide a graded answer sheet to students who request it. Someday other laws may affect employment. While the *Standards for Educational and Psychological Measurement* (AERA, APA, & NCME, 1999) do not require that test items be made public, they do make clear that the individual whose future is affected by a career decision based on test results is among those with a "right to know" the test results used to make the decision. Such information should describe in simple language what the test covers, what the scores mean, common misinterpretations of test scores, and how the scores will be used.

How old must data be before they are removed from employee files? One guideline is to remove all evaluative information that has not been used for HR decisions, especially if it has been updated. When data *have* been used for HR decisions, before destroying them it is desirable to determine their likely usefulness for making future predictions and for serving as evidence of the rationale for prior decisions. Such data should not be destroyed indiscriminately.

Care also should be taken to minimize erroneous rejection and erroneous acceptance decisions. One way to minimize erroneous rejection decisions is to provide a reasonable opportunity for retesting and reconsideration (AERA, APA, & NCMEA, 1999), even to the extent of considering alternative routes to qualification (possibly by an on-the-job trial period or a trial period in on-the-job training if these strategies are feasible). Erroneous acceptances simply may reflect a lack of proper job training. Where remedial assistance is not effective, a change in job assignment (with special training or relevant job experience in preparation for career advancement) should be considered.

A further concern is that employees be treated ethically both during and after evaluation. The most effective way to ensure such ethical treatment is to standardize procedures. Standard procedures should include personal and considerate treatment; a clear explanation of the evaluation process; direct and honest answers to examinees' questions; and, when special equipment is required, as in the case of computer-based testing, practice exercises to make sure examinees understand how to use the equipment.

Obligations to Employers

Ethical issues in this area go beyond the basic design and administration of decision-making procedures. They include

- Conveying accurate expectations for evaluation procedures;
- Ensuring high-quality information for HR decisions;
- Periodically reviewing the accuracy of decision-making procedures;
- Respecting the employer's proprietary rights; and
- Balancing the vested interests of the employer with government regulations, with commitment to the profession, and with the rights of those evaluated for HR decisions.

Accurate information (as conveyed through test manuals and research investigations) regarding the costs and benefits of a proposed assessment procedure or training program, together with the rationale for decision criteria (e.g., cutoff scores) and their likely effects, is the responsibility of the HR expert. He or she also is ethically bound to provide reliable, valid, and fair data, within the limits of the resources (time, support, money) provided by the employer. The following case illustrates this principle (Committee on Professional Standards, 1982).

A small government agency located in a fiscally conservative community hired an I/O psychologist to prepare six promotional exams for police and firefighters over a period of only 18 months. Since the first exam had to be administered in only five months, there was little time for documentation. There was no relevant reference material at the agency, no additional staff resources beyond limited clerical services, and no adequate job-analysis data for any of the jobs. Attempts to conduct a job analysis for the purpose of test development failed because the employees involved feared that the results would be used to downgrade their jobs. Department heads had great concern over the security of the test items and, therefore, refused to allow internal employees to be involved in writing the test items, pretesting them, or reviewing the final test.

In view of these constraints, it was difficult for the I/O psychologist to upgrade the quality of the employment tests, as required by professional and legal standards. He described the limitations of his services to the agency management. He educated his agency on professional and legal requirements and convinced it to have two consultants carry out components of two promotional exams. Further, he successfully promoted the use of two selection devices, an assessment center and a job-related oral examination, which reduced the adverse impact on minority group applicants.

Through the I/O psychologist's efforts, the promotional exams for police and firefighters became more job related than they were before he was hired. Considering the limited budgetary and human resources available to the small jurisdiction, he was delivering the best possible professional services he could while trying to make necessary changes in the system.

Another ethical issue arises when HR professionals are constrained from conducting research because the results may in some way be detrimental to their employer (e.g., they may be discoverable in a future lawsuit). The dilemma becomes especially acute if the HR professional believes that proper practice has been hindered. It is his or her responsibility to resolve the issue by following the employer's wishes, persuading the employer to do otherwise, or changing jobs.

Balancing obligations to the employer, to the profession, and to those evaluated for HR decisions is difficult. These ethical dilemmas are easier to identify than to resolve. The recommendation is first to attempt to effect change by constructive action within the organization before disclosing confidential information to others. As discussed in the next paragraph, maintaining ethical standards is most important, though the need to support the integrity, reputation, and proprietary rights of the host organization is recognized.

So, when organizations request researchers to act in an unethical manner (e.g., reveal the names of individuals providing supervisory evaluations even though participants were promised confidentiality), researchers should make known to these organizations their obligations to follow applicable ethics codes and the parties should seek a compromise that does not involve a violation of the code (Wright & Wright, 1999). An unbalanced way of handling such dilemmas in which the interests of the employer prevail over ethical standards can give the field of I/O psychology, and HR in general, a reputation as "a mere technocratic profession serving the objectives of corporations" (Lefkowitz, 2003, p. 326).

Individual Differences Serving as Antecedents of Ethical Behavior

So far, our discussion has focused on contextual effects on ethical behavior. In other words, we have discussed regulations, policies, and procedures that encourage individuals to behave ethically. However, there are individual differences in the ethical behavior of individuals, even when contextual variables are the same. Consider the following evidence:

- The implementation of ethics codes was most successful among individuals who achieved the conventional level of moral development (note that the preconventional level typifies the moral reasoning of children, the conventional level involves going beyond defining right and wrong in terms of self-interest, and the postconventional level involves defining right and wrong in terms of universal principles such as justice and virtue) (Greenberg, 2002).
- Individuals in the highest group of the moral development distribution exhibited more transformational leadership behaviors (e.g., inspired followers to look beyond their self-interests for the good of the group) than individuals scoring in the lowest group (Turner, Barling, Epitropaki, Butcher, & Milner, 2002).
- Individuals' cognitive ability can affect the level of cognitive effort that can be exerted in considering an ethical issue (e.g., in facing an ethical dilemma) (Street, Douglas, Geiger, & Martinko, 2001).
- Women are more likely than men to perceive specific hypothetical business practices as unethical (Franke, Crown, & Spake, 1997).
- Personal values influence the extent to which an issue will be viewed as moral in nature and the subsequent actions taken (Pierce, Broberg, McClure, & Aguinis, 2004).
- A manager's narcissism (i.e., a broad personality construct that includes an exaggerated sense of self-importance, fantasies of unlimited success or power, need for admiration, entitlement, lack of empathy, and exploitation of others) is negatively related to supervisor ratings of interpersonal performance and integrity (Blair, Hoffman, & Helland, 2008).

Although the above discussion points to individual differences, to improve understanding of individuals' responses to potentially unethical situations at work, there is a need to adopt a person-situation interactionist perspective (Pierce & Aguinis, 2005). In other words, depending on how an individual perceives the moral intensity of a particular event, he or she may react in one way or another. For example, investigators of a sexual-harassment accusation are less apt to attribute blame to a male accused of sexual harassment and less apt to recommend that he receive a punitive action (e.g., suspension or termination), if the features of the romance–harassment scenario are low in moral intensity as follows: A non-extramarital (vs. extramarital) romance that was not in violation (versus in violation) of a written organizational policy and resulted in hostile work environment (versus the more blatant quid pro quo) harassment.

The above admittedly selective evidence points to an important conclusion: Although the implementation of ethics programs can certainly mitigate unethical behavior, the ultimate success of such efforts depends on an interaction between how the system is implemented and individual differences regarding such variables as cognitive ability, moral development, gender, and personal values. Given the variability in these, and other individual-differences variables, one should also expect variability in the success rate of corporate ethics programs.

ETHICAL ISSUES IN ORGANIZATIONAL RESEARCH

In field settings, researchers encounter social systems comprising people who hold positions in a hierarchy and who also have relationships with consumers, government, unions, and other public institutions. Researchers cannot single-handedly manage the ethical dilemmas that arise because they are a weak force in a field of powerful ones, with only limited means for ensuring moral action or for rectifying moral lapses (Mirvis & Seashore, 1979).

Mirvis and Seashore (1979) proposed that most ethical concerns in organizational research arise from researchers' multiple and conflicting roles within the organization where research is being conducted. Indeed, researchers have their own expectations and guidelines concerning research, while organizations, managers, and employees may hold a very different set of beliefs concerning research (Aguinis & Henle, 2002). For example, a researcher may view the purpose of a concurrent validation study of an integrity test as a necessary step to justify its use for selecting applicants. Alternatively, management may perceive it as a way, unbeknown to employees, to weed out current employees who may be stealing. The researcher may argue that this use of the research results violates participants' confidentiality, while management may counter that it will benefit the organization's bottom line to identify and terminate dishonest individuals. Mirvis and Seashore (1979) recommended that researchers clearly define their roles with various contingencies in organizations when doing research in organizations and that they openly and honestly address conflicts between the ethical norms of researchers and organizations before conducting the research.

The consideration of ethical issues in organizational research begins not at the data-collection phase, but at the research-planning stage. These activities must be conducted in a manner that respects participants' rights. Ethical considerations also come into play in the reporting of research results. Let's consider each of these steps in turn, as discussed by Aguinis and Henle (2002).

Ethical Issues at the Research-Planning Stage

Before conducting a study in an organizational setting, researchers must evaluate their competence to conduct the research, their knowledge of ethical guidelines, the soundness of the research design, and the ethical acceptability of their study. For example, poorly designed research will lead to inaccurate conclusions that may hurt the populations to which they are applied. Poorly designed research can also result in a substantial waste of resources on the part of the sponsoring organization.

Regarding ethical acceptability, researchers should attempt to conduct a cost-benefit analysis. Benefits to participants, the sponsoring organization, society, and science (e.g., increased knowledge) must outweigh costs and potential risks to research participants (e.g., wasted time, invasion of privacy, psychological or physical harm). In cases where participants are at risk (e.g., cognitive ability measures that may cause anxiety), steps must be taken to minimize potential harm (e.g., debriefing). It is often useful to seek impartial views regarding the ethical acceptability of the study from peers, potential participants, or similar sources.

An important, yet often overlooked, issue is the cost of *not* conducting the research. Discarding a research idea that has the potential to benefit many others in important ways because it involves some ethical concerns (e.g., not informing participants of the exact nature of the study) may not resolve ethical concerns, but instead exchange one ethical dilemma for another (Rosnow, 1997).

Ethical Issues in Recruiting and Selecting Research Participants

Using volunteers in research has been advocated as a technique to avoid coercion in participation. However, subtle coercion may still exist through inducements offered to volunteers (Kimmel, 1996). While offering inducements (e.g., money) increases participation rates, ethical issues are raised when participants feel they cannot afford to pass up the incentive. To determine if inducements are excessive and, thus, coercive, Diener and Crandall (1979) advised offering the incentive to potential participants for studies involving a varying amount of risk, and, if they acknowledge that they would participate even when there is considerable risk involved, the inducement is too strong.

Subtle coercion may also exist when a supervisor "strongly recommends" that all employees participate in the research in question. This is particularly a concern when studying populations that have been discriminated against (e.g., African Americans exposed to discrimination in hiring practices) or exploited (e.g., women subjected to sexual harassment). Particularly in dealing with these populations, researchers must be careful to avoid false advertising of what their study realistically can do, and not unnecessarily raise the expectations of participants regarding the purported benefits of the research results. It is also beneficial actively to seek minorities to assist with research (as assistants or coinvestigators) to help identify issues of concern to particular minority groups (Gil & Bob, 1999).

Ethical Issues in Conducting Research: Protecting Research Participants' Rights

Although organizational research rarely involves physical and psychological harm, harm can take place. For instance, researchers may design experiments with various levels of stress (e.g., participants are told they failed an employment test or are given an opportunity to steal) or physical discomfort (e.g., physical ability tests). In addition, unanticipated harm can arise. For instance, some participants may become upset when answering questions about their childhood on a biodata inventory. Regardless, researchers must take precautions to protect participants from harm and determine if harm intentionally invoked is justified in terms of the benefits of the research or if other research methods can be used to obtain information in harmless ways.

In addition to protecting participants from harm, researchers must protect the following rights:

- **Right to Informed Consent.**   Provide information about the study in such a way that potential participants are able to understand and determine if they wish to participate. This also includes guaranteeing the right to decline or withdraw participation at any time during the study without negative consequences (as in the case of the supervisor described above who "strongly suggests" that all employees participate in the study). The researcher must prevent employees from perceiving that their employment status will be at risk if they do not participate. In situations where the researcher has authority over potential participants, using a third party to recruit participants may alleviate the pressure to participate. Finally, researchers should describe how confidentiality or anonymity will be guaranteed (this is discussed in detail in the following section), answer any questions participants have after reading the consent form, and inform them of whom they can contact if they have questions or concerns about the research. Participants should sign the consent form as well as receive a copy of it. However, obtaining signed, informed consent may not be necessary in many situations, especially when participants can refuse to participate through their actions (e.g., by choosing to not return an anonymous survey).

• **_Right to Privacy._**   Researchers must respect participants' right to control the amount of information they reveal about themselves. The amount of information participants must reveal about themselves and the sensitivity of this information may affect their willingness to participate in research. The right to privacy is violated when participants are given unwanted information (e.g., graphic details of an incident involving sexual harassment between a supervisor and subordinate), information that would normally be used to make decisions is withheld, or information is released to unauthorized parties (e.g., a supervisor is given information from a study and uses it to make employment decisions; Sieber, 1992).

• **_Right to Confidentiality._**   Participants should have the right to decide to whom they will reveal personal information. Confidentiality differs from privacy because it refers to data (i.e., not individuals). That is, confidentiality refers to decisions about who will have access to research data, how records will be maintained, and whether participants will remain anonymous. Issues of confidentiality should be resolved in the informed consent procedures by stating how participants' identities will be protected and unauthorized disclosures prevented. Ideally, researchers will want to guarantee anonymity because participants are more likely to participate and be honest when they know the results cannot be linked to them individually. Unfortunately, organizational research often requires identifying information to link participants' data to another data set (e.g., supervisory ratings of performance, employment records). In these cases, code names or numbering systems can be used and identifying information promptly destroyed after coding has taken place.

• **_Right to Protection from Deception._**   If researchers are considering the use of deception, they must determine if it is justified through a cost-benefit analysis and consider the feasibility of alternatives to deception (e.g., Aguinis & Henle, 2001b). Researchers must demonstrate that the value of the research outweighs the harm imposed on participants and that the research topic cannot be studied in any other way. Although some research topics may be studied only through the use of deception, given their low base rate, their sensitive nature, and participants' reluctance to disclose honest information, there are serious drawbacks to the approach. It has been argued that deception does not respect participants' rights, dignity, privacy, and freedom to decline participation, and it may result in participants being suspicious of research in general and psychological research in particular (Aguinis & Handelsman, 1997a). Given this, deception should only be used as a last resort.

• **_Right to Debriefing._**   After the study is completed, debriefing must take place to inform participants of the research purpose, to remove any harmful effects brought on by the study, and to leave participants with a sense of dignity and a perception that their time was not wasted (Harris, 1988). Debriefing is the primary method used to ensure that participants receive the scientific knowledge that is often promised as a benefit of participating in research. Debriefing should include information about previous research (i.e., what is known in this particular research area), how the current study might add to this knowledge, how the results of the study might be applied to organizational settings, and the importance of this type of research.

Are these rights protected in practice? Unfortunately, not in many cases. Participant rights such as informed consent, confidentiality, and privacy may be violated in organizational settings due to a perception that research participation is simply part of the job. Moreover, the prevalence of the Internet as a research tool raises unique challenges (Stanton & Rogelberg, 2001, 2002). Take the case of informed consent. While researchers can post consent forms online and have participants click on a button if they consent, some have argued that it is not possible to determine if participants really understand what they are agreeing to do (Azar, 2000). However, concerns participants have about the study could be resolved through phone calls or personal meetings, depending on the geographic locations of the researcher and participants. Researchers should also remind participants that they are free to withdraw at any time and that their participation is voluntary. In addition, confidentiality issues must be resolved. If data are being collected and stored through the Internet, precautions need to be taken to ensure secure transfer and storage of the information so that unauthorized individuals cannot obtain access. Data encryption technology and password protection may help guarantee confidentiality. Finally, debriefing participants may also be of concern. It is difficult to determine if participants will read any statement aimed at debriefing them.

Regardless of the specific research method used to collect data, Mirvis and Seashore (1979) argued that organizations are systems of coercion, which makes protecting participants' rights, as specified by the APA's *Ethical Guidelines*, difficult. Thus, participants may feel pressured to participate in research studies sponsored by their employer, and researchers may not have sufficient control over the research to guarantee the ethical treatment of participants. However, researchers have an ethical obligation to ensure the well-being of multiple research participants in organizational settings. Wright and Wright (1999) called this a "committed-to-participant" approach. They exemplified this approach in a study that examined the effects of different methods of coping behavior on diastolic blood pressure. The researchers informed participants who were engaging in coping methods likely to lead to high blood pressure about the risks of this behavior and recommended appropriate lifestyle changes. Thus, these researchers were able to collect data, participants were warned about risky behaviors, and organizations will hopefully reap the benefits of reducing the number of employees engaging in risky behavior.

Ethical Issues in Reporting Research Results

Ethical considerations do not end with the collection of data, but continue when we write up our research findings in the form of a technical report or submit our research to be reviewed for journal publication. In reporting research results, researchers must be aware of ethical violations regarding each of the following issues: misrepresentation of results, censoring, plagiarism, unjustified authorship credit, and refusal to provide data for replication. We discuss each of these next.

- *Misrepresentation of Results.* Researchers must honestly and accurately report results and not falsify, distort, or omit findings. A classic case involving falsified research results was that of Sir Cyril Burt, a British psychologist studying the inheritance of intelligence. He conducted studies on twins and found substantial evidence of genetic influences on intelligence (for a more detailed description of this incident, see Kimmel, 1996). His findings were not questioned, but, after his death in 1971, it was discovered that much of his research had been fabricated and that coauthors listed on various research studies were fictitious. Less extreme forms of misrepresentation may include recording data without being blind to the hypotheses or participants' treatment condition, errors in data entry, and errors in data analyses (Rosenthal, 1994). If honest errors in data entry or analysis are found, steps should be taken immediately to correct them. For a fascinating account of great frauds in the history of science, see Broad and Wade (1982).
- *Censoring.* Censoring data is especially salient when the results obtained reflect negatively on the organizations in which the data were collected. However, failing to report data that contradict previous research, hypotheses, or beliefs is also deemed

unethical (Rosenthal, 1994). Instead, researchers should provide detailed reports of their methodology, data analyses, findings, and study limitations so that other researchers and organizational practitioners can evaluate the research and determine its value and applicability. Likewise, not reporting findings of unpublished data, especially if the methods used were sound, could be considered unethical because these findings may provide useful information (Rosenthal, 1994).

- *Plagiarism.*   Researchers should be careful to avoid taking credit for work that is not theirs (i.e., plagiarizing). Plagiarism involves putting one's name on another's work, using a large part of someone else's work without citing it, or claiming others' ideas as one's own (Elliott & Stern, 1997). All of these acts are considered stealing. In addition, researchers should avoid self-plagiarism. This refers to making minor modifications to studies previously published so as to publish them again in another outlet; this is considered unacceptable if the data are published as original even though they have been published previously. This practice of "double dipping" can have a biasing effect on subsequent meta-analyses, which may include the same effect size estimate more than once.

- *Authorship Credit.*   The APA's *Ethical Guidelines* state that authorship credit should be given only to those who substantially contribute to the research effort. Thus, conceptualization of the research idea, research design, data analysis, interpretation, preparation of the written description of the study, and so forth would deserve credit, while seniority, status, power, and routine tasks such as data entry or typing would not. The first author is the one who has contributed the most in terms of ideas, design, analyses, writing, and so forth in comparison to the other authors. The decision as to the first author should be based on actual contributions made and not merely reflect status or power. This issue can become important in research involving faculty–student collaborations, where there is a clear status difference. Ethical issues arise not only when faculty or higher-status individuals take first-author credit they have not earned, but also when students are given unearned credit (Fine & Kurdek, 1993). Giving students or others undeserved research credit misrepresents their expertise and abilities and may give them an unfair advantage for employment and promotions.

- *Data Sharing.*   A final ethical issue regarding the reporting of research results is retaining and providing data when requested by other researchers for replication. Replication acts as a safeguard against dishonesty. However, the purpose for requesting existing data should be to reanalyze in order to verify reported findings and not to conduct new research on existing data; if such secondary purpose is intended, then the requester should obtain written permission to do so. If the research is published in an APA journal, data must be retained for five years after publication. Exceptions to providing data are made if confidentiality would be violated or if data are owned by the organization in which the data were collected.

In sum, every researcher in HR, I/O psychology, and related fields has a responsibility to ensure that their research meets established ethical guidelines in order to protect participants' rights and further the advancement and positive societal impact of our fields. This requires thoughtful consideration of ethical issues before, during, and after data collection. As noted above, this may not be easy in many situations. Next, we describe a conceptual scheme and proposed means to investigate ethical issues in organizational research.

Strategies for Addressing Ethical Issues in Organizational Research

Organizations may be viewed as *role systems*—that is, as sets of relations among people that are maintained, in part, by the expectations people have for one another. When communicated, these expectations specify the behavior of organization members and their rights and responsibilities with respect to others in their role system. This implies that, when social scientists, as members of one role system, begin a research effort with organization members, who are members of another role system, it is important to anticipate, diagnose, and treat ethical problems in light of this intersection of role systems. Problems must be resolved through mutual collaboration and appeal to common goals. Ethical dilemmas arise as a result of **role ambiguity** (uncertainty about what the occupant of a particular role is supposed to do), **role conflict** (the simultaneous occurrence of two or more role expectations such that compliance with one makes compliance with the other more difficult), and **ambiguous**, or **conflicting**, **norms** (standards of behavior).

Table 18-1 presents a summary of strategies for resolving such ethical dilemmas. Column 1 of the table provides examples of typical sources of role ambiguity, role conflict, and ambiguous or conflicting norms encountered in organizational research. Column 2 describes strategies for dealing with each of the column 1 dilemmas. While the implementation of these strategies may seem excessively legalistic and rigid, agreements negotiated at the start and throughout research projects serve to affirm ethical norms binding on all parties. These ethical norms include, for example, those pertaining to protection of participants' welfare, preservation of scientific interests, avoidance of coercion, and minimization of risk. Such agreements emphasize that the

TABLE 18-1 Strategies for Addressing Ethical Dilemmas in Organizational Research

Source	Strategy	Ethical Norm
Role ambiguity		Anticipating coercion or co-optation of or by uninvolved parties, researcher, participants, and stakeholders; examining risks and benefits; identifying personal, professional, scientific, organizational, jobholder, and stakeholder interests
Regarding which persons or groups are part of the research	Creating an in-house research group composed of all parties implicated directly or indirectly in the study	
Regarding the researcher's role	Communicating clearly, explicitly, and by example the intended role; clarifying the intended role, the intended means and clarifying ends; examining potential unintended consequences; providing for informed participation	
Regarding the participants' roles	Clarifying role responsibilities and rights; providing for informed consent and voluntary participation; establishing procedures to ensure anonymity, confidentiality, job security, and entitlements; providing for redress of grievances and unilateral termination of the research	
Regarding the stakeholders' roles	Clarifying role responsibilities and rights; establishing procedures to ensure participants' anonymity, confidentiality, job security, and entitlements	
Role conflict		Avoiding coercion of or by uninvolved parties, researcher, participants, and stakeholders; acting with knowledge of risks and benefits; representing personal, professional, scientific, organizational, jobholder, and stakeholder interests through collaborative effort and commitment to ethical basis of the research
Between researcher and participants, between researcher and stakeholders, within researcher	Creating and building role relations, providing for joint examination of intended means and ends and potential unintended consequences, establishing procedures for resolution of conflict through joint effort within established ethical norms	

(*continued*)

TABLE 18-1 Continued

Source	Strategy	Ethical Norm
Between participants, between stakeholders, between participants and stakeholders, within participant or stakeholder	Organizing full role system, providing for collaborative examination of intended means and ends and potential unintended consequences, establishing procedures for resolution of conflict through collaborative effort within established ethical norms	
Ambiguous or conflicting norms		Establishing ethical basis of research
Within or between researcher, participants, and stakeholders	Clarifying ethical norms for research, providing for collaborative examination of unclear or incompatible norms, establishing procedures for resolution of value conflicts through collaborative effort	

Source: Mirvis, P. H., & Seashore, S. E. (1979). Being ethical in organizational research. American Psychologist, 34, 777. Copyright 1979 by the American Psychologist Association. Reprinted by permission of the authors.

achievement of ethical solutions to operating problems is plainly a matter of concern to all parties, not only a matter of the researcher's judgment.

Column 3 of Table 18-1 describes the ethical and social norms that operate to reduce the adverse consequences of ethical dilemmas and at the same time facilitate the achievement of research objectives with a reasonable balance of risk and benefit. Such widely shared norms include, for example, freedom, self-determination, democracy, due process, and equity. So, while roles serve to distinguish the various parties involved in a research effort, shared norms embody general expectations and serve to bind the parties together. In some contexts, however, one set of ethical norms may conflict with another. This can occur, for example, when full and accurate reporting of research to the scientific community might pose an undue risk to the individual welfare of participants (Reese & Fremouw, 1984). In such cases, the researcher bears the responsibility of invoking the additional norm that the conflict be confronted openly, fully, and honestly. While all parties' values may not be honored in its resolution, they should be represented (Baumrind, 1985; Cullen et al., 1989). In short, the conflict should be settled by reason and reciprocity rather than by the preemptive use of power or the selfish reversion to personal whim (Mirvis & Seashore, 1979).

Our final section addresses the controversial issue of the role of a researcher's values and advocacy postures in conducting organizational research. Because values are closely linked to morality, this issue has an important place in any discussion regarding ethics.

Science, Advocacy, and Values in Organizational Research

Organizations frequently use the expertise of university-based professionals to design various HR systems, to evaluate programs, to direct field research efforts, to serve as workshop leaders, and to conduct other similar activities that provide opportunities to influence organizational life. Problems of distortion can arise when a researcher attempts both to extend the base of scientific knowledge in his or her discipline and to promote changes in organizational practice. This is no "ivory-tower" issue, for the problem is relevant to academics as well as to practicing managers.

Many of the ideas in this section come from the excellent discussion by Yorks and Whitsett (1985). When a scientist/practitioner tries to inspire change that runs counter to conventional wisdom, there is pressure to report and present data selectively. Why?

Challenging widely accepted conventional wisdom can generate a strong need to present as convincing a case as possible, without confusing the issue with qualifications. Alternative hypotheses may become adversarial positions to be neutralized, as opposed to alternative interpretations worthy of careful scrutiny. Scientific caution is undermined as one defends prescriptions in managerial forums. (Yorks & Whitsett, 1985, p. 27)

To counter pressures such as these, consider the following guidelines:

- When reporting field studies, lecturing to students, and making presentations to practicing managers, distinguish clearly between what has been observed under certain circumscribed conditions and what is being advocated as a desired state of affairs.
- Avoid use of success stories that managers can expect to duplicate rather painlessly. Doing so has led to the recurring fads that have characterized behavioral science–based management approaches, followed by the inevitable and often unfortunate discrediting of a given approach. This discrediting is almost inevitable when managerial action is based on generalizations from highly specific social situations.
- Respect the limitations of data obtained from a single study. Behavioral science propositions are strongest when they are derived from many situations and are analyzed by a number of independent scholars.
- Do not allow advocacy of certain techniques or organizational policies to masquerade as science, not because such statements do not stimulate useful debate among managers, but because scientific pretensions confuse the issues involved and make it difficult to separate myth from scientific principles. Ultimately, this frustrates the goals both of science and of practice. Managers get tired of hearing still more claims of "scientific conclusions" about how to manage.

What do these guidelines imply?

Hunch and bias provide no basis for decisions, only controlled research and substantiated theory will do. "I don't know" thus becomes not only an acceptable answer to a question, but in many cases a highly valued one. (Miner, 1978, p. 70)

Is there a place for one's values in conducting and reporting research? Lefkowitz (2003) argued that the values of I/O psychologists are congruent with those of the economic system and corporations within which they function. He therefore argued that there is a bias toward serving organizations even when those organizations may stand in opposition to employee rights and well-being. To remedy this situation, he advocated the following changes (p. 327):

- The adoption of a broader model of values—for example, by adding a more humanist dimension
- An interest in and concern for the well-being of individual employees that should be equal in magnitude to the concern for organizational needs, goals, and perspectives
- A consideration of "success" based not only on the narrow criterion of technical competence but also using broader societal concerns as a criterion
- Incorporation of a moral perspective into the field, in addition to the scientific perspective (i.e., descriptive and predictive) and the instrumental perspective (i.e., focused on productivity and organizational effectiveness) that currently predominate

Lefkowitz (2003) raised issues that are increasingly recognized as important (Murphy, 2004) and are currently producing a very heated debate in some HR subfields, such as selection. For example, Chapter 8 described the debate regarding test-score banding and the competing values involved in deciding whether banding should be used in lieu of top–down selection. Some (e.g., Schmidt & Hunter, 2004) argue that HR specialists are faced with the choice of embracing the "values of science" or "other important values." On the other hand, others (Aguinis, 2004a; Zedeck & Goldstein, 2000) argue that both sets of values ought to be considered. To be sure, this is a thorny issue that is likely to generate further debate in the coming years. As noted by an editorial in the *Academy of Management Review* (Donaldson, 2003), "[a]t no time has the legitimacy of business depended so heavily on clarifying its connection to human values. Taking ethics seriously, then, has become the mission more possible" (p. 365).

Evidence-Based Implications for Practice

- Organizational responsibility OR provides a unique and valuable opportunity for HRM practitioners to make contributions consistent with the field's dual mission of enhancing human well-being and maximizing organizational performance
- The preponderance of the evidence suggests that there are clear benefits for organizations that choose to pursue the triple bottom line (i.e., social, environmental, and economic performance) instead of economic performance exclusively
- Strategic Responsibility Management (SRM) is a process that allows organizations to approach responsibility actions in a systematic and strategic manner
- HRM practitioners can help make the business case for OR by extrapolating, adapting, and using measurement and psychometric techniques developed in other areas (e.g., training evaluation, performance management)
- Balancing obligations to the employer, to the profession, and to those evaluated for HR decisions is difficult. The recommendation is first to attempt to effect change by constructive action within the organization before disclosing confidential information to others
- Although the implementation of ethics programs can certainly mitigate unethical behavior, the ultimate success of such efforts depends on an interaction between how the system is implemented and individual differences regarding such variables as cognitive ability, moral development, gender, and personal values.

Ethical choices are rarely easy. The challenge of being ethical in managing human resources lies not in the mechanical application of moral prescriptions, but rather in the process of creating and maintaining genuine relationships from which to address ethical dilemmas that cannot be covered by prescription.

Discussion Questions

1. You work for an advertising agency. Develop a privacy-protection policy for e-mail and voice mail communications.
2. You suspect an employee is stealing company proprietary information. You decide to search his cubicle for evidence. How do you proceed?
3. Describe three specific areas within the general organizational responsibility domain to which HRM researchers can make a contribution and three specific areas to which HRM practitioners can make a contribution.
4. You need to make the case to your CEO regarding the need to hire a "Corporate Responsibility Officer." What arguments can you use to make the case regarding the need for this position given the realities of twenty-first-century organizations and the benefits of organizational responsibility?
5. Discuss the ethical obligations of an employer to job candidates.
6. You learn that a close colleague has misrepresented a research finding to make her organization "look good." What do you do?
7. Is it possible for researchers to be detached from their own personal values in conducting research? Why?
8. What kinds of ethical dilemmas might arise in conducting research in organizations at each stage of the research process? How might you deal with them?

APPENDIX A

Scientific and Legal Guidelines on Employee Selection Procedures—Checklists for Compliance

Both scientific and legal guidelines for selecting employees are available to HR professionals. The purpose of this appendix is to present both sets of guidelines in the form of questions to be answered. Obviously the relevance of each question will vary with the context in which it is asked. Taken together, both sets of guidelines represent key issues to address in any selection situation and, more broadly, with respect to any HR decision.

SCIENTIFIC GUIDELINES—SUMMARY CHECKLIST[1]

PREMISE

The essential principle in the evaluation of any selection procedure is that evidence must be accumulated to support an inference of job relatedness. Selection procedures are demonstrated to be job related when evidence supports the accuracy of inferences made from scores on, or evaluations derived from, those procedures with regard to some important aspect of work behavior (e.g., quality or quantity of job performance, performance in training, advancement, tenure, termination, or other organizationally pertinent behavior) (SIOP, 2003, p. 4).

PLANNING AND ANALYSIS OF WORK

1. Is there a clear statement of the proposed uses of the selection procedures being considered, based on an understanding of the organization's needs and rights and of its present and prospective employees?
2. Has the user identified the sources of evidence most likely to be relevant to the validation effort—that is, relationships to measures of other variables, content-related evidence, and evidence based on the internal structure of the test?
3. Has the design of the validation effort considered (a) existing evidence, (b) design features required by the proposed uses, (c) design features necessary to satisfy the general requirements of sound inference, and (d) the feasibility of particular design features?
4. Has there been a systematic analysis of work that considers, for example, work complexity; work environment; work context; work tasks, behaviors, and activities performed; or worker requirements [e.g., knowledge, abilities, skills, and other personal characteristics (KSAOs)]?
5. Does the analysis of work identify worker requirements, as well as criterion measures, by assembling information needed to understand the work performed, the setting in which the work is accomplished, and the organization's goals?
6. In the analysis of work, is the level of detail appropriate for the intended use and the availability of information about the work?

Sources of Validity Evidence

1. Does the user understand the construct the selection procedure is intended to measure?
2. If criteria other than job performance are used, is there a theory or rationale to guide the choice of these other variables?

---

[1] *Source*: Based on materials found in Society for Industrial-Organizational Psychology, Inc. (2003). *Principles for the Validation and Use of Personnel Selection Procedures* (4th ed.). Bowling Green, OH: SIOP. For more information on the checklist items, consult the subject index.

CRITERION-RELATED EVIDENCE OF VALIDITY

1. Is the choice of predictors and criteria based on an understanding of the objectives for test use, job information, and existing knowledge regarding test validity?
2. Are standardized procedures used? That is, are there consistent directions and procedures for administration, scoring, and interpretation?

Feasibility

1. Is it possible to obtain or develop a relevant, reliable, and uncontaminated criterion measure(s)?
2. Is it possible to do the research on a sample that is reasonably representative of the population of people and jobs to which the results are to be generalized?
3. Does the study have adequate statistical power—that is, a probability of detecting a significant predictor–criterion relationship in a sample if such a relationship does, in fact, exist?
4. Has the researcher identified how design characteristics might affect the precision of the estimate of predictor–criterion relationships (e.g., sample size, the statistic computed, the probability level chosen for the confidence interval, the size of the relationship)?
5. Is the design, predictive or concurrent, appropriate for the population and purpose of the study?

DESIGN AND CONDUCT OF CRITERION-RELATED STUDIES

Criterion Development

1. Are criteria chosen on the basis of work relevance, freedom from contamination, and reliability rather than availability?
2. Do all criteria represent important organizational, team, and individual outcomes, such as work-related behaviors, outputs, attitudes, or performance in training, as indicated by a review of information about the work?
3. Do adequate safeguards exist to reduce the possibility of criterion contamination, deficiency, or bias?
4. Has criterion reliability been estimated?
5. If ratings are used as measures of performance, is the development of rating factors guided by an analysis of the work?
6. Are raters familiar with the demands of the work, as well as the individual to be rated? Are raters trained in the observation and evaluation of work performance?

Choice of Predictors

1. Is there an empirical, logical, or theoretical foundation for each predictor variable chosen?
2. Is the preliminary choice among predictors based on the researcher's scientific knowledge rather than on personal interest or mere familiarity?
3. Have steps been taken to minimize predictor contamination (e.g., by using standardized procedures, such as structured interviews)?
4. If judgment is used in weighting and summarizing predictor data, is the judgment itself recognized as an additional predictor?
5. Has predictor reliability been estimated?

Choice of Participants

1. Is the sample for a validation study representative of the selection situation of interest?
2. If a researcher concludes that a variable moderates validity coefficients, is there explicit evidence for such an effect?

Data Analysis for Criterion-Related Validity

1. Has the method of analysis been chosen with due consideration for the characteristics of the data and the assumptions involved in the development of the method?
2. Has the type of statistical analysis to be used been considered during the planning of the research?
3. Does the data analysis provide information about effect sizes and the statistical significance or confidence associated with predictor–criterion relationships?
4. Have the relative risks of Type I and Type II errors been considered?
5. Does the analysis provide information about the nature of the predictor–criterion relationship and how it might be used in prediction (e.g., number of cases, measures of central tendency, characteristics of distributions, variability for both predictor and criterion variables, and interrelationships among all variables studied)?
6. Have adjustments been made for range restriction and/or criterion unreliability, if appropriate, in order to obtain an unbiased estimate of the validity of the predictor in the population in which it will be used?
7. If adjustments are made, have both adjusted and unadjusted validity coefficients been reported?
8. If predictors are to be used in combination, has careful consideration been given to the method used to combine them (e.g., in a linear manner, by summing scores on different tests, or in a configural manner, by using multiple cutoffs)?
9. If a researcher combines scores from several criteria into a composite score, is there a rationale to support the rules of combination, and are the rules described?
10. Have appropriate safeguards been applied (e.g., use of cross-validation or shrinkage formulas) to guard against overestimates of validity resulting from capitalization on chance?
11. Have the results of the present criterion-related validity study been interpreted against the background of previous relevant research literature?
12. Are unusual findings, such as suppressor or moderator effects, nonlinear regression, or the benefits of configural scoring, supported by an extremely large sample or replication?

EVIDENCE FOR VALIDITY BASED ON CONTENT

1. If a selection procedure has been designed explicitly as a sample of important elements in the work domain, does the validation study provide evidence that the selection procedure samples the important work behaviors, activities, or worker KSAOs necessary for performance on the job or in training?
2. Are the work and worker requirements reasonably stable?
3. Are qualified and unbiased subject matter experts available?
4. Does the content-based procedure minimize elements that are not part of the work domain (e.g., multiple-choice formats or written content when the job does not require writing)?
5. Has each job content domain been defined completely and described thoroughly in terms of what it does and does not include, based on, for example, an analysis of work behaviors and activities, responsibilities of job incumbents, or KSAOs required for effective performance on the job?
6. Has the researcher described the rationale underlying the sampling of the content domain?
7. Is the selection procedure based on an analysis of work that defines the balance between work behaviors, activities, or KSAOs the applicant is expected to have before placement on the job and the amount of training the organization will provide?
8. Does the specificity–generality of the content of the selection procedure reflect the extent to which the job is likely to change as a result of organizational needs, technology, or equipment?

9. Has the researcher established guidelines for administering and scoring the content-based procedure?
10. Has the reliability of performance on content-based selection procedures been determined?
11. Is the job content domain restricted to critical or frequent activities or to prerequisite knowledge, skills, or abilities?

EVIDENCE OF VALIDITY BASED ON INTERNAL STRUCTURE

1. Does the researcher recognize that evidence of internal structure, by itself, is insufficient to establish the usefulness of a selection procedure in predicting future work performance?
2. Are relevant analyses based on the conceptual framework of the selection procedure (typically established by the proposed use of the procedure)?
3. If evidence of validity is based on internal structure, did the researcher consider the relationship among items, components of the selection procedures, or scales measuring constructs?
4. Is the inclusion of items in a selection procedure based primarily on their relevance to a construct or content domain and secondarily on their intercorrelations?
5. If scoring involves a high level of judgment, does the researcher recognize that indices of interrater or scorer consistency, such as generalizability coefficients or measures of interrater agreement, may be more appropriate than internal consistency estimates?

Generalizing Validity Evidence

1. If a researcher wishes to generalize the validity of inferences from scores on a selection procedure to a new situation, based on validation research conducted elsewhere, is such transportability based on job comparability (in content or requirements) or similarity of job context and candidate group?
2. If synthetic or job component validity is used as a basis for generalizing the validity of inferences from scores on a selection procedure, has the researcher documented the relationship between the selection procedure and one or more specific domains of work (job components) within a single job or across different jobs?
3. If meta-analysis is used as a basis for generalizing research findings across settings, has the researcher considered the meta-analytic methods used, their underlying assumptions, the tenability of the assumptions, and artifacts that may influence the results?
4. Are reports that contribute to the meta-analytic research results clearly identified and available?
5. Have researchers fully reported the rules they used to categorize jobs, tests, criteria, and other characteristics of their studies? Have they reported the reliability of the coding schemes used to categorize these variables?
6. Are there important conditions in the operational setting that are not represented in the meta-analysis (e.g., the local setting involves a managerial job and the meta-analytic database is limited to entry-level jobs)?
7. If the cumulative validity evidence in a meta-analysis is relied on for jobs in new settings or organizations, are the following conditions met?
   a. Is the selection procedure to be used as a measure of the trait, ability, or construct studied? Is it a representative sample of the type of selection procedure included in the meta-analysis?
   b. Is the job in the new setting similar to, or a member of, the same job family as the job included in the validity generalization study?
8. Is the researcher attempting to generalize on the basis of a method in general (e.g., interviews, biodata) rather than on the basis of a specific application of the method?

Fairness and Bias

1. Does the researcher recognize that fairness has no single definition, whether statistical, psychometric, or social?
2. Has the researcher tested for predictive bias (consistent nonzero errors of prediction for members of a subgroup) when there are compelling reasons to question whether a predictor and a criterion are related in a comparable fashion for specific subgroups, given the availability of appropriate data?
3. If a test of predictive bias is warranted, has the researcher tested for it using moderated multiple regression?
4. Do tests for predictive bias meet the following conditions: use of an unbiased criterion, sufficient statistical power, and homogeneity of error variances?
5. Has the researcher conducted an item sensitivity review, in which items are reviewed by individuals with diverse perspectives for language or content that might have differing meaning for members of various subgroups and for language that could be demeaning or offensive to members of various subgroups?

Operational Considerations

INITIATING A VALIDATION EFFORT

1. Have all aspects of the research been performed in compliance with the ethical standards of the American Psychological Association?
2. In defining an organization's needs, objectives, and constraints, have the researcher and the organization's representative taken into account the desires of various stakeholders and determined the relative weights to be given to each point of view?
3. Have researchers considered the legal and labor environments when deciding on validation approaches or selection instruments?
4. In choosing a validation strategy, has the researcher considered the number of individuals who currently perform the work and their similarity to the applicant population?
5. Has the researcher considered alternative sources of information for the validation effort, such as workers, managers, supervisors, trainers, customers, archival records, databases, and internal and external reports?
6. Has the researcher explained to decision makers the issues underlying the acceptability of a selection procedure as part of the initial planning effort?
7. Do managers and workers understand in general terms the purpose of the research, the plan for conducting the research, and their respective roles in the development and validation of the selection procedure?

Understanding Work and Worker Requirements

1. In cases where traditional jobs no longer exist, has the researcher considered important requirements for a wider range or type of work activity?
2. Does the sampling plan for data collection take into account the number of workers and their locations, their characteristics (experience, training, proficiency), their shift or other work cycles, and other variables that might influence the analysis of work?
3. In documenting the work-analysis process, has the researcher described the data-collection methods, analyses, results, and implications for the validation effort?

Requirements

SELECTING ASSESSMENT PROCEDURES FOR THE VALIDATION EFFORT

1. Is the researcher familiar with research related to the organization's objectives?
2. In choosing components of a selection battery, has the researcher considered the overall contribution of each component, its relative contribution, and potential construct redundancy?

3. Has the researcher ensured that administration and scoring tasks can be completed consistently across all locations and administrators?
4. Has the researcher carefully considered the format (e.g., multiple-choice, essay) and medium (i.e., the method of delivery) of the content of the selection procedure?
5. Have researchers considered approaches designed to minimize negative perceptions of a selection procedure and to enhance its acceptability to candidates?
6. If alternate forms of a selection procedure are developed, has the researcher taken steps to ensure that candidates' scores are comparable across forms?

SELECTING THE VALIDATION STRATEGY

1. Is the strategy selected feasible in the organizational context, and does it meet project goals within the constraints imposed by the situation?
2. When individual assessment is used (one-on-one evaluations), does the assessor have a rationale for the determination and use of selection procedures?

SELECTING CRITERION MEASURES

1. Has the researcher considered the psychometric characteristics of performance-oriented criteria (those that represent work activities, behaviors, or outcomes, such as supervisory ratings)?
2. Are all criteria representative of important work behaviors, outcomes, or relevant organizational expectations regarding individual behavior or team performance?

DATA COLLECTION

1. Has the researcher communicated relevant information about the data-collection effort to all those affected, including management, test takers, those who provide criterion data, and those who will use the test?
2. Has the researcher determined the extent to which pilot testing is necessary or useful?
3. Have participants in the validation research been given confidentiality unless there are persuasive reasons to proceed otherwise?
4. Have all data been retained at a level of security that permits access only for those with a need to know?

DATA ANALYSES

1. Have all data been checked for accuracy?
2. Is there a documented rationale for treating missing data or outliers?
3. Are data analyses appropriate for the method or strategy undertaken, the nature of the data (nominal, ordinal, interval, ratio), the sample sizes, and other considerations that will lead to correct inferences from the data?
4. If selection procedures are combined, have the algorithm for combination and the rationale for the algorithm been described?
5. Have the rationale and supporting evidence for the use of multiple hurdles or a compensatory model been presented?
6. In recommending the use of a rank-ordering method or a cutoff score, does the recommendation take into account labor-market conditions, the consequences of errors in prediction, the level of a KSAO represented by a chosen cutoff score, and the utility of the selection procedure?
7. If test-score banding is used, has the researcher documented the basis for its development and the decision rules to be followed in its administration?
8. Has the researcher presented normative information relevant to the applicant pool and the incumbent population?

Communicating the Effectiveness of Selection Procedures

1. Has the researcher used expectancy or utility analyses to communicate the effectiveness of selection procedures?
2. Has the researcher identified the results of utility analyses as estimates based on a set of assumptions?
3. Have minimal and maximal point estimates of utility been presented to reflect the uncertainty in estimating various parameters of the utility model?

Appropriate Use of Selection Procedures

1. Has the researcher produced evidence of validity to support individual components as well as the combination of selection procedures?
2. Are selection procedures used only for the purposes for which there is validity evidence?
3. Are the recommendations based on the results of a validation effort consistent with the objectives of the research, the data analyses performed, and the researcher's professional judgment and ethical responsibilities?

TECHNICAL VALIDATION REPORT

1. Do all reports of validation research include the name of the author and date of the study, a statement of the purpose of the research, a description of the analysis of work, and documentation of any search for alternative selection procedures?
2. Are the names, editions, and forms of commercially available selection instruments described? For proprietary instruments, has the researcher described the items, the construct(s) that are measured, and sample items, if appropriate?
3. Does the report describe the methods used by the researcher to determine that the selection procedure is significantly related to a criterion measure or representative of a job content domain?
4. Does the report provide a detailed description of criterion measures; the rationale for their use; data-collection procedures; and a discussion of their relevance, reliability, and freedom from bias?
5. Does the report describe the research sample and the sampling procedure relative to the interpretation of results? Does it provide data regarding restriction in the range of scores on predictors or criteria?
6. Are all summary data available that bear on the conclusions drawn by the researcher and on his or her recommendations?
7. Are the methods used to score items and tasks described fully?
8. Are norm or expectancy tables presented to help guide relevant interpretations?
9. Does the report provide recommendations for implementation and the rationale supporting them (e.g., rank ordering, score bands, cutoff scores)?
10. Have all research findings that might qualify the conclusions or the generalizability of results been reported?
11. Are complete references provided for all published literature and available technical reports (some of which may be proprietary and confidential)?

ADMINISTRATION GUIDE

1. Does the administration guide document completely the information needed to administer the selection procedure, score it, and interpret the score?
2. If the selection procedure is computer based or in a form other than paper and pencil, does the guide include detailed instructions on the special conditions of administration?
3. Is the information developed for users or examinees accurate and complete for its purposes and not misleading?

4. Does the writing style meet the needs of the likely audience?

5. Does the guide include an introduction to inform the reader of the purpose of the assessment procedure and an overview of the research that supports the procedure?

6. Does the guide include contact information, a thorough description of the selection procedures, and an indication of persons to whom the procedure is applicable, and does it state any exceptions to test requirements?

7. Does the administration guide state the necessary qualifications of administrators and the training required to administer the procedures described in the guide?

8. Does the guide provide detailed instructions regarding the actual implementation of the selection procedures, as well as rules and tips for providing an appropriate testing environment and for ensuring the candidate's identity?

9. Does the guide include detailed instructions for scoring and interpreting the results of the selection procedure?

10. Have quality control checks been implemented to ensure accurate scoring and recording?

11. If computer-based test interpretation (CBTI) is used to process responses to a selection procedure, did the researcher provide detailed instructions on how CBTI is to be used in decision making?

12. Does the guide provide detailed information regarding recordkeeping and test-score databases?

13. Does the guide communicate how selection-procedure scores are to be reported and used and who has access to them?

14. Does the guide include information about how to provide feedback to candidates?

15. Does the guide communicate general principles about how persons with disabilities or how deviations from normal procedures (e.g., sessions disrupted by power failures or illness of a candidate) are to be handled?

16. Does the guide explain whether candidates may be reassessed and how reassessment will take place?

17. Does the administration guide emphasize the importance of safeguarding the content, scoring, and validity of the selection procedure, and does it identify practices for ensuring the security of selection-procedure documents?

OTHER CIRCUMSTANCES REGARDING THE VALIDATION EFFORT AND USE OF SELECTION PROCEDURES

1. If advised of changes in organizational functioning, does the researcher examine each situation on its own merits and make recommendations regarding the impact of the change on the validation and use of any selection procedure?

2. Does the researcher periodically review and, if necessary, update selection procedures and their technical or administration guides?

3. For candidates with disabilities, does the user make special accommodations to minimize the impact of a known disability that is not relevant to the construct being assessed?

4. Are researchers and individuals charged with approving accommodations knowledgeable about the availability of modified forms of the selection procedure, psychometric theory, and the likely effect of the disability on selection-procedure performance?

5. Although most employers have too few cases for extensive research, are the principles set forth in this document followed to the extent possible in the preparation of modified selection procedures for candidates with disabilities?

6. Is there documentation of the modifications made, the psychometric characteristics of the modified selection procedures, and the performance of candidates with disabilities on the original form of the procedure (if available)?

7. Does the test user take steps to ensure that a candidate's score on the selection procedure accurately reflects his or her ability rather than construct-irrelevant disabilities?

A "yes" answer to each question in the checklist, while an ideal to strive for, is somewhat unrealistic to expect. This raises the question of relative stringency in adhering to the individual principles.

> It is important to recognize that this document constitutes pronouncements that guide, support, or recommend, but do not mandate specific approaches or actions . . . independent of the professional judgment of those with expertise in the relevant area. (SIOP, 2003, p. 2)

LEGAL GUIDELINES ON EMPLOYEE SELECTION PROCEDURES[2]

1. Adverse Impact

A. Records Relating to Adverse Impact
1. What is the race, sex, or ethnic group of each applicant or candidate who has applied for, or is eligible for, consideration for each job? Sec. 4B, 15A
2. How are data gathered for those who appear in person? Sec. 4B
3. How are data gathered for those who do not appear in person? Sec. 4B
4. What are the operational definitions of "hires," "promoted," or "otherwise selected" and "applicant" or "candidate" used for computing the selection rate? Sec. 16R
5. Where records of race, sex, or ethnic background are kept on a sample, how is the sample selected? Sec. 4A
6. For a user with more than 100 employees what, for the past year, is the adverse impact of the selection procedures for groups that constitute more than 2 percent of the labor force or applicable work force? Sec. 15A(2)(a)

B. Special Record-Keeping Provisions
1. Is the user exempted from keeping records on a race or ethnic group because it constitutes less than 2 percent of the labor force? Sec. 15A(1)
2. Does the user, by virtue of having fewer than 100 employees, qualify for simplified record-keeping procedures? Sec. 15A(1)
3. Where adverse impact has been eliminated, what is the adverse impact for the two succeeding years? Sec. 15A(2)(b)

C. Four-Fifths Rule
1. What is the distribution by race, sex, and ethnic group of applicants, candidates and those hired or promoted for each job for the period in question? Sec. 4B
2. Is the selection rate of any racial, ethnic, or sex group less than four-fifths of that of the group with the highest rate? Sec. 4D
3. Where the total selection process has an adverse impact, what is the adverse impact of the components? Sec. 15A(2)(a)

D. Adverse Impact When User Meets Four-Fifths Rule
1. Does a statistically significant difference in selection rate have a practically significant impact on the employment of members of a race, sex, or ethnic group, even when it does not meet the four-fifths rule? Sec. 4D
2. Is the sample of candidates for promotion used in determining adverse impact restricted by prior selection on a selection procedure that is the same as, similar to, or correlated with, the procedure in question? Sec. 4C
3. Is the selection procedure a significant factor in the continuation of discriminatory assignments? Sec. 4C(1)

---

[2] *Zetetic for Testers II*, © Richard S. Barrett, 1978, is used with the author's permission. Checklist items are keyed to sections in the federal Uniform Guidelines on Employee Selection Procedures (1978).

4. Does the weight of court decisions or administrative interpretations hold that the selection procedure is not job related? Sec. 4C(2)
5. What data are there in the literature or available unpublished sources that bear on the differences in test scores of candidates from different races, sexes, or ethnic groups? Sec. 4D

  E. Qualifying Circumstances Relating to Adverse Impact
1. What procedures are used to recruit minorities and women, and what was their effect on the applicant population? Sec. 4D
2. How does the user's general, long-term posture toward fair employment affect the conclusions regarding adverse impact? Sec. 4E
3. What safeguards are adopted to assure that recorded information about sex, race, or ethnic background is not used adversely against protected minorities and women? Sec. 4B

2. Validation

  A. General Information Regarding Validity
1. What is the purpose of the selection procedure? Sec. 15B(2), 15B(10), 15C(2), 15C(7), 15D(2), 15D(9)
2. What is the rationale for the choice of the validation strategy that is used? Sec. 5A, B, C, 14B(1), 14C(1), 14D(1)
3. How is it determined that specific jobs are included or excluded from the study? Sec. 14B(1), 14C(1), 14D(2), 15B(3), 15D(4)
4. What are the existing selection procedures, and how are they used? Sec. 15B(2), 15C(2), 15D(2)
5. What reasons are advanced, if any, that a criterion-related validity study is not technically feasible? Sec. 14B(1)
6. What reasons are advanced, if any, that a test cannot, or need not, be validated? Sec. 15A(3)(v)
7. Does the user have, or has the user had since the Civil Rights Act applied to the user, records of data that can be or could have been used as predictors or criteria for a criterion-related validity study? Sec. 14B(1)
8. What has been done to change an informal or unscored selection procedure to one which is formal, scored, and quantifiable? Sec. 6B(1)

  B. Identifying Information
1. What are the names and addresses of the contact person or of the researchers who prepared any report on the selection procedure that is used in establishing its job relatedness? Sec. 15B(12), 15C(8), 15D(12)
2. What are the locations and dates of the validity study(ies)? Sec. 15B(1), 15C(1), 15D(1)
3. For each published selection procedure, manual, and technical report, what is the name, author, publisher, date of publication or revision, or form? Sec. 15B(1), 15C(4), 15D(6)
4. What is the content and format of each unpublished selection procedure? Sec. 15B(1), 15C(4), 15D(6)

  C. Job Analysis
1. What job analysis procedure is used? Sec. 14A, 14B(2), 14C(2), 14D(2), 15B(3), 15C(3), 15D(4)
2. When and for what purposes was the job analysis prepared and last revised? Sec. 14A, 14B(2), 14C(2), 14D(2), 15B(3), 15C(3), 15D(4)
3. How does the job analysis describe the work behaviors, their relative frequency, criticality or importance, level of complexity, or the consequences of error? Sec. 14A, 14B(2), 14C(2), 14D(2), 15B(3), 15C(3), 15D(4)

4. How are the relative frequency, criticality or importance, level of complexity, and the consequences of error in job performance determined? Sec. 14A, 14B(2), 14C(2), 14D(2), 15B(3), 15C(3), 15D(4)

D. Professional Control
   1. What professional control is exercised to assure the completeness and accuracy of the collection of the data? Sec. 5E, 15B(13), 15C(9), 15D(10)
   2. What professional control is exercised to assure the accuracy of the data analyses? Sec. 5E, 15B(13), 15C(9), 15D(10)
   3. Was the analysis planned before examination of the data? If not, what changes were made, and why? Sec. 15B(8)

3. Criterion-Related Validity

A. Sample
   1. What is the definition of the population to which the study is to be generalized, and how is the sample drawn from it? Sec. 14B(4), 15B(6)
   2. How does the departure, if any, from a random sample of applicants or candidates affect the interpretation of the results? Sec. 14B(4), 15B(6)
   3. If any members of the population are excluded from the sample, what is the reason for their exclusion? Sec. 14B(4), 15B(6)
   4. If any data on any members of the sample were eliminated after they were collected, what is the reason for their being eliminated, and how does their omission affect the conclusions? Sec. 14B(4), 15B(6), 15B(13)
   5. What are the pertinent demographic data on the sample such as age, sex, education, training, experience, race, national origin, or native language? Sec. 14B(4), 15B(6)
   6. Is the sample used in the validation study representative of the candidates for the job in age, sex, education, training, job experience, motivation, and test-taking experience, or other pertinent characteristics? Sec. 14B(4), 15B(6)
   7. Where samples are combined, what evidence is there that the work performed and the composition of the samples are comparable? Sec. 14B(4)

B. Criterion Measures
   1. What is measured by each criterion? Sec. 14B, 15B(5)
   2. How was criterion performance observed, recorded, and quantified? Sec. 15B(5)
   3. What forms were used for each criterion measure? Sec. 14B(3), 15B(5)
   4. What instructions are given to those who provide the criterion data, and how is it established that the instructions are followed? Sec. 14B(3), 15B(5)
   5. Where an overall measure or a measure of an aspect of work performance is used, what steps were taken to make sure that it measures relevant work behaviors or work outcomes, and not irrelevant information? Sec. 14B(3), 15B(5)
   6. Where several criteria are combined into one overall measure, what is the rationale behind the procedure for combination? Sec. 15B(5)
   7. Where measures of success in training are used as the criterion, what showing is there of the relevance of the training to performance of the work, and of the relationship of performance on the training measures to work performance? Sec. 14B(3), 15B(5)
   8. How is opportunity bias taken into account in the use and interpretation of objective measures? Sec. 14B(3), 15B(5)
   9. Where measures other than those of job performance are used, such as tenure, regularity of attendance, error rate, or training time, what is the utility of predicting performance on these measures? Sec. 14B(3), 15B(5)
   10. Where a paper-and-pencil test is used as a criterion, how is its relevance established? Sec. 14B(3), 15B(5)

11. Where criterion measures are couched in terms that tend to define the subject matter covered by the test, what is the job relatedness of the measures? Sec. 14B(3), 15B(5)

12. What precautions are taken to make sure that judgments of employee adequacy are not contaminated by knowledge of performance on selection procedures? Sec. 14B(3), 15B(5)

13. What are the data bearing on leniency, halo, and reliability of measures of job performance? Sec. 15B(5), 15B(8)

C. Fairness of Criterion Measures

1. What steps are taken to eliminate or take into account possible distortion in performance measures as the result of conscious or unconscious bias on the part of raters against persons of any race, sex, or ethnic group? Sec. 14B(2), 15B(5)

2. Do minorities and women have equivalent assignments, materials, and quality control standards? Sec. 14B(2), 15B(5)

3. Do minorities and women have equal job experience and access to training or help from supervisors? Sec. 14B(2), 15B(5)

4. What comparison is made of rating results, broken down by race, sex, or ethnic group of raters and race, sex, or ethnic group of the workers who are rated? Sec. 15B(11)

D. Results

1. What methods are used for analyzing the data? Sec. 14B(5), 15B(8)

2. What are the validity coefficients for all comparisons between predictors and criteria for all major subgroups? What is the number of cases and significance level associated with each validity coefficient? Sec. 14B(5), 15B(8)

3. For each measure of the selection procedure or criterion, what is the mean and standard deviation for each major group? What is the reliability and standard error of measurement? Sec. 14B(5), 15B(8)

4. When statistics other than the Pearson product moment correlation coefficient (or its derivatives) or expectancy tables or charts are used, what is the reason that they are preferred? Sec. 14B(5)

5. Are validity coefficients and weights verified on the basis of a cross-validation study when one is called for? Sec. 14B(7)

6. How much benefit would accrue to the employer if it were possible to select those who score highest on the performance measure and how much actually accrues through the use of the selection procedure? Sec. 15B(10)

7. What does item analysis show about the difficulty of the items, the effectiveness of distractors (answers keyed as incorrect), and the relation between the items and the test or between the items and the criterion? Sec. 15B(5), 15C(5)

***

E. Corrections and Categorization

1. Where a validity coefficient is corrected for restriction in range of the selection procedure, how is the restriction in range established? Are there any reasons why its use might overestimate the validity? Sec. 15B(8)

2. Where a validity coefficient is corrected for unreliability of the criterion, what is the rationale behind the choice of the reliability measure used? Are there any reasons why its use might overestimate the validity? Sec. 15B(8)

3. What are the levels of significance based on uncorrected correlation coefficients? Sec. 15B(8)

4. Where continuous data are categorized, and particularly where they are dichotomized, what is the rationale for the categorization? Sec. 15B(8)

F. Concurrent Validity
1. Where concurrent validity is used, how does the researcher take into account the effect of training or experience that might influence performance of the research subjects on the selection procedure? Sec. 14B(2), 14B(4), 15B(5)
2. Where concurrent validity is used, what account is taken of those persons who were considered for employment but not hired, or if hired, who left the job before their work performance was measured as part of the research study? Sec. 14B(4), 15B(6)

G. Prediction of Performance on Higher-Level Jobs
1. Where proficiency on the higher-level job is used as a criterion, are the knowledges, skills, and abilities developed by training and experience on that job? Sec. 5I
2. Where proficiency on the higher-level job is used as a criterion, do a majority of the employees advance to the higher level job in less than five years? Sec. 5I

H. Fairness
1. How is fairness defined? Sec. 14B(8), 15B(8)
2. How is the fairness of the selection procedure established? Sec. 14B(8), 15B(8)
3. What steps are taken to eliminate unfairness in performance measurements, and what is the evidence that they were successful? Sec. 14B(8), 15B(8)
4. Where the performance on a selection procedure is relatively poorer for minorities or women than their performance on the job, how is the selection procedure modified to eliminate the disparity? Sec. 14B(8), 15B(8)

4. Content Validity

A. Relevance of a Content Validity Strategy
1. Are the applicants or candidates expected to be trained or experienced in the work? Sec. 14C(1)
2. Are the knowledges, skills, or abilities measured by the selection procedure learned on the job? Sec. 14C(1)
3. Does the selection procedure require inferences about the psychological processes involved? Sec. 14C(1)

B. Relation between Selection Procedure and Work Behaviors
1. Is the selection procedure a representative sample of work behaviors? Sec. 14C(1), 14C(2)
2. How is it shown that the behaviors demonstrated in the selection procedure are representative of the behaviors required by the work? Sec. 14C(4)
3. Does the selection procedure produce an observable work product? Sec. 14C(2)
4. How is it shown that the work product generated by the selection procedure is representative of work products generated on the job? Sec. 14C(4)
5. What is the reliability of the selection procedure, and how is it determined? Sec. 14C(5)

C. Knowledge, Skills, and Abilities
1. What is the operational definition of the knowledge, skill, or ability measured by the selection procedure? Sec. 14C(4)
2. How is it established that the knowledge or skill or ability measured by the test is a necessary prerequisite to successful performance? Sec. 14C(1), 14C(4)

D. Adequacy of Simulation
1. Is that part of the work content represented by each item identified so that it is possible to determine whether the behavior required by the selection procedure is a sample of the behavior required by the job? Sec. 15C(5)

2. Does the test question require a response that implies identifiable behavior? Sec. 14C(4)

3. Is the behavior identified by the keyed answer correct and appropriate to the job and the specific situation described? Sec. 14C(4)

4. Is the behavior identified by the test question accurately perceived by the test taker? Sec. 14C(4)

5. Is it likely that the actual job behavior will conform to the behavior described by the candidate's response? Sec. 14C(4)

6. Does the level of difficulty of the question correspond to the level of difficulty of the work behavior required for satisfactory performance? Sec. 14C(4)

7. Can journey workers who are performing satisfactorily pass the test? Sec. 14C(4)

E. Training

1. Is a requirement for a specified level of training, education, or experience justified on the basis of the relationship between the content of the work and of the training, education, or experience? Sec. 14C(6)

2. Where a measure of success in training is used as a selection procedure, how is it shown that the performance evaluated by the measure is a prerequisite to successful work performance? Sec. 14C(7)

5. Construct Validity

1. What is the operational definition of the construct measured by the test? Sec. 14D(2)

2. How is it determined that the constructs covered by the test underlie successful performance of frequent, important, or critical duties of the job? Sec. 14D(2)

3. What is the psychological or other reasoning underlying the test? Sec. 14D(2)

4. What is the evidence from studies conducted by the user and by other researchers that shows that the selection procedure is validly related to the construct? Sec. 14D(3)

5. What evidence shows that the construct, as it is measured by the selection procedure, is related to work behaviors? Sec. 14D(3)

6. Validity Generalization

1. Where criterion-related validity studies performed elsewhere are used to show the job relatedness of a test that has not been validated locally, what showing is there that:

   • All reasonably accessible studies useful for establishing the weight of evidence of validity are included in the bibliography? (Copies of unpublished studies, or studies reported in journals that are not commonly available, should be described in detail or attached.) Sec. 15E(1)(e)

   • The studies are reasonably current and current research methods are used? Sec. 15E(1)(e)

   • The population and the sample drawn from it, the performance measures and job behaviors and other significant variables are sufficiently similar to permit generalization? Sec. 7B(2), 7D, 8B, 15E(1)(a), 15E(1)(b), 15E(1)(c)

   • The selection procedures are fair and valid for the relevant races, sexes, or ethnic groups? Sec. 7B(1), 7B(3), 7C, 15E

2. Where validity data come from an unpublished source, does the representative of the source assert that there is no evidence from other studies that failed to demonstrate validity or that shows the test to be unfair? Sec. 15E(1)(e)

3. What sources of unpublished research who were contacted indicated a) that they had no relevant information, b) that they had relevant information but would not communicate it, and c) that they communicated some or all of the relevant data? Sec 15E(1)(e)

4. Where validity studies incorporate two or more jobs that have one or more work behaviors in common, how similar are the work behaviors, and how was the similarity established? Sec. 14D(4)(b), 15E(1)

7. Application

A. Use of Selection Procedures

1. How is each of the selection procedures used in the selection decision? Sec. 14B(6), 14C(8), 14C(9), 15B(10), 15C(7), 15D(9), 15E(1)(d)
2. Does the use made of the validated selection procedures conform to the findings of the validity study? Sec. 5G, 14B(6)
3. What is the rationale for the weight given to each element in the employment procedure, including tests, interviews, reference checks, and any other sources of information? Sec. 15B(10)
4. How is it determined that rank ordering, if used, is appropriate for selecting employees? Sec. 14B(6), 14C(9), 15B(10), 15C(7), 15D(9)
5. How is it determined that the passing score, if used, is reasonable and consistent with normal expectations of acceptable proficiency of the work force employed on the job? Sec. 5H, 14B(6), 14C(8), 15B(10), 15C(7), 15D(9)
6. If the passing score is based on the anticipated number of openings, how is the score related to an acceptable level of job proficiency? Sec. 5H

B. Test Administration

1. Under what conditions is the test administered with respect to giving instructions, permitting practice sessions, answering procedural questions, applying time limits, and following anonymous scoring procedures? Sec. 9B
2. What precautions are made to protect the security of the test? Is there any reason to believe that the test is not secure? Sec. 12
3. What steps were taken to assure accuracy in scoring, coding, and recording test results? Sec. 9B, 15B(13), 15C(9), 15D(10)
4. What procedures are followed to assure that the significance of guessing, time limits, and other test procedures are understood? Sec. 9B
5. Are the test takers given practice, warm-up time, and instructions on the mechanics of answering questions? Sec. 9B
6. Do all candidates have equal access to test preparation programs? Sec. 11
7. Under what conditions may candidates retake tests? Sec. 12

C. Selection Decisions

1. What are the qualifications of those who interpret the results of the selection procedure? Sec. 9B, 14B(6), 14C(8)
2. How are HR department receptionists and interviewers selected, trained, and supervised? Sec. 9B
3. What questions do interviewers ask, what records do they keep, and what decision rules do they follow in making recommendations? Sec. 15B(7), 15C(4), 15D(6)
4. What control is exercised, and what records kept, regarding the decisions of supervisors to hire or promote candidates? Sec. 15B(7), 15C(4), 15D(6)
5. What are the procedures used to combine the information collected by the selection process for making the selection decision? Sec. 15B(7), 15C(4), 15D(6)

D. Reduction of Adverse Impact

1. What adjustments are made in selection procedures to reduce adverse impact and to eliminate unfairness? Sec. 13B, 14B(8)(d)
2. Is the job designed in such a way as to eliminate unnecessary difficulties for minorities and women? Sec. 13A
3. In determining the operational use of a selection procedure, how are adverse impact and the availability of other selection procedures with less of an adverse impact taken into account? Sec. 13B

4. What investigation was made to identify procedures that serve the user's legitimate interest in efficient and trustworthy workmanship and have less adverse impact? What are the results? Sec. 3B, 15B(9)

5. Has anyone with a legitimate interest shown the user an alternative procedure that is purported to have less adverse impact? If so, what investigation has the user conducted into its appropriateness? Sec. 3B

6. Have all races, sexes, and ethnic groups of applicants or candidates been subjected to the same standards? Sec. 11

7. Where validation is not feasible, what procedures are used to establish that the selection procedures are as job related as possible and will minimize or eliminate adverse impact? Sec. 6A, 6B

8. Is the person who scores the tests or other selection procedure directly aware of, or able to, infer the sex, race, or national origin of the applicants? Sec. 9B

E. Currency, Interim Use
1. Does a user who is using a test that is not fully supported by a validity study have substantial evidence of validity, or have a study under way? Sec. 5J
2. When was the validity study last reviewed for currency of the validation strategy and changes in the labor market and job duties? Sec. 5K

APPENDIX B

An Overview of Correlation and Linear Regression

THE CONCEPT OF CORRELATION

The degree of relationship between any two variables (in the employment context, predictor and criterion) is simply the extent to which they vary together (covary) in a systematic fashion. The magnitude or degree to which they are related linearly is indicated by some measure of correlation, the most popular of which is the Pearson product moment correlation coefficient, r. As a measure of relationship, r varies between -1.00 and $+1.00$. When r is 1.00, the two sets of scores are related perfectly and systematically to each other (see Figure B-1).

Bivariate plots of predictor and criterion scores, as in Figure B-2, are known as **scatterplots**. In the case of an r of $+1.00$, high (low) predictor scores are matched perfectly by high (low) criterion scores. When r is -1.00, however, the relationship is inverse, and high (low) predictor scores are accompanied by low (high) criterion scores. In both cases, r indicates the extent to which the two sets of scores are ordered similarly. Needless to say, given the complexity of variables operating in applied settings, rs of 1.00 are the stuff of which dreams are made! If no relationship exists between the two variables, then r is 0.0, and the scatterplot is circular in shape. If r is moderate (positive or negative), then the scores tend to cluster in the shape of a football or ellipse (see Figure B-2).

Obviously the wider the football, the weaker the relationship, and vice versa. Note that in predicting job success the *sign* of the correlation coefficient is not important, but the magnitude is. The greater the absolute value of r, the better the prediction of criterion performance, given a knowledge of predictor scores. In fact, the square of r indicates the percentage of criterion variance accounted for, given a knowledge of the predictor. Assuming a predictor–criterion correlation of .40, $r^2 = .16$ indicates that 16 percent of the variance in the criterion may be determined (or explained), given a knowledge of the predictor. The statistic r^2 is known as the **coefficient of determination**.

As an overall measure of relationship, r is simply a summary statistic, like a mean. In fact, both predictor and criterion variables can be put into standard score form:

$$z_x = \frac{x - \bar{x}}{\sigma_x} \quad \text{and} \quad z_y = \frac{y - \bar{y}}{\sigma_y},$$

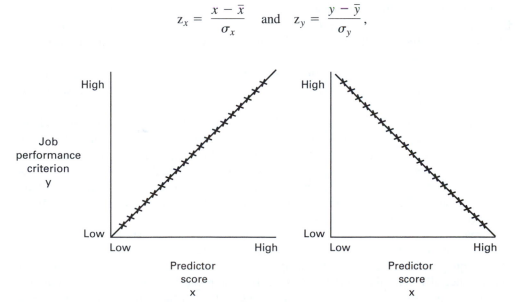

FIGURE B-1 Perfect positive and negative relationships.

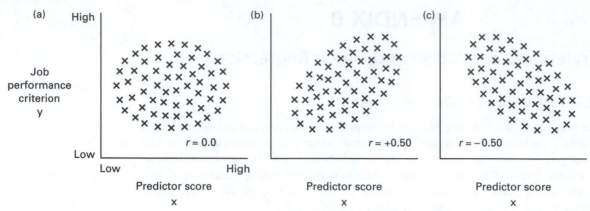

FIGURE B-2   Examples of correlations varying in magnitude and direction.

where σ_x and σ_y are population standard deviations, usually estimated using their sample-based counterparts S_x and S_y. Then r can be interpreted as a mean. It is simply the average of the sum of the cross products of z_x and z_y:

$$r = \frac{\sum z_x z_y}{n} \tag{B-1}$$

Of course, r is only one type of correlational measure. Sometimes the scatterplot of x and y values will indicate that the statistical assumptions necessary to interpret r—namely, bivariate normality, linearity, and homoscedasticity (cf. Chapter 7)—cannot be met. Under these circumstances, other, less restrictive measures of correlation may be computed (cf. Guilford & Fruchter, 1978, chap. 14; also see Appendix C), but, like r, each is a measure of relationship between two variables and may be interpreted as such.

THE CONCEPT OF REGRESSION

Although correlation is a useful procedure for assessing the degree of relationship between two variables, by itself it does not allow us to *predict* one set of scores (criterion scores) from another set of scores (predictor scores). The statistical technique by which this is accomplished is known as **regression analysis**, and correlation is fundamental to its implementation.

The conceptual basis for regression analysis can be presented quite simply by examining a typical bivariate scatterplot of predictor and criterion scores, as in Figure B-2(b). The scatterplot yields several useful pieces of information. The predictor–criterion relationship obviously is positive, moderately strong ($r = +.50$), and linear. In order to predict criterion scores from predictor scores, however, we must be able to describe this relationship more specifically. Prediction becomes possible when the relationship between two variables can be described by means of an equation of the general form $y = f(x)$, read "y is a function of x." In other words, for every value of x, a value of y can be generated by carrying out appropriate mathematical operations on the value of x. In short, if x is the predictor, y (the criterion) can be predicted if we can specify the function f, which serves to relate x and y.

Perhaps the most familiar of all functional relationships is the equation for a straight line: $\hat{y} = a + bx$. Since r always measures only the degree of linear relationship between two variables, the equation describing a straight line (the basis for the general linear model in statistical theory) is especially well suited to our discussion. The interpretation of this equation (in this context termed a **regression line**) is straightforward. For every unit increase in x, there is an increase in y that may be determined by multiplying x by a regression coefficient b (the slope of the

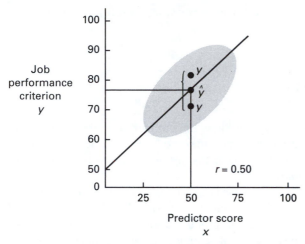

FIGURE B-3   Prediction of job performance from predictor scores.

straight line, Δ_y/Δ_x, which indicates the change in y observed for a unit change in x) and adding a constant a (indicating the point at which the regression line crosses the Y-axis). When this functional relationship is plotted for all individuals in the sample, the result will be a straight line or linear function, as in Figure B-3.

The goodness of fit of the regression line to the data points can be assessed by observing the extent to which actual scores fall on the regression line as opposed to falling either above it or below it. In Figure B-3, for example, note that for a predictor score of 50 we predict a job performance score of 77 for *all* individuals with predictor scores of 50. This y value may be determined by extending a projection upward from the X-axis (predictor score) until it intersects the regression line and then reading off the predicted y value from the Y-axis (criterion score). As the scatterplot in Figure B-3 demonstrates, however, of those individuals with the same predictor score of 50, some score above 77 on the criterion and some score below 77. Since the correlation between predictor and criterion is less than 1.00, prediction will not be perfect, and some errors in prediction are inevitable. The regression line, therefore, is simply a moving average or mean, which summarizes the predictor–criterion relationship at each x value. The difference between observed (y) and predicted ($\hat{y}$) job performance scores at each x value is the amount by which the regression line prediction is in error. By extension, the *average* error in prediction from the regression equation for all individuals could be summarized by $\sum(y - \hat{y})/n$. But, since the regression line is a moving average or mean and since one property of a mean is that deviations above it are exactly compensated by deviations below it (thereby summing to zero), such an index of predictive accuracy is inappropriate. Hence, deviations from the regression line ($y - \hat{y}$) are squared, and the index of predictive accuracy or error variance is expressed as

$$s_{y.x}^2 = \sum(y - \hat{y})^2/n \qquad \text{(B-2)}$$

Note the subscripts $y.x$ in Equation B-2. These are important and indicate that we are predicting y from a knowledge of x (technically we are regressing y on x). In correlation analysis, the order of the subscripts is irrelevant, since we only are summarizing the degree of relationship between x and y and not attempting to predict one value from the other. That is, $r_{xy} = r_{yx}$. In regression analysis, however, $b_{y.x}$ ordinarily will *not* be equivalent to $b_{x.y}$ (unless $r_{xy} = 1.00$). Since the aim is to predict, the designation of one variable as the predictor and the other as the criterion is important (Landis & Dunlap, 2000); so also is the order of the subscripts. For any given problem in bivariate linear regression, therefore, there are two regression lines:

$$\hat{y} = a + bx$$

and

$$\hat{x} = a' + b'y$$

A logical question at this point is "Okay, we know how to measure how accurate our regression line is, but how can we plot it so that it provides the best fit to the data points?" Statisticians generally agree that a line of best fit is one that is cast in such a way that the average error of prediction, $\Sigma(y - \hat{y})^2/n$ is a *minimum*.

When this condition is satisfied, we have achieved a *least-squares* solution of our regression equation $\hat{y} = a + bx$. Although in principle the number of possible values of b that will yield a linear equation is infinite, only one value will produce a line of best fit (in the least-squares sense), since the average error of prediction will be minimized at that value.

How can such a value be determined? Mathematically, the optimum value of b is directly related to r:

$$b_{y.x} = r_{xy}\frac{s_y}{s_x} \tag{B-3}$$

That is, b represents the *slope* of the regression line. The slope is affected by two parameters: (1) r_{xy}, the correlation coefficient; and (2) the variability of criterion scores about their mean (s_y), relative to the variability of predictor scores about their mean (s_x). If both x and y are in standard (z) score form, then both s_x and s_y are equal to 1.0, and the slope of the regression line is equal to r_{xy}. For example, suppose Jerry scores 75 on an aptitude test whose validity with respect to a certain criterion is .50. The mean test score is 60, and the standard deviation of the test scores is 15. Therefore, Jerry's z_x score is

$$\frac{(75 - 60)}{15} = \frac{15}{15} = 1.00$$

Since the test-criterion relationship is .50, Jerry's predicted criterion score is

$$z_{\hat{y}} = r_{xy}z_x = (.50)(1.0) = .50$$

or half a standard deviation above the mean criterion score. Since all scores are in standardized form, $a = 0$; but, when x and y are in raw score (unstandardized) form, then $a \neq 0$. The value of a may be obtained, however, by the following formula:

$$a = \bar{y} - b\bar{x} \tag{B-4}$$

Assume that in Figure B-3 the regression line crosses the Y-axis at a value of 50 (that is, $a = 50$). Assume also that for every unit increase in x there is a half-unit increase in y (that is, $b = 0.5$). The regression equation $\hat{y} = a + bx$ then may be expressed as

$$\hat{y} = 50 + .5x$$

For any given x value, we now have a regression equation that allows us to predict a y value corresponding to it. For example, if x were 80, then

$$\hat{y} = 50 + (.5)(80) = 50 + 40 = 90$$

Let us pause for a moment to answer a question that probably is perplexing you by now: "If we already know the criterion scores of a group, why do we need to predict them?" The answer is that, when we set out initially to determine the degree of predictor–criterion relationship, we do need both sets of scores; otherwise, we could not assess the relationship in the first place. If the relationship is strong, then we may want to use the predictor to forecast the criterion status of all new applicants for whom no criterion data exist, and we probably can do so quite accurately. Accuracy also may be increased by adding one or more predictors to our single predictor. The problem then becomes one of multiple prediction, and we shall consider it further in the next section.

MAKING PREDICTIONS BASED ON MULTIPLE PREDICTORS

Geometrically, the amount of bivariate predictor–criterion association may be visualized in terms of Venn diagrams—that is, in terms of the amount of overlap between two circles that represent, respectively, the total variances of x and y (see Figure B-4).

Since there still exists a fair amount of potentially predictable criterion variance, a stronger relationship (and, therefore, appreciably more accurate criterion prediction) is likely to result if additional valid predictors can be found and incorporated into the regression equation (see Figure B-5). Such a conception is much more representative of real-world job success prediction, since decisions generally are made on the basis of *multiple* sources of information. This more complex state of affairs presents little problem conceptually, representing only a generalization of bivariate correlation and linear regression to the multivariate case. For a more rigorous treatment of these topics, consult any one of several excellent texts (e.g., Cohen, Cohen, West, & Aiken, 2003; Pedhazur, 1982).

In the case of **multiple regression**, we have one criterion variable, but more than one predictor variable. Their combined relationship is called a *multiple correlation* and is symbolized by R. Likewise, R^2, the coefficient of *multiple determination*, analogous to r^2, indicates the proportion of criterion variance that may be explained using more than one predictor. In practice, the degree to which prediction can be improved (i.e., the amount of additional criterion variance that can be accounted for) depends on several factors. A crucial one is the degree of intercorrelation among the predictors themselves. Compare the situation in Figure B-5 with that of Figure B-6.

When the predictors are uncorrelated, as in Figure B-5, R^2 may be computed simply by adding together the individual squared correlation coefficients, r^2:

$$R^2_{y.x_1x_2x_3...x_n} = r^2_{x_1y} + r^2_{x_2y} + r^2_{x_3y} + ... + r^2_{x_ny} \qquad \textbf{(B-5)}$$

When the predictors are correlated with one another, however, the computation of R^2 becomes a bit more involved. In examining Figure B-6, note that the amount of overlap between the criterion and each predictor can be partitioned into two components: (1) that which is unique to a given predictor and (2) that which is shared with the other predictors. In computing R^2, we are concerned only with determining the amount of unique criterion variance explainable by the predictor composite.

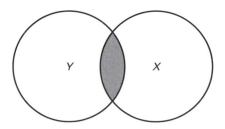

FIGURE B-4 Bivariate predictor/criterion covariation.

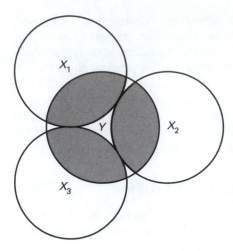

FIGURE B-5 Predictor/criterion covariation, given uncorrelated predictors.

Therefore, for each predictor, that portion of predictor–criterion overlap that is shared with the other predictors must be removed. This can be accomplished (in the two-predictor case) as follows:

$$R^2_{y.x_1x_2} = \frac{r^2_{x_1y} + r^2_{x_2y} - 2r_{x_1x_2}r_{x_1y}r_{x_2y}}{1 - r^2_{x_1x_2}} \tag{B-6}$$

Consider two extreme cases. If $r_{x_1x_2} = 0$, then Equation B-6 reduces to Equation B-5. On the other hand, if x_1 and x_2 are perfectly correlated, then no additional criterion variance can be accounted for over and above that which is accounted for using bivariate correlation. As a general rule of thumb then, *the higher the intercorrelation between predictors, the smaller the increase in R^2 as a result of adding additional predictors to the selection battery.*

In the employment context, we are concerned primarily with generating predictions of job success (using the multiple linear regression model), given knowledge of an individual's standing on several predictor variables. As with bivariate regression, certain statistical assumptions are necessary: linearity, homoscedasticity, and normality. In addition, it is assumed that errors are random (with a mean value of zero and a population variance equal to σ^2_ε) and that any pair of errors will be independent (i.e., the errors corresponding to two observations, y_1 and y_2, do not influence one another).

The multiple-regression model is simply an extension of the bivariate regression model. The general form of the model is as follows:

$$y = a + b_{yx_1.x_2...x_n}x_1 + b_{yx_2.x_1...x_n} + \ldots + b_{y_n.x_1...x_{n-1}}x_n \tag{B-7}$$

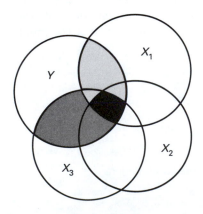

FIGURE B-6 Predictor/criterion covariation in the case of correlated predictors.

The a and b coefficients are interpreted as in bivariate regression, except that $b_{yx_1.x_2...x_n}$ is the regression coefficient for the x_1 values and $b_{yx_2.x_1...x_n}$ is the regression coefficient for the x_2 values. The value of $b_{yx_1.x_2...x_n}$ (known as a **partial regression coefficient**) indicates how many units y increases for every unit increase in x_1 when the effects of x_2 . . . have been held constant. Likewise, the value $b_{yx_2.x_1...x_n}$ indicates how many units y increases for every unit increase in x_2 when the effects of $x_1 . . . x_n$ have been held constant. In short, each partial regression coefficient indicates the unique contribution of each predictor to the prediction of criterion status. As in bivariate regression, the b weights are optimal (in the least-squares sense) and guarantee the maximum possible correlation between predicted and obtained y values. Calculation of the optimal b weights requires the simultaneous solution of a set of linear equations (known as **normal equations**) in which there are as many normal equations as there are predictors. This is a rather complex procedure, but, in view of the wide availability of statistical software programs, it is less of an obstacle today than it once was. The constant a can be computed readily in the multiple regression two-predictor case from

$$a = \hat{y} - \bar{x}_1 b_{yx_1.x_2} - \bar{x}_2 b_{yx_2.x_1} \tag{B-8}$$

Likewise,

$$R^2 = \frac{s_{y.x_1x_2...x_n}^2}{s_y^2}$$

and indicates the proportion of total criterion variance that is accounted for by the predictor variables.

The implementation of the multiple regression model is straightforward, once we have derived our prediction rule (i.e., determined the optimal b weights). Assume we have data on 200 persons hired over a six-month period in a large, expanding manufacturing operation. The data include scores on an aptitude test (x_1) and a work sample test (x_2), as well as job performance measures after the six-month period. After analyzing these data to determine the values of a, $b_{yx_1.x_2}$, and $b_{yx_2.x_1}$ that best describe the relationship between predictors and criterion, suppose our multiple-regression equation assumes the following form:

$$\hat{y} = 8 + .3x_1 + .7x_2$$

This equation says that the most likely criterion score for any new applicant (assuming the applicant comes from the same population as that on whom the equation was derived) is equal to 8 plus .3 times his or her aptitude test score plus .7 times his or her work sample score. If a new applicant scores 60 on the aptitude test and 70 on the work sample test, his or her predicted job performance score six months after hire would be

$$\hat{y} = 8 + (.3)(60) + (.7)(70)$$
$$= 8 + 18 + 49$$
$$= 75$$

PREDICTIVE ACCURACY OF MULTIPLE REGRESSION

The best-fitting regression line may be considered a kind of moving average or mean, but there will be some dispersion of actual criterion scores both above and below those predicted by the regression line. These scores tend to distribute themselves normally (see Figure B-3), with the preponderance of actual criterion scores falling on or near the regression line and fewer scores falling farther away from it. A distribution of these deviations for all individuals would provide a useful index of how far off we are in predicting y from x. The wider the dispersion, the greater the error of prediction. (Conversely the smaller the dispersion, the smaller the error of prediction.) Since the standard deviation is a convenient measure of dispersion, we can use it as an index of the extent of our errors in prediction.

Equation B-2, $s_{y.x}^2 = \Sigma(y - \hat{y})^2/n$, which we referred to earlier as our index of predictive accuracy, is a variance indicating the amount of variability about the regression line. The square root of this expression is a standard deviation—the standard deviation of the errors of estimate—more commonly known as the **standard error of estimate (SEE)**. Although the SEE is computed based on sample data and, therefore, is a statistic, we are interested in the population estimate, symbolized with $\sigma_{y.x}$. It can be shown (Ghiselli, Campbell, & Zedeck, 1981, p. 145) that

$$\sigma_{y.x} = \sqrt{\Sigma(y - \hat{y})^2/n}$$

is equivalent to

$$\sigma_{y.x} = \sigma_y\sqrt{1 - r_{xy}^2}$$

or, in the case of two predictors (which can easily be extended to more than two),

$$\sigma_{y.x_1x_2} = \sigma_y\sqrt{1 - R_{y.x_1x_2}^2} \tag{B-9}$$

The standard error of estimate (σ_{est}) is interpreted in the same way as any standard deviation. It is a most useful measure, for it allows us to create confidence limits around a predicted criterion score within which we would expect some specified percentage of actual criterion scores to fall. Thus, on the average, 68 out of 100 actual criterion scores will fall within $\pm 1\sigma_{est}$ of predicted criterion scores, and 95 out of 100 actual criterion scores will fall within $\pm 1.96\,\sigma_{est}$ of predicted criterion scores. To illustrate, suppose the standard deviation of a sample of job performance scores for recent hires is 8.2 and the multiple R between a battery of three tests and a criterion is .68. The σ_{est} for these data may be computed as follows:

$$\sigma_{est} = 8.2\sqrt{1 - .68^2} = 6.0$$

for all applicants with predicted criterion scores of 86. For example, the limits 80 and 92 (86 ± 6.0) will contain, on the average, the actual criterion scores of 68 percent of the applicants. Likewise, the limits 74.2 and 97.8 ($86 \pm 1.96\,\sigma_{est}$) will contain, on the average, the actual criterion scores of 95 percent of the applicants.

Suppose $R^2 = 0$ for a given predictor–criterion relationship. Under these circumstances, the slope of the regression line is zero (i.e., it is parallel to the X-axis), and the best estimate of criterion status for every value of the predictor is equal to $\bar{y}$. In such a situation, σ_{est} equals

$$\sigma_{y.x_1x_2} = \sigma_y\sqrt{1 - R_{y.x_1x_2}^2}$$
$$\sigma_{est} = \sigma_y\sqrt{1 - 0}$$
$$\sigma_{est} = \sigma_y$$

Thus, even if $R^2 = 0$, criterion status for all individuals still can be predicted with $\sigma_{est} = \sigma_y$ if σ_y is known. Therefore, σ_y serves as a baseline of predictive error from which to judge the degree of improvement in predictive accuracy by any regression equation with $R^2 > 0$. As R^2 increases, σ_{est} decreases, thereby demonstrating enhanced predictive accuracy over baseline prediction.

APPENDIX C

Decision Trees for Statistical Methods

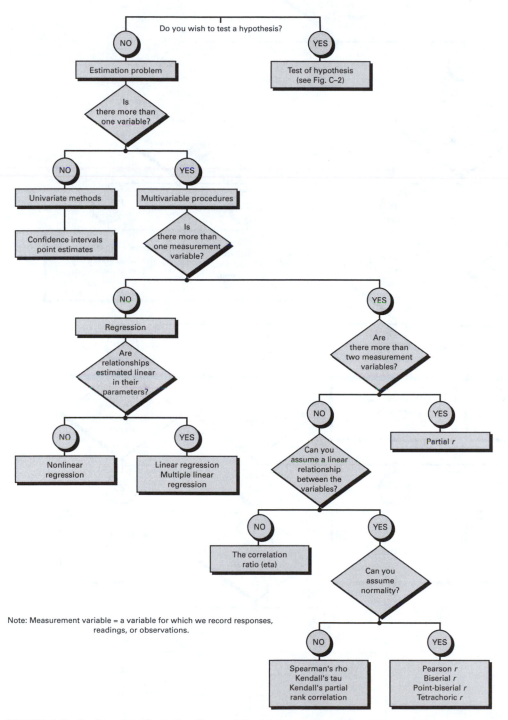

Do you wish to test a hypothesis?

NO → Estimation problem

YES → Test of hypothesis (see Fig. C–2)

Is there more than one variable?

NO → Univariate methods → Confidence intervals point estimates

YES → Multivariable procedures

Is there more than one measurement variable?

NO → Regression

Are relationships estimated linear in their parameters?

NO → Nonlinear regression

YES → Linear regression Multiple linear regression

YES → Are there more than two measurement variables?

NO → Can you assume a linear relationship between the variables?

YES → Partial *r*

Can you assume a linear relationship between the variables?

NO → The correlation ratio (eta)

YES → Can you assume normality?

NO → Spearman's rho Kendall's tau Kendall's partial rank correlation

YES → Pearson *r* Biserial *r* Point-biserial *r* Tetrachoric *r*

Note: Measurement variable = a variable for which we record responses, readings, or observations.

FIGURE C-1 Decision tree for estimation problems.

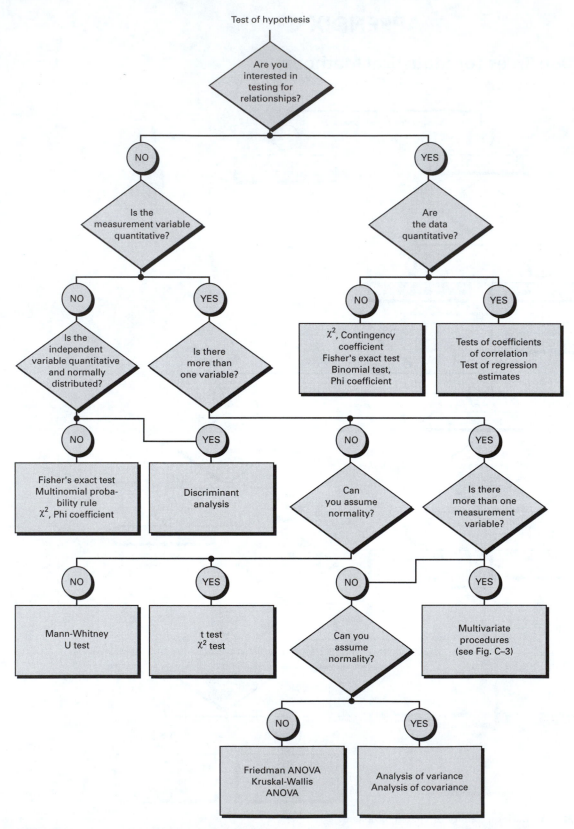

FIGURE C-2 Decision tree for hypothesis testing.

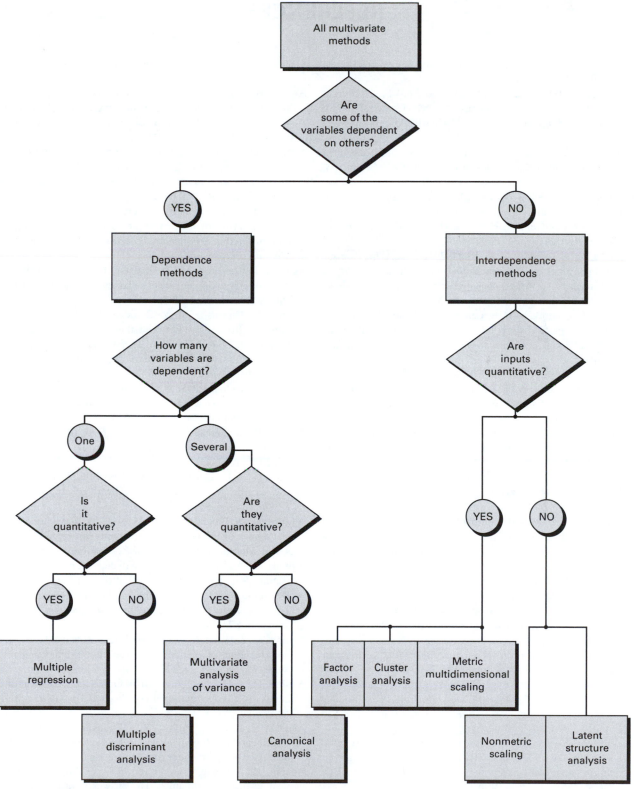

FIGURE C-3   A classification of multivariate methods.   *Source*: Reprinted from J. N. Sheth.
The multivariate revolution in marketing research. Journal of Marketing, 1971, 35, 15.
Published by the American Marketing Association.

REFERENCES

2008 HR trend book. (2008). Alexandria, VA: Society for Human Resource Management.

3M Company, 2008 annual report. Retrieved April 14, 2009, from http://library.corporate-ir.net/library/80/805/80574/items/329750/D57EE3ED-4D21-4ED2-9B46-9FFDCABB9B5D_3M2008AR.pdf.

Academy of Management. (1995). The Academy of Management code of ethical conduct. *Academy of Management Journal, 38,* 573–577.

Ackerman, P. L. (1989). Within-task intercorrelations of skilled performance: Implications for predicting individual differences? (A comment on Henry & Hulin, 1987). *Journal of Applied Psychology, 74,* 360–364.

Adams, S. R., & Thornton, G. C., III. (1989, October). *The assessor judgment process: A review of the reliability and validity of assessment center ratings.* Paper presented at the 1989 National Assessment Conference, Minneapolis, MN.

Adler, N. J., Campbell, N., & Laurent, A. (1989). In search of appropriate methodology: From outside the People's Republic of China looking in. *Journal of International Business Studies, 20,* 61–74.

Aguilera, R. V., Rupp, D. E., Williams, C. A., & Ganapathi, J. (2007). Putting the S back in corporate social responsibility: A multi-level theory of social change in organizations. *Academy of Management Review, 32,* 836–863.

Aguinis, H. (1995). Statistical power problems with moderated multiple regression in management research. *Journal of Management, 21,* 1141–1158.

Aguinis, H. (2001). Estimation of sampling variance of correlations in meta-analysis. *Personnel Psychology, 54,* 569–590.

Aguinis, H. (Ed.). (2004a). Introduction to test score banding in human resource selection. *Test score banding in human resource selection: Legal, technical, and societal issues* (pp. 1–6). Westport, CT: Praeger.

Aguinis, H. (2004b). *Regression analysis for categorical moderators.* New York, NY: Guilford.

Aguinis. H. (Ed.). (2004c). *Test score banding in human resource selection: Legal, technical, and societal issues.* Westport, CT: Praeger.

Aguinis, H. (2009a). *Performance management* (2nd ed.). Upper Saddle River, NJ: Pearson Prentice Hall.

Aguinis, H. (2009b). An expanded view of performance management. In J. W. Smither, M. London (Eds.), *Performance management: Putting research into practice* (pp. 1–43). San Francisco, CA: Jossey-Bass/Wiley.

Aguinis, H. (2009c). Organizational responsibility: Doing good and doing well. In S. Zedeck (Ed.), *APA handbook of industrial and organizational psychology* (Vol. 1). Washington, DC: American Psychological Association.

Aguinis, H., & Adams, S. K. R. (1998). Social-role versus structural models of gender and influence use in organizations: A strong inference approach. *Group and organization management, 23,* 414–446.

Aguinis, H., Beaty, J. C., Boik, R. J., & Pierce, C. A. (2005). Effect size and power in assessing moderating effects of categorical variables using multiple regression: A 30-year review. *Journal of Applied Psychology, 90,* 94–107.

Aguinis, H., Boik, R. J., & Pierce, C. A. (2001). A generalized solution for approximating the power to detect effects of categorical moderator variables using multiple regression. *Organizational Research Methods, 4,* 291–323.

Aguinis, H., Bommer, W. H., & Pierce, C. A. (1996). Improving the estimation of moderating effects by using computer-administered questionnaires. *Educational and Psychological Measurement, 56,* 1043–1047.

Aguinis, H., Cortina, J. M., & Goldberg, E. (1998). A new procedure for computing equivalence bands in personnel selection. *Human Performance, 11,* 351–365.

Aguinis, H., Cortina, J. M., & Goldberg, E. (2000). A clarifying note on differences between the W. F. Cascio, J. Outtz, S. Zedeck, and I. L. Goldstein (1991) and H. Aguinis, J. M. Cortina, and E. Goldberg (1998) banding procedures. *Human Performance, 13,* 199–204.

Aguinis, H., Culpepper, S. A., & Pierce, C. A. (2009). *Revival of test bias research in preemployment testing.* Manuscript submitted for publication.

Aguinis, H., Culpepper, S. A., & Pierce, C. A. (2010). *Revival of test bias research in preemployment testing.* Manuscript submitted for publication.

Aguinis, H., & Handelsman, M. M. (1997a). Ethical issues in the use of the bogus pipeline. *Journal of Applied Social Psychology, 27,* 557–573.

Aguinis, H., & Handelsman, M. M. (1997b). The unique ethical challenges of the bogus pipeline methodology: Let the data speak. *Journal of Applied Social Psychology, 27,* 582–587.

Aguinis, H., & Harden, E. (2004). Will banding benefit my organization? An application of multi-attribute utility analysis. In H. Aguinis (Ed.), *Test score banding in human resource selection: Legal, technical, and societal issues* (pp. 193–216). Westport, CT: Praeger.

Aguinis, H., & Henle, C. A. (2001a). Effects of nonverbal behavior on perceptions of a female employee's power bases. *Journal of Social Psychology, 141,* 537–549.

Aguinis, H., & Henle, C. A. (2001b). Empirical assessment of the ethics of the bogus pipeline. *Journal of Applied Social Psychology, 31,* 352–375.

Aguinis, H., & Henle, C. A. (2002). Ethics in research. In S. G. Rogelberg (Ed.), *Handbook of research methods in industrial and organizational psychology* (pp. 34–56). Malden, MA: Blackwell.

Aguinis, H., & Henle, C. A. (2005). "How is drug testing implemented in this company?" The answer is in the eye of the beholder. *Revue Sciences de Gestion, Management Sciences, 46,* 103–133.

Aguinis, H., Henle, C. A., & Beaty, J. C. (2001). Virtual reality technology: A new tool for personnel selection. *International Journal of Selection and Assessment, 9,* 70–83.

Aguinis, H., Henle, C. A., & Ostroff, C. (2001). Measurement in work and organizational psychology. In N. Anderson, D. S. Ones, H. K. Sinangil, & C. Viswesvaran (Eds.), *Handbook of industrial, work and organizational psychology* (Vol. 1, pp. 27–50). London: Sage.

Aguinis, H., & Kraiger, K. (2009). Benefits of training and development for individuals and teams, organizations, and society. *Annual Review of Psychology, 60,* 451–474.

Aguinis, H., Mazurkiewicz, M. D., & Heggestad, E. D. (2009). Using Web-based frame-of-reference training to decrease biases in personality-based job analysis: An experimental field study. *Personnel Psychology, 62,* 405–438.

Aguinis, H., Michaelis, S. E., & Jones, N. M. (2005). Demand for certified human resources professionals in Internet-based job announcements. *International Journal of Selection and Assessment, 13,* 160–171.

Aguinis, H., Nesler, M. S., Quigley, B. M., Lee, S., & Tedeschi, J. T. (1996). Power bases of faculty supervisors and educational outcomes for graduate students. *Journal of Higher Education, 67,* 267–297.

Aguinis, H., Petersen, S. A., & Pierce, C. A. (1999). Appraisal of the homogeneity of error variance assumption and alternatives to multiple regression for estimating moderating effects of categorical variables. *Organizational Research Methods, 2,* 315–339.

Aguinis, H., & Pierce, C. A. (1998a). Heterogeneity of error variance and the assessment of moderating effects of categorical variables: A conceptual review. *Organizational Research Methods, 1,* 296–314.

Aguinis, H., & Pierce, C. A. (2008). Enhancing the relevance of organizational behavior by embracing performance management research. *Journal of Organizational Behavior, 29,* 139–145.

Aguinis, H., Pierce, C. A., Bosco, F. A., & Muslin, I. S (2009). First decade of Organizational Research Methods: Trends in design, measurement, and data-analysis topics. *Organizational Research Methods, 12,* 69–112.

Aguinis, H., Pierce, C. A., & Culpepper, S. A. (2009). Scale coarseness as a methodological artifact: Correcting correlation coefficients attenuated from using coarse scales. *Organizational Research Methods, 12,* 623–652.

Aguinis, H., Simonsen, M. M., & Pierce, C. A. (1998). Effects of nonverbal behavior on perceptions of power bases. *Journal of Social Psychology, 138,* 455–469.

Aguinis, H., & Smith, M. A. (2007). Understanding the impact of test validity and bias on selection errors and adverse impact in human resource selection. *Personnel Psychology, 60,* 165–199.

Aguinis, H., & Stone-Romero, E. F. (1997). Methodological artifacts in moderated multiple regression and their effects on statistical power. *Journal of Applied Psychology, 82,* 192–206.

Aguinis, H., Sturman, M. C., & Pierce, C. A. (2008). Comparison of three meta-analytic procedures for estimating moderating effects of categorical variables. *Organizational Research Methods, 11,* 9–34.

Aguinis, H., & Whitehead, R. (1997). Sampling variance in the correlation coefficient under indirect range restriction: Implications for validity generalization. *Journal of Applied Psychology, 82,* 528–538.

Aiken, L. R. (1999). *Psychological testing and assessment* (10th ed.). Boston, MA: Allyn & Bacon.

Ailon, G. (2008). Mirror, mirror on the wall: *Culture's consequences* in a value test of its own design. *Academy of Management Review, 33,* 885–904.

Albemarle Paper Company v. Moody, 422 U.S. 405 (1975).

Alexander, R. A. (1988). Group homogeneity, range restriction, and range enhancement effects on correlations. *Personnel Psychology, 41,* 773–777.

Alexander, R. A., Alliger, G. M., & Hanges, P. J. (1984). Correcting for range restriction when the population variance is unknown. *Applied Psychological Measurement, 8,* 431–437.

Alexander, R. A., Barrett, G. V., & Doverspike, D. (1983). An explication of the selection ratio and its relationship to hiring rate. *Journal of Applied Psychology, 68,* 342–344.

Alexander, R. A., & DeShon, R. P. (1994). Effect of error variance heterogeneity on the power of tests for regression slope differences. *Psychological Bulletin, 115,* 308–314.

Alexandrescu, F. (2007). Review of the book Community rights and corporate responsibility: Canadian mining and oil companies in Latin America. *Critical Sociology 33*(3), 593–595.

Allen, D. G., Mahto, R. V., & Otondo, R. F. (2007).Web-based recruitment: Effects of information, organizational brand, and attitudes toward a web site on applicant attraction. *Journal of Applied Psychology, 92,* 1696–1708.

Allen, D. G., Van Scotter, J. R., & Otondo, R. F. (2004). Recruitment communication media: Impact on prehire outcomes. *Personnel Psychology, 57,* 143–171.

Allen, M. J., & Yen, W. M. (1979). *Introduction to measurement theory.* Monterey, CA: Brooks/Cole.

Alliger, G. M., & Janak, E. A. (1989). Kirkpatrick's levels of training criteria: Thirty years later. *Personnel Psychology, 42,* 331–342.

Alliger, G. M., Lilienfeld, S. O., & Mitchell, K. E. (1996). The susceptibility of overt and covert integrity tests to coaching and faking. *Psychological Science, 7,* 32–39.

Alliger, G. M., Tannenbaum, S. I., Bennett, W., Jr., Traver, H., & Shortland, A. (1997). A meta-analysis of the relations among training criteria. *Personnel Psychology, 50*(2), 341–358.

Alsop, R. (2004, February 19). Corporate scandals hit home. *The Wall Street Journal.* Retrieved May 25, 2004, from www.harrisinteractive.com.

Alsop, R. (2007, September 17). The new battle for M.B.A. grads. *The Wall Street Journal,* pp. R1, R3.

Ambec, S., & Lanoie, P. (2008). Does it pay to be green? A systematic overview. *Academy of Management Perspectives, 22*(4), 45–62.

A model employment-privacy policy. (1993, July). *Macworld,* p. 121.

American Educational Research Association, American Psychological Association, and National Council on Measurement in Education. (1999). *Standards for educational and psychological testing.* Washington, DC: American Educational Research Association.

American Management Association. (2001). *Workplace monitoring and surveillance.* New York, NY: Author.

American Psychological Association. (2002). Ethical principles of psychologists and code of conduct. *American Psychologist, 57,* 1060–1073.

American Psychological Association Task Force on Employment Testing of Minority Groups. (1969). Job testing and the disadvantaged. *American Psychologist, 24,* 637–650.

Americans with Disabilities Act of 1990, 42 U.S.C. § 12101 *et seq.*

Anderson, C. W. (1960). The relation between speaking times and decisions in the employment interview. *Journal of Applied Psychology, 44,* 267–268.

Anderson, N. (2003). Applicant and recruiter reactions to new technology in selection: A critical review and agenda for future research. *International Journal of Selection and Assessment, 11,* 121–136.

Anderson, N. (2003). Applicant and recruiter reactions to new technology in selection: A critical review and agenda for future research. *International Journal of Selection and Assessment, 11,* 121–136.

Anderson, J. C., & Gerbing, D. W. (1991). Predicting the performance of measures in a confirmatory factor analysis with a pretest assessment of their substantive validities. *Journal of Applied Psychology, 76,* 732–740.

Anderson, N., & Witvliet, C. (2008). Fairness reactions to personnel selection methods: An international comparison between the Netherlands, the United States, France, Spain, Portugal, and Singapore. *International Journal of Selection and Assessment, 16,* 1–13.

Angarola, R. T. (1985). Drug testing in the workplace: Is it legal? *Personnel Administrator, 30*(9), 79–89.

Angoff, W. H. (1971). Scales, norms, and equivalent scores. In R. L. Thorndike (Ed.), *Educational measurement* (pp. 508–600). Washington, DC: American Council on Education.

Anguish, L. K. (2002, April). OFCCP issues directive for functional affirmative action programs (SHRM White Paper). Available at www.shrm.org.

Ansberry, C. (2003b, June 30). A new blue-collar world. *The Wall Street Journal,* pp. B1, B4.

Ansoff, H. I. (1988). *The new corporate strategy.* New York, NY: Wiley.

Antonioni, D. (1994). The effects of feedback accountability on upward appraisal ratings. *Personnel Psychology, 47,* 349–356.

Antonioni, D., & Park, H. (2001). The effects of personality similarity on peer ratings of contextual work behaviors. *Personnel Psychology, 54,* 331–360.

Applebome, P. (1995, February 20). Employers wary of school system. *The New York Times,* pp. A1, A13.

Armer, P. (1970). The individual: His privacy, self-image and obsolescence. *Proceedings of the meeting of the Panel on Science and Technology,* 11th "Science and Astronautics." U.S. House of Representatives. Washington, DC: U.S. Government Printing Office.

Arnold, H. J., & Feldman, D. C. (1981). Social desirability response bias in self-report choice situations. *Academy of Management Journal, 24,* 377–385.

Arthur, W., Jr., Bennett, W., Jr., Edens, P. S., & Bell, S. T. (2003). Effectiveness of training in organizations: A meta-analysis of design and evaluation features. *Journal of Applied Psychology, 88,* 234–245.

Arthur, W., Day, E. A., McNelly, T. L., & Edens, P. S. (2003). A meta-analysis of the criterion-related validity of assessment center dimensions. *Personnel Psychology, 56,* 125–154.

Arvey, R. D. (1979). Unfair discrimination in the employment interview: Legal and psychological aspects. *Psychological Bulletin, 86,* 736–765.

Avery, D. R. (2003). Reactions to diversity in recruitment advertising—Are differences black and white? *Journal of Applied Psychology, 88,* 672–679.

Arvey, R. D., & Begalla, M. E. (1975). Analyzing the homemaker job using the Position Analysis Questionnaire (PAQ). *Journal of Applied Psychology, 60,* 513–517.

Arvey, R. D., & Campion, J. E. (1982). The employment interview: A summary and review of recent research. *Personnel Psychology, 35,* 281–322.

Arvey, R. D., Cole, D. A., Hazucha, J. F., & Hartanto, F. M. (1985). Statistical power of training evaluation designs. *Personnel Psychology, 38,* 493–507.

Arvey, R. D., Davis, G. A., McGowen, S. L., & Dipboye, R. L. (1982). Potential sources of bias in job analytic processes. *Academy of Management Journal, 25,* 618–629.

Arvey, R. D., Landon, T. E., Nutting, S. M., & Maxwell, S. E. (1992). Development of physical ability tests for police officers: A construct validation approach. *Journal of Applied Psychology, 77,* 996–1009.

Arvey, R. D., & McGowen, S. L. (1982, August). *The use of experience requirements in selecting employees.* Paper presented at the annual meeting of the American Psychological Association, Washington, DC.

Avery, D. R., & McKay, P. F. (2006). Target practice: An organizational impression-management approach to attracting minority and female job applicants. *Personnel Psychology, 59,* 157–187.

Avery, D. R., McKay, P. F., & Wilson, D. C. (2007). Engaging the aging workforce: The relationship between perceived age similarity, satisfaction with coworkers, and employee engagement. *Journal of Applied Psychology, 92,* 1542–1556.

Arvey, R. D., Salas, E., & Gialluca, K. A. (1992). Using task inventories to forecast skills and abilities. *Human Performance, 5,* 171–190.

Aryee, S. (1997). Selection and training of expatriate employees. In N. Anderson, & P. Herriot (Eds.), *International handbook of selection and assessment* (pp. 147–160). Chichester, England: Wiley.

Ash, R. A., & Edgell, S. L. (1975). A note on the readability of the Position Analysis Questionnaire (PAQ). *Journal of Applied Psychology, 60,* 765–766.

Asher, J. J. (1972). The biographical item: Can it be improved? *Personnel Psychology, 25,* 251–269.

Ashforth, E., & Kreiner, G. (1999). "How can you do it?" Dirty work and the challenge of constructing a positive identity. *Academy of Management Review, 24,* 413–434.

Astin, A. W. (1964). Criterion-centered research. *Educational and Psychological Measurement*, *24*, 807–822.

Aston, A. (2007, Jan. 22). Who will run the plants? *BusinessWeek*, p. 78.

Atkins, P. W. B., & Wood, R. E. (2002). Self versus others' ratings as predictors of assessment center ratings: Validation evidence for 360-degree feedback programs. *Personnel Psychology*, *55*, 871–904.

Attewell, P., & Rule, J. (1984). Computing and organizations: What we know and what we don't know. *Communications of the ACM*, *27*, 1184–1192.

Austin, J. R., & Bartunek, J. M. (2003). Theories and practices of organization development. In W. C. Borman, D. R. Ilgen, & R. J. Klimoski (Eds.), *Handbook of psychology: Vol. 12. Industrial and organizational psychology* (pp. 309–332). Hoboken, NJ: Wiley.

Austin, J. T., & Villanova, P. (1992). The criterion problem: 1917–1992. *Journal of Applied Psychology*, *77*, 836–874.

Avery, D. R. (2003). Reactions to diversity in recruitment advertising—Are differences black and white? *Journal of Applied Psychology*, *88*, 672–679.

Avolio, B. J., Sosik, J. J., Jung, D. I., & Berson, Y. (2003). Leadership models, methods, and applications. In W. C. Borman, D. R. Ilgen, & R. J. Klimoski (Eds.), *Handbook of psychology: Vol. 12. Industrial and organizational psychology* (pp. 277–307). Hoboken, NJ: Wiley.

Azar, B. (2000). Online experiments: Ethically fair or foul? *Monitor on Psychology*, *31*(4), 50–52.

Baker, S. (2003, August 25). Where danger lurks. *Business Week*, pp. 114–118.

Baldwin, T. T. (1992). Effects of alternative modeling strategies on outcomes of interpersonal skills training. *Journal of Applied Psychology*, *77*, 147–154.

Baldwin, T. T., & Ford, J. K. (1988). Transfer of training: A review and directions for future research. *Personnel Psychology*, *41*, 63–105.

Baldwin, T. T., & Magjuka, R. J. (1997). Training as an organizational episode: Pre-training influences on trainee motivation. In J. K. Ford, S. W. J. Kozlowski, K. Kraiger, E. Salas, & M. Teachout (Eds.), *Impoving training effectiveness in work organizations* (pp. 99–127). Mahwah, NJ: Lawrence Erlbaum.

Balma, J. J. (1959). The concept of synthetic validity. *Personnel Psychology*, *12*, 395–396.

Balzer, W. K., & Sulsky, L. M. (1992). Halo and performance appraisal research: A critical examination. *Journal of Applied Psychology*, *77*, 975–985.

Bandura, A. (1977). *Social learning theory*. Englewood Cliffs, NJ: Prentice Hall.

Bandura, A. (1986). *Social foundations of thought and action: A social cognitive theory*. Englewood Cliffs, NJ: Prentice Hall.

Bandura, A. (1991). Social-cognitive theory of self-regulation. *Organizational Behavior and Human Decision Processes*, *50*, 248–287.

Bandura, A. (1997). *Self-efficacy: The exercise of control*. New York, NY: Freeman.

Banks, C. G. (2009, April). *Methodological approaches to wage-and-hour cases: I-O expert relevance*. Paper presented at the annual conference of the Society for Industrial and Organizational Psychology, New Orleans, LA.

Banks, C. G, & Roberson, L. (1985). Performance appraisers as test developers. *Academy of Management Review*, *10*, 128–142.

Baranowski, L. E., & Anderson, L. E. (2005). Examining rating sources variation in work behavior to KSA linkages. *Personnel Psychology*, *58*, 1041–1054.

Barber, A. E. (1998). *Recruiting employees: Individual and organizational perspectives*. Thousand Oaks, CA: Sage.

Barber, A. E., Daly, C. L., Giannantonio, C. M., & Phillips, J. M. (1994). Job search activities: An examination of changes over time. *Personnel Psychology*, *47*, 739–766.

Barber, A. E., Hollenbeck, J. R., Tower, S. L., & Phillips, J. M. (1994). The effects of interview focus on effectiveness: A field experiment. *Journal of Applied Psychology*, *79*, 886–896.

Barber, A. E., & Roehling, M. V. (1993). Job postings and the decision to interview: A verbal protocol analysis. *Journal of Applied Psychology*, *78*, 845–856.

Baritz, L. (1960). *The servants of power*. Middletown, CT: Wesleyan University Press.

Barkema, H. G., & Vermuelen, F. (1997). What differences in the cultural backgrounds of partners are detrimental for international joint ventures? *Journal of International Business Studies*, *28*, 845–864.

Barney, J. (1991). Firm resources and sustained competitive advantage. *Journal of Management*, *17*, 99–120.

Baron, R. A. (1983). "Sweet smell of success?" The impact of pleasant artificial scents on evaluations of job applicants. *Journal of Applied Psychology*, *68*, 709–713.

Baron, R. A. (1988). Negative effects of destructive criticism: Impact on conflict, self-efficacy, and task performance. *Journal of Applied Psychology*, *73*, 199–207.

Baron, R. A. (1993). Interviewers' moods and evaluations of applicants: The role of applicant qualifications. *Journal of Applied Social Psychology*, *23*, 253–271.

Barrick, M. R., & Mount, M. K. (2003). Impact of meta-analysis methods on understanding personality-performance relations. In K. R. Murphy (Ed.), *Validity generalization: A critical review* (pp. 197–221). Mahwah, NJ: Lawrence Erlbaum.

Barr, M. A., & Raju, N. S. (2003). IRT-based assessments of rater effects in multiple-source feedback instruments. *Organizational Research Methods*, *6*, 15–43.

Barrett, R. S. (1996). Interpeting the correlation coefficient. In R. S. Barrett (Ed.), *Fair employment strategies in human resource management* (pp. 73–87). Westport, CT: Quorum Books.

Barrett, G. V., & Alexander, R. A. (1989). Rejoinder to Austin, Humphreys, and Hulin: Critical reanalysis of Barrett, Caldwell, and Alexander. *Personnel Psychology*, *42*, 597–612.

Barrett, G. V., Caldwell, M. S., & Alexander, R. A. (1985). The concept of dynamic criteria: A critical reanalysis. *Personnel Psychology*, *38*, 41–56.

Barrett, G. V., & Lueke, S. B. (2004). Legal and practical implications of banding for personnel selection. In H. Aguinis (Ed.), *Test score banding in human resource selection: Legal, technical, and societal issues* (pp. 71–112). Westport, CT: Praeger.

Barrett, G. V., Phillips, J. S., & Alexander, R. A. (1981). Concurrent and predictive validity designs: A critical reanalysis. *Journal of Applied Psychology, 66,* 1–6.

Barrick, M. R., & Mount, M. K. (1991). The Big Five personality dimensions and job performance: A meta-analysis. *Personnel Psychology, 44,* 1–26.

Barrick, M. R., & Mount, M. K. (1996). Effects of impression management and self-deception on the predictive validity of personality constructs. *Journal of Applied Psychology, 83,* 261–272.

Barrick, M. R., & Mount, M. K. (2003). Impact of meta-analysis methods on understanding personality-performance relations. In K. R. Murphy (Ed.), *Validity generalization: A critical review* (pp. 197–221). Mahwah, NJ: Lawrence Erlbaum.

Barrick, M. R., Mount, M. K., & Judge, T. A. (2001). Personality and performance at the beginning of the new millennium: What do we know and where do we go next? *International Journal of Selection and Assessment, 9,* 9–30.

Barrick, M. R., Stewart, G. L., & Piotrowski, M. (2002). Personality and job performance: Test of the mediating effects of motivation among sales representatives. *Journal of Applied Psychology, 87,* 43–51.

Barron, L. G., & Sackett, P. R. (2008). Asian variability in performance rating modesty and leniency bias. *Human Performance, 21,* 277–290.

Bartlett, C. J., Bobko, P., Mosier, S. B., & Hannan, R. (1978). Testing for fairness with a moderated multiple regression strategy: An alternative to differential analysis. *Personnel Psychology, 31,* 233–241.

Bartlett, C. J., & O'Leary, B. S. (1969). A differential prediction model to moderate the effects of heterogeneous groups in personnel selection and classification. *Personnel Psychology, 22,* 1–17.

Barton, J. (1994). Choosing to work at night: A moderating influence on individual tolerance to shift work. *Journal of Applied Psychology, 79,* 449–454.

Barrier, M. (2002, July). A line in the sand. n.d. Retrieved April 17, 2008, www.shrm.org/hrmagazine/articles/0702/0702barrier.asp.

Baskerville, R. F. (2003). Hofstede never studied culture. *Accounting, Organizations, & Society, 28,* 1–14.

Bass, B. M. (1954). The leaderless group discussion. *Psychological Bulletin, 51,* 465–492.

Bass, B. M. (1962). Further evidence on the dynamic nature of criteria. *Personnel Psychology, 15,* 93–97.

Bass, B. M. (1980). Team productivity and individual member competence. *Small Group Behavior, 11,* 431–504.

Bass, B. M. (1983). Issues involved in relations between methodological rigor and reported outcomes in evaluations of organizational development. *Journal of Applied Psychology, 6,* 197–199.

Bass, B. M., Cascio, W. F., McPherson, J. W., & Tragash, H. (1976). Prosper-training and research for increasing management awareness about affirmative action in race relations. *Academy of Management Journal, 19,* 353–369.

Bass, B. M., Cascio, W. F., & O'Connor, E. J. (1974). Magnitude estimations of expressions of frequency and amount. *Journal of Applied Psychology, 59,* 313–320.

Bass, B. M., & Riggio, R. E. (2006). Transformational leadership (2nd ed.). Mahwah, NJ: Lawrence Erlbaum.

Batt, R. (2002). Managing customer services: Human resource practices, quit rates, and sales growth. *Academy of Management Journal, 45,* 587–597.

Bauer, T. N., Truxillo, D. M., Tucker, J. S., Weathers, V., Bertolino, M., Erdogan, B., & Campion, M. A. (2006). Selection in the information age: The impact of privacy concerns and computer experience on applicant reactions. *Journal of Management, 32,* 601–621.

Baumrind, D. (1985). Research using intentional deception: Ethical issues revisited. *American Psychologist, 40,* 165–174.

Becker, B. E. (1989). The influence of labor markets on human resources utility estimates. *Personnel Psychology, 42,* 531–546.

Becker, G. (2000). How important is transient error in estimating reliability? Going beyond simulation studies. *Psychological Methods, 5,* 370–379.

Becker, T. E. (2005). Development and validation of a situational judgment test of employee integrity. *International Journal of Selection & Assessment, 13,* 225–232.

Becker, B. E., & Huselid, M. A. (1992). Direct estimates of Sd_y and the implications for utility analysis. *Journal of Applied Psychology, 77,* 227–233.

Becker, B. E., Huselid, M. A., & Ulrich, D. (2001). *The HR scorecard: Linking people, strategy, and performance.* Boston, MA: Harvard Business School Press.

Becker, T. E., & Klimoski, R. J. (1989). A field study of the relationship between the organizational feedback environment and performance. *Personnel Psychology, 42,* 343–358.

Beehr, T. A., & Gilmore, D. C. (1982). Applicant attractiveness as a perceived job-relevant variable in selection of management trainees. *Academy of Management Journal, 25,* 607–617.

Begley, S. (2003, November 7). Expectations may alter outcomes far more than we realize. *The Wall Street Journal,* p. B1.

Bergeron, D. M. (2007). The potential paradox of organizational citizenship behavior: Good citizens at what cost? *Academy of Management Review, 32,* 1078–1095.

Bergman, M. E., Donovan, M. A., Drasgow, F., Overton, R. C., & Henning, J. B. (2008). Test of Motowidlo et al.'s (1997) theory of individual differences in task and contextual performance. *Human Performance, 21,* 227–253.

Bell, B. S., & Kozlowski, S. W. J. (2002). Adaptive guidance: Enhancing self-regulation, knowledge, and performance in technology-based training. *Personnel Psychology, 55,* 267–306.

Bendell, J. (2007). World review: The responsibility of business schools. *Journal of Corporate Citizenship, 28 (July–September),* 4–14.

Benedict, M. E., & Levine, E. L. (1988). Delay and distortion: Tacit influences on performance appraisal effectiveness. *Journal of Applied Psychology, 73,* 507–514.

Bennett, R. J., & Robinson, S. L. (2000). Development of a measure of workplace deviance. *Journal of Applied Psychology*, *85*, 349–360.

Bennett, R., Aston, A., & Colquhoun, T. (2000). Cross-cultural training: A critical step in ensuring the success of international assignments. *Human Resource Management*, *39*, 239–250.

Berman, F. E., & Miner, J. B. (1985). Motivation to manage at the top executive level: A test of the hierarchic role-motivation theory. *Personnel Psychology*, *38*, 377–391.

Bernard v. Gulf Oil Corp., 890 F.2d 735 (5th Cir. 1989).

Bernardin, H. J., & Beatty, R. W. (1984). *Performance appraisal: Assessing human behavior at work.* Boston, MA: Kent.

Bernardin, H. J., & Beatty, R. W. (1991). *Performance appraisal: Assessing human behavior at work* (2nd ed.). Boston, MA: Kent.

Bernardin, H. J., & Buckley, M. R. (1981). A consideration of strategies in rater training. *Academy of Management Review*, *6*, 205–212.

Bernardin, H. J., & Cooke, D. K. (1993). Validity of an honesty test in predicting theft among convenience store employees. *Academy of Management Journal*, *36*, 1097–1108.

Bernardin, H. J., Cooke, D. K., & Villanova, P. (2000). Conscientiousness and agreeableness as predictors of rating leniency. *Journal of Applied Psychology*, *85*, 232–236.

Benson, M. J., & Campbell, J. P. (2007). To be, or not to be, linear: An expanded representation of personality and its relationship to leadership performance. *International Journal of Selection & Assessment*, *15*, 232–249.

Berry, C. M., Sackett, P. R., & Wiemann, S. (2007). A review of recent developments in integrity test research. *Personnel Psychology*, *60*, 271–301.

Bersoff, D. N. (Ed.). (2003). *Ethical conflicts in psychology* (3rd ed.). Washington, DC: American Psychological Association.

Bertua, C., Anderson, N., & Salgado, J. F. (2005). The predictive validity of cognitive ability tests: A UK meta-analysis. *Journal of Occupational & Organizational Psychology*, *78*, 387–409.

Bhagat, R. S. (2002). Book review of culture's consequences: Comparing values, behaviors, institutions, and organizations across nations (2nd ed.). *Academy of Management Review*, *27*, 460–462.

Bhagwati, J. (2007). *In defense of globalization.* New York, NY: Oxford University Press.

Bhawuk, D. P. S., & Brislin, R. W. (2000). Cross-cultural training: A review. *Applied Psychology: An International Review*, *49*, 162–191.

Billsberry, J. (2007). *Experiencing recruitment and selection.* Hoboken, NJ: Wiley.

Bing, J. W. (2004). Hofstede's consequences: The impact of his work on consulting and business practices. *Academy of Management Executive*, *18*(1), 80–87.

Biskupic, J. (2008, June 20). Court aids older workers alleging discrimination. *USA Today*, 5A.

Binning, J. F., & Barrett, G. V. (1989). Validity of personnel decisions: A conceptual analysis of the inferential and evidential bases. *Journal of Applied Psychology*, *74*, 478–494.

Bing, M. N., LeBreton, J. M., Davison, H., Migetz, D. Z., & James, L. R. (2007). Integrating implicit and explicit social cognitions for enhanced personality assessment. *Organizational Research Methods*, *10*, 136–179.

Black, J. S., & Gregersen, H. B. (1991). When Yankee comes home: Factors related to expatriate and spouse repatriation adjustment. *Journal of International Business Studies*, *22*(4), 671–695.

Black, J. S., Gregersen, H. B., & Mendenhall, M. E. (1992). *Global assignments.* San Francisco, CA: Jossey-Bass.

Blair, C. A., Hoffman, B. J., & Helland, K. R. (2008). Narcissism in organizations: A multisource appraisal reflects different perspectives. *Human Performance*, *21*, 254–276.

Blanchard, P. N., & Thacker, J. W. (2007). *Effective training: Systems, strategies, and practices* (3rd ed.). Upper Saddle River, NJ: Pearson Prentice Hall.

Blanton, H., & Jaccard, J. (2006). Arbitrary metrics redux. *American Psychologist*, *61*, 62–71.

Blau, G., & Andersson, L. (2005). Testing a measure of instigated workplace incivility. *Journal of Occupational & Organizational Psychology*, *78*, 595–614.

Blum, M. L., & Naylor, J. C. (1968). *Industrial psychology, its theoretical and social foundations* (rev. ed.). New York, NY: Harper & Row.

Bobko, P., & Bartlett, C. J. (1978). Subgroup validities: Differential definitions and differential prediction. *Journal of Applied Psychology*, *63*, 12–14.

Bobko, P., & Colella, A. (1994). Employee reactions to performance standards: A review and research propositions. *Personnel Psychology*, *47*, 1–29.

Bobko, P., Roth, P. L., & Buster, M. A. (2005). Work sample selection tests and expected reduction in adverse impact: A cautionary note. *International Journal of Selection and Assessment*, *13*, 1–10.

Bobko, P., Roth, P. L., & Buster, M. A. (2007). The usefulness of unit weights in creating composite scores: A literature review, application to content validity, and meta-analysis. *Organizational Research Methods*, *10*, 689–709.

Bobko, P., & Roth, P. L. (2008). Psychometric accuracy and (the continuing need for) quality thinking in meta-analysis. *Organizational Research Methods*, *11*, 114–126.

Bobko, P., Roth, P. L., & Potosky, D. (1999). Derivation and implications of a meta-analytic matrix incorporating cognitive ability, alternative predictors, and job performance. *Personnel Psychology*, *52*, 561–589.

Bobko, P., & Stone-Romero, E. F. (1998). Meta-analysis may be another useful research tool, but it is not a panacea. *Research in personnel and human resources management* (Vol. 16, pp. 359–397). Stamford, CT: JAI Press.

Boehm, V. R. (1972). Negro-white differences in validity of employment and training selection procedures: Summary of research evidence. *Journal of Applied Psychology*, *56*, 33–39.

Boehm, V. R. (1977). Differential prediction: A methodological artifact? *Journal of Applied Psychology*, *62*, 146–154.

Bolster, B. I., & Springbett, B. M. (1961). The reaction of interviewers to favorable and unfavorable information. *Journal of Applied Psychology*, *45*, 97–103.

Bommer, W. H., Johnson, J. L., Rich, G. A., Podsakoff, P. M., & Mackenzie, S. B. (1995). *Personnel Psychology, 48*, 587–605.

Bond, N. (1973). Auditing change: The technology of measuring change. In M. D. Dunnette (Ed.), *Work and nonwork in the year 2001.* Monterey, CA: Brooks/Cole.

Bono, J. E., & Judge, T. A. (2003). Core self-evaluations: A review of the trait and its role in job satisfaction and job performance. *European Journal of Personality, 17*, S5–S18.

Booth, J. F. (1998). Guest editorial: Uses of PC technology in selection and assessment. *International Journal of Selection and Assessment, 6*, 57–60.

Borman, W. C. (1974). The rating of individuals in organizations: An alternate approach. *Organizational Behavior and Human Performance, 12*, 105–124.

Borman, W. C. (1978). Exploring the upper limits of reliability and validity in job performance ratings. *Journal of Applied Psychology, 63*, 135–144.

Borman, W. C. (1982). Validity of behavioral assessment for predicting military recruiter performance. *Journal of Applied Psychology, 67*, 3–9.

Borman, W. C. (1991). Job behavior, performance, and effectiveness. In M. D. Dunnette, & L. M. Hough (Eds.), *Handbook of industrial and organizational psychology* (2nd ed., Vol. 2, pp. 271–326). Palo Alto, CA: Consulting Psychologists Press.

Borman, W. C., Eaton, N. K., Bryan, D. J., & Rosse, R. (1983). Validity of Army recruiter behavioral assessment: Does the assessor make a difference? *Journal of Applied Psychology, 68*, 415–419.

Borman, W. C., & Hallam, G. L. (1991). Observation accuracy for assessors of work-sample performance: Consistency across task and individual-differences correlates. *Journal of Applied Psychology, 76*, 11–18.

Borman, W. C., Hanson, M. A., Oppler, S. H., Pulakos, E. D., & White, L. A. (1993). Role of early supervisory experience in supervisor performance. *Journal of Applied Psychology, 78*, 443–449.

Borman, W. C., & Motowidlo, S. J. (1997). Task performance and contextual performance: The meaning for personnel selection research. *Human Performance, 10*, 99–109.

Borman, W. C., Penner, L. A., Allen, T. D., & Motowidlo, S. (2001). Personality predictors of citizenship performance. *International Journal of Selection and Assessment, 9*, 52–69.

Borman, W. C., Rosse, R. L., & Abrahams, N. M. (1980). An empirical construct validity approach to studying predictor-job performance links. *Journal of Applied Psychology, 65*, 662–671.

Borman, W. C., White, L. A., & Dorsey, D. W. (1995). Effects of ratee task performance and interpersonal factors on supervisor and peer performance ratings. *Journal of Applied Psychology, 80*, 168–177.

Borman, W. C., White, L. A., Pulakos, E. D., & Oppler, S. H. (1991). Models of supervisory job performance ratings. *Journal of Applied Psychology, 76*, 863–872.

Boswell, W. R., Roehling, M. V., LePine, M. A., & Moynihan, L. M. (2003). Individual job-choice decisions and the impact of job attributes and recruitment practices: A longitudinal field study. *Human Resource Management, 42*, 23–37.

Bottger, P. C., & Yetton, P. W. (1987). Improving group performance by training in individual problem solving. *Journal of Applied Psychology, 72*, 651–657.

Boudreau, J. W. (1983a). Economic considerations in estimating the utility of human resource productivity improvement programs. *Personnel Psychology, 36*, 551–576.

Boudreau, J. W. (1983b). Effects of employee flows on utility analysis of human resource productivity improvement programs. *Journal of Applied Psychology, 68*, 396–406.

Boudreau, J. W. (1988). Utility analysis. In L. Dyer (Ed.), *Human resource management: Evolving roles and responsibilities* (pp. 1-125–1-186). Washington, DC: Bureau of National Affairs.

Boudreau, J. W. (1991). Utility analysis for decisions in human resource management. In M. D. Dunnette, & L. M. Hough (Eds.), *Handbook of industrial and organizational psychology* (2nd ed., Vol. 2, pp. 621–745). Palo Alto, CA: Consulting Psychologists Press.

Boudreau, J. W. (1998). Strategic human resource management measures: Key linkages and the PeopleVantage model. *Journal of Human Resource Costing and Accounting, 3*(2), 29.

Boudreau, J. W., & Berger, C. J. (1985). Decision-theoretic utility analysis applied to employee separations and acquisitions. *Journal of Applied Psychology, 70*, 581–612.

Boudreau, J. W., & Ramstad, P. M. (2003). Strategic industrial and organizational psychology and the role of utility analysis models. In W. C. Borman, D. R. Ilgen, & R. J. Klimoski (Eds.), *Handbook of psychology: Vol. 12. Industrial and organizational psychology* (pp. 193–221). Hoboken, NJ: Wiley.

Boudreau, J. W., & Ramstad, P. M. (2006). Talentship and HR measurement and analysis: From ROI to strategic organizational change. *Human Resource Planning, 29*(1), 25–33.

Boudreau, J. W., & Ramstad, P. M. (2007). *Beyond HR: The new science of human capital.* Boston, MA: Harvard Business School Press.

Boudreau, J. W., & Rynes, S. L. (1985). Role of recruitment in staffing utility analysis. *Journal of Applied Psychology, 70*, 354–366.

Bower, J. L. (2007, November). Solve the succession crisis by growing inside-outside leaders. *Harvard Business Review, 85*, 91–96.

Bower, J. L. (2008, April 15). The leader within your company. *BusinessWeek.* n.d. Retrieved April 28, 2008, from www.businessweek.com.

Bowler, M. C., & Woehr, D. J. (2006). A meta-analytic evaluation of the impact of dimension and exercise factors on assessment center ratings. *Journal of Applied Psychology, 91*, 1114–1124.

Bownas, D. A., Bosshardt, M. J., & Donnelly, L. F. (1985). A quantitative approach to evaluating training curriculum content sampling adequacy. *Personnel Psychology, 38*, 117–131.

Bozeman, D. P. (1997). Interrater agreement in multi-source performance appraisal: A commentary. *Journal of Organizational Behavior, 18*, 313–316.

Bozionelos, N. (2005). When the inferior candidate is offered the job: The selection interview as a political and power game. *Human Relations*, *58*, 1605–1631.

Brady, F. N. (1985). A Janus-headed model of ethical theory: Looking two ways at business/society issues. *Academy of Management Review*, *10*, 568–576.

Brannick, M. T. (2001). Implications of empirical Bayes meta-analysis for test validation. *Journal of Applied Psychology*, *86*, 468–480.

Brannick, M. T., & Hall, S. M. (2003). Validity generalization from a Bayesian perspective. In K. R. Murphy (Ed.), *Validity generalization: A critical review* (pp. 339–364). Mahwah, NJ: Lawrence Erlbaum.

Brannick, M. T., Levine, E. L., & Morgeson, F. P. (2007). *Job and work analysis: Methods, research, and applications for human resource management* (2nd ed.). Thousand Oaks, CA: Sage Publications.

Brass, D. J., & Oldham, G. R. (1976). Validating an in-basket test using an alternative set of leadership scoring dimensions. *Journal of Applied Psychology*, *61*, 652–657.

Bray, D. W., & Campbell, R. J. (1968). Selection of salesmen by means of an assessment center. *Journal of Applied Psychology*, *52*, 36–41.

Bray, D. W., Campbell, R. J., & Grant, D. L. (1974). *Formative years in business: A long-term AT&T study of managerial lives*. New York, NY: Wiley.

Bray, D. W., & Howard, A. (1983). *Longitudinal studies of adult psychological development*. New York, NY: Guilford.

Bray, D. W., & Moses, J. L. (1972). Personnel selection. *Annual Review of Psychology*, *23*, 545–576.

Brealey, R., & Myers, S. (2003). *Principles of corporate finance* (7th ed.). New York, NY: McGraw-Hill.

Breaugh, J. A. (1983). Realistic job previews: A critical appraisal and future research directions. *Academy of Management Review*, *8*, 612–619.

Breaugh, J. A. (1992). *Recruitment: Science and practice*. Boston, MA: PWS-Kent.

Breaugh, J. A. (2008). Employee recruitment: Current knowledge and important areas for future research. *Human Resource Management Review*, *18*, 103–118.

Breaugh, J. A., Greising, L. A., Taggart, J. W., & Chen, H. (2003). The relationship of recruiting sources and pre-hire outcomes: Examination of yield ratios and applicant quality. *Journal of Applied Social Psychology*, *33*, 2267–2287.

Breaugh, J. A., Macan, T. H., & Grambow, D. M. (2008). Employee recruitment: Current knowledge and directions for future research. In G. P. Hodgkinson, & J. K. Ford (Eds.), *International Review of Industrial and Organizational Psychology* (Vol. 23, pp. 45–82). Hoboken, NJ: Wiley.

Breaugh, J. A., & Starke, M. (2000). Research on employee recruitment: So many studies, so many remaining questions. *Journal of Management*, *26*, 405–434.

Brennan, E. (2009). ADA Amendments Act of 2008 takes effect January 1, 2009. n.d. www.americantrails.org/resources/accessible/ADAAA08.html.

Brett, J. M., Tinsley, C. H., Janssens, M., Barsness, Z. I., & Lytle, A. L. (1997). New approaches to the study of culture in industrial/organizational psychology. In P. C. Earley & M. Erez (Eds.), *New perspectives on industrial/organizational psychology* (pp. 75–129). San Francisco, CA: New Lexington Press.

Bretz, R. D., & Judge, T. A. (1998). Realistic job previews: A test of the adverse self-selection hypothesis. *Journal of Applied Psychology*, *83*, 330–337.

Bretz, R. D., Jr., Milkovich, G. T., & Read, W. (1990). The current state of performance appraisal research and practice: Concerns, directions, and implications. *Journal of Management*, *18*, 321–352.

Bretz, R. D., Jr., & Thompsett, R. E. (1992). Comparing traditional and integrative learning methods in organizational training programs. *Journal of Applied Psychology*, *77*, 941–951.

Bridges, W. (1994a, September 19). The end of the job. *Fortune*, pp. 62–64, 68, 72, 74.

Bridges, W. (1994b). *Job shift: How to prosper in a world without jobs*. Reading, MA: Addison-Wesley.

Briscoe, D. R., Schuler, R. S., & Claus, L. (2009). *International human resource management* (3rd ed.). London: Routledge.

Brislin, R. W., & Bhawuk, D. P. S. (1999). Cross-cultural training: Research and innovations. In J. Adamopoulos, & Y. Kashima (Eds.), *Social psychology and cultural context* (pp. 205–216). Thousand Oaks, CA: Sage.

Britt, L. P., III. (1984). Affirmative action: Is there life after *Stotts*? *Personnel Administrator*, *29*, 96–100.

Broad, W., & Wade, N. (1982). *Betrayers of the truth: Fraud and deceit in the halls of science*. New York, NY: Simon & Schuster.

Brogden, H. E. (1946). On the interpretation of the correlation coefficient as a measure of predictive efficiency. *Journal of Educational Psychology*, *37*, 64–76.

Brogden, H. E. (1949). When testing pays off. *Personnel Psychology*, *2*, 171–183.

Brogden, H. E., & Taylor, E. K. (1950a). The dollar criterion—Applying the cost accounting concept to criterion construction. *Personnel Psychology*, *3*, 133–154.

Brogden, H. E., & Taylor, E. K. (1950b). The theory and classification of criterion bias. *Educational and Psychological Measurement*, *10*, 159–186.

Brown, B. (1988, August 4). Succession strategies for family firms. *The Wall Street Journal*, p. 23.

Brown, B. K., & Campion, M. A. (1994). Biodata phenomenology: Recruiters' perceptions and use of biographical information in resume screening. *Journal of Applied Psychology*, *79*, 897–908.

Brown, S. H. (1979). Validity distortions associated with a test in use. *Journal of Applied Psychology*, *64*, 460–462.

Brown, F. G. (1983). *Principles of educational and psychological testing* (3rd ed.). New York, NY: Holt, Rinehart, & Winston.

Brown, S. P. (1996). A meta-analysis and review of organizational research on job involvement. *Psychological Bulletin*, *120*, 235–256.

Brown, K. G. (2001). Using computers to deliver training: Which employees learn and why? *Personnel Psychology*, *54*, 271–296.

Brown, K. G. (2005). An examination of the structure and nomological network of trainee reactions: A closer look at "smile sheets." *Journal of Applied Psychology*, *90*, 991–1001.

Brown, K. G., & Ford, J. K. (2002). Using computer technology in training: Building an infrastructure for active learning. In K. Kraiger (Ed.), *Creating, implementing, and managing effective training and development* (pp. 192–233). San Francisco, CA: Jossey-Bass.

Brown, S. H., Stout, J. D., Dalessio, A. T., & Crosby, M. M. (1988). Stability of validity indices through test score ranges. *Journal of Applied Psychology*, *73*, 736–742.

Browne, M. W. (1975). Predictive validity of a linear regression equation. *British Journal of Mathematical and Statistical Psychology*, *28*, 79–87.

Brugnoli, G. A., Campion, J. E., & Basen, J. A. (1979). Racial bias in the use of work samples for personnel selection. *Journal of Applied Psychology*, *64*, 119–123.

Buckingham, M., & Coffman, C. (1999). *First break all the rules: What the world's greatest managers do differently.* New York, NY: Simon & Schuster.

Bullock, R. J., & Svyantek, D. J. (1985). Analyzing meta-analysis: Potential problems, an unsuccessful replication, and evaluation criteria. *Journal of Applied Psychology*, *70*, 108–115.

Buono, A. F. (2003). The hidden costs and benefits of organizational resizing activities. In K. P. De Meuse, & M. L. Marks (Eds.), *Resizing the organization* (pp. 306–346). San Francisco, CA: Jossey-Bass.

Burchell, J., & Cook, J. (2006). It's good to talk? Examining attitudes towards corporate social responsibility dialogue and engagement processes. *Business Ethics: A European Review 15*, 154–170.

Burke, M. J., & Doran, L. I. (1989). A note on the economic utility of generalized validity coefficients in personnel selection. *Journal of Applied Psychology*, *74*, 171–175.

Burke, M. J., & Frederick, J. T. (1984). Two modified procedures for estimating standard deviations in utility analyses. *Journal of Applied Psychology*, *69*, 482–489.

Burke, M. J., & Frederick, J. T. (1986). A comparison of economic utility estimates for alternative Sd_y estimation procedures. *Journal of Applied Psychology*, *71*, 334–339.

Burke, R. J., Weitzel, W., & Weir, T. (1978). Characteristics of effective employee performance review and development interviews: Replication and extension. *Personnel Psychology*, *31*, 903–919.

Burlington Industries, Inc. v. Ellerth, 118 S. Ct. 2257 (1998).

Burnett, J. R., Fan, C., Motowidlo, S. J., & DeGroot, T. (1998). Interview notes and validity. *Personnel Psychology*, *51*, 375–396.

Buster, M. A., Roth, P. L., & Bobko, P. A. (2005). A process for content validation of education and experienced-based minimum qualifications: An approach resulting in federal court approval. *Personnel Psychology*, *58*, 771–799.

Butler, S. K., & Harvey, R. J. (1988). A comparison of holistic versus decomposed rating of Position Analysis Questionnaire work dimensions. *Personnel Psychology*, *41*, 761–771.

Byham, W. C., & Spitzer, M. E. (1971). *The law and personnel testing.* New York, NY: American Management Association.

Byrnes, N. (2005, October 10). Starsearch: How to recruit, train, and hold on to great people. What works, what doesn't. *BusinessWeek*, pp. 68–78.

Byrne, J. A. (2002, June 24). Restoring trust in corporate America. *Business Week*, pp. 30–42.

Byrnes, N. (2005, October 10). Starsearch. *BusinessWeek*, pp. 68–78.

Cable, D. M., Aiman-Smith, L., Mulvey, P. W., & Edwards, J. R. (2000). The sources and accuracy of job applicants' beliefs about organizational culture. *Academy of Management Journal*, *43*, 1076–1085.

Cable, D. M., & Judge, T. A. (1997). Interviewers' perceptions of person-organization fit and organizational selection decisions. *Journal of Applied Psychology*, *82*, 546–561.

Cabrera, E. F., & Raju, N. S. (2001). Utility analysis: Current trends and future directions. *International Journal of Selection and Assessment*, *9*, 92–102.

Cadrain, D. (2003). Are your employee drug tests accurate? *HRMagazine*, *48*(1), 40–45.

Caldwell, D. F., & Burger, J. M. (1998). Personality characteristics of job applicants and success in screening interviews. *Personnel Psychology*, *51*, 119–136.

California Brewers Association v. Bryant, 444 U.S. 598 (1982).

Caligiuri, P. M. (2000). The big five personality characteristics as predictors of expatriates' desire to terminate the assignment and supervisor-rated performance. *Personnel Psychology*, *53*, 67–88.

Caligiuri, P., & Cascio, W. F. (2000). Sending women on global assignments. *WorldatWork Journal*, *9*(2), 34–40.

Caligiuri, P. M., & Phillips, J. M. (2003). An application of self-assessment realistic job previews to expatriate assignments. *International Journal of Human Resource Management*, *14*, 1102–1116.

Caligiuri, P., & Tarique, I. (2006). International assignee selection and cross-cultural training and development. In G. K. Stahl, & I. Björkman (Eds.), *Handbook of research in international human resource management* (pp. 302–322). Cheltenham, UK: Edward Elgar.

Callinan, M., & Robertson, I. T. (2000). Work sample testing. *International Journal of Selection and Assessment*, *8*, 248–260.

Campbell, J. P. (1971). Personnel training and development. *Annual Review of Psychology*, *22*, 565–602.

Campbell, J. P. (1988). Training design for performance improvement. In J. P. Campbell, & R. J. Campbell (Eds.), *Productivity in organizations* (pp. 177–215). San Francisco, CA: Jossey-Bass.

Campbell, J. P. (1990). Modeling the performance prediction problem in industrial and organizational psychology. In M. D. Dunnette, & L. M. Hough (Eds.), *Handbook of industrial and organizational psychology* (2nd ed., Vol. 1, pp. 687–782). Palo Alto, CA: Consulting Psychologists Press.

Campbell D. J., & Lee, C. (1988). Self-appraisal in performance evaluation: Development versus evaluation. *Academy of Management Review*, *13*, 302–314.

Campbell, D. T., & Fiske, D. W. (1959). Convergent and discrimination validation by the multitrait-multimethod matrix. *Psychological Bulletin*, *56*, 81–105.

Campbell, J. P., Dunnette, M. D., Arvey, R. D., & Hellervik, L. V. (1973). The development and evaluation of behaviorally based rating scales. *Journal of Applied Psychology*, *57*, 15–22.

Campbell, J. P., McHenry, J. J., & Wise, L. L. (1990). Modeling job performance in a population of jobs. *Personnel Psychology*, *43*, 313–333.

Campbell, D. T., & Stanley, J. C. (1963). *Experimental and quasi-experimental designs for research.* Chicago, IL: Rand McNally.

Campion, M. A. (1991). Meaning and measurement of turnover: Comparison of alternative measures and recommendations for research. *Journal of Applied Psychology*, *76*, 199–212.

Campion, M. A., Campion, J. E., & Hudson, J. P., Jr. (1994). *Journal of Applied Psychology*, *79*, 998–1002.

Campion, M. A., Outtz, J. L, Zedeck, S., Schmidt, F. L, Kehoe, J. F., Murphy, K. R, & Guion, R. M. (2001). The controversy over score banding in personnel selection: Answers to 10 key questions. *Personnel Psychology*, *54*, 149–185.

Campion, M. A., Palmer, D. K., & Campion, J. E. (1997). A review of structure in the selection interview. *Personnel Psychology*, *50*, 655–702.

Cannon-Bowers, J. A., Tannenbaum, S. I., Salas, E., & Volpe, C. E. (1995). Defining competencies and establishing team training requirements. In R. A. Guzzo, & E. Salas (Eds.), *Team effectiveness and decision making in organizations* (pp. 333–380). San Francisco, CA: Jossey-Bass.

Cappelli, P. (1999). *The new deal at work: Managing the market-driven workforce.* Boston, MA: Harvard Business School Press.

Cappelli, P. (2001, March). Making the most of online recruiting. *Harvard Business Review*, *78*, pp. 139–146.

Cappelli, P. (2008). *Talent on demand: Managing talent in an age of uncertainty.* Boston, MA: Harvard Business School Press.

Capriotti, P., & Moreno, A. (2007). Communicating corporate responsibility through corporate web sites in Spain. *Corporate Communications: An International Journal 12*(3), 221–237.

Carlson, R. E. (1967). Selection interview decisions: The effect of interviewer experience, relative quota situation, and applicant sample on interviewer decisions. *Personnel Psychology*, *20*, 259–280.

Carlson, K. D., & Schmidt, F. L. (1999). Impact of experimental design on effect size: Findings from the research literature on training. *Journal of Applied Psychology*, *84*, 851–862.

Carlson, K. D., Scullen, S. E., Schmidt, F. L., Rothstein, H., & Erwin, F. (1999). Generalizable biographical data validity can be achieved without multi-organizational development and keying. *Personnel Psychology*, *52*, 731–755.

Carlson, R. E., Thayer, P. W., Mayfield, E. C., & Peterson, D. A. (1971). Improvements in the selection interview. *Personnel Journal*, *50*, 268–275.

Carretta, T. R., & Ree, M. J. (2000). General and specific cognitive and psychomotor abilities in personnel selection: The prediction of training and job performance. *International Journal of Selection and Assessment*, *8*, 227–236.

Carroll, S. J., & Gillen, D. J. (1987). Are the classical management functions useful in describing managerial work? *Academy of Management Review*, *12*, 38–51.

Carson, K. P., Becker, J. S., & Henderson, J. A. (1998). Is utility really futile? A failure to replicate and an extension. *Journal of Applied Psychology*, *83*, 84–96.

Cascio, W. F. (1975). Accuracy of verifiable biographical information blank responses. *Journal of Applied Psychology*, *60*, 767–769.

Cascio, W. F. (1976a). Factor structure stability in attitude measurement. *Educational and Psychological Measurement*, *36*, 847–854.

Cascio, W. F. (1976b). Turnover, biographical data, and fair employment practice. *Journal of Applied Psychology*, *61*, 576–580.

Cascio, W. F. (1980). Responding to the demand for accountability: A critical analysis of three utility models. *Organizational Behavior and Human Performance*, *25*, 32–45.

Cascio, W. F. (1982). Scientific, operational, and legal imperatives of workable performance appraisal systems. *Public Personnel Management Journal*, *11*, 367–375.

Cascio, W. F. (1989). Using utility analysis to assess training outcomes. In I. L. Goldstein (Ed.), *Training and development in organizations* (pp. 63–88). San Francisco, CA: Jossey-Bass.

Cascio, W. F. (1991). *Costing human resources: The financial impact of behavior in organizations* (3rd ed.). Boston, MA: PWS-Kent.

Cascio, W. F. (1993a). Assessing the utility of selection decisions: Theoretical and practical considerations. In N. Schmitt, & W. C. Borman (Eds.), *Personnel selection in organizations* (pp. 310–340). San Francisco, CA: Jossey-Bass.

Cascio, W. F. (1993b, February). Downsizing: What do we know? What have we learned? *Academy of Management Executive*, *7*(1), 95–104.

Cascio, W. F. (1993c, August). *The 1991 Civil Rights Act and the Americans with Disabilities Act of 1990: Requirements for psychological practice in the workplace.* Master lecture presented at the annual convention of the American Psychological Association, Toronto.

Cascio, W. F. (1998). The theory of vertical and horizontal individualism and collectivism: Implications for international human resource management. In J. Cheng, & B. Peterson (Eds.), *Advances in international and comparative management* (pp. 87–103). Greenwich, CT: JAI Press.

Cascio, W. F. (2002a). *Responsible restructuring: Creative and profitable alternatives to layoffs.* San Francisco, CA: Berrett-Kohler.

Cascio, W. F. (2002b). Strategies for responsible restructuring. *Academy of Management Executive*, *16*(3), 80–91.

Cascio, W. F. (2003a). Changes in workers, work, and organizations. In W. C. Borman, D. R. Ilgen, & R. J. Klimoski (Eds.), *Handbook of psychology: Vol. 12. Industrial and organizational psychology* (pp. 401–422). Hoboken, NJ: Wiley.

Cascio, W. F. (2003b). Corporate restructuring and the no-layoff payoff. *Perspectives on Work*, *7*, 4–6.

Cascio, W. F. (2006). Global performance management systems. In I. Bjorkman, & G. Stahl (Eds.), *Handbook of research in international human resource management* (pp. 176–196). Cheltenham, UK: Edward Elgar.

Cascio, W. F. (2010). *Managing human resources: Productivity, quality of work life, profits* (8th ed.). New York, NY: McGraw-Hill/Irwin.

Cascio, W. F. (2008, March). Shifting the paradigm: Work in the 21st century. Keynote address presented at the 29th annual IOOB Conference, Denver, Colorado.

Cascio, W. F. (in press). The changing world of work. In Linley, A., Harrington, S., & Page, N. (Eds.), *Oxford Handbook of Positive Psychology and Work.* Oxford, UK: Oxford University Press.

Cascio, W. F., & Aguinis, H. (2005). Test development and use: New twists on old questions. *Human Resource Management, 44,* 219–235.

Cascio, W. F., & Aguinis, H. (2008). Staffing 21st-century organizations. In J. P. Walsh, & A. P. Brief (Eds.), *Academy of Management Annals* (Vol. 2, pp. 133–165). Mahwah, NJ: Lawrence Erlbaum.

Cascio, W. F., & Boudreau, J. W. (2008). *Investing in people: Financial impact of human resource initiatives.* Upper Saddle River, NJ: Pearson Education.

Cascio, W. F., & Boudreau, J. W. (in press). Utility of selection systems: Supply-chain analysis applied to staffing decisions. In S. Zedeck (Ed.), *Handbook of I/O Psychology.* Washington, DC: American Psychological Association.

Cisco Corporation (2009). Downloaded April 13, 2009, from www.cisco.com.

Cascio, W. F., Alexander, R. A., & Barrett, G. V. (1988). Setting cutoff scores: Legal, psychometric, and professional issues and guidelines. *Personnel Psychology, 41,* 1–24.

Cascio, W. F., & Bernardin, H. J. (1981). Implications of performance appraisal litigation for personnel decisions. *Personnel Psychology, 34,* 211–226.

Cascio, W. F., Goldstein, I. L., Outtz, J., & Zedeck, S. (2004). Social and technical issues in staffing decisions. In H. Aguinis (Ed.), *Test score banding in human resource selection: Legal, technical, and societal issues* (pp. 7–28). Westport, CT: Praeger.

Cascio, W. F., Jacobs, R., & Silva, J. (2010). Validity, utility, and adverse impact: Practical implications from 30 years of data. In J. L. Outtz (Ed.), *Adverse impact: Implications for organizational staffing and high-stakes selection* (pp. 271–288). Hoboken, NJ: Lawrence Erlbaum.

Cascio, W. F., & Kurtines, W. L. (1977). A practical method for identifying significant change scores. *Educational and Psychological Measurement, 37,* 889–895.

Cascio, W. F., & Morris, J. R. (1990). A critical re-analysis of Hunter, Schmidt, and Coggin's "Problems and pitfalls in using capital budgeting and financial accounting techniques in assessing the utility of personnel programs." *Journal of Applied Psychology, 75,* 410–417.

Cascio, W. F., Outtz, J., Zedeck, S., & Goldstein, I. L. (1991). Statistical implications of six methods of test score use in personnel selection. *Human Performance, 4*(4), 233–264.

Cascio, W. F., & Phillips, N. (1979). Performance testing: A rose among thorns? *Personnel Psychology, 32,* 751–766.

Cascio, W. F., & Ramos, R. A. (1986). Development and application of a new method for assessing job performance in behavioral/economic terms. *Journal of Applied Psychology, 71,* 20–28.

Cascio, W. F., & Silbey, V. (1979). Utility of the assessment center as a selection device. *Journal of Applied Psychology, 64,* 107–118.

Cascio, W. F., & Valenzi, E. R. (1977). Behaviorally anchored rating scales: Effects of education and job experience of raters and ratees. *Journal of Applied Psychology, 62,* 278–282.

Cascio, W. F., & Valenzi, E. R. (1978). Relations among criteria of police performance. *Journal of Applied Psychology, 63,* 22–28.

Cascio, W. F., Valenzi, E. R., & Silbey, V. (1978). Validation and statistical power: Implications for applied research. *Journal of Applied Psychology, 63,* 589–595.

Cascio, W. F., Valenzi, E. R., & Silbey, V. (1980). More on validation and statistical power. *Journal of Applied Psychology, 65,* 135–138.

Cascio, W. F., & Zedeck, S. (1983). Open a new window in rational research planning. Adjust alpha to maximize statistical power. *Personnel Psychology, 36,* 517–526.

Casellas, G. F., & Hill, I. L. (1998, Fall). Sexual harassment: Prevention and avoiding liability. *Legal Report,* pp. 1–5.

Casteen, J. T., III. (1984). The public stake in proper test use. In C. W. Daves (Ed.), *The uses and misuses of tests* (pp. 1–11). San Francisco, CA: Jossey-Bass.

Castilla, E. J. (2005). Social networks and employee performance in a call center. *American Journal of Sociology, 110,* 1243–1283.

Cattell, R. B. (1957). *Personality and motivation structure and measurement.* New York, NY: Harcourt, Brace, & World.

Cawley, B. D., Keeping, L. M., & Levy, P. E. (1998). Participation in the performance appraisal process and employee reactions: A meta-analytic review of field investigations. *Journal of Applied Psychology, 83,* 615–633.

Cederblom, D. (1982). The performance appraisal interview: A review, implications, and suggestions. *Academy of Management Review, 7,* 219–227.

Cellar, D. F., & Wade, K. (1988). Effect of behavioral modeling on intrinsic motivation and script-related recognition. *Journal of Applied Psychology, 73,* 181–192.

CEO succession: Has grooming talent on the inside gone by the wayside? (2007, November 28). Retrieved March 9, 2008, from http://knowledge.wharton.upenn.edu.

Cesare, S. J., Blankenship, M. H., & Giannetto, P. W. (1994). A dual focus of Sd_y estimations: A test of the linearity assumption and multivariate application. *Human Performance, 7,* 235–253.

Cesare, S. J., Tannenbaum, R. J., & Dalessio, A. (1990). Interviewers' decisions related to applicant handicap type and rater empathy. *Human Performance, 3,* 157–171.

Chan, K., & Drasgow, F. (2001). Toward a theory of individual differences and leadership: Understanding the motivation to lead. *Journal of Applied Psychology, 86,* 481–498.

Chan, D., & Schmitt, N. (1997). Video-based versus paper-and-pencil method of assessment in situational judgment tests: Subgroup differences in test performance and face validity perceptions. *Journal of Applied Psychology, 82,* 143–159.

Chan, D., Schmitt, N., DeShon, R. P., Clause, C. S., & Delbridge, K. (1997). Reactions to cognitive ability tests: The relationships between race, test performance, face validity perceptions, and test-taking motivation. *Journal of Applied Psychology, 82,* 300–310.

Chan, D., Schmitt, N., Jennings, D., Clause, C. S., & Delbridge, K. (1998). Applicant perceptions of test fairness: Integrating justice and self-serving bias perspectives. *International Journal of Selection and Assessment, 6,* 232–239.

Chan, D., Schmitt, N., Sacco, J. M., & DeShon, R. P. (1998). Understanding pretest and posttest reactions to cognitive ability and personality tests. *Journal of Applied Psychology, 83,* 471–485.

Chapman, D. S., & Rowe, P. M. (2002). The influence of video-conference technology and interview structure on the recruiting function of the employment interview: A field experiment. *International Journal of Selection and Assessment, 10,* 185–197.

Chapman, D. S., Uggerslev, K. L., Carroll, S. A., Piasentin, K. A., & Jones, D. A. (2005). Applicant attraction to organizations and job choice: A meta-analytic review of the correlates of recruiting outcomes. *Journal of Applied Psychology, 90,* 928–944.

Chapman, D. S., & Webster, J. (2003). The use of technologies in the recruiting, screening, and selection process for job candidates. *International Journal of Selection and Assessment, 11,* 113–120.

Chapman, D. S., & Webster, J. (2006). Toward an integrated model of applicant reactions and job choice. *International Journal of Human Resource Management, 17,* 1032–1057.

Chapman, D. S., & Zweig, D. I. (2005). Developing a nomological network for interview structure: Antecedents and consequences of the structured selection interview. *Personnel Psychology, 58,* 673–702.

Chen, G., Thomas, B., & Wallace, J. C. (2005). A multilevel examination of the relationships among training outcomes, mediating regulatory processes, and adaptive performance. *Journal of Applied Psychology, 90,* 827–841.

Cheung, G. W. (1999). Multifaceted conceptions of self-other ratings disagreement. *Personnel Psychology, 52,* 1–36.

Cheung, G. W., & Rensvold, R. B. (1999). Testing factorial invariance across groups: A reconceptualization and proposed new method. *Journal of Management, 25,* 1–27.

Cheung, G. W., & Rensvold, R. B. (2002). Evaluating goodness-of-fit indexes for testing measurement invariance. *Structural Equation Modeling, 9,* 233–255.

Chhokar, J. S., & Wallin, J. A. (1984). A field study of the effect of feedback frequency on performance. *Journal of Applied Psychology, 69,* 524–530.

Chuang, D. T., Chen, J. J., & Novick, M. R. (1981). Theory and practice for the use of cut-scores for personnel decisions. *Journal of Educational Statistics, 6,* 129–152.

Church, A. H., Waclawski, J., & Kraut, A. I. (2001). *Designing and using organizational surveys: A seven-step process.* San Francisco, CA: Jossey-Bass.

Cintas Corporation. (2009). 2008 annual report and corporate website. Accessed at www.cintas.com.

Civil Rights Act of 1991, 42 U.S.C. §§ 1981, 2000e *et seq.*

Civil rights statutes extended to Arabs, Jews. (1987, May 19). *Daily Labor Report,* pp. A-2, A-6.

Clark, M. M. (2002, October). Listen up! Language diversity has ups and downs. *HR News,* p. 17.

Clarke, M. (2003, March). *Taking voluntary redundancy: A retrospective study.* Unpublished doctoral dissertation, International Graduate School of Management, University of South Australia, Adelaide.

Cleary, T. A. (1968). Test bias: Prediction of grades of negro and white students in integrated colleges. *Journal of Educational Measurement, 5,* 115–124.

Clevenger, J., Pereira, G. M., Wiechmann, D., Schmitt, N., & Harvey, V. S. (2001). Incremental validity of situational judgment tests. *Journal of Applied Psychology, 86,* 410–417.

Cliffordson, C. (2002). Interviewer agreement in the judgment of empathy in selection interviews. *International Journal of Selection and Assessment, 10,* 198–205.

Cohen, A. C. (1959). Simplified estimators for the normal distribution when samples are singly censored or truncated. *Technometrics, 1,* 217–237.

Cohen, J. (1960). A coefficient of agreement for nominal scales. *Educational and Psychological Measurement, 10,* 37–46.

Cohen, J. (1988). *Statistical power analysis* (2nd ed.). Hillsdale, NJ: Lawrence Erlbaum.

Cohen, J. (2001, May). Net a job. *Working Mother,* pp. 23–27.

Cohen, J., Cohen, P., West, S. G., & Aiken, L. S. (2003). *Applied multiple regression/correlation analysis for the behavioral sciences* (3rd ed.). Mahwah, NJ: Lawrence Erlbaum.

Colbert, A. E., Kristof-Brown, A. L., Bradley, B. H., & Barrick, M. R. (2008). CEO transformational leadership: The role of goal importance congruence in top management teams. *Academy of Management Journal, 51,* 81–96.

Colihan, J., & Burger, G. K. (1995). Constructing job families: An analysis of quantitative techniques used for grouping jobs. *Personnel Psychology, 48,* 563–586.

Collarelli, S. M., & Beehr, T. A. (1993). Selection out: Firings, layoffs, and retirement. In N. Schmitt, & W. C. Borman (Eds.), *Personnel selection in organizations* (pp. 341–384). San Francisco, CA: Jossey-Bass.

Collins, C. J. (2007). The interactive effects of recruitment practices and product awareness in job-seekers' employer knowledge and applicant behaviors. *Journal of Applied Psychology, 92,* 180–190.

Collins, C. J., & Han, J. (2004). Exploring applicant pool quantity and quality: The effects of early recruitment practices, corporate advertising, and firm reputation. *Personnel Psychology, 57,* 685–717.

Collins, M. W., & Morris, S. B. (2008). Testing for adverse impact when sample size is small. *Journal of Applied Psychology, 93,* 463–471.

Collins, C. J., & Stevens, C. K. (2002). The relationship between early recruitment-related activities and the application decisions of new labor-market entrants: A brand-equity approach to recruitment. *Journal of Applied Psychology, 87,* 1121–1133.

Collings, D., & Scullion, H. (2006). Global staffing. In G. K. Stahl, & I. Björkman (Eds.), *Handbook of research in international human resource management* (pp. 141–157). Cheltenham, UK: Edward Elgar.

Colquitt, J. A., Conlon, D. E., Wesson, M. J., Porter, C. O. L. H., & Ng, K. Y. (2001). Justice at the millennium: A meta-analytic review of 25 years of organizational justice research. *Journal of Applied Psychology, 86,* 425–445.

Colquitt, J. A., LePine, J. A., & Noe, R. A. (2000). Toward an integrative theory of training motivation: A meta-analytic path analysis of 20 years of research. *Journal of Applied Psychology*, *85*, 678–707.

Colquitt, J. A., & Simmering, M. S. (1998). Conscientiousness, goal orientation, and motivation to learn during the learning process: A longitudinal study. *Journal of Applied Psychology*, *83*, 654–665.

Colvin, G. (2003, September 1). The U.S. is falling asleep on the job. *Fortune*, p. 54.

Colvin, G. (2006, June 12). Why dream teams fail. *Fortune*, pp. 87–92.

Committee on Professional Standards. (1982). Casebook for providers of psychological services. *American Psychologist*, *37*, 698–701.

Committee to Review the Scientific Evidence on the Polygraph, National Research Council (2003). *The polygraph and lie detection*. Washington, DC: National Academies Press.

Conaty, W. J. (2007, October). *Leadership development at GE*. Presented at Leadership succession in a changing world, Society for Human Resource Management Foundation. Tampa, FL.

Conley, P. R., & Sackett, P. R. (1987). Effects of using high- versus low-performing job incumbents as sources of job-analysis information. *Journal of Applied Psychology*, *72*, 434–437.

Connecticut v. Teal, 457 U.S. 440 (1982).

Converse, P. D., Oswald, F. L., Imus, A., Hedricks, C., Roy, R., & Butera, H. (2008). Comparing personality test formats and warnings: Effects on criterion-related validity and test-taker reactions. *International Journal of Selection and Assessment*, *16*, 155–169.

Conway, J. M. (1998a). Estimation and uses of the proportion method variance for multitrait-multidimensional data. *Organizational Research Methods*, *1*, 209–222.

Conway, J. M. (1998b). Understanding method variance in multitrait-multirater performance appraisal matrices: Examples using general impressions and interpersonal affect as measured method factors. *Human Performance*, *11*, 29–55.

Conway, J. M. (2002). Method variance and method bias in industrial and organizational psychology. In S. G. Rogelberg (Ed.), *Handbook of research methods in industrial and organizational psychology* (pp. 344–365). Malden, MA: Blackwell.

Conway, J. M., & Huffcutt, A. I. (1997). Psychometric properties of multisource performance ratings: A meta-analysis of subordinate, supervisor, peer, and self-ratings. *Human Performance*, *10*, 331–360.

Conway, J. M., Jako, R. A., & Goodman, D. F. (1995). A meta-analysis of interrater and internal consistency reliability of selection interviews. *Journal of Applied Psychology*, *80*, 565–579.

Conway, J. M., Lombardo, K., & Sanders, K. C. (2001). A meta-analysis of incremental validity and nomological networks for subordinate and peer rating. *Human Performance*, *14*, 267–303.

Cooke, R. A., & Rousseau, D. M. (1983). Relationship of life events and personal orientations to symptoms of strain. *Journal of Applied Psychology*, *68*, 446–458.

Cooper, W. H. (1981). Ubiquitous halo. *Psychological Bulletin*, *90*, 218–244.

Cornelius, E. T., DeNisi, A. S., & Blencoe, A. G. (1984). Expert and naive raters using the PAQ: Does it matter? *Personnel Psychology*, *37*, 453–464.

Cornelius, E. T., & Lane, F. B. (1984). The power motive and managerial succession in a professionally oriented service industry organization. *Journal of Applied Psychology*, *69*, 32–39.

Cortina, J. M. (1993). What is coefficient alpha? An examination of theory and applications. *Journal of Applied Psychology*, *78*, 98–104.

Cortina, J. M. (2003). Apples and oranges (and pears, oh my!): The search for moderators in meta-analysis. *Organizational Research Methods*, *6*, 415–439.

Cortina, J. M., Goldstein, N. B., Payne, S. C., Davison, H. K., & Gilliland, S. W. (2000). The incremental validity of interview scores over and above cognitive ability and conscientiousness scores. *Personnel Psychology*, *53*, 325–351.

Costanza, D. P., Fleishman, E. A., & Marshall-Meis, J. M. (1999). Knowledges. In Peterson, N. G., Mumford, M. D., Borman, W. C., Jeanerette, P. R., & Fleishman. E. A. *An Occupational Information System for the 21st Century: The Development of O*Net* (pp. 75–90). Washington, DC: American Psychological Association.

Court preserves affirmative action. (2003, June 24). *The Wall Street Journal*, pp. A1, A8.

Coward, W. M., & Sackett, P. R. (1990). Linearity of ability-performance relationships: A reconfirmation. *Journal of Applied Psychology*, *75*, 297–300.

Coy, P. (2005, June 27). Old. Smart. Productive. *BusinessWeek*, pp. 78–86.

Coy, P., & Ewing, J. (2007, April 9). Where are all the workers? *BusinessWeek*, pp. 28–31.

Craig, S. B., & Kaiser, R. B. (2003). Applying item response theory to multisource performance ratings: What are the consequences of violating the independent observations assumption? *Organizational Research Methods*, *6*, 44–60.

Cravens, D. W., & Woodruff, R. B. (1973). An approach for determining criteria of sales performance. *Journal of Applied Psychology*, *57*, 242–247.

Crawford, D., & Esterl, M. (2007, January 31). At Siemens, witnesses cite pattern of bribery. *The Wall Street Journal*, pp. A1, A10.

Crew, J. C. (1984). Age stereotypes as a function of race. *Academy of Management Journal*, *27*, 431–435.

Cronbach, L. J. (1951). Coefficient alpha and the internal structure of tests. *Psychometrika*, *16*, 297–334.

Cronbach, L. J. (1975). Five decades of public controversy over mental testing. *American Psychologist*, *30*, 1–14.

Cronbach, L. J. (1990). *Essentials of psychological testing* (5th ed.). New York, NY: HarperCollins.

Cronbach, L. J., & Furby, L. (1970). How should we measure "change"—or should we? *Psychological Bulletin*, *74*, 68–80.

Cronbach, L. J., & Gleser, G. C. (1965). *Psychological tests and personnel decisions* (2nd ed.). Urbana: University of Illinois Press.

Cronbach, L. J., Gleser, G. C., Nanda, H., & Rajaratnam, N. (1972). *The dependability of behavioral measurements: Theory of generalizability for scores and profiles*. New York, NY: Wiley.

Cronbach, L. J., & Meehl, P. E. (1955). Construct validity in psychological tests. *Psychological Bulletin*, *52*, 281–302.

Cronbach. L. J., & Snow, R. E. (1977). *Aptitudes and instructional methods*. New York, NY: Irvington.

Cronshaw, S. F. (1997). Lo! The stimulus speaks: The insider's view on Whyte and Latham's "The futility of utility analysis." *Personnel Psychology*, *50*, 611–615.

Cronshaw, S. F., & Alexander, R. A. (1985). One answer to the demand for accountability: Selection utility as an investment decision. *Organizational Behavior and Human Decision Processes*, *35*, 102–118.

Cronshaw, S. F., & Alexander, R. A. (1991). Why capital budgeting techniques are suited for assessing the utility of personnel programs: A reply to Hunter, Schmidt, and Coggin (1988). *Journal of Applied Psychology*, *76*, 454–457.

Cropanzano, R., Slaughter, J., & Bachiochi, P. (2005). Organizational justice and black applicants' reactions to affirmative action. *Journal of Applied Psychology*, *90*, 1168–1184.

Crosby, F. J., Iyer, A., Clayton, S., & Downing, R. A. (2003). Affirmative action: Psychological data and the policy debates. *American Psychologist*, *58*(2), 93–115.

Crosby, F. J., Stockdale, M. S., & Ropp, S. A. (Eds.). (2007). *Sex discrimination in the workplace.* Malden, MA: Blackwell.

Crossley, C. D., & Stanton, J. M. (2005). Negative affect and job search: Further examination of the reverse causation hypothesis. *Journal of Vocational Behavior*, *66*, 549–560.

Cullen, J. B., Victor, B., & Stephens, C. (1989). An ethical weather report: Assessing the organization's ethical climate. *Organizational Dynamics*, *18*, 50–62.

Cummings, L. L. (1973). A field experimental study of the effects of two performance appraisal systems. *Personnel Psychology*, *26*, 489–502.

Cureton, E. E. (1965), Reliability and validity: Basic assumptions and experimental designs. *Educational and Psychological Measurement*, *25*, 327–346.

Cushner, K., & Brislin, R. W. (1996). *Intercultural interactions: A practical guide* (2nd ed.). Thousand Oaks, CA: Sage.

Czaja, R. F., & Blair, J. (2005). *Designing surveys: A guide to decisions and procedures.* Thousand Oaks, CA: Sage.

Czajka, J. M., & DeNisi, A. S. (1988). Effects of emotional disability and clear performance standards on performance ratings. *Academy of Management Journal*, *31*, 393–404.

Da Costa, P. N. (2009, April 23). U.S. mass layoffs rise to highest on record. Retrieved April 26, 2009, from www.reuters.com.

Dahringer, L. D. (2003). Dean's corner: It's the right thing to do. *ENewsline*, *9*(2). Available at www.aacsb.edu/publications/enewsline/Vol-2/Issue-9/dc-dahringer.asp.

Dalton, D. R., & Dalton, C. M. (2008). Meta-analyses: Some very good steps toward a bit longer journey. *Organizational Research Methods*, *11*, 127–147.

Dalessio, A. T., & Silverhart, T. A. (1994). Combining biodata test and interview information: Predicting decisions and performance criteria. *Personnel Psychology*, *47*, 303–315.

Daubert v. Merrell Dow Pharmaceuticals, 509 U.S. 579 (1993).

Davis, B. L., & Mount, M. K. (1984). Effectiveness of performance appraisal training using computer-assisted instruction and behavior modeling. *Personnel Psychology*, *37*, 439–452.

Davis, D. D. (1998). International performance measurement and management. In J. W. Smither (Ed.), *Performance appraisal: State of the art in practice* (pp. 95–131). San Francisco, CA: Jossey-Bass.

Davis, G. M. (2003, August 22). The Family and Medical Leave Act: 10 years later. Retrieved June 15, 2004, from www.shrm.org/hrresources/lrpt_published/CMS_005127.asp.

Davis, N. (2007, October 7). Database is key to integrated talent management. *HR News.* n.d. Retrieved October 17, 2007, from www.shrm.org/hrnews.

Davis, F. D., & Yi, M. Y. (2004). Improving computer skill training: behavior modeling, symbolic mental rehearsal, and the role of knowledge structures. *Journal of Applied Psychology*, *89*, 509–523.

Dawes, R. M., & Corrigan, B. (1974). Linear models in decision making. *Psychological Bulletin*, *81*, 95–106.

Day, A. L., & Carroll, S. A. (2002). Situational and patterned behavior description interviews: A comparison of their validity, correlates, and perceived fairness. *Human Performance*, *16*, 25–47.

Day, D. V., & Sulsky, L. M. (1995). Effects of frame-of-reference training and information configuration on memory organization and rating accuracy. *Journal of Applied Psychology*, *80*, 158–167.

Dayan, K., Kasten, R., & Fox, S. (2002). Entry-level police candidate assessment center: An efficient tool or a hammer to kill a fly? *Personnel Psychology*, *55*, 827–849.

Deadrick, D. L., & Madigan, R. M. (1990). Dynamic criteria revisited: A longitudinal study of performance stability and predictive validity. *Personnel Psychology*, *43*, 717–744.

Dean, M. A., Roth, P. L., & Bobko, P. (2008). Ethnic and gender subgroup differences in assessment center ratings: A meta-analysis. *Journal of Applied Psychology*, *93*, 685–691.

Dean, M. A., & Russell, C. J. (2005). An examination of biodata theory-based constructs in a field context. *International Journal of Selection and Assessment*, *13*, 139–149.

Deci, E. L. (1972). Work, who does not like it and why. *Psychology Today*, *6*, 57–58, 92.

Decker, P. J. (1983). The effects of rehearsal group size and video feedback in behavior modeling training. *Personnel Psychology*, *36*, 763–773.

Decker, P. J., & Nathan, B. R. (1985). *Behavior modeling training: Principles and applications.* New York, NY: Praeger.

De Corte, W. (1999). A note on the success ratio and the utility of fixed hiring rate personnel selection decisions. *Journal of Applied Psychology*, *84*, 952–958.

DeGroot, T., & Motowidlo, S. J. (1999). Why visual and vocal interview cues can affect interviewers' judgments and predict job performance. *Journal of Applied Psychology*, *84*, 986–993.

De Corte W., Lievens F., & Sackett P. R. (2007). Combining predictors to achieve optimal trade-offs between selection quality and adverse impact. *Journal of Applied Psychology*, *92*, 1380–1393.

De Corte, W., Lievens, F., & Sackett, P. R. (2008). Validity and adverse impact potential of predictor composite formation. *International Journal of Selection and Assessment*, *16*, 183–194.

Deller, J. (1997). Expatriate selection: Possibilities and limitations of using personality scales. In D. M. Saunders (Series Ed.) & Z. Aycan (Vol. Ed.), *Expatriate management: Theory and research* (pp. 93–116). Stamford, CT: JAI Press.

Deming, W. E. (1986). *Out of the crisis*. Cambridge, MA: Center for Advanced Engineering Study, Massachusetts Institute of Technology.

De Meuse, K. P., Marks, M. L., & Dai, G. (in press). Organizational downsizing, mergers and acquisitions, and strategic alliances: Using theory and research to enhance practice. In S. Zedeck (Ed.), *Handbook of industrial and organizational psychology*. Washington, DC: American Psychological Association.

DeNisi, A. S., Cornelius, E. T., III, & Blencoe, A. G. (1987). Further investigation of common knowledge effects on job analysis ratings. *Journal of Applied Psychology, 72*, 262–268.

DeNisi, A. S., & Kluger, A. N. (2000). Feedback effectiveness: Can 360-degree appraisals be improved? *Academy of Management Executive, 14*, 129–139.

DeNisi, A. S., Randolph, W. A., & Blencoe, A. G. (1983). Potential problems with peer ratings. *Academy of Management Journal, 26*, 457–464.

DeNisi, A. S., Robbins, T., & Cafferty, T. P. (1989). Organization of information used for performance appraisals: Role of diary-keeping. *Journal of Applied Psychology, 74*, 124–129.

DeRouin, R. E., Fritzsche, B. A., & Salas, E. (2004). Optimizing e-learning: Research-based guidelines for learner-controlled training. *Human Resource Management Review, 43*, 147–62.

DeShon, R. P. (2003). A generalizability theory perspective on measurement error corrections in validity generalization. In K. R. Murphy (Ed.), *Validity generalization: A critical review* (pp. 365–402). Mahwah, NJ: Lawrence Erlbaum.

Dess, G. D., Lumpkin, G. T., & Eisner, A. B. (2007). *Strategic management* (3rd ed.). Burr Ridge, IL: McGraw-Hill.

Developing business leaders for 2010. (2003). New York, NY: The Conference Board.

Diener, E., & Crandall, R. (1979). *Ethics in social and behavioral research.* Chicago, IL: University of Chicago Press.

Dierdorff, E. C., & Wilson, M. A. (2003). A meta-analysis of job analysis reliability. *Journal of Applied Psychology, 88*, 635–646.

Dill, W. R. (1972). What management games do best. In E. L. Deci, B. V. H. Gilmer, & H. W. Karn (Eds.), *Readings in industrial and organizational psychology* (pp. 442–451). New York, NY: McGraw-Hill.

Dineen, B. R., & Noe, R. A. (2009). Effects of customization on application decisions and applicant pool characteristics in a Web-based recruitment context. *Journal of Applied Psychology, 94*, 224–234.

Dineen, B. R., Noe, R. A., Shaw, J. D., Duffy, M. K. & Wiethoff, C. (2007). Level and dispersion of satisfaction in teams: Using foci and social context to explain the satisfaction-absenteeism relationship. *Academy of Management Journal, 50*, 623–643.

Dineen, D., & Soltis, R. (in press). Recruitment: Updating the literature. In S. Zedeck (Ed.), *Handbook of industrial and organizational psychology*. Washington, DC: American Psychological Association.

Dipboye, R. L. (1982). Self-fulfilling prophecies in the selection-recruitment interview. *Academy of Management Review, 7*, 579–586.

Dipboye, R. L. (1992). *Selection interviews: Process perspectives.* Cincinnati, OH: South-Western.

Dipboye, R. L., Fontanelle, G. A., & Garner, K. (1984). Effects of previewing the application on interview process and outcomes. *Journal of Applied Psychology, 69*, 118–128.

Dipboye, R. L., & Jackson, S. J. (1999). Interviewer experience and expertise effects. In R. W. Eder, & M. M. Harris (Eds.), *The employment interview handbook* (pp. 259–278). Thousand Oaks, CA: Sage.

Dipboye, R. L., Stramler, C. S., & Fontanelle, G. A. (1984). The effects of the application on recall of information from the interview. *Academy of Management Journal, 27*, 561–575.

Distefano, M. K., Pryer, M., & Craig, S. H. (1980). Job-relatedness of a posttraining job knowledge criterion used to assess validity and test fairness. *Personnel Psychology, 33*, 785–793.

Dobbins, G. H., Cardy, R. L., & Truxillo, D. M. (1988). The effects of purpose of appraisal and individual differences in stereotypes of women on sex differences in performance ratings: A laboratory and field study. *Journal of Applied Psychology, 73*, 551–558.

Donaldson, T. (2003). Editor's comments: Taking ethics seriously—A mission now more possible. *Academy of Management Review, 28*, 363–366.

Donovan, J. J., Dwight, S. A., & Hurtz, G. M. (2002). An assessment of the prevalence, severity, and verifiability of entry-level applicant faking using the randomized response technique. *Human Performance, 16*, 81–106.

Detert, J. R., Treviño, L. K., Burris, E. R., & Andiappan, M. (2007). Managerial modes of influence and counterproductivity in organizations: A longitudinal business-unit-level investigation. *Journal of Applied Psychology, 92*, 993–1005.

Dougherty, C. (2008, July 26). Ex-manager at Siemens convicted in bribery scandal. *International Herald Tribune.* Retrieved August 21, 2008, from www.iht.com.

Dougherty, T. W., Turban, D. B., & Callender, J. C. (1994). Confirming first impressions in the employment interview: A field study of interviewer behavior. *Journal of Applied Psychology, 79*, 659–665.

Douthitt, S. S., Eby, L. T., & Simon, S. A. (1999). Diversity of life experiences: The development and validation of a biographical measure of receptiveness to dissimilar others. *International Journal of Selection and Assessment, 7*, 112–125.

Dowling, P. J., Festing, M., & Engle, A. D., Sr. (2009). *International human resource management* (5th ed.). Mason, OH: Thomson-South-Western.

Drasgow, F. (1987). Study of the measurement bias of two standardized psychological tests. *Journal of Applied Psychology, 72*, 19–29.

Drasgow, F., & Kang, T. (1984). Statistical power of differential validity and differential prediction analyses for detecting measurement nonequivalence. *Journal of Applied Psychology, 69*, 498–508.

Driskell, J. E., Willis, R. P., & Copper, C. (1992). Effect of over-learning on retention. *Journal of Applied Psychology, 77*, 615–622.

DuBois, C. L., Sackett, P. R., Zedeck, S., & Fogli, L. (1993). Further exploration of typical and maximum performance criteria: Definitional issues, prediction, and white-black differences. *Journal of Applied Psychology, 78*, 205–211.

Dubois, D. A. (2002). Leveraging hidden expertise: Why, when, and how to use cognitive task analysis. In K. Kraiger (Ed.), *Creating, implementing, and managing effective training and development* (pp. 80–114). San Francisco, CA: Jossey-Bass.

Dudek, E. E. (1963). Personnel selection. In P. R. Farnsworth, O. McNemar, & Q. McNemar (Eds.), *Annual Review of Psychology, 14*, 261–284.

Dudley, N. M., Orvis, K. A., Lebiecki, J. E., & Cortina, J. M. (2006). A meta-analytic investigation of conscientiousness in the prediction of job performance: Examining the intercorrelations and the incremental validity of narrow traits. *Journal of Applied Psychology, 91*, 40–57.

Dunford, B., Boudreau, J., & Boswell, W. (2005). Out-of-the-money: The impact of underwater stock options on executive job search. *Personnel Psychology, 58*, 67–101.

Dugan, K. W. (1989). Ability and effort attributions: Do they affect how managers communicate performance feedback information? *Academy of Management Journal, 32*, 87–114.

Dunham, K. J. (2002, October 15). The jungle: Focus on recruitment, pay, and getting ahead. *The Wall Street Journal*, p. B8.

Dunlap, W. P., Cortina, J. M., Vaslow, J. B., & Burke, M. J. (1996). Meta-analysis of experiments with matched groups or repeated measures designs. *Psychological Methods, 1*, 170–177.

Dunnette, M. D. (1962). Personnel management. In P. R. Farnsworth, O. McNemar, & Q. McNemar (Eds.), *Annual Review of Psychology, 13*, 285–314.

Dunnette, M. D. (1963a). A modified model for test validation and selection research. *Journal of Applied Psychology, 47*, 317–332.

Dunnette, M. D. (1963b). A note on the criterion. *Journal of Applied Psychology, 47*, 251–253.

Dunnette, M. D. (1999). Introduction. In N. G. Peterson, M. D. Mumford, W. C. Borman, & E. A. Fleishman (Eds.), *An occupational information system for the 21st century: The development of O*Net* (pp. 3–7). Washington, DC: American Psychological Association.

Dunnette, M. D., & Borman, W. S. (1979). Personnel selection and classification systems. *Annual Review of Psychology, 30*, 477–525.

Dunnette, M. D., & Kirchner, W. K. (1965). *Psychology applied to industry.* New York, NY: Meredith.

Dvir, T., Eden, D., & Banjo, M. L. (1995). Self-fulfilling prophecy and gender: Can women be Pygmalion and Galatea? *Journal of Applied Psychology, 80*, 253–270.

Earley, P. C. (1985). Influence of information, choice, and task complexity upon goal acceptance, performance, and personal goals. *Journal of Applied Psychology, 70*, 481–491.

Earley, P. C., Connolly, T., & Ekegren, G. (1989). Goals, strategy development, and task performance: Some limits on the efficacy of goal setting. *Journal of Applied Psychology, 74*, 24–33.

Eaton, N. K., Wing, H., & Mitchell, K. J. (1985). Alternate methods of estimating the dollar value of performance. *Personnel Psychology, 38*, 27–40.

Ebel, R. L. (1977). Comments on some problems of employment testing. *Personnel Psychology, 30*, 55–68.

Eckhardt, G. (2002). Book review of culture's consequences: Comparing values, behaviors, institutions, and organizations across nations (2nd ed.). *Australian Journal of Management, 27*, 89–94.

Eddy, E. R., Stone, D. L., & Stone-Romero, E. F. (1999). The effects of information management policies on reactions to human resource information systems: An integration of privacy and procedural justice perspectives. *Personnel Psychology, 52*, 335–358.

Eden, D. (1985). Team development: A true field experiment at three levels of rigor. *Journal of Applied Psychology, 70*, 94–100.

Eden, D. (1988). Pygmalion, goal setting, and expectancy: Compatible ways to boost productivity. *Academy of Management Review, 13*, 639–652.

Eden, D., & Aviram, A. (1993). Self-efficacy training to speed reemployment: Helping people to help themselves. *Journal of Applied Psychology, 78*, 352–360.

Eden, D., & Shani, A. B. (1982). Pygmalion goes to boot camp: Expectancy, leadership, and trainee performance. *Journal of Applied Psychology, 67*, 194–199.

Edwards, J. E., Frederick, J. T., & Burke, M. J. (1988). Efficacy of modified CREPID SD_ys on the basis of archival organizational data. *Journal of Applied Psychology, 73*, 529–535.

Edwards, J. R. (2002). Alternatives to difference scores: Polynomial regression and response surface methodology. In F. Drasgow, & N. Schmitt (Eds.), *Measuring and analyzing behavior in organizations* (pp. 350–400). San Francisco, CA: Jossey-Bass.

Edwards, J. R., & Van Harrison, R. (1993). Job demands and worker health: Three-dimensional reexamination of the relationship between person-environment fit and strain. *Journal of Applied Psychology, 78*, 628–648.

Einhorn, H. J. (1972). Expert measurement and mechanical combination. *Organizational Behavior and Human Performance, 7*, 86–106.

Einhorn, H. J., & Hogarth, R. M. (1975). Unit weighting schemes for decision making. *Organizational Behavior and Human Performance, 13*, 171–192.

Elkins, T. J., & Phillips, J. S. (2000). Job context, selection decision outcome, and the perceived fairness of selection tests: Biodata as an illustrative case. *Journal of Applied Psychology, 85*, 479–484.

Ellingson, J. E., Sackett, P. R., & Hough, L. M. (1999). Social desirability corrections in personality measurement: Issues of applicant comparison and construct validity. *Journal of Applied Psychology, 84*, 155–166.

Elliott, D., & Stern, J. E. (1997). *Research ethics: A reader.* Hanover, NH: University Press of New England.

Elmer-Dewitt, P. (1993, January 18). Who's reading your screen? *Time*, p. 46.

Engardio, P. (2006, January 30). The future of outsourcing. *Business Week*, pp. 50–58.

Engardio, P. (2007, August 20, 27). Managing the new workforce. *BusinessWeek*, pp. 48–51.

England, G. W. (1971). *Development and use of weighted application blanks* (rev. ed.). Minneapolis: University of Minnesota Industrial Relations Center.

Engle, A. D., Sr., Dowling, P. J., & Festing, M. (2008). State of origin: Research in global performance management, a proposed research domain, and emerging implications. *European Journal of International Management, 2,* 153–169.

Epstein, A. (1985, January 26). Employers responsible in sex-harassment cases. *Denver Post,* p. 3A.

Epstein, S. (1979). The stability of behavior: I. On predicting most of the people much of the time. *Journal of Personality and Social Psychology, 37,* 1097–1126.

Epstein, S. (1980). The stability of behavior: II. Implications for psychological research. *American Psychologist, 35,* 790–806.

Equal Employment Opportunity Commission Annual Report. (2009). Downloaded March 27, 2009, from www.eeoc.gov/abouteeoc/plan/par/2008/managements_discussion.html#highlights.

Equal Employment Opportunity Commission. (n.d.). Retrieved March 26, 2009a, from www.eeoc.gov/stats/epa.html..

Equal Employment Opportunity Commission. (n.d.). Retrieved March 26, 2009b, from www.eeoc.gov/stats/adea.html.

Equal Employment Opportunity Commission. (n.d.). Retrieved March 26, 2009c, from www.eeoc.gov/types/ada.html.

Equal Employment Opportunity Commission. Guidelines on discrimination because of sex, 29 CFR 1604.10. Employment policies relating to pregnancy and childbirth. (revised July 1, 2006).

Erez, M., & Earley, P. C. (1987). Comparative analysis of goal-setting strategies across cultures. *Journal of Applied Psychology, 72,* 658–665.

Erez, M., Earley, P. C., & Hulin, C. L. (1985). The impact of goal acceptance and performance: A two-step model. *Academy of Management Journal, 28,* 50–66.

Erez, M., & Zidon, I. (1984). Effect of goal acceptance on the relationship of goal difficulty to performance. *Journal of Applied Psychology, 69,* 69–78.

Erlam, N. A. (2005). Walking the criminal records tightrope. n.d. Retrieved April 17, 2008, www.shrm.org/ema/sm/articles/2005/octdec05Erlam.asp.

Facteau, J. D., & Craig, S. B. (2001). Are performance appraisal ratings from different rating sources comparable? *Journal of Applied Psychology, 86,* 215–227.

Facteau, J. D., Dobbins, G. H., Russell, J. E. A., Ladd, R. T., & Kudisch, J. D. (1995). The influence of general perceptions of the training environment on pre-training motivation and perceived training transfer. *Journal of Management, 21,* 1–25.

Falcone, P. (1995). Getting employers to open up on a reference check. *HRMagazine, 40*(7), 58–63.

Faley, R. H., & Sundstrom, E. (1985). Content representativeness: An empirical method of evaluation. *Journal of Applied Psychology, 70,* 567–571.

Faragher v. City of Boca Raton, 118 S. Ct. 2275 (1998).

Farh, J. L., & Dobbins, G. H. (1989). Effects of comparative performance information on the accuracy of self-ratings and agreement between self- and supervisor ratings. *Journal of Applied Psychology, 74,* 606–610.

Farh, J. L., Dobbins, G. H., & Cheng, B. S. (1991). Cultural relativity in action: A comparison of self-ratings made by Chinese and U.S. workers. *Personnel Psychology, 44,* 129–147.

Farh, J. L., Werbel, J. D., & Bedeian, A. G. (1988). An empirical investigation of self appraisal-based performance evaluation. *Personnel Psychology, 41,* 141–156.

Farr, J. L. (2003). Introduction to the special issue: Stereotype threat effects in employment settings. *Human Performance, 16,* 179–180.

Farr, J. L., & Jacobs, R. (2006). Trust us: New perspectives on performance appraisal. In W. Bennett, C. E. Lance, & D. J. Woehr (Eds.), *Performance measurement: Current perspectives and future challenges* (pp. 321–337). Mahwah, NJ: Lawrence Erlbaum.

Farmer, S., & Aguinis, H. (2005). Accounting for subordinate perceptions of supervisor power: An identity-dependence model. *Journal of Applied Psychology, 90,* 1069–1083.

Farrell, J. N., & McDaniel, M. A. (2001). The stability of validity coefficients over time: Ackerman's (1988) model and the General Aptitude Test Battery. *Journal of Applied Psychology, 86,* 60–79.

Fay, C. H., & Latham, G. P. (1982). Effects of training and rating scales on rating errors. *Personnel Psychology, 35,* 105–116.

Fay, D., & Frese, M. (2001). The concept of personal initiative: An overview of validity studies. *Human Performance, 14,* 97–124.

Ferguson, J., & Fletcher, C. (1989). An investigation of some cognitive factors involved in person-perception during selection interviews. *Psychological Reports, 64,* 735–745.

Ferguson, L. W. (1960). Ability, interest, and aptitude. *Journal of Applied Psychology, 44,* 126–131.

Ferris, G. R., Yates, V. L., Gilmore, D. C., & Rowland, K. M. (1985). The influence of subordinate age on performance ratings and causal attributions. *Personnel Psychology, 38,* 545–557.

Fiedler, F. E. (1967). *A theory of leadership effectiveness.* New York, NY: McGraw-Hill.

Fiedler, F. E., Mitchell, T., & Triandis, H. C. (1971). The culture assimilator: An approach to cross-cultural training. *Journal of Applied Psychology, 55,* 95–102.

Field, A. P. (2001). Meta-analysis of correlation coefficients: A Monte Carlo comparison of fixed- and random-effects methods. *Psychological Methods, 6,* 161–180.

Findley, H. M., Giles, W. F., & Mossholder, K. W. (2000). Performance appraisal process and system facets: Relationships with contextual performance. *Journal of Applied Psychology, 85,* 634–640.

Fine, M. A., & Kurdek, L. A. (1993). Reflections on determining authorship credit and authorship order on faculty-student collaborations. *American Psychologist, 48,* 1141–1147.

Fine, S. A. (1989). *Functional job analysis scales: A desk aid.* Milwaukee, WI: Sidney A. Fine.

Finkelstein, S., & Hambrick, D. C. (1996). *Strategic leadership: Top executives and their effects on organizations.* New York, NY: West.

Finkelstein, L. M., Frautschy Demuth, R. L., & Sweeney, D. L. (2007). Bias against overweight job applicants: Further explorations of when and why. *Human Resource Management, 46,* 203–222.

Firefighters Local Union No. 1784 v. Stotts, 467 U.S. 661 (1984).

Fisher, A. (2002, November 11). What you call old age, I call a lifetime of experience. *Fortune*, p. 218.

Fisher, S. L., & Ford, J. K. (1998). Differential effects of learner effort and goal orientation on two learner outcomes. *Personnel Psychology, 51*, 397–420.

Flanagan, J. C. (1954a). The critical incident technique. *Psychological Bulletin, 51*, 327–358.

Flanagan, J. C. (1954b). Some considerations in the development of situational tests. *Personnel Psychology, 7*, 461–464.

Flanagan, J. C., & Burns, R. K. (1955). The employee performance record: A new appraisal and development tool. *Harvard Business Review, 33*, 95–102.

Fleishman, E. A. (1973). Twenty years of consideration and structure. In E. A. Fleishman, & J. G. Hunt (Eds.), *Current developments in the study of leadership*. Carbondale: Southern Illinois University Press.

Fleishman, E. A. (1975). Toward a taxonomy of human performance. *American Psychologist, 30*, 1127–1149.

Fleishman, E. A. (1988). Some new frontiers in personnel selection research. *Personnel Psychology, 42*, 679–701.

Fleishman, E. A. (1992). *Fleishman Job Analysis Survey Rating Scale Booklet (F-JAS)*. Potomac, MD: Management Research Institute.

Fleishman, E. A. & Mumford, M. D. (1988). Ability-requirement scales. In S. Gael (Ed.), *The job analysis handbook for business, industry, and government* (pp. 917–935). New York, NY: Wiley.

Fleishman, E. A., & Mumford, M. D. (1991). Evaluating classifications of job behavior: A construct validation of the ability requirement scales. *Personnel Psychology, 44*, 523–575.

Fleishman, E. A., & Peters, D. A. (1962). Interpersonal values, leadership attitudes, and managerial "success." *Personnel Psychology, 15*, 127–143.

Fleishman, E. A., & Quaintance, M. K. (1984). Taxonomies of human performance: The description of human tasks. Potomac, MD: Management Research Institute.

Fleishman, E. A., & Reilly, M. E. (1992a). *Fleishman Job Analysis Survey (F-JAS) Administrator's Guide*. Potomac, MD: Management Research Institute.

Fleishman, E. A., & Reilly, M. E. (1992b). *Handbook of human abilities: Definitions, measurements, and job task characteristics*. Potomac, MD: Management Research Institute.

Fletcher, C. (2001). Performance appraisal and management: The developing research agenda. *Journal of Occupational and Organizational Psychology, 74*, 473–487.

Florin-Thuma, B. C., & Boudreau, J. W. (1987). Performance feedback utility in a small organization: Effects on organizational outcomes and managerial decision processes. *Personnel Psychology, 40*, 693–713.

Foley, J. D., Jr. (1969). Determining training needs of department store sales personnel. *Training and Development Journal, 23*, 24–27.

Foldes, H. J., Duehr, E. E., & Ones, D. S. (2008). Group differences in personality: Meta-analyses comparing five U.S. racial groups. *Personnel Psychology, 61*, 579–616.

Fondas, N. (1992, Summer). A behavioral job description for managers. *Organizational Dynamics*, pp. 47–58.

For dual-career expats, economic woes threaten benefits. (2009, January 30). Retrieved February 9, 2009, from www.shrm.org/hrdisciplines/global.

Ford, J. K., & Noe, R. A. (1987). Self-assessed training needs: The effects of attitudes toward training, managerial level, and function. *Personnel Psychology, 40*, 39–53.

Ford, J. K., Quiñones, M. A., Sego, D. J., & Sorra, J. S. (1992). Factors affecting the opportunity to perform trained tasks on the job. *Personnel Psychology, 45*, 511–527.

Ford, J. K., Smith, E. M., Sego, D. J., & Quiñones, M. A. (1993). Impact of task experience and individual factors on training-emphasis ratings. *Journal of Applied Psychology, 78*, 583–590.

Ford, J. K., & Weissbein, D. A. (1997). Transfer of training: An updated review and analysis. *Performance Improvement Quarterly, 10*(2), 22–41.

Forgas, J. P., & George, J. M. (2001). Affective influences on judgments and behavior in organizations: An information processing perspective. *Organizational Behavior and Human Decision Processes, 86*, 3–34.

Forster, S. (2003, September 15). The best way to recruit new workers and to find a job. *The Wall Street Journal*, p. R8.

Fox, S., & Dinur, Y. (1988). Validity of self assessment: A field evaluation. *Personnel Psychology, 41*, 581–592.

Franke, G. R., Crown, D. F., & Spake, D. F. (1997). Gender differences in ethical perceptions of business practices: A social role theory perspective. *Journal of Applied Psychology, 82*, 920–934.

Frase-Blunt, M. (2004, April). Make a good first impression. *HRMagazine, 49*(4), 80–86.

Frayne, C. A., & Latham, G. P. (1987). The application of social learning theory to employee self-management of attendance. *Journal of Applied Psychology, 72*, 387–392.

Fredericksen, N. (1962). Factors in in-basket performance. *Psychological Monographs, 76*(22, Whole No. 541), entire issue.

Freeberg, N. E. (1976). Criterion measures for youth-work training programs: The development of relevant performance dimensions. *Journal of Applied Psychology, 61*, 537–545.

Freeman, R. E. (1984). *Strategic management: A stakeholder approach*. Boston, MA: Pitman.

Frese, M., Beimel, S., & Schoenborn, S. (2003). Action training for charismatic leadership: Two evaluations of studies of a commercial training module on inspirational communication of a vision. *Personnel Psychology, 56*, 671–697.

Fried, Y., Tiegs, R. B., & Bellamy, A. R. (1992). Personal and interpersonal predictors of supervisors' avoidance of evaluating subordinates. *Journal of Applied Psychology, 77*, 462–468.

Friedman, T. L. (2005). *The world is flat*. New York, NY: Farrar, Strauss, & Giroux.

Friedman, T. L. (2008). *Hot, flat, and crowded*. New York, NY: Farrar, Strauss, & Giroux.

Frieling, E., Kannheiser, W., & Lindberg, R. (1974). Some results with the German form of the Position Analysis Questionnaire (PAQ). *Journal of Applied Psychology, 59*, 741–747.

Frost, B. C., Chia-Huei, E. K., & James, L. R. (2007). Implicit and explicit personality: A test of a channeling hypothesis for aggressive behavior. *Journal of Applied Psychology, 92*, 1299–1319.

Furby, L. (1973). Interpreting regression toward the mean in developmental research. *Development Psychology, 8,* 172–179.

Furnco Construction Corp. v. Waters, 438 U.S. 567 (1978).

Furnham, A. (2008). HR professionals' beliefs about, and knowledge of, assessment techniques and psychometric tests. *International Journal of Selection and Assessment, 16,* 300–305.

Fusilier, M. R., & Hoyer, W. D. (1980). Variables affecting perceptions of invasion of privacy in a personnel selection situation. *Journal of Applied Psychology, 65,* 623–626.

Gael, S. (Ed.). (1988). *The job analysis handbook for business, industry, and government.* New York, NY: Wiley.

Gagné, R. M. (1962). Military training and principles of learning. *American Psychologist, 18,* 83–91.

Gagné, R. M. (Ed.). (1967). *Learning and individual differences.* Columbus, OH: Merrill.

Gagné, R. M. (1977). *Conditions of learning* (3rd ed.). New York, NY: Holt, Rinehart, & Winston.

Gagné, R. M., & Briggs, L. J. (1979). *Principles of instructional design* (2nd ed.). New York, NY: Holt, Rinehart, & Winston.

Gagné, R. M., & Rohwer, W. D., Jr. (1969). Instructional psychology. *Annual Review of Psychology, 20,* 381–418.

Ganster, D. C., Williams, S., & Poppler, P. (1991). Does training in problem solving improve the quality of group decisions? *Journal of Applied Psychology, 76,* 479–483.

Ganzach, Y. (1995). Negativity (and positivity) in performance evaluation: Three field studies. *Journal of Applied Psychology, 80,* 491–499.

Ganzach, Y., Kluger, A. N., & Klayman, N. (2000). Making decisions from an interview: Expert measurement and mechanical combination. *Personnel Psychology, 53,* 1–20.

García, M. F., Posthuma, R. A., & Colella, A. (2008). Fit perceptions in the employment interview: The role of similarity, liking, and expectations. *Journal of Occupational and Organizational Psychology, 81,* 173–189.

Garr, D. (2000). *IBM redux: Lou Gerstner and the business turnaround of the decade.* New York, NY: Wiley.

Gaugler, B. B., Rosenthal, D. B., Thornton, G. C., III, & Bentson, C. (1987). Meta-analysis of assessment center validity. *Journal of Applied Psychology, 72,* 493–511.

Gaudine, A. P., & Saks, A. M. (2004). A longitudinal quasi-experiment on the effects of post-training transfer interventions. *Human Resource Development Quarterly, 15,* 57–76.

Gaugler, B. B., & Rudolph, A. S. (1992). The influence of assessee performance variation on assessors' judgments. *Personnel Psychology, 45,* 77–98.

Gaugler, B. B., & Thornton, G. C., III. (1989). Number of assessment center dimensions as a determinant of assessor accuracy. *Journal of Applied Psychology, 74,* 611–618.

Gazur, M. (1994). *Global business challenges: Am I ready?* Boulder, CO: International Concepts, Ltd.

Geisinger, K. F., Spies, R. A., Carlson, J. F., & Plake, B. S. (Eds.) (2007). *The seventeenth mental measurements yearbook.* Lincoln, NE: University of Nebraska Press.

Gelfand, M. J., Erez, M., & Aycan, Z. (2007). Cross-cultural organizational behavior. *Annual Review of Psychology, 58,* 479–514.

Gelfand, M. J., Leslie, L. M., & Fehr, R. (2008). To prosper organizational psychology should . . . Adopt a global perspective. *Journal of Organizational Behavior, 29,* 493–517.

Gentry, W. A., Weber, T. J., & Sadri, G. (2008). Examining career-related mentoring and managerial performance across cultures: A multi-level analysis. *Journal of Vocational Behavior, 72,* 241–253.

George, B. (2007, November 29). An embarrassment of succession fiascoes. Retrieved April 13, 2009, from www.business week.com.

Gerhart, B., & Fang, M. (2005). National culture and human resource management: Assumptions and evidence. *International Journal of Human Resource Management, 16*(6), pp. 971–986.

Geutal, H., & Stone, D. L. (Eds.). (2005). *The brave new world of eHR: Human resources management in the digital age.* San Francisco, CA: Jossey-Bass.

Ghiselli, E. E. (1956). Dimensional problems of criteria. *Journal of Applied Psychology, 40,* 1–4.

Ghiselli, E. E. (1963). Managerial talent. *American Psychologist, 8,* 631–642.

Ghiselli, E. E. (1966). *The validity of occupational aptitude tests.* New York, NY: Wiley.

Ghiselli, E. E. (1973). The validity of aptitude tests in personnel selection. *Personnel Psychology, 26,* 461–477.

Ghiselli, E. E., & Brown, C. W. (1955). *Personnel and industrial psychology* (2nd ed.). New York, NY: McGraw-Hill.

Ghiselli, E. E., Campbell, J. P., & Zedeck, S. (1981). *Measurement theory for the behavioral sciences.* San Francisco, CA: Freeman.

Ghiselli, E. E., & Haire, M. (1960). The validation of selection tests in the light of the dynamic nature of criteria. *Personnel Psychology, 13,* 225–231.

Ghorpade, J. (2000). Managing five paradoxes of 360-degree feedback. *Academy of Management Executive, 14,* 140–150.

Ghorpade, J., & Chen, M. M. (1995). Creating quality-driven performance appraisal systems. *Academy of Management Executive, 9*(1), 32–39.

Gil, E. F., & Bob, S. (1999). Culturally competent research: An ethical perspective. *Clinical Psychology Review, 19,* 45–55.

Gilliland, S. W. (1993). The perceived fairness of selection systems: An organizational justice perspective. *Academy of Management Review, 18,* 694–734.

Gist, M. E., Schwoerer, C., & Rosen, B. (1989). Effects of alternative training methods on self-efficacy and performance in computer software training. *Journal of Applied Psychology, 74,* 884–891.

Gist, M. E., Stevens, C. K., & Bavetta, A. G. (1991). Effects of self-efficacy and post-training intervention on the acquisition and maintenance of complex interpersonal skills. *Personnel Psychology, 44,* 837–861.

Gleason, W. J. (1957). Predicting army leadership ability by modified leaderless group discussion. *Journal of Applied Psychology, 41,* 231–235.

Glennon, J. R., Albright, L. E., & Owens, W. A. (1966). *A catalog of life history items.* Greensboro, NC: Richardson Foundation.

GMAC Global Relocation Services. (2008). *Global relocation trends: 2008 survey report.* Retrieved August 21, 2008, from www.gmacglobalrelocation.com.

Goffin, R. D., & Woychesin, D. E. (2006). An empirical method of determining employee competencies/KSAOs from task-based job analysis. *Military Psychology*, *18*(2), pp. 121–130.

Goldman, B. M. (2001). Toward an understanding of employment discrimination claiming: An integration of organizational justice and social information processing theories. *Personnel Psychology*, *54*, 361–386.

Goldstein, I. L. (1978). The pursuit of validity in the evaluation of training programs. *Human Factors*, *20*, 131–144.

Goldstein, I. L., & Associates. (1989). *Training and development in organizations.* San Francisco, CA: Jossey-Bass.

Goldstein, I. L., & Ford, J. K. (2002). *Training in organizations: Needs assessment, development, and evaluation* (4th ed.). Belmont, CA: Wadsworth.

Goldstein, A. P., & Sorcher, M. (1974). *Changing supervisor behavior.* New York, NY: Pergamon.

Goldstein, H. W., Yusko, K. P., Braverman, E. P., Smith, D. B., & Chung, B. (1998). The role of cognitive ability in the subgroup differences and incremental validity of assessment center exercises. *Personnel Psychology*, *51*, 357–374.

Goldstein, H. W., Zedeck, S., & Goldstein, I. L. (2002). G: Is this your final answer? *Human Performance*, *15*, 123–142.

Gong, Y. (2003a). Toward a dynamic process model of staffing composition and subsidiary outcomes in multinational enterprises. *Journal of Management*, *29*, 259–280.

Gong, Y. (2003b). Subsidiary staffing in multinational enterprises: Agency, resources, and performance. *Academy of Management Journal*, *46*, 728–739.

Goodman, P. S., & Healy, J. (2009, March 7). Job losses hint at vast remaking of the economy. *The New York Times*. Retrieved March 7, 2009, from www.nytimes.com.

Goodman, J. S., & Wood, R. E. (2004). Feedback specificity, learning opportunities, and learning. *Journal of Applied Psychology*, *89*, 809–821.

Gordon, M. E., & Cohen, S. L. (1973). Training behavior as a predictor of trainability. *Personnel Psychology*, *26*, 261–272.

Gordon, M. E., & Johnson, W. A. (1982). Seniority: A review of its legal and scientific standing. *Personnel Psychology*, *35*, 255–280.

Gordon, H. W., & Leighty, R. (1988). Importance of specialized cognitive function in the selection of military pilots. *Journal of Applied Psychology*, *73*, 38–45.

Gottfredson, L. S. (1988). Reconsidering fairness: A matter of social and ethical priorities. *Journal of Vocational Behavior*, *33*, 293–319.

Grant, D. L., Katkovsky, W., & Bray, D. W. (1967). Contributions of projective techniques to assessment of management potential. *Journal of Applied Psychology*, *51*, 226–231.

Gratz v. Bollinger. (2003, June 23). Available at http://laws.findlaw.com/us/000/02–516.html.

Green, D. R. (1975, March). *What does it mean to say a test is biased?* Paper presented at the meeting of the American Educational Research Association, Washington, DC.

Greenberg, J. (2002). Who stole the money, and when? Individual and situational determinants of employee theft. *Organizational Behavior and Human Decision Processes*, *89*, 985–1003.

Greenfield, W. M. (2004). In the name of corporate social responsibility. *Business Horizons*, *47*(1), 19–28.

Greenhouse, L. (1984, June 13). Seniority is held to outweigh race as a layoff guide. *The New York Times*, pp. 1A, 12B.

Greenwood, M. (2007). Stakeholder engagement: Beyond the myth of corporate responsibility. *Journal of Business Ethics*, *74*, 315–327.

Greer, O. L., & Cascio, W. F. (1987). Is cost accounting the answer? Comparison of two behaviorally based methods for estimating the standard deviation of performance in dollars with a cost-accounting-based approach. *Journal of Applied Psychology*, *72*, 588–595.

Gregersen, H. B. (1992). Commitments to a parent company and a local work unit during repatriation. *Personnel Psychology*, *45*, 29–54.

Gregersen, H. B., & Black, J. S. (1996). Multiple commitments upon repatriation: The Japanese experience. *Journal of Management*, *22*, 209–229.

Gregory, D. L. (1998). Reducing the risk of negligence in hiring. *Employee Relations Law Journal*, *14*, 31–40.

Greguras, G. J., & Robie, C. (1998). A new look at within-source interrater reliability of 360-degree feedback ratings. *Journal of Applied Psychology*, *83*, 960–968.

Greguras, G. J., Robie, C., Schleicher, D. J., & Goff, M. (2003). A field study of the effects of rating purpose on the quality of multisource ratings. *Personnel Psychology*, *56*, 1–21.

Greller, M. (1980). Evaluation of feedback sources as a function of role and organizational level. *Journal of Applied Psychology*, *65*, 24–27.

Grey, R. J., & Kipnis, D. (1976). Untangling the performance appraisal dilemma: The influence of perceived organizational context on evaluation processes. *Journal of Applied Psychology*, *61*, 329–335.

Greguras, G. J., Robie, C., Born, M. P., & Koenigs, R. J. (2007). A social relations analysis of team performance ratings. *International Journal of Selection and Assessment*, *15*, 434–448.

Griggs v. Duke Power Company, 401 U.S. 424 (1971).

Griendling, H. (2008, May 2). *World-class recruiting.* n.d. Retrieved May 21, 2008, from www.ere.net/articles/db/514928EADEF748CE98297A69348EEF16.asp.

Griffore, R. J. (2007). Speaking of fairness in testing. *American Psychologist*, *62*, 1081–1082.

Grimsley, G., & Jarrett, H. F. (1973). The relation of managerial achievement to test measures obtained in the employment situation: Methodology and results. *Personnel Psychology*, *26*, 31–48.

Grimsley, G., & Jarrett, H. F. (1975). The relation of past managerial achievement to test measures obtained in the employment situation: Methodology and results—II. *Personnel Psychology*, *28*, 215–231.

Grossman, R. J. (2003, August). Are you ignoring older workers? *HRMagazine*, pp. 40–46.

Grossman, R. J. (2006, January). Developing talent. *HRMagazine*, pp. 40–46.

Grove, A. (2003, August 25). The future of tech: The big picture. *Business Week*, pp. 86–88.

Grutter v. Bollinger. (2003). Available at http://laws.findlaw.com/us/000/02-241.html.

Guardians Assn. of N.Y. City Police Dept. v. Civil Service Comm. of City of N. Y. (1980, November). *The Industrial-Organizational Psychologist*, pp. 44–49.

Guilford, J. P. (1954). *Psychometric methods* (2nd ed.). New York, NY: McGraw-Hill.

Guilford, J. P., & Fruchter, B. (1978). *Fundamental statistics in psychology and education* (6th ed.). New York, NY: McGraw-Hill.

Guion, R. M. (1961). Criterion measurement and personnel judgments. *Personnel Psychology, 14*, 141–149.

Guion, R. M. (1965). *Personnel testing.* New York, NY: McGraw-Hill.

Guion, R. M. (1966). Employment tests and discriminatory hiring. *Industrial Relations, 5*, 20–37.

Guion, R. M. (1976). Recruiting, selection, and job placement. In M. D. Dunnette (Ed.), *Handbook of industrial and organizational psychology* (pp. 777–828). Chicago, IL: Rand McNally.

Guion, R. M. (1987). Changing views for personnel selection research. *Personnel Psychology, 40*, 199–213.

Guion, R. M. (1998). *Assessment, measurement, and prediction for personnel decisions.* Mahwah, NJ: Lawrence Erlbaum.

Guion, R. M. (2002). Validity and reliability. In S. G. Rogelberg (Ed.), *Handbook of research methods in industrial and organizational psychology* (pp. 57–76). Malden, MA: Blackwell.

Guion, R. M. (2004). Banding: Background and general management purpose. In H. Aguinis (Ed.), *Test score banding in human resource selection: Legal, technical, and societal issues* (pp. 49–70). Westport, CT: Praeger.

Guion, R. M., & Cranny, C. J. (1982). A note on concurrent and predictive validity designs: A critical reanalysis. *Journal of Applied Psychology, 67*, 239–244.

Guion, R. M., & Gibson, W. M. (1988). Personnel selection and placement. *Annual Review of Psychology, 39*, 349–374.

Gulliksen, H. (1950). *Theory of mental tests.* New York, NY: Wiley.

Gunz, H., & Peiperl, M. (Eds.). (2007). *Handbook of career studies.* Thousand Oaks, CA: Sage.

Guthrie, J. P., & Olian, J. D. (1991). Does context affect staffing decisions? The case of general managers. *Personnel Psychology, 44*, 263–292.

Guzzo, R. A., Jette, R. D., & Katzell, R. A. (1985). The effects of psychologically-based intervention programs on worker productivity: A meta-analysis. *Personnel Psychology, 38*, 275–291.

Haaland, S., & Christiansen, N. D. (2002). Implications of trait-activation theory for evaluating the construct validity of assessment center ratings. *Personnel Psychology, 55*, 137–163.

Hackman, J. R. (1998). Why teams don't work. In R. S. Tindale, & L. Heath (Eds.), *Theory and research on small groups* (pp. 245–267). New York, NY: Plenum Press

Haccoun, R. R., & Hamtieux, T. (1994). Optimizing knowledge tests for inferring learning acquisition levels in single-group training-evaluation designs: The internal referencing strategy. *Personnel Psychology, 47*, 593–604.

Haigh, M., & Jones, M. T. (2007). A critical review of relations between corporate responsibility research and practice. *Electronic Journal of Business Ethics and Organization Studies 12*(1), 16–28.

Haire, M. (1964). *Psychology of management* (2nd ed.). New York, NY: McGraw-Hill.

Hakel, M. D. (1989). Merit-based selection: Measuring the person for the job. In W. F. Cascio (Ed.), *Human resource planning, employment, and placement* (pp. 2-135–2-158). Washington, DC: Bureau of National Affairs.

Hakel, M. D., Ohnesorge, J. P., & Dunnette, M. D. (1970). Interviewer evaluations of job applicants' resumes as a function of the qualifications of the immediately preceding applicants: An examination of contrast effects. *Journal of Applied Psychology, 54*, 27–30.

Hakstian, A. R., Farrell, S., & Tweed, R. G. (2002). The assessment of counterproductive tendencies by means of the California Psychological Inventory. *International Journal of Selection and Assessment, 10*, 58–86.

Hall, S. M., & Brannick, M. (2002). Comparison of two random effects methods of meta-analysis. *Journal of Applied Psychology, 87*, 377–389.

Hall, D. T., & Mirvis, P. H. (1995). Careers as life-long learning. In A. Howard (Ed.), *The changing nature of work* (pp. 323–361). San Francisco, CA: Jossey-Bass.

Hambleton, R. K. (1994). Guidelines for adapting educational and psychological tests: A progress report. *European Journal of Psychological Assessment, 10*, 229–244.

Hambleton, R. K., & Kanjee, A. (1995). Increasing the validity of cross-cultural assessments: Use of improved methods for test adaptations. *European Journal of Psychological Assessment, 11*, 147–157.

Hamel, G. (2000). *Leading the revolution.* Boston, MA: Harvard Business School Press.

Hanges, P. J., Braverman, E. P., & Rentch, J. R. (1991). Changes in raters' perceptions of subordinates: A catastrophe model. *Journal of Applied Psychology, 76*, 878–888.

Hanisch, K. A., & Hulin, C. L. (1994). Two-stage sequential selection procedures using ability and training performance: Incremental validity of behavioral consistency measures. *Personnel Psychology, 47*, 767–785.

Hanser, L. M., Arabian, J. M., & Wise, L. (1985, October). *Multidimensional performance measurement.* Paper presented at the annual meeting of the Military Testing Association, San Diego, CA.

Harpaz, I. (1996). International management survey research. In B. J. Punnett, & O. Shenkar (Eds.), *Handbook for international management research* (pp. 37–62). Cambridge, MA: Blackwell.

Harrell, A. M., & Stahl, M. J. (1981). A behavioral decision theory approach for measuring McClelland's trichotomy of needs. *Journal of Applied Psychology, 66*, 242–247.

Harris, B. (1988). Key words: A history of debriefing in social psychology. In J. Morawski (Ed.), *The rise of experimentation in American psychology* (pp. 188–212). New York, NY: Oxford University Press.

Harris, H. (2006). Issues facing women on international assignments: A review of the research. In G. K. Stahl, & I. Björkman (Eds.), *Handbook of research in international human resource management* (pp. 265–282). Cheltenham, UK: Edward Elgar.

Harris, M. M., Becker, A. S., & Smith, D. E. (1993). Does the assessment center scoring method affect the cross-situational consistency of ratings? *Journal of Applied Psychology, 78*, 675–678.

Harris, M. M., & Schaubroeck, J. (1988). A meta-analysis of self-supervisor, self-peer, and peer-supervisor ratings. *Personnel Psychology, 41*, 43–62.

Harrison, J. K. (1992). Individual and combined effects of behavior modeling and the cultural assimilator in cross-cultural management training. *Journal of Applied Psychology, 77*, 952–962.

Härtel, C. E. J. (1993). Rating format research revisited: Format effectiveness and acceptability depend on rater characteristics. *Journal of Applied Psychology, 78*, 212–217.

Hartigan, J. A., & Wigdor, A. K. (Eds.). (1989). *Fairness in employment testing: Validity generalization, minority issues, and the General Aptitude Test Battery.* Washington, DC: National Academy Press.

Hartman, E. A., Mumford, M. D., & Mueller, S. (1992). Validity of job classifications: An examination of alternative indicators. *Human Performance, 5*, 191–211.

Harvey, R. J. (1986). Quantitative approaches to job classification: A review and critique. *Personnel Psychology, 39*, 267–289.

Harvey, R. J. (1991). Job analysis. In M. D. Dunnette, & L. M. Hough (Eds.), *Handbook of industrial and organizational psychology* (2nd ed., Vol. 2, pp. 71–163). Palo Alto, CA: Consulting Psychologists Press.

Harvey, R. J., Friedman, L., Hakel, M. D., & Cornelius, E. T., III. (1988). Dimensionality of the Job Element Inventory, a simplified worker-oriented job analysis questionnaire. *Journal of Applied Psychology, 73*, 639–646.

Harvey, R. J., & Lozada-Larsen, S. R. (1988). Influence of amount of job descriptive information on job analysis rating accuracy. *Journal of Applied Psychology, 73*, 457–461.

Hattrup, K., Rock, J., & Scalia, C. (1997). The effects of varying conceptualizations of job performance on adverse impact, minority hiring, and predicted performance. *Journal of Applied Psychology, 82*, 656–664.

Hauenstein, N. M., & Foti, R. J. (1989). From laboratory to practice: Neglected issues in implementing frame-of-reference rater training. *Personnel Psychology, 42*, 359–378.

Hausknecht, J. P., Day, D., & Thomas, S. C. (2004). Applicant reactions to selection procedures: An updated model and meta-analysis. *Personnel Psychology, 57*, 639–683.

Hausknecht, J. P., Halpert, J. A., Di Patio, N. T., & Moriarty Gerrard, M. O. (2007). Retesting in selection: A meta-analysis of coaching and practice effects for tests of cognitive ability. *Journal of Applied Psychology, 92*, 373–385.

Hausknecht, J. P., Trevor, C. O., & Farr, J. L. (2002). Retaking ability tests in a selection setting: Implications for practice effects, training performance, and turnover. *Journal of Applied Psychology, 87*, 243–254.

Hawk, R. H. (1967). *The recruitment function.* New York, NY: American Management Association.

Hayes, T. L., & Macan, T. H. (1997). Comparison of the factors influencing interviewer hiring decisions for applicants with and those without disabilities. *Journal of Business and Psychology, 11*, 357–371.

Hazer, J. T., & Highhouse, S. (1997). Factors influencing managers' reactions to utility analysis: Effects of SD_y method, information

frame, and focal intervention. *Journal of Applied Psychology, 82*, 104–112.

Hedge, J. W., & Kavanagh, M. J. (1988). Improving the accuracy of performance evaluations: Comparison of three methods of performance appraiser training. *Journal of Applied Psychology, 73*, 68–73.

Hedges, L. V., & Olkin, I. (1985). *Statistical methods for meta-analysis.* Orlando, FL: Academic Press.

Hegarty, W. H., & Sims, H. P., Jr. (1979). Organizational philosophy, policies, and objectives related to unethical decision behavior: A laboratory experiment. *Journal of Applied Psychology, 64*, 331–338.

Heilman, M. E., Simon, M. C., & Repper, D. P. (1987). Intentionally favored, unintentionally harmed? The impact of gender based preferential selection on self-perceptions and self-evaluations. *Journal of Applied Psychology, 72*, 62–68.

Helms, J. E. (2006). Fairness is not validity or cultural bias in racial-group assessment: A quantitative perspective. *American Psychologist, 61*, 845–859.

Heneman, H. G., III. (1975). Research roundup. *The Personnel Administrator, 20*(6), 61.

Heneman, R. L. (1986). The relationship between supervisory ratings and results oriented measures of performance: A meta-analysis. *Personnel Psychology, 39*, 811–826.

Heneman, H. G., III, Schwab, D. P., Huett, D. L., & Ford, J. J. (1975). Interviewer validity as a function of interview structure, biographical data, and interviewee order. *Journal of Applied Psychology, 60*, 748–753.

Heneman, R. L., & von Hippel, C. (1995). Balancing individual and group rewards: Rewarding individual contributions to the team. *Compensation and Benefits Review, 27*, 745–759.

Heneman, R. L., & Wexley, K. N. (1983). The effects of time delay in rating and amount of information observed on performance rating accuracy. *Academy of Management Journal, 26*, 677–686.

Henik, A., & Tzelgov, J. (1985). Control of halo error: A multiple regression approach. *Journal of Applied Psychology, 70*, 577–580.

Henkoff, R. (1994, October 3). Finding, training, and keeping the best service workers. *Fortune*, pp. 110–122.

Hennessy, J., Mabey, B., & Warr, P. (1998). Assessment centre observation procedures: An experimental comparison of traditional, checklist and coding methods. *International Journal of Selection and Assessment, 6*, 222–231.

Henry, E. R. (1965). *Research conference on the use of autobiographical data as psychological predictors.* Greensboro, NC: Richardson Foundation.

Henry, R. A., & Hulin, C. L. (1987). Stability of skilled performance across time: Some generalizations and limitations on utilities. *Journal of Applied Psychology, 72*, 457–462.

Henry, R. A., & Hulin, C. L. (1989). Changing validities: Ability-performance relations and utilities. *Journal of Applied Psychology, 74*, 365–367.

Herbst, M. (2007, December 13). Big oil's talent hunt. *BusinessWeek.* n.d. Retrieved January 27, 2008, from www.businessweek.com.

Herold, D. M., & Parsons, C. K. (1985). Assessing the feedback environment in work organizations: Development of the Job

Feedback Survey. *Journal of Applied Psychology*, *70*, 290–305.

Herrnstein, R. J., & Murray, C. (1994). *The bell curve: Intelligence and class structure in American life.* New York, NY: Free Press.

Hersey, R. B. (1932). *Workers' emotions in shop and home.* Philadelphia, PA: University of Pennsylvania Press.

Hesketh, B. (1997a). Dilemmas in training for transfer and retention. *Applied Psychology: An International Review*, *46*, 317–339.

Hesketh, B. (1997b). W(h)ither dilemmas in training for transfer. *Applied Psychology: An International Review*, *46*, 380–386.

Higgins, C. A., & Judge, T. A. (2004). The effect of applicant influence tactics on recruiter perceptions of fit and hiring recommendations. *Journal of Applied Psychology*, *89*, 622–632.

Hillenbrand, C., & Money, K. (2007). Corporate responsibility and corporate reputation: Two separate concepts or two sides of the same coin? *Corporate Reputation Review 10*(4), 261–277.

Hinkin, T. R., & Tracey, J. B. (1999). An analysis of variance approach to content validation. *Organizational Research Methods*, *2*, 175–186.

HiringGateway@yahoo-inc.com. Accessed August 19, 2008.

Hira, N. A. (2007, November 12). The making of a UPS driver. *Fortune*, pp. 118–130.

Hirschman, C. (2007). Putting forecasting in focus. *HRMagazine, 52*(3), 44–49

Hitt, M. A., & Barr, S. H. (1989). Managerial selection decision models: Examination of configural cue processing. *Journal of Applied Psychology*, *74*, 53–61.

Hitt, M. A., Ireland, R. D., & Hoskisson, R. D. (2009). *Strategic management: Competitiveness and globalization, concepts* (8th ed.). Florence, KY: South-Western.

Hitt, M. A., Miller, C. C., & Collela, A. (2009). *Organizational behavior* (2nd ed.). Hoboken, NJ: Wiley.

Hobbs, N., & Stoops, N. (2002). *Demographic trends in the 20th century: Census 2000 special report* (CENSR–4). Washington, DC: U.S. Census Bureau.

Hobson, C. J., & Gibson, F. W. (1983). Policy capturing as an approach to understanding and improving performance appraisal: A review of the literature. *Academy of Management Review*, *8*, 640–649.

Hoenig, J. M., & Heisey, D. M. (2001). The abuse of power: The pervasive fallacy of power calculations for data analysis. *American Statistician*, *55*, 19–24.

Hof, R. D. (2005, June 20). The power of us. *BusinessWeek*, pp. 74–82.

Hoffman, C. C. (1999). Generalizing physical ability test validity: A case study using test transportability, validity generalization, and construct-related validation evidence. *Personnel Psychology*, *52*, 1019–1041.

Hoffman, C. C., Holden, L. M., & Gale, K. (2000). So many jobs, so little "N": Applying expanded validation models to support generalization of cognitive test validity. *Personnel Psychology*, *53*, 955–991.

Hoffman, C. C., & McPhail, S. M. (1998). Exploring options for supporting test use in situations precluding local validation. *Personnel Psychology*, *51*, 987–1003.

Hoffman, C. C., & Thornton, G. C. (1997). Examining selection utility where competing predictors differ in adverse impact. *Personnel Psychology*, *50*, 455–470.

Hoffman, D. A., Jacobs, R., & Baratta, J. E. (1993). Dynamic criteria and the measurement of change. *Journal of Applied Psychology*, *78*, 194–204.

Hofstede, G. (2001). *Culture's consequences: Comparing values, behaviors, institutions, and organizations across nations* (2nd ed.). Thousand Oaks, CA: Sage.

Hofstede, G., & Hofstede, G. J. (2005). *Cultures and organizations: Software of the mind* (revised & expanded 2nd ed.). New York: McGraw-Hill.

Hogan, E. A. (1987). Effects of prior expectations on performance ratings: A longitudinal study. *Academy of Management Journal*, *30*, 354–368.

Hogan, J., Barrett, P., & Hogan, R. (2007). Personality measurement, faking, and employment selection. *Journal of Applied Psychology*, *92*, 1270–1285.

Hogan, J., & Hogan, R. (1989). How to measure employee reliability. *Journal of Applied Psychology*, *74*, 273–279.

Hogan, J., & Holland, B. (2003). Using theory to evaluate personality and job-performance relations: A socioanalytic perspective. *Journal of Applied Psychology*, *88*, 100–112.

Hogan, P. M., Hakel, M. D., & Decker, P. J. (1986). Effects of trainee-generated versus trainer-provided rule codes on generalization in behavior-modeling training. *Journal of Applied Psychology*, *71*, 469–473.

Hogan, R., & Shelton, D. (1998). A socioanalytic perspective on job performance. *Human Performance*, *11*, 129–144.

Holladay, C. L., & Quiñones, M. A. (2003). Practice variability and transfer of training: The role of self-efficacy generality. *Journal of Applied Psychology*, *88*, 1094–1103.

Holland, K. (2008, January 27). When English is the rule at work. *The New York Times.* Downloaded August 24, 2008, from www.nytimes.com.

Hollenbeck, G. P. (2002). Coaching executives: Individual leader development. In R. Silzer (Ed.), *The 21st century executive* (pp. 137–167). San Francisco, CA: Jossey-Bass.

Hollenbeck, J. R., Ilgen, D. R., Tuttle, D. B., & Sego, D. J. (1995). Team performance on monitoring tasks: An examination of decision errors in contexts requiring sustained attention. *Journal of Applied Psychology*, *80*, 685–696.

Hollender, J. (2004). What matters most: Corporate values and social responsibility. *California Management Review*, *46*(4), 111–119.

Holstein, W. J. (2008, January 10). McCormick's successful succession plan. *BusinessWeek.* n.d. Retrieved April 28, 2008, from www.businessweek.com.

Holton, E. F., III. (1996). The flawed four-level evaluation model. *Human Resource Development Quarterly*, *7*, 5–21.

Holton, E. F., III, Chen, H. C., & Naquin, S. S. (2003). An examination of learning transfer system characteristics across organizational settings. *Human Resource Development Quarterly*, *14*, 459–482.

Horst, P. (1941). *The prediction of personal adjustment.* New York, NY: Social Science Research Council.

Hough, L. M. (1984). Development and evaluation of the "Accomplishment Record" method of selecting and promoting professionals. *Journal of Applied Psychology*, *69*, 135–146.

Hough, L. M. (1992). The "Big Five" personality variables-construct confusion: Description versus prediction. *Human Performance*, *5*, 139–155.

Hough, L. M. (1998). Effects of intentional distortion in personality measurement and evaluation of suggested palliatives. *Human Performance, 11,* 209–244.

Hough, L. M., & Oswald, F. L. (2000). Personnel selection: Looking toward the future—Remembering the past. *Annual Review of Psychology, 51,* 631–664.

Hough, L. M., Oswald, F. L., & Ployhart, R. E. (2001). Determinants, detection and amelioration of adverse impact in personnel selection procedures: Issues, evidence and lessons learned. *International Journal of Selection and Assessment, 9,* 152–194.

House, R. J., Hanges, P. W., Javidan, M., Dorfman, P., & Gupta, V. (Eds.). (2004). *Culture, leadership, and organizations: The GLOBE study of 62 societies.* Thousand Oaks, CA: Sage.

House, R. J., & Mitchell, T. R. (1974). Path-goal theory of leadership. *Journal of Contemporary Business, 3,* 81–97.

House, R. J., Wright, N. S., & Aditya, R. N. (1997). Cross-cultural research on organizational leadership: A critical analysis and a proposed theory. In P. C. Earley, & M. Erez (Eds.), *New perspectives on international industrial and organizational psychology* (pp. 535–625). San Francisco, CA: New Lexington Press.

Howard, A. (1986). College experiences and managerial performance. *Journal of Applied Psychology, 71,* 530–552.

Howard, A. (1995). Rethinking the psychology of work. In A. Howard (Ed.), *The changing nature of work* (pp. 513–555). San Francisco, CA: Jossey-Bass.

Howard, J. L., & Ferris, G. R. (1996). The employment interview context: Social and situational influences on interviewer decisions. *Journal of Applied Social Psychology, 26,* 112–136.

Hoyt, W. T. (2000). Rater bias in psychological research: When is it a problem and what can we do about it? *Psychological Methods, 5,* 64–86.

Hufcutt, A. J., & Arthur, W., Jr. (1994). Hunter and Hunter (1984) revisited: Interview validity for entry-level jobs. *Journal of Applied Psychology, 79,* 184–190.

Huffcutt, A. I. (2002). Research perspectives on meta-analysis. In S. G. Rogelberg (Ed.), *Handbook of research methods in industrial and organizational psychology* (pp. 198–215). Malden, MA: Blackwell.

Huffcutt, A. J., & Arthur, W., Jr. (1994). Hunter and Hunter (1984) revisited: Interview validity for entry-level jobs. *Journal of Applied Psychology, 79,* 184–190.

Huffcutt, A. I., Conway, J. M., Roth, P. L., & Stone, N. J. (2001). Identification and meta-analytic assessment of psychological constructs measured in employment interviews. *Journal of Applied Psychology, 86,* 897–913.

Huffcutt, A. I., & Roth, P. L. (1998). Racial group differences in employment interview evaluations. *Journal of Applied Psychology, 83,* 179–189.

Huffcutt, A. I., Weekley, J. A., Wiesner, W. H., Degroot, T. G., & Jones, C. (2001). Comparison of situational and behavior description interview questions for higher-level positions. *Personnel Psychology, 54,* 619–644.

Hughes, G. L., & Prien, E. P. (1989). Evaluation of task and job skill linkage judgments used to develop test specifications. *Personnel Psychology, 42,* 283–292.

Huint, H., & Saks, A. M. (2003). Translating training science into practice: A study of managers' reactions to post-training transfer interventions. *Human Resource Development Quarterly, 14,* 181–198.

Hulin, C. L., Henry, R. A., & Noon, S. L. (1990). Adding a dimension: Time as a factor in the generalizability of predictive relationships. *Psychological Bulletin, 107,* 328–340.

Hülsheger, U. R., Maier, G. W., & Stumpp, T. (2007). Validity of general mental ability for the prediction of job performance and training success in Germany: A meta-analysis. *International Journal of Selection & Assessment, 15,* 3–18.

Humphreys, L. G. (1973). Statistical definitions of test validity for minority groups. *Journal of Applied Psychology, 58,* 1–4.

Hunter, J. E., & Hunter, R. F. (1984). Validity and utility of alternative predictors of job performance. *Psychological Bulletin, 96,* 72–98.

Hunter, J. E., & Schmidt, F. L. (1990). *Methods of meta-analysis: Correcting error and bias in research findings.* Newbury Park, CA: Sage.

Hunter, J. E., & Schmidt, F. L. (2000). Racial and gender bias in ability and achievement tests: Resolving the apparent paradox. *Psychology, Public Policy, and Law, 6,* 151–158.

Hunter, J. E., & Schmidt, F. L. (2004). *Methods of meta-analysis: Correcting error and bias in research findings* (2nd ed.). Thousand Oaks, CA: Sage.

Hunter, J. E., Schmidt, F. L., & Coggin, T. D. (1988). Problems and pitfalls in using capital budgeting and financial accounting techniques in assessing the utility of personnel programs. *Journal of Applied Psychology, 73,* 522–528.

Hunter, J. E., Schmidt, F. L., & Hunter, R. (1979). Differential validity of employment tests by race: A comprehensive review and analysis. *Psychological Bulletin, 86,* 721–735.

Hunter, J. E., Schmidt, F. L., & Jackson, G. B. (1982). *Meta-analysis: Cumulating research findings across studies.* Beverly Hills, CA: Sage.

Hunter, J. E., Schmidt, F. L., & Judiesch, M. K. (1990). Individual differences in output variability as a function of job complexity. *Journal of Applied Psychology, 75,* 28–42.

Hunter, J. E., Schmidt, F. L., & Le, H. (2006). Implications for direct and indirect range restriction for meta-analysis methods and findings. *Journal of Applied Psychology, 91,* 594–612.

Hurley, A. E., & Sonnenfeld, J. A. (1998). The effect of organizational experience on managerial career attainment in an internal labor market. *Journal of Vocational Behavior, 52,* 172–190.

Hurtz, G. M., & Alliger, G. M. (2002). Influence of coaching on integrity test performance and unlikely virtues scale scores. *Human Performance, 15,* 255–273.

Huselid, M. A., Becker, B. E., & Beatty, R. W. (2005). *The workforce scorecard.* Boston, MA: Harvard Business School Press.

Hutcheson, J. O. (2007, March 19). Building a family business to last. *BusinessWeek.* n.d. Retrieved May 7, 2008, from www.businesseek.com.

Hyland v. Fukada, 580 F.2d 977 (9th Cir. 1978).

Iacono, W. G., & Lykken, D. T. (1997). The validity of the lie detector: Two surveys of scientific opinion. *Journal of Applied Psychology, 82,* 426–433.

ICE Annual Report, fiscal Year 2007. (2008). Downloaded from www.ice.gov/pi/reports/annual_report/2008/ar_2008_page3.htm.

Ilgen, D. R., & Favero, J. L. (1985). Limits in generalization from psychological research to performance appraisal processes. *Academy of Management Review, 10*, 311–321.

Ilgen, D. R., Fisher, C. D., & Taylor, M. S. (1979). Consequences of individual feedback on behavior in organizations. *Journal of Applied Psychology, 64*, 349–371.

Ilgen, D. R., & Moore, C. F. (1987). Types and choices of performance feedback. *Journal of Applied Psychology, 72*, 401–406.

Imada, A. S., & Hakel, M. D. (1977). Influence of nonverbal communication and rater proximity on impressions and decisions in simulated employment interviews. *Journal of Applied Psychology, 62*, 295–300.

Intel Corporation. (2008). 2008 annual report. Retrieved May 12, 2009, from www.intc.com.

Irvine, S. H., & Kyllonen, P. C. (Eds.). (2002). *Item generation and test development*. Mahwah, NJ: Lawrence Erlbaum.

Ivancevich, J. M. (1983). Contrast effects in performance evaluation and reward practices. *Academy of Management Journal, 26*, 465–476.

Jackson, D. N., Harris, W. G., Ashton, M. C., McCarthy, J. M., & Tremblay, P. F. (2000). How useful are work samples in validational studies? *International Journal of Selection and Assessment, 8*, 29–33.

Jacobs, A. N. (2004, July 27). An instant message from the Supreme Court: Are you listening? *Employment Source Newsletter*. n.d. www.epexperts.com.

Jacobs, R., & Baratta, J. E. (1989). Tools for staffing decisions: What can they do? What do they cost? In W. F. Cascio (Ed.), *Human resource planning, employment, and placement* (pp. 2-159–2-199). Washington, DC: Bureau of National Affairs.

Jacobs, R., Kafry, D., & Zedeck, S. (1980). Expectations of behaviorally anchored rating scales. *Personnel Psychology, 33*, 595–640.

Jacoby, J., Mazursky, D., Troutman, T., & Kuss, A. (1984). When feedback is ignored: The disutility of outcome feedback. *Journal of Applied Psychology, 69*, 531–545.

Jordan, M. (2005, November 8). Testing "English-only" rules. *The Wall Street Journal*, pp. B1, B13.

James, L. R. (1998). Measurement of personality via conditional reasoning. *Organizational Research Methods, 1*, 131–163.

James, L. R., Demaree, R. G., Mulaik, S. A., & Ladd, R. T. (1992). Validity generalization in the context of situational models. *Journal of Applied Psychology, 77*, 3–14.

James, L. R., Demaree, R. G., & Wolf, G. (1993). *r*ws: An assessment of within-group interrater agreement. *Journal of Applied Psychology, 78*, 306–309.

James, L. P., McIntyre, M. D., Glisson, C. A., Green, P. D., Patton, T. W., LeBreton, J. M., Frost, B. C., Russell, S. M., Sablynski, C. J., Mitchell, T. R., & Williams, L. J. (2005). A conditional reasoning measure for aggression. *Organizational Research Methods, 8*, 69–99.

Janove, J. W. (2003, March). Skating through the minefield. *HRMagazine*, pp. 107–113.

Jansen, P. G. W., & Vinkenburg, C. J. (2006). Predicting management career success from assessment center data: A longitudinal study. *Journal of Vocational Behavior, 68*, 253–266.

Jansen, P. G. W., & Stoop, B. A. M. (2001). The dynamics of assessment center validity: Results of a 7-year study. *Journal of Applied Psychology, 86*, 741–753.

Jansen, P. G. W., & Vinkenburg, C. J. (2006). Predicting management career success from assessment center data: A longitudinal study. *Journal of Vocational Behavior, 68*, 253–266.

Janssens, M. (1994). Evaluating international managers' performance: Parent country standards as control mechanisms. *International Journal of Human Resource Management, 5*, 853–873.

Janz, T. (1982). Initial comparisons of patterned behavior description interviews versus unstructured interviews. *Journal of Applied Psychology, 67*, 577–580.

Jattuso, M. L., & Sinar, E. F. (2003). Source effects in internet-based screening procedures. *International Journal of Selection and Assessment, 11*, 137–140.

Jawahar, I. M. (2001). Attitudes, self-monitoring, and appraisal behaviors. *Journal of Applied Psychology, 86*, 875–883.

Jawahar, I. M., & Williams, C. R. (1997). Where all the children are above average: The performance appraisal purpose effect. *Personnel Psychology, 50*, 905–925.

Jelley, R. B., & Goffin, R. D. (2001). Can performance-feedback accuracy be improved? Effects of rater priming and rating-scale format on rating accuracy. *Journal of Applied Psychology, 86*, 134–144.

Jenkins, J. G. (1946). Validity for what? *Journal of Consulting Psychology, 10*, 93–98.

Jennings, E. E. (1953). The motivation factor in testing supervisors. *Journal of Applied Psychology, 37*, 168–169.

Jereb, E., Rajkovic, U., & Rajkovic, V. (2005). A hierarchical, multi-attribute system approach to personnel selection. *International Journal of Selection and Assessment, 13*, 198–205.

Jerry, W., & Borman, W. C. (2002). Predicting adaptive performance: Further tests of a model of adaptability. *Human Performance, 15*, 299–324.

Jick, T. D. (1979). Mixing qualitative and quantitative methods: Triangulation in action. *Administrative Science Quarterly, 24*, 602–611.

Jobs, S., cited in Morris, B. (2008, March 17). What makes Apple golden. *Fortune*, p. 74.

Job sites reviews. (2008, January). n.d. Retrieved May 22, 2008, from www.consumersearch.com/www/internet/jobsites.

Jones, D. A., Shultz, J. W., & Chapman, D. S. (2006). Recruiting through job advertisements: The effects of cognitive elaboration on decision-making. *International Journal of Selection and Assessment, 11*, 167–179.

Johnson, J. T., & Ree, M. J. (1994). RANGEJ: A Pascal program to compute the multivariate correction for range restriction. *Educational and Psychological Measurement, 54*, 693–695.

Johnson, J. W., Carter, G. W., Davison, H. K., & Oliver, D. H. (2001). A synthetic validity approach to testing differential prediction hypotheses. *Journal of Applied Psychology, 86*, 774–780.

Johnson v. Railway Express Agency, 421 U.S. 454 (1975).

Johnson, R. E., Rosen, C. C., & Levy, P. E. (2008). Getting to the core of core self-evaluation: a review and recommendations. *Journal of Organizational Behavior, 29*, 391–413.

Joinson, C. (2001). Refocusing job descriptions. *HRMagazine*, *46*(1), 66–72.

Jones, G. R. (2009). *Organizational theory, design, and change* (6th ed.). Upper Saddle River, NJ: Prentice Hall.

Jones, R. G., & Born, M. P. (2008). Assessor constructs in use as the missing component in validation of assessment center dimensions: A critique and directions for research. *International Journal of Selection and Assessment, 16*, 229–238.

Jones, J. W., & Dages, K. D. (2003). Technology trends in staffing and assessment: A practice note. *International Journal of Selection and Assessment, 11*, 247–252.

Jose, J. R. (2001). Evaluating team performance. In M. J. Fleming, & J. B. Wilson (Eds.), *Effective HR measurement techniques* (pp. 107–112). Alexandria, VA: Society for Human Resource Management.

Joyce, L. W., Thayer, P. W., & Pond, S. B., III. (1994). Managerial functions: An alternative to traditional assessment center dimensions? *Personnel Psychology, 47*, 109–121.

Judge, T. A., & Bono, J. E. (2001). Relationship of core self-evaluations traits—self-esteem, generalized self-efficacy, locus of control, and emotional stability—with job satisfaction and job performance: A meta-analysis. *Journal of Applied Psychology, 86*, 80–92.

Judge, T. A., Bono, J. E., Ilies, R., & Gerhardt, M. W. (2002). Personality and leadership: A qualitative and quantitative review. *Journal of Applied Psychology, 87*, 765–780.

Judge, T. A., Cable, D. M., Boudreau, J. W., & Bretz, R. D., Jr. (1995). An empirical investigation of the predictors of executive career success. *Personnel Psychology, 48*, 485–519.

Judge, T. A., & Higgins, C. A. (1998). Affective disposition and the letter of reference. *Organizational Behavior and Human Decision Processes, 75*, 207–221.

Judge, T. A., & Hurst, C. (2008). How the rich (and happy) get richer (and happier): Relationship of core self-evaluations to trajectories in attaining work success. *Journal of Applied Psychology, 93*, 849–863.

Judge, T. A., & Ilies, R. (2002). Relationship of personality to performance motivation: A meta-analytic review. *Journal of Applied Psychology, 87*, 797–807.

Judge, T. A., Piccolo, R. F., & Ilies, R. (2004). The forgotten ones? The validity of consideration and initiating structure in leadership research. *Journal of Applied Psychology, 89*, 36–51.

Judge, T. A., LePine, J. A., & Rich, B. L. (2006). Loving yourself abundantly: Relationship of the narcissistic personality to self- and other perceptions of workplace deviance, leadership, and task and contextual performance. *Journal of Applied Psychology, 91*, 762–776.

Judiesch, M. K., Schmidt, F. L., & Mount, M. K. (1992). Estimates of the dollar value of employee output in utility analyses: An empirical test of two theories. *Journal of Applied Psychology, 77*, 234–250.

Kacmar, K. M., & Ferris, G. R. (1989). Theoretical and methodological considerations in the age-job satisfaction relationship. *Journal of Applied Psychology, 74*, 201–207.

Kadlec, D. (2007, October). You oughta be in Facebook. *Money*, p. 44.

Kaess, W. A., Witryol, S. L., & Nolan, R. E. (1961). Reliability, sex differences, and validity in the leaderless group discussion technique. *Journal of Applied Psychology, 45*, 345–350.

Kahneman, D., & Ghiselli, E. E. (1962). Validity and nonlinear heteroscedastic models. *Personnel Psychology, 15*, 1–12.

Kaiser, R. B., Lindberg, J. T., & Craig, S. B. (2007). Assessing the flexibility of managers: A comparison of methods. *International Journal of Selection & Assessment, 15*, 40–55.

Kane, J. S., Bernardin, H. J., Villanova, P., & Peyrfitte, J. (1995). Stability of rater leniency: Three studies. *Academy of Management Journal, 38*, 1036–1051.

Kane, J. S., & Kane, K. F. (1993). Performance appraisal. In H. J. Bernardin, & J. E. A. Russell (Eds.), *Human resource management: An experimental approach* (pp. 377–404). New York, NY: McGraw-Hill.

Kane, J. S., & Lawler, E. E., III. (1978). Methods of peer assessment. *Psychological Bulletin, 85*, 555–586.

Kane, J. S., & Lawler, E. E., III. (1980). In defense of peer assessment: A rebuttal to Brief's critique. *Psychological Bulletin, 88*, 80–81.

Katz, D., & Kahn, R. L. (1978). *The social psychology of organizations* (2nd ed.). New York, NY: Wiley.

Katzell, R. A. (1994). Contemporary meta-trends in industrial and organizational psychology. In H. C. Triandis, M. D. Dunnette, & L. M. Hough (Eds.), *Handbook of industrial and organizational psychology* (2nd ed., Vol. 4, pp. 1–89). Palo Alto, CA: Consulting Psychologists Press.

Keeping, L. M., & Levy, P. E. (2000). Performance appraisal reactions: Measurement, modeling, and method bias. *Journal of Applied Psychology, 85*, 708–723.

Kehoe, J. F. (2002). General mental ability and selection in private sector organizations: A commentary. *Human Performance, 15*, 97–106.

Kehoe, J. F. (2008). Commentary on Pareto-optimality as a rationale for adverse impact reduction: What would organizations do? *International Journal of Selection and Assessment, 16*, 195–200.

Keil, C. T., & Cortina, J. M. (2001). Degradation of validity over time: A test and extension of Ackerman's model. *Psychological Bulletin, 127*, 673–697.

Keith, N., & Frese, M. (2005). Self-regulation in error-management training: Emotion control and meta-cognition as mediators of performance effects. *Journal of Applied Psychology, 90*, 677–691.

Keith, N., & Frese, M. (2008). Effectiveness of error-management training: A meta-analysis. *Journal of Applied Psychology, 93*, 59–69.

Kelloway, E. K., Loughlin, C., Barling, J., & Nault, A. (2002). Self-reported counterproductive behaviors and organizational citizenship behaviors: Separate but related constructs. *International Journal of Selection and Assessment, 10*, 143–151.

Kelly, G. A. (1958). The theory and technique of assessment. *Annual Review of Psychology, 9*, 323–352.

Kerlinger, F. N., & Lee, H. B. (2000). *Foundations of behavioral research* (4th ed.). Stamford, CT: Thomson Learning.

Kerr, S., & Jermier, J. M. (1978). Substitutes for leadership: Their meaning and measurement. *Organizational Behavior and Human Performance, 22,* 375–403.

Keys, B., & Wolfe, J. (1988). Management education and development: Current issues and emerging trends. *Journal of Management, 14,* 205–229.

Kiker, D. S., & Motowidlo, S. J. (1999). Main and interaction effects of task and contextual performance on supervisory reward decisions. *Journal of Applied Psychology, 84,* 602–609.

Kimmel, A. J. (1996). *Ethical issues in behavioral research: A survey.* Cambridge, MA: Blackwell.

King, R. (2008, May 2). The (virtual) global office. *BusinessWeek.* Downloaded from www.businessweek.com.

King, L. M., Hunter, J. E., & Schmidt, F. L. (1980). Halo in a multi-dimensional forced-choice performance evaluation scale. *Journal of Applied Psychology, 65,* 507–516.

Kingsbury, F. A. (1933). Psychological tests for executives. *Personnel, 9,* 121–133.

Kinicki, A. J., Prussia, G. E., Bin, J. W., & McKee-Ryan, F. M. (2004). A covariance structure analysis of employees' response to performance feedback. *Journal of Applied Psychology, 89,* 1057–1069.

Kinslinger, H. J. (1966). Application of projective techniques in personnel psychology since 1940. *Psychological Bulletin, 66,* 134–150.

Kirchner, W. K., & Dunnette, M. D. (1957). Applying the weighted application blank technique to a variety of office jobs. *Journal of Applied Psychology, 41,* 206–208.

Kirchner, W. K., & Reisberg, D. J. (1962). Differences between better and less effective supervisors in appraisal of subordinates. *Personnel Psychology, 15,* 295–302.

Kirkman, B. L., Lowe, K. B., & Gibson, C. B. (2006). A quarter century of *Culture's consequences*: A review of empirical research incorporating Hofstede's cultural values framework. *Journal of International Business Studies, 37,* 285–320.

Kirkpatrick, D. L. (1977). Evaluating training programs: Evidence vs. proof. *Training and Development Journal, 31,* 9–12.

Kirkpatrick, D. L. (1983). Four steps to measuring training effectiveness. *Personnel Administrator, 28*(11), 19–25.

Kirkpatrick, D. L. (1994). *Evaluating training programs: The four levels.* San Francisco, CA: Berrett-Kohler.

Kirkpatrick, J. J., Ewen, R. B., Barrett, R. S., & Katzell, R. A. (1968). *Testing and fair employment.* New York, NY: New York University Press.

Kirnan, J. P., Farley, J. A., & Geisinger, K. F. (1989). The relationship between recruiting source, applicant quality, and hire performance: An analysis by sex, ethnicity, and age. *Personnel Psychology, 42,* 293–308.

Kirsch, I., Jungeblut, A., Jenkins, L., & Kolstad, A. (2002). *Adult literacy in America: A first look at the results of the National Adult Literacy survey* (3rd ed.). Washington, DC: U.S. Government Printing Office (NCES 1993-275).

Kisamore, J. L., & Brannick, M. T. (2008). An illustration of the consequences of meta-analysis model choice. *Organizational Research Methods, 11,* 35–53.

Kitayama, S. (2002). Culture and basic psychological processes— Toward a system view of culture: Comment on Oyserman et al. (2002). *Psychological Bulletin, 128,* 89–96.

Kiviat, B. (2009, February 1). After Layoffs, There's Survivor's Guilt. *Time magazine.* Available at http://www.time.com/time/business/article/0,8599,1874592,00.html?imw=Y.

Klehe, U., & Anderson, N. (2007). Working hard and working smart: motivation and ability during typical and maximum performance. *Journal of Applied Psychology, 92,* 978–992.

Klein, K. E. (2007, June 20). Succession planning without an heir. *BusinessWeek.* n.d. Retrieved April 28, 2008, www.businesseek.com.

Klein, H. J., Noe, R. A., & Wang, C. (2006). Motivation to learn and course outcomes: the impact of delivery mode, learning-goal orientation, and perceived barriers and enablers. *Personnel Psychology, 59,* 665–702.

Kleinman, M. (1993). Are rating dimensions in assessment centers transparent for participants? Consequences for criterion and construct validity. *Journal of Applied Psychology, 78,* 988–993.

Kleingeld, A., Van Tuijl, H., & Algera, J. A. (2004). Participation in the design of performance management systems: A quasi-experimental field study. *Journal of Organizational Behavior, 25,* 831–851.

Klimoski, R., & Brickner, M. (1987). Why do assessment centers work? The puzzle of assessment center validity. *Personnel Psychology, 40,* 243–260.

Klimoski, R. J., & Strickland, W. J. (1977). Assessment centers— Valid or merely prescient? *Personnel Psychology, 30,* 353–361.

Kluger, A. N., & Colella, A. (1993). Beyond the mean bias: The effect of warning against faking on biodata item variances. *Personnel Psychology, 46,* 763–780.

Kluger, A. N., & DeNisi, A. S. (1996). The effects of feedback interventions on performance: Historical review, a meta-analysis, and a preliminary feedback intervention theory. *Psychological Bulletin, 119,* 254–284.

Kluger, A. N., Reilly, R. R., & Russell, C. J. (1991). Faking biodata tests: Are option-keyed instruments more resistant? *Journal of Applied Psychology, 76,* 889–896.

Knouse, S. B. (1987). An attribution theory approach to the letter of recommendation. *International Journal of Management, 4*(1), 5–13.

Kohn, L. S., & Dipboye, R. L. (1998). The effects of interview structure on recruiting outcomes. *Journal of Applied Social Psychology, 28,* 821–843.

Kolk, N. J., Born, M. P., van der Flier, H., & Olman, J. M. (2002). Assessment center procedures: Cognitive load during the observation phase. *International Journal of Selection and Assessment, 10,* 271–278.

Kolstad v. American Dental Association, 119 S. Ct. 2118 (1999).

Komaki, J. L., Desselles, M. L., & Bowman, E. D. (1989). Definitely not a breeze: Extending an operant model of effective supervision to teams. *Journal of Applied Psychology, 74,* 522–529.

Konovsky, M. A., & Cropanzano, R. (1991). Perceived fairness of employee drug testing as a predictor of employee attitudes and job performance. *Journal of Applied Psychology, 76,* 698–707.

Kontoghiorghes, C. (2004). Reconceptualizing the learning transfer conceptual framework: Empirical validation of a new systemic model. *International Journal of Training and Development*, 8, 210–221.

Komar, S., Brown, D. J., Komar, J. A., & Robie, C. (2008). Faking and the validity of conscientiousness: A Monte Carlo investigation. *Journal of Applied Psychology*, 93, 140–154.

Korb, L. D. (1956). How to measure the results of supervisory training. *Personnel*, 32, 378–391.

Korman, A. K. (1968). The prediction of managerial performance: A review. *Personnel Psychology*, 21, 295–322.

Korsgaard, M. A., Roberson, L., & Rymph, R. D. (1998). What motivates fairness? The role of subordinate assertive behavior on manager's interactional fairness. *Journal of Applied Psychology*, 83, 731–744.

Kozlowski, S. W. J., & Bell, B. S. (2003). Work groups and teams in organizations. In W. C. Borman, D. R. Ilgen, & R. J. Klimoski (Vol. Eds.), *Handbook of psychology: Vol. 12. Industrial and organizational psychology* (pp. 333–375). Hoboken, NJ: Wiley.

Kozlowski, S. W. J., & Hattrup, K. (1992). A disagreement about within-group agreement: Disentangling issues of consistency versus consensus. *Journal of Applied Psychology*, 77, 161–167.

Kraiger, K. (2002). Decision-based evaluation. In K. Kraiger (Ed.), *Creating, implementing, and managing effective training and development* (pp. 331–375). San Francisco, CA: Jossey-Bass.

Kraiger, K. (2003). Perspectives on training and development. In W. C. Borman, D. R. Ilgen, & R. J. Klimoski (Eds.), *Handbook of psychology: Vol. 12. Industrial and organizational psychology* (pp. 171–192). Hoboken, NJ: Wiley.

Kraiger, K., & Aguinis, H. (2001). Training effectiveness: Assessing training needs, motivation, and accomplishments. In M. London (Ed.), *How people evaluate others in organizations* (pp. 203–220). Mahwah, NJ: Lawrence Erlbaum.

Kraiger, K., Ford, J. K., & Salas, E. (1993). Application of cognitive, skill-based, and affective theories of learning outcomes to new methods of training evaluation. *Journal of Applied Psychology*, 78, 311–328.

Kraiger, K., & Jerden, E. (2007). A new look at learner control: Meta-analytic results and directions for future research. In S. M. Fiore, & E. Salas (Eds.), *Where is the learning in distance learning? Towards a science of distributed learning and training* (pp. 65–90). Washington, DC: APA Books.

Kraiger, K., McLinden, D., & Casper, W. J. (2004). Collaborative planning for training impact. *Human Resource Management Review*, 43, 337–351.

Kraimer, M. L., Shaffer, M. A., Harrison, D. A., & Ren, H. (2007, November). Examining international assignment success from a psychological contracts and careers perspective. *Executive summary presented to the SHRM Foundation* (funding agency).

Kraimer, M. L., Wayne, S. J., & Jaworski, R. A. (2001). Sources of support and expatriate performance: The mediating role of expatriate adjustment. *Personnel Psychology*, 54, 71–99.

Kraut, A. I. (1975). Prediction of managerial success by peer and training staff ratings. *Journal of Applied Psychology*, 60, 14–19.

Kraut, A. I., & Scott, G. J. (1972). Validity of an operational management assessment program. *Journal of Applied Psychology*, 56, 124–129.

Kravitz, D. A. (2008). The diversity-validity dilemma: Beyond selection-The role of affirmative action. *Personnel Psychology*, 61, 173–193.

Kravitz, D. A., & Klineberg, S. L. (2000). Reactions to two versions of affirmative action among whites, blacks, and Hispanics. *Journal of Applied Psychology*, 85, 597–611.

Krell, E. (2007, December). Unmasking illegal workers. *HRMagazine*, pp. 49–52.

Kromrey, J. D., & Hines, C. V. (1995). Use of empirical estimates of shrinkage in multiple regression: A caution. *Educational and Psychological Measurement*, 55, 901–925.

Kronholz, J., Tomsho, R., & Forelle, C. (2003, June 30). High court's ruling on race could affect business hiring. *The Wall Street Journal*, pp. A1, A6.

Krzystofiak, F., Cardy, R., & Newman, J. (1988). Implicit personality and performance appraisal: The influence of trait inferences on evaluations of behavior. *Journal of Applied Psychology*, 73, 515–521.

Kuder, G. F., & Richardson, M. W. (1937). The theory of the estimation of test reliability. *Psychometrika*, 2, 151–160.

Kuder, G. F., & Richardson, M. W. (1939). The calculation of test reliability coefficients based on the method of rational equivalence. *Journal of Educational Psychology*, 30, 681–687.

Kulas, J. T., & Finkelstein, L. M. (2007). Content and reliability of discrepancy-defined self-awareness in multisource feedback. *Organizational Research Methods*, 10, 502–522.

Kuncel, N. R., & Borneman, M. J. (2007). Toward a new method of detecting deliberately faked personality tests: The use of idiosyncratic item responses. *International Journal of Selection & Assessment*, 15, 220–231.

Kuncel, N. R., & Sackett, P. R. (2007). Selection citation mars conclusions about test validity and predictive bias. *American Psychologist*, 62, 145–146.

Kurecka, P. M., Austin, J. M., Jr., Johnson, W., & Mendoza, J. L. (1982). Full and errant coaching effects on assigned role leaderless group discussion performance. *Personnel Psychology*, 35, 805–812.

Kurtzberg, T. R., Naquin, C. E., & Belkin, L. Y. (2005). Electronic performance appraisals: The effects of e-mail communication on peer ratings in actual and simulated environments. *Organizational Behavior and Human Decision Processes*, 98, 216–226.

Laczo, R. M., & Sackett, P. R. (2004). Effects of banding on performance and minority hiring: Further Monte Carlo simulations. In H. Aguinis (Ed.), *Test score banding in human resource selection: Legal, technical, and societal issues* (pp. 133–150). Westport, CT: Praeger.

Lado, A. A., & Wilson, M. C. (1994). Human resource systems and sustained competitive advantage: A competency-based perspective. *Academy of Management Review*, 19, 699–727.

Ladika, S. (2006, October). Trouble on the hiring front. *HRMagazine*, pp. 56–61.

LaFasto, F. M., & Larson, E. C. E. (2001). *When teams work best: 6,000 team members and leaders tell what it takes to succeed.* Thousand Oaks, CA: Sage.

LaHuis, D. M., & Avis, J. M. (2007). Using multilevel random coefficient modeling to investigate rater effects in performance ratings. *Organizational Research Methods, 10,* 97–107.

Lance, C. E., & Bennett, W. (2000). Replication and extension of models of supervisory job performance ratings. *Human Performance, 13,* 139–158.

Lance, C. E., Foster, M. R., Gentry, W. A., & Thoresen, J. D. (2004). Assessor cognitive processes in an operational assessment center. *Journal of Applied Psychology, 89,* 22–35.

Lance, C. E., Foster, M. R., Nemeth, Y. M., Gentry, W. A., & Drollinger, S. (2007). Extending the nomological network of assessment center construct validity: Prediction of cross-situationally consistent and specific aspects of assessment center performance. *Human Performance, 20,* 345–362.

Lance, C. E., Johnson, C. D., Douthitt, S. S., Bennett, W., & Harville, D. L. (2000). Good news: Work sample administrators' global performance judgments are (about) as valid as we've suspected. *Human Performance, 13,* 253–277.

Lance, C. E., Lambert, T. A., Gewin, A. G., Lievens, F., & Conway, J. M. (2004). Revised estimates of dimension and exercise variance components in assessment center post-exercise dimension ratings. *Journal of Applied Psychology, 89,* 377–385.

Lance, C. E., LaPointe, J. A., & Stewart, A. M. (1994). A test of the context dependency of three causal models of halo rating error. *Journal of Applied Psychology, 79,* 332–340.

Lance, C. E., Teachout, M. S., & Donnelly, T. M. (1992). Specification of the criterion construct space: An application of hierarchical confirmatory factor analysis. *Journal of Applied Psychology, 77,* 437–452.

Lance, C. B., Woehr, D. J., & Meade, A. W. (2007). Case study: A Monte Carlo investigation of assessment center construct validity models. *Organizational Research Methods, 10,* 430–448.

Landis, D., & Bhagat, R. (Eds.). (1996). *Handbook of intercultural training.* Newbury Park, CA: Sage.

Landis, R. S., & Dunlap, W. P. (2000). Moderated multiple regression tests are criterion specific. *Organizational Research Methods, 3,* 254–266.

Landis, R. S., Fogli, L., & Goldberg, E. (1998). Future-oriented job analysis: A description of the process and its organizational implications. *International Journal of Selection and Assessment, 6*(3), 192–197.

Landon, T. E., & Arvey, R. D. (2007). Ratings of test fairness by human resource professionals. *International Journal of Selection and Assessment, 15,* 185–196.

Landy, F. J. (1986). Stamp collecting versus science: Validation as hypothesis testing. *American Psychologist, 41,* 1183–1192.

Landy, F. J. (2003). Validity generalization: Then and now. In K. R. Murphy (Ed.), *Validity generalization: A critical review* (pp. 155–195). Mahwah, NJ: Lawrence Erlbaum.

Landy, F. J., & Bates, F. (1973). Another look at contrast effects in the employment interview. *Journal of Applied Psychology, 58,* 141–144.

Landy, F. J., & Farr, J. L. (1980). Performance rating. *Psychological Bulletin, 87,* 72–107.

Landy, F. J., & Conte, J. M. (2007). *Work in the 21st century: An introduction to industrial and organizational psychology* (2nd ed.). Malden, MA: Blackwell.

Landy, F. J., & Conte, J. M. (2009). *Work in the 21st century: An introduction to industrial and organizational psychology* (3rd ed.). Malden, MA: Blackwell.

Landy, F. J., & Vasey, J. (1991). Job analysis: The composition of SME samples. *Personnel Psychology, 44,* 27–50.

Lane, C. (2003, June 24). Affirmative action for diversity is upheld. *The Washington Post.* Retrieved June 25, 2003, from www.washingtonpost.com.

Langan-Fox, J., Waycott, J., Morizzi, M., & McDonald, L. (1998). Predictors of participation in performance appraisal: A voluntary system in a blue-collar work environment. *International Journal of Selection and Assessment, 6,* 249–260.

Lapolice, C. C., Carter, G. W., & Johnson, J. W. (2008). Linking O*NET descriptors to occupational literacy requirements using job component validation. *Personnel Psychology, 61,* 405–441.

Larson, S. C. (1931). The shrinkage of the coefficient of multiple correlation. *Journal of Educational Psychology, 22,* 45–55.

Larson, J. R., Jr. (1989). The dynamic interplay between employees' feedback-seeking strategies and supervisors' delivery of performance feedback. *Academy of Management Review, 14,* 408–422.

Latham, G. P. (1988). Human resource training and development. *Annual Review of Psychology, 39,* 545–582.

Latham, G. P. (2007). *Work motivation: History, theory, and practice.* Thousand Oaks, CA: Sage.

Latham, G. P., Budworth, M., Yanar, B., & Whyte, G. (2008). The influence of a manager's own performance appraisal on the evaluation of others. *International Journal of Selection and Assessment, 16,* 220–228.

Latham, G. P., & Frayne, C. A. (1989). Self-management training for increasing job attendance: A follow-up and a replication. *Journal of Applied Psychology, 74,* 411–416.

Latham, G. P., & Locke, E. A. (2006). New directions in goal-setting theory. *Current Directions in Psychological Science, 15*(5), 265–268.

Latham, G. P., & Saari, L. M. (1979). Application of social-learning theory to training supervisors through behavioral modeling. *Journal of Applied Psychology, 64,* 239–246.

Latham, G. P., Saari, L. M., Pursell, E. D., & Campion, M. A. (1980). The situational interview. *Journal of Applied Psychology, 65,* 422–427.

Latham, G. P., Wexley, K. N., & Pursell, E. D. (1975). Training managers to minimize rating errors in the observation of behavior. *Journal of Applied Psychology, 60,* 550–555.

Latham, G. P., & Whyte, G. (1994). The futility of utility analysis. *Personnel Psychology, 47,* 31–46.

Lau, S. (2008, February). U.S. laws abroad. *HRMagazine*, p. 33.

Lauricella, T. (2007, September 16). How old are you? As old as your skills. *The Wall Street Journal Sunday*, p. 2.

Lautenschlager, G. J., & Mendoza, J. L. (1986). A step-down hierarchical multiple regression analysis for examining hypotheses about test bias in prediction. *Applied Psychological Measurement, 10*, 133–139.

Lavelle, L. (2003, September 29). After the jobless recovery, the war for talent. *Business Week*, p. 92.

Law, K. S., & Myors, B. (1993). Cutoff scores that maximize the total utility of a selection program: Comment on Martin and Raju's (1992) procedure. *Journal of Applied Psychology, 78*, 736–740.

Lawler, E. E., III. (1967). The multitrait-multirater approach to measuring managerial job performance. *Journal of Applied Psychology, 51*, 369–381.

Lawler, E. E., III. (1969). Job design and employee motivation. *Personnel Psychology, 22*, 435–436.

Lawley, D. N. (1943). A note on Karl Pearson's selection formulae. *Proceedings of the Royal Society of Edinburgh, LXII*–Part I, 19–32.

Lawshe, C. H. (1975). A quantitative approach to content validity. *Personnel Psychology, 28*, 563–575.

Lawshe, C. H., & Balma, M. J. (1966). *Principles of personnel testing* (2nd ed.). New York, NY: McGraw-Hill.

Lawshe, C. H, & Bolda, R. A. (1958). Expectancy charts. I. Their use and empirical development. *Personnel Psychology, 11*, 353–365.

Lawshe, C. H., Bolda, R. A., Brune, R. L., & Auclair, G. (1958). Expectancy charts. II. Their theoretical development. *Personnel Psychology, 11*, 545–559.

Lawshe, C. H., & Schucker, R. E. (1959). The relative efficiency of four test weighting methods in multiple prediction. *Educational and Psychological Measurement, 19*, 103–114.

Lawler, E. E., III, & O'Toole, J. (2006). *The new American workplace.* New York, NY: Palgrave Macmillan.

LeBreton, J. M., Burgess, J. R. D., Kaiser, R. B., Atchley, E. K., & James, L. R. (2003). The restriction of variance hypothesis and interrater reliability and agreement: Are ratings from multiple sources really dissimilar? *Organizational Research Methods, 6*, 80–128.

LeBreton, J. M., & Senter, J. L. (2008). Answers to 20 questions about interrater reliability and interrater agreement. *Organizational Research Methods, 11*, 815–852.

Ledvinka, J. (1979). The statistical definition of fairness in the federal selection guidelines and its implications for minority employment. *Personnel Psychology, 32*, 551–562.

Le, H., Schmidt, F. L., & Putka, D. J. (2009). The multifaceted nature of measurement artifacts and its implications for estimating construct-level relationships. *Organizational Research Methods, 12*, 165–200.

Lee, R., & Foley, P. P. (1986). Is the validity of a test constant through the test score range? *Journal of Applied Psychology, 71*, 641–644.

Lee, R., Miller, K. J., & Graham, W. K. (1982). Corrections for restriction of range and attenuation in criterion-related validation studies. *Journal of Applied Psychology, 67*, 637–639.

Lefkowitz, J. (2003). *Ethics and values in industrial-organizational psychology.* Mahwah, NJ: Lawrence Erlbaum.

Lent, R. H., Aurbach, H. D., & Levin, L. S. (1971). Predictors, criteria, and significant results. *Personnel Psychology, 24*, 519–533.

Leonard, B. (2008, January). Bush signs military leave FMLA expansion into law. n.d. Retrieved April 15, 2008, from www.shrm.org/hrnews_published/archives/CMS_024440.asp.

LePine, J. A. (2003). Team adaptation and postchange performance: Effects of team composition in terms of members' cognitive ability and personality. *Journal of Applied Psychology, 88*, 27–39.

LePine, J. A., & Van Dyne, L. (2001). Peer responses to low performers: An attributional model of helping in the context of groups. *Academy of Management Review, 26*, 67–84.

Lester, S. W., Kickul, J. R., Bergmann, T. J., & De Meuse, K. P. (2003). The effects of organizational resizing on the nature of the psychological contract and employee perceptions of contract fulfillment. In K. P. De Meuse, & M. L. Marks (Eds.), *Resizing the organization* (pp. 78–107). San Francisco, CA: Jossey-Bass.

Leung, A. (2003). Different ties for different needs: Recruitment practices of entrepreneurial firms at different developmental phases. *Human Resource Management, 42*, 303–320.

Levering, R., & Moskowitz, M. (2008, February 4). 100 Best companies to work for. *Fortune.* Accessed March 14, 2008, at http://money.cnn.com/magazines/fortune/bestcompanies/2008/snapshots/1.html.

Levering, R., & Moskowitz, M. (2009, February 2). 100 Best companies to work for. *Fortune*, pp. 67–78.

Levitz, J., & Shishkin, P. (2009, March 11). More workers cite age bias after layoffs. *The Wall Street Journal*, p. D1.

Levine, E. L., May, D. M., Ulm, R. A., & Gordon, T. R. (1997). A methodology for developing and validating minimum qualifications (MQs). *Personnel Psychology, 50*, 1009–1023.

Lewin, A. Y., & Zwany, A. (1976). Peer nominations: A model, literature critique, and a paradigm for research. *Personnel Psychology, 29*, 423–447.

Lievens, F. (1998). Factors which improve the construct validity of assessment centers: A review. *International Journal of Selection and Assessment, 6*, 141–152.

Lievens, F. (2001). Assessor training strategies and their effects on accuracy, interrater reliability, and discriminant validity. *Journal of Applied Psychology, 86*, 255–264.

Lievens, F. (2002). Trying to understand the different pieces of the construct validity puzzle of assessment centers: An examination of assessor and assessee effects. *Journal of Applied Psychology, 87*, 675–686.

Lievens, F., & Conway, J. M. (2001). Dimension and exercise variance in assessment center scores: A large-scale evaluation of multitrait-multimethod studies. *Journal of Applied Psychology, 86*, 1202–1222.

Lievens, F., Conway, J. M., & De Corte, W. (2008). The relative importance of task, citizenship and counterproductive performance to job performance ratings: Do rater source and team-based culture matter? *Journal of Occupational and Organizational Psychology, 81*, 11–27.

Lievens, F., & Harris, M. M. (2003). Research on internet recruitment and testing: Current status and future directions. In C. L. Cooper, & I. T. Robertson (Eds.), *International review of industrial and organizational psychology*. Chichester, England: Wiley.

Lievens, F., Harris, M. M., Van Keer, E., & Bisqueret, C. (2003). Predicting cross-cultural training performance: The validity of personality, cognitive ability, and dimensions measured by an assessment center and a behavior description interview. *Journal of Applied Psychology, 88*, 476–489.

Lievens, F., & Peeters, H. (2008). Interviewers' sensitivity to impression-management tactics in structured interviews. *European Journal of Psychological Assessment, 24*, 174–180.

Lievens, F., Reeve, C. L., & Heggestad, E. D. (2007). An examination of psychometric bias due to retesting on cognitive ability tests in selection settings. *Journal of Applied Psychology, 92*, 1672–1682.

Lievens, F., & Sackett, P. R. (2007). Situational judgment tests in high-stakes settings: Issues and strategies with generating alternate forms. *Journal of Applied Psychology, 92*, 1043–1055.

Lilienfeld, S. O., Alliger, G., & Mitchell, K. (1995). Why integrity testing remains controversial. *American Psychologist, 50*, 457–458.

Lin, T. R., Dobbins, G. H., & Farh, J. L. (1992). A field study of race and age similarity effects on interview ratings in conventional and situational interviews. *Journal of Applied Psychology, 77*, 363–371.

Linn, R. L. (1978). Single-group validity, differential validity, and differential prediction. *Journal of Applied Psychology, 63*, 507–512.

Linn, R. L., & Gronlund, N. E. (1995). *Measurement and assessment in teaching* (7th ed.). Englewood Cliffs, NJ: Prentice Hall.

Linn, R. L., & Werts, C. E. (1971). Considerations for studies of test bias. *Journal of Educational Measurement, 8*, 1–4.

Lipsey, M. S., & Wilson, D. B. (1993). The efficacy of psychological, educational, and behavioral treatment. *American Psychologist, 48*, 1181–1209.

Lissitz, R. W., & Green, S. B. (1975). Effects of the number of scale points on reliability: A Monte Carlo approach. *Journal of Applied Psychology, 60*, 10–13.

Littrell, L. N., Salas, E., Hess, K. P., Paley, M., & Riedel, S. (2006). Expatriate preparation: A critical analysis of 25 years of cross-cultural training research. *Human Resource Development Review, 5*, 355–388.

Locke, E. A. (1968). Toward a theory of task motivation and incentives. *Organizational Behavior and Human Performance, 3*, 157–189.

Locke, E. A., Frederick, E., Buckner, E., & Bobko, P. (1984). Effect of previously assigned goals on self-set goals and performance, *Journal of Applied Psychology, 69*, 694–699.

Locke, E. A., & Latham, G. P. (1990). *A theory of goal setting and task performance*. Englewood Cliffs, NJ: Prentice Hall.

Locke, E. A., & Latham, G. P. (2002). Building a practically useful theory of goal setting and task motivation. *American Psychologist, 57*, 705–717.

Locke, E. A., Latham, G. P., & Erez, M. (1988). The determinants of goal commitment. *Academy of Management Review, 13*, 23–39.

Locke, E. A., Shaw, K. N., Saari, L. M., & Latham, G. P. (1981). Goal setting and task performance: 1969–1980. *Psychological Bulletin, 90*, 125–152.

London, M. (2003). *Job feedback: Giving, seeking, and using feedback for performance improvement* (2nd ed.). Mahwah, NJ: Lawrence Erlbaum.

London, M., & Bray, D. W. (1980). Ethical issues in testing and evaluation for personnel decisions. *American Psychologist, 35*, 890–901.

London, M., & Stumpf, S. A. (1983). Effects of candidate characteristics on management promotion decisions: An experimental study. *Personnel Psychology, 36*, 241–259.

London, M., Mone, E. M., & Scott, J. C. (2004). Performance management and assessment: Methods for improved rater accuracy and employee goal setting. *Human Resource Management, 43*, 319–336.

Longenecker, C. O., & Gioia, D. A. (1994, Winter). Delving into the dark side: The politics of executive appraisal. *Organizational Dynamics*, pp. 47–58.

Longenecker, C. O., Sims, H. P., & Gioia, D. A. (1987). Behind the mask: The politics of employee appraisal. *Academy of Management Executive, 1*, 183–193.

Lopez, F. M., Jr. (1966). *Evaluating executive decision making* (Research Study 75). New York, NY: American Management Association.

LoPresto, R. L., Mitcham, D. E., & Ripley, D. E. (1986). *Reference checking handbook*. Alexandria, VA: American Society for Personnel Administration.

Lord, F. M. (1962). Cutting scores and errors of measurement. *Psychometrika, 27*, 19–30.

Lord, J. S. (1989). External and internal recruitment. In W. F. Cascio (Ed.), *Human resource planning, employment, and placement* (pp. 2-73–2-102). Washington, DC: Bureau of National Affairs.

Lowell, R. S., & DeLoach, J. A. (1982). Equal employment opportunity: Are you overlooking the application form? *Personnel, 59*(4), 49–55.

Lublin, J. S. (2006, May 15). Harassment law in U.S. is strict, foreigners find. *The Wall Street Journal*, pp. B1, B3.

Lubinski, D. (2000). Scientific and social significance of assessing individual differences: Sinking shafts at a few critical points. *Annual Review of Psychology, 51*, 405–444.

Lubinski, D., Benbow, C. P., & Ryan, J. (1995). Stability of vocational interests among the intellectually gifted from adolescence to adulthood: A 15-year longitudinal study. *Journal of Applied Psychology, 80*, 196–200.

Lyness, K. S., & Heilman, M. E. (2006). When fit is fundamental: Performance evaluations and promotions of upper-level female and male managers. *Journal of Applied Psychology, 91*, 777–785.

Mabe, P. A., III, & West, S. G. (1982). Validity of self-evaluation of ability: A review and meta-analysis. *Journal of Applied Psychology, 67*, 280–296.

Macan, T. H., Avedon, M. J., Paese, M., & Smith, D. E. (1994). The effects of applicants' reactions to cognitive ability tests and an assessment center. *Personnel Psychology, 47,* 715–738.

MacDonald, R. (2008, November 6). *Talent management in IBM.* Paper presented at the annual meeting of the National Academy of Human Resources, New York, NY.

Machin, M. A. (2002). Planning, managing, and optimizing transfer of training. In K. Kraiger (Ed.), *Creating, implementing, and managing effective training and development* (pp. 263–301). San Francisco, CA: Jossey-Bass.

MacMillan, D. (2007, May 7). The art of the online résumé. *BusinessWeek,* p. 86.

MacMillan, I. C., & Selden, L. (2008, December). Change with your customers—and win big. *Harvard Business Review, 86*(12), 24.

Mael, F. A. (1991). A conceptual rationale for the domain and attributes of biodata items. *Personnel Psychology, 44,* 763–792.

Mael, F. A., & Ashforth, B. E. (1995). Loyal from day one: Biodata, organizational identification, and turnover among newcomers. *Personnel Psychology, 48,* 309–333.

Mager, R. F. (1984). *Preparing instructional objectives* (2nd ed.). Belmont, CA: Pitman Learning.

Magjuka, R. J., & Baldwin, T. T. (1991). Team-based employee involvement programs: Effects of design and administration. *Personnel Psychology, 44,* 793–812.

Maher, K. (2003a, January 14). Corporations cut middlemen and do their own recruiting. *The Wall Street Journal,* p. B10.

Maher, K. (2003b, June 17). The jungle: Focus on recruitment, pay, and getting ahead. *The Wall Street Journal,* p. B8.

Maher, K., & Silverman, R. E. (2002, January 2). Online job sites yield few jobs, users complain. *The Wall Street Journal,* pp. A7, A13.

Mahoney, L., & Thorne, L. (2005). Corporate social responsibility and long term compensation: Evidence from Canada. *Journal of Business Ethics, 57,* 241–253.

Maier, M. H. (1988). On the need for quality control in validation research. *Personnel Psychology, 41,* 497–502.

Makiney, J. D., & Levy, P. E. (1998). The influence of self-ratings versus peer ratings on supervisors' performance judgments. *Organizational Behavior and Human Decision Processes, 74,* 212–222.

Mann, R. B., & Decker, P. J. (1984). The effect of key behavior distinctiveness on generalization and recall in behavior modeling training. *Academy of Management Journal, 27,* 900–910.

Mantwill, M., Kohnken, G., & Aschermann, E. (1995). Effects of the cognitive interview on the recall of familiar and unfamiliar events. *Journal of Applied Psychology, 80,* 68–78.

Marchese, M. C., & Muchinsky, P. M. (1993). The validity of the employment interview: A meta-analysis. *International Journal of Selection and Assessment, 1,* 18–26.

Marcus, B., Goffin, R. D., Johnston, N. G., & Rothstein, M. G. (2007). Personality and cognitive ability as predictors of typical and maximum managerial performance. *Human Performance, 20,* 275–285.

Marcus, B., Schuler, H., Quell, P., & Hümpfner, G. (2002). Measuring counterproductivity: Development and initial validation of a German self-report questionnaire. *International Journal of Selection and Assessment, 10,* 18–35.

Marks, M. A., Sabella, M. J., Burke, C. S., & Zaccaro, S. J. (2002). The impact of cross-training on team effectiveness. *Journal of Applied Psychology, 87,* 3–13.

Marsh, H. W., & Hocevar, D. (1988). A new, more powerful approach to multitrait-multimethod analyses: Application of second-order confirmatory factor analysis. *Journal of Applied Psychology, 73,* 107–117.

Marshall, J., & Heffes, E. (2007, January/February). New group pushes "responsibility officer". *Financial Executive, 23*(1), 11–11.

Martell, R. F., & Borg, M. R. (1993). A comparison of the behavioral rating accuracy of groups and individuals. *Journal of Applied Psychology, 78,* 43–50.

Martell, R. F., & Leavitt, K. N. (2002). Reducing the performance-cue bias in work behavior ratings: Can groups help? *Journal of Applied Psychology, 87,* 1032–1041.

Martin, D. C., & Bartol, K. M. (1991). The legal ramifications of performance appraisal: An update. *Employee Relations Law Journal, 17*(2), 257–286.

Martin, C. L., & Nagao, D. H. (1989). Some effects of computerized interviewing on job applicant responses. *Journal of Applied Psychology, 74,* 72–80.

Martin, S. L., & Raju, N. S. (1992). Determining cutoff scores that optimize utility: A recognition of recruiting costs. *Journal of Applied Psychology, 77,* 15–23.

Martocchio, J. J. (1992). Microcomputer usage as an opportunity: The influence of context in employee training. *Personnel Psychology, 45,* 529–552.

Martocchio, J. J., & Dulebohn, J. (1994). Performance feedback effects in training: The role of perceived controllability. *Personnel Psychology, 47,* 358–373.

Martocchio, J. J., Harrison, D. A., & Berkson, H. (2000). Connections between lower back pain, interventions, and absence from work: A time-based meta-analysis. *Personnel Psychology, 53,* 595–624.

Martocchio, J. J., & Judge, T. A. (1997). Relationship between conscientiousness and learning in employee training: Mediating influences of self-deception and self-efficacy. *Journal of Applied Psychology, 82,* 764–773.

Martocchio, J. J., & Webster, J. (1992). Effects of feedback and cognitive playfulness on performance in microcomputer software training. *Personnel Psychology, 45,* 553–578.

Marx, R. D. (1982). Relapse prevention for managerial training: A model for maintenance of behavior change. *Academy of Management Review, 7,* 433–441.

Maslach, C., & Leiter, M. P. (2008). Early predictors of job burnout and engagement. *Journal of Applied Psychology, 93,* 498–512.

Masterson, S. S., Lewis, K., Goldman, B. M., Taylor, M. S. (2000). Integrating justice and social exchange: The differing effects of fair procedures and treatment on work relationships. *Academy of Management Journal, 43,* 738–748.

Mathieu, J. E., & Leonard, R. L., Jr. (1987). Applying utility concepts to a training program in supervisory skills: A time-based approach. *Academy of Management Journal, 30,* 316–335.

Mathieu, J. E., Martineau, J. W., & Tannenbaum, S. I. (1993). Individual and situational influences on the development of self-efficacy: Implications for training effectiveness. *Personnel Psychology, 46,* 125–147.

Matsui, T., Kakuyama, T., & Onglatco, M. L. U. (1987). Effects of goals and feedback on performance in groups. *Journal of Applied Psychology, 72,* 407–415.

Mattioli, D. (2009, February 10). Training, amid cutbacks. *The Wall Street Journal,* p. 17.

Mattson, B. W. (2003). The effects of alternative reports of human resource development results on managerial support. *Human Resource Development Quarterly, 14*(2), 127–151.

Maurer, S. D. (2002). A practitioner-based analysis of interviewer job expertise and scale format as contextual factors in situational interviews. *Personnel Psychology, 55,* 307–327.

Maurer, T. J., & Alexander, R. A. (1992). Methods of improving employment test critical scores derived by judging test content: A review and critique. *Personnel Psychology, 45,* 727–762.

Maurer, T. J., Alexander, R. A., Callahan, C. M., Bailey, J. J., & Dambrot, F. H. (1991). Methodological and psychometric issues in setting cutoff scores using the Angoff method. *Personnel Psychology, 44,* 235–262.

Maurer, S. D., Palmer, J. K., & Ashe, D. K. (1993). Diaries, checklists, evaluations, and contrast effects in measurement of behavior. *Journal of Applied Psychology, 78,* 226–231.

Maurer, T. J., Raju, N. S., & Collins, W. C. (1998). Peer and subordinate performance appraisal measurement equivalence. *Journal of Applied Psychology, 83,* 693–702.

Maurer, T. J., Solomon, J. M., Andrews, K. D., & Troxtel, D. D. (2001). Interviewee coaching, preparation strategies, and response strategies in relation to performance in situational employment interviews: An extension of Maurer, Solomon, and Troxtel (1998). *Journal of Applied Psychology, 86,* 709–717.

Maurer, T. J., & Solomon, J. M. (2007). The science and practice of a structured employment-interview coaching program. *Personnel Psychology, 59,* 433–456.

Maurer, T. J., Solomon, J., & Troxtel, D. (1998). Relationship of coaching with performance in situational employment interviews. *Journal of Applied Psychology, 83,* 128–136.

Maxwell, S. E., & Arvey, R. D. (1993). The search for predictors with high validity and low adverse impact: Compatible or incompatible goals? *Journal of Applied Psychology, 78,* 433–437.

May, G. L., & Kahnweiler, W. M. (2000). The effect of a mastery practice design on learning and transfer in behavior modeling training. *Personnel Psychology, 53,* 353–373.

Mayer, J. D. (2005). A tale of two visions: Can a new view of personality help integrate psychology? *American Psychologist, 60,* 294–307.

Mayer, R. C., & Davis, J. H. (1999). The effect of the performance appraisal system on trust for management: A field quasi-experiment. *Journal of Applied Psychology, 84,* 123–136.

Mayfield, E. C. (1970). Management selection: Buddy nominations revisited. *Personnel Psychology, 23,* 377–391.

Mayfield, E. C. (1972). Value of peer nominations in predicting life insurance sales performance. *Journal of Applied Psychology, 56,* 319–323.

McBride, S. (2003, August 7). In corporate Asia, a looming crisis over succession. *The Wall Street Journal,* pp. A1, A6.

McCarthy, J., & Goffin, R. (2004). Measuring job interview anxiety: Beyond weak knees and sweaty palms. *Personnel Psychology, 57,* 607–637.

McCall, M. W., Jr., Lombardo, M., & Morrison, A. (1988). Lessons of experience. New York, NY: Lexington Books.

McCall, M. W., Jr. (2004, August). Leadership development through experience. *Academy of Management Executive, 18*(3), 127–130.

McClelland, D. C. (1975). *Power: The inner experience.* New York, NY: Irvington-Halsted-Wiley.

McClelland, D. C., & Boyatzis, R. E. (1982). Leadership motive pattern and long-term success in management. *Journal of Applied Psychology, 67,* 737–743.

McClelland, D. C., & Burnham, D. (1976, March–April). Power is the great motivator. *Harvard Business Review, 51,* pp. 159–166.

McClenahen, J. S. (1997, January 20). To go—Or not to go? *Industry Week,* pp. 33, 36.

McConnon, A. (2007, September 10). Social networking is graduating—and hitting the job market. How do the online Rolodexes stack up? *Business,* p. 49.

McCormick, E. J. (1979). *Job analysis: Methods and applications.* New York, NY: AMACON.

McCormick, E. J., & Ilgen, D. R. (1985). *Industrial and organizational psychology* (8th ed.). Englewood Cliffs, NJ: Prentice Hall.

McCormick, E. J., & Jeanneret, P. R. (1988). Position analysis questionnaire (PAQ). In S. A. Gael (Ed.), *The job analysis handbook for business, industry, and government* (Vol. 2, pp. 825–842). New York, NY: Wiley.

McCormick, E. J., Jeanneret, P. R., & Mecham, R. C. (1972). A study of job characteristics and job dimensions as based on the Position Analysis Questionnaire (PAQ). *Journal of Applied Psychology, 56,* 347–368.

McDaniel, M. A., Hartman, N. S., Whetzel, D. L., & Grubb, W. L. (2007). Situational judgment tests, responses instructions, and validity: A meta-analysis. *Personnel Psychology, 60,* 63–91.

McDaniel, M. A., Morgeson, F. P., Finnegan, E. B., Campion, M. A., & Braverman, E. P. (2001). Use of situational judgment tests to predict job performance: A clarification of the literature. *Journal of Applied Psychology, 86,* 730–740.

McDaniel, M. A., & Nguyen, N. T. (2001). Situational judgment tests: A review of practice and constructs assessed. *International Journal of Selection and Assessment, 9,* 103–113.

McDaniel, M. A., Schmidt, F. L., & Hunter, J. E. (1988). A meta-analysis of the validity of methods for rating training and experience in personnel selection. *Personnel Psychology, 41,* 283–314.

McDaniel, M. A., Whetzel, D. L., Schmidt, F. L., & Maurer, S. (1994). The validity of employment interviews: A comprehensive review and meta-analysis. *Journal of Applied Psychology, 79,* 599–616.

McDonald, T., & Hakel, M. D. (1985). Effects of applicant race, sex, suitability, and answers on interviewer's questioning strategy and ratings. *Personnel Psychology, 38,* 321–334.

McDonald v. Santa Fe Transportation Co., 427 U.S. 273 (1976).

McEvoy, G. M., & Beatty, R. W. (1989). Assessment centers and subordinate appraisals of managers: A seven-year examination of predictive validity. *Personnel Psychology, 42*, 37–52.

McEvoy, G. M., & Buller, P. F. (1987). User acceptance of peer appraisals in an industrial setting. *Personnel Psychology, 40*, 785–797.

McEvoy, G. M., & Cascio, W. F. (1985). Strategies for reducing employee turnover: A meta-analysis. *Journal of Applied Psychology, 70*, 342–353.

McEvoy, G. M., & Cascio, W. F. (1987). Do good or poor performers leave? A meta-analysis of the relationship between performance and turnover. *Academy of Management Journal, 30*, 744–762.

McEvoy, G. M., & Cascio, W. F. (1989). Cumulative evidence of the relationship between employee age and job performance. *Journal of Applied Psychology, 74*, 11–17.

McFarland, L. A., & Ryan, A. M. (2000). Variance in faking across noncognitive measures. *Journal of Applied Psychology, 85*, 812–821.

McFarland, L. A., Ryan, A. M., Sacco, J., & Kriska, S. D. (2004). Examination of structured interview ratings across time: The effects of applicant race, rater race, and panel composition. *Journal of Management, 30*, 435–452.

McGehee, W., & Thayer, P. W. (1961). *Training in business and industry.* New York, NY: Wiley.

McGregor, D. (1957). An uneasy look at performance appraisal. *Harvard Business Review, 35*(3), 89–94.

McKay, P. F., & Avery, D. R. (2006). What has race got to do with it? Unraveling the role of racio-ethnicity in job seekers' reactions to site visits. *Personnel Psychology, 59*, 395–429.

McKinnon, D. W. (1975). Assessment centers then and now. *Assessment and Development, 2*, 8–9.

McLinden, D. J. (1995). Proof, evidence, and complexity: Understanding the impact of training and development in business. *Performance Improvement Quarterly, 8*(3), 3–18.

McMorris, F. A. (1995, February 28). Is office voice mail private? Don't bet on it. *The Wall Street Journal*, p. B1.

McPhail, S. M. (Ed.). (2007). *Alternative validation strategies.* San Francisco, CA: Jossey-Bass.

Meehl, P. E. (1954). *Clinical vs. statistical prediction.* Minneapolis: University of Minnesota Press.

Meehl, P. E., & Rosen, A. (1955). Antecedent probability and the efficiency of psychometric signs, patterns, or cutting scores. *Psychological Bulletin, 52*, 194–216.

Meglino, B. M., DeNisi, A. S., Youngblood, S. A., & Williams, K. J. (1988). Effects of realistic job previews: A comparison using an enhancement and a reduction preview. *Journal of Applied Psychology, 73*, 259–266.

Mendenhall, M. E., & Oddou, G. (1995). The overseas assignment: A practical look. In M. E. Mendenhall, & G. Oddou (Eds.), *Readings and cases in international human resource management* (2nd ed., pp. 206–216). Cincinnati, OH: South-Western.

Mendoza, J. L., Bard, D. E., Mumford, M. D., & Ang, S. (2004). Criterion-related validity in multiple-hurdle designs: Estimation and bias. *Organizational Research Methods, 7*, 418–441.

Meritor Savings Bank v. Vinson, 477 U.S. 57 (1986).

Meritt-Haston, R., & Wexley, K. N. (1983). Educational requirements: Legality and validity. *Personnel Psychology, 36*, 743–753.

Mero, N. P., & Motowidlo, S. J. (1995). Effects of rater accountability on the accuracy and the favorability of performance ratings. *Journal of Applied Psychology, 80*, 517–524.

Mero, N. P., Guidice, R. M., & Brownlee, A. L. (2007). Accountability in a performance appraisal context: The effect of audience and form of accounting on rater response and behavior. *Journal of Management, 33*, 223–252.

Merriam-Webster Dictionary (2009). Available at www.merriam-webster.com.

Mersman, J. L., & Donaldson, S. I. (2000). Factors affecting the convergence of self-peer ratings on contextual and task performance. *Human Performance, 13*, 299–322.

Messick, S. (1980). Test validity and the ethics of assessment. *American Psychologist, 35*, 1012–1027.

Messick, S. (1995). Validity of psychological assessment. *American Psychologist, 50*, 741–749.

Meyer, H. H. (1987). Predicting supervisory ratings versus promotional progress in test validation studies. *Journal of Applied Psychology, 72*, 696–697.

Meyer, H. H. (1991). A solution to the performance appraisal feedback enigma. *Academy of Management Executive, 5*(1), 68–76.

Middendorf, C. H., & Macan, T. H. (2002). Note-taking in the employment interview: Effects on recall and judgments. *Journal of Applied Psychology, 87*, 293–303.

Mihalevsky, M., Olson, K. S., & Maher, P. T. (2007). *Behavioral competency dictionary.* La Puente, CA: Bassett Unified School District.

Milkovich, G. T., & Newman, J. M. (2005). *Compensation management* (8th ed.). Burr Ridge, IL: McGraw-Hill/Irwin.

Milkovich, G. T., & Newman, J. M. (2008). *Compensation management* (9th ed.). Burr Ridge, IL: McGraw-Hill/Irwin.

Miller, C. C., & Cardinal, L. B. (1994). Strategic planning and firm performance: A synthesis of more than two decades of research. *Academy of Management Journal, 37*, 1649–1665.

Miller, E. C. (1980). An EEO examination of employment applications. *Personnel Administrator, 25*(3), 63–69, 81.

Miner, J. B. (1978a). *The management process: Theory, research, and practice.* New York, NY: Macmillan.

Miner, J. B. (1978b). The Miner Sentence Completion Scale: A reappraisal. *Academy of Management Journal, 21*, 283–294.

Miner, J. B., & Crane, D. P. (1981). Motivation to manage and the manifestation of a managerial orientation in career planning. *Academy of Management Journal, 24*, 626–633.

Miner, J. B., & Smith, N. R. (1982). Decline and stabilization of managerial motivation over a 20-year period. *Journal of Applied Psychology, 67*, 297–305.

Miner, J. B., Smith, N. R., & Bracker, J. S. (1994). Role of entrepreneurial task motivation in the growth of technologically innovative firms: Interpretations from follow-up data. *Journal of Applied Psychology, 79*, 627–630.

Mirvis, P. H., & Seashore, S. E. (1979). Being ethical in organizational research. *American Psychologist, 34,* 766–780.

Mitchell, T. W. (1994). *Catalog of biodata items.* San Diego, CA: MPORT.

Mitchell, T. R., Harman, W. S., Lee, T. W., & Lee, D. Y. (2009). Self-regulation and multiple deadline goals. In R. Kanfer, G. Chen, & R. D. Pritchard (Eds.), *Work motivation: Past, present, and future* (pp. 199–232). Mahwah, NJ: CRC Press, for the society for Industrial and Organizational Psychology.

Mitchell, M. L., & Jolley, J. M. (2010). *Research design explained* (7th ed.). Belmont, CA: Wadsworth.

Mitsch, R. J. (1983). Ensuring privacy and accuracy of computerized employee records. *Personnel Administrator, 28*(9), 37–41.

Moir, L. (2007, Autumn). Measuring the business benefits of corporate responsibility. *Management Services, 51*(3), 46–47.

Moir, L., Kennerley, M., & Ferguson, D. (2007). Measuring the business case: Linking stakeholder and shareholder value. *Corporate Governance, 7,* 388–400.

Mook, J. (2007, January). Accommodation paradigm shifts. *HRMagazine,* pp. 115–120.

More normal nonsense. (1989, July 17). *Fortune,* p. 118.

Morgan, J. P. (1989, August 20). Employee drug tests are unreliable and intrusive. *Hospitals,* p. 42.

Morgan, R. B., & Casper, W. (2001). Examining the factor structure of participant reactions to training: A multi-dimensional approach. *Human Resource Development Quarterly, 11,* 301–317.

Morgeson, F. P., & Campion, M. A. (1997). Social and cognitive sources of potential inaccuracy in job analysis. *Journal of Applied Psychology, 82,* 627–655.

Morgeson, F. P., Campion, M. A., Dipboye, R. L., Hollenbeck, J. R., Murphy, K., & Schmitt, N. (2007). Are we getting fooled again? Coming to terms with limitations in the use of personality tests in personnel selection. *Personnel Psychology, 60,* 1029–1049.

Morgeson, F. P., Delaney-Klinger, K. A., Mayfield, M. S., Ferrara, P., & Campion, M. A. (2004). Self-presentation processes in job analysis: A field experiment investigating inflation in abilities, tasks, and competencies. *Journal of Applied Psychology, 89,* 674–686.

Morris, B. (2000, October 16). Can Michael Dell escape the box? *Fortune,* pp. 92–110.

Morris, S. B., & Lobsenz, R. (2000). Significance tests and confidence intervals for the adverse impact ratio. *Personnel Psychology, 53,* 89–111.

Morris, M. A., & Robie, C. (2001). A meta-analysis of the effects of cross-cultural training on expatriate performance and adjustment. *International Journal of Training and Development, 5,* 112–125.

Morrow, C. C., Jarrett, M. Q., & Rupinski, M. T. (1997). An investigation of the effect and economic utility of corporate-wide training. *Personnel Psychology, 50,* 91–119.

Moscoso, S. (2000). A review of validity evidence, adverse impact and applicant reactions. *International Journal of Selection and Assessment, 8,* 237–247.

Mossholder, K. W., & Arvey, R. D. (1984). Synthetic validity: A conceptual and comparative review. *Journal of Applied Psychology, 69,* 322–333.

Motowidlo, S. J., Carter, G. W., Dunnette, M. D., Tippins, N., Werner, S., Burnett, J. R., & Vaughn, M. J. (1992). Studies of the structured behavioral interview. *Journal of Applied Psychology, 77,* 571–587.

Mount, M. K., Witt, L. A, & Barrick, M. R. (2000). Incremental validity of empirically keyed biodata scales over GMA and the five factor personality constructs. *Personnel Psychology, 53,* 299–323.

Mowday, R. T., Porter, L. W., & Steers, R. M. (1982). *Employee-organization linkages: The psychology of commitment, absenteeism, and turnover.* San Diego, CA: Academic Press.

Moyer, D. (2009, January). Is experience enough? *Harvard Business Review, 87*(1), p. 120.

Mueller-Hanson, R., Heggestad, E. D., & Thornton, G. C. (2003). Faking and selection: Considering the use of personality from select-in and select-out perspectives. *Journal of Applied Psychology, 88,* 348–355.

Muir, C. (2005). Managing the initial job interview: Smile, schmooze, and get hired? *Academy of Management Executive, 19,* 156–158.

Mullins, W. C., & Kimbrough, W. W. (1988). Group composition as a determinant of job analysis outcomes. *Journal of Applied Psychology, 73,* 657–664.

Mullins, C., & Ratliff, F. R. (1979, March). *Application of a generalized development curve to problems in human assessment.* Paper presented at the U.S. Air Force Human Resources Laboratory Conference on Human Assessment, Brooks Air Force Base, TX.

Mumford, M. D. (1983). Social comparison theory and the evaluation of peer evaluations: A review and some applied implications. *Personnel Psychology, 36,* 867–881.

Mumford, M. D., Connelly, M. S., Helton, W. B., Strange, J. M., & Osburn, H. K. (2001). On the construct validity of integrity tests: Individual and situational factors as predictors of test performance. *International Journal of Selection and Assessment, 9,* 240–257.

Mumford, M. D., & Owens, W. A. (1987). Methodology review: Principles, procedures, and findings in the application of background data measures. *Applied Psychological Measurement, 11,* 1–31.

Mumford, M. D., & Stokes, G. S. (1992). Developmental determinants of individual action: Theory and practice in applying background measures. In M. D. Dunnette, & L. M. Hough (Eds.), *Handbook of industrial and organizational psychology* (2nd ed., Vol. 3, pp. 61–138). Palo Alto, CA: Consulting Psychologists Press.

Murphy, K. R. (1986). When your top choice turns you down: Effect of rejected offers on the utility of selection tests. *Psychological Bulletin, 99,* 133–138.

Murphy, K. R. (1987). Detecting infrequent deception. *Journal of Applied Psychology, 72,* 611–614.

Murphy, K. R. (2000). Impact of assessments of validity generalization and situational specificity on the science and practices of personnel selection. *International Journal of Selection and Assessment, 8,* 194–206.

Murphy, K. R. (2002). Can conflicting perspectives on the role of g in personnel selection be resolved? *Human Performance, 15,* 173–186.

Murphy, K. R. (2003). The logic of validity generalization. In K. R. Murphy (Ed.), *Validity generalization: A critical review* (pp. 1–29). Mahwah, NJ: Lawrence Erlbaum.

Murphy, K. R. (2004). Conflicting values and interests in banding research and practice. In H. Aguinis (Ed.), *Test score banding in human resource selection: Legal, technical, and societal issues* (pp. 175–192). Westport, CT: Praeger.

Murphy, K. R., & Balzer, W. K. (1989). Rater errors and rating accuracy. *Journal of Applied Psychology, 74,* 619–624.

Murphy, K. R., & Cleveland, J. N. (1995). *Understanding performance appraisal: Social, organizational, and goal-based perspectives.* Thousand Oaks, CA: Sage.

Murphy, K. R., & Constans, J. I. (1987). Behavioral anchors as a source of bias in ratings. *Journal of Applied Psychology, 72,* 573–577.

Murphy, K. R., Cronin, B. E., & Tam, A. P. (2003). Controversy and consensus regarding the use of cognitive ability testing in organizations. *Journal of Applied Psychology, 88,* 660–671.

Murphy, K. R., & DeShon, R. (2000a). Interrater correlations do not estimate the reliability of job performance ratings. *Personnel Psychology, 53,* 873–900.

Murphy, K. R., & DeShon, R. (2000b). Progress in psychometrics: Can industrial and organizational psychology catch up? *Personnel Psychology, 53,* 913–924.

Murphy, K. R., & Dzieweczynski, J. L. (2005). Why don't measures of broad dimensions of personality perform better as predictors of job performance? *Human Performance, 18,* 343–357.

Murphy, K. R., Jako, R. A., & Anhalt, R. L. (1993). Nature and consequences of halo error: A critical analysis. *Journal of Applied Psychology, 78,* 218–225.

Murphy, K. R., & Myors, B. (2003). *Statistical power analysis* (2nd ed.). Mahwah, NJ: Lawrence Erlbaum.

Murphy, K. R., & Pardaffy, V. A. (1989). Bias in behaviorally anchored rating scales: Global or scale-specific? *Journal of Applied Psychology, 74,* 343–346.

Murphy, K. R., & Shiarella, A. H. (1997). Implications of the multidimensional nature of job performance for the validity of selection tests: Multivariate frameworks for studying test validity. *Personnel Psychology, 50,* 823–854.

Murphy, K. R., Thornton, G. C., III, & Prue, K. (1991). Influence of job characteristics on the acceptability of employee drug testing. *Journal of Applied Psychology, 76,* 447–453.

Nagle, B. F. (1953). Criterion development. *Personnel Psychology, 6,* 271–288.

Nakache, P. (1997, September 29). Cisco's recruiting edge. *Fortune,* pp. 275, 276.

Nam, I., Mengersen, K., & Garthwaite, P. (2003). Multivariate meta-analysis. *Statistics in Medicine, 22,* 2309–2333.

Napier, N. K., & Taylor, S. (2002). Experiences of women professionals abroad: Comparisons across Japan, China, and Turkey.

International Journal of Human Resource Management, 13, 837–851.

Naquin, C. E., & Tynan, R. O. (2003). The team halo effect: Why teams are not blamed for their failures. *Journal of Applied Psychology, 88,* 332–340.

Nathan, B. R., & Cascio, W. F. (1986). Technical and legal standards for performance assessment. In R. A. Berk (Ed.), *Performance management* (pp. 1–50). Baltimore: Johns Hopkins University Press.

Naylor, J. C., & Shine, L. C. (1965). A table for determining the increase in mean criterion score obtained by using a selection device. *Journal of Industrial Psychology, 3,* 33–42.

Needed: Leadership. (2003, October 20). *Business Week,* p. 92.

Nesler, M. S., Aguinis, H., Quigley, B. M., Lee, S., & Tedeschi, J. T. (1999). The development and validation of a scale measuring global social power based on French and Raven's (1959) power taxonomy. *Journal of Applied Social Psychology, 29,* 750–771.

Neuman, G. A., & Wright, J. (1999). Team effectiveness: Beyond skills and cognitive ability. *Journal of Applied Psychology, 84,* 376–389.

Newstrom, J. W. (1978). Catch 22: The problems of incomplete evaluation of training. *Training and Development Journal, 32,* 22–24.

Newman, D. A., Jacobs, R. R., & Bartram, D. (2007). Choosing the best method for local validity estimation: Relative accuracy of meta-analysis versus a local Study versus Bayes-analysis. *Journal of Applied Psychology, 92,* 1394–1413.

Nicholas, J. M. (1982). The comparative impact of organization development on hard criteria measures. *Academy of Management Review, 7,* 531–542.

Nicholas, J. M., & Katz, M. (1985). Research methods and reporting practices in organization development: A review and some guidelines. *Academy of Management Review, 10,* 737–749.

Nikolaou, I., & Judge, T. A. (2007). Fairness reactions to personnel selection techniques in Greece: The role of core self-evaluations. *International Journal of Selection and Assessment, 15,* 206–219.

Nobile, R. J. (1985). Employee searches in the workplace: Developing a realistic policy. *Personnel Administrator, 30*(5), 89–98.

Noe, R. A. (1986). Trainees' attributes and attitudes: Neglected influences on training effectiveness. *Academy of Management Review, 11,* 736–749.

Noe, R. A. (2008). *Employee training and development* (4th ed.). Burr Ridge, IL: McGraw-Hill.

Noe, R. A., & Colquitt, J. A. (2002). Planning for training impact: Principles of training effectiveness. In K. Kraiger (Ed.), *Creating, implementing, and managing effective training and development* (pp. 53–79). San Francisco, CA: Jossey-Bass.

Noe, R. A., & Wilk, S. L. (1993). Investigation of the factors that influence employees' participation in development activities. *Journal of Applied Psychology, 78,* 291–302.

Noonan, L. E., & Sulsky, L. M. (2001). Impact of frame-of-reference and behavioral observation training on alternative training effectiveness criteria in a Canadian military sample. *Human Performance, 14,* 3–26.

Northrop, L. C. (1989). *The psychometric history of selected ability constructs.* Washington, DC: U.S. Office of Personnel Management.

Nunnally, J. C., & Bernstein, I. H. (1994). *Psychometric theory* (3rd ed.). New York, NY: McGraw-Hill.

Obdyke, L. K. (2002). *Searches and surveillance in today's workplace.* Alexandria, VA: Society for Human Resource Management.

O'Brien, J. M. (2009, February 2). Zappos knows how to kick it. *Fortune,* pp. 54–60.

O'Connell, M. S., Hartman, N. S., McDaniel, M. A., Grubb, W. L., & Lawrence, A. (2007). Incremental validity of situational judgment tests for task and contextual job performance. *International Journal of Selection and Assessment, 15,* 19–29.

Oddou, G., & Mendenhall, M. E. (2000). Expatriate performance appraisal: Problems and solutions. In M. E. Mendenhall, & G. Oddou (Eds.), *Readings and cases in international human resource management* (3rd ed., pp. 213–223). Cincinnati, OH: South-Western.

Office of Strategic Services (OSS) Assessment Staff. (1948). *Assessment of men.* New York, NY: Rinehart.

Officers for Justice v. Civil Service Commission of the City and County of San Francisco, 979 F. 2d 721 (9th Cir.), cert. denied, 61 U.S.L.W. 3667, 113 S. Ct. 1645 (1993, March 29).

Ogden, D., & Wood, J. (2008, March 25). Succession planning: A Board imperative. Retrieved April 28, 2008, from www.businessweek.com.

Olson-Buchanan, J. B. (2002). Computer-based advances in assessment. In F. Drasgow, & N. Schmitt (Eds.), *Measuring and analyzing behavior in organizations* (pp. 44–87). San Francisco, CA: Jossey-Bass.

Olson-Buchanan, J. B., Drasgow, F., Moberg, P. J., Mead, A. D., Keenan, P. A., & Donovan, M. A. (1998). Interactive video assessment of conflict resolution skills. *Personnel Psychology, 51,* 1–24.

Ones, D. S., Dilchert, S., Viswesvaran, C., & Judge, T. A. (2007). In support of personality assessment in organizational settings. *Personnel Psychology, 60,* 995–1027.

Ones, D. S., & Viswesvaran, C. (1998). Gender, age, and race differences on overt integrity tests: Results across four large-scale job applicant datasets. *Journal of Applied Psychology, 83,* 35–42.

Ones, D. S., & Viswesvaran, C. (2007). A research note on the incremental validity of job knowledge and integrity tests for predicting maximal performance. *Human Performance, 20,* 293–303.

Ones, D. S., Viswesvaran, C., & Schmidt, F. L. (1993). Comprehensive meta-analysis of integrity test validities: Findings and implications for personnel selection and theories of job performance. *Journal of Applied Psychology, 78,* 679–703.

Online technologies and their impact on recruitment strategies. (2008, September). Alexandria, VA: Society for Human Resource Management.

Oppler, S. H., Campbell, J. P., Pulakos, E. D., & Borman, W. C. (1992). Three approaches to the investigation of subgroup bias in performance measurement: Review, results, and conclusions. *Journal of Applied Psychology, 77,* 201–217.

O'Brien, K. E., & Allen, T. D. (2008). The relative importance of correlates of organizational citizenship behavior and counterproductive work behavior using multiple sources of data. *Human Performance, 21,* 62–88.

Ordóñez, L. D., Schweitzer, M. E., Galinsky, A. D., & Bazerman, M. H. (2009). Goals gone wild: the systematic side effects of overprescribing goal setting. *Academy of Management Perspectives, 23*(1), 4–16.

O'Reilly, B. (2000, February 7). They've got mail! *Fortune,* pp. 101–112.

O'Reilly, C. A., & Pfeffer, J. (2000). *Hidden value: How great companies achieve extraordinary results with ordinary people.* Boston, MA: Harvard Business School Press.

Orlitzky, M. (2001). Does firm size confound the relationship between corporate social performance and firm financial performance? *Journal of Business Ethics, 33,* 167–180.

Orlitzky, M., Schmidt, F. L., & Rynes, S. L. (2003). Corporate social and financial performance: A meta-analysis. *Organization Studies, 24,* 403–441.

Orr, J. M., Sackett, P. R., & Mercer, M. (1989). The role of prescribed and nonprescribed behaviors in estimating the dollar value of performance. *Journal of Applied Psychology, 74,* 34–40.

Ostroff, C. (1991). Training effectiveness measures and scoring schemes: A comparison. *Personnel Psychology, 44,* 353–374.

Osterman, P. (2009). The truth about middle managers. Boston, MA: Harvard Business School Press.

Oswald, F. L., Saad, S., & Sackett, P. R. (2000). The homogeneity assumption in differential prediction analysis: Does it really matter? *Journal of Applied Psychology, 85,* 536–541.

Oswald, F. L., Friede, A. J., Schmitt, N., Kim, B. K., & Ramsay, L. J. (2005). Extending a practical method for developing alternate test forms using independent sets of items. *Organizational Research Methods, 8,* 149–164.

Outtz, J. L. (2002). The role of cognitive ability tests in employment selection. *Human Performance, 15,* 161–171.

Overman, S. (2008, April). The CEO as recruiter. *HRMagazine,* pp. 81–84.

Overton, R. C., Harms, H. J., Taylor, L. R., & Zickar, M. J. (1997). Adapting to adaptive testing. *Personnel Psychology, 50,* 171–185.

Owens, W. A. (1976). Background data. In M. D. Dunnette (Ed.), *Handbook of industrial and organizational psychology.* Chicago, IL: Rand McNally.

Oyserman, D., Coon, H., & Kemelmeier, M. (2002). Rethinking individualism and collectivism: Evaluation of theoretical assumptions and meta-analyses. *Psychological Bulletin, 128,* 3–72.

Paauwe, J., Williams, R., & Keegan, A. (2002). *The importance of the human resource management function in organizational change* (Working Paper). Rotterdam, The Netherlands: Department of Business and Organization, Rotterdam School of Economics, Erasmus University.

Paradise, A. (2007). *State of the industry: ASTD's annual review of trends in workplace learning and performance.* Alexandria, VA: ASTD.

Parloff, R. (2007, October 15). The war over unconscious bias. *Fortune,* pp. 90–102.

Parsons v. Pioneer Hi-Bred Int'l Inc., 8th Cir., No. 05–3496 (2006, May 19).

Parsons, C. K., & Liden, R. C. (1984). Interviewer perceptions of applicant qualifications: A multivariate field study of demographic characteristics and nonverbal cues. *Journal of Applied Psychology, 69,* 557–568.

Payne, S. C, Culbertson, S., & Boswell, W. R. (2008). Newcomer psychological contracts and employee socialization activities: Does perceived balance in obligations matter? *Journal of Vocational Behavior, 73,* 465–472.

Pearce, J. A., II, & R. B. Robinson, Jr. (2009). *Strategic management: Strategy formulation, implementation, and control* (11th ed.), Chicago, IL: Irwin.

Pearlman, K. (1980). Job families: A review and discussion of their implications for personnel selection. *Psychological Bulletin, 87,* 1–28.

Pearlman, K., & Barney, M. F. (2000). Selection for a changing workplace. In J. F. Kehoe (Ed.), *Managing selection in changing organizations* (pp. 3–72). San Francisco, CA: Jossey-Bass.

Peikes, L., & Mitchell, C. M. (2006, August). 2nd Circuit: Employee working abroad has no remedy for extraterritorial discriminatory conduct. *HR News,* p. 1.

Peiperl, M., & Jonsen, K. (2007). Global careers. In H. Gunz, & M. Peiperl (Eds.), *Handbook of career studies* (pp. 350–372). Thousand Oaks, CA: Sage.

Pennsylvania State Police v. Suders. (2004). 93 Fair Employment Practices Cases (BNA) 1473.

Personnel Administrator of Mass. v. Feeney, 442 U.S. 256 (1979).

Peters, C. C., & van Voorhis, W. R. (1940). *Statistical procedures and their mathematical bases.* New York, NY: McGraw-Hill.

Peterson, N. G., Mumford, M. D., Borman, W. C., Jeanneret, P. R., & Fleishman, E. A. (Eds.). (1999). *An occupational information system for the 21st century: The development of O*Net.* Washington, DC: American Psychological Association.

Peterson, N. G., Mumford, M. D., Borman, W. C., Jeanneret, P. R., Fleishman, E. A., Levin, K. Y., Campion, M. A., Mayfield, M. S., Morgeson, F. P., Pearlman, K., Gowing, M. K., Lancaster, A. R., Silver, M. B., & Dye, D. M. (2001). Understanding work using the Occupational Information Network (O*Net): Implications for practice and research. *Personnel Psychology, 54,* 451–492.

Petty, M. M. (1974). A multivariate analysis of the effects of experience and training upon performance in a leaderless group discussion. *Personnel Psychology, 27,* 271–282.

Pfeffer, J., & Sutton, R. I. (2000). *The knowing-doing gap: How smart companies turn knowledge into action.* Boston, MA: Harvard Business School Press.

Phillips, J. M. (1998). Effects of realistic job previews on multiple organizational outcomes: A meta-analysis. *Academy of Management Journal, 41,* 673–690.

Phillips, J. M., & Gully, S. M. (1997). Role of goal orientation, ability, need for achievement, and locus of control in the self-efficacy and goal-setting process. *Journal of Applied Psychology, 82,* 792–802.

Pidd, K. (2004). The impact of workplace support and identity on training transfer: A case study of drug and alcohol safety training in Australia. *International Journal of Training and Development, 8,* 274–288.

Piekkari, R. (2006). Language effects in multinational corporations: A review from an international human resource management perspective. In G. K. Stahl, & I. Björkman (Eds.), *Handbook of research in international human resource management* (pp. 536–550). Cheltenham, UK: Edward Elgar.

Pierce, C. A., & Aguinis, H. (1997). Using virtual reality technology in organizational behavior research. *Journal of Organizational Behavior, 18,* 407–410.

Pierce, C. A., & Aguinis, H. (2001). A framework for investigating the link between workplace romance and sexual harassment. *Group and Organization Management, 26*(2), 206–229.

Pierce, C. A., & Aguinis, H. (2005). Legal standards, ethical standards, and responses to social-sexual conduct at work. *Journal of Organizational Behavior, 26,* 727–732.

Pierce, C. A., & Aguinis, H. (2009). Moving beyond a legal-centric approach to managing workplace romances: Organizationally sensible recommendations for HR leaders. *Human Resource Management, 48,* 447–464.

Pierce, C. A., Aguinis, H., & Adams, S. K. R. (2000). Effects of a dissolved workplace romance and rater characteristics on responses to a sexual harassment accusation. *Academy of Management Journal, 43,* 869–880.

Pierce, C. A., Broberg, B. J., McClure, J. R., & Aguinis, H. (2004). Responding to sexual harassment complaints: Effects of a dissolved workplace romance on decision-making standards. *Organizational Behavior & Human Decision Processes, 95,* 66–82.

Piller, C. (1993a, July). Bosses with X-ray eyes. *Macworld,* pp. 118–123.

Piller, C. (1993b, July). Privacy in peril. *Macworld,* pp. 124–130.

Pingitore, R., Dugoni, B. L., Tindale, R. S., & Spring, B. (1994). Bias against overweight job applicants in a simulated employment interview. *Journal of Applied Psychology, 79,* 909–917.

Ployhart, R. E. (2006). Staffing in the 21st century: New challenges and strategic opportunities. *Journal of Management, 32,* 868–897.

Ployhart, R. E., & Ehrhart, M. G. (2002). Modeling the practical effects of applicant reactions: Subgroup differences in test-taking motivation, test performance, and selection rates. *International Journal of Selection and Assessment, 10,* 258–270.

Ployhart, R. E., & Holz, B. C. (2008). The diversity-validity dilemma: Strategies for reducing racioethnic and sex subgroup differences and adverse impact in selection. *Personnel Psychology, 61,* 153–172.

Ployhart, R. E., Lim, B., & Chan, K. (2001). Exploring relations between typical and maximum performance ratings and the five factor model of personality. *Personnel Psychology, 54,* 809–843.

Ployhart, R. E., Weekley, J. A., Holtz, B. C., & Kemp, C. (2003). Web-based and paper-and-pencil testing of applicants in a proctored setting: Are personality, biodata, and situational judgment tests comparable? *Personnel Psychology, 56,* 733–752.

Ployhart, R. E., Schneider, B., & Schmitt, N. (2006). *Staffing organizations: Contemporary practice and theory* (3rd ed.). Mahwah, NJ: Lawrence Erlbaum.

Plumlee, L. B. (1980, February). *A short guide to the development of work sample and performance tests* (2nd ed.). Washington, DC: U.S. Office of Personnel Management, Personnel Research and Development Center.

Podsakoff, P. M., & MacKenzie, S. B. (1994). An examination of the psychometric properties and nomological validities of some revised and reduced substitutes for leadership scales. *Journal of Applied Psychology, 79,* 702–713.

Podsakoff, P. M., MacKenzie, S. B., Lee, J-Y., & Podsakoff, N. P. (2003). Common method biases in behavioral research: A critical review of the literature and recommended remedies. *Journal of Applied Psychology, 88,* 879–903.

Posthuma, R. A, Morgeson, F. P., & Campion, M. A. (2002). Beyond employment interview validity: A comprehensive narrative review of recent research and trends over time. *Personnel Psychology, 55,* 1–81.

Postovit, B. (2002, January 14). *Monsanto's integrated expatriation and repatriation policy.* Presentation to class in University of Colorado Executive MBA Program.

Potosky, D., Bobko, P., & Roth, P. L. (2005). Forming composites of cognitive ability and alternative measures to predict job performance and reduce adverse impact: Corrected estimates and realistic expectations. *International Journal of Selection and Assessment, 13,* 304–315.

Potosky, D., Bobko, P., & Roth, P. L. (2008). Some comments on Pareto thinking, test validity, and adverse impact: When "and" is optimal and "or" is a trade-off. *International Journal of Selection and Assessment, 16,* 201–205.

Powell, G. N. (1991). Applicant reactions to the initial employment interview: Exploring theoretical and methodological issues. *Personnel Psychology, 44,* 67–83.

Power & Precision: A computer program for statistical power analysis and confidence intervals. (2000). Englewood, NJ: Biostat.

Prahalad, C. K., & Hamel, G. (1994). *Competing for the future.* Boston, MA: Harvard Business School Press.

Premack, S. L., & Wanous, J. P. (1985). A meta-analysis of realistic job preview experiments. *Journal of Applied Psychology, 70,* 706–719.

Prengaman, P. (2003, August 21). Language barrier a peril on fire lines. *Denver Post,* p. 16A.

Pregnancy discrimination. (2009). Downloaded March 27, 2009, from www.eeoc.gov/types/pregnancy.html on.

Pritchard, R. D., Jones, S. D., Roth, P. L., Stuebing, K. K., & Ekeberg, S. E. (1988). Effects of group feedback, goal setting, and incentive on organizational productivity. *Journal of Applied Psychology, 73,* 337–358.

Probst, T., Brubaker, T., & Barsotti, A. (2008). Organizational injury rate underreporting: The moderating effect of organizational safety climate. *Journal of Applied Psychology, 93,* 1147–1154.

Proskauer Rose LLP. (2002, October). Supreme Court clarifies employer liability for supervisor sex harassment. Accessed August 22, 2003, at www.shrm.org.

Pulakos, E. D. (1984). A comparison of rater training programs: Error training and accuracy training. *Journal of Applied Psychology, 69,* 581–588.

Pulakos, E. D. (1986). The development of training programs to increase accuracy with different rating tasks. *Organizational Behavior and Human Decision Processes, 38,* 76–91.

Pulakos, E. D., Arad, S., Donovan, M. A., & Plamondon, K. E. (2000). Adaptability in the workplace: Development of a taxonomy of adaptive performance. *Journal of Applied Psychology, 85,* 612–624.

Pulakos, E. D., Borman, W. C., & Hough, L. M. (1988). Test validation for scientific understanding: Two demonstrations of an approach to studying predictor-criterion linkages. *Personnel Psychology, 41,* 703–716.

Pulakos, E. D., & Schmitt, N. (1995). Experience-based and situational interview questions: Studies of validity. *Personnel Psychology, 48,* 289–308.

Putka, D. J., Le, H., McCloy, R. A., & Diaz, T. (2008). Ill-structured measurement designs in organizational research: Implications for estimating interrater reliability. *Journal of Applied Psychology, 93,* 959–981.

Pyburn, K. M., Jr., Ployhart, R. E., & Kravitz, D. A. (2008). The diversity-validity dilemma: Overview and legal context. *Personnel Psychology, 61,* 143–151.

Quiñones, M. A. (1995). Pretraining context effects: Training assignment as feedback. *Journal of Applied Psychology, 80,* 226–238.

Quiñones, M. A. (1997). Contextual influences on training effectiveness. In M. A. Quiñones, & A. Ehrenstein (Eds.), *Training for a rapidly changing workplace* (pp. 177–200). Washington, DC: American Psychological Association.

Rafaeli, A., Hadomi, O., & Simons, T. (2005). Recruiting through advertising or employee referrals: Costs, yields, and the effects of geographic focus. *European Journal of Work and Organizational Psychology, 14,* 355–366.

Raju, N. S., Bilgic, R., Edwards, J. E., & Fleer, P. F. (1997). Methodology review: Estimation of population validity and cross-validity, and the use of equal weights in prediction. *Applied Psychological Measurement, 21,* 291–305.

Raju, N. S., Bilgic, R., Edwards, J. E., & Fleer, P. F. (1999). Accuracy of population validity and cross-validity estimation: An empirical comparison of formula-based, traditional empirical, and equal weight procedures. *Applied Psychological Measurement, 23,* 99–115.

Raju, N. S., & Brand, P. A. (2003). Determining the significance of correlations corrected for unreliability and range restriction. *Applied Psychological Measurement, 27,* 52–71.

Raju, N. S., Burke, M. J., & Maurer, T. J. (1995). A note on direct range restriction corrections in utility analysis. *Personnel Psychology, 48,* 143–149.

Raju, N. S., Burke, M. J., & Normand, J. (1990). A new approach for utility analysis. *Journal of Applied Psychology, 75,* 3–12.

Raju, N. S., & Drasgow, F. (2003). Maximum likelihood estimation in validity generalization. In K. R. Murphy (Ed.), *Validity generalization: A critical review* (pp. 263–285). Mahwah, NJ: Lawrence Erlbaum.

Raju, N. S., Pappas, S., & Williams, C. P. (1989). An empirical Monte Carlo test of the accuracy of the correlation, covariance, and regression slope models for assessing validity generalization. *Journal of Applied Psychology, 74*, 901–911.

Rambo, W. W., Chomiak, A. M., & Price, J. M. (1983). Consistency of performance under stable conditions of work. *Journal of Applied Psychology, 68*, 78–87.

Rasmussen, K. G., Jr. (1984). Nonverbal behavior, verbal behavior, resume credentials, and selection interview outcomes. *Journal of Applied Psychology, 69*, 551–556.

Rau, B. L., & Adams, G. A. (2005). Attracting retirees to apply: Desired organizational characteristics of bridge employment. *Journal of Organizational Behavior, 26*, 649–660.

Rauschenberger, J. M., & Schmidt, F. L. (1987). Measuring the economic impact of human resource programs. *Journal of Business and Psychology, 2*, 50–59.

Raymark, P. H., Balzer, W. K., & De La Torre, F. (1999). A preliminary investigation of the sources of information used by raters when appraising performance. *Journal of Business and Psychology, 14*, 317–337.

Raymark, P. H., Schmit, M. J., & Guion, R. M. (1997). Identifying potentially useful personality constructs for employee selection. *Personnel Psychology, 50*, 723–736.

Reber, R. A., & Wallin, J. A. (1984). The effects of training, goal setting, and knowledge of results on safe behavior: A component analysis. *Academy of Management Journal, 27*, 544–560.

Reb, J., & Cropanzano, R. (2007). Evaluating dynamic performance: The influence of salient gestalt characteristics on performance ratings. *Journal of Applied Psychology, 92*, 490–499.

Ree, M. J., & Carretta, T. R. (1998). Computerized testing in the United States Air Force. *International Journal of Selection and Assessment, 6*, 82–89.

Ree, M. J., & Carretta, T. R. (2002). g2K. *Human Performance, 15*, 3–23.

Ree, M. J., & Carretta, T. R. (2006). The role of measurement error in familiar statistics. *Organizational Research Methods, 9*, 99–112.

Ree, M. J., Carretta, T. R., & Earles, J. A. (1999). In validation sometimes two sexes are one too many: A tutorial. *Human Performance, 12*, 79–88.

Ree, M. J., Carretta, T. R., Earles, J. A., & Albert, W. (1994). Sign changes when correcting for range restriction: A note on Pearson's and Lawley's selection formulas. *Journal of Applied Psychology, 79*, 298–301.

Ree, M. J., & Earles, J. A. (1991). Predicting training success: Not much more than g. *Personnel Psychology, 44*, 321–332.

Reese, H. W., & Fremouw, W. J. (1984). Normal and normative ethics in behavioral sciences. *American Psychologist, 39*, 863–876.

Reilly, R. R., & Chao, G. T. (1982). Validity and fairness of some alternative employee selection procedures. *Personnel Psychology, 35*, 1–62.

Reilly, R. R., & Manese, W. R. (1979). The validation of a minicourse for telephone company switching technicians. *Personnel Psychology, 32*, 83–90.

Reilly, R. R., & McGourty, J. (1998). Performance appraisal in team settings. In J. W. Smither (Ed.), *Performance appraisal: State of the art in practice* (pp. 244–277). San Francisco, CA: Jossey-Bass.

Reilly, R. R., Zedeck, S., & Tenopyr, M. L. (1979). Validity and fairness of physical ability tests for predicting performance in craft jobs. *Journal of Applied Psychology, 64*, 262–274.

Reingold, J. (2009, January 22). Jim Collins: How great companies turn crisis into opportunity. Downloaded April 13, 2009, from http://money.cnn.com/2009/01/15/news/companies/Jim_Collins_Crisis.fortune/index.htm on.

Rich, L. L. (1995). Right to privacy in the workplace in the information age. *Colorado Lawyer, 24*(3), 539–540.

Richards, S. A., & Jaffee, C. L. (1972). Blacks supervising whites: A study of inter-racial difficulties in working together in a simulated organization. *Journal of Applied Psychology, 56*, 234–240.

Richman, W. L., Kiesler, S., Weisband, S., & Drasgow, F. (1999). A meta-analytic study of social desirability distortion in computer-administered questionnaires, traditional questionnaires, and interviews. *Journal of Applied Psychology, 84*, 754–775.

Ricks, J. R., Jr. (1971). *Local norms: When and why* (Test Service Bulletin No. 58). New York, NY: Psychological Corporation.

Riggio, R. (2008). *Introduction to industrial and organizational psychology* (5th ed.). Upper Saddle River, NJ: Prentice Hall.

Riordan, C. M., & Vandenberg, R. J. (1994). A central question in cross-cultural research: Do employees of different cultures interpret work-related measures in an equivalent manner? *Journal of Management, 20*, 643–671.

Ritchie, R. J., & Moses, J. L. (1983). Assessment center correlates of women's advancement into middle management: A 7-year longitudinal analysis. *Journal of Applied Psychology, 68*, 227–231.

Robbins, T., & DeNisi, A. S. (1994). A closer look at interpersonal affect as a distinct influence on cognitive processing in performance evaluations. *Journal of Applied Psychology, 79*, 341–353.

Roberson, Q. M., Collins, C. J., & Oreg, S. (2005). The effects of recruitment message specificity on applicant attraction to organizations. *Journal of Business and Psychology, 19*, 319–339.

Roberson, L., Deitch, E. A., Brief, A. P., & Block, C. J. (2003). Stereotype threat and feedback seeking in the workplace. *Journal of Vocational Behavior, 62*, 176–188.

Roberts, K., Kossek, E. E., & Ozeki, C. (1998). Managing the global workforce: Challenges and strategies. *Academy of Management Executive, 12*(4), 93–106.

Robertson, I., & Downs, S. (1979). Learning and the prediction of performance: Development of trainability testing in the United Kingdom. *Journal of Applied Psychology, 64*, 42–50.

Robertson, I. T., & Downs, S. (1989). Work-sample tests of trainability: A meta-analysis. *Journal of Applied Psychology, 74*, 402–410.

Robinson, S. L., & Bennett, R. J. (1995). A typology of deviant workplace behaviors: A multidimensional scaling study. *Academy of Management Journal, 38*, 555–572.

Roch, S. G. (2006). Discussion and consensus in rater groups: Implications for behavioral and rating accuracy. *Human Performance, 19*, 91–115.

Roch, S. G., Sternburgh, A. M., & Caputo, P. M. (2007). Absolute vs. relative performance rating formats: Implications for fairness and organizational justice. *International Journal of Selection and Assessment, 15*, 302–316.

Rodgers, R., & Hunter, J. E. (1991). Impact of management by objectives on organizational productivity. *Journal of Applied Psychology, 76*, 322–336.

Rodgers, R., Hunter, J. E., & Rogers, D. L. (1993). Influence of top management commitment on management program success. *Journal of Applied Psychology, 78*, 151–155.

Roehling, M. V., & Wright, P. M. (2006). Organizationally sensible versus legal-centric approaches to employment decisions. *Human Resource Management, 45*, 605–627.

Rogers, W. M., Schmitt, N., & Mullins, M. E. (2002). Correction for unreliability of multifactor measures: Comparison of alpha and parallel forms of approaches. *Organizational Research Methods, 5*, 184–199.

Ronan, W. W., & Prien, E. P. (1966). *Toward a criterion theory: A review and analysis of research and opinion.* Greensboro, NC: Richardson Foundation.

Ronan, W. W., & Prien, E. P. (1971). *Perspectives on the measurement of human performance.* New York, NY: Appleton-Century-Crofts.

Rosato, D. (2009, April). Networking for people who hate to network. *Money*, pp. 25, 26.

Rose, G. L., & Brief, A. P. (1979). Effects of handicap and job characteristics on selection evaluations. *Personnel Psychology, 32*, 385–392.

Rosenthal, R. (1994). Science and ethics in conducting, analyzing, and reporting psychological research. *Psychological Science, 5*, 127–134.

Rosenthal, R. (1995). Writing meta-analytic reviews. *Psychological Bulletin, 118*, 83–192.

Rosenthal, R., & Rosnow, R. L. (1991). *Essentials of behavioral research: Methods and data analysis* (2nd ed.). New York, NY: McGraw-Hill.

Rosnow, R. L. (1997). Hedgehogs, foxes, and the evolving social contract in psychological science: Ethical challenges and methodological opportunities. *Psychological Methods, 2*, 345–356.

Rosnow, R. L., & Rosenthal, R. (2008). *Beginning behavioral research: A conceptual primer* (6th ed.). Upper Saddle River, NJ: Prentice Hall.

Rosse, J. G., Stecher, M. D., Miller, J. L., & Levin, R. A. (1998). The impact of response distortion on preemployment personality testing and hiring decisions. *Journal of Applied Psychology, 83*, 634–644.

Roth, P. L., Bevier, C. A., Bobko, P., Switzer, F. S., & Tyler, P. (2001). Ethnic group differences in cognitive ability in employment and educational settings: A meta-analysis. *Personnel Psychology, 54*, 297–330.

Roth, P. L., Bevier, C. A., Switzer, F. S., & Schippmann, J. S. (1996). Meta-analyzing the relationship between grades and job performance. *Journal of Applied Psychology, 81*, 548–556.

Roth, P. L., & Bobko, P. (1997). A research agenda for multi-attribute utility analysis in human resource management. *Human Resource Management Review, 7*, 341–368.

Roth, P. L., & Bobko, P. (2000). College grade point average as a personnel selection device: Ethnic group differences and potential adverse impact. *Journal of Applied Psychology, 85*, 399–406.

Roth, P. L., Bobko, P., & McFarland, L. A. (2005). A meta-analysis of work sample test validity: Updating and integrating some classic literature. *Personnel Psychology, 58*, 1009–1037.

Roth, P., Bobko, P., McFarland, L., & Buster, M. (2008). Work sample tests in personnel selection: A meta-analysis of Black-White differences in overall and exercise scores. *Personnel Psychology, 61*, 637–661.

Roth, P. L., Van Iddekinge, C. H., Huffcutt, A. I., Eidson, C. E., & Bobko, P. (2002). Corrections for range restriction in structured interview ethnic group differences: The values may be larger than researchers thought. *Journal of Applied Psychology, 87*, 369–376.

Rothaus, P., Morton, R. B., & Hanson, P. G. (1965). Performance appraisal and psychological distance. *Journal of Applied Psychology, 49*, 48–54.

Rothstein, H. R. (2003). Progress is our most important product: Contributions of validity generalization and meta-analysis to the development and communication of knowledge in I/O psychology. In K. R. Murphy (Ed.), *Validity generalization: A critical review* (pp. 115–154). Mahwah, NJ: Lawrence Erlbaum.

Rothstein, H. R., McDaniel, M. A., & Borenstein, M. (2002). Meta-analysis: A review of quantitative cumulation methods. In F. Drasgow, & N. Schmitt (Eds.), *Measuring and analyzing behavior in organizations* (pp. 534–570). San Francisco, CA: Jossey-Bass.

Rothstein, H. R., Schmidt, F. L., Erwin, F. W., Owens, W. A., & Sparks, C. P. (1990). Biographical data in employment selection: Can validities be made generalizable? *Journal of Applied Psychology, 75*, 175–184.

Rotundo, M., & Sackett, P. R. (1999). Effect of rater race on conclusions regarding differential prediction in cognitive ability tests. *Journal of Applied Psychology, 84*, 815–822.

Rousseau, D. M. (1995). *Psychological contracts in organizations: Written and unwritten agreements.* Newbury Park, CA: Sage.

Rowe, P. M. (1960). *Individual differences in assessment decisions.* Unpublished doctoral dissertation, McGill University, Montreal.

Rowe, P. M. (1963). Individual differences in selection decisions. *Journal of Applied Psychology, 47*, 304–307.

Rucci, A. J. (2002). What the best business leaders do best. In R. Silzer (Ed.), *The 21st century executive: Innovative practices for building leadership at the top* (pp. 1–42). San Francisco, CA: Jossey-Bass.

Rupp, D. E., Ganapathi, J., Aguilera, R. V., & Williams, C. A. (2006). Employee reactions to corporate social responsibility: An organizational justice framework. *Journal of Organizational Behavior, 27*, 537–543.

Rush, C. H., Jr. (1953). A factorial study of sales criteria. *Personnel Psychology, 6*, 9–24.

Rushton, J. P., & Jensen, A. R. (2005). Thirty years of research on race differences in cognitive ability. *Psychology, Public Policy, and Law, 11*, 235–294.

Russell, C. (2001). A longitudinal study of top-level executive performance. *Journal of Applied Psychology, 86*, 560–573.

Russell, C. J., Colella, A., & Bobko, P. (1993). Expanding the context of utility: The strategic impact of personnel selection. *Personnel Psychology, 46*, 781–801.

Russell, J. S., & Goode, D. L. (1988). An analysis of managers' reactions to their own performance appraisal feedback. *Journal of Applied Psychology*, *73*, 63–67.

Russell, J. S., Wexley, K. N., & Hunter, J. E. (1984). Questioning the effectiveness of behavior modeling training in an industrial setting. *Personnel Psychology*, *37*, 465–481.

Ryan, A. M. (2001). Explaining the black-white test score gap: The role of test perceptions. *Human Performance*, *14*, 45–75.

Ryan, A. M., & Lasek, M. (1991). Negligent hiring and defamation: Areas of liability related to preemployment inquiries. *Personnel Psychology*, *44*, 293–319.

Ryans, D. G., & Fredericksen, N. (1951). Performance tests of educational achievement. In E. F. Lindquist (Ed.), *Educational measurement*. Washington, DC: American Council on Education.

Rynes, S. L. (1991). Recruitment, job choice, and post-hire consequences: A call for new research directions. In M. D. Dunnette, & L. M. Hough (Eds.), *Handbook of industrial and organizational psychology* (2nd ed., Vol. 2, pp. 399–444). Palo Alto, CA: Consulting Psychologists Press.

Rynes, S. L., Bretz, R. D., & Gerhart, B. (1991). The importance of recruitment in job choice: A different way of looking. *Personnel Psychology*, *44*, 487–521.

Rynes, S. L., & Cable, D. M. (2003). Recruitment research in the twenty-first century. In W. C. Borman, D. R. Ilgen, & R. J. Klimoski (Eds.), *Handbook of psychology: Vol. 12. Industrial and organizational psychology* (pp. 55–76). Hoboken, NJ: Wiley.

Rynes, S. L., Orlitzky, M. O., & Bretz, R. D. (1997). Experienced hiring versus college recruiting: Practices and emerging trends. *Personnel Psychology*, *50*, 309–339.

Saad, A. (2009, April). *Filling the data vacuum in wage-and-hour litigation: The example of misclassification cases, emphasis on class certification*. Paper presented at the annual conference of the Society for Industrial and Organizational Psychology, New Orleans, LA.

Saad, S., & Sackett, P. R. (2002). Investigating differential prediction by gender in employment-oriented personality measures. *Journal of Applied Psychology*, *87*, 667–674.

Saal, F. E., Downey, R. G., & Lahey, M. A. (1980). Rating the ratings: Assessing the psychometric quality of rating data. *Psychological Bulletin*, *88*, 413–428.

Saari, L. M., Johnson, T. R., McLaughlin, S. D., & Zimmerle, D. M. (1988). A survey of management training and education practices in U.S. companies. *Personnel Psychology*, *41*, 731–743.

Sackett, P. R. (1987). Assessment centers and content validity: Some neglected issues. *Personnel Psychology*, *40*, 13–25.

Sackett, P. R. (1991). On interpreting measures of change due to training or other interventions: A comment on Cascio (1989, 1991). *Journal of Applied Psychology*, *76*, 590–591.

Sackett, P. R. (2003). The status of validity generalization research: Key issues in drawing inferences from cumulative research findings. In K. R. Murphy (Ed.), *Validity generalization: A critical review* (pp. 91–114). Mahwah, NJ: Lawrence Erlbaum.

Sackett, P. R., Borneman, M. J., & Connelly, B. S. (2008). High-stakes testing in higher education and employment. *American Psychologist*, *63*, 215–227.

Sackett, P. R., & DuBois, C. L. Z. (1991). Rater-ratee race effects on performance evaluation: Challenging meta-analytic conclusions. *Journal of Applied Psychology*, *76*, 873–877.

Sackett, P. R., DuBois, C. L. Z., & Noe, A. W. (1991). Tokenism in performance evaluation: The effects of work group representation on male-female and white-black differences in performance ratings. *Journal of Applied Psychology*, *76*, 263–267.

Sackett, P. R., & Hakel, M. D. (1979). Temporal stability and individual differences in using assessment information to form overall ratings. *Organizational Behavior and Human Performance*, *23*, 120–137.

Sackett, P. R., & Laczo, R. M. (2003). Job and work analysis. In W. C. Borman, D. R. Ilgen, & R. J. Klimoski (Eds.), *Handbook of psychology: Vol. 12. Industrial and organizational psychology* (pp. 21–37). Hoboken, NJ: Wiley.

Sackett, P. R., Laczo, R. M., & Arvey, R. D. (2002). The effects of range restriction on estimates of criterion interrater reliability: Implications for validation research. *Personnel Psychology*, *55*, 807–825.

Sackett, P. R., & Lievens, F. (2008). Personnel selection. *Annual Review of Psychology*, *59*, 419–450.

Sackett, P. R., & Mullen, E. J. (1993). Beyond formal experimental design: Towards an expanded view of the training evaluation process. *Personnel Psychology*, *46*, 613–627.

Sackett, P. R., & Wilk, S. L. (1994). Within-group norming and other forms of score adjustment in preemployment testing. *American Psychologist*, *49*, 929–954.

Sackett, P. R., & Yang, H. (2000). Correction for range restriction: An expanded typology. *Journal of Applied Psychology*, *85*, 112–118.

Sackett, P. R., Zedeck, S., & Fogli, L. (1988). Relations between measures of typical and maximum job performance. *Journal of Applied Psychology*, *73*, 482–486.

Saks, A. M. (1995). Longitudinal field investigation of the moderating and mediating effects of self-efficacy on the relationship between training and newcomer adjustment. *Journal of Applied Psychology*, *80*, 211–225.

Salas, E., Burke, C. S., & Cannon-Bowers, J. B. (2002). What we know about designing and delivering team training: Tips and guidelines. In K. Kraiger (Ed.), *Creating, implementing, and managing effective training and development* (pp. 234–259). San Francisco, CA: Jossey-Bass.

Salas, E., & Cannon-Bowers, J. B. (2000). Designing training systems systematically. In E. A. Locke (Ed.), *The Blackwell handbook of principles of organizational behavior* (pp. 43–59). Malden, MA: Blackwell.

Salas, E., & Cannon-Bowers, J. B. (2001). The science of training: A decade of progress. *Annual Review of Psychology*, *52*, 471–499.

Salas, E., Wilson, K. A., & Burke, C. S. (2006). Does crew resource management training work? An update, an extension, and some critical needs. *Human Factors*, *48*, 392–412.

Salgado, J. F. (1997). The five-factor model of personality and job performance in the European Community. *Journal of Applied Psychology*, *82*, 30–43.

Salgado, J. F., & Anderson, N. (2002). Cognitive and GMA testing in the European Community: Issues and evidence. *Human Performance*, *15*, 75–96.

Salgado, J. F., Anderson, N., Moscoso, S., Berua, C., de Fruyt, F., & Rolland, J. P. (2003). A meta-analytic study of general mental ability validity for different occupations in the European Community. *Journal of Applied Psychology*, *88*, 1068–1081.

Salgado, J. F., Viswesvaran, C., & Ones, D. S. (2001). Predictors used for personnel selection: An overview of constructs, methods, and techniques. In N. Anderson, D. S. Ones, H. K. Sinangil, & C. Viswesvaran (Eds.), *Handbook of industrial, work, and organizational psychology: Vol. 1. Personnel psychology* (pp. 165–199). London: Sage.

Sanchez, J. I., & Fraser, S. L. (1992). On the choice of scales for task analysis. *Journal of Applied Psychology*, *77*, 545–553.

Sanchez, J. I., & Levine, E. L. (2001). The analysis of work in the 20th and 21st centuries. In N. Anderson, D. S. Ones, H. K. Sinangil, & C. Viswesvaran (Eds.), *Handbook of industrial, work, and organizational psychology: Vol. 1. Personnel psych* (pp. 70–90). London: Sage.

Sands, W. A. (1973). A method for evaluating alternative recruiting-selection strategies: The CAPER model. *Journal of Applied Psychology*, *57*, 222–227.

Sawyer, J. (1966). Measurement and prediction, clinical and statistical. *Psychological Bulletin*, *66*, 178–200.

Saxe, L., Dougherty, D., & Cross, T. (1985). The validity of polygraph testing. *American Psychologist*, *40*, 355–366.

Schein E. H. (1980). *Organizational psychology* (3rd. ed.). Englewood Cliffs, NJ: Prentice Hall.

Scherbaum, C. A. (2005). Synthetic validity: Past, present, and future. *Personnel Psychology*, *58*, 481–515.

Schippmann, J. S., Ash, R. A., Battista, M., Carr, L., Eyde, L. D., Hesketh, B., Kehoe, J., Pearlman, K., Prien, E. P., & Sanchez, J. I. (2000). The practice of competency modeling. *Personnel Psychology*, *53*, 703–740.

Schleicher, D. J., & Day, D. V. (1998). A cognitive evaluation of frame-of-reference rater training: Content and process issues. *Organizational Behavior and Human Decision Processes*, *73*, 76–101.

Schleicher, D. J., Day, D. V., Mayes, B. T., & Riggio, R. E. (2002). A new frame for frame-of-reference training: Enhancing the construct validity of assessment centers. *Journal of Applied Psychology*, *87*, 735–746.

Schmieder, R. A., & Frame, M. C. (2007). Competency modeling. In S. G. Rogelberg (Ed.), *Encyclopedia of industrial and organizational psychology* (Vol. 1, pp. 85–87). Thousand Oaks, CA: Sage.

Schmidt, F. L. (1971). The relative efficiency of regression and simple unit predictor weights in applied differential psychology. *Educational and Psychological Measurement*, *31*, 699–714.

Schmidt, F. L. (1988). The problem of group differences in ability test scores in employment selection. *Journal of Vocational Behavior*, *33*, 272–292.

Schmidt, F. L. (1991). Why all banding procedures in personnel selection are logically flawed. *Human Performance*, *4*(4), 265–277.

Schmidt, F. L. (1993). *Personnel psychology* at the cutting edge. In N. Schmitt, & W. C. Borman (Eds.), *Personnel selection* in organizations (pp. 497–515). San Francisco, CA: Jossey-Bass.

Schmidt, F. L. (2002). The role of general cognitive ability and job performance: Why there cannot be a debate. *Human Performance*, *15*, 187–210.

Schmitt, N. (2007). The value of personnel selection: Reflections on some remarkable claims. *Academy of Management Perspectives*, *21*, 19–23.

Schmidt, F. L. (2008). Meta-analysis: A constantly evolving research integration tool. *Organizational Research Methods*, *11*, 96–113.

Schmidt, A., & Ford, J. K. (2003). Learning within a learner-control training environment: The interactive effects of goal orientation and metacognitive instruction on learning outcomes. *Personnel Psychology*, *56*, 405–430.

Schmidt, F. L., Greenthal, A. L., Hunter, J. E., Berner, J. G., & Seaton, F. W. (1977). Job sample vs. paper-and-pencil trades and technical tests: Adverse impact and examinee attitudes. *Personnel Psychology*, *30*, 187–197.

Schmidt, F. L., & Hunter, J. E. (1977). Development of a general solution to the problem of validity generalization. *Journal of Applied Psychology*, *62*, 529–540.

Schmidt, F. L., & Hunter, J. E. (1981). Employment testing: Old theories and new research. *American Psychologist*, *36*, 1128–1137.

Schmidt, F. L., & Hunter, J. E. (1983). Individual differences in productivity: An empirical test of estimates derived from studies of selection procedure utility. *Journal of Applied Psychology*, *68*, 407–414.

Schmidt, F. L., & Hunter, J. E. (1996). Measurement error in psychological research: Lessons from 26 research scenarios. *Psychological Methods*, *1*, 199–223.

Schmidt, F. L., & Hunter, J. E. (1998). The validity and utility of selection methods in personnel psychology. Practical and theoretical implications of 85 years of research findings. *Psychological Bulletin*, *124*, 262–274.

Schmidt, F. L., & Hunter, J. E. (2003a). History, development, evolution, and impact of validity generalization and meta-analysis methods, 1975–2001. In K. R. Murphy (Ed.), *Validity generalization: A critical review* (pp. 31–65). Mahwah, NJ: Lawrence Erlbaum.

Schmidt, F. L., & Hunter, J. E. (2003b). Meta-analysis. In J. A. Schinka, & W. F. Velicer (Eds.), *Handbook of psychology: Research methods in psychology* (Vol. 2, pp. 533–554). Hoboken, NJ: Wiley.

Schmidt, F. L., & Hunter, J. E. (2004). SED banding as a test of scientific values in I/O psychology. In H. Aguinis (Ed.), *Test score banding in human resource selection: Legal, technical, and societal issues* (pp. 151–174). Westport, CT: Praeger.

Schmidt, F. L., Hunter, J. E., McKenzie, R. C., & Muldrow, T. W. (1979). Impact of valid selection procedures on work-force productivity. *Journal of Applied Psychology*, *64*, 609–626.

Schmidt, F. L., Hunter, J. E., & Pearlman, K. (1982). Assessing the economic impact of personnel programs on productivity. *Personnel Psychology*, *35*, 333–347.

Schmidt, F. L., Hunter, J. E., & Urry, V. W. (1976). Statistical power in criterion-related validity studies. *Journal of Applied Psychology*, *61*, 473–485.

Schmidt, F. L., & Kaplan, L. B. (1971). Composite vs. multiple criteria: A review and resolution of the controversy. *Personnel Psychology, 24*, 419–434.

Schmidt, F. L., Le, H., & Ilies, R. (2003). Beyond alpha: An empirical examination of the effects of different sources of measurement error on reliability estimates for measures of individual-differences constructs. *Psychological Methods, 8*, 206–224.

Schmidt, F. L., Oh, I., & Le, H. (2006). Increasing the accuracy of corrections for range restriction: Implications for selection procedure validities and other research results. *Personnel Psychology, 59*, 281–305.

Schmidt, F. L., Pearlman, K., & Hunter, J. E. (1980). The validity and fairness of employment and educational tests for Hispanic Americans: A review and analysis. *Personnel Psychology, 33*, 705–724.

Schmidt, F., & Rader, M. (1999). Exploring the boundary conditions for interview validity: Meta-analytic validity findings for a new interview type. *Personnel Psychology, 52*, 445–464.

Schmitt, N. (1977). Interrater agreement in dimensionality and combination of assessment center judgments. *Journal of Applied Psychology, 62*, 171–176.

Schmitt, N., & Chan, D. (1998). *Personnel selection: A theoretical approach.* Thousand Oaks, CA: Sage.

Schmitt, N., & Cohen, S. A. (1989). Internal analyses of task ratings by job incumbents. *Journal of Applied Psychology, 73*, 96–104.

Schmitt, N., Cortina, J. M., Ingerick, M. J., & Wiechmann, D. (2003). Personnel selection and employee performance. In W. C. Borman, D. R. Ilgen, & R. J. Klimoski (Eds.), *Handbook of psychology: Vol. 12. Industrial and organizational psychology* (pp. 77–105). Hoboken, NJ: Wiley.

Schmitt, N., & Coyle, B. W. (1979). Applicant decisions in the employment interview. *Journal of Applied Psychology, 61*, 184–192.

Schmitt, N., Gilliland, S. W., Landis, R. S., & Devine, D. (1993). Computer-based testing applied to selection of secretarial applicants. *Personnel Psychology, 46*, 149–165.

Schmitt, N., Gooding, R. Z., Noe, R. A., & Kirsch, M. (1984). Meta-analysis of validity studies published between 1964 and 1982 and the investigation of study characteristics. *Personnel Psychology, 37*, 407–422.

Schmit, M. J., Kihm, J. A., & Robie, C. (2000). Development of a global measure of personality. *Personnel Psychology, 53*, 153–193.

Schmitt, N., & Kunce, C. (2002). The effects of required elaboration of answers to biodata questions. *Personnel Psychology, 55*, 569–587.

Schmitt, N., Mellon, P. M., & Bylenga, C. (1978). Sex differences in validity for academic and employment criteria, and different types of predictors. *Journal of Applied Psychology, 63*, 145–150.

Schmitt, N., & Oswald, F. L. (2004). Statistical weights of ability and diversity in selection decisions based on various methods of test score use. In H. Aguinis (Ed.), *Test score banding in human resource selection: Legal, technical, and societal issues* (pp. 113–132). Westport, CT: Praeger.

Schmitt, N., Oswald, F. L., Kim, B. H., Gillespie, M. A., & Ramsay, L. J. (2003). Impact of elaboration on socially desirable responding and the validity of biodata measures. *Journal of Applied Psychology, 88*, 979–988.

Schmitt, N., Pulakos, E. D., Nason, E., & Whitney, D. J. (1996). Likability and similarity as potential sources of predictor-related criterion bias in validation research. *Organizational Behavior and Human Decision Processes, 68*, 272–286.

Schmitt, N., Rogers, W., Chan, D., Sheppard, L., & Jennings, D. (1997). Adverse impact and predictive efficiency of various predictor combinations. *Journal of Applied Psychology, 82*, 719–730.

Schmitt, N., & Stults, D. (1986). Methodology review: Analysis of multitrait-multimethod matrices. *Applied Psychological Measurement, 10*, 1–22.

Schmidt, F. L., & Zimmerman, R. D (2004). A counterintuitive hypothesis about employment interview validity and some supporting evidence. *Journal of Applied Psychology, 89*, 553–561.

Schmimmack, U., Oishi, S., & Diener, E. (2005). Individualism: A valid and important dimension of cultural differences between nations. *Personality and Social Psychology Review, 9*, 17–31.

Schneider, B. (2007). Evolution of the study and practice of personality at work. *Human Resource Management, 46*, 583–610.

Schneider, J., & Mitchel, J. O. (1980). Functions of life insurance agency managers and relationships with agency characteristics and managerial tenure. *Personnel Psychology, 33*, 795–808.

Schoenfeldt, L. F., Schoenfeldt, B. B., Acker, S. R., & Perlson, M. R. (1976). Content validity revisited: The development of a content-oriented test of industrial reading. *Journal of Applied Psychology, 61*, 581–588.

Schriesheim, C. A., Powers, K. J., Scandura, T. A., Gardiner, C. C., & Lankau, M. J. (1993). Improving construct measurement in management research: Comments and a quantitative approach for assessing the theoretical adequacy of paper-and-pencil survey-type instruments. *Journal of Management, 19*, 385–417.

Schuler, R. S., & Jackson, S. E. (1989). Determinants of human resource management priorities and implications for industrial relations. *Journal of Management, 15*, 89–99.

Schwab, D. P., & Heneman, H. G., III. (1978). Age stereotyping in performance appraisal. *Journal of Applied Psychology, 63*, 573–578.

Schwager v. Sun Oil Co. of Pa., 591 F.2d 58 (10th Cir. 1979).

Schwartz, N. D. (2009, February 15). Job losses pose a threat to stability worldwide. *The New York Times.* Downloaded from www.NYTimes.com.

Scott, S. G., & Einstein, W. O. (2001). Strategic performance appraisal in team-based organizations: One size does not fit all. *Academy of Management Executive, 15*, 107–116.

Scullen, S. E. (1999). Using confirmatory factor analysis of correlated uniqueness to estimate method variance in multitrait-multimethod matrices. *Organizational Research Methods, 2*, 275–292.

Scullen, S. E., Mount, M. K., & Goff, M. (2000). Understanding the latent structure of job performance ratings. *Journal of Applied Psychology, 85*, 956–970.

Seeing forward: Succession planning and leadership development at 3M. (2008, August). DVD produced by the Society for Human Resource Management Foundation, Alexandria, VA.

Segal, J. A. (2002). Searching for answers: Don't search employees in a way that leaves them questioning your legal authority. *HRMagazine, 47*(3). Available at http://www.shrm.org/hrmagazine/articles/0302/0302legal.asp#jas.

Segal, J. A. (2006, April). They go and come . . . and go. *HRMagazine,* pp. 127–133.

Segrest Purkiss, S. L., Perrewé, P. L., Gillespie, T. L., Mayes, B. T., & Ferris, G. R. (2006). Implicit sources of bias in employment interview judgments and decisions. *Organizational Behavior and Human Decision Processes, 101,* 152–167.

Senge, P. (1999). *The fifth discipline: The art and practice of the learning organization.* New York, NY: Bantam.

Senge, P. M. (1990). *The fifth discipline: The art and practice of the learning organization.* Garden City, NY: Doubleday.

Sewell, C. (1981). Pre-employment investigations: The key to security in hiring. *Personnel Journal, 60*(5), 376–379.

Shadish, W. R., Cook, T. D., & Campbell, D. T. (2002). *Experimental and quasi-experimental designs for generalized causal inference.* Boston, MA: Houghton Mifflin.

Shalley, C. E., Oldham, G. R., & Porac, J. F. (1987). Effects of goal difficulty, goal-setting method, and expected external evaluation on intrinsic motivation. *Academy of Management Journal, 30,* 553–563.

Shapira, Z., & Shirom, A. (1980). New issues in the use of behaviorally anchored rating scales: Level of analysis, the effects of incident frequency, and external validation. *Journal of Applied Psychology, 65,* 517–523.

Sharf, J. C. (1988). Litigating personnel measurement policy. *Journal of Vocational Behavior, 33,* 235–271.

Shaw, K. N. (2004). Changing the goal-setting process at Microsoft. *Academy of Management Executive, 18*(4), 139–142.

Shen, W., & Cannella, A. A., Jr. (2002). Revisiting the performance consequences of CEO succession: The impacts of successor type, post-succession senior executive turnover, and departing CEO tenure. *Academy of Management Journal, 45,* 717–733.

Shore, L. M., & Tetrick, L. E. (1991). A construct validity study of the Survey of Perceived Organizational Support. *Journal of Applied Psychology, 76,* 637–643.

Shore, T. H., Shore, L. M., & Thornton, G. C., III. (1992). Construct validity of self- and peer evaluations of performance dimensions in an assessment center. *Journal of Applied Psychology, 77,* 42–54.

Shotland, A., Alliger, G. M., & Sales, T. (1998). Face validity in the context of personnel selection: A multimedia approach. *International Journal of Selection and Assessment, 6,* 124–130.

SHRM Foundation. (2007, October). *SHRM Foundation research on human capital challenges.* Alexandria, VA: Author.

Sieber, J. E. (1992). *Planning ethically responsible research: A guide for students and internal review boards.* Newbury Park, CA: Sage.

Siegel, L. (1982). Paired comparison evaluations of managerial effectiveness by peers and supervisors. *Personnel Psychology, 37,* 703–710.

Siehl, C., & Hessell, S. (1999). *Cadet Uniform Services: Cleaning up in the cleaning business* (Case No. A08-99-0017). Phoenix, AZ: Thunderbird—The American Graduate School of International Management.

Siero, S., Boon, M., Kok, G., & Siero, F. (1989). Modification of driving behavior in a large transport organization: A field experiment. *Journal of Applied Psychology, 74,* 417–423.

Silverman, S. B., & Wexley, K. N. (1984). Reaction of employees to performance appraisal interviews as a function of their participation in rating scale development. *Personnel Psychology, 37,* 703–710.

Silvester, J., & Anderson, N. (2003). Technology and discourse: A comparison of face-to-face and telephone employment interviews. *International Journal of Selection and Assessment, 11,* 206–214.

Silvester, J., Anderson, N., Haddleton, E., Cunningham-Snell, N., & Gibb, A. (2000). A cross-modal comparison of telephone and face-to-face selection interviews in graduate recruitment. *International Journal of Selection and Assessment, 8,* 16–21.

Simms, J. (2002). Business: Corporate social responsibility—You know it makes sense. *Accountancy, 130*(1311), 48–50.

Sinangil, H. K., & Ones, D. S. (2001). Expatriate management. In N. Anderson, D. S. Ones, H. K. Sinangil, & C. Viswesvaran (Eds.), *Handbook of industrial, work, and organizational psychology: Vol. 1. Personnel psychology* (pp. 425–443). London: Sage.

Singer, M. S., & Bruhns, C. (1991). Relative effect of applicant work experience and academic qualification on selection interview decisions: A study of between-sample generalizability. *Journal of Applied Psychology, 76,* 550–559.

Sisson, D. E. (1948). Forced choice, the new Army rating. *Personnel Psychology, 1,* 365–381.

Sitzmann, T., Kraiger, K., Stewart, D., & Wisher, R. (2006). The comparative effectiveness of Web-based and classroom instruction: A meta-analysis. *Personnel Psychology, 59,* 623–664.

Slaughter, J. E., Zickar, M. J., Highhouse, S., & Mohr, D. C. (2004). Personality trait inferences about organizations: Development of a measure and assessment of construct validity. *Journal of Applied Psychology, 89,* 85–103.

Smith, A. (2007, March 1). Beer distributor ordered to pay nearly $200,000 for age discrimination. Downloaded March 28, 2009, from http://moss07.shrm.org/LegalIssues/StateandLocalResources/Pages/1CMS_016033.aspx.

Smith, A. (2008, May 27). *Supreme Court permits retaliation claims under two more federal laws.* Downloaded May 29, 2008, from www.shrm.org/law/library.

Smith, P. C., & Kendall, L. M. (1963). Retranslation of expectations: An approach to the construction of unambiguous anchors for rating scales. *Journal of Applied Psychology, 47,* 149–155.

Smither, J. W., Collins, H., & Buda, R. (1989). When ratee satisfaction influences performance evaluations: A case of illusory correlation. *Journal of Applied Psychology, 74,* 599–605.

Smither, J. W., London, M., Vasilopoulos, N. L., Reilly, R. R., Millsap, R., & Salvemini, N. (1995). An examination of the effects of an upward feedback program over time. *Personnel Psychology, 48,* 1–34.

Smither, J. W., Reilly, R. R., Millsap, R. E., Pearlman, K., & Stoffey, R. W. (1993). Applicant reactions to selection procedures. *Personnel Psychology, 46,* 49–76.

Snyder, R. A., Raben, C. S., & Farr, J. L. (1980). A model for the systematic evaluation of human resource development programs. *Academy of Management Review, 5,* 431–444.

Soares, C. (2003). Corporate versus individual moral responsibility. *Journal of Business Ethics, 46*(2), 143–150.

Society for Industrial and Organization Psychology, Inc. (2003). *Principles for the validation and use of personnel selection procedures* (4th ed.). Bowling Green, OH: Author.

Society for Human Resource Management. (2007). *FMLA: An overview of the 2007 FMLA survey.* Alexandria, VA: SHRM.

Solomon, R. L. (1949). An extension of a control group design. *Psychological Bulletin, 46,* 137–150.

Solomon, J. (1989, April 4). As firms' personnel files grow, worker privacy falls. *The Wall Street Journal,* p. B1.

Solomonson, A. L., & Lance, C. E. (1997). Examination of the relationship between true halo and halo error in performance ratings. *Journal of Applied Psychology, 82,* 665–674.

Somaya, D., Williamson, I. O., & Lorinkova, N. (2008). Gone but not lost: The different performance impacts of employee mobility between cooperators versus competitors. *Academy of Management Journal, 51*(5), 936–953.

Sondergaard, M. (1994). Research note: Hofstede's consequences: A study of reviews, citations, and replications. *Organization Studies, 15,* 447–456.

Southwest Airlines named No. 7 in *Fortune* magazine's "Top 50 Most Admired Companies." (2009, March 2). Downloaded April 13, 2009, from www.reuters.com/article/pressRelease/idUS243125+02-Mar-2009+PRN20090302.

Spector, P. E. (1976). Choosing response categories for simulated rating scales. *Journal of Applied Psychology, 61,* 374–375.

Spector, P. E., Fox, S., & Penney, L. M. (2006). The dimensionality of counterproductivity: Are all counterproductive behaviors created equal? *Journal of Vocational Behavior, 68,* 446–460.

Spitzer, D. R. (2005). Learning-effectiveness measurement: A new approach for measuring and managing learning to achieve business results. *Advances in Developing Human Resources, 7,* 55–70.

Sprangers, M., & Hoogstraten, J. (1989). Pretesting effects in retrospective pretest-posttest designs. *Journal of Applied Psychology, 74,* 265–272.

Spreitzer, G. M., McCall, M. W., Jr., & Mahoney, J. D. (1997). Early identification of international executive potential. *Journal of Applied Psychology, 82,* 6–29.

Spychalski, A. C., Quiñones, M. A., Gaugler, B. B., & Pohley, K. (1997). A survey of assessment center practices in organizations in the United States. *Personnel Psychology, 50,* 71–90.

Srinivas, S., & Motowidlo, S. J. (1987). Effects of raters' stress on the dispersion and favorability of performance ratings. *Journal of Applied Psychology, 72,* 247–251.

Srivastava, A., Bartol, K. M., & Locke, E. A. (2006). Empowering leadership in management teams: Effects on knowledge-sharing, efficacy, and performance. *Academy of Management Journal, 49,* 1239–1251.

St. John, C. H., & Roth, P. L. (1999). The impact of cross-validation adjustments on estimates of effect size in business policy and strategy research. *Organizational Research Methods, 2,* 157–174.

Stahl, M. J. (1983). Achievement, power, and managerial motivation: Selecting managerial talent with the job choice exercise. *Personnel Psychology, 36,* 775–789.

Stahl, M. J., Grigsby, D. W., & Gulati, A. (1985). Comparing the Job Choice Exercise and the multiple-choice version of the Miner Sentence Completion Scale. *Journal of Applied Psychology, 70,* 228–232.

Stahl, M. J., & Harrell, A. M. (1982). Evolution and validation of a behavioral decision theory measurement approach to achievement, power, and affiliation. *Journal of Applied Psychology, 67,* 744–751.

Staines, G. L., & Pleck, J. H. (1984). Nonstandard work schedules and family life. *Journal of Applied Psychology, 69,* 515–523.

Stajkovic, A. D., & Luthans, F. (2003). Behavioral management and task performance in organizations: Conceptual background, meta-analysis, and test of alternative models. *Personnel Psychology, 56,* 155–194.

Stamoulis, D. T., & Hauenstein, N. M. (1993). Rater training and rating accuracy: Training for dimensional accuracy versus training for ratee differentiation. *Journal of Applied Psychology, 78,* 994–1003.

Stanton, J. M. (2000). Reactions to employee performance monitoring: Framework, review, and research directions. *Human Performance, 13,* 85–113.

Stanton, J. M., & Rogelberg, S. G. (2001). Using Internet/intranet Web pages to collect organizational research data. *Organizational Research Methods, 4,* 200–217.

Stanton, J. M., & Rogelberg, S. G. (2002). Beyond online surveys: Internet research opportunities for industrial-organizational psychology. In S. G. Rogelberg (Ed.), *Handbook of research methods in industrial and organizational psychology* (pp. 275–294). Malden, MA: Blackwell.

Stark, S., Chernyshenko, O. S., & Drasgow, F. (2006). Detecting differential item functioning with confirmatory factor analysis and item response theory: Toward a unified strategy. *Journal of Applied Psychology, 91,* 1292–1306.

Steel, E. (2007, October 9). Job-search sites face a nimble threat. *The Wall Street Journal,* p. B10.

Steel, P. D. G., Huffcutt, A. I., & Kammeyer-Mueller, J. (2006). From the work one knows the worker: A systematic review of the challenges, solutions, and steps to creating synthetic validity. *International Journal of Selection & Assessment, 14,* 16–36.

Steel, P. D., & Kammeyer-Mueller, J. D. (2002). Comparing meta-analytic moderator estimation techniques under realistic conditions. *Journal of Applied Psychology, 87,* 96–111.

Steel, P. D. G., & Kammeyer-Mueller, J. (2008). Bayesian variance estimation for meta-analysis. *Organizational Research Methods, 11,* 54–78.

Steele-Johnson, D., & Hyde, B. G. (1997). Advanced technologies in training: Intelligent tutoring systems and virtual reality. In M. A. Quiñones, & A. Ehrenstein (Eds.), *Training for a rapidly changing workplace* (pp. 225–248). Washington, DC: American Psychological Association.

Steele-Johnson, D., Osburn, H. G., & Pieper, K. F. (2000). A review and extension of current models of dynamic criteria. *International Journal of Selection and Assessment*, *8*, 110–136.

Steers, R. M., & Porter, L. W. (Eds.). (1975). *Motivation and work behavior.* New York, NY: McGraw-Hill.

Steiner, D. S., & Gilliland, S. W. (1996). Fairness reactions to personnel selection techniques in France and the United States. *Journal of Applied Psychology*, *81*, 134–141.

Sternberg, R. J. (1997). The concept of intelligence and its role in lifelong learning and success. *American Psychologist*, *52*, 1030–1037.

Sternberg, R. J., & Hedlund, J. (2002). Practical intelligence, g, and work psychology. *Human Performance*, *15*, 143–160.

Stevens, S. S. (1951). Mathematics, measurement, and psychophysics. In S. S. Stevens (Ed.), *Handbook of experimental psychology* (pp. 1–49). New York, NY: Wiley.

Stevens, C. K. (1997). Effects of preinterview beliefs on applicants' reactions to campus interviews. *Academy of Management Journal*, *40*, 947–966.

Stevens, C. K. (1998). Antecedents of interview interactions, interviewers' ratings, and applicants' reactions. *Personnel Psychology*, *51*, 55–85.

Stevens, C. K., & Kristof, A. L. (1995). Making the right impression: A field study of applicant impression management during job interviews. *Journal of Applied Psychology*, *80*, 587–606.

Stewart, S. M., Bing, M. N., Davison, H. K., Woehr, D. J., & McIntyre, M. D. (2009). In the eyes of the beholder: A non-self-report measure of workplace deviance. *Journal of Applied Psychology*, *94*, 207–215.

Stewart, G. L., Dustin, S. L., Barrick, M. R., & Darnold, T. C. (2008). Exploring the handshake in employment interviews. *Journal of Applied Psychology*, *93*, 1139–1146.

Stewart, M. M., & Shapiro, D. L. (2000). Selection based on merit versus demography: Implications across race and gender lines. *Journal of Applied Psychology*, *85*, 219–231.

Stites, J. (2005, May). Equal pay for the sexes. *HRMagazine*, pp. 64–69.

Stockford, L., & Bissel, H. W. (1949). Factors involved in establishing a merit rating scale. *Personnel*, *26*, 94–116.

Stokes, G. S., & Cooper, L. A. (2001). Content/construct approaches in life history form development for selection. *International Journal of Selection and Assessment*, *9*, 138–151.

Stokes, G. S., Hogan, J. B., & Snell, A. F. (1993). Comparability of incumbent and applicant samples for the development of biodata keys: The influence of social desirability. *Personnel Psychology*, *46*, 739–762.

Stokes, G. S., & Searcy, C. A. (1999). Specification of scales in biodata form development: Rational vs. empirical and global vs. specific. *International Journal of Selection and Assessment*, *7*, 72–85.

Stone, D. L., Gueutal, H. G., & McIntosh, B. (1984). The effects of feedback sequence and expertise of the rater on perceived feedback accuracy. *Personnel Psychology*, *37*, 487–506.

Stone, E. F., & Hollenbeck, J. R. (1984). Some issues associated with the use of moderated regression. *Organizational Behavior and Human Performance*, *34*, 195–213.

Stone, D. L., & Stone, E. F. (1987). Effects of missing application-blank information on personnel selection decisions: Do privacy protection strategies bias the outcome? *Journal of Applied Psychology*, *72*, 452–456.

Stone-Romero, E. F., Alliger, G. M., & Aguinis, H. (1994). Type II error problems in the use of moderated multiple regression for the detection of moderating effects in dichotomous variables. *Journal of Management*, *20*, 167–178.

Strategic planning. (2009). *Wikipedia.* Downloaded April 13, 2009, from http://en.wikipedia.org/wiki/Strategic_planning.

Street, M. D., Douglas, S. C., Geiger, S. W., & Martinko, M. J. (2001). The impact of cognitive expenditure on the ethical decision-making process: The cognitive elaboration model. *Organizational Behavior and Human Decision Processes*, *86*, 256–277.

Streufert, S., Pogash, R., & Piasecki, M. (1988). Simulation-based assessment of managerial competence: Reliability and validity. *Personnel Psychology*, *41*, 537–557.

Stuit, D. B., & Wilson, J. T. (1946). The effect of an increasingly well defined criterion on the prediction of success at naval training school (tactical radar). *Journal of Applied Psychology*, *30*, 614–623.

Sullivan, J. (2008, May 19). Understanding why fast hiring is critical to recruitment success. n.d. Retrieved May 21, 2008, from www.ere.net/articles/db/4EE49B909CC040D391C6275116B111 F8.asp.

Sugrue, B., & Rivera, R. J. (2005). *State of the industry: ASTD's annual review of trends in workplace learning and performance.* Alexandria, VA: American Society for Training & Development.

Sulsky, L. M., & Balzer, W. K. (1988). Meaning and measurement of performance rating accuracy: Some methodological and theoretical concerns. *Journal of Applied Psychology*, *73*, 497–506.

Sulsky, L. M., & Day, D. V. (1992). Frame-of-reference training and cognitive categorization: An empirical investigation of rater memory issues. *Journal of Applied Psychology*, *77*, 501–510.

Sun, L., Aryee, S., & Law, K. S. (2007). High-performance human resource practices, citizenship behavior, and organizational performance: A relational perspective. *Academy of Management Journal*, *50*, 558–577.

Sundstrom, E., McIntyre, M., Halfhill, T., & Richards, H. (2000). Work groups: From the Hawthorne studies to work teams of the 1990s and beyond. *Group Dynamics*, *4*(1), 44–67.

Sundvik, L., & Lindeman, M. (1998). Performance rating accuracy: Convergence between supervisor assessment and sales productivity. *International Journal of Selection and Assessment*, *6*, 9–15.

Switzer, K. C., Nagy, M. S., & Mullins, M. E. (2005). The influence of training reputation, managerial support, and self-efficacy on pre-training motivation and perceived training transfer. *Applied HRM Research*, *10*, 21–34.

Taft, R. (1959). Multiple methods of personality assessment. *Psychological Bulletin*, *56*, 333–352.

Tannenbaum, S. (2002). A strategic view of organizational training and learning. In K. Kraiger (Ed.), *Creating, implementing, and managing effective training and development* (pp. 10–52). San Francisco, CA: Jossey-Bass.

Tannenbaum, R. J., & Wesley, S. (1993). Agreement between committee-based and field-based job analyses: A study in the context of licensure testing. *Journal of Applied Psychology, 78*, 975–980.

Task Force on Assessment Center Guidelines (1989). Guidelines and ethical considerations for assessment center operations. *Public Personnel Management, 18*, 457–470.

Taylor, M. S., & Bergmann, T. J. (1987). Organizational recruitment activities and applicants' reactions at different stages of the recruitment process. *Personnel Psychology, 40*, 261–285.

Taylor, M. S., Masterson, S. S., Renard, M. K., & Tracy, K. B. (1998). Managers' reactions to procedurally just performance management systems. *Academy of Management Journal, 41*, 568–579.

Taylor, P. J., Pajo, K., Cheung, G. W., & Stringfield, P. (2004). Dimensionality and validity of a structured telephone reference check procedure. *Personnel Psychology, 57*, 745–772.

Taylor, H. C., & Russell, J. T. (1939). The relationship of validity coefficients to the practical effectiveness of tests in selection. *Journal of Applied Psychology, 23*, 565–578.

Taylor, P. J., Russ-Eft, D. F., & Chan, D. W. L. (2005). A meta-analytic review of behavior modeling training. *Journal of Applied Psychology, 90*, 692–709.

Taylor, P. J., Russ-Eft, D. F., & Taylor, H. (2009). Transfer of management training from alternative perspectives. *Journal of Applied Psychology, 94*, 104–121.

Taylor, P. J., & Small, B. (2002). Asking applicants what they would do versus what they did do: A meta-analytic comparison of situational and past behavior employment interview questions. *Journal of Occupational and Organizational Psychology, 75*, 277–294.

Tellegen, A. (in press). *MPQ (Multidimensional Personality Questionnaire): Manual for administration, scoring, and interpretation.* Minneapolis: University of Minnesota Press.

Templer, K. J., Tay, C., & Chandrasekar, N. A. (2006). Motivational cultural intelligence, realistic job preview, realistic living-condition preview, and cross-cultural adjustment. *Group and Organization Management, 31*, 154–173.

Tenopyr, M. L. (1977). Content-construct confusion. *Personnel Psychology, 30*, 47–54.

Tenopyr, M. L. (1984, November). *So let it be with content validity.* Paper presented at the Content Validity III Conference, Bowling Green, OH.

Tenopyr, M. L. (2002). Theory versus reality: Evaluation of g in the workplace. *Human Performance, 15*, 107–122.

Tepper, B. J. (1994). Investigation of general and program-specific attitudes toward corporate drug-testing policies. *Journal of Applied Psychology, 79*, 392–401.

Terpstra, D. E, Mohamed, A. A., & Kethley, R. B. (1999). An analysis of federal court cases involving nine selection devices. *International Journal of Selection and Assessment, 7*, 26–34.

Tesluk, P. E., Farr, J. L., Mathieu, J. E., & Vance, R. J. (1995). Generalization of employee involvement training to the job setting: Individual and situational effects. *Personnel Psychology, 48*, 607–632.

Tesluk, P. E., & Jacobs, R. R. (1998). Toward an integrated model of work experience. *Personnel Psychology, 51*, 321–355.

Tesluk, P. E., & Mathieu, J. E. (1999). Overcoming roadblocks to effectiveness: Incorporating management of performance barriers into models of work group effectiveness. *Journal of Applied Psychology, 84*, 200–217.

Tett, R. P., & Burnett, D. D. (2003). A personality trait-based interactionist model of job performance. *Journal of Applied Psychology, 88*, 500–517.

Tett, R. P., & Christiansen, N. D. (2007). Personality tests at the crossroads: A response to Morgeson, Campion, Dipboye, Hollenbeck, Murphy, and Schmitt (2007). *Personnel Psychology, 60*, 967–993.

Tett, R. P., Jackson, D. N., & Rothstein, M. (1991). Personality measures as predictors of job performance: A meta-analytic review. *Personnel Psychology, 44*, 703–742.

Thaler-Carter, R. (2001, June). Diversify your recruitment advertising. *HRMagazine*, pp. 92–100.

Theaman, M. (1984). The impact of peer review on professional practice. *American Psychologist, 39*, 406–414.

Thelen, J. (2006, March–April). Workplace rights for service members: The USERRA regulations deconstructed. *Legal Report*, pp. 1–8.

The Global Economic Downturn: Why the UN Global Compact and Corporate Sustainability are Needed More than Ever. (2009). Retrieved March 2, 2009, from http://www.unglobalcompact.org/NewsAndEvents/news_archives/2008_10_17.html

The Responsible Endowment Coalition. (2009). Retrieved March 2, 2009, from http://www.endowmentethics.org/.

The world's most admired companies. (2009, March 16). *Fortune*, pp. 75–88.

Thompson, R. W. (1998, March). Study refutes perception that expatriation often fails. *HR News*, p. 2.

Thompson, C. (2008, March). Standard should not have been applied to hearing test. *HRMagazine*, p. 88.

Thorndike, E. L. (1920). A constant error in psychological ratings. *Journal of Applied Psychology, 4*, 25–29.

Thorndike, R. L. (1949). *Personnel selection: Test and measurement techniques.* New York, NY: Wiley.

Thornton, G. C., & Zorich, S. (1980). Training to improve observer accuracy. *Journal of Applied Psychology, 65*, 351–354.

Thornton, E. (2009, March 2). The hidden perils of layoffs. *BusinessWeek*, pp. 52, 53.

Thurstone, L. L. (1931). *The reliability and validity of tests.* Ann Arbor, MI: Edwards.

Tillema, H. H. (1998). Assessment of potential, from assessment centers to development centers. *International Journal of Selection and Assessment, 6*, 185–191.

Tippins, N. T., Beaty, J., Drasgow, F., Gibson, W. M., Pearlman, K., Segall, D. O., & Shepherd, W. (2006). Unproctored Internet testing in employment settings. *Personnel Psychology, 59*, 189–225.

Tonidandel, S., Quiñones, M. A., & Adams, A. A. (2002). Computer-adaptive testing: The impact of test characteristics on perceived performance and test takers' reactions. *Journal of Applied Psychology, 87*, 320–332.

Toops, H. A. (1944). The criterion. *Educational and Psychological Measurement, 4,* 271–297.

Tracey, J. B., Hinkin, T. R., Tannenbaum, S., & Mathieu, J. E. (2001). The influence of individual characteristics and the work environment on varying levels of training outcomes. *Human Resource Development Quarterly, 12,* 5–23

Tracey, J. B., Tannenbaum, S. I., & Kavanagh, M. J. (1995). Applying trained skills on the job: The importance of the work environment. *Journal of Applied Psychology, 80,* 239–252.

Trattner, M. H. (1982). Synthetic validity and its application to the Uniform Guidelines' validation requirements. *Personnel Psychology, 35,* 383–397.

Trattner, M. H., & O'Leary, B. S. (1980). Sample sizes for specified statistical power in testing for differential validity. *Journal of Applied Psychology, 65,* 127–134.

Triandis, H. (1971). *Attitude and attitude change.* New York, NY: Wiley.

Triandis, H. (1994). Cross-cultural industrial and organizational psychology. In H. Triandis, M. D. Dunnette, & L. M. Hough (Eds.), *Handbook of industrial and organizational psychology* (Vol. 4, pp. 103–172). Palo Alto, CA: CPP, Inc.

Triandis, H. C. (1998). Vertical and horizontal individualism and collectivism: Theory and research implications for international comparative management. In J. L. Cheng, & R. B. Peterson (Eds.), *Advances in international and comparative management* (pp. 7–35). Greenwich, CT: JAI Press.

Triandis, H. C. (2002). Generic individualism and collectivism. In M. Gannon, & K. Newman (Eds.), *The Blackwell handbook of cross-cultural management* (pp. 16–45). Oxford: Blackwell Business.

Triandis, H. C. (2004). The many dimensions of culture. *Academy of Management Executive, 18*(1), pp. 88–93.

Triandis, H. C., Kurowski, L. L., & Gelfand, M. J. (1994). Workplace diversity. In H. Triandis, M. D. Dunnette, & L. M. Hough (Eds.), *Handbook of industrial and organizational psychology* (Vol. 4, pp. 769–827). Palo Alto, CA: CPP, Inc.

Trotter, R., Zacur, S. R., & Greenwood, W. (1982). The pregnancy disability amendment: What the law provides, Part II. *Personnel Administrator, 27,* 55–58.

Tross, S. A., & Maurer, T. J. (2008). The effect of coaching interviewees on subsequent interview performance in structured experience-based interviews. *Journal of Occupational and Organizational Psychology, 81,* 589–605.

Truxillo, D. M. & Bauer, T. N. (1999). Applicant reactions to test scores banding in entry-level and promotional contexts. *Journal of Applied Psychology, 84,* 322–339.

Truxillo, D. M., Bauer, T. N., Campion, M. A., & Paronto, M. E. (2002). Selection fairness information and applicant reactions: A longitudinal field study. *Journal of Applied Psychology, 87,* 1020–1031.

Truxillo, D. M., Bauer, T. N., Campion, M. A., & Paronto, M. E. (2006). A field study of the role of Big Five Personality in applicant perceptions of selection fairness, self, and the hiring organization. *International Journal of Selection and Assessment, 14,* 269–277.

Truxillo, D. M., Donahue, L. M., & Sulzer, J. L. (1996). Setting cutoff scores for personnel selection tests: Issues, illustrations, and recommendations. *Human Performance, 9,* 275–295.

Tsaousis, I., & Nikolaou, I. E. (2001). The stability of the five-factor model of personality in personnel selection and assessment in Greece. *International Journal of Selection and Assessment, 9,* 290–301.

Tsui, A. S., & Ohlott, P. (1988). Multiple assessment of managerial effectiveness: Interrater agreement and consensus in effectiveness models. *Personnel Psychology, 41,* 779–803.

Tucker, D. H., & Rowe, P. M. (1977). Consulting the application form prior to the interview: An essential step in the selection process. *Journal of Applied Psychology, 62,* 283–287.

Tullar, W. D., Mullins, T. W., & Caldwell, S. A. (1979). Effects of interview length and applicant quality on interview decision time. *Journal of Applied Psychology, 64,* 669–674.

Turban, D. B., & Jones, A. P. (1988). Supervisor subordinate similarity: Types, effects, and mechanisms. *Journal of Applied Psychology, 73,* 228–234.

Turban, D. B., & Keon, T. L. (1993). Organizational attractiveness: An interactionist perspective. *Journal of Applied Psychology, 78,* 184–193.

Turnage, J. J., & Muchinsky, P. M. (1984). A comparison of the predictive validity of assessment center evaluations versus traditional measure in forecasting supervisory job performance: Interpretive implications of criterion distortion for the assessment paradigm. *Journal of Applied Psychology, 69,* 595–602.

Turner, N., Barling, J., Epitropaki, O., Butcher, V., & Milner, C. (2002). Transformational leadership and moral reasoning. *Journal of Applied Psychology, 87,* 304–311.

Turner, S. M., DeMers, S. T., Fox, H. R., & Reed, G. M. (2001). APA's guidelines for test user qualifications: An executive summary. *American Psychologist, 56,* 1099–1113.

Twitchell, S., Holton, E. F., III, & Trott, J. R., Jr. (2001). Technical training evaluation practices in the United States. *Performance Improvement Quarterly, 13*(3), 84–109.

Tyler, K. (2004, January). I say potato, you say patata. *HRMagazine,* pp. 85–87.

Tyler, K. (2008, September). 15 ways to train on the job. *HRMagazine,* pp. 105–108.

Tziner, A., & Dolan, S. (1982). Validity of an assessment center for identifying future female officers in the military. *Journal of Applied Psychology, 67,* 728–736.

Tziner, A., Murphy, K. R., & Cleveland, J. N. (2002). Does conscientiousness moderate the relationship between attitudes and beliefs regarding performance appraisal and rating behavior? *International Journal of Selection and Assessment, 10,* 218–224.

Uggerslev, K. L., & Sulsky, L. M. (2002). Presentation modality and indirect performance information: Effects on ratings, reactions, and memory. *Journal of Applied Psychology, 87,* 940–950.

Underhill, B. O., McAnally, K., & Koriath, J. J. (2008). *Executive coaching for results.* San Francisco, CA: Berrett-Kohler.

Uniform guidelines on employee selection procedures. (1978). 43 Fed. Reg. 38, 290–38, 315.

United States Commission on Civil Rights. (1977). *Statement on affirmative action.* Washington, DC: U.S. Government Printing Office.

U.S. Airways, Inc. v. Barnett, 535 U.S. 391 (2002) 228 F. 3d 1105.

U.S. Department of Labor. (1972). *Handbook for analyzing jobs.* Washington, DC: U.S. Government Printing Office.

U.S. Department of Labor. (1982). *A guide to job analysis: A "how to" publication for occupational analysts.* Washington, DC: U.S. Government Printing Office.

U.S. Department of Labor (2009). Downloaded March 27, 2009, from www.dol.gov/esa/ofccp/regs/compliance/ofcpcomp.htm.

U.S. Immigration and Customs Enforcement. (n.d.). Retrieved March 26, 2009, from www.ice.gov/pi/news/factsheets/worksite.htm.

Upton, G. J. G. (1982). A comparison of alternative tests for the 2×2 comparative trial. *Journal of the Royal Statistical Society, Series A, 145*, 86–105.

Useem, J. (1999, July 5). For sale online: You. *Fortune*, pp. 67–78.

Valbrun, M. (2003, August 7). EEOC sees rise in intra-race complaints of color bias. *The Wall Street Journal*, pp. B1, B3.

Vancouver, J. B., & Day, D. V. (2005). Industrial and organization research on self-regulation: From constructs to applications. *Applied Psychology, 54*, 155–185.

Van der Zee, K. I., Bakker, A. B., & Bakker, P. (2002). Why are structured interviews so rarely used in personnel selection? *Journal of Applied Psychology, 87*, 176–184.

Vance, R. J., Coovert, M. D., MacCallum, R. C., & Hedge, J. W. (1989). Construct models of task performance. *Journal of Applied Psychology, 74*, 447–455.

Vance, R. J., Winne, P. S., & Wright, E. S. (1983). A longitudinal examination of rater and ratee effects in performance ratings. *Personnel Psychology, 36*, 609–620.

Vandenberg, R. J. (2002). Toward a further understanding of an improvement in measurement invariance methods and procedures. *Organizational Research Methods, 5*, 139–158.

Van Hoye, G., & Lievens, F. (2007). Investigating web-based recruitment sources: Employee testimonials vs word-of-mouse. *International Journal of Selection and Assessment, 15*, 372–382.

Van Iddekinge, C. H., & Ployhart, R. E. (2008). Developments in the criterion-related validation of selection procedures: A critical review and recommendations for practice. *Personnel Psychology, 61*, 871–925.

Van Iddekinge, C. H., Raymark, P. H., & Roth, P. L. (2005). Assessing personality with a structured employment interview: Construct-related validity and susceptibility to response inflation. *Journal of Applied Psychology, 90*, 536–552.

Van Iddekinge, C. H., Raymark, P. H., Roth, P. L., & Payne, H. S. (2006). Comparing the psychometric characteristics of ratings of face-to-face and videotaped structured interviews. *International Journal of Selection and Assessment, 14*, 347–359.

Vardi, Y., & Weitz, E. (2004). *Misbehavior in organizations: Theory, research and management.* Mahwah, NJ: Lawrence Erlbaum.

Varela, O. E., & Premeaux, S. F. (2008). Do cross-cultural values affect multisource feedback dynamics? The case of high power distance and collectivism in two Latin American countries. *International Journal of Selection & Assessment, 16*, 134–142.

Verschoor, C. C. (2003). Corporate responsibility: High priority for CEOs. *Strategic Finance, 85*(4), 20, 22.

Varley, P. (Ed.). (1998). *The sweatshop quandary: Corporate responsibility on the global frontier.* Washington, DC: Investor Responsibility Research Center.

Vella, M. (2008, April 28). White-collar workers shoulder together—Like it or not. *BusinessWeek*, p. 58.

Vicino, F. C., & Bass, B. M. (1978). Lifespace variables and managerial success. *Journal of Applied Psychology, 63*, 81–88.

Vigneau, J. D. (1995). To catch a thief—and other workplace investigations. *HRMagazine, 40*(1), 90–95.

Vinchur, A. J., Schippmann, J. S., Smalley, M. D., & Rothe, H. F. (1991). Productivity consistency of foundry chippers and grinders: A 6-year field study. *Journal of Applied Psychology, 76*, 134–136.

Vinchur, A. J., Schippmann, J. S., Switzer, F. S., & Roth, P. L. (1998). A meta-analytic review of predictors of job performance for salespeople. *Journal of Applied Psychology, 83*, 586–597.

Viswesvaran, C., Deller, J., & Ones, D. S. (2007). Personality measures in personnel selection: Some new contributions. *International Journal of Selection and Assessment, 15*, 354–358.

Viswesvaran, C., & Ones, D. S. (2000). Perspectives on models of job performance. *International Journal of Selection and Assessment, 8*, 216–226.

Viswesvaran, C., Ones, D. S., & Schmidt, F. L. (1996). Comparative analysis of the reliability of job performance ratings. *Journal of Applied Psychology, 81*, 557–574.

Viswesvaran, C., Schmidt, F. L., & Ones, D. S. (2002). The moderating influence of job performance dimensions on convergence of supervisory and peer ratings of job performance: Unconfounding construct-level convergence and rating difficulty. *Journal of Applied Psychology, 87*, 345–354.

Von Drehle, D. (2003, June 24). Court mirrors public opinion. *The Washington Post.* Retrieved June 29, 2003, from www.washingtonpost.com.

Vranica, S., & Steel, E. (2006, October 23). Wanted: On-line media expertise. *The Wall Street Journal*, p. B4.

Vroom, V. H., & Yetton, P. W. (1973). *Leadership and decision making.* Pittsburgh, PA: University of Pittsburgh Press.

Wagner, S. H., & Goffin, R. D. (1997). Differences in accuracy of absolute and comparative performance appraisal methods. *Organizational Behavior and Human Decision Processes, 70*, 95–103.

Waldman, D. A., & Avolio, B. J. (1991). Race effects in performance evaluations: Controlling for ability, education, and experience. *Journal of Applied Psychology, 76*, 897–901.

Waldman, D. A., Ramirez, G., House, R., & Puranam, P. (2001). Does leadership matter? CEO leadership attributes and profitability under conditions of perceived environmental uncertainty. *Academy of Management Journal, 44*, 134–143.

Walker, J. W. (1980). *Human resource planning.* New York, NY: McGraw-Hill.

Walker, H. J., Feild, A. H., Giles, W. F., Armenakis, A. A., & Bernerth, J. (2008, August). *Employee testimonials on recruitment Web sites: Differences in important job-seeker reactions.* Paper presented at the annual meeting of the Academy of Management, Anaheim, CA.

Wallace, S. R. (1965). Criteria for what? *American Psychologist, 20,* 411–417.

Wanberg, C. R., Kanfer, R., & Banas, J. T. (2000). Predictors and outcomes of networking intensity among unemployed job seekers. *Journal of Applied Psychology, 85,* 491–503.

Wanek, J. E. (1999). Integrity and honesty testing: What do we know? How do we use it? *International Journal of Selection and Assessment, 7,* 183–195.

Wang, G. (2002). Control groups for human performance technology (HPT) evaluation and measurement. *Performance Improvement Quarterly, 15*(2), 34–48.

Wang, G. G., & Wilcox, S. (2006). Training evaluation: knowing more than is practiced. *Advances in Developing Human Resources, 8,* 528–539.

Wanous, J. P. (1977). Organizational entry: Newcomers moving from outside to inside. *Psychological Bulletin, 84,* 601–618.

Wanous, J. P., & Hudy, M. J. (2001). Single-item reliability: A replication and extension. *Organizational Research Methods, 4,* 361–375.

Wanous, J. P., Sullivan, S. E., & Malinak, J. (1989). The role of judgment calls in meta-analysis. *Journal of Applied Psychology, 74,* 259–264.

Wards Cove Packing v. Atonio, 490 U.S. 642 (1989).

Warr, P., & Bunce, D. (1995). Trainee characteristics and the outcomes of open learning. *Personnel Psychology, 48,* 347–376.

Washington v. Davis, 426 U.S. 229 (1976).

Watson v. Fort Worth Bank & Trust, 108 S. Ct. 299 (1988).

Wayne, S. J., & Liden, R. C. (1995). Effects of impression management on performance ratings: A longitudinal study. *Academy of Management Journal, 38,* 232–260.

Webb, E. J., Campbell, D. T., Schwartz, R. D., & Sechrest, L. (2000). *Unobtrusive measures* (rev. ed.). Thousand Oaks, CA: Sage.

Webster, E. C. (1964). *Decision making in the employment interview.* Montreal: Eagle.

Webster, E. C. (1982). *The employment interview: A social judgment process.* Ontario, Canada: S.I.P.

Weekley, J. A., Frank, B., O'Connor, E. J., & Peters, L. H. (1985). A comparison of three methods of estimating the standard deviation of performance in dollars. *Journal of Applied Psychology, 70,* 122–126.

Weekley, J. A., & Gier, J. A. (1989). Ceilings in the reliability and validity of performance ratings: The case of expert raters. *Academy of Management Journal, 32,* 213–222.

Weekley, J. A., & Jones, C. (1997). Video-based situational testing. *Personnel Psychology, 50,* 25–49.

Weekley, J. A., & Jones, C. (1999). Further studies of situational tests. *Personnel Psychology, 52,* 679–700.

Weinzimmer, L. G., Mone, M. A., & Alwan, L. C. (1994). An examination of perceptions and usage of regression diagnostics in organization studies. *Journal of Management, 20,* 179–192.

Weiss, D. J., & Dawis, R. V. (1960). An objective validation of factual interview data. *Journal of Applied Psychology, 40,* 381–385.

Weiss, D. J., England, G. W., & Lofquist, L. H. (1961). *Validity of work histories obtained by interview* (Minnesota Studies in Vocational Rehabilitation No. 12). Minneapolis: University of Minnesota.

Weiss, R. S., & Rein, M. (1970). The evaluation of broad aim programs: Experimental design, its difficulties, and an alternative. *Administrative Science Quarterly, 15,* 97–109.

Weitz, J. (1961). Criteria for criteria. *American Psychologist, 16,* 228–231.

Welch, J., & Byrne, J. A. (2001). *Jack: Straight from the gut.* New York, NY: Warner Books.

Wells, S. J. Counting on workers with disabilities. (2008, April). *HRMagazine,* pp. 44–49.

Wellins, R. S., Byham, W. C., & Wilson, J. M. (1991). *Empowered teams: Creating self-directed workgroups that improve quality, productivity, and participation.* San Francisco, CA: Jossey-Bass.

Welsh, E. T., Wanberg, C. R., Brown, K. G., & Simmering, M. J. (2003). E-learning: emerging uses, empirical results and future directions. *International Journal of Training and Development, 7,* 245–258.

Werner, J. M. (1994). Dimensions that make a difference: Examining the impact of in-role and extrarole behaviors on supervisory ratings. *Journal of Applied Psychology, 79,* 98–107.

Werner, J. M., & Bolino, M. C. (1997). Explaining U.S. courts of appeals decisions involving performance appraisal: Accuracy, fairness, and validation. *Personnel Psychology, 50,* 1–24.

Wernimont, P. F., & Campbell, J. P. (1968). Signs, samples, and criteria. *Journal of Applied Psychology, 52,* 372–376.

Wesman, A. G. (1952). *Reliability and confidence* (Test Service Bulletin No. 44). New York, NY: Psychological Corporation.

Wesman, A. G. (1966). *Double-entry expectancy tables* (Test Service Bulletin No. 56). New York, NY: Psychological Corporation.

Wessel, D. (1989, September 7). Evidence is skimpy that drug testing works, but employers embrace practice. *The Wall Street Journal,* pp. B1, B8.

Westen, D., & Weinberger, J. (2004). When clinical description becomes statistical prediction. *American Psychologist, 59,* 597–613.

Westphal, J. D., & Clement, M. B. (2008). Sociopolitical dynamics in relations between top managers and security analysts: Favor rendering, reciprocity, and analyst stock recommendations. *Academy of Management Journal, 51,* 873–897.

Wexley, K. N., Alexander, R. A., Greenawalt, J. P., & Couch, M. A. (1980). Attitudinal congruence and similarity as related to interpersonal evaluations in manager-subordinate dyads. *Academy of Management Journal, 23,* 320–330.

Wexley, K. N., & Baldwin, T. T. (1986). Management development. *Journal of Management, 12*, 277–294.

Wexley, K. N., & Latham, G. P. (2002). *Developing and training human resources in organizations* (3rd ed.). Upper Saddle River, NJ: Prentice Hall.

Wexley, K. N., Sanders, R. E., & Yukl, G. A. (1973). Training interviewers to eliminate contrast effects in employment interviews. *Journal of Applied Psychology, 57*, 233–236.

Whetzel, D. L., McDaniel, M. A., & Nguyen, N. T. (2008). Subgroup differences in situational judgment test performance: A meta-analysis. *Human Performance, 21*, 291–309.

White, R. W. (1959). Motivation reconsidered: The concept of competence. *Psychological Bulletin, 66*, 297–333.

White, E. (2005, February 1). The jungle: Focus on recruitment, pay, and getting ahead. *The Wall Street Journal*, p. B6.

Whitney, D. J., & Schmitt, N. (1997). Relationship between culture and responses to biodata employment items. *Journal of Applied Psychology, 82*, 113–129.

Whitten, J. L., & Bentley, L. D. (2006). *Introduction to systems analysis and design.* Burr Ridge, IL: McGraw-Hill/Irwin.

Whyte, G., & Latham, G. (1997). The futility of utility analysis revisited: When even an expert fails. *Personnel Psychology, 50*, 601–610.

Wiersner, W., & Cronshaw, S. (1988). A meta-analytic investigation of the impact of interview format and degree of structure on the validity of the employment interview. *Journal of Occupational Psychology, 61*, 275–290.

Wiesen, J. P. (2001, April). Some possible reasons for adverse impact. In S. D. Kriska, T. Lin, & J. P. Wiesen (Eds.), *Reducing adverse impact while maintaining validity: The public sector experience.* Practitioner forum conducted at the meeting of the Society for Industrial and Organizational Psychology, San Diego, CA.

Wigdor, A. K., & Garner, W. R. (Eds.). (1982). *Ability testing: Use, consequences, and controversies.* Washington, DC: National Academy Press.

Wiggins, J. S. (1973). *Personality and prediction: Principles of personality assessment.* Reading, MA: Addison-Wesley.

Williams, C. R., Labig, C. E., Jr., & Stone, T. H. (1993). Recruitment sources and posthire outcomes for job applicants and new hires: A test of two hypotheses. *Journal of Applied Psychology, 78*, 163–172.

Williams, J. R., & Levy, P. E. (1992). The effects of perceived system knowledge on the agreement between self-ratings and supervisor ratings. *Personnel Psychology, 45*, 835–847.

Williams, L. J., & Anderson, S. E. (1994). An alternative approach to method effects using latent variable models: Applications in organizational behavior research. *Journal of Applied Psychology, 79*, 323–331.

Williams, L. J., Cote, J. A., & Buckley, M. R. (1989). Lack of method variance in self-reported affect and perceptions at work: Reality or artifact? *Journal of Applied Psychology, 74*, 462–468.

Williams, L. J., Ford, L. R., & Nguyen, N. (2002). Basic and advanced measurement models for confirmatory factor analysis. In S. G. Rogelberg (Ed.), *Handbook of research methods in industrial and organizational psychology* (pp. 366–389). Malden, MA: Blackwell.

Williamson, L. G., Campion, J. E., Malos, S. B., Roehling, M. V., & Campion, M. A. (1997). Employment interview on trial: Linking interview structure with litigation outcomes. *Journal of Applied Psychology, 82*, 900–912.

Williamson, I. O., Lepak, D. P., & King, J. (2003). The effect of company recruitment web site orientation on individuals' perceptions of organizational attractiveness. *Journal of Vocational Behavior, 63*, 242–263.

Willman, S. K. (2003, January–February). Tips for minimizing abuses of the Americans with Disabilities Act. *Legal Report*, pp. 3–8 (Available from Society for Human Resource Management, 1800 Duke Street, Alexandria, VA).

Wills, J. L. (1993). Job analysis. In U.S. Department of Education. *Skill systems in education and industry* (Vol. 1). Washington, DC: U.S. Department of Education. Retrieved January 22, 2004, from www.dol.gov.

Witkiewitz, K., & Marlatt, G. A. (2004). Relapse prevention for alcohol and drug problems: That was Zen, this is Tao. *American Psychologist, 59*, 224–235.

Witt, L. A. (1998). Enhancing organizational goal congruence: A solution to organizational politics. *Journal of Applied Psychology, 83*, 666–674.

Witt, L. A., & Spitzmuller, C. (2007). Person-situation predictors of maximum and typical performance. *Human Performance, 20*, 305–315.

Woehr, D. J., & Arthur, W. (2003). The construct-related validity of assessment center ratings: A review and meta-analysis of the role of methodological factors. *Journal of Management, 29*, 231–258.

Woehr, D. J., & Huffcutt, A. I., (1994). Rater training for performance appraisal: A quantitative review. *Journal of Occupational and Organizational Psychology, 67*, 189–205.

Wohlers, A. J., & London, M. (1989). Ratings of managerial characteristics: Evaluation, difficulty, co-worker agreement, and self-awareness. *Personnel Psychology, 42*, 235–261.

Wollowick, H. B., & McNamara, W. J. (1969). Relationship of the components of an assessment center to management success. *Journal of Applied Psychology, 53*, 348–352.

Wood, R. E., Mento, A. J., & Locke, E. A. (1987). Task complexity as a moderator of goal effects: A meta-analysis. *Journal of Applied Psychology, 72*, 416–425.

Woodward, N. H. (2007, August). Using "cost of living adjustments" to compensate expats. *Global HR News.* Retrieved August 15, 2007, from www.shrm.org.

Wright, P. M. (2008). *Human resource strategy: Adapting to the age of globalization.* Alexandria, VA: Society for Human Resource Management Foundation.

Wright, T. A., & Wright, V. P. (1999). Ethical responsibility and the organizational researcher: A committed-to-participant research perspective. *Journal of Organizational Behavior, 20*, 1107–1112.

Wygant v. Jackson Board of Education, 476 U.S. 261 (1986).

Wymer, J. F., III. (1999, May–June). Reasonable accommodation and undue hardship. *Legal Report*, pp. 6–8 (Available from Society for Human Resource Management, 1800 Duke Street, Alexandria, VA).

Yakubovich, V., & Lup, D. (2006). Stages of the recruitment process and the referrer's performance effect. *Organization Science, 17*, 710–723.

Yang, J. L. (2009, April 13). How to get a job. *Fortune*, pp. 49–56.

Yang, H., Sackett, P. R., & Nho, Y. (2004). Developing a procedure to correct for range restriction that involves both institutional selection and applicants' rejection of job offers. *Organizational Research Methods, 7*, 442–455.

Yorks, L., & Whitsett, D. A. (1985). Hawthorne, Topeka, and the issue of science versus advocacy in organizational behavior. *Academy of Management Review, 10*, 21–30.

Yuki, M., Maddux, W. W., Brewer, M. B., & Takemura, K. (2005). Cross-cultural differences in relationship-and group-based trust. *Personality & Social Psychology Bulletin, 31*, 48–62.

Yun, G. J., Donahue, L. M., Dudley, Ni. M., & McFarland, L. A. (2005). Rater personality, rating format, and social context: Implications for performance appraisal ratings. *International Journal of Selection and Assessment, 13*, 97–107.

Zalkind, S. S., & Costello, T. W. (1962). Perception: Some recent research and implications for administration. *Administrative Science Quarterly, 7*, 218–235.

Zedeck, S., & Cascio, W. F. (1982). Performance appraisal decisions as a function of rater training and purpose of the appraisal. *Journal of Applied Psychology, 67*, 752–758.

Zedeck, S., & Cascio, W. F. (1984). Psychological issues in personnel decisions. *Annual Review of Psychology, 35*, 461–518.

Zedeck, S., Cascio, W. F., Goldstein, I. L., & Outtz, J. (1996). Sliding bands: An alternative to top-down selection. In R. S. Barrett (Ed.), *Handbook of fair employment strategies* (pp. 222–234). Westport, CT: Quorum Books.

Zedeck, S., & Goldstein, I. L. (2000). The relationship between I/O psychology and public policy: A commentary. In J. F. Kehoe (Ed.), *Managing selection in changing organizations* (pp. 371–398). San Francisco, CA: Wiley.

Zedeck, S., & Kafry, D. (1977). Capturing rater policies for processing evaluation data. *Organizational Behavior and Human Performance, 18*, 269–294.

Zhao, Y., Lei, J., Lai, B. Y. C., & Tan, H. S. (2005). What makes the difference? A practical analysis of research on the effectiveness of distance education. *Teachers College Record, 107*, 1836–1884.

Zohar, D. (1980). Safety climate in industrial organizations: Theoretical and applied implications. *Journal of Applied Psychology, 65*, 96–102.

Zottoli, M. A., & Wanous, J. P. (2000). Recruitment source research: Current status and future directions. *Human Resource Management Review, 10*, 353–383.

SUBJECT INDEX

AUTHOR INDEX